Towards an Archaeology of the Nain Region, Labrador

BRYAN C. HOOD

EDITED BY WILLIAM W. FITZHUGH

Published by the
Arctic Studies Center
National Museum of Natural History
Smithsonian Institution
Washington, D.C.

Printed in the United States of America

ISBN: 10: 0-9816142-0-5
ISBN 13: 978-0-9816142-0-5

Library of Congress Cataloging-in-Publication Data

Hood, Bryan C., 1955-
    Towards an archaeology of the Nain Region, Labrador / Bryan C. Hood ; edited by William W. Fitzhugh.
        p. cm. — (Contributions to circumpolar anthropology ; v. 7)
    Includes bibliographical references and index.

    ISBN-13: 978-0-9816142-0-5 (pbk. : alk. paper)
    ISBN-10: 0-9816142-0-5 (pbk. : alk. paper)

    1. Indians of North America—Newfoundland and Labrador—Nain Region—Antiquities. 2. Eskimos—Newfoundland and Labrador—Nain Region—Antiquities. 3. Inuit—Newfoundland and Labrador—Nain Region—Antiquities. 4. Nain Region (N.L.)—Antiquities. 5. Excavations (Archaeology)—Newfoundland and Labrador—Nain Region. 6. Ethnoarchaeology—Newfoundland and Labrador—Nain Region. 7. Environmental archaeology—Newfoundland and Labrador—Nain Region. 8. Material culture—Newfoundland and Labrador—Nain Region—History. 9. Historic buildings—Newfoundland and Labrador—Nain Region. 10. Land settlement patterns—Newfoundland and Labrador—Nain Region—History. I. Fitzhugh, William W., 1943- II. Arctic Studies Center (National Museum of Natural History) III. Title.

    E78.N72H66 2008
    971.8004'97—dc22
                                    2008012674

The paper used in this publication meets the minimum requirements of the American National Standard for Information Sciences—Permanence of Paper for Printed Library Materials, Z39.48-1992.

Technical Editor: Cara Seitchek
Layout and Typography: Jody Billert / Design Literate, Inc.
Production editor: Abigail McDermott
Printed by United Book Press, Inc., Baltimore, MD

This publication is Volume 7 in the Arctic Studies Center series, *Contributions to Circumpolar Anthropology*, produced by the Arctic Studies Center, National Museum of Natural History, Smithsonian Institution.

THIS SERIES IS MADE POSSIBLE IN PART BY THE JAMES W. VANSTONE (1925-2001) ENDOWMENT. ADDITIONAL SUPPORT FOR THIS VOLUME HAS BEEN PROVIDED BY THE INSTITUTE FOR ARCHAEOLOGY, UNIVERSITY OF TROMSØ, NORWAY.

Front Cover: *Duncan Strong at Nukasusutok Island, August 1928. W. D. Strong collection © Smithsonian Institution, National Anthropological Archives, Negative No. 99-10592.*

Back Cover: *Bryan Hood at Nukasusutok-5, Area 3, in 1980 (Photo: Morten Meldgaard).*

contents

foreword

BY WILLIAM W. FITZHUGH

In 1969 while in the second field season of my PhD work in Hamilton Inlet, Geoff Conrad, Peter Wells, and I flew 200 miles north to survey two locations at the forest-tundra boundary in northern Quebec-Labrador. One of these locations was on the George River, where Dillon Wallace, Mina Hubbard, and W. B. Cabot had described Naskapi (today's Innu) camped in the early 1900s to intercept the annual caribou migration in August and September at Indian House Lake (Hutte de la Sauvage) near the Labrador border in northeastern Quebec. Here we found many historic Innu camps at the northern edge of the forest. This country was harsh and its scoured surface still bore the scars of continental ice sheets. For the Innu who lived here, starvation was always just a breath away, for if the 'deer' migration changed the Innu were often too weak to re-locate.

After a few days we flew east to the comparative paradise of Village Bay, where Port Manvers Run joins the Labrador Sea at the southeast side of the Kiglapait Mountains. To the north lay the Okak archipelago; to the south the island archipelago east of Nain, then the northernmost town in Labrador, settled by Moravian missionaries in 1771. As we waded ashore in the blisteringly cold water, the contrast with the interior barrens was stark indeed. It wasn't that the land was so different, for it had the same stunted spruce trees and tangled alder thickets, the same patches of wind-blown sand and winter-killed tree stumps. What was different was the wealth of resources provided by the ocean. The bountiful Labrador coast waters made the barrens seem like the most desolate place on earth. If you had a choice – and in the competitive world of early Labrador history, one often did not – you would choose the coast, and if you know how to hunt sea mammals and navigate a treacherous coastline, it could sustain larger and more sedentary communities.

Our brief visit to Village Bay and Thalia Point demonstrated great archaeological potential, with finds of Inuit camps dating to the past 5-600 years, the first Pre-Dorset and Dorset sites to be found in Labrador, and scattered traces of yet-to-be defined early Indian cultures. The region was well-described in detailed annual reports of the Moravians in the 18-19th C. and some ethnographic work had been done by geologist E.P. Wheeler, whose student, Stearns (Tony) Morse, and Peter Johnson had studied its geology and geomorphology. Wheeler and Morse were still working in the Nain area when we arrived, as was Terje Brantenberg, a social anthropologist. My brief excursion to Thalia Point convinced me that Nain, which lay just south of the coastal tree-line, was more central to the question of Indian-Eskimo boundary dynamics than Hamilton Inlet, where I had been working on this problem since 1968.

Beginning in 1973 I acquired a boat and started making excursions to Nain from Hamilton Inlet, and in 1975 I began to focus exclusively on this area. In 1977-78 I undertook a large survey of the coast north of Nain, as far as Killinek and Port Burwell at the northern tip of Labrador. By this time Bryan Hood had become part of the field team, and when we returned to continue work in Nain in the early 1980s, Bryan began his own project at a large Maritime Archaic site at Nukasusutok 5. In later years he researched other sites at Nukasusutok and explored the inner fjords north of

Nain. Hood's work more than complements our earlier studies; he has advanced it in important ways, making the first detailed published test of the Maritime Archaic longhouse model, exploring Maritime Archaic-Paleoeskimo contacts, and expanding knowledge of Dorset settlement patterns. This volume is the first detailed description of Nain culture history to be published, spans a period of 6000 years, and includes a large number of sites from different environmental zones, from outer coast to interior bays and fjords. Hood's analytical study of settlement data using *k*-means and other methods is a model approach to the study of settlement information and the first such study to appear for any arctic or subarctic region. Description of Duncan Strong's finds from the early historic Inuit village at Nukasusutok, housed at the R.S. Peabody Foundation in Andover, Massachusetts, brings his study up toward the present day. While not a complete scenario of the early history of Nain it is a fine start at creating an accessible published literature on the archaeology of northern Labrador.

I thank Bryan for his long and continuing dedication to the peoples and cultures of Nain, and for his meticulous description and analysis of hard-won field data. It gives me great pleasure to publish this work through the Arctic Studies Center as the first of several future monographs on Smithsonian-related Labrador research. We dedicate this volume to the people of Nain in gratitude for the support and encouragement they have provided our collective efforts for many years.

Heading home to Nain over the sea ice east of Strathcona Run, April 1996. (Photo: B. Hood)

preface

The research described herein was undertaken in two phases separated by twelve years. The first phase transpired on Nukasusutok Island in 1979 and 1980 as fieldwork directed towards an M.A. degree at Trent University (Hood 1981). During subsequent years I pursued my Ph.D. at the University of Massachusetts, Amherst. That research was directed primarily towards north Norwegian Stone Age archaeology, but a prominent underlying theme was that comparison between Norway and Labrador could provide useful insight concerning hunter-gatherer complexity. Having eventually acquired a teaching position at Memorial University of Newfoundland, I returned to Nukasusutok in 1992 and 1993 to reevaluate the previous work. I also expanded my geographical scope to include a modest program in the Webb Bay and Port Manvers Run area from 1992 to 1994.

This temporal split presented some problems when it was time to proceed with the final analysis of the material from the Nukasusutok-5 site. There was always the nagging question as to whether or not the observations made by naive eyes in 1979 could reliably be compared with those made on the basis of more experience in 1992. Should inconsistencies in observations between the two periods be attributed to inexperienced omissions in 1979 rather than to real behavioral differences? There were also some differences in recording techniques between the two research phases which had an impact on the methods chosen for the final analyses. For example, in 1979-1980 debitage was collected in 1 m^2 units while 50 cm^2 units were used in 1992-1993. Or, in 1979-80 utilized flakes and bipolar cores were not point plotted systematically in the field, so many of them were only provenienced within 1 m^2 units. Thus, the distribution patterns of these types could not be studied at the level of detail I would prefer today. These and other problems were annoying and frustrating, but hardly fatal. Although hitches remain they are not sufficient to subvert the main conclusions reached herein.

Despite the intensity of fieldwork in Labrador during the 1970s and 1980s, very little has been published beyond preliminary reports and some doctoral dissertations. This situation imposes significant limitations on the extent to which the material presented here can be used to elucidate broader culture-historical problems. Consequently, this volume will not offer a new synthesis of Labrador archaeology, although one is badly needed. The task of integration lies with others. Instead, the main purpose of the volume is to provide a detailed descriptive report that will be useful to other researchers. Of course, there is more to it than that; the material is also used to direct attention towards broader methodological and conceptual issues. The unifying theme for several of the chapters is the social structuration of space, which is treated at two different scales. The first scale is site structure, for which a set of methodological strategies is outlined. The second scale is regional and inter-regional, which is played out in general discussions of settlement patterns and theorization of the Pre-Dorset/Maritime Archaic social boundary relationship. In both cases the discussions feed on the tensions between processual and post-processual archaeologies. Thus the worm's eye view opens onto the wider world.

Bryan Hood

acknowledgments

This text has been many years in the making and has involved perambulations on both sides of the Atlantic such that the assistance of a rather wide range of people and institutions must be acknowledged.

During the 1979-80 field seasons financial support was received from the Arctic Institute of North America, the Committee for Research and Department of Anthropology, Trent University, and the Historic Resources Division, Government of Newfoundland and Labrador. The 1992-1994 field seasons were supported by grants from Memorial University (Vice-President's Research Grant and internal SSHRC funds), the Institute of Social and Economic Research and the Historic Resources Division of the Government of Newfoundland and Labrador. Much of the cataloguing and lab work performed by students was supported by the Memorial University MUCEP program. The Archaeology Unit, Memorial University, kindly kept me employed from 1990-1995.

Over the years, many people participated in this research in one capacity or another. In 1979 I was accompanied in the field by Jack Contin and Charles Curtis and in 1980 by William Fitzhugh, Eric Loring, Stephen Loring, Morten Meldgaard and Douglas Sutton. From 1992 to 1994 Edward Flowers of Nain served as my field assistant, joined in 1994 by Elias Henoche, also of Nain. Also joining the crew on a memorable survey/hunting trip to Hebron in 1997 were Kitti Flowers, Chesley Ittulak and Sam Kalleo. Lab assistance in cataloguing and related matters was provided by Marcus Anderson, Patricia Barefoot, Stephanie Barry, Marie-Claire Goyer, Randolph Lawlor, Sandy Ste. Croix and Robin Tuck.

Specialized analytical assistance was performed by Rodolfe Fecteau (University of Western Ontario; charcoal species identification), Dosia Layendecker (Smithsonian; charcoal species identification), Brian Ritchie (Trent University, soils analysis), Michael Deal (Memorial University, botanical identification) and Ann Rick (Canadian Museum of Nature, zoological analysis). Most of the lithic artifact photos were taken by John Bourne (Photo Services, Memorial University).

Once upon a time (1981, precisely), a preliminary look at the Maritime Archaic material reported here was presented as an M.A. thesis at Trent University (Hood 1981). I would like to thank the members of my thesis committee, Morgan Tamplin and the late Richard Johnston, for their guidance in thesis preparation and Romas Vastokas and Paul Healy for assistance in acquiring funding from Trent sources.

A special thanks is due to William Fitzhugh (Smithsonian). His invitation to participate in the Torngat Archaeological Project in 1978 was the stepping stone to everything that has happened since. He also suggested the work on Nukasusutok-5, provided subsistence and logistical support in 1980 and served as an outside committee member for the M.A. thesis. In recent years he has provided valuable commentary on my attempts to theorize the Maritime Archaic.

I also appreciate the efforts of the staff of the Cultural Heritage Division, province of Newfoundland and Labrador, and the Newfoundland Museum, for authorizing research and export permits, providing valuable information from site records, and sending me copies of unpublished manuscripts. Specifically:

Martha Drake, Ken Reynolds, Delphina Mercer, Stephen Hull, Elaine Anton and Kevin McAleese.

My access to W. D. Strong's collection at the Robert S. Peabody Museum of Archaeology, Phillips Academy, Andover, Massachusetts, was kindly arranged by Malinda Blustain. The material and photographs are used by permission of the Peabody Museum. I would also like to thank the staff of the National Anthropological Archives at the Smithsonian Institution for making available Strong's field notes and photographs. Some of Strong's photos are used here with permission of the Smithsonian Institution.

Over the past several years the financial and infrastructural support of the University of Tromsø, Norway, has been instrumental in bringing this work to completion. Additionally, without tutoring in the basics of Autocad from Tor Mikalsen, I would never have managed to produce the maps and floor plans herein. Anne Tommervåg and Geir Davidsen provided pointers on digital photo retouching.

I would also like to thank the manuscript peer reviewers for pointing out various errors and omissions and for suggesting improvements. The remaining blemishes are my own fault.

Last but not least, much gratitude must be extended to the Labradorians who assisted in imple-menting the fieldwork and invited me into their homes. In 1979 Henry Webb of Nain provided boat transportation to and from Nukasusutok and Sue Webb provided radio communications. Winston White was most gracious in supplying accommodation during our sojourns in Goose Bay and provided us with some memorable mid-summer rest and recreation at his summer home at Kauk in 1979 and 1980. Gary Baikie of the Torngâsok Cultural Center (Nain), in his capacity as the community liason for archaeological matters, approved the 1992-94 fieldwork and provided assistance with logistics in 1992. Joe Webb and Dennis Wyatt provided boat transportation to our field sites in 1992. Edward Flowers kindly contributed the use of his boat and his father's motor in 1993 and Gus Flowers provided us with transportation out to Webb Bay in 1994. Thanks to Christine Denniston for providing accommodation in Nain in 1992 and 1993.

A special thanks to the Flowers family for taking me into their home, and to Gus and Edward for giving me the opportunity to travel with them on summer hunting trips and an especially memorable winter trip to Nutak in April 1993. Not to mention other forays since then. Without their support my ignorance would have been much worse and I might truly have gone *isumaitsik*....

Motoring up Port Manvers Run with Edward Flowers, 1993. (Photo: B. Hood)

figures

tables

Nain, July 1978. (Photo: B.Hood)

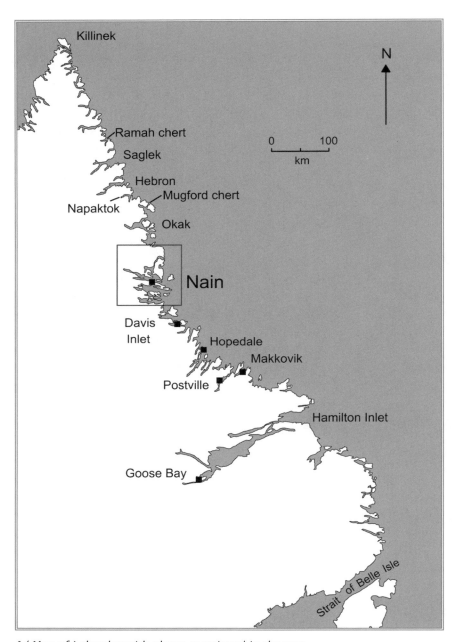

1/ Map of Labrador with places mentioned in the text.

Introduction

The Nain region is home to the currently northernmost permanent settlement in Labrador (Figure 1). Although the settlement itself was established in 1771 by the Moravian missionaries, occupation of the island-studded coast extends back at least 7000 years. The region contains a rich archaeological record of Inuit, Pre-Inuit (Paleoeskimo), Innu and pre-contact Indian occupations, as well as post-contact European activity. Concerted archaeological research began in the area during the early 1970s and it could probably be said that the region is now the most thoroughly investigated portion of Labrador. Relatively little of this archaeological research has been published to date other than as preliminary reports, so the present volume is an attempt to provide more substantial documentation of several localities pertaining to a variety of time periods and cultural contexts.

The Goals of this Text

This book is entitled "Towards an Archaeology of the Nain Region" and not "The Archaeology of the Nain Region" because it is not intended to be a synthetic culture-historical work. Its primary purpose is to bring together the results of several years of research in two portions of the Nain area: Nukasusutok Island and Webb Bay/Port Manvers Run. Since most of the archaeological data from the Nain region have been collected by others, it is to them that the task of synthesis belongs. The goals of this monograph are both broader and narrower than a culture-historical account.

Broader, because the text endeavors to articulate some of the archaeological material with theoretical and methodological issues of wider significance. Narrower, because detailed descriptive reports are presented on a limited range of material that will constitute primary documentation for use in a future integration. This case study approach has the consequence that certain cultural periods are omitted (Intermediate and Late Pre-Contact Indian). Another consequence is that the chapter sequencing is not by chronological or cultural period but by geographical sub-region (Nukasusutok Island, Webb Bay/Port Manvers Run).

The theoretical theme that runs throughout the book is the social structuration of space. By this is meant the view that space is not a passive adaptive stage, but an affordance that is actively constructed through social practice, becoming a meaningful landscape imbued with social and ideological significance. This socially constructed affordance acts back upon the practice of human agents, presenting them with an array of constraints and opportunities for action and plays a generative role in the formation of individual and social identities. Material ecological properties and social action are thus enfolded in each other (for related but not necessarily isomorphic views see Giddens 1979, 1984; Hood 1988; Ingold 1996, 2000; Tilley 1994). In this volume the structuration of space is discussed on two scales: the spatial configuration of individual settlements and the organization of regional and supra-regional landscapes.

As far as the spatial organization of individual settlements is concerned, the focus is the role of dwellings in the structuration of social life: dwellings as material components of social practice. More specifically, Maritime Archaic and Paleoeskimo dwellings are considered here. Previous discussions of the Maritime Archaic have drawn somewhat divergent social inferences from dwelling structures (Fitzhugh 1981, 1984, 1985a; Hood 1993, 1995), but the methodological basis for these inferences has never been spelled out explicitly. There have been discussions of methodologies for analyzing Paleoeskimo dwellings (e.g., Dekin 1976; Jensen 1996; McGhee 1979; Stapert and Johanson 1996), but in many other cases spatial distributions are illustrated but not analyzed. Consequently, the main concern in Chapter 3 will be to formulate a strategy to connect some of our interpretive conventions with the data by means of fairly explicit analytical arguments. Some would call this middle-range theory (Binford 1980), but here it is simply considered as methodological strategy. An explicit discussion of methodology is necessary because "interpretive archaeology" (which is linked with some of the views mentioned above) has often presented narratives that lack adequate justification of their claims to have recognized a meaningful pattern in the archaeological record. Such interpretations constitute weak assertions or advocacy statements rather than analytical arguments and are thus subject to accusations that they present a "past as wished for" (Renfrew 1989:36). They leap to interpret cultural context, but often fail to engage the archaeological record as an *archaeological* phenomenon.

The methodological strategy outlined in Chapter 3 is applied to some, but not all of the material discussed herein. It is most systematically applied in analyses of the two sites with the best data bases: an Early-Middle Maritime Archaic site, Nukasusutok-5 (Chapters 5, 6 and 7), and a Pre-Dorset site, Attu's Point (Chapter 13). More limited in scope are the analyses of an Early/Middle Dorset locality, Nukasusutok 12

(Chapter 10) and the Pre-Dorset site Port Manvers Run-1 (Chapter 12). Other chapters are more descriptive in character, providing brief overviews of the smaller or less well-investigated sites on Nukasusutok Island (Chapter 4) and in the Webb Bay Port-Manvers Run area (Chapter 12).

The discussion of regional landscape organization is taken up primarily in Chapter 14, which considers the problem of Pre-Dorset/Maritime Archaic social boundary relations. This chapter is also a reflection upon how a specific problem in subarctic archaeology resonates with implications for the broader debates between the competing archaeological ontologies of humans as adaptive beings in nature versus humans as cultural beings constructing their own worlds of significance. The problem of working in the area of tension between these "paradigms" is highlighted. Regional and supra-regional spatial relations are also briefly touched upon in Chapter 11, which outlines data concerning the 18th and early 19th century Inuit occupation of Nukasusutok Island. The primary goal of the chapter is to present an overview of collections made in 1928 by William Duncan Strong and relate them to the ethnohistorically documented Inuit settlement. In the process, some fascinating yet highly fragmentary glimpses can be had of Inuit life during a time of marked changes in settlement and society during the contact period. These changes played out on both the local and supra-regional spatial scales, and were linked with the global expansion of the European capitalist World System.

The remainder of this introductory chapter provides a background to the descriptive and analytical components to follow. First up is a brief overview of archaeological research history in northern Labrador that focuses on what is most relevant for contextualizing the issues dealt with in the present volume. The aim is to show how the present work grew out of the existing tradition and how some of the questions handled here were formulated within this tradition. This overview is followed by a short outline of north-central

Labrador culture-history to provide the reader with a framework into which the empirical fragments of this volume can be inserted. Thereafter, Chapter 2 describes the environmental context of the Nain region.

A Brief History of Archaeological Research in the Nain Region and Adjacent Areas

The first professional archaeological fieldwork in the Nain region was undertaken by William Duncan Strong in conjunction with the Rawson-MacMillan Subarctic Expedition of 1927-28. Strong conducted ethnographic research among the Davis Inlet and Barren Ground Innu (Naskapi) (Leacock and Rothschild 1994; VanStone 1985) and undertook archaeological surveys along the central coast between Hopedale and Nain. Three archaeological sites near Hopedale produced distinctive artifacts that led Strong to postulate the existence of an "Old Stone Culture" for Labrador (Strong 1930). He concluded that this "Old Stone Culture" was an early Indian complex from which Eskimo culture developed. In the course of his work Strong also investigated prehistoric and historic Inuit sites, including those on Nukasusutok Island, but this material was never published except for osteological material taken from graves (Stewart 1939). In 1933 and 1934, Junius B. Bird (1945) investigated early contact period Inuit houses in the Hopedale area. Many years later, ethnohistorian J. Garth Taylor (1966) visited the Nukasusutok settlement as part of his survey of 18th century Labrador Inuit settlements in the Nain and Okak regions·

Until the late 1960s there existed only a sketchy outline of Labrador prehistory based on Elmer Harp's (1963) work in the Strait of Belle Isle, in which he defined the "Boreal Archaic." William Fitzhugh's research in the Hamilton Inlet region between 1968 and 1972 (Fitzhugh 1972, 1975, 1976, 1978) provided the first culture-history for central Labrador. Fitzhugh also conducted surveys at Thalia Point north of Nain in 1971 and 1973, which revealed the first evidence for Pre-Dorset in the Nain region (Fitzhugh 1976:103). Between 1967-1969, James Tuck excavated the important cemetery at Port au Choix, Newfoundland, which led him to define the Maritime Archaic Tradition (Tuck 1971, 1976a). Tuck then undertook a project at Saglek Bay in northern Labrador from 1969-71, an important result of which was evidence for the temporal and geographical overlap of Maritime Archaic and Pre-Dorset. Tuck (1975:195-196) speculated on the possibility of technological exchanges between the two cultures.

From 1973 to 1975 the scale of Fitzhugh's efforts expanded considerably. In 1973 Fitzhugh (1973) conducted a survey of the central coast from Hamilton Inlet to Nain. The Nain area was the center of surveys and excavations from 1974-1976, punctuated by the excavation of a Maritime Archaic cemetery at Rattlers Bight in Hamilton Inlet in 1975 and additional surveys of the central coast (Fitzhugh 1976). Related to Fitzhugh's work was Richard Jordan's investigation of contact period Inuit houses at Hamilton Inlet in 1973 and 1975 (R. Jordan 1974, 1978), which focused on socio-economic changes from the 17th to 19th centuries. Jordan's work provided an archaeological context for J. Garth Taylor's (1974) ethnohistoric research on the 18th century communal house period. Additionally, Steven Cox conducted surveys and excavations in the Okak region in 1974 and 1975. Cox's (1977) work continued the theme of settlement pattern analysis begun by Fitzhugh at Hamilton Inlet and made important contributions to Maritime Archaic, Pre-Dorset and Dorset culture-history.

Elsewhere, in 1973 and 1974 Robert McGhee and James Tuck (1975) built upon Harp's earlier surveys along the Strait of Belle Isle and pushed the occupation history of the region back to at least 8500 B.P. (Renouf 1977). Their work also provided evidence of early Maritime Archaic mortuary ceremonialism at 7500 B.P. (McGhee and Tuck 1975; Tuck and McGhee 1975; Tuck 1975). From 1973 to 1977, Gilles Samson followed up Geoffrey Conrad's initial reconnaissance at Indian

House Lake in the Quebec-Labrador interior with further surveys, excavations and paleoenvironmental research. Although settlement seems to have been sporadic until the Innu occupation of the historic period, Samson (1978) discovered several sites attributable to the Maritime Archaic Tradition.

By the late 1970s, Smithsonian fieldwork had produced a solid outline of central and north-central coast culture-history (e.g., Cox 1978; Fitzhugh 1977, 1978a,b; R. Jordan 1978; Nagle 1978). In 1977 and 1978 the Smithsonian Torngat Archaeological Project extended research northwards along the Torngat Mountain coast all the way to Killinek and the Button Islands (Fitzhugh 1980). Major concentrations of Maritime Archaic and Pre-Dorset settlement were identified in the more southerly section of the project area near Hebron Fiord. It was on the 1978 season of the Torngat project that the author was initiated into Labrador archaeology, acquiring a particular taste for the Maritime Archaic and Pre-Dorset. The author returned to Labrador in 1979 to undertake a small scale excavation on a Maritime Archaic site in the Nain area, which was continued in 1980 (Hood 1981).

In 1980 Fitzhugh began the first of several seasons of fieldwork devoted primarily to further study of the Maritime Archaic. An important focus of this work was the development of Maritime Archaic dwelling structures from small single-family boulder-pits to multi-family longhouses (Fitzhugh 1981, 1984, 1985a, 1985b, 1986). The question of Maritime Archaic/Pre-Dorset cultural boundaries was also explored (Fitzhugh 1984). During the 1980s a number of other Smithsonian-related researchers were active in Labrador. Stephen Loring undertook surveys of the inner bays and islands of the Davis Inlet and Nain regions, focussing on late pre-contact Innu archaeology (Loring 1983, 1985, 1989, 1992), while Susan Kaplan continued her research on historic Labrador Inuit settlement and socio-economic change, which included investigations of a Thule component on Iglosiatik Island southeast of Nain (Kaplan 1983).

Callum Thomson conducted several years of surveys and excavations at Saglek Bay in the Torngat region (Thomson 1981, 1982, 1983, 1984, 1986, 1989), uncovering further evidence of Maritime Archaic and Pre-Dorset occupation, as well as data pertaining to other cultures and periods, particularly Late Dorset. Cox (1988) investigated an important Pre-Dorset locale at Nuasornak Island in the Okak region.

Compared with earlier periods, during the late 1980s and early 1990s northern Labrador archaeology was relatively quiescent. Kaplan continued with investigations of historic Inuit occupation in the Nain and Okak regions, and Loring conducted excavations of contact period Inuit material at the Nain Moravian mission and in the Torngats (Loring 1998) as well as working with the Innu at interior locations. The author undertook small scale investigations in the Nain area from 1992-1994, which constitute the basis for some of the chapters in this volume.

The nature of Labrador archaeology changed dramatically in 1995 with the first phase of environmental impact studies associated with the Voisey's Bay nickel find. An intensive survey of the mining concession area between Voisey's Bay and Anaktalak Bay was undertaken in 1996 (Hood and Baikie 1998a; Labrèche et al. 1997) and exploratory drilling sites all over the Nain area and in other parts of Labrador were investigated by contract archaeologists. Mitigation-related fieldwork has been sporadic in the Nain area in recent years, but Loring has continued with fieldwork directed towards pre-contact and Innu sites in the interior (Loring 2001) and historic Inuit material in the Makkovik region, while Kaplan has continued her work with Inuit occupation at Okak. In 1997 the author undertook survey work in the Hebron and Napartok Bay regions aimed at supplementing data on Maritime Archaic/Pre-Dorset social boundaries (Hood 1998a).

The research tradition outlined here has emphasized a number of themes that provide a context for the discussions in this volume. Of primary importance is Fitzhugh's (1984, 1985a) work on the Maritime

Archaic, including dwelling site organization and social inferences from temporal changes in dwelling structures, mortuary ceremonialism and Ramah chert procurement and exchange. The spatial analyses of the Early-Middle Maritime Archaic site Nukasusutok-5 presented in Chapter 6 are formulated in light of these discussions of social organization. A second theme in the research tradition is Fitzhugh's (1984) and Tuck's (1975) interpretations of Maritime Archaic and Pre-Dorset social boundary relationships, which reflects the concern for Indian/Inuit contacts that has been a constant *leitmotif* since the genesis of discourse on northern archaeology and anthropology (Fitzhugh 1987; Hood 1998b). The discussion of Maritime Archaic/Pre-Dorset boundary relations in Chapter 14 is an elaboration on that established theme.

Another primary structuring element in Labrador archaeology has been the focus on cultural adaptations, as seen through settlement patterns and the lense of Steward's (1955) cultural ecology (Fitzhugh 1972) and biogeographic theory (Fitzhugh 1997). During the early- to mid-1970s a series of hypotheses was proposed which related changes in Indian and Paleoeskimo/Inuit population distributions to environmental change (e.g., Fitzhugh 1972, 1977). Although accumulating research eventually suggested the postulated links between culture change and environmental change were too simplistic (Fitzhugh and Lamb 1985), much of northern archaeology continues to pursue a rather reductionist ecological program (Hood 1998b). Consequently, one of the strands woven into this volume is a desire to place greater emphasis on internal social process and agency, while at the same time situating social strategies within the natural world. Thus, a portion of Chapter 14 uses the Pre-Dorset/ Maritime Archaic boundary issue to reflect upon the possibilities of an ecology of social practice.

The next section is an overview of northern Labrador culture-history that provides a framework for positioning the data and interpretations presented in the following chapters. There has been no systematic updated overview of Labrador culture-history since a series of papers published in 1978 (*Arctic Anthropology*) and 1980 (*Arctic*), so that 25 year old framework must still be used as a point of reference. But since the goal of this volume is primarily analysis and interpretation rather than revamping the culture-history, this basic framework is adequate for the task at hand.

Outline of Central and Northern Labrador Culture-History

Figure 2 presents an outline of central and northern Labrador culture-history. Following the tradition with such charts, there is a basic division between Innu/pre-contact Indian and Inuit/Paleoeskimo cultures as well as a distinction between the central coast (Hamilton Inlet) and north coast sequences. The textual overview is weighted towards the north coast and some of the problems discussed in this volume. It is divided into separate Innu/pre-contact Indian and Inuit/Pre-Inuit ("Eskimo") sequences.

Innu/Pre-Contact Indian Sequence
Maritime Archaic
Whether considered as late Paleo-Indian or Early Archaic, populations ancestral to the Maritime Archaic probably colonized southern Labrador by ca. 8500 B.P.. Their assemblages are marked by triangular points of quartz and quartzite, small quartz scrapers and bipolar cores (McGhee and Tuck 1975; Renouf 1977). The archaeological record of the Labrador side of the Strait of Belle Isle shows a subsequent continuous development through the Middle and Late Archaic, as seen in a shift from nipple-based points to forms with well-defined stems (McGhee and Tuck 1975). The distinctive mortuary ceremonialism that is one of the defining characteristics of the Maritime Archaic first appears at the L'Anse Amour burial mound, dated ca. 7500 B.P. (McGhee and Tuck 1975). By 7500-7000 B.P., Early Maritime Archaic populations were present on the central coast of Labrador at Hamilton Inlet

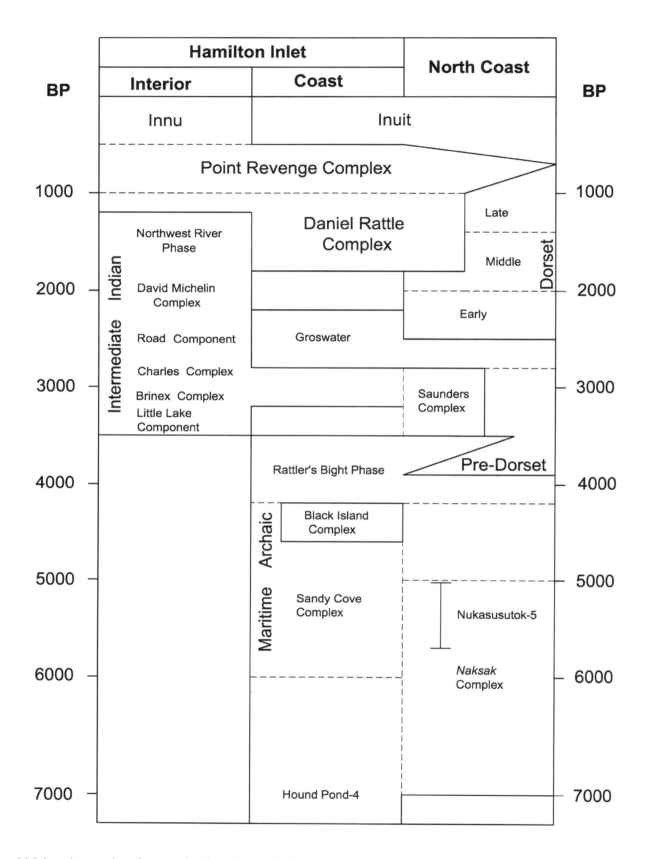

2/ Culture-history chart for central and northern Labrador.

(Fitzhugh 1978a:69) and in the Nain region at Ballybrack-10, where two burial mounds resembling those at L'Anse Amour were excavated (Fitzhugh 1978a:82, 86-87). Ballybrack Mound-2 was dated 7065±70 B.P..

The Early to Middle Maritime Archaic in the Nain and Okak regions was grouped within a vaguely defined *Naksak Complex* (Fitzhugh 1978a:72) which extended from 7000-5000 B.P.. The earliest components contain nipple-based points, lanceolate bi-pointed bifaces, triangular points and side-notched bifaces of Ramah chert, quartz and quartzite, endscrapers of Mugford chert, a ground slate component of celts, adzes and gouges, with occasional ulus and projectile points, and a high frequency of bipolar cores *(pièces esquillées)*. Lithic raw materials are dominated by quartz, although this is mostly used for flake production through bipolar percussion, but there are also varying quantities of Ramah chert, Mugford cherts, slate and quartzite (Fitzhugh 1978a:72). Sites of the partly overlapping Sandy Cove Complex (6000-4500 B.P.) at Hamilton Inlet exhibit similarities in stemmed points and in the predominance of quartz debitage and bipolar cores, but they lack endscrapers. Moderate frequencies of Ramah chert in the Nain area sites indicate regular excursions to the chert sources at Ramah Bay 300 km to the north, but the paucity of Ramah chert at Hamilton Inlet suggests that supply lines were mostly restricted to the north at this time.

A raised beach sequence at Aillik, near Makkovik, in combination with several other localities, produced evidence of temporal changes in the form of Maritime Archaic dwelling structures (Fitzhugh 1984). Prior to 6000 B.P., dwellings consisted of small boulder pit-houses, 3.0-3.5 m in diameter, and rectangular surface tent rings partitioned into two to five segments by rock dividers. Fitzhugh (2002:7) reports a radiocarbon date of 6870±180 B.P. for a 10 m long, four segment structure at Aillik, and a date of 6400±110 B.P. from an 8 m long, five segment structure from the same beach level. During the course of the sixth millennium B.P.

there was a development towards larger rectangular structures 9-16 m long divided into three or four segments (Fitzhugh 1984, 1985a). The pit-houses and rectangular structures may represent spring and fall sites (Fitzhugh 1985a:88), but the settlement pattern of the Early-Middle Maritime Archaic is by no means clear. The general model has been one of outer coastal settlement from spring to fall and inner bay settlement in fall and winter (Fitzhugh 1978a:83-84), but the limited work in the inner bays and near interior has not produced evidence for probable winter sites, although new Maritime Archaic localities have been identified (Labrèche et al. 1997; Loring 2001).

The period between 5000-4200 B.P. is perhaps the most poorly known part of the northern Labrador Maritime Archaic sequence. Components dated to this time have been identified in the Nain and Okak regions (Cox 1977:184-194; Fitzhugh 1978a:77), with the general impression that they exhibit stylistic development towards later Rattlers Bight Phase tool forms. At Hamilton Inlet there is an intrusion of southern Labrador-affiliated Maritime Archaic material between 4500-4200 B.P.— the Black Island Complex (Fitzhugh 1975, 1978a:69-70)— marked by side-notched projectile points and rhyolitic chert raw materials. Linear distributions of hearths at Okak-2 and Black Island-2 suggest the use of longhouse tent dwellings ranging from 30-50 m long (Fitzhugh 1981:17-18).

The Late Maritime Archaic Rattlers Bight Phase (4200-3500 B.P.) is the most thoroughly investigated part of the Maritime Archaic time sequence, mainly through excavations of large habitation sites at Hamilton Inlet (Fitzhugh 1972, 1975, 1978a) and at Nulliak Cove north of Hebron Fjord (Fitzhugh 1981, 1984, 1985a). At Rattlers Bight in Hamilton Inlet a small cemetery consisting of nine red ocher burials had grave goods that included chunks and tools of Ramah chert, soapstone implements, ground slate tools, mica sheets and copper. Differences in the distribution of grave goods between the burials led Fitzhugh (1978a:85, 2002) to suggest some degree of status differentiation. At Nulliak Cove, two of four boulder-constructed burial mounds were excavated. Mound 1 contained ca. 90 artifacts in a red ocher-lined pit, including Ramah chert points and bifaces, slate celts and mica sheets, while Mound 2 contained fewer grave goods: a Ramah chert point, a copper pendant, mica and a walrus tusk (Fitzhugh 1981:12, 2002). From the same period, the Port au Choix cemetery on the west coast of Newfoundland contained the remains of 100 individuals (Tuck 1976). During this phase the Labrador flaked stone technology was almost totally composed of Ramah chert. The occurrence of Ramah chert in contemporary sites along the U.S. east coast, as well as the presence in Labrador Maritime Archaic sites of non-local materials such as soapstone, mica and copper, indicates the operation of widespread exchange systems.

The apparent increase in the size of Maritime Archaic dwellings noted after 5000 B.P. reached its peak in the Rattlers Bight Phase, with longhouse features ranging in size from 15-100 m long. In most cases these have been inferred from linear distributions of hearths and lithic materials representing the remains of surface tent structures, but in one exemplary case at Aillik (Makkovik) a 28 m long structure divided into seven internal segments was excavated into a cobble beach (Fitzhugh 1981, 1984, 1985a). If the marked segments and hearth-centered lithic distributions can be interpreted as individual family living floors, then these longhouses may have housed 50-100 individuals (Fitzhugh 1984:20). At Nulliak Cove, north of Hebron Fjord, there are traces of 27 such structures, suggesting the site was a repeatedly used staging area for expeditions to the Ramah chert quarries (Fitzhugh 1985b:49-50). Seen as a whole, the evidence for large co-residential groups, mortuary distinctions and exchange systems has suggested some form of social "complexity" had developed during the Late Maritime Archaic, although it is by no means clear how that complexity should be characterized (Fitzhugh 1981, 1985a, 2002, 2006; Hood 1993, 1995).

The disappearance of the northern Labrador Maritime Archaic from the archaeological record after 3500 B.P. remains one of the most vexing problems in Labrador prehistory. This occurred after a several hundred year co-existence with the Pre-Dorset Paleoeskimo people, who colonized Labrador ca. 4000 B.P.. About the time the Maritime Archaic disappeared another Indian sequence began: a series of Intermediate Indian complexes.

Intermediate Indians

The Intermediate Indian period of Labrador began ca. 3500 B.P. and continued until 1500 B.P. at Hamilton Inlet, but only until 2800 B.P. on the north-central coast (Fitzhugh 1972; Nagle 1978). The Hamilton Inlet sequence is marked by a discontinuous series of six archaeological units. Most of these assemblages are dominated by interior cherts and quartzites which, together with implement styles, suggest affiliation with interior-based cultural traditions. On the north-central coast another archaeological unit has been defined: the Saunders Complex (3500-2800 B.P.). This complex has stylistic similarities with the Brinex and Charles Complexes at Hamilton Inlet, but contains considerable quantities of chert from the Cape Mugford region north of Okak Bay. Sites consist of cobble hearths and lithic scatters and occur mostly in inner bay and inner island contexts. Traces of the Saunders Complex have been found as far north as Hebron Fjord (Hood 1998a; Nagle 1978). This coastal activity opens up the possibilities for interactions with Late Pre-Dorset peoples. After the disappearance of the Saunders Complex there is, as yet, no archaeological evidence for Indian occupation of the north-central coast until the Late Pre-Contact Period.

Late Pre-Contact Indians

The Late Pre-Contact Indian occupation of central and northern Labrador has been divided into two archaeological units. The Daniel Rattle Complex (1800-1000 B.P.) differs from the earlier Intermediate Indian complexes in its near exclusive use of Ramah chert for stone tools. Its settlement pattern is broadly similar to the preceding Saunders Complex, with most sites situated in inner bay and inner island locations, but there are also sites on exposed headlands suggestive of greater use of marine resources. No sites have been found north of the Nain area. Traces of large tent structures resembling the ethnographically documented Innu *shaputuan* have been identified; these were multi-family longhouses that could be used for ritual purposes. Given the contemporary presence of Middle Dorset occupation in the Nain region and the rest of northern Labrador, the heavy use of Ramah chert by Daniel Rattle groups raises questions concerning the role of Dorset peoples in chert acquisition (Loring 1992:329-342).

The Point Revenge Complex (1000-400 B.P.) developed out of the Daniel Rattle Complex and must represent an ancestral Innu population. Settlement sites are found as far north as Nain, while trace occurrences of Point Revenge material are found as far north as Saglek Bay. Settlement remains include a large tent ring (Fitzhugh 1978b), hearths and concentrations of crushed calcined bone. Like Daniel Rattle, Point Revenge sites are also marked by near-exclusive use of Ramah chert, so questions of cultural interaction with Late Dorset and Thule populations are pertinent (Loring 1992:343-408).

Inuit/Pre-Inuit Sequence

Pre-Dorset
The Pre-Dorset colonization of northern Labrador ca. 4000 B.P. (Fitzhugh (2002:142, 145; 2006) marks the first arrival of Paleoeskimo people in northern Labrador. They brought with them an Arctic Small Tool Tradition technology composed of microblades, burins and harpoon delivery systems that differed radically from their Maritime Archaic contemporaries. Their choice of lithic materials was heavily weighted towards the fine-grained cherts found in the Cape Mugford region north of Okak, although varying amounts of

Ramah chert and slate were also employed. Early Pre-Dorset materials are mostly found in northern Labrador as far south as the Nain area; the southern-most site is situated at Windy Tickle north of Hopedale (Fitzhugh 1977:21). Late Pre-Dorset sites (3500-2800 B.P.) are relatively few, but this may be partly a visibility problem resulting from limited typological change over time and few radiocarbon dates (Cox 1978, 1988). By 3000-2800 B.P. there are clear indications that Pre-Dorset began developing *in situ* into what is termed the Groswater Phase.

Pre-Dorset settlement patterns are assumed to be similar to those of the Maritime Archaic, involving spring-fall occupation of outer coastal areas and fall-winter use of the inner bay areas. But as with the Maritime Archaic there are no convincing candidates for inner bay winter sites. Compared with the Late Maritime Archaic multi-family longhouse settlements, Pre-Dorset sites are small, consisting of 1-3 tent dwellings. In some cases Pre-Dorset sites consist only of lithic scatters, in other cases traces of a hearth or tent ring may be present. Several well-preserved axial structures with box-hearths and heating rocks have been identified.

Pre-Dorset and Maritime Archaic populations overlapped between 4000-3500 B.P.. The social boundary relationship between the two cultures is one of the important questions of Labrador archaeology and may be an significant factor in the eventual disappearance of the Maritime Archaic. Similar boundary questions might be raised regarding Pre-Dorset and the Intermediate Indian Saunders Complex.

Groswater Phase
By 2800 B.P. the stylistic changes in Late Pre-Dorset are sufficient to mark the emergence of the Groswater Phase. Microblades increase in frequency, distinctive side-notched flat-based harpoon endblades appear, as does an array of side-notched bifaces, while burins are now side-notched and facially ground. Lithic materials consist of a combination of radiolarian cherts from the

Newfoundland west coast and Ramah chert. Groswater settlement is concentrated in Newfoundland, southern Labrador and the central Labrador coast north to Postville. Relatively few Groswater localities have been registered on the north coast of Labrador. Settlement patterns are characterized as similar to Pre-Dorset, with spring-fall occupation of the outer coast and fall-winter sites in the inner bays. In this case, however, there is at least one good candidate for an inner bay winter site, at Postville on Kaipokok Bay (Loring and Cox 1986). Groswater dwellings consist of slab pavements with box-hearths (Cox 1978; Fitzhugh 1972; Loring and Cox 1986). Labrador Groswater has been dated as late as 2200 B.P..

Dorset

About 2500 B.P., populations similar to central Arctic Early Dorset colonized northern Labrador, moving as far south as the Nain-Okak regions. Early Dorset differed substantially from Groswater, with whom they overlapped for a few hundred years. The Early Dorset (2500-2000 B.P.) tool assemblage included tip-fluted harpoon endblades, nephrite burin-like tools, soapstone vessels and near-exclusive use of Ramah chert for flaked tools. They also utilized semi-subterranean winter houses (Cox 1978). Relatively few Early Dorset sites have been registered; the major localities are located at Okak and Seven Islands Bay in the northern Torngat Mountain region (Fitzhugh 1980). It is not certain whether Early Dorset developed locally into the Middle Dorset phase (2000-1400 B.P.), but the large number of Middle Dorset sites constitute the most extensive Dorset occupation of the Labrador coast. Traces between Nain and Hamilton Inlet are limited, but several sites are known along the coast south of Hamilton Inlet (Stopp 1997). This was also a period of major Dorset activity on the island of Newfoundland (Renouf 1993). Middle Dorset settlement patterns were anchored at winter semi-subterranean house sites, often in outer island locations within several kilometers of the landfast ice-edge. Some of these sites seem to have been based on fall-early winter sealing, with mid-winter to early spring movement to camps closer to the ice-edge, while others contain significant components of walrus that suggest occupation in mid-winter and spring (Cox and Spiess 1980). Cox and Spiess (1980) suggested that Middle Dorset lacked breathing hole sealing techniques. Spring-fall settlement, associated with tent ring dwellings, was spread over outer and inner coastal islands in the Nain and Okak areas. The degree to which the inner bays and fjords were used seems to vary regionally, although this may be an artifact of survey coverage. Middle Dorset sites are virtually absent from the inner bays of the Nain region and are sparse on the inner islands. At Okak sites are also lacking in the inner bays but they are common on the inner islands. There is little evidence of Dorset activity in the inner reaches of Saglek Bay (Thomson 1986), but sod houses are known from inner fjord locations at Nachvak and Hebron (Cox and Spiess 1980; Fitzhugh 1980; Hood 1998a). Analysis of the distribution patterns of Ramah chert, soapstone, and Newfoundland cherts indicates the operation of exchange networks and population movement along the Labrador coast (Nagle 1984).

Late Dorset (1400-800 B.P.) occupation of Labrador was less extensive than during the Middle Dorset Period, being limited to the Nain region and northwards. There were shifts in tool types and settlement characteristics that raise questions about cultural continuity with Middle Dorset. Semi-subterranean houses were shallower and lacked middens, suggesting use limited to fall and early winter, with mid-winter to spring use of snow houses (Cox 1978; Fitzhugh 1980). The presence of Ramah chert-using Late Pre-Contact Indian groups along the central coast and in the Nain-Okak areas during both the Middle and Late Dorset periods means that questions of social boundaries and interaction need to be considered.

Thule/Inuit

The earliest dates attributed to the Thule colonization of Labrador range between 800-600 B.P. (AD 1000-1400; Fitzhugh 1994), but the tendency of Thule to re-occupy Late Dorset house sites raises problems of dating context. At present it seems best to regard the earliest dates as uncertain and the Thule arrival in Labrador as dating sometime after AD 1250-1300. Given the dating problems it is uncertain whether early Thule peoples would have encountered Late Dorset populations in northern Labrador. The Thule culture brought to Labrador a very different organizational system than that found in Dorset, marked by bowhead whale hunting and the expanded transport possibilities of dog sleds and large boats *(umiaks)*. During the earliest period of Thule/Inuit occupation (AD 1300-1600), their winter settlements were marked by round houses constructed of stone, wood, whalebone and sod, with entrance passages, cold traps and rear sleeping platforms. Sometimes houses shared a common entrance passage. Snow houses were also used during the winter and in the spring, and tent dwellings and stone-walled shelters from spring to fall. Lack of bone preservation in the middens limits the range of inferences that can be drawn concerning subsistence-settlement patterns, but sea mammal exploitation was probably central. Tools of organic materials are also poorly preserved, but the lithic material is marked by drilled slate harpoon endblades, ulus, nephrite tools, and soapstone vessels (Kaplan 1983:216-230). Early Contact Period Thule is represented in the Nain region by sod houses at the Iglosiatik-1 site, some with traces of metal, that apparently date to the early 16th century (Fitzhugh 1994:258; Kaplan 1983:216, 455-462).

R. Jordan (1977, 1978) and Jordan and Kaplan (1980) maintained that the 17th century Inuit settlement in Hamilton Inlet represented the southernmost permanent Inuit occupation and that Inuit activity in southern Labrador during the 16th-18th centuries was limited to seasonal trading with Europeans and the raiding of their establishments. But documentary information and archaeological data suggest the Inuit presence in southern Labrador was a more substantial year-round occupation that began in the mid-1500s, concomitant with expanding European fishing and whaling (Basque, French, English, Portugese and Spanish) and lasted until the mid-1700s, when the increasing scale of European activity may have led to a contraction of Inuit occupancy towards Hamilton Inlet (Auger 1991; Martijn and Clermont 1980; Stopp 2002). The 17th century Inuit settlement of the north-central coast was marked by houses similar to Thule forms and the continued use of lithic tools, except at Hamilton Inlet where slate and nephrite were replaced by metal. European goods, possibly Basque and Dutch, were common at Hamilton Inlet and Hopedale, but generally rare further north (Kaplan 1983:230-235).

During the 18th century a series of changes occurred, with a shift towards larger multi-family communal houses in northern Labrador and increasing replacement of traditional material culture with European goods. These goods were obtained from French traders at Chateau Bay and Hamilton Inlet and then later from English traders in the Cape Charles region and the Moravian missionary centers that were established in north-central Labrador in the years after 1771. The multi-family households were sometimes led by "big-man" traders, middlemen in the baleen trade with the Europeans (R. Jordan 1978; Jordan and Kaplan 1980; Kaplan 1983, 1985; Taylor 1974). Christianization of most of the north-central coast Inuit occurred by the second decade of the 19th century, which resulted in a seasonal centralization of settlement at the missions and a shift to single-family housing. But non-Christian Inuit continued to dominate northernmost Labrador until the gradual establishment of more northerly missions in 1830 and thereafter (Loring 1998).

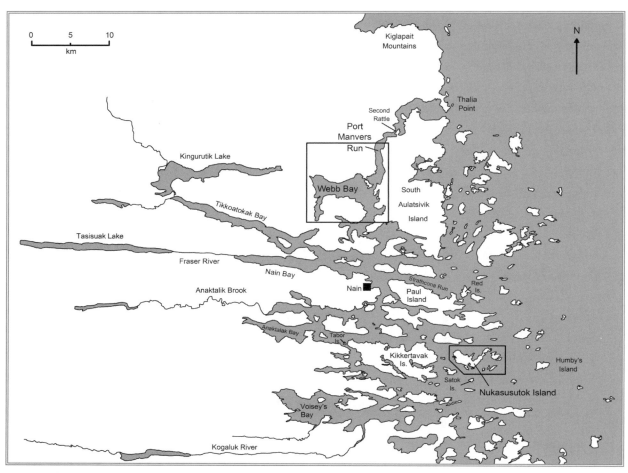

3/ Map of the Nain Region. Original map © 2004 produced under licence from Her Majesty the Queen in Right of Canada, with permission of Natural Resources Canada.

Environment of the Nain Region

Labrador is a land of sharp contrasts. Its coast is an almost 1200 km long ecotone in which arctic and sub-arctic environments are juxtaposed. The cold south-ward flowing Labrador Current carries pack ice along the coast and contributes to the formation of extensive landfast ice during the winter. A narrow coastal strip of tundra vegetation extends all the way from Killinek in the north to the Strait of Belle Isle in the south. In con-trast, the vast interior is covered with boreal forest, bogs and innumerable lakes. The present northern limit of trees is located at Napartok Bay, 130 km north of Nain (Figure 1; Elliott and Short 1979).

Paralleling this environmental contrast is a cultur-al juxtaposition. Broadly speaking, during the post-contact period, Inuit people have been associated pri-marily with the coastal tundra zone, although they have used the interior seasonally. Innu ("Naskapi") peo-ple have focused their land use on the subarctic interi-or and the inner bays and islands of the coastal zone. The shifting relationship between these ecological and cultural boundaries is a central theme in Labrador archaeology.

This chapter begins with a geographical overview of the Nain region, then moves on to outline its bedrock and Quaternary geology. After a brief synop-sis of paleoenvironmental changes evident in pollen core data, a summary of historic land-use in the Nain region is presented. This is followed by more specific descriptions of two areas: Nukasusutok Island and Webb Bay/Port Manvers Run.

OVERVIEW OF THE NAIN REGION

The town of Nain is presently the northernmost perma-nent community in Labrador. The surrounding coastal region (Figure 3) is an archipelago of over two hundred islands that range in size from the smallest of skerries to the massive bulk of 140 km long South Aulatsivik Island. The higher elevations on these islands mostly range from 250-500 m, although Mt. Thoresby at the north end of South Aulatsivik Island rises to ca. 900 m. Passages between the islands vary from wide expans-es of deep water to narrow, shoal, tidal "rattles." The region can be categorized into three major ecological zones: outer islands, inner islands and bays, and the interior plateau. The outer island fringe is composed of numerous windswept islands with predominantly tundra vegetation. The inner island belt consists of several large and numerous small islands which bear scrub birch and willow vegetation and stands of black spruce in sheltered areas. The spruce-forested inner bays cut into the edge of the interior plateau and sev-eral river valleys extend inland from the bays, provid-ing transportation routes into the interior. The most important of these are the Fraser River, west of Nain, and the Kogaluk River (*Emish-shipu* is the Innu toponym) to the southwest of Nain in the Voisey's Bay region. Most of the interior plateau ranges in elevation from 250-350 m and has a predominantly tundra veg-etation. The Kiglapait Mountains constitute a border with the Okak region to the north; these peaks range over 800 m.

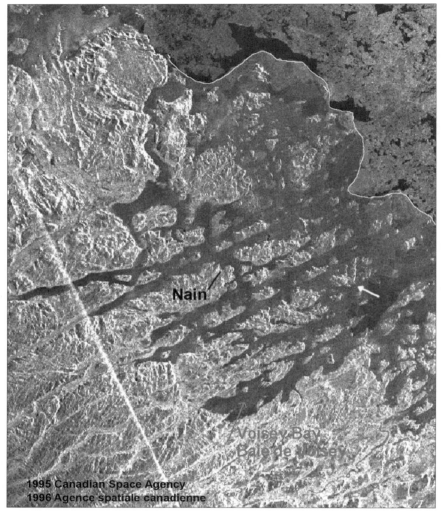

4/ RADARSAT synthetic aperture radar satellite photo of the Nain district. Taken March 20, 1996. Open water areas in black; gray line marks the edge of the landfast ice (sîna); white arrow indicates Nukasusutok Island. Photo supplied by the Canadian Ice Service, © Canadian Space Agency

Tanner (1944:289) described summers on the Labrador coast as "characterized by exceedingly unstable weather" because of the constant shift between warm continental and cold maritime conditions. Although this was certainly the case during the 1979 fieldwork, during the 1990s there have been extended periods of warm dry conditions. Late in August and into September northeasterly gales occur frequently. Snow may begin to fall in mid-September.

One of the most important environmental factors for humans along the Labrador coast is ice distribution. There are two different types of ice: pack ice and landfast ice. Pack ice drifts southward along the Labrador Current. The position of the pack ice is dependent on wind conditions; westerlies disperse the ice, pushing it out to sea, but easterlies push it against the coastline and the landfast ice. Pack ice generally disappears by early to mid-July, although with consistent onshore winds it can persist into August. Besides being a navigational hazard, pack ice is important because seals, walrus and polar bears usually follow its movements.

Climatically, the north coast of Labrador is affected by both continental and maritime air masses. During the summer westerly winds may bring warm dry weather from the interior; during the winter they are usually the purveyors of cold and predominantly clear conditions. Easterly winds bring cold weather in summer, relatively warm conditions in winter and carry most of the precipitation in both seasons (Tanner 1944:302-308). The January temperature at Hopedale (the closest long-term meteorological station to Nain) averages -16.4 C and the August average is 10.6 C. Total precipitation amounts to 822 mm annually and the average winter snowfall is 445 cm (Environment Canada 2002).

Landfast ice is attached to the landmass of the bays and islands and extends seaward after freeze-up. In Nain the average freeze-up occurs by December 10, while an early freeze-up could occur in late November. Ice that is safe for human travel by dog sled or snowmobile may extend 40 to 50 km east from Nain, depending on the presence of islands which facilitate anchoring. At the outer edge of the landfast ice there may be open water, known as the *sîna*, in which sea mammals may be hunted from the ice edge or with kayaks. Frequently, however, the pack ice may drift up against the landfast ice and eliminate these open water areas. The position of the *sîna* varies annually and monthly; Figure 4 is a RADARSAT synthetic aperture radar satellite photo that shows the contact zone between the landfast and pack ice on March 20, 1996. Strong currents in tidal "rattles" maintain polynyas, open areas within the landfast ice. In the Nain area such regular open water areas can be found near the eastern ends of Strathcona and Harmony Runs, the "Second Rattle" on Port Manvers Run, near Tabor Island and the narrows at Tikkoatokak Bay. More variable openings occur in other areas. The satellite photo shows that the area between Nukasusutok Island, Humby's Island and Iglosiatik Island had relatively thin ice in March. The ice in this area tends to thin out quickly in the spring sun and develop early openings because of ocean swells. Break-up of the landfast ice generally occurs in mid-June, but pack ice can block navigation well after this date. In both 1992 and 1993 it was almost August before the first coastal freight boat could make its way up the coast to Nain.

Bedrock Geology of the Nain Region

The earliest rocks of the northern Labrador coast are the gneisses of the Archean Nain Province (> 2.5 Ga). In the Nain region, these outcrop primarily in a band between Okak and Webb Bay. Otherwise, most of the rocks that make up the Nain archipelago are part of the Middle Proterozoic Nain Plutonic Suite (1.6-1.0 Ga), which consists mostly of anorthosite, troctolite, diorite and granite (Ryan 1990; Ryan et al. 1995). This bedrock geology does not provide a great deal of raw material that would be sought after by stone knappers. Vein quartz is abundant throughout the region and was used frequently in the Early-Middle periods of the Maritime Archaic. A particularly large quartz vein occurs on one of the Red Islands, east of Paul Island. A

prehistorically quarried quartz crystal outcrop, possibly used by Pre-Dorset, is located on "No-Name Island" just east of Nukasusutok Island (Fitzhugh 1981:30).

Aside from those mentioned above, virtually all the lithic materials required for prehistoric technology had to be acquired from outside the Nain region. Ramah chert, used extensively by the Maritime Archaic, Dorset and Pre-Innu peoples, is derived from the Ramah Group, which outcrops between Ramah Bay and Nachvak Fiord, ca. 300 km north of Nain (Gramly 1978; Lazenby 1980). Mugford chert, used extensively by Pre-Dorset, but also by Early/Middle Maritime Archaic and Intermediate Indian peoples, is found in the Mugford Group, 150 km north of Nain between Okak and Napartok Bay (Gramly 1978; Lazenby 1980). Slates were used for ground tools by the Maritime Archaic, the Thule/Inuit and occasionally by Dorset peoples. Specific slate sources have not been identified, but it is likely that many slates were derived from the Mugford Group.

Soapstone sources in central and northern Labrador have been documented from an archaeological perspective by Nagle (1984) and from an economic geology perspective by Meyer and Montague (1993, 1994, 1995). No soapstone sources are currently known in the Nain area. The place name Soapstone Tickle, between the Red Islands, hints at a possible source, but the location is not known to local carvers. Otherwise, the nearest sources of soapstone are either 100 km north of Nain in the Okak region or 80 km to the south at Freestone Harbour near Utshimassits (Davis Inlet).

Paleoenvironmental Change

The post-glacial marine emergence chronology of the Nain area is based largely on radiocarbon dated archaeological sites on raised beaches (Fitzhugh 1977, Clark and Fitzhugh 1990, 1992). The oldest radiocarbon date in the area is 7800±130 B.P. (reservoir corrected 7760±65 B.P.) on a geological sample of marine shells from 36 m on South Aulatsivik Island (Johnson

1985:75; Clark and Fitzhugh 1990:301). The earliest archaeological radiocarbon date is 7065±70 B.P. from the Early Maritime Archaic Ballybrack-10 site, located at 41 m on South Aulatsivik Island (Fitzhugh 1978:85; Clark and Fitzhugh 1990:301). When these dates and elevations are linked with later dates from archaeological sites as well as a marine limit determination of 71 m, the estimated uplift curve suggests a date of ca. 8500 B.P. for the marine limit and the deglaciation of the outer coast of the Nain archipelago (Clark and Fitzhugh 1990:302).

There have been suggestions that uplift rates differ between the outer coast and the inner bays. According to Clark and Fitzhugh (1992:200) for Hamilton Inlet and Johnson (1985:74) for the Torngat Mountain region, the inner bay marine limit is younger and lower. In the Nain area, Johnson (1969:110) identified the marine limit at Webb Bay as lying at 41 m, substantially lower than the 71 m determined ca. 22 km to the east on South Aulatsivik Island. More recent investigations along Reid Brook between inner Voisey's Bay and inner Anaktalak Bay— south and 15 km west of Johnson's research area— place the marine limit at 93±2 m and provide a radiocarbon date of 7580±70 B.P. (7485±45 B.P., reservoir corrected) for marine shell at 50 m (Bell 1997). Johnson's marine limit must therefore be incorrect and the proposed differences in outer/inner coast uplift regimes are contradicted by the new data from Voisey's Bay.

Figure 5 depicts the relative sea level curve presented by Clark and Fitzhugh (1990) together with Bell's (1997) suggested curve for Voisey's Bay. The latter should be treated with caution since it is a simple exponential projection based on the local marine limit, the single radiocarbon date and undated marine terrace elevations. Nonetheless, the Voisey's Bay curve suggests greater uplift in the inland area, which would be expected from an ice sheet that was thicker inland and thinning towards the coast. The archaeological

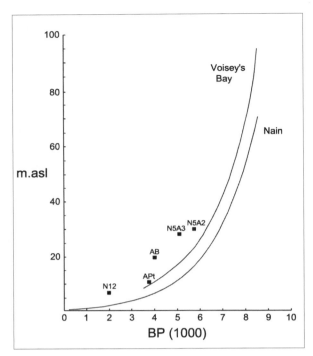

5/ Relative sea level curves for Nain and inner Voisey's Bay (after Clark and Fitzhugh 1990 and Bell 1997). Sites marked: Nukasusutok-5, Area 2 (N5A2), Nukasusutok-5, Area 3 (N5A3), Attu's Bight (AB), Attu's Point (AP) and Nukasusutok 12 (N12).

study area at Webb Bay probably lies somewhere between these uplift profiles. Some of the archaeological sites discussed in the text are marked on the diagram; their positioning will be discussed later.

During the 1970s, interest in the relationship between climate change and culture change (e.g., Fitzhugh 1972, 1977a) was pursued through the collection of pollen data from several locations in northern and central Labrador. As part of this program, one core was taken from Nain Pond (Short 1978), but it proved problematic because of reversed datings in the stratigraphic sequence. Similarities with cores taken in the Okak area, however, permitted reasonable extrapolations. Cores were also taken in 1939 by Wenner (1947), but these are of limited utility since they predate the use of radiocarbon dating. Generally, the pollen data indicate the area was deglaciated by 10,500 B.P. and that by 9000 B.P. the ice front stood

[1]cf. Tanner's (1944:245) determination of the marine limit at 83 m on Sandy Island, 20 km east of South Aulatsivik Island.

on the interior plateau, at least 100 km from the coast. The post-glacial period was marked by tundra vegetation until a transition to shrub tundra with a strong birch and alder component ca. 6700-6500 B.P.. After 4500 B.P., an open spruce woodland was present. Climatic cooling is indicated after 3500 B.P. (Short 1978:32).

Initial efforts at dendrochronology in the Nain area began in the early 1970s, but the information only extended back to 1769 (H.E. Wright, International Dendrochronological Data Base, National Oceanic and Atmospheric Administration [NOAA] 2003). Additional data are currently being collected, but the work is still at a preliminary stage. The other source of climate-related information is the oxygen isotope data from the Greenland ice cores. These data provide much higher chronological resolution than the pollen cores, but their high frequency variations can be difficult to interpret and attempts to correlate them with coarsely dated archaeological entities are problematic. In Chapter 14, ice core and pollen data are combined to discuss environmental changes relevant to understanding shifts in Maritime Archaic settlement and the social boundary problems subsequent to Pre-Dorset colonization.

Recent Seasonal Resource Use in the Nain Region

Brice-Bennett (1977) outlines the seasonal variations in Nain region fauna and the concomitant patterning of human activities during the 20th century. The following discussion is based on her account as well as Taylor (1974), with supplemental information derived from local informants and personal observation. The coastal resources are discussed first, followed by inner bay/interior species.

In early spring Canada geese and various migratory duck species return north and are hunted in early to mid-May. Later in the spring and the early summer, eggs are collected from duck and gull nesting areas. After break-up in mid-June, the migratory harp seal

moves north from its whelping grounds off Newfoundland following schools of capelin. Large numbers can be netted or shot as they enter the bays traveling in herds. Although most of the harps summer off west Greenland they can occasionally be found in Labrador waters during the summer. The ringed seal is present year round in the Nain area, although ecological studies by Boles et al. (1980:54) suggest that during the summer some may migrate from the central coast to locations north of Okak. Harbor and grey seals haul out on seaward islands in the spring and break-up is said to be a good time for hunting bearded seals. During the open water season seals are most frequently encountered in the outer island areas, but many move up the bays with high tide.

Fishing was the major summer activity in the Nain area until the recent downturn in fish stocks. Arctic char begin their seaward runs from the rivers in early June and spend the summer among the islands until mid-August, when they return upriver to spawn. Salmon are fished in late July and August and cod in August and September. Minke and white whales are seen occasionally. Bowhead whales once frequented the Labrador coast, although they were rarely hunted by 18th century Inuit in the Nain area, possibly because poor bathymetric conditions reduced the likelihood of their entering the bays (Taylor 1988:125).

In the fall, Canada geese are pursued beginning the last week of August. Their main southward movement occurs in mid-September and few remain after October 25. Ducks and various sea birds are also exploited. In September, ringed, young bearded, grey and harbour seals move into the bays to feed. Brice-Bennett (1977:144) notes that the beginning of the harp seal southern migration varies from late September or October to late November or December. The later the commencement of the migration the more likely it is that the harps will stay seaward to avoid the already frozen coastal areas. Late 18th and early 19th century Inuit settlements tended to be located in good locations for fall harp sealing (Taylor

1974:51) and numerous references in the Moravian Periodical Accounts make clear the importance of the fall seal hunt for storing up supplies for the winter.

When ice formation begins in the bays, most of the seals that had previously been feeding there shift seaward. Those that are trapped in the bays after freeze-up are hunted basking on the ice, through their breathing holes or in patches of open water. During the winter, ringed seals are found in open water at the *sîna* and at breathing holes. March is the worst month for sealing because pack ice jams against the landfast ice and eliminates the leads of open water. Come April, ringed seals may be encountered basking on the ice beside their breathing holes or at the *sîna*.

Walrus are rare today in the Nain region, but they formerly appeared at the *sîna* in February and March. Polar bears move south with the pack ice, inhabiting the *sîna* and coastal headlands from March until May. If the pack ice lingers until later in the summer, both polar bears and walrus may be found occasionally near the outer islands, although the bears sometimes wander as far up the bays as Tikkoatokak.

Caribou is the main resource exploited by humans in the inner bays and on the interior plateau. Although they may be hunted at any time of the year, their hides are best for clothing in September and October. Brice-Bennett (1977:158-159) notes the winter core areas for interior caribou herds, the nearest concentrations to Nain being in the Kiglapait Mountains, near Kingurutik Lake and between Tasisuak Lake and Anaktalik Brook. The geographical range of caribou varies over time. Prior to the mid-1960s, caribou primarily frequented the interior plateau, requiring lengthy hunting trips inland (Brice-Bennett 1977:155). For example, in 1780 Moravian missionary William Turner accompanied Inuit caribou hunters on two trips up the Fraser River valley and onto the plateau, up to 80 km inland from Nain (Taylor 1969). At this time, prior to the Inuit accessing firearms, the Inuit brought kayaks inland on their late summer hunt (August-September) and travelled with dog sleds on a winter hunt (February). Meat might be cached for emergency use later in the winter. In more recent years, large caribou herds have moved out towards the coast, crossing over the sea ice to the outer islands. Most of these animals return inland before break-up, but some are trapped on the islands for the summer. Caribou are also encountered sporadically in the inner bays between spring and fall.

Other animal species found in the interior or along the inner bays include: black bear, fox, wolf, arctic hare, wolverine, otter, mink, muskrat and lynx. Black bears, hare and fox can also be found on some of the larger coastal islands. During the winter, wolves may move over the sea ice to the islands in pursuit of caribou. The economically significant terrestrial birds are rock and spruce ptarmigan, which today are hunted in April/May when there is a heavy snow cover and it is still possible to travel over the sea ice.

Nukasusutok Island

Nukasusutok Island (*NaKasêtjutôk* in the current orthography) is located about 30 km southeast of Nain. According to Wheeler (1953:62-63), the island's Inuktitut name means "the place where the brothers quarreled." That name may be illuminated by ethnohistoric information suggesting that during the 18th century brothers rarely shared households because of conflicts over authority within multi-family communal houses (Taylor 1974:82).

The island (Figures 3, 16) is approximately 10 km in length (east-west). It is indented on the north and the south by two bays; the southern bay is commonly known as Wyatt Harbour. According to geologist E. P. Wheeler II (cited in Morse 1971:94), Commander A.B. N. Wyatt of the British Navy survey ship *Challenger* (see Wyatt 1934) attested to the fine anchoring qualities of these embayments by maintaining— doubtless with a degree of exaggeration— that the entire British Navy could be accommodated here. Less expansive, Morse (1971:95) noted that Wyatt Harbour is among the finest on the coast of Labrador. These bays effectively divide the island at its mid-point into two somewhat physiographically different portions. The western end of Nukasusutok is 3 km in width, contains the highest point on the island (298 m) and is generally rugged and mountainous. The eastern end is a thin northeast trending arm that ranges from 0.3 to 1.3 km in width. This extremity is less rugged than the western tip of the island, has more flat low-lying areas, and elevations do not exceed ca. 152 m. At both ends of the island most of the shoreline plunges precipitously down to the sea.

Geologically, Nukasusutok Island is part of the Middle Proterozoic Nain Plutonic Suite and is underlain by gneiss, anorthosites, intrusive troctolites, diorites and monzonites (Davies 1974; Ryan 1990; Ryan et al. 1995). A combination of faulting, intrusions and weathering has produced a topography of rounded hills punctuated in places by parallel-walled "passes." The only lithic material on the island that was of possible utility to prehistoric peoples is vein quartz, which outcrops in several places on the island.

The vegetation of Nukasusutok is primarily that of a tundra community with plant species such as lichen, willow, dwarf birch, alder, Labrador tea, crowberry, blueberry, cranberry, cloudberry and various grasses. Although the exposed eastern arm of the island is strictly a tundra environment, certain well sheltered areas on the western end maintain substantial groves of black spruce. Spruce trees at the head of Wyatt Harbour have attained heights in the neighborhood of 3.0 to 4.5 m.

The *raison d'etre* of any human occupation of Nukasusutok would be exploitation of the sea mammals, aquatic birds and fish found within the island's catchment area. Good spring sealing may be had to the southeast between Satok and Humby's Island. During the summer, seals are common in the "Bridges" passage to the west, off the east side of Kikkertavak Island and among the small islands immediately to the east of Nukasusutok. Numerous aquatic birds may be had in the area during the open water season: black and eider ducks, teals, scoters, black guillemots, loons and gulls. The small islands to the east of Nukasusutok are a particularly good area for these waterfowl. Geese are seasonal visitors and may be encountered in the larger ponds on Nukasusutok. Ptarmigan also occur there. Arctic char, tom cod and occasionally salmon may be caught in the waters surrounding Nukasusutok. Minke whales sometimes move into Wyatt Harbour to feed.

In contrast to the diverse and abundant marine fauna, Nukasusutok exhibits a paucity of terrestrial game. The arctic hare is a resident of the barren hills and several Inuit stone traps testify to the presence of fox. Caribou are known to frequent the island on rare occasions (such as 5-6 animals in 1992), crossing over the sea ice during the winter and becoming stranded after break-up. Several black bears were resident at the western end of the island in 1992.

Webb Bay/Port Manvers Run

Webb Bay is located 25 km north of the town of Nain (Figures 3 and 159). It is named after the settler family Webb, that maintains cabins at the head of the bay, but it is also known by the Inuktitut name *Udjuktôk*, place of bearded seals (Wheeler 1953:94-95). Extending 15 km east-west by 3-7 km wide, Webb Bay is separated from the outer coast by South Aulatsivik Island, the largest island in the Nain archipelago. Access by boat is either from the south through the "First Rattle" at the tip of the Itilialuk Peninsula, or from the north via Port Manvers Run. The latter is a fjord-like passage that swings around the western side of South Aulatsivik and enters the sea at Thalia Point *(Tikigâtsuk)*. The Run is significant as a transportation route because it constitutes an "inner passage" that can be used by boat travelers to avoid the exposed outer coast to the east of South Aulatsivik Island. During the winter, hunters can travel northwards to Okak by snowmobile or dogsled, either by going to the head of Webb Bay and following the Webb Brook Valley into Tasiuyak Bay, or by moving north up Port Manvers Run and then crossing the plateau behind the Kiglapait Mountains and thence down into Tasiuyak.

As far as game resources are concerned, Webb Bay is considered to be a "core area" for hunting ringed seals (Brice-Bennett 1977:125), particularly in the spring. During the summer seals tend to be scarce, but ringed and harbor seals may be shot occasionally, particularly off the point at the southern entrance to Port Manvers Run. The most important location for sealing along Port Manvers Run is the "Second Rattle," a narrowing of the Run which has such a strong tidal current that it remains an ice free polynya throughout the winter. This is also a "core area" for harbor seals (Brice-Bennett 1977:125). The narrow "tickle" between Igloo Island and the north shore of Webb Bay sometimes does not freeze over until February, providing extended open water sealing possibilities, and it may be a good sealing location in spring and fall.

The aforementioned winter travel routes can be used to access either the Kiglapait Mountain caribou herd to the north, or the Kinguritik herd to the west. Caribou may frequent the Webb Bay/Port Manvers area throughout the year, although they can be hard to find during the summer when they tend to be up the stream valleys and at relatively high elevations. In mid-April 1994 a small caribou herd was present in the interior valleys of South Aulatsivik Island. In late April tracks indicated a recent westward movement of this herd across Port Manvers Run and back towards the interior, presumably a shift towards spring calving areas.

Black bears are also very common in the region, inhabiting forested areas near streams and wandering up to fairly high elevations on the mountains. Polar bears move through Port Manvers Run during the winter and may be found there occasionally in the summer, especially in the northern portion from the Second Rattle to Thalia Point. Wolves and arctic hare also occur in the area, as well as porcupine and otter.

Webb Bay is a good location for wildfowl in the spring and fall, particularly geese and ducks (black and harlequin). Webb Brook at the head of the bay is an important salmon and char spawning stream (Brice-Bennett 1977:133), but summer fishing can be variable in the bay. In 1992-94 the summer fishing was poor, while in early summer 2002 there was good char fishing near the southern entrance to Port Manvers Run.

The bedrock at the western end of Webb Bay is Archean gneiss, while most of the remainder of the Webb Bay/Port Manvers Run area consists of anorthosites of the Middle Proterozoic Nain Plutonic Suite. At the north end of the Run, extending north towards Okak, is the Kiglapait layered intrusion, a gabbroic body also dating to the Middle Proterozoic (Ryan 1990; Ryan et al. 1995). The only rock type of use to prehistoric peoples would have been vein quartz, which outcrops sporadically throughout the area.

Scattered observations concerning the glacial geology of the Webb Bay/Port Manvers Run region were made by Väinö Tanner (1944) and his associates, but the only detailed study is that of Peter Johnson (1969). Johnson studied the extensive glacio-fluvial and glacio-marine sand and gravel terraces on the north side of Webb Bay and identified six phases in their formation. Early phases involved the wasting of ice into separate units centered on Webb Bay and Attu's Brook, then the development of a series of ice-dammed lakes and kame terraces at progressively lower elevations with runoff towards the east. A large marginal lake then formed from ice meltwater and runoff from the deglaciated highlands, contributing to subglacial drainage down Port Manvers Run. According to Johnson, the ice then withdrew sufficiently such that the eustatically rising sea cut a terrace at 41 m, which he considered to be the local marine limit. As noted previously, however, more recent data from Voisey's Bay (Bell 1997) suggest Johnson's 41 m marine limit is incorrect. If we situate Webb Bay between the Voisey's Bay and Nain uplift curves shown in Figure 5, then a terrace cut at 40 m would date ca. 7000 B.P.

Scenes from a bygone era: trapboats in Nain Harbour, 1978. (Photo: B. Hood)

"Wet-site excavation," Nukasusutok-5, Area 2C, 1980, with Doug Sutton and Morten Meldgaard (right). (Photo: B. Hood)

Theory and Method in the Analysis of Social Space

3

One of the central themes of this text is the analysis of social space. In this chapter the theme is addressed at the scale of site structure and individual features. First up is a general discussion of the status of spatial analysis in archaeology, which focuses on some of the main trends relevant to the set of problems outlined here. Current interpretations of Maritime Archaic social relations and dwelling space are then outlined and their explicit or implicit theoretical and methodological approaches are assessed. Given these considerations, a methodological strategy for the analysis of Maritime Archaic dwelling spaces is presented. A similar treatment of Paleoeskimo material follows.

Spatial Analysis in Archaeology

Spatial analysis of archaeological sites became an important theme in the late 1960s as part of the New Archaeology's program of finding appropriate methods for addressing conceptual problems. Much of the initial impetus was related to studies of functional variation within and between sites, which involved identifying functionally distinct tool kits. Simple quantitative techniques based on grid counts and point data were borrowed from geography and ecology, such as nearest neighbor analysis and tool type correlation studies (e.g., Hodder and Orton 1976). It became evident, however, that archaeological data were not a direct reflection of behavior and that the attempt to identify tool kits through correlation studies was problematic (Speth and Johnson 1976). Recognizing the complex

relationship between what Schiffer (1972) termed the archaeological and systemic contexts, attention turned to documenting the formation processes of the archaeological record. Much of this involved ethnoarchaeological studies of site structure (e.g., Yellen 1977; Binford 1978, 1983), which sought to identify "translation rules" for inferring systemic context from archaeological context. At the same time, a more varied range of quantitative methods was developed for recognizing patterns in complex spatial data, such as *k*-means cluster analysis, unconstrained clustering, correspondence analysis etc. (e.g., Blankholm 1991; Carr 1984; Hietala 1984; Kintigh and Ammerman 1982). Subsequent work investigated site structure in terms of formation history, considering specific problems such as the effects of site maintenance behavior on patterning (Binford 1983, 1987; O'Connell 1987). As noted by Wandsnider (1996), monitoring such processes may require dropping traditional analytical entities such as artifact types in favor of novel units of analysis that are more relevant to formation processes, such as size-sorting indices employed as indicators of site maintenance behavior (Wandsnider 1996:353-359), or refitting studies used to reveal the micro-behaviorial level of site structure (Cziesla 1989, 1990).

Whatever the methodological sophistication of spatial analysis, the central problem is the inferential process of connecting the observable archaeological context with the unobservable past cultural system. Ethnoarchaeological studies have been crucial for

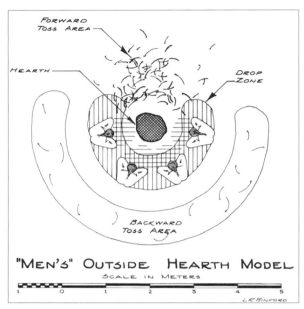

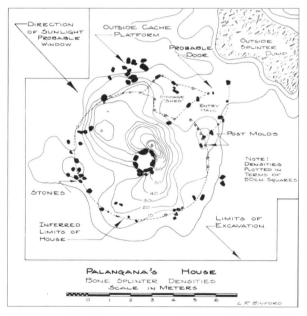

6/ Binford's external/internal hearth models. (6a) external hearth model (from Binford 1983:153).

6b/ internal hearth model, Palanga's house (from Binford 1983:177). Reproduced by permission.

understanding the relationship between archaeological traces of behavior and the organizational variables generating those traces (Binford 1987). The most frequently cited ethnoarchaeological work on hunter-gatherer site structure is that of Binford (1978a, b, 1983, 1987). From the late 1970s through the 1980s Binford focused on human body mechanics as a univer-

sal constraint that would produce consistent spatial patterns. The most well known example is the so-called "hearth-centered" model (Binford 1978b, 1983). According to Binford, the positioning of individuals around an outdoor hearth results in a characteristic pattern of a "drop zone" containing small items in the vicinity of the hearth and the seated individuals and a "toss zone" in front of the hearth and behind the hearth-users, where larger items are discarded (Figure 6a). Hearths inside dwelling structures do not exhibit this pattern since they are subjected to regular maintenance procedures of gathering debris and dumping it outside the dwelling (Figure 6b). The methods used for developing and presenting these models were largely qualitative and visual, with the goal of defining general spatial patterns that could be regarded as behavioral configurations. Nonetheless, Binford (1981:286) emphasized that spatial data should be collected at as detailed a level as possible, since we do not yet know enough about spatial structures to justify coarser-grained recording.

Binford used the hearth-centered model to provide an alternative interpretation of the French Paleolithic site Pincevent. According to Binford (1983:147-148), Leroi-Gourhan and Brézillion (1972) imposed certain unevaluated assumptions when they concluded that the spatial patterning of debris associated with hearths indicated the presence of several tent structures. Instead, Binford (1983:158-159) suggested the patterns derived from a rotation of seating positions around *outdoor* hearths. Debate continues as to how the spatial organization of Pincevent and other Upper Paleolithic sites should be interpreted (e.g., Audouze 1987; Carr 1991; Enloe et al. 1994; Julien et al. 1987; Koetje 1987, 1994; Simek 1984). Meanwhile, some researchers attempted to develop methodological tools for the analysis of hearth-centered distributions (Stapert 1989), while others discussed additional site formation considerations that complicate Binford's hearth-centered model (e.g., O'Connell 1987; Stevenson 1991).

One of the problems with Binford's studies is that they mostly attribute spatial patterning in sites to "etic" behavioral factors such as body mechanics or practical "maintenance" strategies that determine disposal decisions. Although processualists eventually paid more attention to social factors such as the role of sharing, kinship and cooperative labor in the spacing of dwellings (e.g., Binford 1991; Gargett and Hayden 1991; Whitelaw 1991, 1994), there was no concern for the symbolic dimension of site structure. Symbolic meaning was taken up in Hodder's (1982, 1987) ethnoarchaeological research in east Africa, which explored the structuring effect of social relations, such as gender, and the symbolic aspects of discard related to concepts of dirt and purity (see D. Gordon [1980] for an earlier eastern subarctic example). In subsequent post-processual studies, dwelling structures were seen as both the medium and outcome of social structuration processes, simultaneously channeling the physical movements of individuals and serving as symbolic metaphors encoding aspects of ideology (e.g., Hodder 1990:44-70; Parker-Pearson and Richards 1994; Yates 1989). Recent research takes a phenomenological rather than structuralist approach to constructed space, theorizing how "the body" subjectively experiences movement through dwellings and other aspects of the inhabited environment (Tilley 1994, 1999:40-49).

The upshot of this discussion is that there are two main methodological approaches to spatial analysis (although these are not mutually exclusive). The first approach is *model-centered* (Carr 1991). This generally involves linking the observed archaeological context with an ethnoarchaeological model that provides insight into the unobserved past behavioral context. The model employed could be either an "etic" behavioral model or an "emic" socio-ideological model. The question of evaluating a model's correspondence with the spatial data is a central problem. There is a constant danger that model-centered approaches will assume what they set out to prove, and that fitting the

model to the data will result in an uncritical accommodation argument (Binford 1981:284-285) in which the model becomes an unevaluated interpretative convention or a rhetorical device used to construct a past-as-wished for. From the neo-positivist perspective, although data are recognized as constructed through a theoretical lens it is believed that independent middle-range methods can be applied to provide a measure of goodness of fit (Binford 1981:21-30, 1982). The hermeneutic perspective, on the other hand, sees method as inseparable from theory, such that evaluating goodness of fit is a negotiation process marked by fluidity and a lack of firm foundations for determining the plausibility of arguments. While data can in some sense "confront" theory, emphasis is placed on enhancing interpretive coherence and reducing inconsistencies (Hodder 1999:39, 60-62). Nonetheless, there seems to be agreement that some kinds of methodological strategies are necessary to provide challenges to interpretative models and to prevent arguments from becoming self-serving tautologies. These strategies may involve contrasting arguments developed from different paradigmatic positions, applying different types of methods (quantitative and qualitative) with different assumptions to the same data set, and considering several different types of contextual information and different scales of analysis (e.g., Binford 1987:503; Blankholm 1991; Carr 1991; Hodder 1999:130-131). In this process, quantitative analysis can be used as a pattern recognition exercise aimed at exposing possible anomalies between models and data, a tool for resisting premature accommodations. Such flexible methodological strategies might be considered part of a critical realist epistemology (Sayer 1992, 2000).

The other approach to spatial analysis can be termed *empirical pattern recognition*. Instead of taking its point of departure in a conceptual model, this approach uses exploratory quantitative methods to identify statistically meaningful associations in spatial data. These patterns may then be interpreted post hoc

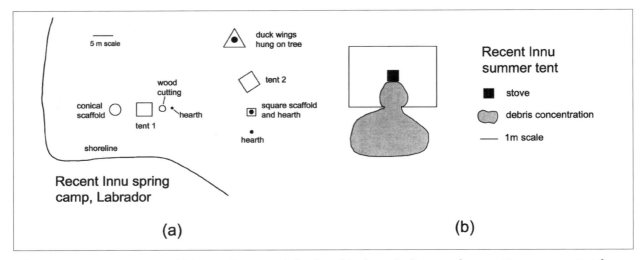

 = Recent Innu spring camp, Labrador: 5 m scale, duck wings hung on tree, wood cutting, tent 2, conical scaffold, hearth, square scaffold and hearth, tent 1, hearth, shoreline. (a). Recent Innu summer tent: stove, debris concentration, 1m scale. (b).

7/ Recent Innu camp structure. (a) Innu spring camp, Labrador. (b) schematic diagram of a recent Innu summer tent feature, Labrador.

in relation to a model. The assumption is that statistical techniques can provide results that are independent of model premises, such that unanticipated patterns might be recognized (Carr 1991:226). While this property has some virtue, the important objection is that no statistical tool provides guidelines as to how the resulting patterns should be interpreted in terms of behavior. So, while a technique may provide a means of revealing patterning that is inherent in the data itself rather than an artifact of model conventions, the interpretations of the patterning are ultimately model dependent. There is also the danger that the elegance of a technique, such as the popular k-means cluster analysis (Kintigh and Ammerman 1982; Simek 1984), may promote its use as a cookbook solution.

This general discussion has implications for the methodology used in the spatial analysis of habitation areas undertaken in this text. The methodological strategy employed here involves the recursive use of models and empirical pattern recognition studies. Theory is used to frame models of Maritime Archaic and Paleoeskimo dwelling space, while the methods serve two roles: (1) evaluating the goodness of fit between models and data— their degree of accommodation or "coherence," and (2) as exploratory tools for partitioning complex data sets so as to expose unanticipated aspects of variation— *anomalies* between

models and data that could require re-evaluation of the model assumptions. Methodological discussions for the Maritime Archaic and Paleoeskimo cases are presented separately, since each cultural context presents its own specific problems of analysis.

The Maritime Archaic: Longhouse Models and Spatial Muddles

During the 1970s, excavations at Maritime Archaic habitation sites in central and northern Labrador failed to identify distinct traces of dwelling structures. Hearths were sometimes arranged in a linear fashion along raised beach terraces (e.g., Rattlers Bight and Black Island Cove, Fitzhugh 1975, 1978a; Okak-2, Cox 1977), but these and other features (Hood 1981) were generally interpreted as the remains of individual family tent structures. Although the Maritime Archaic seemed "different" from the historically known Innu, the viewing lens for perceiving and interpreting these spatial patterns was traditional subarctic ethnography. This ethnographic model generated assumptions of nuclear family organizational units with modest tent structures as dwellings. For example, modern Innu spring-summer camps leave remains such as those sketched in Figure 7. Individual tents may be spaced at varying distances, dependent on both terrain and social relationships, and may be associated with exter-

8/ Innu summer tent site, 1980. Small stakes mark stove location, door immediately to the right. Exterior midden between tent site and scaffold. Photo: W. Fitzhugh.

nal features such as hearths, wooden scaffolds, skin-stretching frames, wood chopping areas and the symbolic placement of animal bones in adjacent trees. Dwelling remains may consist of small, single family tent floors with a central stove, along with trash distributions centered on the doorway and exterior area immediately outside the tent (Figures 7 and 8). Larger tents are also used, however.

During the 1978 season of the Smithsonian Institution's Torngat Archaeological Project, probable Maritime Archaic rectangular structures were noted briefly at Aillik, near Makkovik on the central coast, while several linear structures up to 100 m long and associated with Late Maritime Archaic artifacts were identified at Nulliak Cove, north of Hebron Fjord (Fitzhugh 1980). The break-through came in 1980, when Smithsonian investigations at Aillik revealed the clearly defined remains of a "longhouse" embedded in a cobble beach. The feature measured in at 28 m long, 4 m wide, and was segmented into seven compart-

ments with raised rock dividers. It was associated with several external conical cache pits (Figures 9 and 10). The longhouse was actually the latest in a sequence of structures that began on a higher and earlier raised beach. There appeared to be an "evolutionary" development over time from small, single-family pit-houses and rectangular structures towards progressively larger segmented rectangular structures, culminating in the longhouse. (Fitzhugh 2006).

This remarkably clear longhouse and the sequence of earlier structures became a paradigm or interpretative model that could be used to make sense of the previously excavated hearth rows, the linear features at Nulliak Cove and other ambiguous spatial distributions. The "longhouse model" revolutionized Maritime Archaic archaeology, revealing how the ethnographically derived expectations had hindered recognition of the pattern. The model made visible what was previously hidden and helped make sense out of spatial muddles. We cannot do without it.

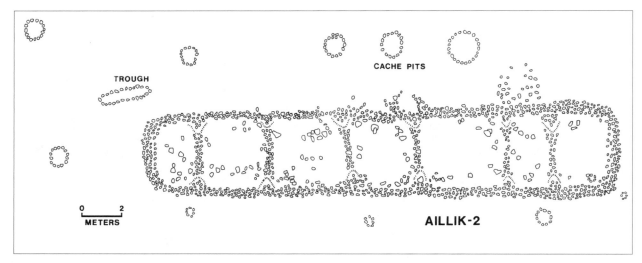

9/ Maritime Archaic longhouse, Aillik-2 (after Fitzhugh 1984:33).

Nonetheless, the model also poses certain dangers when applied as a handy template to data that are considerably more ambiguous than the "classic" feature at Aillik. At the descriptive or pattern recognition level, accurate delineation of dwelling size and configuration could be compromised by naive application of the longhouse template. There may be a temptation to interpret any linear distribution as a longhouse, particularly distributions encountered on surveys and not subjected to substantive analysis. Such pattern recognition errors snowball on the inferential level when correlations of structure size and social composition are based on faulty description. Consequently, we have the ingredients for potentially deceptive accommodation arguments in which the longhouse model becomes a taken-for-granted interpretative convention. So, when dealing with ambiguous spatial data we have to balance carefully between using the longhouse model as a necessary guide to pattern recognition and employing methodological strategies to prevent unjustified reproduction of the model and to expose unanticipated patterning.

The Functional and Social Dimensions of Maritime Archaic Dwellings

There appear to be at least three different forms of Maritime Archaic dwellings: (1) small pit-houses of ca. 3.0-3.5 m in diameter (either circular or oval double-room features, Fitzhugh 2006), (2) rectangular surface structures, and (3) "longhouses." The latter may be either surface structures or slightly excavated into cobble beaches. The current chronology, based on a combination of radiocarbon dating and elevation above sea-level, has pit-houses pre-dating 6000 B.P.. Rectangular surface structures are also found prior to 6000 B.P.; these measure ca. 8-12 m in length and are partitioned into two to five segments by rock dividers (Fitzhugh 1984, 1985a, 1985b:62, 1986:56, 2006). Between 6000-5500 B.P., rectangular surface structures at Aillik and in the Nain area range from 9-16 m long and contain two to four internal segments (Fitzhugh 1984:10, 13). A three-segment structure at Aillik West-1 is dated 5210±270 B.P. (Fitzhugh 1984:8). Between 5000-4200 B.P., a 30-40 m line of hearths at Okak-2 (Cox 1977:184-185) has been interpreted as a longhouse (Fitzhugh 1981:18), while at Black Island-2, in Hamilton Inlet, 12 evenly spaced hearths suggest a 50 m long structure with 12-13 segments (Fitzhugh 1975:122-125, 1981:17, 1984:13). Longhouse development reached its peak during the Rattlers Bight Phase (4200-3500 B.P.), with a 70 m linear arrangement of hearths at Rattlers Bight in Hamilton Inlet, 27 surface longhouses ranging in length from 15-100 m at Nulliak Cove near Hebron,

10/ Maritime Archaic longhouse, Aillik-2, excavated into a cobble beach. Photo: W. Fitzhugh.

and the classic 28 m long seven segment semi-subterranean structure at Aillik (Fitzhugh 1981:18, 1984, 1986:56, 1985a:88-89). The time of appearance of the first longhouses is unclear, but likely occurs between 5000-4500 B.P.. One possible conclusion to be drawn from this sequence is that longhouses developed by "accretion" (Fitzhugh, personal communication). Beginning with the basal units of single compartment pit-houses and two segment rectangular dwellings, additional compartments were simply added on in a geometric progression, as clones of the basal units.

The question, however, is what constitutes a "longhouse"? What is the archaeological signature of such a feature and how does it differ from a "rectangular structure" and a linear arrangement of completely independent tents or outdoor hearths? First of all, "rectangular structure" seems to designate surface features that exhibit tent-ring-like rock borders and internal stone segment dividers. The term "longhouse" is ambiguous since it denotes a feature that is also rectangular, but longer— with an unspecified minimum length threshold— and which may or may not display the aforementioned architectural features of rectangular structures. Additionally, the term longhouse may be a misleading metaphor since it denotes certain ethnographically well-known dwellings (e.g., Iroquoian) that are not applicable to the Labrador case. Rather than being continuous architectural constructions, Maritime Archaic longhouses probably consisted of a linear series of linked individual tents. In the case of the 28 m long structure at Aillik there is clearly an architectural unity defined by its semi-subterranean excavation into a cobble beach, but this may simply have been the foundation for several closely packed tent dwellings. In cases that lack obvious architectural components, such as the surface features at Nulliak, the longhouse is an *inference* based on several lines of evidence, not all of which may be present or of equal quality in a given case: a linear series of regularly spaced hearths, a bounded linear distribution of lithic material (3.5-4.0 m wide), segment divider rocks and traces of wall border rocks.

It is impossible to be more precise about the nature of the spatial patterning associated with rectangular structures and longhouses because no detailed distribution maps have been published. Partial plans of longhouses from Nulliak Cove and Rattlers Bight (Fitzhugh 1981: Figures 7 and 10, 1985a:96-97) indicate fairly regularly spaced (3-4 m) clusters of charcoal and fire-cracked rock (not always mutually associated) running down the center of the structures (Figure 11a). In some cases, though, charcoal concentrations also occur close to the presumed walls. Tool and debitage distributions are described as being hearth-centered (Fitzhugh 1981:17-18, 1985a:98, 1985b:49), but the details of this spatial configuration are not specified. A schematic diagram of a longhouse from Nulliak Cove shows lithic distributions that are not always associated with possible hearths (Figure 11b; Fitzhugh 1985a:97). Some of the lithic concentrations are spatially independent, but most of them are joined along one side of the structure, suggesting an overlapping arc configuration or "ribbons" connecting separate concentrations. These examples should at least raise some questions as to how we might distinguish longhouses from lines of independent tents or outdoor hearths.

In sum, our knowledge of Maritime Archaic dwelling structures is constrained by ill-defined terms and piecemeal information. The term "longhouse" originated as an *ad hoc* category (Barsalou 1983) formulated to make sense of linear spatial distributions. Although useful for that initial purpose, the category needs to evolve further because considerable ambiguity results from its status as a conceptual combination in which archaeological attributes are mapped onto analog models from other contexts. It should also be pointed out that in addition to pit-houses, rectangular structures and longhouses, there are other types of Maritime Archaic features on the landscape that might be dwelling-related, such as isolated rock pavements (Fitzhugh 1978: Figure 14 illustrates one from Big Island, Saglek Bay; the author has observed similar features on Uigortlek Island in the Nain region). Reducing ambiguity and error in our inferences will require a systematic study of Maritime Archaic features that documents their range of variation and provides firmer criteria for distinguishing dwelling types with and without traces of architecture.

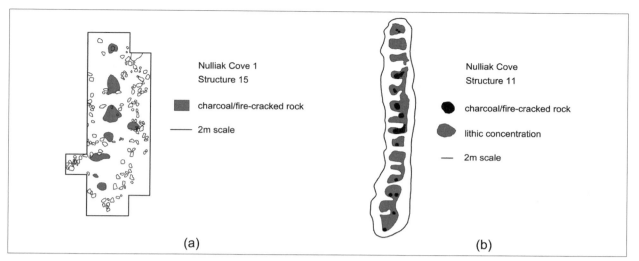

11/ Maritime Archaic longhouses from Nulliak Cove-1. (a) Structure 15, (b) Structure 11 (after Fitzhugh 1985a:97; reproduced by permission, Arctic Anthropology, University of Wisconsin Press).

If we restrict ourselves to the established dwelling features, the question is: to what extent are these different types or sizes of structures part of an evolutionary development over time versus functional or seasonal variants? In the pre-6000 B.P. period, the coexistence of pit-houses and rectangular surface structures suggests they may be seasonal variants, with pit-houses used in colder periods (Fitzhugh 1985a:89). If that was the case, however, the outer coast locations of the pit-houses do not correspond well with the postulated interior-maritime settlement pattern, in which fall-winter settlement is posited for the inner bays or near interior (Fitzhugh 1978:83-84). However, pit-houses might have been used on the coast in the colder spring or fall periods while exploiting migrating harp seal herds, and rectangular structures during the summer. Alternatively, the lack of pit-houses after 6000 B.P. might be explained by a shift of winter settlement from the outer coast to the near-interior (Fitzhugh 1985a:88). Questions could also be raised concerning the contrast between the virtually semi-subterranean longhouse feature at Aillik and the surface longhouses at Nulliak Cove. Is this a seasonal difference, or is the Aillik feature merely a situational variant used on rocky cobble beaches?

We have very little information concerning how Maritime Archaic dwellings were constructed. Few details have been published, aside from hints of postholes at the Aillik longhouse (Fitzhugh 1984:33). The assumption is that the rectangular surface structures were tent dwellings and that the longhouses represent a series of individual tent structures placed adjacent to each other. The pit-houses and longhouses excavated into cobble beaches may also have been roofed in this manner; there is no evidence that they were covered with sod.

Estimates of the duration of dwelling occupations is problematic in the absence of preserved bone material. Fitzhugh (1985a:98) suggests the Nulliak Cove longhouses were used for short periods of days or weeks on the basis of low rates of debris accumulation inside the structures and the absence of middens. This short occupation is related to Nulliak Cove's role as a repeatedly-used staging area for trips to the Ramah Bay chert sources, part of an "expeditionary" model of chert procurement involving pronounced long-distance seasonal mobility (Fitzhugh 1985b:50). On the other hand, longhouses used as seasonal base camps within a local settlement system may have been occupied longer, resulting in greater accumulation as seen in the "sheet midden" deposits at Rattlers Bight (Fitzhugh

1981:18, 1985b:49). Consequently, we might expect seasonal, functional, and geographical differences in the nature of longhouses and their duration of occupation. In the absence of bone material these differences might be reflected in the types of features and lithic assemblages present, the ratio of primary versus secondary refuse (Schiffer 1987:58-72) and the degree to which peripheral areas of the sites exhibit build-ups of external activity areas (Binford 1983:190). Of course, these variables are complicated by other factors such as group size and composition and culturally codified disposal practices.

The social significance of longhouses has been discussed from somewhat different directions. Although reliance on subarctic Innu ethnography as an analogy source led to difficulties in recognizing the longhouse pattern in the first place, Fitzhugh (1981, 1984, 1985a) turns to this analogy again when interpreting social space in longhouses, but it should be emphasized that he has not presented a full and explicit account of his position. He characterizes Maritime Archaic society in line with ethnographic interpretations of subarctic Algonkian society as egalitarian, with emphasis on individual families and the personal autonomy of individuals (Fitzhugh 1985a:104-105). Nonetheless, when seen in terms of the temporal development from small pit-houses to longhouses, there appears to have been an increase in co-residential group size over time, from single family units (or small groups of two or three families, if clusters of two or three pit-houses indicate contemporary use), towards large multi-family co-residential longhouses consisting of 50-100 individuals (Fitzhugh 1984:20). Additionally, variation in mortuary treatment may indicate some degree of status distinction in Maritime Archaic society (Fitzhugh 1978:85, 1981:32).

A consequence of this social model is that when analyzing architecturally distinct Maritime Archaic dwelling features, Fitzhugh emphasizes the significance of the individual segments or compartments of the structures, which he considers to be individual family living floors. In the case of the more ambiguous linear distributions of hearths and lithics, he views hearth-centered distributions as indicative of individual family living floors (Fitzhugh 1984:18, 1985a:98). The individual family floor areas can be thought of as structural "modules" (Binford 1983:147). A pit-house then consists of a single such module while a longhouse is a linear accretion of multiple modules. In earlier published papers, Fitzhugh (1984:8-9, 1985a:96) argued that the regular spacing of hearths and debris distributions related to longhouse segments is strongly repetitive, indicating the dwelling compartments were used simultaneously. More recently, however, Fitzhugh (2006: 12-13) suggests that perhaps not all longhouse modules were contemporary. The central segments of longhouses tend to have greater accumulations of debris than the peripheral segments, suggestive of longer occupation. Dwellings may have been organized around a stable central unit, with additional segments being added or subtracted on an "accordion" basis in relation to the arrival and departure of families. In this reading, the overall configuration of a longhouse is largely determined by repetitive "microscale" patterns at the module level.

Modular organization plays a conceptual and methodological role in how spatial patterning in dwellings is linked to possible social distinctions in Maritime Archaic societies. Fitzhugh (1985a:98) views Maritime Archaic social organization as "generally egalitarian" because the contents of longhouse segments are repetitive in terms of household activities and material culture. Nonetheless, there are indications that some artifact production and discard, particularly that involving Ramah chert, slate and soapstone, may be concentrated in particular parts of a longhouse. The possibility that these segments were communal work areas is dismissed, since the content and configuration of these areas is similar to the other segments. In any event, the implication is that relative social equality/distinction might be investigated through the degree of module redundancy or variability (Fitzhugh 1984:11).

Modular organization is one analytical framework we can use in analyzing Maritime Archaic dwellings but, as indicated, it is also linked to ethnographically derived premises about individual family-focused social organization as well as the assumption that the overall configuration of a longhouse results from repeated replication of microscale processes at the modular level. As an alternative, the continuous linear pattern may be generated by *macroscale* processes which unite several modular units into a spatial logic partly determined by the meaning of the dwelling as a whole. This unifying spatial logic may be social and ideological rather than simply a functional consequence of dwelling geometry— the cloning of individual family modules. Structural linearity may be an organizational principle in which the practical ordering of domestic space in the course of daily life is a vehicle for actively structuring social relations, as well as being a symbolic representation of those relations.

The unifying linear principle could indicate an emphasis on connected space, a merging of private and public space that expresses a corporate social logic rather than a logic of familial segmentation. Elsewhere, the author suggested that:

> The spatial logic of the longhouse, consisting of an extremely contrived linear ordering of individual social units, conveyed a tension within Maritime Archaic society between the autonomy of individual household units and the collective organization of emergent corporate groups. Maritime Archaic seasonal mobility might have entailed tendencies towards group fission, flexible autonomous social units and temporary settlements. Household autonomy was spatially encoded in the segmentation of longhouses into multiple compartments representing individual household floors. These individual social

modules were incorporated into a larger collective unit by the overall structure of the dwelling. The longhouse structure physically created a corporate unit and gave that unit a temporary (seasonal) material existence through the organization of domestic space. Furthermore, the longhouse helped establish an ideological fiction of collectivity in a social world which otherwise tended towards seasonal fragmentation. I suggest that this pattern signifies the emergence of situational rather than permanent corporate principles and expresses flux in Maritime Archaic complexity processes (Hood 1995:95).

The methodological consequence of such a social model is that spatial analysis must be multiscalar. At the microscale level the focus is on patterning within individual modules. At the mesoscale level the patterns that cross-cut or unite modules are considered. At the macroscale, patterns at the level of the dwelling as a whole are investigated.

One of the main practical problems in developing accurate descriptions of Maritime Archaic dwelling structures is delimiting them in size. This is particularly the case for ambiguous linear distributions without clear architectural demarcation. Longhouse interpretation may be complicated by overlapping between non-contemporary structures and the resulting palimpsest accumulations. Without systematic radiocarbon dating of hearths, combined with refitting studies, we have no firm grounds for assuming that longhouse segments constitute a contemporaneous unity. This methodological problem has broader interpretative significance in that lacking good control over segment contemporaneity we have no grounds for accurate dwelling size estimates, thus no grounds for inferring the demographic and social composition of a settlement or for postulating symbolic order and meaning.

The foregoing discussion focused on identifiable dwelling structures, but it is obviously not the case that all patterns at Maritime Archaic sites are the consequence of activities conducted within the confines of dwellings. To avoid unwarranted accommodation arguments we need alternative models for identifying distribution patterns unrelated to dwelling structures. Binford's (1983:156-159;165-170) well-known distinction between patterns connected with indoor and outdoor hearths and his discussion of "extensive" activity areas is one point of departure.

Expanding the View: Other Archaeological Contexts

Longhouses are an unusual dwelling form among ethnographically known hunter-gatherers. North American subarctic ethnography contains examples of large communal structures (see below), but none of these had linear dimensions approaching those of Late Maritime Archaic dwellings and there is little documentation of their spatial patterning. Otherwise, longhouses are better represented in the ethnography of sedentary agricultural societies such as the Iroquoians. Since the latter analogy is problematic for northern hunter-gatherers, it may be useful to take a comparative archaeological view and consider the spatial patterning associated with longhouse-like features in the eastern subarctic, arctic and elsewhere. What spatial patterns result when people are enclosed in linear structures? This will hardly be comprehensive, but will attempt to develop a sense of the variability in spatial patterning.

Beginning close to Labrador, an interesting example is Séguin's (1995) work on sites dating 700-1000 B.P. in the James Bay region of northern Québec. Séguin applied Binford's hearth-centered model and Cree ethnography to the interpretation of hearth-centered distributions lacking evidence of structural remains. Archaeologically, she distinguished between external hearths, small structures with single central hearths and longhouses with two or multiple hearths. Her brief consideration of the ethnographic material suggested there are regional variations among Cree groups in the positioning of activities and persons vis

à vis hearths. In the Mistassini area, men's and women's activities are conducted on the same side of the hearth, while in the Chisasibi area they are conducted on opposite sides. The longhouse structure posited for site GdFc-2 (Figure 12a; Séguin 1995:44) consisted of four hearths placed in a ca. 9 m long line, spaced at ca. 1 m intervals; lithic concentrations were found on opposite sides of two hearths and on one side of the other two. Séguin interpreted this distribution as a ca. 13 m long, 5.5 m wide longhouse, with the lithic concentrations representing activities conducted between the hearths and the dwelling walls.

In contrast, Loring (1992:245, 250-260) described a probable longhouse (shaputuan) dated 1800-1500 B.P. at Daniel Rattle-1, Area IV, near Davis Inlet on the Labrador coast. There was no trace of walls; the feature consisted of a 4.5 m long, 1.0 m wide, raised linear hearth with two smaller cobble hearths slightly distant at both ends. The central hearth was tightly packed with calcined bone fragments, bone ash, thermally-altered Ramah chert flakes and heat-shattered biface fragments, and fire-cracked rocks. Lithic tools and flakes occurred in a major concentration extending 3.5 m outwards on one of the long sides of the hearth feature, with a two diffuse clusters on the opposite side and minor concentrations associated with the small end-hearths.

Returning to Québec, at site GbFd-9 (Figure 12b) Séguin (1995:43) identified two features (B and E) as external hearths, although the excavated area was too small to identify possible drop/toss zones. Six other hearths (A, C, D, F-H) were placed in a 30 m long line, spaced at intervals of 4.4 to 6.6 m. Lithic remains were concentrated within 1.0 to 1.5 m of the hearth centers, in five cases on opposite sides of the hearths, in one case as two clusters on the same side. Each hearth is interpreted as the focus of a separate tent structure, but little justification is given for this conclusion. Hearths C, D and F are closely positioned and are aligned on the same axis, hearths G and H lie slightly apart from the first group and are aligned on a slight-

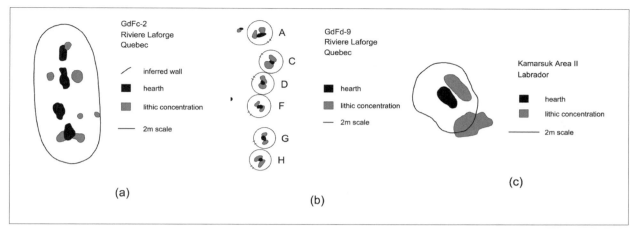

12/ Pre-contact Recent Indian dwelling features. (a) longhouse, GdFc-2, Rivière Laforge, Québec (after Séguin 1995:44). (b) individual tent structures, GbFd-9, Rivière Laforge, Québec (after Séguin 1995:43). (c) tent dwelling, Kamarsuk Area II, Labrador (after Loring 1992:266, 270). Figures a and b reproduced by permission, l'Association des archéologues du Québec.

ly different axis, and hearth A is out of alignment with the C-D-F group. It is unclear why the C-D-F and G-H groups could not be considered longhouses; the only difference appears to be that their lithic concentrations are oriented towards what would be the middle of a longhouse rather than lying between the hearths and the walls. This would seem to be a weak criterion given the ethnographic observations on variability in the placement of activities around hearths. Indeed, with Fitzhugh's longhouse model in mind, one might even consider the possibility of a larger structure, given a refit between hearth areas A and F. Nonetheless, Séguin's material is very relevant to the Maritime Archaic longhouse discussion, since it provides some concrete archaeological examples of alternatives in spatial patterning and it attempts to apply an ethnoarchaeologically-derived behavioral model.

Séguin's individual structure interpretation can be compared with Loring's (1992:266-276) discussion of a Late Prehistoric dwelling from Kamarsuk Area II, north of Davis Inlet, Labrador (Figure 12c). The feature was a slightly semi-subterranean oval tent structure, 4 by 5 m in size, with a raised central cobble hearth. The hearth contained calcined bone fragments and thermally altered Ramah chert. There was a pronounced concentration of debitage on one side of the hearth, but relatively little on the opposite side, sug-

gesting the latter was used as a sleeping area. A second concentration of Ramah chert debitage at one end of the structure and extending outside suggested a doorway midden. This spatial pattern is broadly similar to that identified by Séguin and bears a strong resemblance to Binford's "archetype" model for hearth-centered patterns expected in enclosed and maintained spaces (i.e., Palanga's House, Figure 6b).

A distinctly different pattern was found at the late Point Revenge Complex Winter Cove-4 site (ca. 500 B.P.) in Hamilton Inlet, Labrador (Fitzhugh 1978b). This feature was a 4 by 8 m oval tent ring with a single central internal hearth and nine external hearths. Some of the external hearths were almost superimposed by the tent ring such that, in contrast to Fitzhugh's interpretation, they may represent earlier activity. Very little lithic material was found inside the tent ring; only a small concentration adjacent to the well-constructed hearth and along the southeastern wall of the feature. This seems consistent with Binford's inside-hearth model. Most of the lithics were concentrated around the external hearths, which were less substantial cobblestone clusters. The tools and flakes mostly lay adjacent to the hearths (akin to drop zones), but in one case there was a wide scatter of debitage extending out at least 3 m from a hearth, evidently a "non-maintained" zone. Fitzhugh (1978b:158-159) suggested the structure represents a warm weather occupation by a multi-family group.

Returning to the spatial structure of longhouses, another archaeological case of such features can be found in Late Dorset Paleoeskimo society (ca. 500-1000/1200 AD). These features range from 10 to 45 m in length, 5-7 m wide, and sometimes incorporate stone walls up to 1 meter in height. The central corridors may lack distinctive hearths, although there may be traces of a central "passage" with rock constructions and burned fat. The walls sometimes contain small niches with traces of burned fat and possible domestic activities. In some cases, lines of external hearths and caches run parallel to the structures (Appelt and Gulløv 1998:148-149, 1999:24-35; Damkjar 2000; McGhee 1971; Plumet 1985; Schledermann 1990:202-251). Investigators agree that these structures represent the communal ritual activities of multi-family groups, probably conducted during the summer, but they disagree on whether the structures were roofed tent dwellings or whether the walls were merely symbolic. Plumet (1985:228-229, 366-367, 371) argues that the spatial logic was of individual family floor spaces along the walls, with a linear central communal area that was a symbolic spatial transformation of the axial structure principle used in smaller Dorset sod-house dwellings.

Perhaps the clearest example of longhouse spatial patterning is found in a 15.5 m long feature at the David site in northwest Greenland (Appelt and Gulløv 1999:36-40; Figure 13a), where a series of separate lithic concentrations were closely linked to a central passage feature. Some of the concentrations lay adjacent to stone-slab pits of unknown function. Four of these clusters were regularly spaced along the east side of the passage (ca. 7 m between center points); the clusters were all somewhat oval and of broadly similar dimensions (4-6 m long, 3-4 m wide). On the west side of the passage were two linear distributions of similar dimensions (5-6 m long, 2 m wide) and a small flake concentration at one end of the passage.

There were also four small clusters of tools lying outside the main concentrations. Thus, there were slight differences in depositional patterns on either side of the passage such that the configuration was somewhat asymmetric. The eastern wall contained traces of at least six regularly spaced (1.5 m) slabs with burned fat suggestive of hearth areas. It may be significant that the largest debris concentrations occurred on this side of the structure.

Schledermann's (1990:209-211, 239, 245) spatial distribution data from Ellesmere Island exhibit generally similar tendencies. At the Longhouse site, partial excavation of a 45 m long feature suggested a pattern of paired lithic/bone clusters on opposite sides of the central area. The clusters were of similar size (mostly 2.0 by 1.0-1.5 m) and fairly evenly spaced along each side (mostly 2.0-2.5 m between their center points). Although there were sporadic traces of charcoal and burned bone there were no distinct hearths. The pattern in the 14.5 m long structure at the Cove site suggests seven clusters of variable dimensions on each side of the passage. The clusters along the southern half of the structure seem semi-regularly spaced (1.5-2.7 m between center points) and have higher find densities than those on the northern side of the structure. Although those on the northern side are also regularly spaced (1.5 m between center points), they are arranged in two groups separated by 4.5 m of low density: four at the western end of the structure, two at the eastern end. Again, there is a hint of slight asymmetry in cluster placement and deposition, as at the David site feature.

A slightly different pattern was found in Late Dorset House B at the UNG-11 site in the Ungava region (Plumet 1985:105-134, 209-231, *hors texte* 9 and 10). The feature was ca. 36 m long and 5 m wide (Figure 13b). The central axis of the structure had a slightly raised ridge containing stone-lined boxes and pits with traces of burned fat and red ocher. In the wall area there were several niches consisting of flat slabs and burned fat that were spaced at 2-3 m intervals. A schematic summary indicates the lithic distribution was primarily concentrated in the southern end of the structure. Debris occurred along the walls as near-continuous distributions, with hints of separate but overlapping clusters spaced about two meters apart, evidently associated with the wall niches. Seven smaller clusters (mostly 1.5-2.0 m in diameter) occurred closer to the center, adjacent to the box and pit features.

The spatial patterning in these structures is reasonably consistent, with small, relatively discrete, sometimes regularly spaced, debris clusters along both sides of the central axis of the features. These clusters are associated with rock constructions and traces of burning. Possible hearth niches in the walls at the David site and UNG-11 seem to be associated with larger and denser debris accumulations. Hence, although we lack evidence for "classic" hearth-centered distributions there are strong indications that the distributions are feature-related, probably to cooking/heating/ illumination areas with oil lamps. A slight exception to the pattern of relatively discrete debris clusters is UNG-11, where there was greater accumulation of material adjacent to the walls and overlap between niche-related distributions. It should be kept in mind, however, that although these feature-centered distributions seem similar to those associated with domestic hearths, the spatial organization of Late Dorset longhouses was likely structured by special ritual practices.

A final archaeological example comes from farther afield: the well-known, although not well understood, "longhouse" structures from the Russian Upper Paleolithic site Kostenki (Grigor'ev 1967; Klein 1969:114-117, 170-177). The three structures described by Klein had similar features: lines of 9-10 hearths, mostly spaced ca. 1.5-2.0 m apart. Distributions of the associated artifactual materials suggested one dwelling 35 m in length by 10-15 m in width, a second 35 m in length by 5 m in width, and a third 23 m in length by 5 m in width. Cache pits with mammoth bone and smaller circular structures that

might have been house-pits were also present. These features, and the complex sites of which they are a part, present similar analytical problems, and then some, to the Maritime Archaic longhouses that lack clear architectural features. Grigor'ev (1993:58-59) notes that delineation of the dwelling boundaries is arbitrary line-drawing through density distributions, but the lithic distributions from Kostenki I, Horizon 1 (Grigor'ev 1967:345; Klein 1969:117) at least provide a sense of the spatial structure at the site (Figure 13c). Taking into account that some excavation units were destroyed, the most dense flake concentrations were located primarily within a 1-3 m distance of the central hearths, although towards the southern end of the proposed dwelling the debitage extended up to 4 meters distant. The concentrations were all on the eastern side of the dwelling, with the exception of two small clusters on western side of the hearth line. The southern portion of the dwelling had a near continuous distribution of flakes paralleling four of the hearths and there may have been a separate concentration in the middle near two hearths, as well as a separate concentration paralleling the three northernmost hearths. If, for the sake of argument, we accept Grigor'ev's dwelling boundary, it would appear that the longhouse dwelling was surrounded by storage pits and there might have been some external lithic reduction or dumping of waste from inside the dwelling.

It is interesting to compare the spatial patterns of the archaeological longhouses described above. There are obvious parallels between Séguin's northern Québec longhouse, the Late Dorset structures and the Kostenki situation— clusters of debris on either side of central hearths (or central "features" in the case of Late Dorset)— although the Kostenki pattern is one of less discrete clusters with much more overlap between what may or may not have been individual hearth-centered distributions. The more continuous distributions at Kostenki are similar to the wall-related concentrations in the Ungava Late Dorset longhouse. Each of these cases varies somewhat in the position of relative-

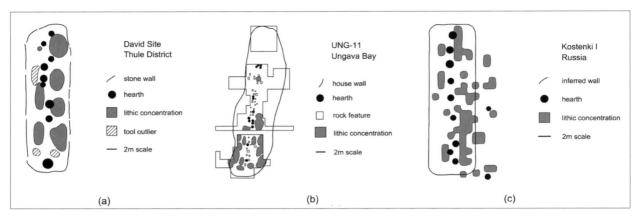

13/ Late Dorset and Russian Upper Paleolithic longhouses. (a) Late Dorset longhouse, David site, Thule district, Greenland (after Appelt et al. 1999:36-40). (b) Late Dorset longhouse, UNG-11, Ungava, Québec (after Plumet 1985: hors texte 9, 10); reproduced by permission of author). (c) Upper Paleolithic longhouse, Kostenki I, Russia (after Grigor'íev 1967:345; reproduced by permission, Current Anthropology, University of Chicago Press).

ly empty or maintained space: in the Québec Late Pre-Contact case it is near the walls, in the Late Dorset longhouses it may occur in the center, near the walls, or at one end of the structures, while at Kostenki it consists of most of one entire side of the structure.

In sum, these archaeological examples exhibit similar micro-scale patterns involving feature-centered distributions that probably result from commonalities in body mechanics. But they also suggest that feature-centered distributions were organized into macro-level configurations through different kinds of social practices or cultural logics. In the case of Maritime Archaic longhouses we might anticipate that micro-level feature-centered distributions will be similar to those in the behavioral models, but that their integration into the dwelling as a whole will be culturally idiosyncratic. We should now briefly consider some ethnographic examples that illustrate the mutual structuring of spatial practice and cultural logic.

Ethnography: Social Space and Meaning

The preceding discussion of archaeological spatial patterning identified some micro-level behavioral consistencies, but the interpretive scope of these observations is limited: "We are left with a bunch of pieces, but cannot explain why they are assembled the way they are" (Whitelaw 1994:219). The integration of micro-patterns into macro-configurations is structured by differing social and cultural logics that were hinted at but not illuminated in the preceding discussion. The behavioral dimensions of dwelling space will now be related to social and ideological aspects of spatial organization using ethnographic analogies, beginning with social organization linkages then shifting towards the symbolic.

The strongly behavioral ethnoarchaeological studies of spatial patterns have been supplemented by greater attention to the role of social organization in community patterning. To a great extent this has focused on the degree to which dwelling proximity in settlement layouts correlates with social relationships such as kinship, sharing and labor cooperation (e.g., Binford 1991; Gargett and Hayden 1991; Whitelaw 1991; Yellen 1977). Whitelaw's (1991) cross-cultural study of hunter-gatherer community space concluded that there are clear linkages between spatial and social proximity, and that increases in social scale result in more organization or patterning of community structure. In situations involving cooperation in labour or resource sharing, close spacing of habitations facilitates interaction, but also the monitoring of behavior and possessions (Whitelaw 1991:168), which plays into the regulation of cooperation and sharing. Whitelaw (1991:165) notes that linear spatial arrangements are primarily found in arctic and subarctic regions; strangely, he relates this to dispersal of social units along shorelines and claims that "...because linear arrangements allow only one or two neighbors, they do not particularly emphasize the coherence of a group." Such a conclusion is thin, to say the least, and it seems absurd to suggest that linear arrangements such as Maritime Archaic longhouses contribute little to group coherence. Although cross-cultural generalizations can point to general patterns to be investigated, they are not very context sensitive and in a case such as hunter-gatherer longhouses, which are very rare in the ethnographic record, they completely fail us. It is necessary, therefore, to explore specific contextual studies in order to arrive at a more dynamic view of spatial patterning.

Archaeological treatment of the meaningful dimensions of space has built on the seminal work of Bourdieu (1979) and Lévi-Strauss (1963) on dwelling organization, combined with Giddens' (1984) structuration theory, the work of diverse human geographers and influences from phenomenology. At the risk of oversimplifying, the common thread is that space is organized in accordance with symbolic principles, but spatial meanings are invoked, reproduced or changed through human practice (Parker Pearson and Richards 1994:5). Meaningful space is constructed through social action and, in turn, that construction acts back upon social action: meaning-laden space is both a product and precedent of agency. This holds for the small scale of dwelling sites as well as for large scale landscapes (Tilley 1994). The following is a nice summary statement of this view, as applied to the organization of housing space:

> The house and the body are intimately linked. The house is an extension of the person; like an extra skin, carapace or second layer of clothes, it serves as much to reveal and display as it does to hide and protect. House, body and mind are in continuous interaction,

the physical structure, furnishing, social conventions and mental images of the house at once enabling, moulding, informing and constraining the activities and ideas which unfold within its bounds. A ready-made environment is fashioned by a previous generation and lived in long before it becomes an object of thought, the house is a prime agent of socialization (Carsten and Hugh-Jones 1995:2).

A focus on the interplay of mind, architecture and action leads to consideration of the metaphorical role played by housing as a material representation of social structure and ideology, either as a mirror or transformation. Seen from the structuralist tradition, components of houses can represent social divisions and hierarchies, while the dwelling as a whole can give the appearance of unity to opposing principles (Carsten and Hugh-Jones 1995:8, 12) or encode cosmological metaphors. As emphasized above, however, these are not static abstract structures but codes and materials that are produced and reproduced through daily practice.

An example of this perspective is Yates' (1989) structuralist analysis of social space in Sami tents. Gender was structured by divisions into male (back) and female (front) space, while the generations (parents and young children, versus older children) were distinguished laterally. In both cases the central hearth served as the fulcrum of the spatial differentiation. These socio-spatial divisions were paralleled by conceptual divisions based on Sami cosmology, such that a series of binary oppositions were played out within the horizontal dwelling space: male/female, back/front, north/south, winter/summer, sacred/profane, clean/unclean, death/life, hunting/milking, hunting blood/menstrual blood. The hearth was the crucial center that mediated these oppositions. Furthermore, the vertical space of the tent was divided into levels associated with divisions of the heavens, with different spiritual personages associated with each level. Consequently, the tent was a locus in which gender and other structures were produced and reproduced in daily practices.

Siberian Nenets tent interiors and camp lay-outs are also structured by gender divisions and rules for movement (Golovnev and Osherenko 1999:32-39; Haakanson 2000:82-89). Tent doors normally face east. Within the tent the central hearth is the anchor point for an invisible symbolic *siyangi* line that extends westwards across the floor and continues outside the tent in the opposite direction from the entrance. Movement of all people within the tent is restricted to the front and sides of the hearth because it is not permitted to cross the *siyangi* line behind the hearth. Outside the tent, adult women are not permitted to cross the *siyangi* line when they are within sight of the camp. This means that women cannot move behind the tents and must instead depart and return from the front entrances by following the same path. Women's work areas are therefore in front of the tents. Although the movement of adult men is restricted within the tent it is not restricted outside; the men's work area is behind the tent where the *siyangi* line projects westwards. These symbolic orientation and movement regulation principles have consequences for the lay-out of multi-tent camps (Figure 14). The tents must be set up in a line along a north-south axis in order to maintain the principle that women cannot cross the multiple *siyangi* lines that extend from the western (back) sides of the dwellings (Haakanson 2000:219). The spacing between the tents is related to the nature and closeness of personal relationships (Haakanson 2000:221). It is interesting to compare this rule-structured linearity of individual dwellings with the linear organization of Maritime Archaic longhouses.

Tanner (1979:73-107) discusses the symbolic dimensions of space among the Mistassini Cree. For much of the year the Cree use single-family tent dwellings. When they are used at winter aggregation sites, Tanner (1979:83) notes they are arranged in a line. He suggests that a location on one end of the line will be chosen by the hunting group leader. Single-fam-

ily dwellings display a consistent pattern of internal organization. A central hearth is placed back from the doorway and a living area is positioned at the back of the dwelling behind the hearth and opposite the door. Each individual has their own place at the rear of the dwelling, while the front of the dwelling is communal space. The tent space is also divided by gender, with one side associated with women, the other with men. Within the gender divisions there are further spatial positionings in relation to marital status and age. Household items and foods are also ordered in relation to the gender division. The meat of large animals (moose, caribou, bear) is stored on the male side, while that of smaller animals (beaver, etc.) is stored on the women's side and each gender attends to the proper ritual treatment and disposal of the bones.

This basic pattern recurs when the Cree move to winter communal dwellings, which are shared by several families. Divisions of male and female space are maintained, with the proviso that adjacent families cannot place members of the same gender adjacent to each other. The hunting party leader selects a position near the doorway. Tanner (1979:86-87) notes that "...the move to a communal dwelling brings about a minimal alteration in the use of domestic space by the individual commensal group, and the relative autonomy of each group is preserved." This is consistent with Fitzhugh's (1985a) interpretations of Maritime Archaic longhouses. It should be noted, however, that unlike other frequently cited ethnographic cases (e.g., Bourdieu 1970; Carsten and Hugh-Jones 1995; Yates 1989), the organization of Cree interior space is not structured by geographic or cosmological symbolism (Tanner 1979:87).

The eastern subarctic ethnographic record contains sporadic references to large dwellings that could be called "longhouses." Among the Labrador Innu and the Québec Cree a large multi-hearth tent (Innu: *shaputuan*) was associated with the *makushan* caribou feast (Henriksen 1973:35-39; Tanner 1979:162-169, 180). Among the Ojibway, bark longhouses were

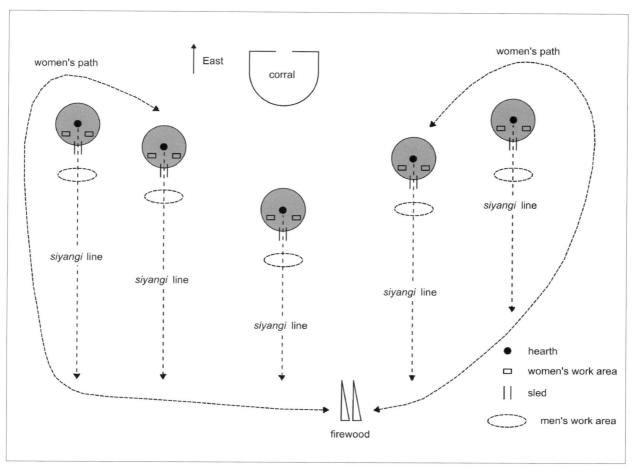

women's path

East

corral

women's path

siyangi line

siyangi line

siyangi line

siyangi line

siyangi line

●   hearth

▭   women's work area

‖   sled

⬭   men's work area

firewood

14/ Spatial organization of a Nenets summer camp (after Haakanson 2000:87; reproduced by permission of author).

used by the *Midéwiwin* ritual societies (Landes 1968:133; Steinbring 1981:252). An interesting (but not very well documented) example of symbolic spatial structures in the eastern subarctic is depicted in an eighteenth century painting by Major George Seton of a ritual feature constructed by the Cree (illustrated in McGhee 1996:176). The feature is an enclosure constructed of tightly-packed, shoulder-high branches embedded in the ground; judging by the size of the Cree figures, it must have been at least 25 m long and 5 m wide. At each end of the feature is an opening framed by arched tree branches while the central portion of the interior contains one or two hearths, a wooden post embedded upright in the ground and three presumably dead animals. The Cree (approximately 55 people are depicted within and around the feature) are mostly seated along the interior walls.

The feature seems to be a ritual transformation of a *shaputuan* structure.

The foregoing discussion points to several dimensions of variation beyond the strictly behavioral that may contribute to spatial patterning in dwellings. The problem for many will be: so what? These social and ideological dimensions are so culturally specific that they cannot be inferred reliably from archaeological data. But although signifying practices cannot be inferred *reliably,* they are obviously an important source of spatial structure that cannot be ignored. We can at least engage in contextual studies of spatial patterning that are open to such interpretive issues. With all the foregoing considerations in mind, methodological strategies for exploring different dimensions of spatial patterning in Maritime Archaic and Paleoeskimo sites will now be drafted.

Methodological Strategy for the Spatial Analysis of Maritime Archaic Sites

As emphasized above, a multi-scalar approach is required if we are to link social interpretations with patterning in Maritime Archaic dwellings. Three levels are discussed: micro-, meso- and macro-scales. In each case model-based interpretation and pattern recognition studies are played off against each other. The operation of site formation processes must also be considered.

Inside vs Outside Patterns

The first step in analyzing ambiguous distributions lacking clear architectural features is to distinguish between patterns likely to have been produced within dwelling structures versus those indicative of outdoor activities. According to Binford (1983:156-158, 176-184), distributions characteristic of dwelling interiors may exhibit the following characteristics: the outer border of the distribution is sharply constrained (indicative of a tent wall), hearths are carefully constructed to avoid uncontrolled burning and dispersal of ash and coals, no drop-toss zones are associated with hearths due to repeated maintenance activity, and outdoor dumps may accumulate as a consequence of maintenance procedures (Figure 6b). Maintenance activities may result in size-sorting of artifactual remains with a tendency towards smaller items remaining inside dwellings and larger items being transferred to external dumps (O'Connell 1987). While these suggestions seem to be a reasonable baseline, there are different ways of organizing internal space and the degree of maintenance activity may vary with the length of occupation.

Outdoor activities may be less spatially bounded than indoor activities; indeed some activities are conducted outdoors because of a need for unconstrained space or because the activities would be too messy or disruptive to be conducted within a dwelling (Binford 1983:170). Binford's (1978, 1983:153-156) model of activities conducted around outdoor hearths postu-

lates the presence of distinct depositional zones related to the features (Figure 6a). Drop zones should occur in an arc close to the hearths and contain small items that fell beside the hearth-users. On the opposite side of the hearth might be a forward toss zone where larger objects were thrown, while behind the hearth-users is a backward toss zone for larger items. The general configuration thus includes a size-sorting of objects. Additionally, the outer edge of the hearth-centered distribution will exhibit a gradual fall-off rather than clear bounding. Broadly similar patterns may be associated with other features related to "extensive" activity areas, such as butchering locales and cooking pits (Binford 1983:165-170). Another characteristic of outside distributions may be a relative lack of maintenance activity, which may result in mostly primary rather than secondary refuse. Nonetheless, a variety of formation processes may contribute to the "smearing" of these patterns, resulting in considerable ambiguity (Stevenson 1991).

Micro-scale Analysis

Initially, micro-scale analysis is directed towards the identification of relatively discrete behavioral units defined empirically through pattern recognition studies involving tool and debitage distributions and their relationships with features. Identification may involve visual inspection of point plots and density contours, or the use of quantitative techniques such as k-means cluster analysis and correspondence analysis. The contents of k-means clusters can be compared using contingency table analysis. The distribution patterns should be interpreted in terms of their status as primary/secondary refuse and be related to body mechanics and daily practices. These micro-scale patterns can then be coordinated to identify possible behavioral modules, at which point the ethnoarchaeological models for feature-centered distributions can be applied. These behavioral modules then become social-analytical units for defining possible family floor spaces or longhouse segments.

Meso-scale Analysis

Meso-scale analysis is directed towards phenomena which link modules together, both behaviorally and socially. Continuous linear distributions of primary refuse are probably the best indicators of supra-module behavioral patterning, since they are most likely to be the product of *in situ* social action. Cross-module distributions of secondary refuse would be more ambiguous, as secondary refuse is indicative of maintenance behavior rather than *in situ* social action. For example, continuous distributions of small-sized debitage might be a better meso-scale indicator than fire-cracked rock, since the latter is more likely to be secondary refuse. Cross-module links might also be identified through refitting analyses or more general technological organization studies aimed at mapping the staging of lithic reduction in different parts of a dwelling. Other characteristics, such as rock constructions and even the orientation of empty spaces, may also play a role in identifying meso-scale patterning.

Macro-scale Analysis

Macro-scale analysis is concerned with the overall form of the dwelling: how its structural logic channels practice, its role as both a material precedent for and product of social action, and how the dwelling form may represent conceptual structures. These questions may be addressed qualitatively by identifying patterns of symmetry, order, repetition and relationships between communal and private space. Quantitatively, the focus is on comparing the contents of individual modules to identify patterns of repetition or variability that may be related to social similarities or differences. These patterns can be assessed using simple contingency table comparisons of module content, or in the case of larger structures, correspondence analysis.

Although these three analytical levels have been presented in a sequence from micro-analysis to macro-analysis, this does not imply that one must begin with the former and end with the latter. Indeed, as will be shown in Chapter 6, it may be useful to begin with an assessment of overall structural patterns at the macro-level before turning to micro-level analysis. Consequently, the analytical process requires a multi-scalar circularity that might be considered "hermeneutic" (Hodder 1999).

Formation Processes

The analytical strategy discussed above would be incomplete without discussion of relevant site formation processes. To some extent these will be specific to individual localities, but several general observations can be made. Natural formation processes are the best understood. The properties of the sediment matrix in which the cultural material is deposited is a major factor complicating spatial relationships. The Maritime Archaic selection of sandy beaches raises problems because sand is an unstable surface subject to deflation and redeposition. Such instability may result in considerable vertical movement, possibly size-sorting of artifacts, and the destruction of certain features. Stable gravel surfaces may present fewer problems, but on cobble beaches there may be a pronounced trickle-down effect of smaller objects between the rocks. Horizontal movement related to occupation activity is more likely to "smear" distributions in sand deposits than in gravel or cobble sediments. Aeolian processes in sandy sediments may also displace artifacts horizontally. Other natural formation processes of relevance to the study area include tree-falls and frost action, both of which may cause vertical and horizontal shifts in artifacts and obliterate features.

As far as cultural formation processes are concerned, most ethnoarchaeological research has focused on the implications of site maintenance for generating different patterns of primary and secondary refuse accumulation. Maintenance behavior is expected within dwellings, but the degree of implementation may vary with the length of occupation. Preventive maintenance (Binford 1983:177) would involve periodic clearing of primary refuse from dwelling floors and deposition of the waste outside or in less-used portions of the dwelling. This behavior may be recognizable in dump formation and size-sorting of artifactual material (Binford 1983:177; O'Connell 1987). However, refuse disposal patterns may also be affected by symbolic rules for the preferential deposition of certain items. At frequently re-occupied sites, such as the tombolo beaches used during the Early-Middle Maritime Archaic, there is a high likelihood of palimpsest deposits. Additionally, there might be repeated cannibalization of earlier dwelling structures for construction materials, although this might be difficult to identify in ambiguous spatial distributions.

Paleoeskimos: Axial Features and Bilateral Organization

A large collection of papers in the journal *Études/Inuit/Studies* (LeBlanc and Nagy 2003) provides a good overview of the range of variation in Paleoeskimo architecture. Paleoeskimo dwellings consisted of four principle types: (1) tent structures, often associated with central hearths, which occur in both Early and Late Paleoeskimo contexts, (2) semi-subterranean houses, found only in Dorset, (3) longhouses, also found only in Dorset (although Susan Rowley mentions a three-roomed "longhouse-like" Pre-Dorset feature— cited in Ramsden and Murray 1995:106; also Rowley and Rowley 1997:274), and 4) snowhouses, for which archaeological traces are absent or enigmatic. The present discussion is oriented primarily towards tent structures, since these are the focus of the analyses to follow, but semi-subterranean features are mentioned to the extent that they display features in common with the tent dwellings. Longhouses were discussed previously in the Maritime Archaic section.

Early Paleoeskimo tent dwellings display a variety of morphological characteristics. They may be ephemeral, consisting of little more than a cluster of rocks and associated lithics and bone, but in other cases they are more distinct features consisting of a box-hearth with or without a surrounding tent ring. The most discussed dwelling form is the mid-passage or axial feature, which is best known from the High Arctic, Greenland, Labrador and Ungava. These features consist of a central box-hearth, sometimes packed with cooking/heating stones, from which double lines of rock dividers extend outwards to separate a structure into two halves. They may or may not include an encompassing tent ring (e.g., Figure 15a). In Greenland there are also finds of what have been termed "platform dwellings," consisting of box-hearths associated with rock pavements (Olsen 1998). These structural variations have been treated largely in terms of seasonal differences, with some researchers arguing that the more substantial features with hearths and tent rings represent winter dwellings while the more ephemeral features indicate summer dwellings or winter snowhouses (Cox 1978:98; Maxwell 1985:98; cf., Savelle 1984). Analyzing Pre-Dorset structures from Prince of Wales Island, Ramsden and Murray (1995) suggested that faunal associations imply the opposite inference: substantial features were used during the summer while ephemeral features represent winter dwellings. Knuth (1967:43) concluded from his work in northern Greenland that it was impossible to distinguish summer/winter dwellings; the housing tradition was by nature insubstantial and highly transportable. A recent integration of Knuth's data underlines the difficulties of seasonal interpretation (Grønnow and Jensen 2003:337).

Less attention has been paid to Dorset tent dwellings. In some cases these also incorporate an axial feature principle, sometimes with slab pavements and soapstone vessel support rocks, and they may or may not be encompassed by tent rings (e.g., R. Jordan 1980:611; Lemoine et al. 2003; Sutherland 2003; Chapter 9 in this volume). Such features were presumably used from spring to fall.

Detailed studies of the spatial patterning associated with Paleoeskimo structures have been limited. Researchers often publish floor plans of structures with their associated artifacts, but these are generally presented as site documentation, with little attention

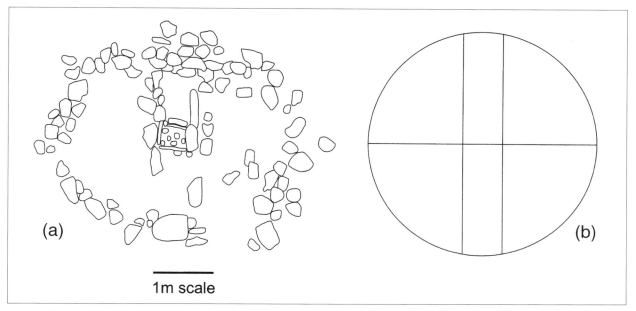

15/ Early Paleoeskimo axial features. (a) Peary Land, North Greenland (after Knuth 1967: plate 7; reproduced by permission of EHESS/CNRS), (b) bilateral model analytical subdivisions.

to behavioral or social analysis. The first attempt to address spatial analysis problems was that of Dekin (1976), who used simple quantitative methods in what he termed "elliptical analysis" to explore spatial patterning at the Pre-Dorset Closure site on south Baffin Island. Dekin addressed several questions: (1) the general nature of the locality (dwelling, outdoor), (2) the nature of the dwelling (tent, snow house, etc.), (3) the shape and configuration of the tent, (4) the entrance location, and (5) internal activity organization. These questions were constructed with the help of general ethnographic expectations and then presented as hypotheses to be tested. His method consisted of constructing two ellipses around the distribution, one representing the hypothesized outer edge of a tent, the other a possible internal tent skirt. The ellipses were then divided into four quadrants that were used as analytical units for the exploration of internal activity variation. Dekin suggested the internal spatial pattern might indicate a division of labor by sex. He concluded that the ellipse-quadrant principle, which began as an analytical technique, fit well enough with the Pre-Dorset data that it could be used as a general model for Pre-Dorset activity partitioning.

Although valuable as a first attempt at explicit spatial analysis, the method is highly model dependent. The use of four quadrants as analytical units is rather coarse-grained, since each quadrant consists of a ca. 4 m^2 block. Consequently, more subtle patterns on a smaller scale are overlooked and distributions that overlap quadrants risk analytical amputation. With these simple quantitative comparisons one would not expect to be able to "see" much variation other than that anticipated by the model. More fine-grained pattern recognition techniques might permit a fuller exploration of the spatial structure and they would be less model dependent.

Besides Dekin's effort, perhaps the most explicit attempt to develop a methodology for the analysis of Paleoeskimo structures is that of Stapert and Johansen's (1996) application of "ring and sector" analysis and refitting to the early Dorset site Ikkarlussuup Tima in Disko Bay, Greenland. The site consisted of two tent rings and what was interpreted as a sod house. Ring and sector analysis was first developed for analysing hearth-centered distributions on European Upper Paleolithic sites. The technique plots histograms of item frequencies within concentric rings at various intervals (50 cm seemed optimal) extending out from hearth features. The method was linked explicitly with Binford's hearth-centered models in that outdoor hearths were expected to produce unimodal ring distributions of debris reflective of gradual fall-off, while debris distributions associated with hearths inside dwellings would produce multimodal distributions reflective of wall effects. The rings could also be divided into horizontal sectors to detect variations in object frequencies that might depart from the "wall effect" and thereby indicate dwelling entrances. While innovative, the technique tends to assume what it sets out to prove— it is very model dependent. Since it is based on quadrat counts, such coarse resolution may hamper critical evaluation of model expectations. Furthermore, inconsistencies between the ring and sector analysis and the refitting results in the study were downplayed as an "optical illusion" resulting from the use of different data types (Stapert and Johansen 1996:64-65). One might conclude, however, that refitting provided more robust results.

Following on the heels of Dekin's analysis was McGhee's (1979:52-55) discussion of the spatial organization of Independence I dwelling features at the Cold site on Devon Island. McGhee divided these features into quadrants, with the central point on a hearth or presumed hearth area, thus creating front/back and left/right analytical units. Combining the artifactual material from several features at the site, he used a chi-square test to conclude that, overall, there were no significant differences between front/back, but that there were significant differences between left/right. He attributed the lateral differences to men's tool kits (right side: burins, burin spalls, hunting weapons) vs women's tool kits (left side: microblades, needles). McGhee (1979:255) extended this inference by suggesting that non-dwelling sites ("camps" and "work stations") which tend to have high percentages of possibly male tools may indicate primarily male activities.

A serious methodological problem with McGhee's analysis is that he lumped the material from several different dwelling features into a single contingency table in order to avoid small sample size problems. This procedure masks the scope of variation to the degree that the meaningfulness of the lumped sample must be questioned. Another problem is McGhee's use of the same coarse quadrat technique as Dekin, which renders the analysis insensitive to finer-grained spatial patterning, some of which is clearly evident in the Cold site floor plans. Finally, the assumptions regarding gender specific tools are problematic, although they are useful for drawing out possible dimensions of social variation.

Jensen's (1994, 1996) discussion of Paleoeskimo sites in the Skjoldungen District of southeast Greenland presented a spatial analysis of a Dorset locality that also considered site formation factors such as distinctions between primary and secondary refuse. Lithic raw materials proved to be particularly useful for the analysis, since each raw material type seemed to have its own depositional history (Jensen 1996:156). Different types of raw materials tended to be found on either side of the axial feature, which Jensen suggested may indicate a division of space by gender. Analysis of the circulation and deposition of lithic raw materials was developed further by Desrosiers and Rahmani (2003), who used the *chaîne opératoire* method to link lithic reduction sequences to spatial patterning at a Middle Dorset site in Nunavik, northern Québec .

A recent unpublished thesis by Mikalsen (2001) focused on spatial analysis of two Saqqaq sites from Disko Bay, west Greenland. One locality consisted of a single tent ring structure while the other contained five features: one distinct axial feature, a "platform" structure, two hearths and a possible cache. The analysis employed two approaches: simple cross-tabulations were used to evaluate bilateral left/right, front/back patterning, while *k*-means cluster analysis was used to search for other aspects of patterning. There was a tendency for burins, points and knives to be deposited separately from microblades and scrapers, although the distinction was not strictly bilateral. This pattern was interpreted as indicating functional and possibly gender differences in the use of space. At one of the sites, flakes of chalcedony and crystal quartz seemed to have more restricted spatial distributions than the predominant *killiaq*. The cluster analyses seemed most useful for identifying specific activity or depositional areas, while the cross-tabulations based on the bilateral model revealed patterns in the raw material distribution that were not so evident in the cluster analyses.

While many researchers view the apparent bilateral structure of Paleoeskimo axial feature dwellings as reflecting a division of labor and space by gender, others have suggested the dualism may indicate a partitioning of space between two co-residential families. This is unlikely for most Early Paleoeskimo structures. On the one hand, they seem too small for two families. On the other hand, two families arranged on opposite sides of a mid-passage should result in functionally redundant tool assemblages on each side, but in some cases there are functional differences in tools that depart from these expectations and seem more consistent with a gender interpretation (Jensen 1996). The co-residential family hypothesis seems more appropriate for Dorset; Harp (1976:132) suggested that Dorset semi-subterranean dwellings housed joint household units. A Late Dorset structure at Okak-3 in Labrador was rather large (7-8 m by 6 m) and had an axial feature with three hearths (Cox 1978:111); the large floor area and multiple hearths are suggestive of a joint household. Some Labrador Dorset tent rings are large (6 by 3.25 m) and bisected by a central rock alignment, leading R. Jordan (1980:612) to propose they were used by two families. It seems beyond doubt that Late Dorset longhouses were used by multiple households, although the precise nature of that use is unclear.

The possible symbolic meanings of the axial feature have also been considered. Knuth (1983:8-12) observed that Pearyland Independence I and Independence II axial features were oriented consistently towards water. He noted that the two halves of the dwelling structures bisected by an axial feature could be referred to by Greenlandic terms as: *avangnâ*, ("the side on your right when you sit in the tent facing the water") and *kujatâ*, the left side. A consistent conceptual division was implied, but the point was not developed further. Knuth simply suggested that: "The hearth passage of the Independence culture seems to be a kind of universal furniture unit serving as lamp, heating installation, cooking stove, kitchen cupboard, firewood box, and clothes chest" (Knuth 1983:12; Jensen [1996:156] makes a similar observation).

Plumet (1989:323-324) developed the idea of the axial feature and bilateral symmetry as a central conceptual theme in Paleoeskimo dwelling organization for over 3000 years. He suggested a metaphor of the axial feature as the "backbone" of the dwelling, uniting a family group within individual structures. With a spatial transformation of the small tent axial principle into the central axis of the Dorset longhouse, a series of individual family floor areas were united into a band unit. Furthermore, Plumet drew a comparison with the depictions of bilateral symmetry in Dorset art, in which animal anatomy is often depicted in "x-ray" style in terms of a backbone with ribs extending outwards. Following Knuth (1967a:48, 1967b:199), Plumet compared the axial concept with the Sami fireplace and tent structure, and their symbolic associations. Thus, through the back door (so to speak), we come to the relevance of Yates' (1989) structuralist interpretation of the Sami tent as an analogy for the analysis of Paleoeskimo axial structures.

Odgaard (2001:164, 2003:369-370) associated the axial feature with circumpolar shamanistic ideas of the hearth as a gateway to other worlds, such as mythological "clan rivers." She also suggested that hearths and axial features were physical markers that socialized the arctic landscape and served as conduits for cultural memory, symbolically relating human groups to the land.

A final suggestion for possible symbolic meaning of the axial feature originated from a photograph shown at a 1999 Arctic archaeology meeting in Copenhagen. The photo, taken by Knud Rasmussen in southern Greenland, showed a child's play-model of a kayak made from rocks. There was a prominent central box made of flat slabs, representing the cockpit, while rocks extended outwards in opposite directions to indicate the bow and stern. The construction bore an interesting resemblance to an axial feature.

Methodological Strategy for the Analysis of Paleoeskimo Spatial Patterns

Most of the Paleoeskimo analyses undertaken herein will be conducted at the micro-scale level since the volume deals with probable tent dwellings rather than semi-subterranean houses or longhouses. Individual dwellings can probably be considered as behavioral modules, but if some structures contained joint families on opposite sides of an axial feature the opposed floor areas might be considered as individual behavioral modules. The kinds of patterns discussed on the multi-modular macro-scale for the Maritime Archaic longhouse— symmetry, repetition etc.— will thus be treated on the single module level for most of the Paleoeskimo structures. The discussion here will be somewhat briefer than for the Maritime Archaic, since some of the general observations made for that case apply here as well.

The model-based analysis takes its point of departure in a theme discussed repeatedly by researchers: bilateral organization centered on the hearth and axial feature. To what extent can patterns in tool types and raw materials on either side of and within the axial feature be indicative of joint family composition, gender differences or symbolic organization? Two families inhabiting different sides of the same dwelling may produce redundant deposits of tool types on each side of an axial feature, at least insofar as they are engaged in similar productive and maintenance activities. Division of the bilateral dwelling space by gender may

produce different and complementary distributions of tool types on either side of an axial feature. One might assume, following McGhee (1979) that tool types such as burins, burin spalls and hunting weapons could be associated with men's activities, while women's activities could be represented by microblades and scrapers. Linkages of particular lithic tools with gender is, unfortunately, rather problematic (cf., Gero 1991), but the interpretation might be more robust if a consistent pattern was repeated across multiple dwelling structures. Expectations for symbolic patterning are difficult to specify in advance, except insofar as the previously mentioned social and gender structuring of dwellings is embedded in the symbolic practices of daily life. One possibility is consistent bilateral patterning in the deposition of lithic raw material types. While this might simply reflect the practicalities of positioning reduction activities, repeated patterns of spatial contrasts in raw material types across many dwellings could be attributable to the symbolic meanings attached to different materials.

Methodologically, the bilateral model can be explored using simple contingency tables. The analytical units for dwelling space can be categorized as the axial feature and two lateral sides, or front and back zones (Figure 15b). An important limitation on such analyses is that tool frequencies are often so low that significance tests are impractical, thus conclusions remain impressionistic and highly vulnerable to sampling error. Reliance on the bilateral model limits interpretive scope, however, by locking us into preconceived analytical units. The broad spatial divisions used may not be sensitive to smaller scale patterns which may be significant for understanding behavioral and formational questions. Site plans often exhibit small clusters of tools and debitage that might represent discrete depositional and behavioral processes. These clusters must be understood at the microscale level and then integrated into the modular analysis. Lithic clusters could be considered using the hearth-centered model, but the presence of an axial feature may inhibit free rotation of bodies around the hearth, resulting in a distinctly bilateral distribution pattern rather than the expected arc-like distribution. Also, we sometimes assume that distinct hearths and axial features were used inside dwellings, but this need not have been the case where tent anchoring rocks are absent. Thus the inside-outside hearth question should be addressed in those cases where structural evidence is lacking.

The behavioral-formational agenda requires different analytical tools than the bilateral model approach: pattern recognition techniques that are less dependent on preconceived analytical units. As was the case for the Maritime Archaic strategy, k-means cluster analysis can be used as a model-independent pattern recognition technique for tool distributions. Because it is not particularly constrained by sample size, the method seems fairly well suited for Paleoeskimo sites, which typically consist of relatively small numbers of tools spread over fairly compact areas. Clustering techniques will be employed to recognize micro-level item groupings that may be useful for identifying behavior such as discrete drop or dump zones. The contents of the resulting clusters can then be compared using contingency table analysis. Point-plotted tools and debitage will be used to consider distribution boundary questions related to the inside-outside hearth problem (i.e., the wall effect). Additionally, point-plotted debitage will be used directly to analyze spatial variation in lithic raw materials, as well as to identify the appropriate quadrat groupings for contingency table analysis of raw materials. Where possible, tool refits can be used to point to behavioral connections within and outside of dwelling structures. The use of size-sorting to distinguish primary/secondary refuse is of minimal utility for Paleoeskimo material given the consistently small size of the tools and debitage.

Formation Processes

Most of the formation processes discussed for the Maritime Archaic are also relevant for Pre-Dorset. A slight contrast is the tendency for Pre-Dorset sites to be located on gravel beaches rather than sand. These more stable surfaces might be characterized by less horizontal smearing and less likelihood of palimpsest deposits caused by deflation and redeposition. Dwelling structure cannibalization and recycling of construction materials is to some extent recognizable from disturbance of the expected patterns of formalized box-hearths and axial features that are sometimes present on Pre-Dorset sites.

Notes on the Quantitative Methods

Given that a wide array of quantitative techniques is readily available for spatial analysis, a few words should be said regarding the choice of techniques used here. Besides the obvious requirement that the techniques should provide information on patterning relevant to the models being evaluated, the techniques must be appropriate to the data collection format. At the Maritime Archaic site Nukasusutok-5, much of the provenience data for two abundant tool classes, utilized flakes and bipolar cores, is limited to quadrat frequencies. This situation necessitates reliance on quadrat-based analytical methods. Another requirement—partly self-imposed rather than conceptually grounded—was that the techniques should be methodologically transparent and empirically rich. That is, they should be relatively simple mathematically and easy for most readers to grasp, involve minimal statistical transformation of the data and provide a description of the patterning that would enhance the empirical detail rather than cloak it with mathematical abstraction. The two main techniques used here meet these demands: k-means cluster analysis and contingency table analysis. A third technique, multivariate correspondence analysis, is less easy to grasp mathematically, but as a data reduction technique it provides graphic output that can be useful for understanding the underlying dimensions of variation in complex data sets. A fourth technique involving a size-sorting index is more problematic and is used experimentally.

K-means cluster analysis (Kintigh and Ammerman 1982) is employed frequently for the analysis of point distributions. The technique uses measured distances (Euclidean) between item types to define circular clusters of cultural material. The clusters are formed by subdividing the total data set such that intra-cluster variance is minimized while inter-cluster distance is maximized using the sum squared error (SSE). Cluster centroids indicate the mean x and y values of the items assigned to the cluster. There is a degree of subjectivity in determining how many clusters constitute the best statistical solution. Inflection points on graphic plots of the %SSE plotted against the number of clusters provide some "objective" indication of the number of clusters in the best solution. Ultimately, however, it is our understanding of site context, which is embedded in our model-related preconceptions, that screens the possible solutions and guides the final decision. An important shortcoming is that *k*-means has the built-in requirement of circular clusters. Refuse distributions are, of course, rather more irregular in shape, but the technique appears to provide fairly robust results (Blankholm 1991:75). Since *k*-means analysis does not include a statistical technique for comparing the contents of the clusters, this function is fulfilled by contingency tables.

Correspondence analysis (Greenacre 1993) is a multivariate data reduction technique used for identifying patterning in categorical data, in this case the contents of site quadrats. It is based on a chi-square distance measure applied to a table of units (quadrats) and variables (tool types, flake raw materials, etc.) and can be regarded as: "...a method for decomposing the overall Chi-square statistic...by identifying a small number of dimensions in which the deviations from the expected values can be represented" (StatSoft Inc. 2002). In practice this involves projection of perpendicular axes through the observed frequency profiles such that deviations from the expected profiles are expressed as geometric distances. Each axis accounts for a different part of the total variation. In a robust

solution the first two axes should explain most of the variation. The most important output is a bivariate plot of units and variables in which their distances from the origin express their deviations from their expected profiles. Units positioned closely in the plot share similar relative frequencies of variables. But the physical distances between unit and variable points in the plots cannot be interpreted directly because of the way statistical distances are computed; units can be compared with units and variables with variables, but their spacing relative to each other cannot be given a simple geometric reading. A general principle, however, is that each axis of the plot orders the points from one end to the other such that points at opposite ends of an axis display contrasting properties. Correspondence analysis is well-suited for quadrat-distributed data as long as item frequencies are sufficient relative to the number of units and variables, but only the Maritime Archaic site Nukasusutok-5 had a large enough sample and excavated area to justify application of the technique and then only to a limited degree.

In many situations simple contingency table comparisons of grouped quadrats are sufficient to reveal important dimensions of spatial patterns. This is perhaps the simplest, most methodologically transparent and empirically descriptive analytical technique in the existing arsenal. Its main drawback is that it requires cutting spatial distributions into categories and assumptions must be made as to which categories are relevant or justifiable. In the analyses to follow, spatial categories are defined in terms of model-derived units, by model-independent *k*-means clustering results and occasionally by visual assessment of the distributions. Where item frequencies warrant, the chi-square significance test is used to check for non-random relationships. Where item frequencies are so high that chi-square inevitably would produce a statistically significant result, as in the case of debitage frequencies from the Maritime Archaic site Nukasusutok-5, the test is omitted and the observed and expected frequencies are compared

Inuit fish camp at Comfort Cove, Snyder Bay. (Photo: W. Fitzhugh 1983)

to identify which table cells deviate most from expected values.

Given the role of size-sorting patterns in the site formation studies outlined above, Wandsnider (1996:353-354) formulated a size-sorting index (SSI) that can be used to monitor spatial variations in object size. The SSI summarizes the representation of small and large items in a quadrat, with high negative values indicating a dominance of large items, high positive values a dominance of small items, and values near 0 indicating a mixture of sizes. There are some obvious drawbacks to this index. First, the cut-off point for small versus large items is subjective. Second, the index does not make much sense for the Pre-Dorset lithic assemblages since they are composed almost entirely of rather small items. Even in assemblages with somewhat wider size-ranges a limited number of items in the large category can be overwhelmed by "noise" from an abundant small category. Third, the

utility of the index may be limited by the total number of items used. Debitage assemblages might provide enough material for meaningful spatial comparisons, but in assemblages with few tools the index might be highly susceptible to random effects and it may be difficult to compare widely distributed excavation units with low item frequencies. Given all these considerations, the index was only applied to the large quartz debitage assemblage from the Maritime Archaic site Nukasusutok-5.

Conclusion: Behavioral Space and Signifying Practices

Most of the discussion to be presented in other chapters of this volume is couched in terms of identifying the behavioral dimensions that might account for observed spatial patterns. Some of these behavioral dimensions involve the unintended consequences of body mechanics while others involve intentional actions related to site maintenance considerations. These are dimensions for which ethnoarchaeological middle-range theory building has provided a reasonably robust interpretive framework. The approaches to the social dimensions of space that were outlined previously mostly fit within the structuralist tradition in which pre-existing cultural schemas are construed as generating material culture patterns. This is a cultural constructionist position in which a frame of meaning is imposed on practice and on nature. Meaning is not strictly pre-programmed, however, it is activated through practice. Practice draws upon cognitive schemas but it also responds to precedent practices and the need for situational improvisation. Although constructionist approaches are useful counterpoints to myopic behaviorism they fail to capture the "work in progress" nature of social action as signifying practice (cf. Ingold 1993:162). The social structuration of space is an ongoing and always incomplete work and individual components or sites are only partial sedimentations of processes that stretch over variable scales of space and time. Spatial patterns therefore may be ambiguous with respect to both function and meaning. Nonetheless, it is hoped that the methodological strategies outlined above will help reduce ambiguity and lead to useful proposals regarding the behavioral and social dimensions of Maritime Archaic and Paleoeskimo dwelling space.

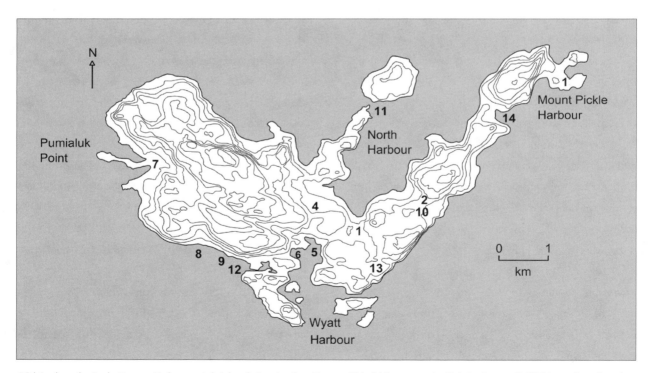

16/ Archaeological sites on Nukasusutok Island. Precise locations withheld by request. Original map © 2004 produced under licence from Her Majesty the Queen in Right of Canada, with permission of Natural Resources Canada.

CHAPTER 3

Nukasusutok Island: Overview and Surveyed Sites

The first archaeological fieldwork undertaken on Nukasusutok Island was in 1928 when William Duncan Strong excavated Inuit communal houses at the site now designated as Nukasusutok-8 and collected from graves at several locations on the western end of the island, including Nukasusutok-7. J. Garth Taylor revisited Nukasusutok-8 during his 1966 field study of Labrador Inuit settlements (Taylor 1966). In 1973, Warren Hofstra, associated with the Smithsonian Institution, conducted a brief survey of the island and recorded Nukasusutok-1 to 7 and Nukasusutok-9. William Fitzhugh's Smithsonian crew returned in 1975 and 1976 to conduct further surveys, test Nukasusutok-5 and excavate the Late Pre-Dorset structures at Nukasusutok-2.

In 1979 and 1980 the author conducted several investigations on the island. The Maritime Archaic site Nukasusutok-5 was excavated in both years and the Dorset locality Nukasusutok-12 was excavated in 1980. Surveys were carried out in both years in order to revisit previously recorded sites and identify new ones. Nukasusutok-9 (HcCh-11) was the only site that was not relocated. The area surveyed in 1979 was restricted to the central portion of the island between Nukasusutok 8 and 10; the eastern end of the island near Mount Pickle Harbour was surveyed in 1980. Additional excavations were conducted by the author at Nukasusutok-5 in 1992 and 1993 and Nukasusutok-8 was test-pitted in 1993. In 1997 contract surveys related to mineral exploration were undertaken by

Gerald Penney (1997), who identified previously unrecorded features at Nukasusutok-7 on the southwest corner of the island. These features were revisited by the author in 2004.

Table 1 lists the archaeological sites that have been registered on Nukasusutok Island and their approximate locations are depicted in Figure 16. Precise point locations are withheld at the request of the provincial Culture Heritage Division. A total of 14 sites has been recorded, of which eight components are attributable to the Maritime Archaic, five to the Labrador Inuit, two to Dorset and one to Late Pre-Dorset. This chapter provides brief descriptions of the minor surveyed sites, most of which are Maritime Archaic flake scatters. Four sites will be described in separate chapters: the excavated localities of Nukasusutok-5 (Maritime Archaic), Nukasusutok-12 (Early/Middle Dorset), and W. D. Strong's and the author's activities at Nukasusutok-7 and 8. One significant site will not be considered in detail: Nukasusutok-2. This important Late Pre-Dorset locality is described by Fitzhugh (2002), so only a brief summary is provided as follows.

Nukasusutok-1 (HcCh-4)

This locality includes a small Maritime Archaic occupation and two large Inuit fox traps. The Maritime Archaic component is located on a flat gravel ridge on the south side of a rock outcrop and has clear views to the northeast and southwest. To the north the topog-

Table 1. List of Archaeological Sites Registered on Nukasusutok Island.

Site Name	Borden No.	Culture	Site Type
Nukasusutok-1	HcCh-4	Maritime Archaic; Inuit	lithic scatter; fox traps
Nukasusutok-2*	HcCh-5	Late Pre-Dorset	axial feature dwellings
Nukasusutok-4	HcCh-6	Maritime Archaic	lithic scatter
Nukasusutok-5	HcCh-7	Maritime Archaic	habitation site
Nukasusutok-6	HcCh-8	Maritime Archaic	lithic scatter
Nukasusutok-7	HcCi-8	Inuitsod house,	tent rings, graves
Nukasusutok-8	HcCh-10	Inuit	communal sod houses, graves
Nukasusutok-9	HcCh-11	Maritime Archaic(?)	lithic scatter
Nukasusutok-10	HcCh-12	Maritime Archaic	lithic scatter
Nukasusutok-11	HcCh-13	Inuit	tent rings
Nukasusutok-12	HcCh-14	Early/Middle Dorset	axial feature dwellings
Nukasusutok-13	HcCh-15	Maritime Archaic	lithic scatter
Nukasusutok-14	HcCh-16	Maritime Archaic; Inuit	lithic scatter; pinnacles
Mount Pickle Harbour-1	HcCh-17	Early Dorset	lithic scatter

*Nukasusutok-3 was combined with Nukasusutok-2

raphy drops quite steeply down to the North Harbour while in all other directions the site is bordered by lower marshy areas. No elevation above sea level was taken, but according to the topographic map it must lie at roughly 65 m asl. The site was first reported in 1973 by Hofstra, who surface collected a single ground slate flake. The cultural material observed in 1979 was scattered sparsely across a deflated area about 8 m by 8 m in size. A biface blank of Ramah chert was surface collected. Flakes of quartz, Ramah chert, slate and black chert were noted on the surface.

The lithic raw materials and high elevation suggest a Maritime Archaic *Naksak* Complex affiliation. The biface blank (Figure 17:c) is large (133 mm long), asymmetric in form, with partial flaking of the dorsal surface (mostly on the margins), and a largely unretouched flat ventral surface with cortex. The unusually high elevation suggests the locality was probably used when the shoreline was lower, perhaps as low as 30 m asl., for which a date of ca. 6800 B.P. would be expected, although an even later date is possible.

The two Inuit fox traps are positioned on top of a rock outcrop. They are constructed of large rocks and boulders and contain sliding door openings.

Nukasusutok-2 (HcCh-5)

This important Late Pre-Dorset locality was visited by the Smithsonian Institution in 1975 and two axial feature dwellings were excavated in 1976 (Cox 1978:101; Fitzhugh 1976:135). The site is located on a broad gravel beach at roughly 60-65 m asl., about 30 m northwest of the Maritime Archaic site Nukasusutok-10, which is situated higher up on the crest of the beach sequence. The material has recently been published by Fitzhugh (2002); the following site description summarizes his report.

The two axial feature dwellings lay virtually side-by-side, only 14 m apart. Both were oval, bi-lobed in form, with their axial features oriented towards the north (seaward). Most of the tent anchor rocks at Structure 1 had been removed and piled on top of the axial feature, but Structure 2 was intact, with a sur-

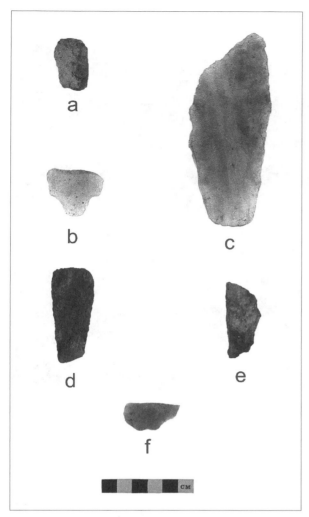

17/ Tools from surveyed Maritime Archaic Sites on Nukasusutok Island. a: bipolar core, Nukasusutok-4; b: stemmed point, Nukasusutok-4; c: asymmetric biface blank, Nukasusutok-1; d: miniature celt, Nukasusutok-13; e: celt fragment, Nukasusutok-6; f: bipolar core, Nukasusutok-14.

Small lithic assemblages were associated with each dwelling. Structure 1 had only 7 tools, all inside the structure. Structure 2 had 61 tools and 282 flakes, most of which were located outside the front of the dwelling. Those lithics deposited inside the structure were primarily associated with the axial feature and hearths; few were found in the lateral compartments. Tool types included: burins (ground and unground, some with waisted hafting constrictions), burin spalls, bifaces (two side-notched), an endscraper, microblades, microblade cores of crystal quartz, celts and utilized flakes. The most remarkable characteristic of the assemblage was the 10 celts associated with Structure 2, an unusually large number for an outer coast Pre-Dorset site.

The ground and waisted burin forms and side-notched bifaces are Late Pre-Dorset types. The axial feature dwellings are similar to the Independence II structures described by Knuth (1968). A single radiocarbon date run on burned fat procured from the hearth in Structure-1 was assayed at 3315 ± 85 B.P., or 3055 ± 85 B.P. with C-12/13 correction.

Cox (1978:98) suggested the more substantial Pre-Dorset axial feature structures, such as those at Nukasusutok-2, may be fall or winter dwellings (cf., Ramsden and Murray 1995). Fitzhugh (2002:153-155) concluded that Nukasusutok-2 might have been a winter settlement used from October to December, based on several characteristics of the site: (1) its unusually high elevation and great distance from the contemporary shoreline, (2) the solid and carefully planned construction of the dwellings as well as the presence of fire-cracked rock and burned fat, (3) the abundance of celts, presumably used for chopping firewood and frozen meat, and (4) the lack of lithics in the lateral compartments may indicate the presence of bedding. On the other hand, Fitzhugh (2002:155) also noted several features that might militate against a lengthy winter occupation: a small lithic assemblage indicative of minimal accumulation, a lack of storage caches, and predominantly outdoor lithic reduction activities. A

rounding ring of anchoring rocks (Figure 18). Both structures were ca. 4 m front-to-back along their axial features and ca. 5 m wide. In both cases the axial features consisted of three main components placed in a front-to-back sequence: (1) an enclosed box-hearth of vertical flat slabs containing "boiling stones," (2) a slab-lined hearth depression for heating the stones, and (3) a semi-open hearth bordered by inclined rock slabs and containing burned fat, interpreted as a lamp/cooking hearth. Both structures also had small wing pavements extending from one side of the axial feature at the rear of the dwelling.

18/ Nukasusutok-2: Structure 2.

summary of Pre-Dorset settlement patterns emphasized the general assumption that winter settlement was located in the inner bays or interior, in light of which Nukasusutok-2 is a singular anomaly (Fitzhugh 2002:155-156).

Nukasusutok-4 (HcCh-6)

Recorded by Hofstra in 1973, this Maritime Archaic site was revisited in 1979. It is located at the western end of a long tombolo beach near the center of the island and is probably ca. 70 m asl., near the marine limit. Exceptional views may be had northeastwards down North Harbour and across Wyatt Harbour to the south. The eastern portion of the beach surface is extremely rocky while the western end is vegetated with crowberry, lichen and small groves of spruce trees. Several small gravel-cobble blow-outs in the center of the beach were probably the source of the tools collected by Hofstra: a large Ramah chert biface midsection, a quartz biface tip, two quartz bipolar cores, five utilized flakes (two slate, three quartz) and one

ground slate flake. The 1979 surface collection consisted of the basal fragment of a Ramah chert point with a relatively compact stem (Figure 17:b) which seems stylistically earlier than those from the Nukasusutok-5 components believed to date 5600-5300 B.P. (Chapter 8).

A small test excavation of 7 m^2 was placed in the central portion of the beach and a 1 m^2 test pit was located 32 m to the south near the edge of the beach. The *in situ* deposits consisted of a thin (4-5 cm) mantle of vegetation and humus underlain by an intermixture of cobbles and brown sand. A small charcoal sample was procured in the central excavated area from a possible hearth associated with a faint red ocher stain, but the sample was insufficient for conventional radiocarbon dating. The only implements recovered from the excavated units were a Ramah chert biface fragment, a utilized flake of the same raw material and a quartz bipolar core (Figure 17:a). The small debitage collection, totalling 103 flakes, was composed of 73.5% quartz, 19.6% Ramah chert and 6.9% "others" (the latter including slate, gray quartzite and an igneous material). The paucity of cultural material indicates this site was a small temporary camp, with the wide separation of the surface scatters suggesting several discrete occupation loci.

About 100 m east of the excavation was a low rock mound situated 20 m back from the northern terrace edge. The mound lay on top of a sand-gravel beach and was oval, 3.50-3.75 m by 4.0-4.5 m in size and ca. 0.50 m high. It was bordered by seven large boulders and filled in with loosely packed 40-60 cm and larger boulders, heavily encrusted with black lichen. Since the feature resembled a Maritime Archaic burial mound it was photographed vertically with a bipod, after which the upper mantle of rocks was removed. This revealed a "box" formed by five very large boulders embedded in the beach with smaller rocks placed within. After additional bipod photography more rocks were removed from the box until sandy gravel was encountered and excavation continued through silt and rocks, terminating at 1.25 m below the surface since no trace of cultural material was found. It is uncertain whether this was a cultural feature.

Nukasusutok-6 (HcCh-8)

Nukasusutok-6 was recorded by Hofstra in 1973 and was revisited in 1979. It is located on the western side of Wyatt Harbour at the opening of an east-west trending pass and lies on a partially deflated raised beach at ca. 30 m asl., which can be maximum dated to ca. 6800 B.P.. The topographic location of the site suggests the terrace was inhabited when the pass was a narrow marine passage that separated what is now a peninsula from the mainland. This constriction may have been a good spot for sealing or fishing, but the sparse cultural remains indicate the site was only used briefly.

The cultural materials occurred in three small localities that extended along the terrace front for about 25 m. Each locality was a debitage scatter of 6-8 m^2 in size. Flake raw material data were collected at each locus by counting the items found within a 1 m diameter sampling circle at the center of each distribution (Table 2). Quartz constituted 91-96% of the flakes sampled, slate 4-15%. Slate varieties present included green, red, mauve and gray-banded materials. Only one Ramah chert flake was observed, but being outside the sampling units it was not included in the table counts.

Table 2. Nukasusutok-6 Flake Raw Materials

	L-1 N %	L-2 N %	L-3 N %	N % TOTAL
Quartz	71 (95.9)	50 (84.7)	6 (92.4)	182 (91.5)
Slate	3 (4.1)	9 (15.3)	5 (7.6)	17 (8.5)
TOTAL	74	59	66	199

Hofstra's 1973 surface collection included a celt fragment, two quartz utilized flakes and two quartz bipolar cores. The only tool was found in 1979 was a badly weathered miniature celt bit made of yellow-green slate (Figure 17:e), which is comparable to those from the Maritime Archaic *Naksak Complex*.

Nukasusutok-9 (HcCh-11)

Nukasusutok-9 was registered by Hofstra in 1973 but it was not possible to relocate it in 1979. According to the scanty site records it was located at the western end of the pass that separates the Wyatt Harbour Peninsula from the mainland. The only materials collected from the site were two utilized flakes of Ramah chert.

Nukasusutok-10 (HcCh-12)

Nukasusutok-10 is a Maritime Archaic occupation located on a raised gravel-boulder beach on the eastern arm of the island, ca. 75 m asl., near the marine limit. It is situated slightly above and about 30 m southeast of the Late Pre-Dorset structures at Nukasusutok-2. The best view from the locality is across the North Harbour. The site was discovered during the 1976 Smithsonian excavations at Nukasusutok-

2. A revisit in 1979 indicated that surface traces of Maritime Archaic activity were limited to two small concentrations of quartz debitage and numerous large chunks of quartz scattered intermittently among the boulders along the crest of the beach. Few Ramah chert flakes were observed. A large vein of quartz, 18 m long, 1 m wide, was exposed on the side of the hill to the northeast. This, and the large quantity of shattered quartz, suggested that one of the functions of Nukasusutok-10 might have been as a quarry site. Smithsonian surface collections included a small oval quartz biface and two biface fragments of Ramah chert. No tools were found during the 1979 visit. Fitzhugh (personal communication) suggested there might be a Maritime Archaic boulder structure at the crest of the raised beach, but observations in 1979 and a brief visit in 1992 failed to identify any structural remains. The high elevation and the quartz-dominated lithic material suggest an early *Naksak* Complex affiliation.

Nukasusutok-11 (HcCh-13)

This site consists of Inuit tent rings located at the tip of the peninsula that forms the western boundary of North Harbour.

Nukasusutok-13 (HcCh-15)

Nukasusutok-13 is a small Maritime Archaic site located on the south side of the island, ca. 1 km east of Wyatt Harbour, on a 65 m asl. raised beach that may have been a tombolo beach at the time of occupation. A good view of the sea is available to the south. Cultural materials consisted of a dense oval concentration of quartz debitage ca. 3 m in diameter with other flakes scattered about more diffusely for a total exposed area of 20 m². Two meters west of the quartz concentration was a 4 by 3 m oval alignment of cobbles that may have been a structural feature. A 1 m² test pit was excavated into a vegetated area adjacent to the quartz concentration, but only two quartz flakes were encountered. Two 1 m diameter circular sampling

units were used to generate raw material counts for the lithic scatter. Table 3 shows that 96 % of the material was quartz and 3 % Ramah chert. Outside the sample units two red quartzite flakes were also observed.

Table 3. Nukasusutok-13 Flake Raw Material Frequencies

	L-1 N %	L-2 N %	TOTAL N %
Quartz	210 (96.3)	14 (100.0)	224 (96.6)
Ramah Chert	8 (3.7)		8 (3.4)
TOTAL	218	14	232

The only tool recovered from the site was a virtually complete miniature celt of green slate (Figure 17:d), which was found on the surface 2 m south of the test pit. The lateral edges of the implement are bifacially flaked and grinding is concentrated at the bit, although it also extends over three-quarters of the tool. This form is typical of the *Naksak* Complex. The high elevation of 65 m suggests the site is fairly early in the Maritime Archaic sequence, but the locality was probably occupied when sea level was substantially lower than the beach terrace.

Nukasusutok-14 (HcCh-16)

This small Maritime Archaic locality is situated on a bare gravel tombolo beach near the middle of the island, 1 km west of Mount Pickle Harbor. No precise elevation was taken, but the site probably lies at 30-35 m asl. It consists of a 5 m diameter scatter of quartz debitage at the easternmost end of the raised beach. A Ramah chert bipolar core (Figure 17:f) and a slate flake were surface collected. No Ramah chert flakes were observed on the surface.

Mount Pickle Harbour-1 (HcCh-17)

The 1980 survey registered a Dorset site on a terrace overlooking the small harbour on the eastern end of Nukasusutok Island. A surface collection of 24 tools was procured. Four Ramah chert flakes and four

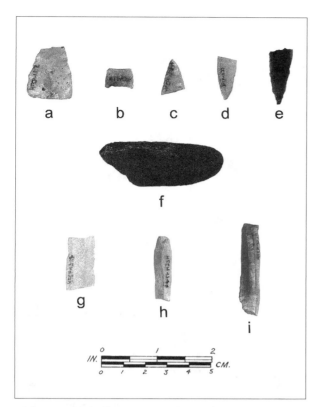

19/ Dorset Tools from Mount Pickle Harbour-1. a, b: triangular endblades; c: endblade on microblade; d, e: distally retouched microblades; f: ground schist; g-i: microblades.

Microblades (n=13) Twelve of the 13 microblades are made of Ramah chert, one is made of crystal quartz; examples are illustrated in Figure 19:g-i. Four are proximal fragments, five are medial fragments and three are distal elements. For the five specimens from which reliable measurements can be obtained, width ranges from 7.9-11.3 mm. Six specimens exhibit traces of utilization, while two are deliberately retouched. The retouched specimens are both distal fragments and both have been modified to create pointed tips. One example has one lateral edge retouched mostly on the dorsal side with less retouch ventrally, while the other lateral edge is mostly retouched ventrally (Figure 19:d). The other implement has slight ventral retouch on both edges, limited to the tip (Figure 19:e). It is unclear whether these are finished products or whether they were intended to be retouched points on microblades similar to Figure 19:c.

Utilized Flakes (n=3) All three utilized flakes are made of Ramah chert.

Ground Schist (n=1) A small bar of ground schist is illustrated in Figure 19:f.

Discussion

This small surface collection does not provide a solid basis for dating, but certain characteristics can be pointed out. The relatively straight-based endblades, together with the tip-fluting spalls, suggest an Early Dorset or early Middle Dorset date. The retouched point on a microblade (and possibly the distally retouched microblades) may also indicate a relatively early Dorset phase.

nephrite flakes (one ground) were also collected. The tool classes are described below.

Tool Descriptions

Triangular Endblades (n=3) All three triangular endblades are made of Ramah chert. Two are proximal fragments. One of these, which may be unfinished, has a straight, bifacially-thinned base (Figure 19:a). The other is small (12.8 mm wide) with a straight-edged indentation at the base that produces small spurs at each corner (Figure 19:b). The third specimen is a bifacially flaked distal fragment; its plano-convex cross-section and width suggest it was made on a microblade (Figure 19:c).

Tip-Fluting Spalls (n=4) All four tip-fluting spalls are made of Ramah chert. Two are complete or nearly complete, one is a proximal fragment, another a medial fragment. All are primary spall removals.

20/ *Nukasusutok-5 in its landscape. View to the west.*

Nukasusutok-5: Descriptive Overview

5

Nukasusutok-5 (HcCh-7) was discovered in 1973 by Warren Hofstra (associated with the Smithsonian Institution). The site was test-pitted in 1975 by William Fitzhugh (1976:132-133, 1978:77) and additional surface collections were made in 1976. These surveys indicated the site was large, extending for at least 100 m along a tombolo beach, with rich deposits of tools, debitage and charcoal. A hard soil deposit observed in one of the test pits was initially thought to be fat-consolidated sand (Fitzhugh 1978:66). Radiocarbon dates of 5575±90 B.P. and 4645±65 B.P. suggested the site pertained to the Middle Maritime Archaic period, although the spread of the dates implied the presence of more than one component. All of these factors indicated the site was a prime candidate for more intensive investigation, so the author undertook excavations there in 1979 and 1980 (Hood 1981). During the early 1980s, Fitzhugh built up a more detailed picture of Maritime Archaic dwelling structures. By the early 1990s, when the author began to re-evaluate his previous work, it was evident that some of the conclusions regarding spatial patterning were faulty. Consequently, in 1992 and 1993 additional excavations were implemented in order to clarify the spatial patterning at the site. This report combines the results of all field seasons and supercedes all previous interpretations.

Discussion of Nukasusutok-5 extends over five chapters. The primary function of this chapter is to provide a general background for the spatial analyses to follow. It begins with an overview of the site and its physical surroundings, moves on to an outline of the excavation layout and methods, then presents a description of the excavation results from the central subarea of the site, focusing on the features identified. Spatial patterning at the central subareas is discussed in Chapter 6, while description and analysis of the other subareas is found in Chapter 7. A description of the tool assemblages is provided in Chapter 8. Finally, Chapter 9 compares the subareas and draws general conclusions regarding the significance of Nukasusutok-5 for the study of the Early/Middle Maritime Archaic.

The Site and its Environs

Nukasusutok-5 is positioned in an extremely well-protected location deep inside Wyatt Harbour (Figure 16). Situated on raised beach terraces 28-31 m asl. (Figure 20), the site is surrounded by hills to the east, west and north that provide fair protection from the prevailing westerly wind, but northeasterly gales are liable to sweep the beach ridge since their force is only partially deflected. The southwest side of the raised beach drops steeply down to Wyatt Harbour, while the northeast slope is of moderate gradient. A paleoshoreline projected along the lowest occupied elevation of 28 m produces a tombolo beach that would provide access to the sea from both sides of the site. This tombolo beach would have been an attractive settlement space with shorelines even lower than 28 m because its grad-

21/ Nukasusutok-5 main beach terrace. Area 1 in foreground, Area 2 in center. View to the north.

ual northeast slope would continue to provide good boat landing possibilities.

The beach upon which the main part of site is located is about 120 m long, trending northwest-southeast, and ranges from 30-40 m wide across its crest (Figures 21 and 22). The northwestern end terminates at the base of a 150 m high hill and the southeastern end is bordered by a lower knoll, the summit of which is perhaps 15-20 m higher than the beach surface. The central and southeastern portions of the beach are dominated by lichen vegetation while the northwestern end is endowed with thicker growth, including dwarf birch and dwarf spruce. Towards the central and western parts of the steep slope along the south side of the beach, moister conditions and a somewhat sheltered location in the lee of the beach ridge have facilitated the growth of fairly dense clusters of dwarf spruce and a number of full-sized spruce trees. On the crest of the raised beach (31 m asl.), several boulders are exposed on the central surface of the beach and a few tongues of

bedrock are visible at the terrace edge. A small blow-out, covering about 50 m^2, is located near the southeastern end of the beach and is the only indication of serious erosion at the site. Otherwise, the deposits are undisturbed.

A small vein of quartz runs along the face of the northern hill, not far from its summit. Brief inspection of this geological feature did not reveal any obvious signs of quarrying activity, but it is possible that some of the quartz used by the inhabitants of Nukasusutok-5 was procured here. Quartz outcrops are also found at other places on the island, notably beside Nukasustok-10 (Chapter 4).

Archaeological Activities and Field Methods

1975 Smithsonian Institution Survey A total of 37 artifacts was surface collected during the Smithsonian surveys of 1973 and 1975, most presumably originating in the blow-out at the southeastern end of the raised beach. Among these artifacts were: four bifacial points, three flake points, one micropoint, two bifaces, three endscrapers, four flake knives, 25 utilized flakes and one bipolar core.

Three 1 m^2 test pits were excavated during the 1975 survey. Test Pit A was situated in the central portion of the beach and came down directly on a hearth that lay in "greasy" black sand mixed with charcoal and red ocher. Recovered from the unit were a biface tip, bipolar cores, utilized flakes and 161 flakes of quartz, Ramah chert, slate and Mugford chert. A charcoal sample from the hearth was dated to 5575±90 B.P. (SI-2626). Test Pit B was located 19 m northwest of "A" and contained a quartz biface tip, utilized flakes and 130 flakes of quartz, Ramah chert, slate, and Mugford chert. Black sand at the base of the deposits, 20 cm below ground surface, was interpreted as burned fat. Test Pit C was located 32 m northwest of "B" near the northwestern end of the beach. It contained a flake knife of Ramah chert and two utilized flakes, along with 5 unretouched flakes. The most remarkable feature of this test unit was a cemented soil horizon encountered 23-30 cm below the surface, which continued down to 55 cm where it terminated on sterile beach gravel. This horizon was interpreted as fat-consolidated sand. The cemented zone contained charcoal and flakes only in its upper 5-7 cm. A charcoal sample from the cemented horizon was dated to 4645±65 B.P. (SI-2527).

1979-80 Excavations The 1979 fieldwork addressed four main problems: (1) clarification of the divergent radiocarbon dates, (2) evaluating whether the cemented soil horizon was a cultural deposit of fat-consolidated sand, (3) the collection of intra-site activity patterning data, and (4) elucidation of the relationship between the Naksak, Sandy Cove and Rattlers Bight Complexes. A brief return to the site in 1980 aimed to resolve questions generated by the previous year's fieldwork: (1) were there two habitation structures, (2) was there a second, later, component in the central portion of the site, and (3) were a set of red ocher feature burials?

After the initial mapping procedures were completed a grid was installed on the site using a baseline running the length of the tombolo beach. Over the two field seasons, three-person crews excavated a total of ca. 124 m^2 in three separate subareas (Figure 22): the edge of the blow-out at the eastern end of the site (Area 1), the center of the beach (Area 2) and the south-facing beach slope (Area 3). An open-area excavation was conducted using 2 by 2 m fields subdivided into 1 m^2 quadrats as the basic working and recording units. In 1979, formal tools, utilized flakes and ground slate flakes were recorded *in situ*. Flake distribution patterns were recorded on floor plans by a combination of direct measurement and "eyeballing," and the debitage was collected by 1 m^2 quadrats. The excavation proceeded using arbitrary vertical levels ranging from 5-15 cm. Vertical depths were taken from the ground surface by line level. Virtually all of the excavation back-dirt was sifted through a 6.4 mm (1/4 inch) screen. In 1980 the excavation at Area 2 was extended, but because of poor weather conditions and limited time, debitage was not recorded *in situ* and very little back-dirt was screened. Fortunately, only a small area was excavated and the finds were much sparser than in the central part of Area 2. After these two field seasons it was concluded that: 1) Area 2 had evidence for two tent rings with external hearth areas, 2) the red ocher features at Area 3 were unlikely to have been burials, and 3) the supposed fat-consolidated sand was an extremely well developed iron pan (Hood 1981).

1992-93 Excavations In 1991-92 a re-evaluation of the original data in light of accumulated information on Maritime Archaic dwelling structures indicated that the previous interpretation positing two tent rings was incorrect. Instead, it seemed possible that some kind of rectangular structure was present. A report from Fitzhugh's brief visit to the site in 1985 (Smithsonian site record files) speculated on the presence of a longhouse structure running down the center of the beach.

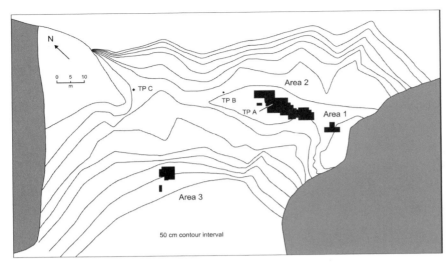

22/ Nukasusutok-5 excavation layout.

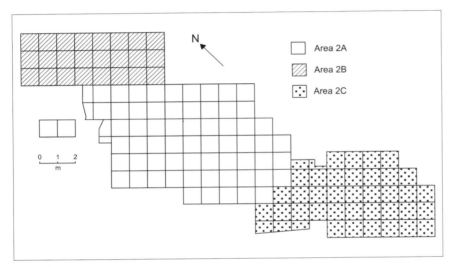

23/ Area 2 subareas.

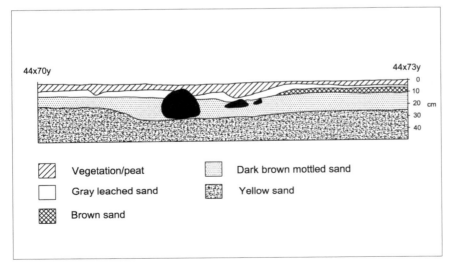

24/ Area 2A soil profile.

Consequently, the goal of the 1992-93 fieldwork was to extend the original Area 2 excavation towards the northwest and southeast to evaluate the possibility that the spatial patterns reflected the presence of a longhouse.

The field methods employed in 1992-93 were slightly different than those used in 1979-80. Debitage was collected in 50 cm² quadrats and the vertical depths of all retouched artifacts, rocks and other features were determined with an engineer's level. As in 1979, the flake distribution patterns were recorded through a combination of direct measurement and "eyeballing" and all back-dirt was screened through 6.4 mm mesh. In 1992 the excavation consisted of a rectangular field of 24 m² (Area 2B) which formed a northwestward extension of the original Area 2 excavation, while the 1993 effort opened up 27 m² (Area 2C) to the southeast of Area 2. In each year the work was accomplished by a two person crew.

Descriptions of the features, pedology, formation processes and dating of Area 2 are preconditions for making sense of the spatial patterns. Because the Area 2 spatial analysis in Chapter 6 is long and complex, the text is divided into manageable units by using most of the present chapter to describe the archaeological context of Area 2. Since the analyses of Areas 1 and 3 are more limited in scope, these subareas are only mentioned briefly here for the sake of general orientation; details can be found in Chapter 7.

Area 1

Area 1 was defined as the central and eastern portions of the blow-out located at the southeastern end of the tombolo beach, ca. 31 m asl. (Figures 21 and 22). Clusters of rocks exposed in the blow-out suggested the presence of five or six hearths. In 1979 a T-shaped excavation field totalling 16 m^2 was positioned at the edge of the blow-out. Since the excavation did not produce much in the way of tools or additional features, attention was shifted to the central part of the beach.

Area 2

Area 2 was positioned near the center of the tombolo beach, 25 m west of Area 1 and at a similar elevation of 31 m asl. (Figures 21 and 22). A total of ca. 124 m^2 was excavated over four field seasons. The largest single excavation was in 1979, when ca. 54 m^2, was opened. The 1979 work constitutes most of what is defined as Area 2A (Figure 23). In 1980 an additional 16.5 m^2 was excavated southwards; this includes the northern portion of Area 2C. In 1992, 26 m^2 was excavated north of the original excavation; this subarea is referred to as Area 2B. The 1993 excavation of 27 m^2 expanded south of the 1980 limit, extending subarea 2C.

The results of the 1992-1993 fieldwork revealed that these two extensions differed from the central area excavated in 1979-1980 in that both Areas 2B and 2C exhibited thinner deposits, fewer features, and less artifactual material. Additionally, Area 2B contained deposits of fire-cracked rock quite unlike anything in Areas 2A and 2C. Furthermore, the radiocarbon dates (see below) indicated chronological differences: Area 2A ca. 5300-5700 B.P. and Areas 2B and 2C both ca. 6000 B.P.. It was apparent that different settlement phases were represented at Area 2, not a continuous longhouse structure.

Stratigraphy

A representative soil profile for Area 2A is shown in Figure 24. In the central portion of the excavation the vegetation and humus zone (lfh horizon) ranged from about 3 to 12 cm in thickness with its deepest deposits found above sub-surface depressions. The base of this horizon was generally a thin layer of greasy black humified peat. Cultural material was found occasionally among the roots of the undecomposed vegetation but was more frequent in the humified peat. A thin, discontinuous leaching zone (Ae horizon) was found in most of the excavated units. This gray sand layer was thickest and most prominent above sub-surface depressions and it contained moderate quantities of cultural material. Next in the profile was a dark brown sand, which contained most of the cultural material. Its distinct dark coloring is mostly the result of humic acid and sesquioxide translocation downwards from the leached horizon. The depth of this deposit varied considerably. It was quite thin near the northwestern end of Area 2A (79y line), ranging from 4-8 cm thick, but at the southeastern end, in the vicinity of several hearths (44x 70-73y), it ranged from 20-25 cm thick. Among the boulders along the northern periphery of the excavation the dark brown sand graded into a very black sand, which overlay the basal beach deposit. Beneath the dark brown sand was a layer of culturally sterile yellow sand that graded into a surface of rounded beach cobbles and gravel. This sterile horizon commenced 8 cm below surface level at the northwestern end of Area 2A, 14-16 cm below the surface at the eastern end, and 25-30 cm below the surface in one of the hearth areas (44x70-73y). In sum, the initial Maritime Archaic occupation at Area 2A probably occurred on a sand layer overlying a gravel-cobble surface. Areas 2B and 2C exhibited thinner sand deposits and markedly less development of a dark B horizon.

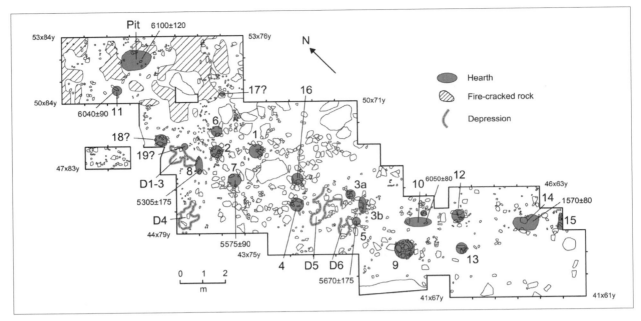

25/ Area 2 features.

During the 1979 excavation at Area 2A there seemed to be a predominantly sterile layer (9-14 cm below surface) between two different cultural levels near 46x69y. The upper level tended to have a higher frequency of Ramah chert flakes. In the first analysis of the site, several upper levels of adjacent excavation units for which a later component seemed possible were separated analytically and termed "Occupation 2." At the time, the grounds for this distinction were ambiguous and the present re-analysis does not clarify the matter. A later component cannot be ruled out, but the apparent superposition could also be the result of wind redeposition. In the spatial analysis (Chapter 6) the debitage patterning in this area is interpreted as being derived primarily from the 5300-5700 B.P. occupation.

Features

Four classes of features were identified at Area 2: rock constructed surface hearths, pit-hearths, irregular depressions and fire-cracked rock concentrations. There was also a large flat boulder in the middle of Area 2A which, despite being a natural feature, seems significant for the spatial organization of the site and

thus worthy of brief consideration here. The three sub-areas are treated separately; each feature is described along with its relevant contextual information. Feature locations and configurations can be found in Figure 25, while Figure 26 shows a vertical bipod photo of part of Area 2A.

Area 2A

The Area 2A features occurred in two groups. At the northern end of the subarea were hearths 1, 2, 6, 7, 8 and possible hearths 18 and 19, along with depressions 1 to 3. Towards the south were hearths 3a, 3b, 4, 5 and possible hearth 16. In the middle was the large boulder. These feature groups will be described from north to south.

Hearth 1 (Figure 27) was situated 25 cm north of the central boulder and was composed of eight rounded and flat cobbles and a large, slightly inclined, flat slab. Faint traces of red ocher and a small amount of charcoal were found among the rocks.

Hearth 2 was located at the north end of Smithsonian Test Pit A. It consisted of a 75 cm wide flower petal-like arrangement of large and small flat slabs. This feature had been exposed to the wind since

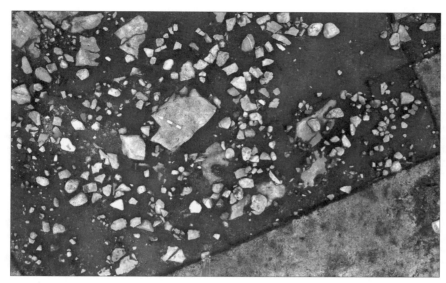

26/ Area 2A bipod photo.

27/ Area 2A hearth-1.

of charcoal. A crude flake point of Ramah chert, a utilized flake of Ramah chert and large numbers of Ramah chert, quartz and slate flakes were contained within the pit fill. Nearby the feature were a flake knife of Ramah chert and a schist tablet.

Hearth 7 was positioned in the southwest corner of Smithsonian Test Pit A. According to their field notes, the hearth was 50-75 cm in diameter and was composed of numerous small flat slabs and a single inclined flat slab, accompanied by red ocher and charcoal fill. A Ramah chert biface fragment, two utilized Ramah chert flakes and a Ramah chert bipolar core were found in direct association. Charcoal from this hearth was radiocarbon dated to 5575±90 B.P. (SI-2526).

Hearth 8 was the easternmost component of what was interpreted as a series of three interlocking pits. The pits were first identified as shallow depressions filled with humified peat that stood out clearly from the surrounding dark brown sand matrix. The hearth was a pit, 85 cm long, 35 cm wide, 25 cm deep, with a roughly bowl-shaped cross-section. Several small cobbles were positioned along the rim of the pit and a large rock lay at its base near the southwestern end. The pit fill of dark brown sand was virtually indistinguishable from the surrounding matrix except for red ocher and a large amount of charcoal. Charcoal from the hearth was dated 5305±175 B.P. (UGa-3160). Artifacts found within the pit included a

1975, so if any charcoal or red ocher had been present, it was gone by 1979. Adjacent to the hearth were an unstemmed flake point of Ramah chert, a Ramah chert biface preform, a stemmed flake of Ramah chert, two biface fragments of Ramah chert, a flake knife of black chert and a schist tablet.

Hearth 6 was 75 cm in diameter and consisted of a 15 cm deep pit surrounded on three sides by four large rocks, with a small flat slab wedged between two of the rocks on the southern edge of the pit. The pit was stained with red ocher and filled with a great deal fragment of a ground slate tool, a Ramah chert micro-point, a slate point tip and a Ramah chert utilized flake. The hearth basin also contained a large number of small Ramah chert retouch flakes.

Depressions 1 and 2 formed a linear series with Hearth 8, but it was difficult to define precisely their boundaries and thus specify the temporal relationship of the features by cross-cutting. Depression 1 was 50 cm in width, roughly 10 cm deep and was bordered by, and contained, several small cobbles. It did not contain charcoal or red ocher. Artifacts found within the pit were a utilized flake of Ramah chert and a ground slate flake. Depression 2 was approximately 1 m long, 75 cm wide, about 10 cm deep, with an irregular bi-lobed shape. No charcoal or red ocher was present. Artifacts from the feature included a black chert endscraper and part of an asymmetric biface of Ramah chert, which joined with another fragment found just outside the pit. The irregular nature of these depressions as well as their lack of charcoal and red ocher suggests they were of natural origin, perhaps related to wind deflation or tree-throw disturbance.

Near the western edge of the excavation was depression 3, a shallow irregular feature, 1.4 m long, 90 cm wide and 7 cm deep. It contained several cobbles, a few flecks of charcoal, but no red ocher. A small number of flakes (30-40) were found within its boundaries and two small bipolar cores were located nearby. Given its amorphous shape and relative lack of charcoal and lithic material this feature is most likely a vestige of deflation or tree-throw activity.

During re-analysis of the site two features were identified as possible hearths. Near the northwestern edge of Area 2A was a circular cluster of rocks, ca. 60 cm in diameter, which included a flat slab but lacked charcoal. This feature was designated as possible hearth 18. Just north of depressions 1 and 2 was a 35 cm by 25 cm oval stain of red ocher mixed with flecks of charcoal. Cross-sectioning indicated the feature was bowl-shaped and 6 cm deep. It contained only a few flakes. Given vague similarities with the central pit

identified in Area 2B, the feature was designated possible hearth 19.

The boulder at the center of Area 2A was a large flat-topped rock, 1.25 m long, 75 cm wide and 50 cm high. As discussed in the spatial analysis (Chapter 6), this natural feature seems to have served as a central fulcrum in structuring the arrangement of two possible dwelling modules on the beach. Its surface was inspected carefully for signs of cultural modification, but none were identified.

Hearths 3a and 3b were probably two separate features, but since their degree of interlocking was unclear in the field they were designated as components 3a and 3b of a single feature. Hearth 3a was a pit, 0.5 m in diameter, capped on its surface with several cobbles and excavated to a depth of 7 cm to the top of the sterile yellow sand. Charcoal was found at the base of the pit and three small red ocher stains ringed the periphery of the pit bottom. Also at the base of the pit were three artifacts: a black chert endscraper, a side-notched biface of Ramah chert and a utilized flake of Ramah chert. The surface of hearth 3b, which measured 0.75 m in diameter, was a rough semi-circle of rocks that surrounded a 10 cm deep charcoal-filled pit. Several cobbles and flat slabs capped the pit surface and a stain of red ocher was present on the northern edge. At the surface of the feature were a biface preform of Ramah chert, a bipolar core of Ramah chert, an endscraper of black chert and a schist tablet.

Hearth 4 was ca. 75 cm in diameter and consisted of an oval ring of cobbles surrounding a thin scatter of charcoal. No pit was apparent and no red ocher was found within or adjacent to the feature. Artifacts in proximity to the feature included a biface tip of Ramah chert, a quartz block core, a Ramah chert utilized flake and a ground slate flake.

Hearth 5 (Figure 28) was marked by an oval alignment of cobbles and consisted of an oval pit 40 cm in diameter and 15 cm deep. The pit contained a large quantity of charcoal as well as red ocher, which

28/ Area 2A hearth-5.

29/ Area 2B under excavation. Fire-cracked rock concentrations in foreground and on northern edge of excavation.

flakes. Its irregular form and lack of cultural material suggests it may have been of natural rather than cultural origin. Depression 5, adjacent to hearth 5, was 60 by 40 cm in size and contained small rocks and a considerable quantity of Ramah chert flakes along one edge. Although a cultural origin cannot be ruled out, its position in the upper portion of the sediment and its similarity to depression 4 suggest a natural disturbance.

During re-analysis of the site, a possible hearth (no.16) was inferred from a rock feature 1 m northeast of hearth 4. This feature, 80 by 50 cm in extent, consisted of a petal-like arrangement of four flat slabs along with several other rocks, but no charcoal association was reported.

Area 2B
Fire-cracked rock concentrations were the most distinctive characteristic of Area 2B, covering almost 35% of the excavation surface (Figures 25 and 29). The rock occurred in thin (<5 cm) "carpets," the most extensive of which occurred along the northwestern edge of the excavation (83-84y), 1.8 m northwest of the central pit feature and 1.2 m southeast of the pit (77-79y units). The configuration of these carpets strongly suggests they extend into the unexcavated areas beyond Area 2B. Two smaller concentrations lay immediately adjacent to the western and eastern sides of the central pit. The concentration to the east partly superimposed the

was more granular than the powdery textured material found in the other features. A single rounded cobble was placed at the base of the pit. Charcoal from the feature was dated 5670 ±175 B.P. (UGa-3161). Only one artifact was found in the vicinity of the hearth: a utilized flake of Ramah chert.

Depression 4 lay south of hearth 4 and was an irregular arc roughly 2 m long, ranging between 20-60 cm wide and several centimeters deep. Although it contained some rocks there were relatively few

30/ Area 2C overview looking North. Area 2A in background.

31/ Area 2C hearth-9.

throughout the pit, but were mostly concentrated on the western side. A total of 46 tiny burned bone fragments were also present in the northwestern portion of the feature. Flakes of quartz, Ramah chert, Mugford chert and slate were found within the basin. Artifacts found within or adjacent to the pit included a quartz block core, utilized flakes and ground slate flakes. Charcoal from the pit returned a radiocarbon date of 6100±120 B.P. (Beta-58173).

Hearth 11 was positioned 60-80 cm west of the central pit. It consisted of a cluster of rocks associated with small patches of charcoal; some flecks of red ocher were present a short distance from the feature. The dispersed nature of the rocks suggested the feature was disturbed. Charcoal from the hearth area was dated 6040±90 B.P. (Beta-57124). A concentration of black chert flakes lay 25 cm southwest of the feature's largest component rock. Nearby artifacts included a quartz block core, utilized flakes, a bifacial point base of quartz, a biface fragment of Ramah chert and ground slate flakes.

Both the radiocarbon dates and the behavioral patterning suggest that Area 2B represents an occupation phase separate from Area 2A. Nonetheless, an important point to consider is the degree of overlap between the southwestern edge of Area 2B and the Area 2A occupation, since a tongue of fire-cracked rock extends over the 50x line into Area 2A. This issue will be considered in more detail in Chapter 6, but suf-

edge of the feature, so it must post-date the infilling of the pit.

In the center of Area 2B was a large pit. The boundaries of this feature were difficult to discern within the dark and, at the time of excavation, water-soaked soil matrix. It consisted of an oval basin, 1.25 m long, 0.90 m wide and 5 cm deep. A few small flat rock slabs were found in its northwestern section and a small cluster of rocks lay in its southeastern portion. Red ocher stains were present on the western edge and within the feature. Tiny charcoal flecks were found

CHAPTER 5

fice it to say that while there is a high likelihood of a palimpsest deposit in the 49-50x area, there are reasonable grounds to use the 50x line as a practical boundary between the two occupations.

Area 2C

As will be established in Chapter 6, south of the southernmost hearths at Area 2A there was a radical decrease in the density of lithic material that continued until a concen-

32/ Area 2C hearth-12.

tration of lithics was encountered in the southeastern corner of Area 2C. This pattern, along with a radiocarbon date, suggests that Area 2C is an occupation phase separate from Area 2A. Six hearth features were present at Area 2C and these will be described in sequence from north to south (Figures 25 and 30).

Hearth 9 (Figure 31) stood out as the most unique and well constructed (or perhaps best preserved) hearth feature at the site. It was roughly circular, 1.0 m in diameter, consisting of an interior floor with several flat stones that was surrounded on three sides by flat slabs, the tops of which were inclined inwards towards the center of the feature. These inclined slabs were backed by cobbles. The placement of the rocks suggests the inclined flat slabs may have been wedged upright to form a three-sided hearth box open to the north. Very little charcoal was found within the feature, but a thick stain was situated just east of its open side. This charcoal deposit may have resulted from intentional removal of the hearth contents. The vicinity of hearth 9 was virtually devoid of tools and debitage. A utilized flake of black chert was found in the hearth interior and a large schist tablet lay to the east of the feature.

The feature designated hearth 10 had two components. On the east side was a small pit, 40 cm in diameter, 15 cm deep, the base of which contained a small

pocket of charcoal beneath a flat cobble. It was similar in form to hearth 5. No cultural materials were associated with this feature. Ca. 60 cm to the west was an elongated pit, 1.2 m long, 40 cm wide and 15 cm deep; a large rock was positioned at its northwestern end and a couple of smaller rocks were present in the southeastern end. The pit fill contained small pieces of charcoal, two small spots of red ocher and a utilized flake of Ramah chert. Charcoal from this feature was dated 6050±80 B.P. (Beta-71475).

Hearth 12 (Figure 32) consisted of a slightly dispersed group of rocks, including two large flat slabs and several smaller fire-cracked rocks. Associated with the feature was a small concentration of burned bone fragments (n=294) and some very sparse charcoal flecks. Roughly 80 cm to the east of the cluster were several small clumps of red ocher.

Hearth 13 should be treated as rather questionable, consisting of little more than a cluster of six rocks. Yet its association with a few flakes and its placement relative to the other features strongly suggested a hearth function.

Hearth 14 was composed of an arc-shaped midden-like deposit between, and extending out from, two large rocks. This unusual deposit was 1.3 m long and 0.6 m wide and consisted of "greasy" red-brown mottled sand (the reddish coloration caused by a combination of iron translocation through the soil, fire oxidation, and red ocher stains). The deposit contained faint charcoal flecks, small pockets of burned bone (n=651), and small particles of red ocher. Several small fire-cracked rocks were also present, slightly to the east of the feature. A large quantity of flakes was associated with hearth 14. Burned Ramah chert flakes were particularly frequent between and immediately adjacent to the two rocks at the center of the feature. A charcoal sample from the feature was dated 1570±80 B.P. (Beta-71474). About 1.0-1.2 m north of hearth 14 was an outlier patch of charcoal, 70 cm by 15-20 cm in size, adjacent to a small cluster of rocks. It was unclear whether this was related to hearth 14 or whether it represented an earlier, disturbed feature.

Hearth 15 was partly exposed at the southern limit of the excavation, 1 m southeast of hearth 14. In a cleft between two rocks was a red ocher and charcoal smear on top of a small flat slab. A small cluster of fire-cracked rocks lay immediately adjacent to the northeast. A few other nearby rocks may have belonged to the feature. Within the hearth were quartz and Ramah chert flakes, while several quartz block cores, utilized flakes and ground slate flakes lay nearby.

Summary: Area 2 Chronology and Feature Variation

Chronology Table 4 lists the seven radiocarbon dates from Area 2 and one from Test Pit C at the extreme northwestern end of the same beach level. The date of 1570±80 B.P. from hearth 14 at Area 2C is problematic. It should probably be rejected because it seems too

Table 4: Radiocarbon Dates from Nukasusutok-5: Area 2 and Main Beach Calibrated with OxCal 3.10 (Bronk-Ramsey 2005)

Feature	Date B.P.	Calibrated BC	Lab No.	Material	Comment
TP-A/hearth 7 (2A)	5575±90	4500-4330	SI-2526	unidentified charcoal	
Hearth 5 (2A)	5670±175	4710-4340	UGa-3161	unidentified charcoal	
Hearth 8 (2A)	5305±175	4330-3960	UGa-3160	unidentified charcoal	
Hearth 11 (2B)	6040±90	5060-4790	Beta-57124	unidentified charcoal	
Pit (2B)	6100±120	5210-4850	Beta-58173	unidentified charcoal	
Hearth 10 (2C)	6050±80	5060-4830	Beta-71475	unidentified charcoal	^{13}C adjusted: -28.1
Hearth 14 (2C)	1570±80		Beta-71474	unidentified charcoal	unacceptably late; low density "different" material
TP-C (north terrace)	4645±65	3520-3350	SI-2527	unidentified charcoal	possibly too young; iron pan formation may result in accumulation of younger humic acids

recent for the associated lithic material. Also, the radiocarbon laboratory reported the charcoal sample consisted of low density wood different in appearance from the other samples. On the other hand, there is always the possibility that the sample might date a Late Prehistoric Indian or Dorset component, although there is no evidence for this in the lithic material.

Taken at face value, the remaining dates from Area 2 suggest the presence of two occupation phases. Phase 1, dated ca. 6000 B.P., occurs in Areas 2B and 2C. These two subareas were separated by a distance of over 10 m and although there were some similarities in associated features (i.e., hearth-pit complexes, see below), there are marked behavioral differences (discussed in greater detail in Chapter 6). Phase 2, with dates ranging from ca. 5700-5300 B.P. (note the large standard deviations for two of the dates), is limited to Area 2A. This occupation lies between the two earlier components, so it is reasonable to ask if the Phase 2 occupation was superimposed on the earlier Phase 1 occupation. As will be discussed in Chapter 8, there are no obvious aspects of the tool typology that would indicate superposition, but Chapter 6 identifies a small area of probable overlap between the northern end of Area 2A and Area 2B: fire-cracked rock deposits along the 49-50x lines. Chapter 6 argues that the spatial patterning of lithics and hearths at Area 2A exhibits certain consistencies suggestive of two "behavioral modules", one on either side of the large central rock, but the number of hearths associated with each module raises questions about possible re-occupation. So far, a phase post-dating ca. 5300 B.P. has not been identified clearly at Area 2. As noted previously, during the 1979 excavation a flake scatter was observed at a higher level than the main Area 2A occupation, although it was not possible to elaborate upon this in the subsequent analysis. There are also later radiocarbon dates from other contexts at the site: 4645±65 B.P. from Test Pit C at the northwestern end of the site terrace and 5090±95 B.P. from Area 3 (see

Chapter 7). Consequently, the likelihood of a third occupation phase at Area 2 should be kept in mind.

Looking more critically at the radiocarbon dates, three possible sources of error can be suggested. The first is inter-laboratory variation. All of the 6000+ B.P. dates were run by Beta Analytic, while the later dates were provided by the Smithsonian and the University of Georgia. A second possible source of error is the old wood factor; none of the charcoal dated 6000+ B.P. was identified to species so it is possible that it could have been derived from old driftwood. The third source of error is soil chemistry. As discussed in Chapter 7, Area 3 and the western end of the main beach terrace were subject to extreme podzolization processes leading to the formation of an impressive iron pan. These pedological processes may contribute to the accumulation of younger humic acids that may effect radiocarbon dates (cf., Lascelles et al. 2000). Although Area 2 did not exhibit iron pan formation there was very strong podzolization, especially at Area 2A where the sand sediments were considerably deeper than Areas 2B and 2C. If so, it is possible the radiocarbon dates from Area 2A are too young and that the subarea may actually date closer to 2B and 2C (6000 B.P.).

Shoreline dating does not provide much assistance in assessing the radiocarbon dates. The displacement curve for the Nain region (Figure 5) indicates that the 31 m asl. beach terrace upon which Area 2 is situated could have emerged by ca. 7000 B.P.. The curve also suggests that if a 6000 B.P. occupation, such as Areas 2B and 2C, was located near its contemporary shoreline it should lie at ca. 20 m asl., while a 5500 B.P. occupation, such as Area 2A, should lie ca. 15 m asl. Consequently, assuming the displacement curve is accurate, it is likely that both the Area 2 occupation phases were located a considerable distance above their contemporary shorelines, 10 m in the case of Areas 2B and 2C, 15 m in the case of Area 2A. Other Nain area Maritime Archaic localities dated ca. 6000 B.P. lie between 26-22 m asl., suggesting a general tendency for sites to be placed well above their contemporary shorelines. This placement is likely related to the practical advantages of using tombolo beaches: two-sided access for boat landing, large settlement surfaces and excellent views.

A final chronological element can be mentioned. Although none of the charcoal samples submitted for radiocarbon dating were identified as to wood type, a series of charcoal samples from both the northern and southern parts of Area 2A as well as from near hearth 10 at Area 2C were identified by Dosia Laeyendecker of the Smithsonian Institution. All these samples contained alder/birch (probably mostly alder) and willow; coniferous wood was absent. The lack of coniferous wood suggests these occupations pre-date 4500-4200 B.P., when spruce woodland became established in the area (Short 1978:32).

Feature Variation

At this point, a brief summary of the Area 2 features is in order. Their range of formal and functional variation will be evaluated to foreshadow their significance for the spatial analysis and interpretation to be presented in Chapter 6.

Two major hearth types were found at Area 2: surface hearths associated with rock clusters (hearths 1, 2, 4, 6, 7, 9, 11, 12, 13, 14 and possibly 15) and shallow pit-hearths with surface rock clusters and at least one or two rocks within the pit basins (hearths 3a, 3b, 5, 8). Both types were generally associated with flat rock slabs and red ocher was often, though not always, present. Among the surface hearths, hearth 9 stood out as unique in its robust construction with a paved floor and inclined slabs, although this impression may simply be a result of better preservation than the other features. Nonetheless, some functional difference may be signaled by the box-like form.

At Area 2B a large pit lay adjacent to hearth 11. A similar arrangement was found at Area 2C, with an elongated pit lying between hearths 9 and 10. This could indicate a paired pit/hearth functional unit, although the contemporaneity of the features cannot be determined. Area 2A's hearths 2 and 8 might also be seen in this light, since the latter has a pit-like form, although it is considerably smaller than the aforementioned pit features.

At Area 2A the hearths were clustered in two groups on opposite sides of the large central rock. The possibility that these groupings represent separate activity modules will be taken up in the next chapter, where the features are contextualized with their associated lithic distributions.

The large quantity of fire-cracked rock at Area 2B stands out from the other two subareas. This statement should perhaps be qualified, since insufficient attention may have been paid to the presence of fire-cracked rock during the 1979-80 fieldwork at Area 2A. Nonetheless, a significant qualitative difference between these two subareas is a reasonable assumption. Area 2B is unquestionably different from Area 2C; in the latter subarea, fire-cracked rock occurs only as small scatters associated with three of the hearths. The spatial pattern of the rock distribution at Area 2B is also distinctive: a roughly concentric ring around a central pit/hearth complex. The next chapter discusses the possible behavioral linkages between these features.

Area 3

Area 3 lay 38 m west of Area 2, slightly downslope on a narrow terrace lying at 28 m asl. (Figure 22). The locality was discovered in 1979 during shovel testing aimed at determining the boundaries of the site. As luck would have it, a shovel-test penetrated the center of an impressively thick and bright red ocher deposit. An area of 28 m^2 was opened, revealing four features, two consisting of remarkable oval concentrations of red ocher and rocks and two more consisting of rock clusters, one with a restricted red ocher deposit, the other with a charcoal patch. At first, these features were believed to be burials, but

Wyatt Harbor, view to the southeast over Nukasusutok-5 site (Photo: W. Fitzhugh 1975)

subsurface investigation did not confirm this. Shovel tests conducted elsewhere along the terrace provided negative results except in one area 4.5 m southwest of the main excavation. A 1 by 3 m unit was opened there, but very little cultural material was encountered. A detailed analysis of Area 3 is presented in Chapter 7.

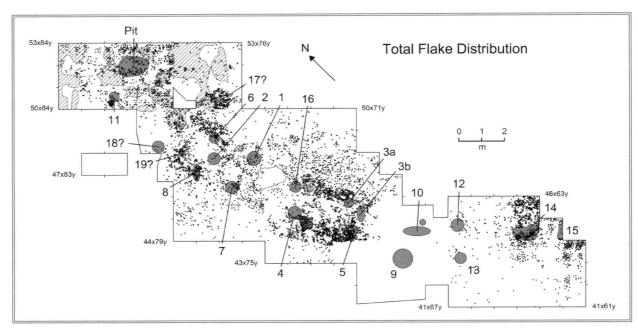

33/ Area 2: total flake distribution in relation to features.

Nukasusutok-5: Spatial Analysis

Chapter 3 outlined interpretations of Maritime Archaic social relations and their behavioral consequences and discussed methodological strategies for linking these behavioral consequences with spatial patterning in the archaeological record. This discussion constitutes a platform for the analysis of spatial patterning at Area 2 that will be undertaken here.

Limitations and Complications

In choosing the most appropriate analytical methods it was necessary to recognize the limitations of the Area 2 data. The first problem was the quality of the provenience data. For the 1979 excavation a significant proportion of the utilized flakes, bipolar cores and block cores were only provenienced within 1 m^2 units, so these tool classes could only be handled by quadrat analysis. The other classes could be presented in both point-plotted and quadrat form. Regarding the debitage analysis, there were good "eyeball" plots of flakes by major raw material types for all excavation seasons except 1980. Weather conditions were so poor in 1980 that flakes were simply collected by quadrats. Fortunately, the area excavated was small (12 m^2) and the quantity of debitage very low, so the plotted flake distributions from adjacent units could still be used for a meaningful visual analysis. Indeed, the debitage point patterns provide some of the strongest support for the interpretations presented herein. The quantitative analyses of debitage raw materials were conducted with quadrats. Area 2A and part of 2C, excavated in

1979-80, were analysed using 1 m^2 quadrats. Area 2B and most of 2C, excavated in 1992 and 1993, were analysed using 50 cm^2 quadrats.

Another potential limitation is the effect of site formation processes. The first issue involves the analytical implications of having at least three occupation phases at the site as a whole and at least two phases at Area 2, dated ca. 6000 B.P. and 5500 B.P.. To what degree can we be assured that any patterns we observe are not simply the result of a messy palimpsest accumulation? Chapter 5 pointed out that the radiocarbon dating of the features at Area 2 suggests the two occupation periods are spatially separated. Furthermore, the discussion of debitage distributions to be presented in this chapter will demonstrate that while a small area of overlap probably exists between Areas 2A and 2B, this does not significantly compromise the analytical results.

Harder to evaluate is the possibility of a later component overlying the southern portion of Area 2A. As noted in Chapter 5, this possibility was indicated by the presence in several units of Ramah chert flakes close to the surface, separated from the main occupation horizon by a thin sterile zone. Given the lack of consistent stratigraphic control in these units it was impossible to make a clear distinction of this upper level material in order to check the effects of its removal on the spatial patterning.

The other problem is the cumulative effect of various natural formation processes on the deposit, particularly when combined with the multiple-component issue. One phenomena is vertical movement in the sand deposits of objects of different density. At Area 2 quartz flakes and chunks sometimes lay deeper than Ramah chert or other flakes. But probably the more important disturbance factor was wind deflation and redeposition of the sand sediments, a process visible today in the blow-out between Areas 1 and 2. As noted in Chapter 5, some of the irregular peat-filled depressions observed at Area 2 might be the result of deflation. This process may produce a mixed deposit of cultural material from different occupation levels at the bottom of a blow-out. Wind action may also displace cultural material along a horizontal plane. Another potential disturbance factor is tree-throws, which might uproot and mix cultural material from separate levels and result in short lateral movements of material. Presently there are no trees at Area 2, but they grow further west on the terrace and their distribution might have been more extensive previously.

Preliminary Overview

The spatial analysis begins with a presentation of the overall feature, debitage and tool distributions, since these provide the essential framework upon which the subsequent analyses and interpretations build. The main goals are to identify the boundaries of the three analytical subareas and to establish preliminary behavioral interpretations that will provide direction for the analyses.

Flake and Feature Distributions

As noted in Chapter 5, the three subareas can be distinguished chronologically, with centrally positioned Area 2A dated 5600-5300 B.P. sandwiched between Areas 2B and 2C, both dated 6000-6100 B.P.. A plot of the distribution pattern of all flakes at Area 2, irrespective of raw material type, also reinforces the impression that the three subareas can be treated as separate analytical units (Figure 33). The low flake frequency between Areas 2A and 2C suggests there is minimal likelihood of significant spatial overlap and palimpsest problems. On the other hand, the units between Areas 2A and 2B (48-50x) contained a fairly high frequency of flakes. Spatial overlap is likely here, since the high frequency of Ramah chert in the border area is more akin to the flake raw material frequencies in 2B than the northern portion of 2A and because there is a slight extension of the Area 2B fire-cracked rock "carpets" into the border area, especially in 49x78-79y. Nonetheless, the amount of overlap is not extensive.

The flake distribution patterns at Area 2A display two double linear or perhaps horseshoe-like configurations (Figure 34)— hereafter referred to as "lobes"— one on each side of a large flat-topped rock. Parts of these configurations display sharp boundaries[2], perhaps indicative of a limiting factor. The eastern boundary of the southernmost lobe is diffuse, although there is an identifiable shift in the density of the points. This is the area in which there might be a later occupation and thus a palimpsest effect (units 45-47x70-73y), a possibility which is discussed further below.

The north lobe is comprised of two parallel north-south trending distributions, each ca. 4 m long, 1-1.2 m wide, which are separated by a near-empty "corridor" 60-80 cm wide. There appears to be a narrow 50-60 cm opening at the northern end of the lobe. The southern end is linked by a sparse distribution of flakes and terminates at the edge of the large central rock. The flake concentration marking the slightly projecting northeastern corner of the lobe might be a consequence of overlap with Area 2B, since fire-cracked rock extends into this area (49x78y).

Five hearths are contained within the north lobe. Hearth 2 is positioned in the corridor near the middle of the lobe and is flanked on either side by hearths 6 and 8, which lie slightly within the linear flake distributions. Hearth 7 is situated on the inner edge of the

[2]Note that the seemingly sharp boundary at 44x 72-71y is artificial; in 1980 flakes were not plotted in this area.

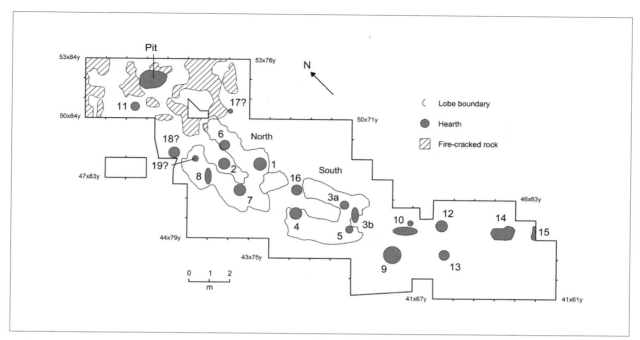

34/ Area 2A: inferred flake lobes in relation to features.

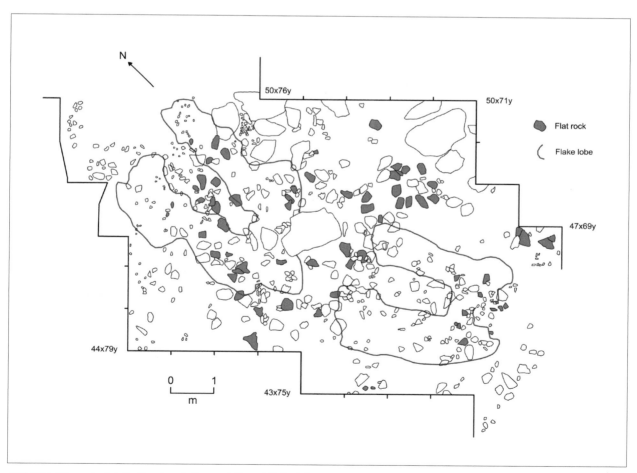

35/ Area 2A: rock distribution in relation to inferred flake lobes.

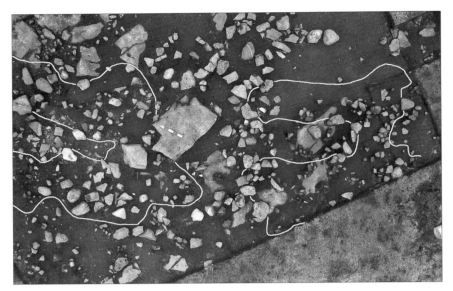

36/ Area 2A: flake lobes superimposed on vertical bipod photo.

flanked on both sides by hearths 3a and 5, which lie at the inner edges of the linear flake distributions. Hearth 4 lies slightly within the corridor and on the edge of the open space between the south lobe and the central rock. Additionally, a rock cluster in 46x73y might have been a hearth (H-16), given its association with a red ocher patch and its position relative to the flake distribution. If so, the hearth locations at the south lobe would be more similar to those at the north lobe. As at the north lobe, the varying forms of the hearths suggest functional differences. Hearths 3a and 5 were circular pits, hearth 3b an elongated pit and hearth 4 as well as possible hearth 16 were surface cobble/slab features.

The pattern becomes more complex when overlaid with the rock distribution (Figures 35 and 36). Rocks occurring within the lobes are generally hearth-related. Most of the flat slabs are spatially associated with hearths, suggesting they were connected with hearth construction and cooking/heating practices. Other small rocks are scattered around the lobes; some of these were probably displaced or discarded from hearths while others may simply be part of the sediment matrix. The northeast tip of the north lobe shows a minor cluster of rather small rocks; these might be outliers of the fire-cracked rock concentration at Area 2B.

Most of the other rocks occur in the area between the lobes, concentrated on the western and eastern sides of the large central rock. The western side contains a diffuse scatter of over two dozen rocks, most of which are moderately large and rounded in form, but a number of flat slabs are also present. Some of the large rocks are positioned directly against the northwestern tip of the south lobe (the vertical photo in

flake distribution and beside the corridor while hearth 1 is located close to the eastern edge of the lobe. A cluster of rocks that might be a hearth (H-18) lies just outside the north lobe in 48x79y. As described in Chapter 5, the hearths exhibited varying forms, perhaps indicative of functional differences. Hearths 1, 2 and 7 were surface cobble and slab hearths, hearth 6 was a pit surrounded by large rocks, while hearth 8 was an elongated pit.

The south lobe also consists of two parallel linear flake distributions, the eastern one 3.7 m long by 0.75-1.0 m wide, the western one 3.7 m long by 1.2 m wide, which are separated by a corridor 0.70-1.0 m wide. The northern end of the lobe is entirely open while the southern end has a narrow 60 cm opening between two hearths. The northern end of the eastern linear distribution terminates 70 cm southeast of the large flat central rock. Depending on where the boundaries of the flake distribution are drawn, the northern end of the western linear distribution terminates 50-80 cm south of the limit of the north lobe. This configuration creates an area of low flake density (2.0 by 1.5 m in size) between the central rock and the south lobe.

The south lobe contains four definite hearths, of which three are located near the southern end. Hearth 3b is positioned in the middle of the corridor and is

Figure 36 shows this more clearly than the drawings). On the eastern side of the large central rock is a distinctive group of moderately large rocks, including quite a few flat slabs, that extends eastwards from the central rock. Some of the larger rocks directly border the northeastern tip of the south lobe while a few lie within 50 cm of the southeastern edge of the north lobe. The western and eastern rock alignments therefore seem structurally similar in their positioning against the ends of the lobes and their extension across the gaps between the two lobes.

At the northern end of the north lobe there is a small cluster of rocks just outside and west of the gap in the flake distribution. Although these may be the remains of a hearth (H-18), they might also have been ejected from the activity space within the north lobe. Nearby is a small pit containing charcoal and red ocher that might have been a hearth (H-19). Just east of the north lobe there is a small concentration of probable fire-cracked rocks nestled between four boulders (49x76y); their association with either the north lobe or Area 2B is unclear. Other fire-cracked rocks were scattered here and there at Area 2A, but they were not recorded systematically. It seems clear, however, that there were no major concentrations as at Area 2B.

The preceding description of the spatial patterning can now be integrated into a preliminary interpretation. There are two debitage lobes, each 4 m long by 3 m wide, on either side of a central rock. The overall pattern does not resemble that of the drop/toss-zone distinctions of the external hearth model. Each lobe contains five hearths that are spaced similarly, as well as a triple hearth alignment, in both cases located towards the end of the lobe furthest from the central rock. Rock clusters occur on both the eastern and western sides of the central rock in the between-lobe space. These spatial configurations suggest the lobes share a marked degree of organizational symmetry. Consequently, there are reasonable grounds to consider the lobes as possible dwelling-related behavioral modules that can be treated as distinct analytical units.

Area 2B is distinguished by its pattern of fire-cracked rock carpets surrounding a pit and a disturbed hearth. This quasi-concentric feature-centered distribution bears a general resemblance to the drop/toss zone model, with flakes mostly occurring in what might be a drop zone close to the central features and fire-cracked rock lying in a surrounding toss-zone-like ring. In contrast, Area 2C is marked by generally low flake density, except for sharply bounded clusters on opposite sides of hearth 14. There were no significant accumulations of fire-cracked rock. Too little was excavated at Area 2C to contextualize the pattern, but there is a clear behavioral contrast with Area 2B. The bounded flake distributions at Area 2C are reminiscent of the lobes at Area 2A.

A Preliminary Look at the Tool Distribution

Having defined what seem to be meaningful overall patterns in the distribution of debitage and features, we should take a preliminary look at the tool distribution to see how it fits with the initial interpretations. As noted previously, point pattern analysis of the tool distributions is hampered by the imprecise proveniencing of many utilized flakes, bipolar cores and block cores. Although the provenienced portion of these types cannot be taken as a random sample of the overall distributions of the types, eliminating them entirely from a point pattern analysis or shifting the entire analysis to quadrats might lose useful information. Consequently, the provenienced portion of the offending types was considered to have at least rough representative value and a *k*-means cluster analysis of the tool assemblage was undertaken. The results should be viewed as illustrative of general tendencies and the overall logic of the analysis, not as the basis for robust conclusions.

Several different numbers of clusters could fit this material depending on the degree of splitting/lumping one is willing to accept, but some of the tool clusters were stable through different runs. Figure 37 illustrates 12- and 9-cluster solutions in relation to the flake and feature distributions. In most cases the tool

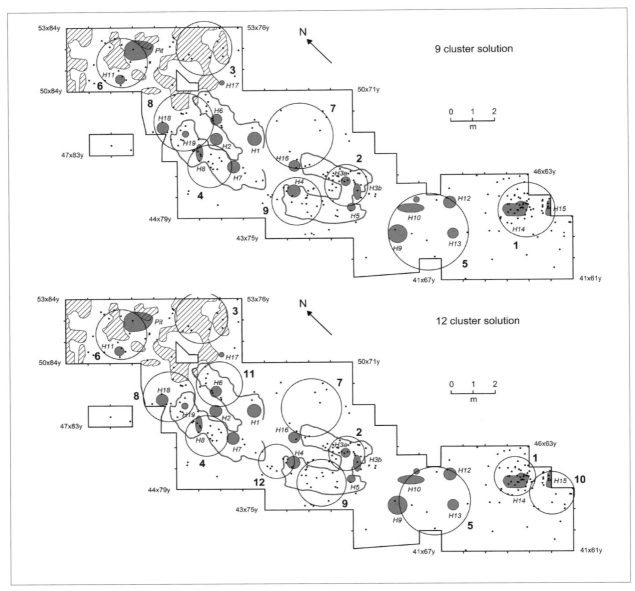

37/ *Area 2 k-means cluster analysis. nine-cluster solution. 12 twelve-cluster solution.*

clusters are associated with hearths, either centered directly on the features or adjacent to them. In Area 2A, clusters 2, 4, 5, and 7 are stable in both solutions. The positioning of cluster 8 is roughly similar in the two solutions, but in the 12-cluster solution its centroid is displaced slightly north, with several items being split off to form a new cluster (11) centered on hearth 6. This seems to be a reasonable adjustment. Additionally, in the 12-cluster solution the centroid of cluster 9 is shifted south such that its tool contents are split with new cluster 12. Each of these two clusters is

positioned adjacent to a hearth (hearths 5 and 4, respectively). This corresponds better with expectations of hearth-centered distributions, but it may be somewhat artificial given the diffuse nature of the tool distributions. Taken at face value, the stability of most clusters over both solutions indicates a pattern, but the differences suggest it would be worthwhile to run additional analyses for Area 2A separate from the other two sub-areas. This is discussed further below.

In Area 2B, clusters 3 and 6 are stable in both solutions, with the former encompassing the central

CHAPTER 6

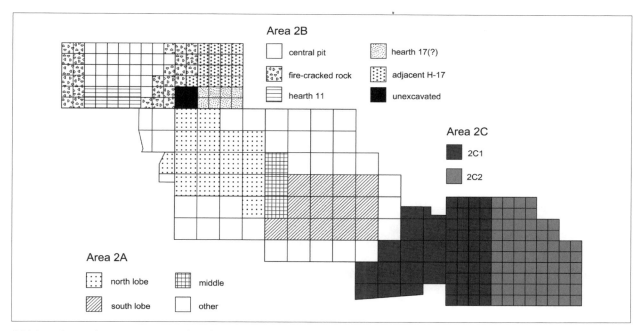

38/ Area 2: quadrat groupings used in the analyses.

pit-hearth complex and the latter situated in an area of fire-cracked rock to the east. In Area 2C, cluster 5 remains stable between hearths 9, 10, 12 and 13. In the 9-cluster solution cluster 1 includes both hearths 14 and 15, but in the 12-cluster solution cluster 1 splits, with a new cluster 10 emerging by hearth 15 and cluster 1 centered on hearth 14. Unfortunately, too little was excavated around hearth 15 to evaluate the significance of this splitting.

Overall, the relative lack of cluster overlap between the three subareas reinforces the impression derived from the flake distributions that the three areas can be treated as independent units for analysis. The following pages will present more detailed interpretations of the spatial structure within each subarea.

Area 2A

The preceding section used the overall distribution of flakes and tools in relation to features at Area 2 to establish a basic framework for analysis. Two behavioral modules were postulated for Area 2A. This initial interpretation will now be investigated systematically through an analysis of the distribution patterns of all data classes. Figure 38 provides an overview of how

quadrats were grouped into larger model-based analytical units for some of the analyses.

Flake Distributions

The most valuable information comes from the point-plotted flakes: quartz, Ramah chert, fine-grained cherts and slate (the latter two materials treated generically). Quadrat data are also provided for the various raw material types, since these counts include flakes found during screening and provide more secure identifications of color variants for Mugford chert and slate than was possible in the field.

The point plots for quartz and Ramah chert exhibit similar forms (Figures 39 and 40), but quartz provides a stronger demarcation of the north lobe while Ramah chert gives a clear definition of the south lobe. Quartz flakes are concentrated close to hearths 6 and 8 at the north lobe and hearths 3b and 5 at the south lobe. With the exception of hearth 3b, these concentrations lie mostly on one side of the hearths. Other clusters, particularly in the south lobe, are independent of the hearths. At the north lobe, Ramah chert has slight concentrations within and adjacent to hearths 7 and 8, but is otherwise rather diffuse except for a clustering

39/ Area 2: distribution of quartz flakes.

at the northwest corner of the lobe. At the south lobe, there is a tight concentration of hundreds of Ramah chert flakes on one side of hearth 4 and a broader, probably overlapping, concentration on one side of hearth 5. The 3-4 m² area between these two hearths contains a total of ca. 1500 Ramah chert flakes, making it the most intensive point of Ramah chert reduction/discard at Nukasusutok-5. A less voluminous clustering (ca. 600 flakes) occurs on one side of hearth 3a, extending into what initially appeared to be a hearth-independent concentration at the northeast corner of

the south lobe. In retrospect, however, the adjacent rock cluster associated with a red ocher stain may be a hearth (H-16, Figures 25 and 33), although no charcoal was recorded in the field notes.

In sum, the distribution patterns of both raw materials are partially, but not exclusively, hearth-centered. Each material exhibits fairly clear outer boundaries rather than a density gradient, consistent with the impression derived from the total flake distribution. There is also a fairly clear inner boundary in each case, resulting in a markedly lower flake density in the

CHAPTER 6

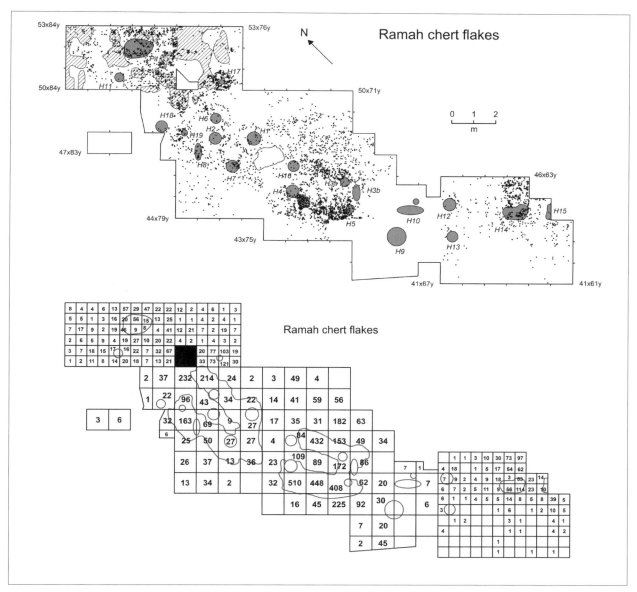

40/ Area 2: distribution of Ramah chert flakes.

middle of each lobe. Consequently, the overall pattern does not correspond with the exterior hearth model.

As noted previously, however, the scatter of Ramah chert flakes to the east of the south lobe creates some interpretive problems. There is a reasonably clear, albeit narrow, break in the density gradient between the south lobe and the eastern scatter, but there may be a palimpsest effect from a later occupation. To control for this possibility, Figure 41 presents a plot of the Ramah chert flake distribution for the south lobe with the uppermost level 1 flakes eliminat-

ed. This is not an ideal solution since level 1 was sufficiently deep that it probably combined some flakes from the two possible components. Nevertheless, the modified plot strongly reinforces the idea of a clear boundary along this side of the lobe and reveals a linear distribution with a width very similar to that of the western side of the lobe.

Patinated Ramah chert has a white and sometimes cracked surface indicative of thermal alteration. The quadrat diagram (Figure 42) indicates that patinated Ramah chert clusters strongly in the south lobe

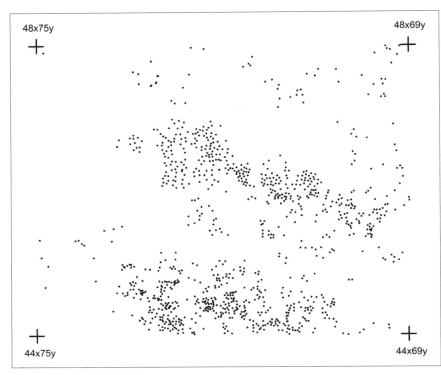

48x75y

48x69y

44x75y

44x69y

41/ Area 2A south lobe, lower level: distribution of Ramah chert flakes.

with Area 2B. Since patination is the result of thermal stress it is not surprising to find the material concentrated near hearths, but its occurrence some distance from hearths implies that in those cases it must have been removed from the hearths and redeposited elsewhere. This possibility is discussed further below.

The point-pattern distribution of fine-grained cherts, along with a quadrat breakdown by gray Mugford and black chert variants (Figure 43) indicates they are mainly associated with the south lobe and are

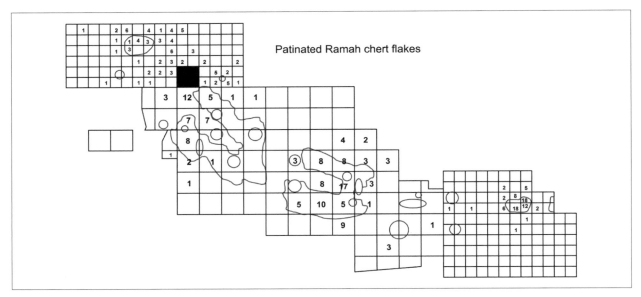

Patinated Ramah chert flakes

42/ Area 2: distribution of patinated Ramah chert flakes.

adjacent to hearths and at the northernmost end of the north lobe associated with hearths 2, 6 and 8, but not with the other two hearths. It is absent from the "middle" area between the lobes. The patinated Ramah chert in units 49x78-79y north of the north lobe may be partly or entirely the result of overlap

absent from the "middle" area. In the south lobe, both materials cluster around hearth 4, with lesser amounts near hearth 5. The black chert distribution is interesting since its highest frequencies (10 flakes) are found in symmetric opposition at both ends of the lobe near the "middle" area. In the north lobe, both cherts are

CHAPTER 6

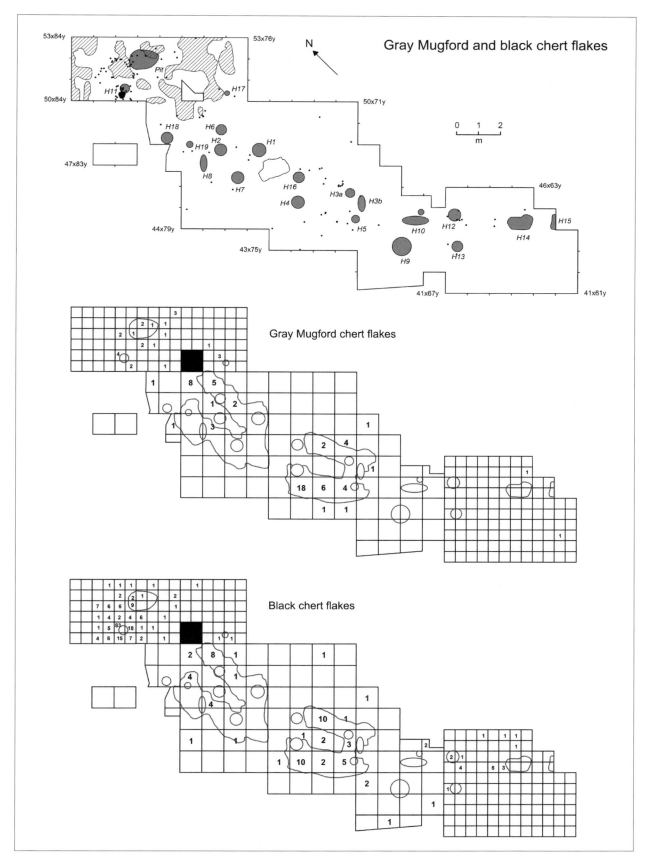

43/ Area 2: distribution of gray Mugford and black chert flakes.

Table 5: Area 2A Flake Raw Material Frequencies by Model Units

	North Lobe	Middle	South Lobe	Other	TOTAL
	N (%)	N (%)	N (%)	N (%)	N (%)
Quartz	1159 (47.0)	63 (58.3)	1065 (26.0)	301 (19.1)	2588 (31.4)
Ramah chert	1097 (44.5)	44 (40.7)	2634 (64.3)	1182 (74.8)	4957 (60.1)
Patinated Ramah	42 (1.7)		71 (1.7)	25 (1.6)	138 (1.7)
Gray Mugford chert	20 (0.8)		35 (0.9)	4 (0.3)	59 (0.7)
Green Mugford chert			2 (0.0)		2 (0.0)
Black chert	19 (0.8)		35 (0.9)	7 (0.4)	61 (0.7)
Slate—total	129 (5.2)	1 (0.9)	252 (6.2)	61(3.9)	443 (5.4)
Beige	7 (0.3)		19 (0.5)	3 (0.2)	
Green	11 (0.4)	1 (0.9)	87 (2.1)	31 (2.0)	
Gray	99 (4.0)		138 (3.4)	20 (1.3)	
Gray-banded	8 (0.3)			1 (0.1)	
Red-brown	3 (0.1)		3 (0.1)	6 (0.4)	
Indet.	1 (0.0)		5 (0.1)		
TOTAL	2466	108	4094	1580	8248

primarily associated with hearths 2, 6 and 8, while they are absent from hearths 1 and 7. The small cluster of both materials in units 49x77-78y north of the north lobe may be a result of overlap with Area 2B.

Figure 44 shows the distribution of plotted slate flakes (undifferentiated by color variant). Once again the pattern is one of concentration in the two lobes and virtual absence from the middle. It is also clear that within each lobe the outer boundaries of the slate distributions fit closely with those of quartz and Ramah chert. At the south lobe slate occurs as two roughly parallel distributions on either side of the central corridor. Closer inspection suggests it clusters adjacent to hearths 3a, 4, 5, with another apparently hearth-independent concentration at the northeastern edge of the lobe. The latter is consistent with the tendencies noted in the quartz and Ramah chert distributions.

To pull this together, Table 5 compares the proportions of the flake raw material types by grouping the quadrats into model-based units: the north and south lobes representing behavioral modules, the "middle" consisting of units near the large central rock between the lobes and "other" defined as all remaining units outside the lobes. There is a clear difference between the north lobe and middle subareas, with their somewhat even proportions of quartz to Ramah chert, and the south lobe and "other" subareas, which have much higher proportions of Ramah chert to quartz. Comparison with chi-square expected frequencies confirms the importance of the aforementioned proportional differences, although the frequency of Ramah chert in the south lobe and "other" subareas may be inflated by palimpsest effects from a Ramah chert-rich later component. The expected frequencies also indicate a slight over-representation of slate flakes at the south lobe. If we consider flake raw materials by weight (Table 6), quartz clearly dominates in all subareas, but the proportional weight of Ramah chert is greater in the south lobe and "other" subareas, consistent with the frequency data.

The middle subarea's relatively balanced frequency of quartz and chert resembles the north lobe proportions (although by weight the Ramah chert propor-

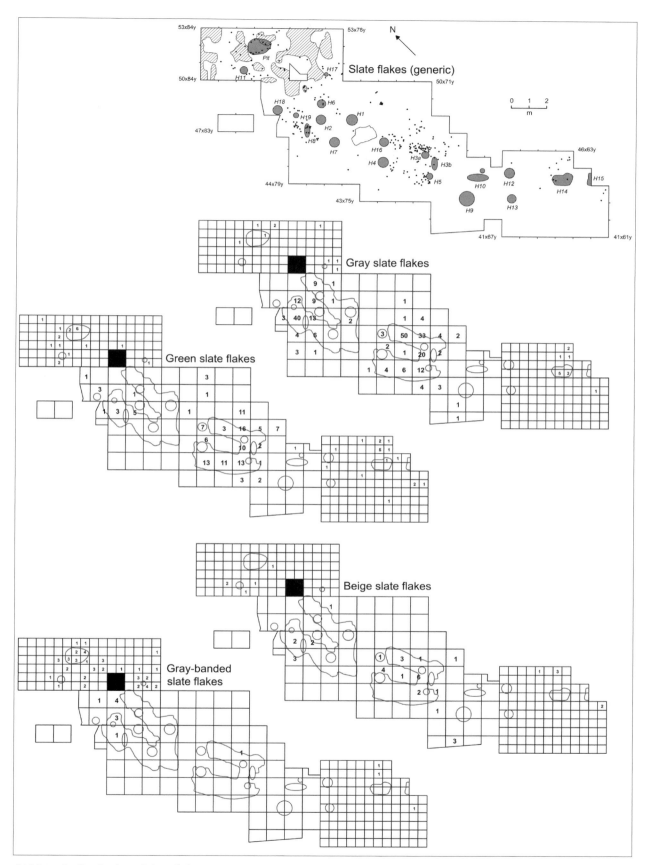

44/ Area 2: distribution of slate flakes.

Table 6: Area 2A Flake Raw Material Weights by Model Units in Grams

	North Lobe N (%)	Middle N (%)	South Lobe N (%)	Other N (%)
Quartz	4309 (87.8)	184 (78.2)	3751 (70.4)	1886 (68.3)
Ramah chert	475 (9.7)	51 (21.7)	1280 (24.0)	770 (27.9)
Patinated Ramah	19.3 (0.4)		44.7 (0.8)	9.7 (0.4)
Gray Mugford chert	4 (0.1)		8 (0.2)	1.7 (0.1)
Black chert		3.3 (0.1)	18.6 (0.3)	1.8 (0.1)
Green Mugford			0.2 (0.0)	
Slate—total	96.5 (2.0)	0.2 (0.1)	271.7 (5.1)	91.4 (3.3)
Beige	1.3 (0.0)		5.2 (0.1)	1.4 (0.1)
Green	39.3 (0.8)	0.2 (0.1)	130.7 (2.5)	67.4 (2.4)
Gray	33 (0.7)		133.2 (2.5)	19.9 (0.7)
Gray-banded	3 (0.1)		0.1 (0.0)	0.1 (0.0)
Red-brown	0.9 (0.0)		0.5 (0.0)	2.6 (0.1)
Indet.	19 (0.4)		2 (0.0)	

tion in the middle is somewhat higher), but the middle has an extremely low overall flake total, entirely lacks patinated Ramah chert and Mugford chert, and has only a single slate flake. Thus, the low intensity of lithic reduction in the middle subarea stands as a marked contrast to the two lobes and is also consistent with its low frequency of retouched implements (n =14, see Table 7), though not with the relatively high proportion of quartz cores (see below). The "other" subarea has quartz/Ramah chert proportions similar to the south lobe.

If we consider slate color variants by frequency, both lobes are dominated by gray slate, while green slate is the second most frequent variant. Nonetheless, a chi-square test (χ^2 = 80.92) indicates there are significant differences in the spatial distributions of the slate variants, the expected frequencies pointing to a slight over-representation of gray slate in the north lobe and slight a over-representation of green slate in the south lobe and "other" subarea. The frequency of green slate in the "other" subarea— most being concentrated east of the south lobe— could imply a behavioral link between the south lobe and the "external"

area to the east. If the comparison is conducted by weight, however, there is parity in gray and green slate between the two lobes, but a repeated over-proportional amount of green slate in the "other" subarea (Table 6). Thus, the similarities in slate type proportions between the south lobe and the "other" subarea parallel the similarities in quartz/Ramah chert proportions between the same subareas.

Variation in flake raw materials can also be evaluated independent of the model units. Although it cannot be assumed that the distributions of tools and debitage are conditioned by the same depositional variables, a tool-cluster based quadrat grouping of flakes might reveal additional dimensions of spatial variation. The quadrats were grouped according to the 9-cluster solution, but the 1 m^2 units did not coincide perfectly with the clusters. The resulting table (not shown) was not particularly enlightening, since the frequency variations were fairly consistent with the model-based analysis. A better way of handling the debitage distribution independent of model assumptions was exploratory correspondence analysis of raw material frequencies by quadrats. The correspondence plot in

Table 7: Area 2A Tool Classes by Model Units.

	PT	BI	PR	FP	SC	UF	SP	CA	SB	ST	BC	CO	TM	OTH	TOTAL
N	2.5	6	3	7	6	25	2	2	2	8	13	13	1	1	91.5
MID	0.5	2			1	4				1		4.5		1	14
S	8	6	2	2	11	41	2	1	4	35	32	11.5*		1	158.5
OTH	2	2	1	1	4	27			6	7	12	8	5	2	77
TOTAL	13	16	6	10	22	97	4	3	12	51	57	37	7	6	341
%	3.8	4.7	1.8	2.9	6.5	28.4	1.2	0.9	3.5	15.0	16.7	10.9	2.1	1.8	

a fragment conjoining with another in a different unit was assigned a value of .5

PT: points (bifacial), BI: bifaces, PR: preforms (biface), FP: flake points, SC: scrapers (endscrapers and flake knives), UF: utilized flakes, SP: slate points, CA: celt/adze, SB: slate blanks (unmodified plates and blanks), ST: slate tool fragments (ground slate flakes and unidentified tool fragments), BC: bipolar cores, CO: block cores (quartz), TM: tool manufacturing (hammerstones, schist tablets, whetstones), and OTH: other (stemmed flakes, linear flakes, graver).

Figure 45 indicates that the first axis (horizontal) accounts for 75.2% of the variation, seriating the quadrats relative to their proportions of Ramah chert and quartz. The units on the left side of the axis are dominated by Ramah chert while the units on the right side are dominated by quartz. The second axis (vertical) accounts for 18.2% of the variation, scaling the quadrats relative to slate proportions. Units placed towards the top of the axis have unusually high frequencies of slate. Symbol coding of quadrats by the model-based units indicates a clear pattern. Most of the north lobe quadrats and all the middle quadrats are pulled right by high quartz frequencies, while most of the south lobe quadrats are pulled left by abundant Ramah chert (although several are pulled by quartz). "Other" quadrats are distributed in both the quartz and Ramah chert groups, although three quadrats are outliers pulled by high frequencies of slate. Ten of the 13 "other" quadrats that group with the south lobe are actually adjacent to that lobe, while 10 of the 15 "other" quadrats that group with the north lobe lie adjacent to that lobe. Mugford chert has very little influence on the plot. Thus, the correspondence analysis indicates that the model-based units are to a great extent replicated by model-independent analysis.

Tool Distribution

The spatial distribution of tool classes may indicate something about functional or depositional variation within Area 2A. The analyses are conducted using 14 largely functional classes, some of which (e.g., bifacial points) could be further subdivided into formal/functional variants (see Chapter 8 for a description of the tool material). Table 7 outlines the tool class frequencies in relation to the model-based units introduced in the debitage analysis. Variation in the table can be scaled by correspondence analysis and visualized in a plot (Figure 46). The first axis of the plot accounts for 44.9% of the variation and primarily contrasts the south lobe on the right side with the north lobe slightly towards the left. The south lobe is positioned with bipolar cores, bifacial points, scrapers, utilized flakes and slate tool fragments. The north lobe is only distinguished by flake points. Common to both lobes are block cores, bifaces and preforms. The middle subarea is pulled to the extreme left of the plot, probably because of a modest frequency of block cores combined with an absence of bipolar cores. Along the second axis, accounting for 34.9% of the variation, the "other" subarea is distinguished towards the bottom of the plot by slate blanks and tool manufacturing items. Although the low tool frequencies limit the robustness of the analysis, it does point to contrasts between the subareas. The lobes are not replicate behavioral modules, but they do share broad similarities.

A more detailed assessment of tool class variation can be had by combining the quantitative data with the spatial distribution diagrams. While some of the tool classes can reasonably be evaluated in terms of their point distributions, others— specifically, utilized flakes, block cores and bipolar cores— lack systematic point proveniencing and are best evaluated by quadrats. Both types of information are provided here. There are some interesting patterns in the distributions of block and bipolar cores (Figures 47 and 48). The largely unworked quartz block cores are frequent in the middle area between the lobes, suggesting they were cached or dumped there. Half of the cores in this area are located in quadrats with few quartz flakes, while the

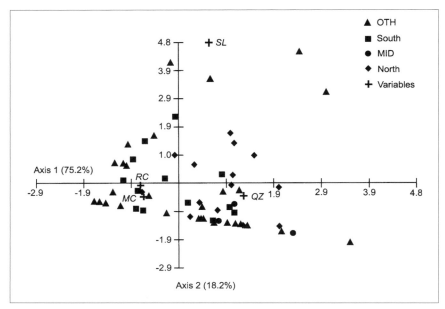

45/ Area 2A: correspondence analysis plot of flake raw materials by quadrat, coded by analytical model units.

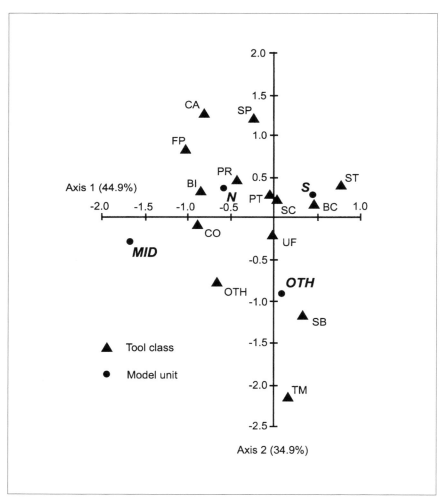

46/ Area 2A: correspondence analysis plot of tool classes by analytical model units.

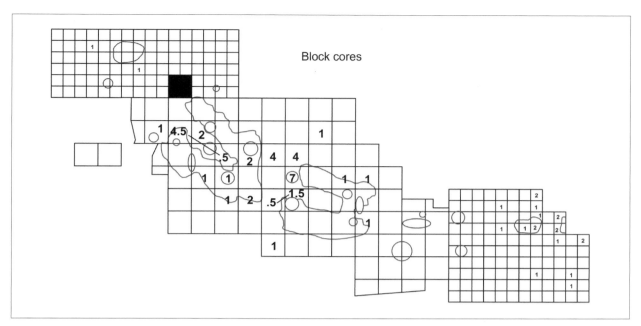

47/ Area 2: distribution of block cores by quadrat.

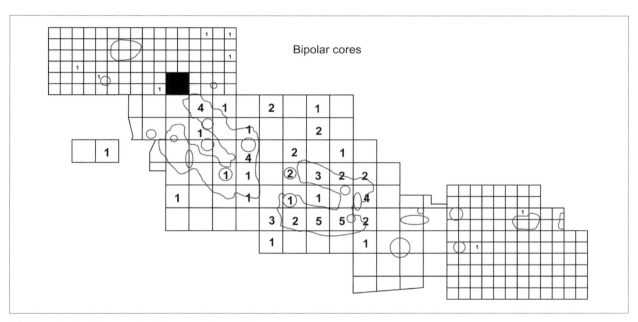

48/ Area 2: distribution of bipolar cores by quadrat.

other half are positioned within or adjacent to a cluster of quartz debitage at the northeastern corner of the south lobe. Consequently, the placement of block cores is partly independent of quartz reduction locations. There is also a slight concentration of block cores at the northern end of the north lobe. Here, however, the cores are clearly associated with quartz flake concentrations. In contrast, bipolar cores, the intermediary and final product of quartz reduction, are mostly found within the south lobe, where they are associated with the greatest densities of quartz flakes but are largely independent of the distribution of block cores. At the north lobe there are small clusters of bipolar cores at each end of the eastern side; the cluster near the northern end is associated with a concentration of quartz flakes, but the southern cluster is not. Both

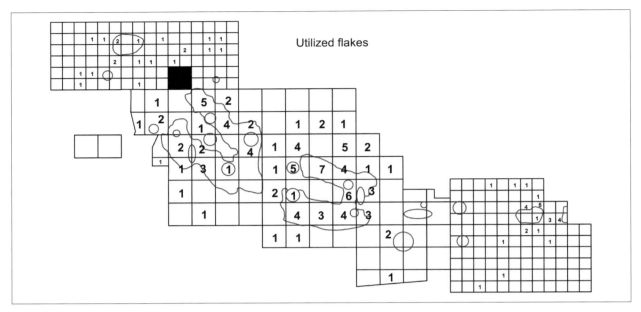

Utilized flakes

49/ Area 2: distribution of utilized flakes by quadrat.

clusters are associated with or are adjacent to concentrations of block cores. In the quadrats east of the middle area between the lobes there are several bipolar cores that are largely independent of the distribution of both block cores and quartz debitage. This placement might suggest they are secondary refuse rather than the products of *in situ* reduction. In sum, with the exception of the eastern exterior area, the associations suggest primary refuse accumulation combined with some degree of caching or dumping of block cores separate from reduction areas. It is noteworthy that possible caching areas are found in similar locations at the northern end of both lobes.

Utilized flakes (Figure 49) are generally found adjacent to the hearth features, although they are also frequent near the eastern edge of the middle area and in the corridor of the south lobe. There is also a small concentration in the area east of the south lobe.

The distribution of bifacial points is plotted in Figure 50, biface preforms in Figure 51, and bifaces and fragments thereof in Figure 52. Most of the items from the three classes are associated with one or the other lobes, generally lying within 1 m of a hearth. Both preforms and biface fragments are fairly evenly distributed between the two lobes, but bifacial points are more frequent in the south lobe. The reverse pattern is seen for flake points (Figure 53); seven points are associated with the north lobe, while only two are associated with the south lobe.

Endscrapers are made exclusively of fine-grained chert, both gray Mugford and black chert. They occur in both lobes, although they are somewhat more frequent in the south lobe, particularly adjacent to Hearth 3a (Figure 54). Three are found near the western edge of the middle area. Two endscrapers lie near the open northern end of the north lobe, although one is in the area of presumed overlap with Area 2B. The distribution of endscrapers is only partly consistent with the distribution of fine-grained chert flakes (Figure 43). On the eastern side of the south lobe there are seven tools and only 23 flakes, while on the western side there is only one tool but 46 flakes. Thus, discard/use and production/retouch are not always correlated.

Ground slate tools are distributed fairly evenly between the two lobes, with slate points and adzes present in each lobe (Figure 55). The distribution of raw slate plates and partially formed tool blanks (Figure 56) is fairly even between the two lobes (two vs three), but four are scattered in the area east of the lobes. Overall, ca. 73% of all ground slate flakes and

CHAPTER 6

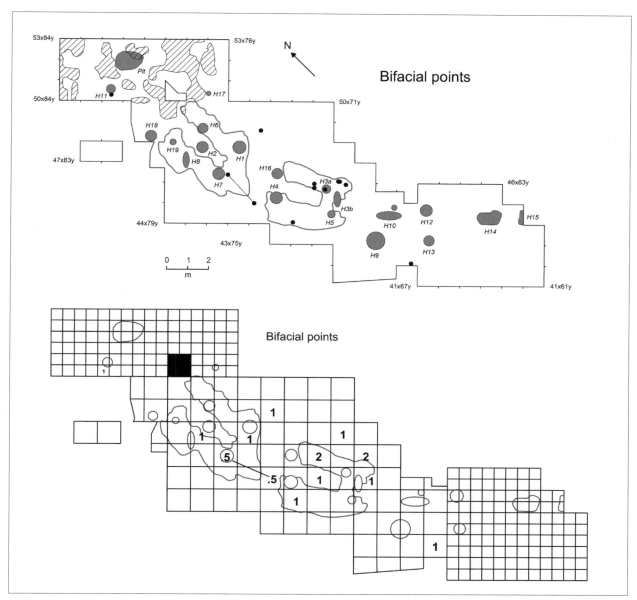

50/ Area 2: distribution of bifacial points.

unidentifiable ground tool fragments are associated with the south lobe (Table 7, Figure 57). The distribution of ground slate flakes struck from tool edges is shown in Figure 57. All but one of these are found in the south lobe and in units adjacent to hearths. One specimen from inside the south lobe conjoins with a non-edge- struck slate flake in the area east of the south lobe. A single edge-struck flake occurs in the north lobe, adjacent to a hearth. In sum, although the deposition of slate tools within each lobe is roughly equivalent, the south lobe seems to exhibit a greater

degree of slate tool production and reworking, as indicated by the high frequency of unground and ground slate flakes (Table 5; Figures 44 and 57). The area east of the south lobe contains a modest number of ground and unground slate flakes, plates/blanks and tools.

The residual category "miscellaneous tools" (Figure 58) tends to be associated with the hearths and is fairly evenly distributed between the lobes. An exception is the clustering of a flake knife, a graver/scraper and a stemmed flake near the eastern edge of the middle area. Seen in conjunction with a cluster of utilized

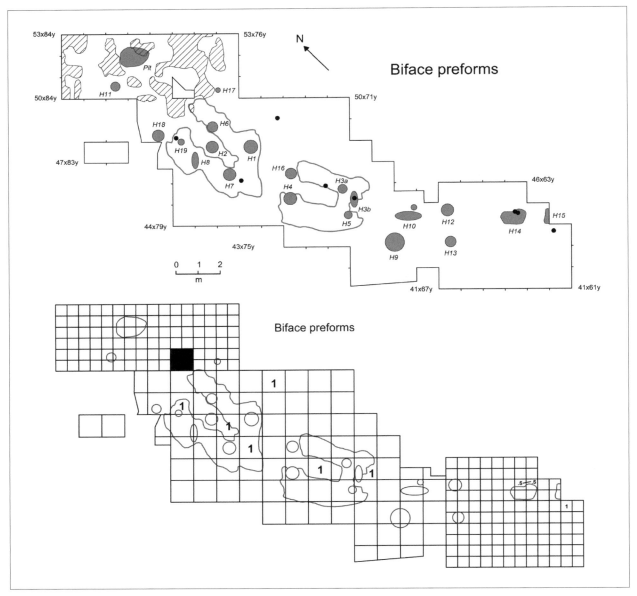

51. Area 2: distribution of biface preforms

flakes in the same area (Figure 49), this might indicate some scraping/cutting functions were undertaken there. A schist tablet is associated with hearth 6 in the north lobe, while a hard slate whetstone lies adjacent to hearth 3a in the south lobe. These may have been associated with grinding slate or bone implements, but the implement at hearth 6 is only associated with a single ground slate flake, while hearth 3a is adjacent to several ground slate flakes and tools.

The stories told by tool raw material frequencies and weights are quite different (Tables 8 and 9). By fre-

quency, the proportion of Ramah chert to quartz tools is 2:1 across all the subareas except for the middle, where they are even. This proportion would be much higher if quartz cores were eliminated from the figures. By weight, however, quartz constitutes ca. 75% of the material in all subareas except the middle, where it is nearly 98%. This is much the same pattern as seen with the flakes (Tables 5 and 6), where Ramah chert is high in frequency but low in weight.

At this point it would be useful to consider the tool distribution with the model-independent

CHAPTER 6

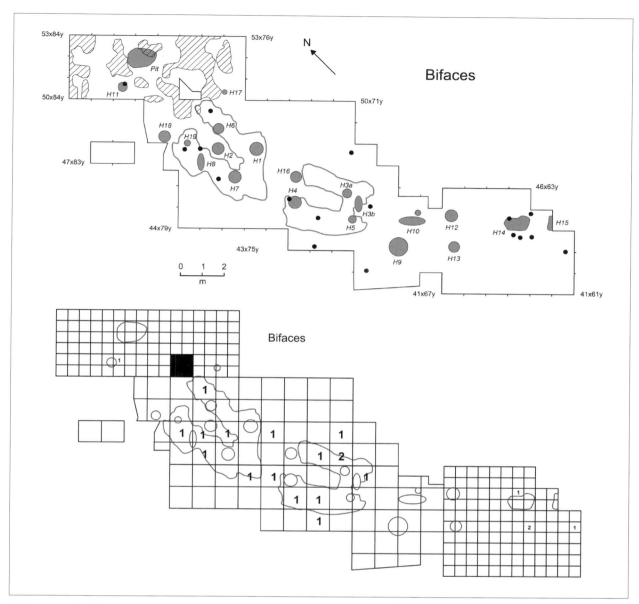

52/ Area 2: distribution of bifaces.

approach, using *k*-means derived groupings. To supplement the overall 9- and 12-cluster solutions presented previously (Figure 37), a separate analysis of Area 2A was conducted. The best result is a 12-cluster solution (Figure 59) which is broadly similar to the overall Area 2 12-cluster solution, but some new clusters are split off. While this may be a slightly better grouping seen from the perspective of identifying hearth-centered distributions, some of the new smaller clusters may be spurious. However, as mentioned above, a serious problem is that the inadequate point-

proveniencing of certain tool types limits the utility of point pattern analysis. We could try to group the quadrats according to the clusters defined by *k*-means analysis, but we run into difficulties, since the 1 m^2 quadrats can overlap different clusters, particularly in the more fine-grained 12-cluster solution. In an attempt to maintain some form of model-independent approach, the earlier 9-cluster solution (Figure 37) was chosen for illustrative purposes. This still poses some difficulties in that the clusters do not conform neatly to the quadrat boundaries, although the number of prob-

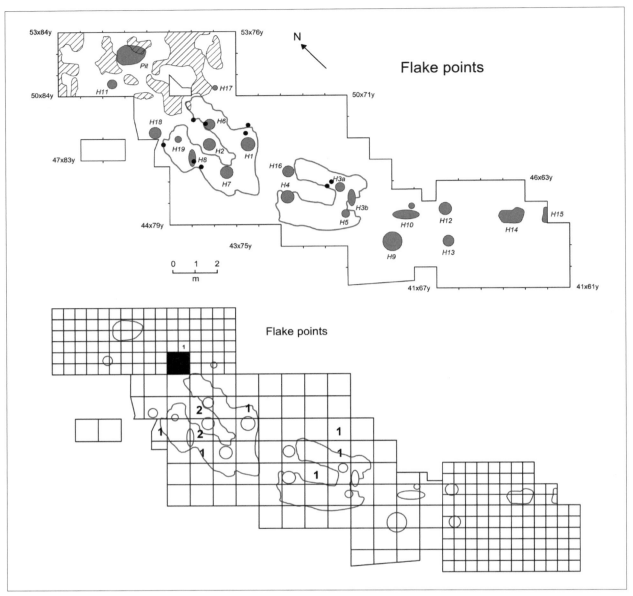

53. Area 2: distribution of flake points.

lem areas is relatively small. Difficult quadrats were assigned to a cluster based on degree of overlap and the relative density of plotted tools. The resulting cluster groupings are very similar to the model-based subareas, so it is questionable whether this approach provides much information beyond that of the model-based analysis. Nonetheless, the resulting tool frequency distribution is presented in Table 10.

The many low cell frequencies in Table 10 render analysis problematic, but Figure 60 presents a correspondence analysis plot to visualize possible varia-

tions between the clusters. The clusters lie in a ring around the origin of the plot and their positioning relative to the tool classes does not suggest groupings. There are minor differences between the clusters, but the variation only involves one or two tool classes and small numbers of items. Nuances can be identified by considering the cells for which observed frequencies depart somewhat from expected values. Bipolar cores are slightly over-represented in cluster 2 (south lobe, hearths 3a,b), concomitant with an under-representation of quartz block cores. In cluster 9 (middle, with

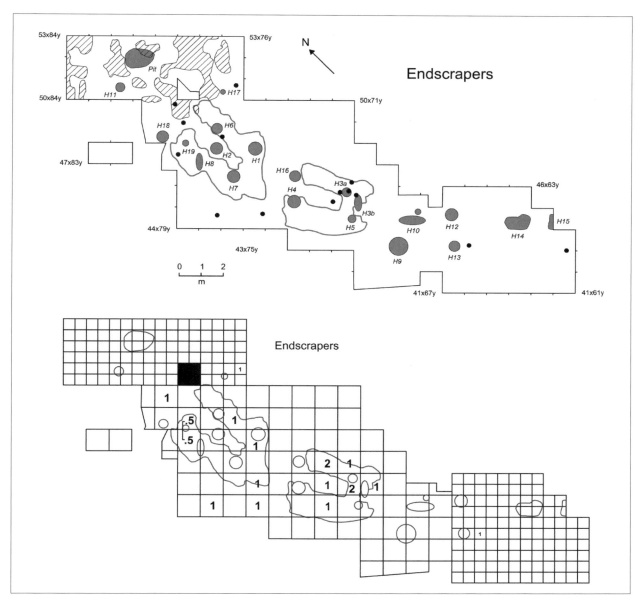

54/ Area 2: distribution of endscrapers.

overlaps from both lobes and the area east of the lobes), block cores and slate tool fragments are over-represented. There is a less-marked overweight of scrapers and bifacial projectile points in cluster 2 and of block cores and slate blanks in cluster 7 (east of the lobes). Cluster 8, lying at the northern "entrance" to the north lobe, exhibits a slight overweight of flake points. There is a slight over-representation of utilized flakes in cluster 9, but this does not seem terribly significant when the quadrat distribution pattern is inspected (Figure 49). There is also an over-represen-

tation of ground slate flakes and unidentifiable slate tool fragments in cluster 9, particularly in association with hearth 4 (Figure 57). Ground slate flakes are also concentrated near hearth 5 (Cluster 2), although this is not statistically disproportional.

If we consider tool raw material frequencies by cluster unit (Table 11), there are few differences between observed and expected frequencies other than somewhat more than expected quartz in cluster 7 (east of the lobes)— mostly accounted for by cores— and a slight over-representation of quartz and slate

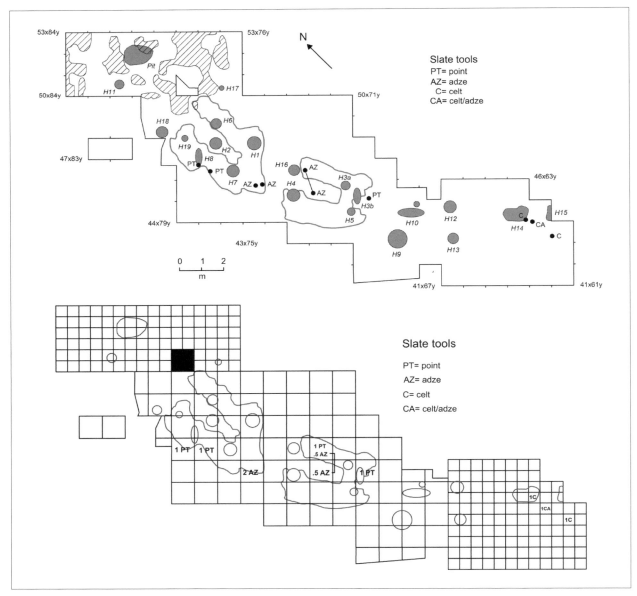

55/ Area 2: distribution of slate tools.

(treated generically) in cluster 9. For the latter, the quartz is accounted for by cores, while the slate consists of ground flakes— most of which are associated with the edge of the south lobe. Thus, the cluster-based division provides little information beyond that derived from the model-based units.

In sum, the *k*-means approach does not provide much information to supplement or contradict the model-based analysis. The 12-cluster solution for Area 2A alone (Figure 59) provides a schematic overview of the hearth-centered distributions, while the "lumped" 9-cluster solution for Area 2 as a whole (Figure 37) indicates that the major and most stable clusters strongly parallel the divisions used in the model-based analyses. Clearly, however, the necessity of using large and coarsely grouped quadrats undermines the possibility of isolating patterns that might be revealed by more precise point-provenience analysis or smaller quadrats.

Table 8: Area 2A Tool Raw Material Frequencies by Model Units.

	North Lobe N (%)	Middle Lobe N (%)	South Lobe N (%)	Other N (%)	TOTAL N (%)
Quartz	23 (25.1)	5.5* (39.3)	35.5 (22.4)	16 (20.8)	80 (23.5)
Ramah chert	48.5 (46.0)	7.5 (53.6)	66 (41.6)	36 (46.8)	158 (46.3)
Gray Mugford	3 (3.3)		3 (1.9)	2 (2.6)	8 (2.3)
Black chert	2 (2.2)		11 (6.9)	5 (6.5)	18 (5.3)
Slate—total	14 (15.3)	1 (7.1)	42 (26.5)	13 (16.9)	70 (20.5)
Green	8	1	15	6	30
Gray	1		22	5	28
Red-brown	3		1	2	6
Gray-banded	1		3		4
Indet.	1		1		2
Schist	1 (1.1)			4 (5.2)	5 (1.5)
Other			1 (0.6)	1 (1.3)	2 (0.6)

*.5 denotes a conjoining fragment

Table 9: Area 2A Tool Raw Material Weights by Model Units. In Grams.

	North Lobe N (%)	Middle Lobe N (%)	South Lobe N (%)	Other N (%)
Quartz	1751 (68.8)	1161 (94.7)	1759 (76.4)	1475.6 (58.2)
Ramah chert	284.2 (11.2)	64.4 (5.3)	302.3 (13.1)	165 (6.5)
Black chert	12 (0.5)		32 (1.4)	15 (0.6)
Gray Mugford	25.3 (1.0)		16 (0.7)	4 (0.2)
Slate—total	294.7 (11.6)	0.3 (0.0)	160.6 (7.0)	155.1 (6.1)
Green	111.5	0.3	98.7	144.1
Gray	16		19.8	9.9
Red-brown	167		3	1.1
Gray-banded	0.2		6.1	
Gray/schist			33	
Schist	177 (7.0)		33 (1.4)	554.5 (21.9)
Other			0.3 (0.0)	167 (6.6)

Distribution of Red Ocher and Bone Fragments

Figure 61 depicts the distribution of red ocher stains and bone fragments. It is possible that more red ocher stains were present but went undocumented given the difficulty of identifying them in the very dark brown podzolized sand or because some were erased by deflation. Taking the data at hand, red ocher stains are found almost exclusively within the lobes, where they occur within or closely adjacent to hearths. Stains are associated with both

Table 10: Area 2A Tool Classes; Quadrats Grouped by *K*-Means Cluster.

	PT	BI	PR	FP	SC	UF	SP	CA	SB	ST	BC	CO	TM	OTH	TOTAL
Cluster 2	7	6	2	2	11	32	2	1	4	19.5*	25	3	4	2	120.5
Cluster 4	0.5	1	1	1	2	8	2		1	2	3	3			24.5
Cluster 7	3	2	1	2	2	22			4	7	13	11	2	1	70
Cluster 8	1	4	2	5	4	20			1	6	6	8	1	1	59
Cluster 9	1.5	3			3	15		2	2	16.5	10	12		2	67
TOTAL	13	16	6	10	22	97	4	3	12	51	57	37	7	6	341

* .5 denotes a conjoining fragment

PT: points (bifacial), **BI**: bifaces, **PR**: preforms (biface), **FP**: flake points, **SC**: scrapers (endscrapers and flake knives), **UF**: utilized flakes, **SP**: slate points, **CA**: celt/adze, **SB**: slate blanks (unmodified plates and blanks), **ST**: slate tool fragments (ground slate flakes and unidentified tool fragments), **BC**: bipolar cores, **CO**: block cores (quartz), **TM**: tool manufacturing (hammerstones, schist tablets, whetstones), and **OTH**: other (stemmed flakes, linear flakes, graver).

Table 11: Area 2A Tool Raw Material Frequencies by *K*-Means Cluster.

	Cluster 2		Cluster 4		Cluster 7		Cluster 8		Cluster 4	
	N	(%)	N	(%)	N	(%)	N	(%)	N	(%)
Quartz	22	(18.3)	4	(16.3)	21	(30.0)	13	(22.0)	20	(29.9)
Ramah chert	55	(45.6)	13.5	(55.1)	35	(50.0)	33	(55.9)	21.5	(32.1)
Black chert	10	(8.3)	1	(4.1)			4	(6.8)	3	(4.5)
Gray Mugford	3	(2.5)	1	(4.1)	1	(1.4)	1	(1.7)	2	(3.0)
Slate—total	26.5*	(22.0)	5	(20.4)	11	(15.7)	7	(11.9)	19.5	(29.1)
Green	11		3		4		3		9	
Gray	12.5				5		1		8.5	
Red-brown	1		2		2		1			
Gray-banded	2						1		1	
Gray/schist										
Indet.							1		1	
Schist	3	(2.5)			2	(2.9)	1	(1.7)		
Other	1	(0.8)							1	(1.5)
TOTAL	120.5		24.5		70		59		67	

* .5 denotes a conjoining fragment

surface and pit hearths, although they seem most intensive with pit features. Deviating from this pattern is a patch 1 m north of hearth 8 at the north lobe and two small stains just south of the south lobe. No uncrushed ocher fragments were observed at Area 2A.

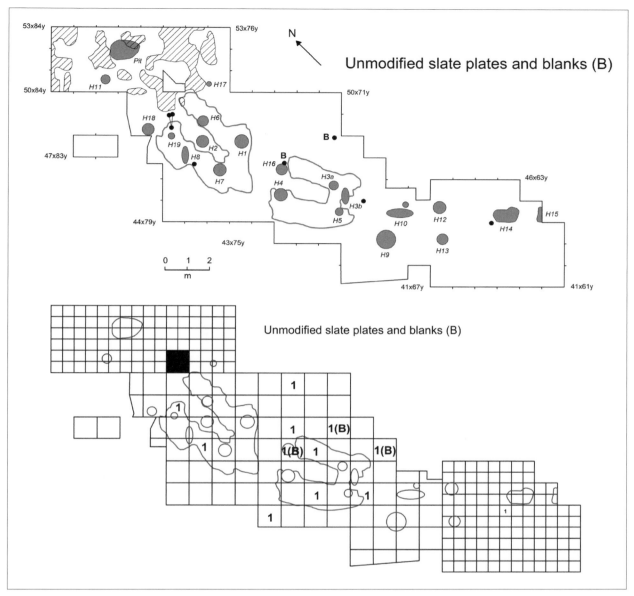

56/ Area 2: distribution of unmodified slate plates and blanks.

The paucity of bone is a consequence of both taphonomic factors and recovery techniques. The extremely acidic soil (pH 4.0-5.0) destroyed all but a few fragments of highly calcined bone. On the other hand, it is possible that more fragments could have been recovered with fine-screening (only 1/4 inch mesh was used). All bone fragments at Area 2A are associated with the two lobes. At the north lobe, a single fragment is found in the pit of hearth 8, another single fragment lies 1 m to the southeast and another single piece lies between hearths 1 and 6. At the south

lobe, six fragments are associated with hearth 5. None of these bone fragments could be identified to taxon.

Feature-Centered Distributions, Size-Sorting, and Cultural Formation Processes

Since the behavioral modules suggested in the Area 2A material might imply dwelling structures we should consider more explicitly the ethnoarchaeologically derived feature-centered models. As discussed in Chapter 3, we might expect to find different types of distribution patterns associated with exterior and inte-

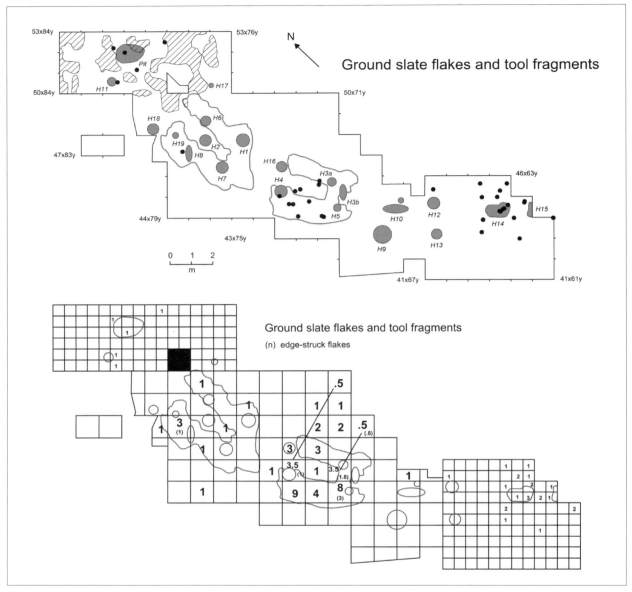

57/ Area 2: distribution of ground slate flakes and ground tool fragments.

rior hearths. In general, exterior hearths may have more extensive debris distributions with drop- and toss-zones characterized by size-sorting of cultural material: smaller items in the drop-zones adjacent to hearths, larger items in the toss-zones further away— a roughly concentric zonation. Interior hearths may exhibit an adjacent concentration of cultural material but may lack clear drop- and toss-zones because of periodic maintenance of dwelling interiors designed to prevent the accumulation of material in the sleeping areas near the dwelling walls. Maintenance of dwelling

interiors may result in the development of exterior secondary refuse deposits such as "door dumps" (Binford 1983:177). Thus, instead of concentric size-sorting there is a distinction between small-sized items near interior hearths and larger items in exterior dumps.

Evaluation of the total debitage distribution as well as distributions of individual raw materials does not indicate the concentric and gradual "distance decay" patterning expected at exterior hearths. Flakes are obviously clustered adjacent to hearths, but they are generally concentrated on one side of

CHAPTER 6

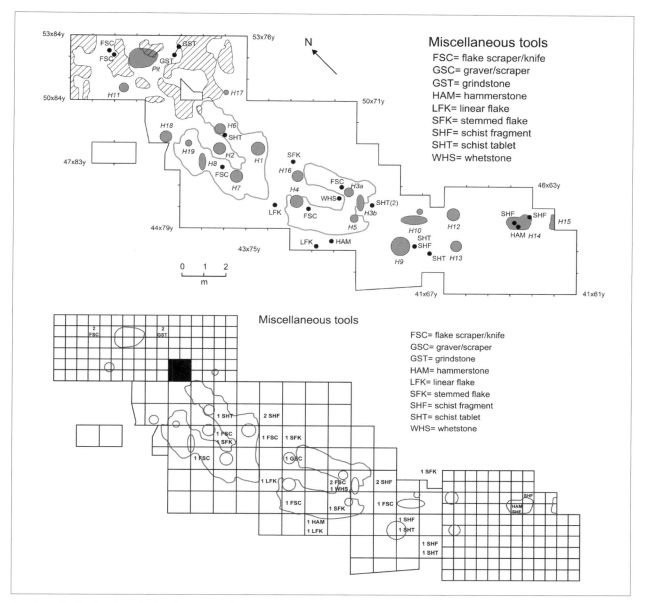

58/ Area 2: distribution of miscellaneous tools.

the hearths rather than forming a ring around them. The overall distributions are bounded in linear "lobe" patterns which, to some extent, may be the result of overlapping hearth-centered distributions. The outer edges of the lobes (particularly the southern one) are fairly sharp, suggestive of a boundary effect. At the same time, the inner edges of the lobes indicate central areas with minimal debitage accumulation, either a consequence of differential activity placement or maintenance of the central areas. The tool distribution patterns are also closely linked to hearths,

although the concentration of block cores in the "middle" and the area east of the lobes deviates from the overall pattern.

If the overall configuration of the debitage and tool distributions seems more in line with an interior hearth model, what about the size-sorting criterion? One problem in assessing size-sorting is that lithics may be less sensitive to the discard and maintenance practices noted ethnoarchaeologically for bones and implements of organic materials, given much less variation in size dimensions. Nonetheless, since lithics are

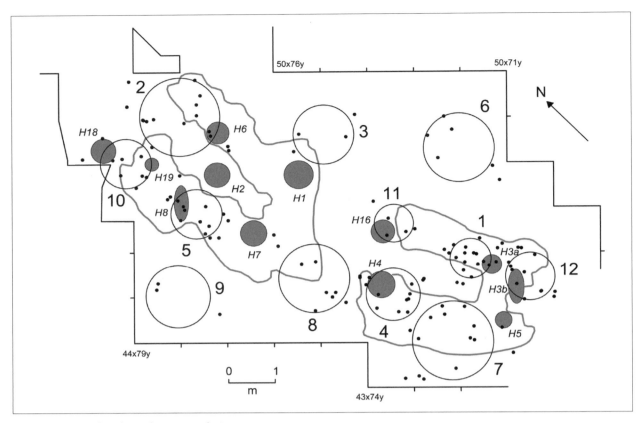

59/ Area 2A: twelve-cluster k-means solution.

the only available data class their potential for reveal-ing relevant patterning should be explored. A distinc-tion between large/small tools and tool fragments was made with reference to a histogram of all tool maxi-mum lengths for Area 2. Given a skewed distribution with over 60% of the tools less than 40 mm long, small was defined as <39.9 mm, large as >40.0 mm. Given the relatively small number of tools and their variable numbers across the units, it did not seem advisable to calculate a size-sorting index. Instead, a subjective evaluation was made in which units with either high absolute numbers of large tools or high proportions of large to small tools were identified and marked on Figure 62. At the north lobe, units with large tools lie between hearths 7 and 8, adjacent to hearths 2 and 6, and associated with possible hearth 19. The latter con-centration is strongly affected by the presence of sev-eral quartz block cores. There are no units with con-centrations of large tools outside the open northern side of the lobe, as might be expected from a "door

dump." At the south lobe, a unit with large tools is directly associated with hearths 3a and 3b while anoth-er lies in the relatively debitage-free "corridor" between hearths 3a and 4. Large tool units also occur at both the eastern and western edges of the middle area. Most of the large implements on the eastern side are unused quartz block cores. As discussed previously, these may represent a raw material cache rather than a discard dump. In sum, there is little evidence for the systematic removal of larger tools from within the modules to secondary deposits elsewhere.

Debitage might also have been subject to mainte-nance related size-sorting, especially quartz, the expe-dient reduction of which produced a wide array of large chunks. Quartz chunks might be more annoying on a dwelling floor than small Ramah chert retouch flakes and the larger quartz fragments would be easi-er to collect and discard outside a dwelling. However, size-sorted patterns of debitage might also reflect the spatial staging of lithic reduction sequences. Initial

CHAPTER 6

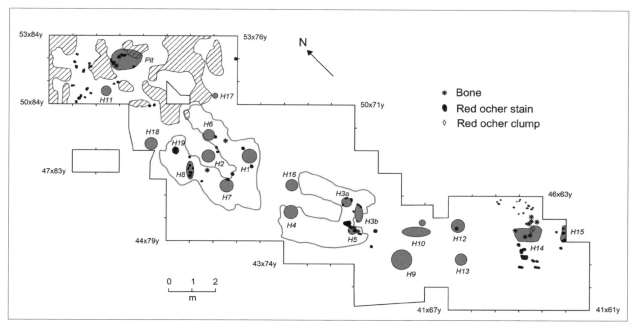

61/ Area 2: distribution of red ocher and bone fragments.

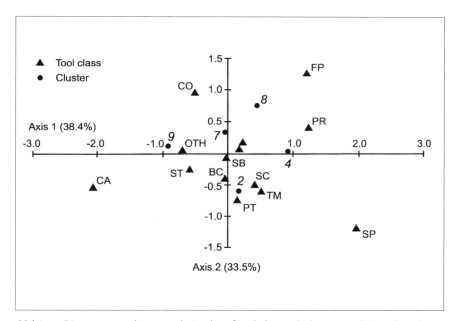

60/ Area 2A: correspondence analysis plot of tool classes by k-means cluster, based on the overall Area 2 nine-cluster solution.

reduction of quartz block cores resulting in the production of large fragments might occur in one area, then some of those fragments could be removed to another location for further bipolar reduction, producing a concentration of small fragments. Nonetheless, it might be possible to distinguish between maintenance related and reduction related size-sorting by consider-

ing the associated tool context. Reduction related size-sorting might be indicated by associations between block cores and larger debitage fragments and bipolar cores and smaller debitage fragments, while maintenance related size-sorting might be signaled by the co-occurrence of both core types and larger debitage sizes. If all reduction stages occurred at the same locale the entire range of core types and debitage sizes would be present.

Investigation of quartz size-sorting was undertaken by calculating a size-sorting index (SSI; Wandsnider 1996, see Chapter 3) for each of the 1 m² quadrats at Area 2A. The SSI summarizes the representation of small and large items in a quadrat, with high negative values indicating a dominance of large items, high positive values a dominance of small items, and values near 0 indicating a mixture of sizes. The large and small flake

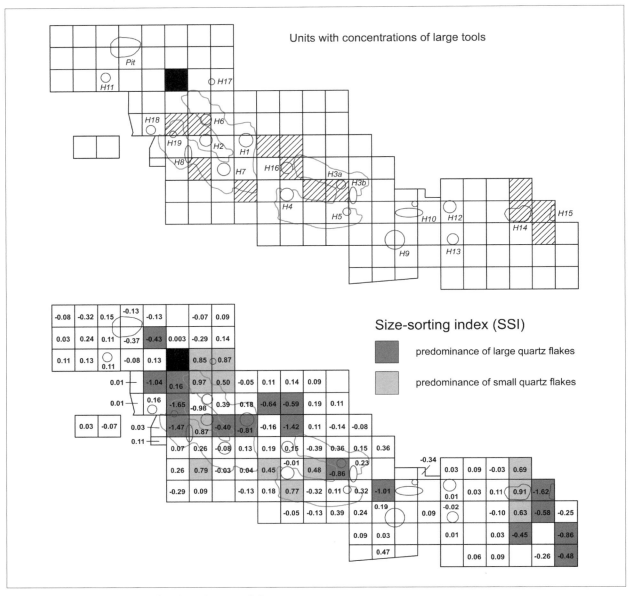

62/ Area 2: size distribution of tools and quartz flakes.

categories were constructed with reference to a line graph of quartz flake sizes for Area 2 as a whole. Around 85% of the flakes were <35 mm in size and the graph flattened out markedly above 35 mm, so "large" was defined as >35 mm. Figure 62 displays the size-sorting indices; units dominated by small or large flakes are highlighted. At the north lobe there is a unit with predominantly small flakes that lies between hearths 2, 7 and 8. On its northern flank are three units with a predominance of large flakes; two of these also have significant numbers of large tools, as does

one unit to the southwest. Hearth 6 lies in one of the aforementioned units dominated by large flakes, but adjacent units to the north and east are dominated by small flakes. Hearth 1 is situated in a unit with primarily large flakes and adjacent to a unit in the middle subarea with mainly large tools (quartz cores). One unit north of the north lobe (49x79y) has a preponderance of large flakes, but its location in the area of probable overlap between Areas 2a and 2b renders it problematic. At the south lobe the unit containing hearth 3a is dominated by large quartz flakes while an

CHAPTER 6

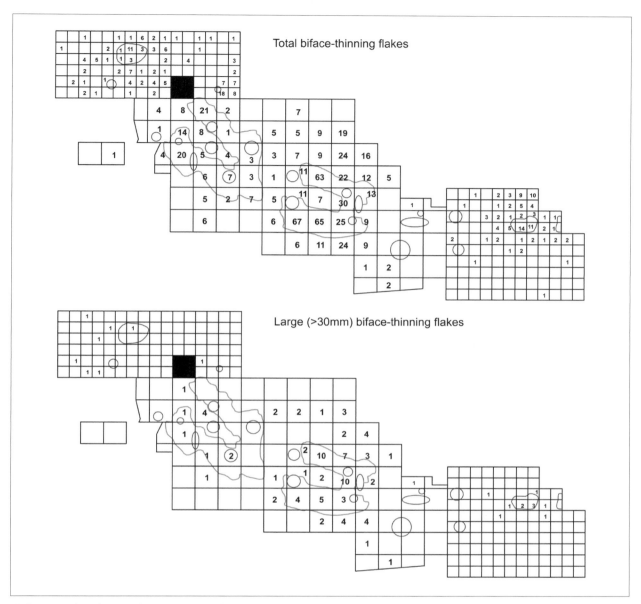

63/ Area 2: distribution of Ramah chert biface-thinning flakes.

adjacent unit is dominated by small flakes; both these units also contain significant numbers of large tools. Two units on opposite sides of hearth 5 have a tendency towards mostly small flakes, while one nearby unit at the western entrance of the middle subarea has a concentration of large tools. An interesting pattern is the presence of three units with large flakes just outside the eastern edge of the middle subarea, accompanied by three units near that edge with concentrations of large tools (mostly quartz cores). This distribution suggests that quartz blocks cached in the middle sub-

area may have been reduced in a location immediately to the east; the cores may have been reduced mostly by direct percussion (there are few bipolar cores), which produced relatively large flakes.

The bounded nature of the overall flake distributions has already been used to argue against an exterior hearth model. It is clear that the size-sorting data do not fit very well with the expectations of the exterior model: concentric zones of small items in drop zones near the hearths, larger items in more distant toss zones. Only the area around hearth 8 in the north lobe appears to conform. Hearth 3a at the south lobe actually exhibits the opposite pattern: large quartz flakes and tools adjacent to the hearths, small flakes somewhat distant. This opposite pattern may represent spatial differences in the staging of quartz reduction: initial direct percussion adjacent to the hearth, selection of desired fragments, then bipolar reduction conducted a short distance from the hearth. Hearth 5 at the south lobe is ambiguous; it lies beside two units with a preponderance of small quartz flakes, one of which (44x74y) is adjacent to a more hearth-distant unit with a very slight tendency towards larger flake sizes. One of these hearth-adjacent units (44x74y) also contained the largest concentration of small Ramah chert flakes at Area 2.

Nor do these data provide much clear evidence for maintenance related size-sorting. Within the north lobe there are four or five units with predominantly large quartz flakes and three or four units with large tools. The south lobe has less in the way of large quartz flakes, but has three units with many large tools. Besides the area directly east of the middle zone, there are no units outside the lobes with concentrations of large tools or flakes that might suggest dumps. Thus, the general impression is that if the lobes represent dwelling structures there was not much effort devoted to maintenance in the form of removing large-sized lithic clutter (although the floors could be the result of less fastidious pre-abandonment behavior [Stevenson 1991]). In sum, the quartz flake size-sorting data are ambiguous, but there are indications that some of the variation might be related to spatial positioning of reduction stages.

A final variable that might point to maintenance activity is the distribution of thermally altered (patinated) Ramah chert flakes. These flakes must have been transformed by direct contact with hearth areas, so their occurrence in locations distant from hearths would indicate secondary deposition. Figure 42 indicates that patinated Ramah chert is strongly associated with hearths and that secondary deposits are most-

ly within an arm's length of a hearth. A concentration occurs outside the northern end of the north lobe, but it is possible that this is associated with the activities that produced the fire-cracked rock concentrations at Area 2B. Otherwise, several patinated flakes occur in the exterior area to the east of the south lobe. These might indicate dumping, but a cluster of rocks at the edge of the excavation (Figure 35) could represent a hearth. In sum, the distribution of thermally altered Ramah chert does not provide much evidence for maintenance activity at Area 2A.

Refitting

Up to this point, micro-scale analysis has been used to establish the presence of two behavioral modules. It is now time to consider the meso-scale question of their relationship to each other and to other parts of Area 2A by looking at lithic refitting patterns. If we consider broken tools, virtually all conjoining tool fragments are found nearby each other within the same quadrat. The only cross-quadrat refits are two fragments of a leaf-shaped (bipointed) biface that reconnect between the southwestern portion of the north lobe and the edge of the south lobe and the middle subarea (Figure 50), a quartz block core with one piece in the inner portion of the north lobe and its conjoining piece at the northern end of the lobe (Figure 47), and two ground slate flakes joining between the inside of the south lobe and the area to the east of that lobe (Figure 57). The latter connection between the south lobe and eastern exterior area parallels previous observations of similarities between the two areas in slate flake raw materials and quartz/Ramah chert proportions.

To supplement this meager evidence an attempt was made to refit the quartz block cores with some of the larger quartz "chunks" from the debitage. This proved to be futile, perhaps due to insufficient effort, but also because of the tendency for quartz to be found either as minimally modified block cores, bipolar cores, or thoroughly shattered flakes, such that there were few easily refitted intermediate forms. A

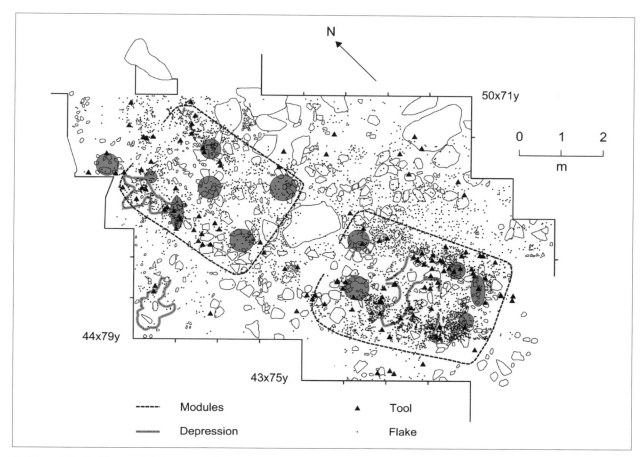

64/ Area 2A: dwelling module interpretation.

Putting the Pieces Together

The multiple lines of evidence presented so far suggest the two lobes are distinct behavioral modules that share similar general activity patterns, but which vary somewhat in tool types and raw material use. Both modules exhibit similar patterns of debitage distribution, each have roughly the same number of hearths and the hearths are positioned similarly at opposite ends of the modules, although the north lobe also has a central hearth. Defined in relation to the debitage distributions the modules are of very similar size: ca. 4 by 3 m. The sharply bounded debitage distributions and the lack of the concentric drop/toss-zone pattern

more systematic refitting study of the Area 2A material might help clarify the spatial organization of the site, but the bulk of the evidence at hand suggests the two lobes were behaviorally independent units.

hypothesized to characterize external hearths could suggest the modules were associated with tent dwellings. The lack of refits between the modules indicates a degree of behavioral independence. Two alternative dwelling configurations can be considered.

The first alternative (Figure 64) considers the sharp external bounding of the debitage lobes to be the consequence of a tent wall edge-effect and postulates two separate dwelling modules on the north and south sides of the large central rock. In this scenario debitage deposition is concentrated along the tent walls, extending 1.0-1.2 m from the walls towards the middle of the dwelling. Most of the hearths are located rather close to the postulated dwelling walls (ca. 0.5 m), with the exception of hearth 2 (centrally located) and hearths 4 and 16 (ca. 1 m from the wall). In the middle is a low flake/tool density area, which in the north lobe is 0.5-1.0 by 3.0 m in size (although it is

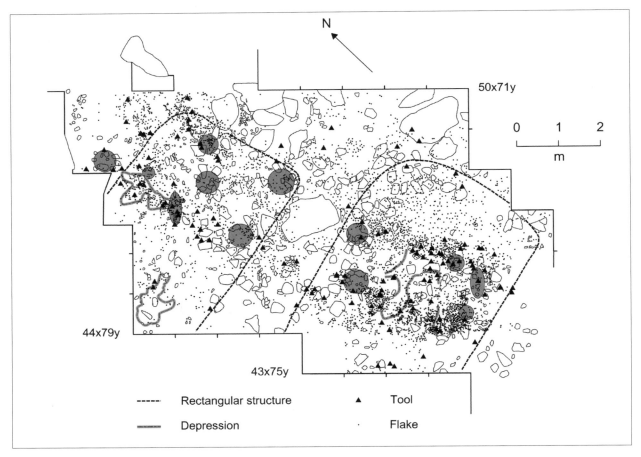

65/ Area 2A: rectangular structure interpretation.

punctuated by hearth 2) and in the south lobe 0.7-1.0 by 2.5 m. These central spaces were either used for activities that did not accumulate lithic refuse (e.g., sleeping) or were kept clean by maintenance procedures (which did not result in lithic size-sorting). Openings at the northern ends of each lobe might indicate entrances. The hearth locations might suggest that certain practices were focused on the inner and outer portions of the dwellings.

Although the modules seem to be independent behavioral units, the overall similarities and symmetries in spatial patterning are striking. At the macro-scale level, the modules might represent independent structures deliberately aligned in tandem with the large flat central rock as a spatial fulcrum point. The clustering of rocks in the middle subarea on both the eastern and western sides of the large central rock might indicate deliberate placement with reference to

two contemporary structures. This apparent common conceptual plan could imply a cooperative relationship between two households. The dwellings were not physically connected, but the total living space would have measured 10 by 3 m in size and run north-south parallel to the beach front.

There are several objections to this alternative. First, some of the apparent boundaries in the flake distribution patterns might be the result of wind deflation and redeposition processes. The possible superposition noted near the eastern edge of the south lobe might also be attributable to such processes. Additionally, the descriptive overview presented in Chapter 5 noted the presence of several depressions at Area 2A that might indicate deflation; two of these are directly associated with the south lobe (Figure 64). Depression 5 cuts across the middle of the lobe in an east-west direction; its orientation cannot account for the empty "corridor space" in the lobe, although it might have contributed to the accumulation of flakes near hearth 4. Depression 6 lies beside hearth 5; it is filled with flakes and seems to contribute little to accumulation or smearing of the distribution. Although less obvious aeolian formation effects cannot be ruled out, the similar configuration of both lobes suggests there is some integrity to the pattern. On the other hand, neither size-sorting patterns nor the distribution of patinated Ramah chert suggest the operation of maintenance practices that might have been responsible for creating bounded distributions.

Perhaps a more significant objection is the spatial structure. The floor areas are rather small: 12-15 m². That is not unusual for hunter-gatherer tent dwellings, but the small area is punctuated by multiple hearths and the cleared central areas are of extremely limited dimensions (0.5-1.0 by 3.0 m, 0.7-1.0 by 2.5 m) such that very few people could be accommodated. The proximity of several hearths to the hypothesized dwelling walls is problematic given the potential for igniting a tent covering. Additionally, the spatial configuration is different from most of the ethnographic and archaeological examples discussed in Chapter 3, in which hearths and debris accumulations are situated towards the center of the dwellings and the cleared living space is positioned at the sides or the back.

In sum, the multiple hearths raise the problem of feature contemporaneity, thus challenging the behavioral unity of the modules.

The second alternative also sees the two modules as components of separate dwellings, but it requires a gestalt switch to see them as parts of larger rectangular structures extending east-west, parallel to each other and perpendicular to the beach front (Figure 65). In this scenario the linear arms of the lobes are activity concentrations that divide the rectangular structures into segments in a manner consistent with the long-

house model. The south lobe provides the best illustration of this interpretation, although it implies a structure that extends beyond the western boundary of the excavation. The north-south ends of the south lobe define the width of the structure (3.7-4.0 m). The northern end of the structure is indicated by the drop-off in flake density between 47-48x, which occurs short of the large boulders in 48-49x71y that constitute a natural limit for a dwelling, and by a set of smaller rocks in 47x71-72y that arc along the edge of the flake density shift and which might be tent anchor rocks. Some of the rocks in the "middle" subarea might relate to the northern wall of the dwelling, while the south side lacks indications of wall rocks. The overall length of the structure is at least 6 meters and it contains at least three segments separated by the two linear lithic concentrations associated with hearths. Two hearths lie within 50 cm of the north wall and two are a similar distance from the south wall; the fifth lies 1.2 m in from the south wall. Lithic reduction activities and tool deposition are concentrated in the area within and between the lobe arms; the eastern and western flanks or segments have markedly fewer flakes and tools and could therefore be sleeping areas. Refits of two sets of ground slate flakes between the center of the lobe and the eastern flank or segment provide a behavioral linkage consistent with this interpretation.

The north lobe provides a weaker exemplification of the interpretation. Its eastern boundary abuts directly on several large boulders that are natural dwelling limits. The sparse flake distribution towards the west is not inconsistent with the interpretation, but it is too meager to be strongly convincing. A dwelling of 3.7-4.0 m in width and at least 5 m in length is implied. Two hearths are located within 50 cm of the south wall while two are positioned 1.2-1.5 m in from the north wall. A fifth hearth is centrally located between the lobe arms. A possible sixth

---

[4]The wall-centered deposition would be most like the pattern noted at one of the Ungava Bay Late Dorset longhouses (Figure 13b; Plumet 1985).

hearth lies 50 cm from the north wall. This configuration implies that the eastern end of the dwelling was the focus of lithic reduction and tool deposition around the hearths while the western portion was an open area with little depositional activity. Consequently, in contrast to the hypothesized southern dwelling, the northern structure was divided into two clearly contrasting sides: an eastern portion with hearth activity and lithic reduction and a western portion with minimal deposition, perhaps a sleeping area. Along the south wall a tongue of flakes protrudes slightly into the middle subarea just west of the large central rock, suggesting an extension of deposition outside the dwelling (perhaps a doorway?).

The segmented structure alternative requires a slight reorganization of the previously presented data. Table 12 outlines the distribution of tool classes with the excavation units grouped as closely as possible to the hypothesized rectangular structures. A chi-square test indicates no significant differences in tool class representation between the two structures at the .05 level (χ^2 = 21.53); but note the many low cell values). Looking at the expected frequencies, flake points and block cores are over-represented at the northern structure while ground slate flakes and tool fragments are over-represented at the southern structure. Tool raw material frequencies and weights (Table 13) exhibit broadly similar proportions at the two structures; as far as frequencies are concerned, there is no statistically significant difference between the structures (χ^2 = 7.48). Slate is proportionally greater by frequency at the southern structure, but slightly greater by weight at the northern structure. Table 14 compares the flake raw materials. In relation to expected frequencies, quartz is over-represented at the northern structure and Ramah chert is over-represented at the southern structure. Among the slates, gray slate dominates by frequency at the northern structure while both gray and green slates are well represented at the southern structure. By weight, quartz dominates at both structures, although there is a substantial weight percent of Ramah chert (28%) at the southern structure. The frequency dominance of gray slate at the northern structure is offset by relatively even proportions of gray and green slate by weight. Consequently, although there is variation between the hypothesized segmented dwellings, there are no grounds to posit distinct contrasts in social practices.

This second interpretation of the modules is subject to the same objections as the first. Changing the

Table 12: Area 2A Tool Classes by Hypothesized Rectangular Structure

	PT	BI	PR	FP	SC	UF	SP	CA	SB	ST	BC	CO	TM	OTH	TOTAL
North	2.5	6	3	7	7	28	2	2	2	9	14	14	1	1	98.5
South	8	8	2	3	11	51	2	1	7	39.5	35	12.5	2	3	185
TOTAL	10.5	14	5	10	18	79	4	3	9	48.5	49	26.5	3	4	283.5

.5 denotes a conjoining fragment

PT: points (bifacial), **BI**: bifaces, **PR**: preforms (biface), **FP**: flake points, **SC**: scrapers (endscrapers and flake knives), **UF**: utilized flakes, **SP**: slate points, **CA**: celt/adze, **SB**: slate blanks (unmodified plates and blanks), **ST**: slate tool fragments (ground slate flakes and unidentified tool fragments), **BC**: bipolar cores, **CO**: block cores (quartz), **TM**: tool manufacturing (hammerstones, schist tablets, whetstones), and **OTH**: other (stemmed flakes, linear flakes, graver).

Table 13: Area 2A Tool Raw Material Frequencies and Weights (in grams) by Hypothesized Rectangular Structure

	North N	North (%)	North Wt (g)	North (%)	South N	South (%)	South Wt (g)	South (%)
Quartz	24	(24.4)	1869.0	(69.8)	39.5	(21.4)	1923.5	(72.3)
Ramah chert	51.5*	(52.3)	292.2	(10.9)	78	(42.2)	341.3	(12.8)
Gray Mugford chert	4	(4.1)	28.3	(1.1)	4	(2.2)	16.0	(0.6)
Black chert	3	(3.0)	15.0	(0.6)	12	(6.5)	33.0	(1.2)
Slate—total	15	(15.2)	294.8	(11.0)	49.5	(26.8)	178.6	(6.7)
Green	9		111.6		17		107.7	
Gray	1		16.0		26.5		61.3	
Red-brown	3		167.0		2		3.5	
Gray-banded	1		0.2		3		6.1	
Indet.	1		n.a.		1		n.a.	
Schist	1	(1.0)	177.0	(6.6)				
Other					2	(1.1)	167.3	(6.3)
TOTAL	98.5				185			

.5 denotes a conjoining fragment

gestalt does not resolve the problem of multiple hearths within a small area, with their potential implication of re-occupation. The modules present interesting patterns, but their interpretation is problematic.

Consumption of Lithic Raw Materials and Technological Organization.

Given the presence of two behavioral modules and possible rectangular structures we can consider what might be inferred about variations in raw material consumption and the spatial dimension of technological organization. The undifferentiated "other" subarea used in the previous analyses is now subdivided so as to accommodate the rectangular dwelling interpretation: quadrats associated with the hypothesized rectangular dwellings are categorized as "north-other" or "south-other" while the remaining units are classed as "other." Thus, the north lobe and north-other taken together constitute the northern rectangular structure and the south lobe and south-

other constitute the southern rectangular structure. Table 15 provides a breakdown of total raw material weights (tools and flakes) by spatial position at Area 2A. Quartz is used prodigiously: 6 kg at the north lobe (6.4 kg for the northern rectangular structure) and ca. 4.5 kg at the south lobe (4.8 kg for the southern rectangular structure). In contrast, the total quantity of Ramah chert consumed (or discarded) at each lobe/structure is quite modest, although the figure for the south lobe (1.6 kg) is over double that of the north lobe (0.7 kg), as is the figure for the southern structure (2.3 kg) versus the northern structure (0.8 kg). Fine-grained cherts are rare and/or highly conserved, with a total of only 49 g discarded at the north lobe/structure and 76 g at the south lobe/structure. Slate is also used quite modestly, with ca. 0.4 kg used at the north lobe/structure and 0.5 kg at the south lobe/structure. Slate type weights vary spatially, however; while both lobes use roughly similar amounts of green slate, the

Table 14: Area 2A Flake Raw Material Frequencies and Weights (in grams) by Hypothesized Rectangular Structure

	North N	North (%)	North Wt (g)	North (%)	South N	South (%)	South Wt (g)	South (%)
Quartz	1273	(46.8)	4678.0	(87.2)	1214	(24.3)	4035.2	(65.3)
Ramah chert	1228	(45.2)	558.2	(10.4)	3322	(66.6)	1732.0	(28.0)
Patinated Ramah	44	(1.6)	19.9	(0.4)	84	(1.7)	49.2	(0.8)
Gray Mugford chert	20	(0.7)	4.0	(0.1)	38	(0.8)	9.6	(0.2)
Black chert	21	(0.8)	3.9	(0.1)	38	(0.8)	19.7	(0.3)
Green Mugford	·				2	(0.0)	0.2	(0.0)
Slate—total	133	(4.9)	99.5	(1.9)	291	(5.8)	330.7	(5.4)
Beige	7		1.3		21		6.1	
Green	11		39.3		110		173.1	
Gray	103		36.0		152		146.9	
Gray-banded	8		3.0				0.1	
Red-brown	3		0.9		3		2.5	
Indet.	1		19.0		5		2.0	
TOTAL	2719				4989			

* .5 denotes a conjoining fragment

south lobe uses much more gray slate and the north lobe more red-brown slate.

The variations in the quantity of quartz and Ramah chert outlined in Table 12 point to slight differences in raw material management and discard practices at the two modules. Practices related to one of the materials, however, cannot be directly compared with those related to the other since they constitute different kinds of reduction systems. Quartz was reduced both by free-hand percussion on raw blocks and bipolar percussion, while Ramah chert was organized in a bifacial reduction system based on large preforms. A summary of the products of each reduction system is presented in Table 16.

As far as quartz is concerned, the total weight of the material is greater in the north lobe. Both lobes have about the same amount of flakes and block cores. The south lobe has somewhat more tools, but this is largely a consequence of the frequency of bipolar cores, of which there are twice as many at the south

lobe as at the north. This might suggest less intensive reduction at the north lobe without the discard of intermediate stage bipolar cores, or simply greater reliance on direct percussion rather than the bipolar technique. As noted earlier, the spatial distribution of cores is sometimes independent of the debitage. Several block cores occur in the debitage-poor middle subarea, seemingly cached or dumped there unrelated to in situ reduction. Just east of the middle area there are several bipolar cores that are independent of both block cores and quartz debitage, which suggests they are secondary refuse. Otherwise, the core/debitage associations are suggestive of primary refuse from in situ reduction.

For Ramah chert, the inhabitants of the south lobe consumed over twice as much material by weight as those of the north lobe, with a corresponding difference in flake production. The quantities of biface fragments and preforms are similar, while the south lobe has three times the quantity of bifacial points,

Table 15: Area 2A Total Lithic Raw Material Weights (Tools and Flakes) by Model Units. Rounded to the Nearest Gram.

	North Lobe		North-Oth		Middle		South Lobe		South-Oth		Other	
	g	(%)	g	(%)	g	(%)	g	(%)	g	(%)	g	(%)
Quartz	6072	(83.3)	369	(78.5)	1244	(94.5)	4483	(67.5)	337	(28.2)	2438	(83.6)
Ramah chert	757	(10.4)	91	(19.4)	72	(5.5)	1608	(24.2)	723	(60.5)	339	(11.6)
Patinated Ramah	20	(0.3)	1	(0.2)			45	(0.7)	5	(0.4)	5	(0.2)
Black chert	15	(0.2)	3	(0.6)			47	(0.7)	3	(0.3)	11	(0.4)
Gray Mugford	28	(0.4)	3	(0.6)			22	(0.3)	2	(0.2)	0.1	(0.0)
Green Mugford									2	(0.2)		
Slate—total	394	(5.4)	3	(0.6)	0.2	(0.0)	435	(6.6)	123	(10.3)	122	(4.2)
green	157		0.1		2		233		55		115	
gray	49		3		186		51		5			
beige	1		5		14	1						
red-brown	167		4		3	1						
gray-banded	1		5			0.1						
indet.	19		2									
Schist	744		555		179							
Other			167	167								

consistent with the differences in overall raw material and flake quantities. On the other hand, despite having twice the amount of raw material, the south lobe has only ca. 30% more tools than the north lobe; this disparity suggests that some tools or preforms were produced for curation to other localities. At both lobes 70-75% of the discarded Ramah chert tools could be considered expedient (i.e., utilized flakes, flake knives, flake points), while 24-25% are curatable bifaces. Unlike quartz, bipolar cores of Ramah chert do not represent a fundamental part of the reduction system. Instead, they are most likely the product of recycling tool fragments. A chi-square test indicates there is no significant difference in the frequencies of quartz and Ramah chert bipolar cores between the subareas ($\chi^2 = 0.46$).

The distribution of Ramah chert bifaces and preforms may be more a consequence of discard behaviour than an indication of activity areas or spatial staging in tool production. A variable that may be more sensitive to tracking the spatial positioning of biface reduction is the distribution of biface-thinning flakes (BTFs). Archaeological data from quarry and site contexts (Gramly 1978; Lazenby 1980, 1984) indicate that Ramah chert was often transported in the form of large bifaces and preforms. Reduction of these implements produces large quantities of BTFs and variation in the size of these flakes is partly related to reduction stage. The spatial concentration of BTFs of different sizes may therefore indicate spatial staging in biface reduction. The approach is not without its methodological problems (Andrefsky 1998:118), however, and the effects of maintenance activity on size-sorting must be considered.

All excavation units with significant quantities of Ramah chert produced considerable numbers of BTFs (defined following House and Ballenger 1976; Raab et al. 1979). In order to set a size threshold for identifying the products of initial stage biface reduction, a "large" thinning flake category was defined as flakes

Table 16: Summary of the Quartz and Ramah Chert Reduction Systems at Area 2A

QUARTZ

	Tools	Block Cores	Bipolar	Flakes	Total Weight (g)
North lobe	23	12	9	1159	6072
North-other	1		1	114	369
Middle	5.5*	4.5		63	1244
South lobe	35.5	14.5	21	1065	4483
South-other	4	1	1	154	555
Other	12	6	3	165	2438

RAMAH CHERT

	Tools	Points	Biface. Frags.	Preforms	Bipolar Cores	Biface- Thinning	Flakes	Total Weight (g)
North Lobe	48.5*	2.5	6	3	4	111	1139	757
North-other	3					13	131	91
Middle	7.5	0.5	2			9	44	64
South Lobe	66	8	6	2	8	341	2705	1608
South-other	14	1	1		2	104	688	505
Other	18	1		1	5	59	369	339

.5 denotes a conjoining fragment

with one dimension in excess of 30 mm. This limit was not entirely arbitrary in that: a) the overall Ramah chert flake size distribution falls mostly less than 25 mm, and b) observations from prehistoric workshops and experimental reduction of Ramah chert bifaces suggests that the reduction of large transportable quarry blanks and biface preforms will probably produce considerable debitage in the over 30 mm size range.

Figure 63 indicates that the distribution of large and small BTFs is fairly consistent with the overall distribution of Ramah chert flakes, since units with several BTFs tend to be units with relatively many Ramah chert flakes, although this is not always the case. By frequency, most of the BTFs are found in the south lobe, which also has the most Ramah chert debitage. The overall distributions of small and large BTFs are similar and most of the major concentrations of each size class

occur adjacent to hearths. An exception to the latter is the cluster of BTFs in 46x74y near the northeast corner of the south lobe; this was also a locus of quartz reduction. There is also a slight concentration of BTFs in the area east of the lobes, particularly at the eastern end of the hypothesized southern structure. By and large, the distribution of BTFs is consistent with the distributions of bifacial points and preforms, except in the area east of the lobes where there are relatively few implements in relation to the number of BTFs. In sum, there is not much evidence for spatial variations in the staging of Ramah chert reduction. Tool production and discard generally are spatially associated, except in the area east of the lobes where production activity is associated with minimal tool discard.

Fine-grained cherts (mostly gray Mugford and black chert) occur in minor quantities by frequency and weight and the size of the debitage is uniformly small (see Chapter 9). This does not mean that these materials were insignificant; their near-exclusive use for endscrapers implies a high degree of selectivity. The three bipolar cores of these materials likely represent recycled tool fragments. The spatial distribution of both tools and flakes made from these cherts is strongly, though not exclusively, limited to within the two lobes.

Slates exhibit distribution patterns that are generally similar to the fine-grained cherts, but slate processing and discard is not as spatially restricted. Finished slate tools and fragments thereof are all found within the lobes as are the majority of ground slate flakes, which represent the reworking of finished tools. However, several ground slate flakes and two blanks lie outside the south lobe in what would be the eastern end of the hypothesized southern structure; two of the ground flakes conjoin with pieces within the south lobe. Otherwise, modified plates of slate raw material and tool blanks occur both within and outside the lobes. Slate flakes of all color types occur primarily within the lobes, but small concentrations of green and gray slate flakes are also found in the eastern end of the southern structure.

Area 2A Conclusion

Neither the two module nor the rectangular dwelling interpretation fit precisely with reports from other Early/Middle Labrador Maritime Archaic dwellings, but the segmented structure model comes closest, given the pattern of linear feature-centered distributions running across the width of a rectangular dwelling, flanked by floor-areas with limited deposition. The segmented structure interpretation is also consistent with the ethnoarchaeological and other archaeological examples of interior dwelling space considered in Chapter 3, which generally exhibited centrally located hearth-centered debris distributions flanked by relatively debris-free habitation areas. On the other hand, the orientation of the hypothesized dwellings perpendicular to the beach front departs from most of the documented Maritime Archaic dwellings, which have their long walls oriented parallel to a beach.

The dwelling sizes implied by both interpretations (modules: 4 by 3 m, rectangular: 4 by 6+ m) are broadly consistent with the current picture of Early/Middle Maritime Archaic structures. At Aillik-2 (near Makkovik), several structures were found on shorelines originally estimated to date 6000-5500 B.P.: a one segment structure 3 m in length, a two segment structure 6 m in length and a four segment structure 10 m in length (Fitzhugh 1984:10). More recently, Fitzhugh (2002:7) reports a radiocarbon date of 6870±180 B.P. for the latter 10 m structure and an additional five segment structure 8 m in length from the same beach level is dated 6400±110 B.P.. At Aillik West-1, a three segment structure 9 m in length is radiocarbon dated to 5210±270 B.P. (Fitzhugh 1984:10). At Hamilton Inlet, Sandy Cove Complex sites (ca. 5000 B.P.) apparently contain structures with two or three hearths and lengths of 12-16 m (Fitzhugh 1984:13). More detailed investigations of Early/Middle Maritime Archaic sites will be necessary to clarify the functional and cultural parameters of these different spatial configurations and to assess how the Area 2A features fit into the range of variation.

Area 2B

Area 2B consists of a central pit and hearth complex surrounded by extensive deposits of fire-cracked rock (Figure 33, 66). Radiocarbon dates of 6100-6000 B.P. indicate this subarea is slightly earlier than Area 2A. Defining the southern boundary of Area 2B is somewhat problematic. As discussed previously, some of the quadrats in the 49-50x76-80y area may contain palimpsest deposits resulting from an overlap between the Area 2A and 2B occupations (see Figure 33). In particular, the high frequency of Ramah chert flakes plus the presence of fire-cracked rock and clusters of other small rocks in 49x76-80y strongly suggest this area is part of the Area 2B occupation. Nonetheless, given this overlap problem and the predominant limitation of *k*-means cluster 8 to the area south of the 50x line, the latter is used as a convenient, if imperfect, southern boundary for the Area 2B analysis.

The central pit is a vaguely defined oval basin 1.25 by 0.9 m in size, 5 cm deep, containing charcoal, red ocher and calcined bone fragments. About 60-80 cm to the west is hearth 11, a disturbed feature that may or may not have been contemporary with the pit. These central features are surrounded by an area of 1.2-1.6 m radius that for the most part contains a diffuse scatter of small to medium-sized rocks. This relatively rock-free central area is ringed by fire-cracked rock deposits distributed as thin "carpets," some of which extend beyond the boundaries of the excavation. The smaller concentrations of the rock debris probably represent discrete depositional events while the larger concentrations may be accretions of several depositional episodes. A small rock deposit overlaps the eastern edge of the central pit feature such that this deposit must partially post-date the feature. Another lesser concentration lies immediately to the west of the pit, implying a close association. The largest continuous rock concentrations lie 1.6 m to the northwest and 1.2 m to the southeast of the pit. The southeastern concentration has a peculiar distribution around a large boulder; the rock-free area adjacent to the boulder indicates that for some reason the fire-cracked rock was not deposited directly up against the boulder. Lithic debitage is mainly concentrated in the central area that is relatively free of fire-cracked rock. An exception is an almost circular flake concentration in the southern corner of the excavation (50x 76-77y), which is discussed further below.

A preliminary interpretation of this pattern is that the central hearth-pit area was employed in multiple episodes of using rocks for cooking or heating, a process involving the positioning of people in the largely rock-free area surrounding the pit. Some of the small-medium size rocks plotted in this zone may represent unused raw materials for the heating process.

The fragmentary debris produced by the heating process was then collected and discarded a short distance beyond the central features, creating the continuous carpets of fire-cracked rocks east and west of the pit. The smaller concentrations immediately adjacent to the pit may indicate the last cleaning phase prior to the cessation of heating activity. Two alternative models could account for this concentric configuration: 1) Binford's (1983:153, 167-169) "drop/toss-zone" model for patterning associated with external hearths and activity areas, and 2) an external discard model, in which fire-cracked rock produced within a dwelling was discarded in a ring immediately outside the dwelling walls. These two models provide the underlying framework for the analysis.

There is more to Area 2B than a concentric pattern, however; two additional features complicate the analysis. The aforementioned circular concentration of flakes in 50x76-77y is directly associated with a cluster of rocks and adjacent to a tongue of fire-cracked rock that extends out from the main mass, as well as another smaller fire-cracked rock dump. Although no charcoal was recorded in the area of the flake/rock concentration, the pattern of all these elements is very similar to that noted at other hearths. The unusual tongue-like configuration of the adjacent fire-cracked rock deposit could be better explained as a result of dumping from this possible hearth (H-17), rather than from the central hearth-pit complex. Thus there could be two different feature-centered complexes at Area 2B. A second possible anomaly is the concentration of fire-cracked rock on the west side of the boulder in unit 50x79y; the concentration extends tongue-like towards the north lobe at Area 2A. The shape of this deposit and its orientation with respect to the boulder suggests that instead of being thrown north to south from the central portion of Area 2B, it could have accumulated by dumping from a location slightly to the west. Two features 1 m to the west and south are possible source areas: a rock cluster (lacking charcoal) suggestive of a possible hearth (H-18) and a small pit with charcoal and red ocher which might have been a hearth (H-19). The following discussion provides a more detailed analysis of these patterns.

Tool Distribution

Detailed information on the distribution of tool classes can be had in Figures 47 to 58. Beginning with a model-based analysis, the tools are grouped using the following units: central pit, hearth 11, fire-cracked rock zone, possible hearth 17, and units adjacent to hearth 17 (Figure 38). As shown in Table 17, all the formal tools are found either in the central pit/hearth area (points, bifaces, flake knives) or near possible hearth 17 (flake point, endscraper). Despite the large number of fine-grained chert flakes adjacent to hearth 11 and the central pit (see below), no endscrapers— which are made almost exclusively of this material— were found in the central area. Utilized flakes are most frequent in the central pit/hearth area, but they are also found in the fire-cracked rock zone and adjacent to possible hearth 17. Two quartz block cores occur in the central area near the pit. Three bipolar cores are present in the central area and another three are found

in the extreme southeastern corner of Area 2B, an area with very few quartz flakes (Figure 39). Given the association between bipolar cores and quartz reduction at Area 2A, the latter isolated bipolar cores might have been tossed there from locations of quartz reduction in the central area or at possible hearth 17. No finished ground slate tools or slate plates/blanks were found in Area 2B, but there were several ground slate flakes, all but one of which were associated with the pit or hearth 11. Given the presence of a modest number of slate flakes (of four different raw material types) and a possible sandstone grindstone, this could suggest an emphasis on reworking curated tools rather than production activity.

Table 18 outlines the distribution of tool raw material frequencies in relation to the model-based units. No patterning is evident besides the lack of slate tools in the hearth 17 units.

Of the 42 tools from Area 2B, 39 have point provenience. Consequently, although the sample size is small, a *k*-means cluster analysis may be more robust than at Area 2A. The overall 12-cluster *k*-means solution computed for Area 2 as a whole (Figure 37) indicat-

Table 17: Area 2B Tool Classes by Model Units

	Center	H-11	Fire-Cracked	H-17	Adjacent H-17	TOTAL N (%)
Stemmed points		1				1 (2.4)
Bifaces		1				1 (2.4)
Flake points					1	1 (2.4)
Endscrapers				1		1 (2.4)
Flake knives	2					2 (4.8)
Utilized flakes	9	3	5		4	21 (50.0)
Bipolar cores	1	1	1		3	6 (14.3)
Block Cores	2					2 (4.8)
Ground slate flakes	3	2	1			6 (14.3)
Grindstones (?)	1					1 (2.4)
TOTAL	**18**	**8**	**7**	**1**	**8**	**42**

Table 18: Area 2B Tool Raw Material Frequencies by Model Units

	Center	H-11	Fire-Cracked	H-17	Adjacent H-17	TOTAL N (%)
Quartz	4	2			3	9 (21.4)
Ramah chert	7	2	6		5	20 (47.6)
Black chert	2	2				4 (9.5)
Gray Mugford chert				1		1 (2.4)
Slate—total	4	2	1			7 (16.7)
Green	2	2	1			5
Gray	1					1
Indet.	1					1
Sandstone	1					1 (2.4)
TOTAL	**18**	**8**	**7**	**1**	**8**	**42**

ed two clusters at Area 2B. Cluster 6 lies in the middle of the central pit-hearth complex while cluster 3 is a northeastern outlier to possible hearth 17. Inspection of the tool distribution constituting cluster 6, however, suggested this cluster lumps together several possibly independent tool groupings. Consequently, a separate k-means analysis was conducted on the Area 2B materials. Three and 5-cluster solutions seemed best, but the 5-cluster solution was preferred because it provided a good separation of what seemed like intuitively reasonable groups (Figure 67). Clusters 1 and 4 are associated with the pit, suggesting two depositional positions on opposite sides of the feature, while cluster 5 is associated with Hearth 11. Cluster 3 includes items lying within or near the fire-cracked rock ring southwest of the pit. Cluster 2 consists of implements lying east of possible hearth 17.

Table 19 shows the tool classes associated with each of these five clusters. The number of tools in each cluster is similar. Although there are differences in the

Table 19: Area 2B Tool Classes by K-Means Cluster

	C-1	C-2	C-3	C-4	C-5	TOTAL
Stemmed point					1	1
Biface					1	1
Endscraper		1				1
Flake knife	2					2
Utilized flake	3	4	4	5	3	19
Bipolar core		3		1	2	6
Block core	1			1		2
Ground slate flake	1		1	2	2	6
Grindstone (?)			1			1
TOTAL	**7**	**8**	**6**	**9**	**9**	**39**

Three items without point provenience: a utilized flake near Cluster 1, a utilized flake near Cluster 4 and a flake point equidistant west of Clusters 2 and 3.

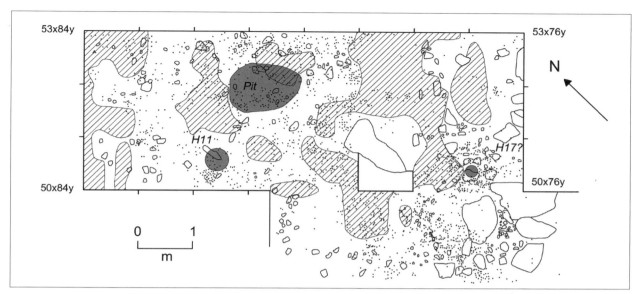

66/ Area 2B: features and total flake distribution.

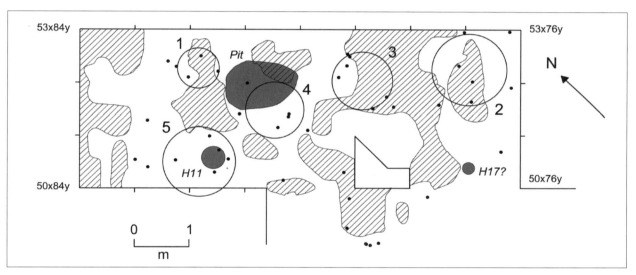

67/ Area 2B: five-cluster k-means solution.

types represented in each cluster, the low frequencies make it difficult to assess the meaning of the variations. The best that can be said is that utilized flakes are evenly distributed across the clusters while formal tools have more restricted distributions. Five of the six bipolar cores are associated with hearths (either hearth 11 or adjacent to possible hearth 17). These cluster results may provide a more nuanced view of spatial distributions within the model-based units, but they reveal little about the nature of these patterns. The same might be said of the distribution of tool raw materials by cluster (Table 20). Tools of Ramah chert (mostly utilized flakes) are fairly evenly distributed across the clusters, while black chert tools (all utilized flakes) and green ground slate flakes are mostly limited to clusters 4 and 5 (the central subarea).

Table 20: Area 2B Tool Raw Material Frequencies by *K*-Means Cluster.

	C-1	C-2	C-3	C-4	C-5	TOTAL N (%)	Weight (g)
Quartz	2	3		1	3	9 (23.1)	973
Ramah chert	3	4	4	4	2	17 (43.6)	104
Black chert				2	2	4 (10.3)	18
Gray Mugford chert		1				1 (2.6)	2
Slate—total	2		1	2	2	7 (17.9)	
Green			1	2	2	5	9
Gray	1					1	1
Indet.	1					1	1
Sandstone			1			1	n.a.
TOTAL	7	8	6	9	9	39	

Three items without point provenience, all of Ramah chert: one near Cluster 1, one near Cluster 4, the other equidistant west of Clusters 2 and 3.

Flake Distribution

As noted above, the majority of the flakes at Area 2B are concentrated in the central fire-cracked rock-free area (Figure 66). Ramah chert is the most abundant flake material. A significant quantity of these flakes is found within the central pit and the vast majority lie within a 1.8 m radius of the pit edge, with the highest density on the eastern and southern sides of the feature (Figure 40). The coterminous boundary between the flakes and fire-cracked rocks is most clear along the 79y line south and east of the pit. In some areas, however, the distributions overlap: the extreme northwest corner of Area 2B, west and north of the pit, west of the large boulder and in unit 49x78y. Nonetheless, given the overall pattern of marked drop-off in flake frequency beyond 1.8 m from the pit, the clustering of many Ramah chert flakes associated with fire-cracked rock in 49-50x78-79y (west of the boulder) may be the result of overlapping deposition with Area 2A.

The circular concentration of Ramah chert flakes in 50x76-77y at the southern corner of Area 2B appears to be a depositional unit quite separate from the debitage associated with the central pit-hearth complex. The concentration is 90 cm in diameter, with a hollow center 30-40 cm wide. Several rocks occur near the center of the flake distribution as well as on its edges. Although no charcoal was noted here, the configuration of flakes and rocks is strongly suggestive of a hearth (possible hearth 17). The Ramah chert flakes on the northwest side of the concentration are partially overlapped by a fire-cracked rock deposit that seems to extend out from the main mass. This extension may have originated from activities centered on hearth 17 rather than being the result of dumping actions associated with the central features. A similar interpretation could also apply to the discrete fire-cracked rock cluster to the northeast of hearth 17 (51x76-77y).

Patinated Ramah chert (Figure 42) is mostly concentrated in a 1 m wide arc to the north, to the east and south of the central pit. It is also associated with the carpet of fire-cracked rocks south of the pit (51-53x77-78.5y), which contains little unpatinated Ramah chert. Since patination is the result of thermal alteration the presence of patinated flake concentrations in units entirely outside the pit and hearth features implies they are secondary refuse dumped there after removal from the combustion features. This contrasting distribution of unpatinated and patinated Ramah chert is consistent with the argument of a central drop-zone (mostly unpatinated chert from tool retouch) and an encircling toss zone (fire-cracked rock and patinated chert removed from the central hearth). The other major concentration of patinated Ramah chert is directly associated with possible hearth 17.

The distribution of large Ramah chert biface-thinning flakes (BTFs; Figure 63) is limited to the quadrats north and west of the central pit and hearth features, with the exception of one flake east of the pit and a single flake associated with possible hearth 17. Most of the small BTFs are located on the opposite (south) side of the pit. This contrast hints at differences in the spatial positioning of biface reduction stages. Overall, the proportion of BTFs is greatest in the central pit-hearth area (42.9%) and in association with possible hearth 17 (27.2%; Table 20, below). Notably, however, no Ramah chert points or preforms and only a single biface were found at Area 2B (Table 20, Figures 50 to 52). Keeping in mind the limited excavation area, this might suggest preparation of bifaces curated for use elsewhere.

The distribution of quartz flakes (Figure 39) is generally consistent with that of Ramah chert, although much less dense. With the exception of units 50x76-77y (associated with possible hearth 17), most of the quartz flakes are located in the central area within 1.8-2.0 m of the pit. In contrast to Ramah chert, quartz flakes are rare within the pit itself.

The distributions of slate (Figure 44) and fine-grained cherts (Figure 43) are similar; both occur mostly in the central area, especially south and west of the pit. This is opposite the trend for Ramah chert, suggesting the materials were reduced at different locations. Slate occurs mostly within the pit itself and within a 1.2 m radius of the pit edge, with the faint suggestion of two scatters, one south and one west of the pit. A few flakes are also associated with possible hearth 17. Beige slate is clustered near hearth 11, while the other types are mostly associated with the pit. Black chert was mostly located outside the pit and within a 1.6 m radius of its edge and, like slate, is clus-

tered in two scatters, one west and one southwest of the pit. The latter cluster lies beside hearth11, indicating an activity locus unassociated with the pit. There are few gray Mugford chert flakes, but their distribution is more balanced between the eastern and western sides of the pit. A very few black chert and gray Mugford chert flakes are associated with possible hearth 17.

Given the preceding considerations, the flake distributions at Area 2B can be analysed by grouping the 50 cm^2 quadrats into analytical units based on the feature-centered model (Figure 38, Table 21). A general category of "central" units could be defined from quadrats associated with the pit and hearth 11, an area mostly free from fire-cracked rock except for the clusters immediately adjacent to the features. But in order to identify possible spatial variations the central area was subdivided by treating quadrats associated with hearth 11 as a separate analytical unit. The "peripheral" area consists of the surrounding quadrats containing deposits of fire-cracked rock. Hearth 17 includes those units closely associated with that feature, while "adjacent" refers to those units northeast of hearth 17 that could represent a depositional zone related to the feature. Ramah chert is the most dominant material by frequency (64-79%) in all the subareas except for at hearth 11, where black chert and Ramah chert constitute 40% and 45%, respectively. Otherwise, green slate is fairly restricted to the central area, a pattern similar to the distribution of green slate tools. When expected frequencies are calculated there is a clear over-representation of black chert at hearth 11 and of patinated Ramah chert in the periphery subarea. The latter supports the toss-zone dumping interpretation. When the five spatial categories are collapsed into three broader units (central/hearth 11, periphery, hearth17/adjacent), black chert remains over-represented in the central subarea and patinated Ramah chert is still over-represented in the periphery, but there is also a slight over-representation of unpatinated Ramah chert in the hearth 17/adjacent subarea.

Table 21: Area 2B Flake Raw Material Frequencies by Model Units

	Central	H-11	Periphery	H-17	Adjacent	TOTAL	Weight (g) (%)
Quartz	131 (16.6)	32 (9.1)	60 (12.6)	88 (14.5)	21 (19.8)	332	1006 (56.7)
Ramah chert	505 (63.9)	159 (45.2)	365 (76.5)	476 (78.7)	72 (67.9)	1577	608 (34.3)
Patinated Ramah	36 (4.6)	2 (0.6)	32 (6.7)	16 (2.6)	6 (5.7)	92	30.4 (1.7)
Black chert	57 (7.2)	142 (40.3)	4 (0.8)	2 (0.3)		205	47.5 (2.7)
Gray Mugford chert	11 (1.4)	6 (1.7)	4 (0.8)	3 (0.5)	1 (0.9)	25	4.8 (0.3)
Green Mugford chert	1 (0.1)		1 (0.2)			2	0.2 (0.0)
White/patinated Mug.	2 (0.3)	2 (0.6)	1 (0.2)			5	0.4 (0.0)
Slate—total	47 (5.9)	9 (2.6)	10 (2.1)	20 (3.3)	6 (5.7)	92	76.4 (4.3)
Beige	1	4				5	5
Green	15	3		1	1	20	31.1
Gray	6			3	1	10	3.9
Gray-banded	22	2	10	13	4	51	29.9
Red-brown	3			2		5	6.5
TOTAL	790	352	477	605	106	2330	

Distribution of Red Ocher and Bone

Figure 61 illustrates the distribution of red ocher and bone fragments. Virtually all the red ocher stains occur within the central rock-free area. Besides the distinct stains within the pit there are two other major clusters of stains, one 1.0-1.5 m northwest of the pit, the other 0.5-1.2 m northwest of hearth 11. Smaller patches occur east of hearth 11, near the southeastern extremity of Area 2B (76y line) and close to the overlap zone with Area 2A. A total of 46 tiny calcined bone fragments were found within the pit, primarily on its western and northern sides near the red ocher patches. Among these was a tiny piece of worked bone that appears to be a pendant fragment with remnants of a gouged hole and striations on each face (see Chapter 8). None of the bone fragments were identifiable to taxon.

Refitting

The only refit accomplished at Area 2B involved two fragments of a sandstone plate (possible grindstone) that lay only a few centimeters apart (Figure 58).

Feature-Centered Distributions, Size-Sorting and Cultural Formation Processes

The previous discussion provides a plausible basis for concluding that there are two feature-centered distributions. The first is the pit-hearth complex, which seems to be associated with a central drop-zone and peripheral toss-zone. The second is possible hearth 17, which has a restricted distribution of Ramah chert debitage and adjacent dumping areas for fire-cracked rock, but lacks further indications of a central drop zone and peripheral toss zone. If these interpretations are reasonable, we might expect to find some evidence for artifact size-sorting associated with the first distribution, but perhaps not with the second.

Tool size-sorting is difficult to quantify at Area 2B because of the low frequencies. If consideration is limited to the relatively large quartz block cores, there are only two items and both are associated with the hypothesized central drop-zone (Figure 47). Quartz flake size distributions are of limited use since quartz occurs in relatively low frequencies (332 flakes) such that size-sorting indices may not be very meaningful.

Additionally, since most quartz flakes were either concentrated in the central area, or were associated with possible hearth 17 in the southern corner of Area 2B, drop/toss-zone comparisons are difficult. In any event, calculation of size-sorting indices for quartz flakes (Figure 62) results in low values for almost all of the quadrats, in principal indicating little size-sorting. Somewhat higher positive values suggesting a tendency towards smaller flakes are associated with possible hearth 17, but this may only indicate intensive reduction. In sum, there is little evidence for size-sorting related to either maintenance activity or reduction staging.

The best evidence for drop/toss-zone behavior comes from the distributions of fire-cracked rock and patinated Ramah chert. As discussed previously, the association of thermally altered Ramah chert flakes with the fire-cracked rock carpets south of the pit (Figure 42) is a clear indication that material was removed from the central hearth/pit area and redeposited a short distance away.

Consumption of Lithic Materials and Technological Organization

The total weight of tool and flake raw materials from Area 2B is presented in Table 22 as a rough estimate of raw material consumption. The area is subdivided into its two main behavioral units: the central pit-hearth area with its surrounding ring of fire-cracked rock, and possible hearth 17 and its adjacent area. Quartz dominates the central area with ca. 1.7 kg despite a low frequency of both flakes and tools; only 0.4 kg of Ramah chert is present. Quartz and Ramah are more evenly represented at the hearth 17 subarea. The total amounts of black chert and slate at Area 2B are in both cases under 100 g. The other materials are represented by trace quantities.

Table 22. Area 2B Total Lithic Raw Material Weights (Tools and Flakes).

	Central (g) (%)	H-17 (g) (%)
Quartz	1707.0 (73.8)	272.0 (58.5)
Ramah chert	430.0 (18.6)	178.0 (38.3)
Patinated Ramah chert	23.1 (1.0)	7.3 (1.6)
Black chert	65.3 (2.8)	0.2 (0.0)
Gray Mugford chert	6.1 (0.3)	0.7 (0.2)
Green Mugford chert	0.2 (0.0)	
White/patinated Mug.	0.4 (0.0)	
Slate—total	79.8 (3.5)	6.6 (1.4)
Beige	5.0	
Green	28.6	2.5
Gray	2.4	1.5
Gray-banded	27.5	2.4
Red-brown	6.3	0.2

Table 23 provides a breakdown of variables relevant to the technological organization of quartz and Ramah chert at Area 2B. Given the paucity of quartz materials there is little that can be said concerning the relationship between cores and flakes. For Ramah chert the lack of points, bifaces, and preforms, despite considerable numbers of biface-thinning flakes (BTFs), suggests the curation of finished products to other locations or discard elsewhere on the site. As noted previously, while most of the BTFs are located within the central "drop-zone", almost all of the large BTFs lie to the north and west of the pit-hearth complex, implying differences in the spatial positioning of biface reduction stages.

Table 23. Summary of the Quartz and Ramah Chert Reduction Systems at Area 2B.

QUARTZ					
	Tools	Block Cores	Bipolar	Flakes	Total Weight (g)
Central	6	2	2	223	1707
H-17	3		3	109	272

RAMAH CHERT							
	Tools	Points	Biface. Frags.	Preforms	Bipolar Cores	Biface-Thinning	Flakes	Total Weight (g)
Central	15		1		1	96	1099	453
H-17	5					53	570	185

* includes patinated flakes

Area 2B Conclusions

It is unlikely that the extensive deposits of fire-cracked rock at Area 2B accumulated *within* a dwelling structure because such waste probably would be removed by regular maintenance activities. But the concentric distribution pattern could be interpreted in two ways. The first alternative sees the configuration as similar to Binford's (1983:153-159, 165-170) outdoor hearth or extensive activity area model. The space within a 1.8 m radius of the pit was used by individuals engaged in cooking-heating practices involving thermally stressed rocks, as well as lithic tool production and maintenance activities. This central core was a drop-zone for flakes accumulating around knappers seated adjacent to the pit. Shattered rocks resulting from cooking-heating within the pit were removed periodically and dumped behind the individuals working around the hearth, forming a roughly concentric toss-zone. Since the flake distribution southeast of the pit seems coterminous with the edge of the fire-cracked rock, prior placement of the rock determined the limit of the debitage. The spatial distribution of thermally altered Ramah chert— directly associated with the hearths and as probable secondary refuse among the fire-cracked rocks— is consistent with this hearth cleaning and peripheral dumping interpretation. The fire-cracked rock concentrations immediately adjacent to the pit represent the last sequence of pit use, since one of the concentrations is partly superimposed on the pit.

The second alternative interprets the concentric pattern as dwelling-related. The sharply bounded flake distribution associated with the central hearth/pit feature is seen as internal to a dwelling and bounded by a tent wall, similar to the modules at Area 2A. This interpretation implies a 4 m wide dwelling running southwest to northeast. In this case, however, there is a second edge-effect in which the inner boundary of the fire-cracked rock is partly coterminous with the outer boundary of the flakes. This contact zone could imply that the fire-cracked rock was redeposited outside a dwelling, partly along the outer edge of a tent wall.

The overall pattern is complicated by three factors. First, it cannot be established whether or not hearth 11 and the central pit were used contemporaneously and thus whether they constitute a paired activity unit. Second, there may be another hearth (no.17) in the southern corner of Area 2B. This feature appears to

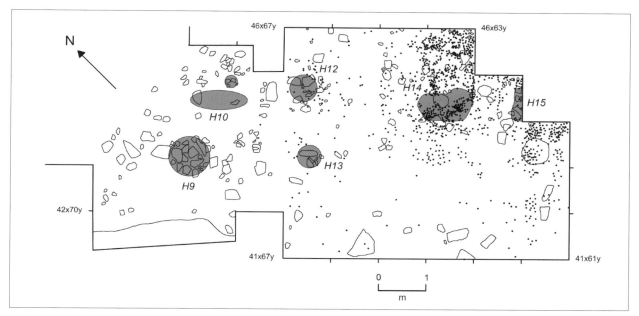

68/ Area 2C: features and total flake distribution.

involve spatially restricted behavior with adjacent rock dumping activity, but without the development of clearly marked drop-toss zones. Further excavation to the southeast would be required to clarify this. Third, the nature of the distributions in the area of overlap with Area 2A are unclear. Some of the fire-cracked rocks in the overlap area might have originated at possible hearth 18 just north of the north lobe, but the contribution of activities related to the lobe itself cannot be ruled out. Given the possibility of overlapping deposits, as well as the limited excavation area, it is difficult to regard one or the other of these alternative interpretations as more robust.

Area 2C

The boundary between Areas 2C and 2A (Figure 38) was partly defined by behavioral discontinuity. The entire northwestern end of Area 2C exhibits a very low density of flakes and tools compared with the south lobe at Area 2A. Indeed, there is a 6-7 m distance between the terminal edge of the south lobe and the next major flake concentration at the southeastern end of Area 2C (Figure 33). The other discontinuity is chronological; the pit associated with hearth 10 (2 m

south of the south lobe) produced a radiocarbon date of 6100±80 B.P.. At the extreme eastern end of Area 2C hearth 14 produced an unacceptable date of 1600±80 B.P.. Although the lack of an acceptable date from the southeastern end of Area 2C means that contemporaneity with Area 2A cannot be ruled out, the behavioral discontinuity and the date from hearth 10 suggest that Area 2C can be treated independently of Area 2A.

Hearths 9, 10, 12 and 13 at the western end of the subarea are all associated with an extremely low lithic density (Figure 68). Furthermore, their orientation and spacing seems rather regular, arranged in a rough rectangle 2 m by 2 m in size. Interestingly, this layout is comparable in size and configuration with the "lobes" at Area 2A, such that the hearth grouping might be interpreted as part of a dwelling module. Unfortunately, the sparse flake and tool distributions provide little additional information. The hearths exhibit different forms, presumably indicative of different functions or practices, an attribute that was also noted at Area 2A. Hearths 12 and 13 are simple clusters of cobbles. Hearth 10 seems to be a composite feature consisting of a small circular pit flanked by an

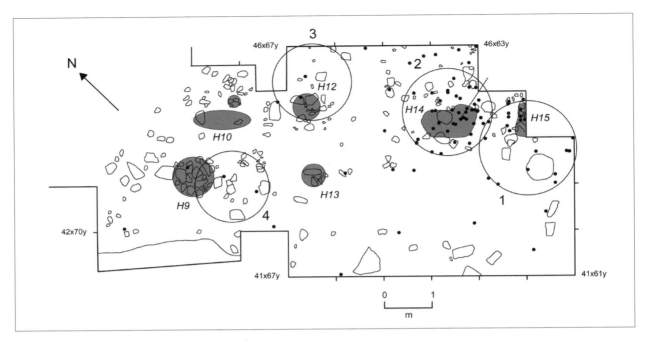

69/ Area 2C: modified four-cluster k-*means solution.*

elongated pit. Hearth 9 was a large stone-floored feature surrounded on three sides by inclined slabs, giving the impression of a box-hearth used for controlling the dispersal of debris or for heat reflection.

Hearths 14 and 15 at the eastern end of Area 2C may be another hearth pairing, since they are spaced 2 m apart, similar to the Area 2A module pattern. Hearth 14 consists of a large (1.2 m diameter) and diffuse scatter of charcoal associated with a pair of large rounded rocks.

Hearth 15, only partially excavated, appears to be an elongated pit containing rocks and red ocher. Towards the southern boundary of the excavation (41x62-63y), three large rocks associated with charcoal and a flake concentration may be evidence for another hearth, although the configuration is unclear.

The flakes at hearth 14 exhibit abrupt density changes on either side of the feature, creating a 1.2 m wide band very similar to the widths of the linear flake distributions at the Area 2A lobes. The flakes associated with hearth 15 suggest a similar pattern, but further excavation is needed to evaluate this. It should also be noted that Area 2C is adjacent to a blow-out containing rock clusters that probably represent hearths

(Figure 71). Thus, the eastern portion of Area 2C and the adjacent deflated area could constitute connected activity areas.

The overall Area 2 *k*-means cluster analysis (Figure 37) identified two tool clusters in Area 2C, one related to hearths 9, 10, 12 and 13 (cluster 5), the other associated with hearths 14 and 15 (cluster 1). It seems reasonable to divide Area 2C into two broad analytical subunits based on the spacing of the hearth features, the marked differences in flake densities and the two *k*-means clusters (Figure 38). Area 2C1 will refer to the northwestern portion of the area (units between 69-71Y and 65Y) and Area 2C2 to the southeastern portion (units between 61-65Y). The analysis could be more nuanced, however, with additional feature-related subdivisions.

Tool Distribution

Figures 47 to 58 depict the tool class distributions. Little can be said about the 2C1 distribution, except that there is an unusually high proportion of schist tablets and fragments. One bar-shaped chlorite schist object and one flat plate of phylite schist lay adjacent to hearth 9, the box-like feature. These implements

Table 24: Area 2C Tool Classes by *K*-Means Cluster and Subarea.

	C-1	C-2	C-3	C-4	Outliers	2C1	2C2	TOTAL N (%)
Stemmed points				1		1		1 (1.0)
Bifaces	1	3			1	1	4	5 (5.2)
Biface preforms	1	1					2	2 (2.1)
Endscrapers	1				1	1	1	2 (2.1)
Stemmed flakes						1		1 (1.0)
Utilized flakes	6	17	3	1	1	7	24	31 (32.0)
Celts/adzes	2	1					3	3 (3.1)
Slate blanks		1					1	1 (1.0)
Ground slate flakes	3	17	1		1	2	20	22 (22.7)
Bipolar cores		1			1	1	1	2 (2.1)
Block cores	6	9			2	1	18	19 (19.6)
Disc cores	1						1	1 (1.0)
Hammerstones		1					1	1 (1.0)
Schist tablets/frags		2		3		4	2	6 (6.2)
TOTAL	21	53	4	5	5	19	79	97

might have been used in the polishing of ground slate tools, although there is a paucity of ground slate tools, slate blanks, as well as ground and unground slate flakes in the subarea. At 2C2 the distributions of almost all the tool types are closely associated with hearths 14 and 15. The exception is endscrapers (Figure 54), one of which is associated with hearth 13, the other which lies 1 m distant from hearth 15. Ground slate flakes (Figure 57) also cluster around Hearths 14 and 15.

Of the 98 tools from Area 2C, 91 have point provenience. A *k*-means analysis was run for Area 2C alone, producing slightly better cluster resolution than in the overall Area 2 analysis. The 5-cluster solution seemed best, isolating small clusters associated with hearths 9 and 12 (four items in each) and separate clusters associated with hearths 14 and 15, but it also created a fifth cluster west of hearth 14 that was diffuse and probably not behaviorally relevant. Consequently, a modified version of this cluster solution was used (Figure 69) in which the fifth cluster was dissolved, with two of its members being reassigned by reason-

able proximity to cluster 2, while the other four members, plus an outlier of cluster 1, were placed in an "outlier" category, denoting lack of clear relation to the feature-centered distributions. Table 24 presents the tool frequencies resulting from this cluster analysis.

The low tool frequencies hinder the identification of statistically significant patterns, but at hearth 14 (cluster 2) several types are prominent: bifaces, utilized flakes, ground slate flakes and perhaps tool manufacturing implements such as a hammerstone and schist tablets. A more general picture can be had by combining clusters 1 and 2 with their adjacent outliers (Area 2C2) and comparing this with combined clusters 3 and 4 (Area 2C1), with the addition of quadrat provenienced items. Low tool frequencies still plague the comparison (Area 2C1= 19 items, vs Area 2C2= 81 items) such that it is difficult to discern any statistically significant differences. About all that can be said is that Area 2C2 has high frequencies of utilized flakes, quartz block cores, bifaces, biface preforms, and ground slate flakes and tool fragments. Notable, however, is the relative lack of quartz bipolar cores (n=1)

Table 25: Area 2C Tool Raw Material Frequencies and Weights by Cluster and Subarea

	C-1	C-2	C-3	C-4	Outliers	2C1	2C2
Quartz	8	8	1		3	2 (290)	21 (2693)
Ramah chert	8	24	2	1	1	9 (66)	29 (584)
Black chert				1	1	2 (4)	
Slate—total	6	17	1			2 (1)	22 (395)
Beige		5	1			1 (0.8)	5 (3)
Green	5	5					10 (335)
Gray	1	2					4 (28)
Gray-banded		2					2 (2)
Red-brown		2				1 (0.2)	3 (1.6)
Green-gray speckled		1					1 (25)
Schist		4		3		4 (664)	4 (30)
Other	1	2					3 (145)
TOTAL	23	54	4	5	5	19	79

in contrast to the abundance of quartz block cores and quartz debitage.

When tool raw materials and weights are considered (Table 25), Area 2C2 has an overwhelming domination of quartz by weight, but Ramah chert and green slate are also important by both weight and frequency.

Flake Distribution

Point-plots are lacking for the westernmost portion of Area 2C1. Fortunately, however, the quadrat counts from that subarea are so low that the information loss is not critical for assessing the spatial patterning. High frequencies of quartz flakes are associated with hearths 14 and 15 (Figure 39). Small numbers of quartz flakes lie immediately north and west of hearths 9 and 10; the southern and eastern sides of these features are virtually devoid of quartz. Hearths 12 and 13 are also virtually devoid of quartz flakes. Ramah chert (Figure 40) exhibits virtually the same pattern as quartz except for a small cluster associated with hearth 12. Virtually all the patinated Ramah chert (Figure 42) is associated with hearth 14. Small clusters of black chert flakes (Figure 43) are found adjacent to hearth 14 and directly associated with

hearth 12. Gray Mugford chert is virtually absent from Area 2C. Slate flakes (Figure 44) of all color variants are mostly associated with hearth 14. Table 26 contrasts the flake raw material frequencies and weights by the two subareas. By frequency there is little difference between the subareas, but by weight Area 2C1 has a relatively high proportion of Ramah chert.

A more nuanced view might be provided by a breakdown of flake materials by hearth feature, essentially paralleling the k-means cluster analysis of tools. Quadrats were grouped by feature proximity and in relation to breaks in flake density; outlying quadrats were eliminated (Table 27). The numbers for hearths 9 and 10 are uncertain, since the 1 m^2 quadrats in this area cannot be as closely related to the features as the 50 cm^2 quadrats further south. Hearths 10, 12, 13 and 14 all display high percentages of Ramah chert, in contrast to hearths 9 and 15 which have high percentages of quartz. Taking into account the small sample sizes from some of the hearths and the incomplete excavation at the southern end of Area 2C, there is at least a suggestion of variations within each of the broader subareas used previously.

Table 26: Area 2C Flake Raw Material Frequencies and Weights by Subarea

	FREQUENCY			WEIGHT		
	2C2 N (%)	2C2 N (%)	TOTAL N (%)	2C2 N (%)	2C2 N (%)	TOTAL N (%)
Quartz	94 (39.9)	630 (40.1)	724 (40.0)	285 (65.4)	2416 (87.1)	2701 (74.6)
Ramah chert	115 (48.7)	825 (52.4)	940 (52.0)	139 (31.9)	293 (10.6)	432 (11.9)
Patinated Ramah	6 (2.5)	60 (3.8)	66 (3.6)	2.4 (0.6)	24 (0.9)	26.4 (0.7)
Black chert	13 (5.5)	11 (0.7)	24 (1.3)	3.8 (0.9)	2.4 (0.1)	62 (1.7)
Gray Mugford chert		3 (0.2)	3 (0.2)		1.3 (0.0)	13 (0.4)
Slate—total	8 (3.4)	44 (2.8)	52 (2.9)	5.7 (1.3)	37 (1.3)	387 (10.7)
Beige	3	9	12	4	22	26
Green	3	17	20	31	252	283
Gray	2	13	15	22	42	64
Gray- banded		3	3		14	14
Red-brown		2	2		4	
TOTAL	**236**	**1573**	**1809**			

Table 27: Area 2C Flake Raw Material Frequencies by Hearth Feature

	H-9 N (%)	H-10 N (%)	H-12 N (%)	H-13 N (%)	H-14 N (%)	H-15 N (%)
Quartz	79 (82.3)	2 (10.0)	5 (7.0)		310 (28.8)	255 (71.0)
Ramah chert	6 (6.3)	15 (75.0)	55 (77.5)	15 (93.8)	671 (62.3)	96 (26.7)
Patinated Ramah	4 (4.2)		2 (2.8)		58 (5.4)	
Black chert	2 (2.1)	2 (10.0)	7 (9.9)	1 (6.3)	6 (0.6)	
Gray Mugford chert					1 (0.1)	
Slate—total	5 (5.2)	1 (5.0)	2 (2.8)		31 (2.9)	8 (2.2)
Beige	3				5	2
Green		1			11	3
Gray	2				12	1
Gray-banded					2	1
Red-brown					1	1
TOTAL	**96**	**20**	**71**	**16**	**1077**	**359**

Red Ocher and Bone Distribution

Figure 61 shows the distribution of red ocher stains and clumps as well as bone fragments. Some of the red ocher stains occur inside hearth 15, but most are concentrated in two areas on opposite sides of hearth 14. The patches on the southwest side are larger and their configuration is virtually identical to the shape of the flake distribution present in the same area (Figure 68), suggesting their spatial extents were limited by the same factors. The red ocher stains on the northeast side of hearth 14 are smaller, but they also fit fairly well with the accompanying flake distribution. Together, these two patches are consistent with the tendency for a bounded linear distribution of debitage running southwest-northeast across hearth 14. Small clumps of red ocher lay within the bounds of hearth 14.

A total of 651 tiny and unidentifiable calcined bone fragments occurred within and adjacent to hearth 14; most of these were recovered by fine-sieving the charcoal samples. Associated with hearth 12 were 294 tiny and equally unidentifiable bone fragments.

Refitting

Only broken tools were considered for refitting. A total of three items was refitted, but all the pieces lay within a few centimeters of each other. Thus, no connection can be drawn between Areas 2C1 and 2C2 or between 2C and other parts of Area 2.

Feature-Related Distributions, Size-Sorting and Cultural Formation Processes

The small amount of lithic material from Area 2C1 renders difficult any analysis of size-sorting. At 2C2, quartz block cores are concentrated around hearths 14

and 15, although several are found in quadrats up to 2 m southwards where they may have been cached or thrown. The distribution of large-sized tools tends to be centered around hearths 14 and 15 (Figure 62); to some extent this is correlated with a high frequency of quartz cores. When quartz flake size distributions are considered using the size-sorting index (Figure 62) there are three units with predominantly small flakes directly associated with and adjacent to hearth 14, and two units with tendencies towards larger flakes between hearths 14 and 15. Three other units to the south also have tendencies towards larger flakes; each of these units were associated with a quartz core. Thus, as at Area 2A, there is a tendency to find both small and large flake units in what might be expected to be drop zones around hearths. This may indicate a lack of maintenance or a spatial repositioning of quartz reduction from the initial reduction of block cores in one place (producing larger debitage) to secondary reduction of bipolar cores in another place (producing smaller debitage). The tendency of units

Table 28: Area 2C Total Lithic Raw Material Weights (Tools and Flakes). In Grams

	2C1 (g)	2C2 (g)	TOTAL (g)	(%)
Quartz	575	5109	5684	(70.3)
Ramah chert	205	877	1082	(13.4)
Patinated Ramah	2.4	24	26.4	(0.3)
Black chert	7.8	2.4	10.2	(0.1)
Gray Mugford chert		1.3	1.3	(0.0)
Slate—total	6.5	407	439	(5.4)
Beige	4.8	25	29.8	
Green	31	587	618	
Gray	22	70	92	
Gray-banded		16	16	
Red-brown	1	5.6	6.6	
Gray-green speckled		25	25	
Schist	665	30.6	695	(8.6)
Other		145	145	(1.8)

with larger flake sizes to be associated with unreduced quartz block cores may support this.

Consumption of Lithic Materials and Technological Organization.

Given the paucity of material from Area 2C1 and the incomplete excavation of what seems to be a possible dwelling module at Area 2C2, there is not much point in drawing particular conclusions concerning raw material consumption and technological organization. The most relevant observation is that if Area 2C1 represents a dwelling module then it indicates very little deposition of lithic materials, in sharp contrast to Area 2C2 and especially to the inferred dwellings at Area 2A. Table 28 outlines the total raw material weights (tools and flakes) from the Area 2C subareas.

Variations in quartz and Ramah chert reduction patterns between Area 2C1 and 2C2 are outlined in Table 29. Perhaps the most striking observation is the almost complete lack of quartz bipolar cores (n=1) in contrast to an abundance of block cores. This might indicate quartz reduction by free hand percussion rather than by the bipolar technique. A second bipolar core is of Ramah chert. There is also a single small disc core of Ramah chert; its sharp edges and lack of crushing indicate that it was not a product of bipolar percussion; it is probably an extremely reduced tool fragment. Most of the Ramah chert biface-thinning flakes (Figure 63) are concentrated within a 1 m radius of hearth 14. The distribution of large biface-thinning flakes (Figure 63) is similar.

As far as the other raw materials are concerned, the paucity of slate plates and blanks (n=1), combined with the modest representation of ground slate flakes, might indicate emphasis on tool maintenance rather than production. The extremely low frequency of black and Mugford chert also suggests a similar maintenance pattern.

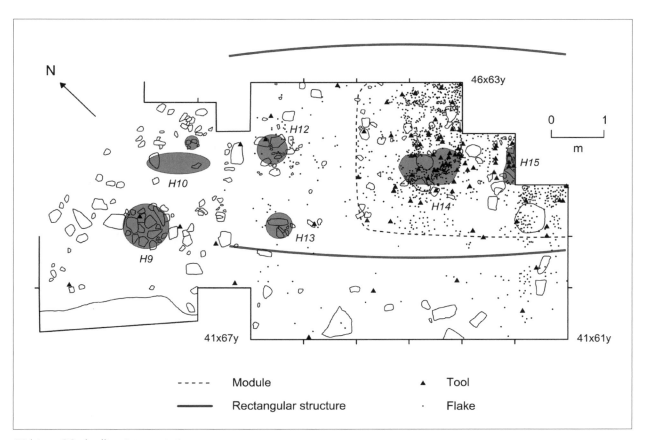

70/ Area 2C: dwelling interpretations.

Table 29: Summary of the Quartz and Ramah Chert Reduction Systems at Area 2C

QUARTZ

	Tools	Block Cores	Bipolar	Flakes	Total Weight (g)
Area 2C1	2	1		94	575g
Area 2C2	20	16	1	630	5109 g

RAMAH CHERT

	Tools	Points	Biface. Frags.	Preforms	Bipolar Cores	Disc Cores	Biface-Thinning	Flakes	Total Weight (g)
Area 2C1	7	1	1		1		16	121	207 g
Area 2C2	34		4	4		1	98	885	901 g

Area 2C Conclusions

Area 2C received insufficient excavation to draw many robust conclusions about spatial patterning. The visual impression is that the four form/function differentiated hearths at Area 2C1 may constitute a dwelling module in a pattern reminiscent of Area 2A. Unfortunately, the sparse lithics provide little additional contextual material to evaluate this. On the other hand, the low density lithic distribution, combined with a 6100 B.P. radiocarbon date, militate against this configuration being part of a longhouse structure affiliated with Area 2A. At Area 2C2 the hearths and linear flake distributions strongly suggest a dwelling module similar to those inferred from the "lobes" at Area 2A (Figure 70). If the Area 2C2 hearth/flake configurations represent dividers in a segmented rectangular structure, then that structure would be aligned northwest-southeast, parallel with the beach front (Figure 70), in contrast to the perpendicular orientation at Area 2A. The area of sparse deposition between hearth 14 and hearths 12 and 13 could then be viewed as a flanking floor space similar those inferred for the southern rectangular structure at Area 2A. It might even be possible to suggest that the hearths at 2C1 (at least hearths 12 and 13) are part of the same longhouse structure, although this would require that the longhouse is partitioned into large segments of high and low deposition intensity. Clarification of these alternatives can only be had by extending the Area 2C2 excavation towards the southeast.

Nukasusutok-5, Area 2A, 1979, with Jack Contin and Chuck Curtis. (Photo: B. Hood)

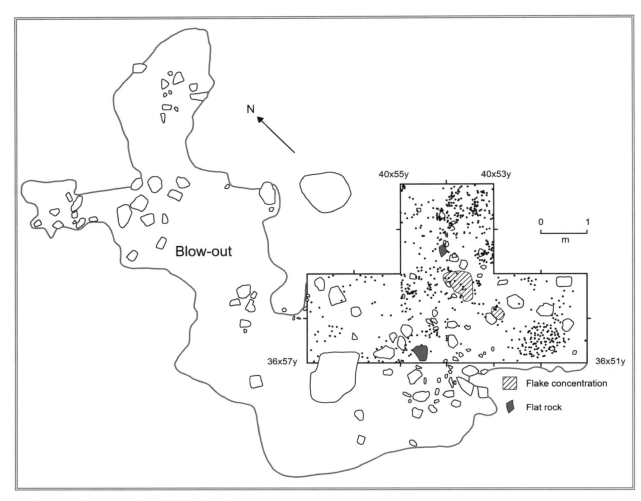

71/ Area 1: features and total flake distribution.

Nukasusutok-5: Areas 1 and 3

This chapter presents analyses of Areas 1 and 3 at Nukasusutok-5. The treatment of Area 1 is brief since the size of the excavation field was small and there were few features and formal tools. Area 3 is discussed more in-depth, given the presence of unusual red ocher features.

Area 1

Area 1 was a small 16 m² excavation field at the edge of the blow-out towards the eastern end of the site (Figures 21, 22, 71). On the southwest side of the excavation was a cluster of rocks, half of which were inside the bounds of the excavation, half outside. Measuring 1.5 m in diameter, the cluster consisted of small cobbles and a few flat slabs. The feature was entirely deflated and no tools, charcoal or red ocher were associated with it, only a few flakes. To the north-west in the blow-out were rock clusters that may represent three or four hearths. The most northerly of these was 1 m in diameter and consisted of eight cobbles and one flat slab. It was accompanied by charcoal flecks and small granules of red ocher as well as by Ramah chert, quartz, slate and black chert flakes. The other features had no visible cultural material.

The *in situ* deposits showed that beneath the surface vegetation and humus there were fine mottled brown sands extending to about 30 cm below the surface, where they contacted beach gravel. A thin, discontinuous leaching zone was present. Lithic material occurred from just below the humus to about 25 cm

below the surface. The area was excavated in 5 cm levels, which were lumped together for analytical purposes.

Flakes

The total flake distribution is shown in Figure 71, while Figures 72 to 74 depict the distribution of individual raw material types by plots and quadrat counts. Quartz is frequent in the eastern extension of Area 1 and occurs in a major concentration near the center of the excavation. There is also a dense concentration of mostly fingernail-sized fragments beside a rock at 37.30x 52.80y. This concentration was probably the result of a single reduction event involving one or more quartz cores. There is also a more diffuse oval concentration of quartz in 36x51-52y. Ramah chert frequencies are modest over most of the excavation, but there is a higher frequency cluster in 36x51-52y, the same location as the diffuse quartz concentration. Only one flake of patinated Ramah chert and two biface-thinning flakes of Ramah were identified. A few black chert flakes are present, mostly towards the center of the excavation, and only two slate flakes were recovered. Table 30 summarizes the flake raw material frequencies and weights.

Tools

The excavated tool distribution is shown by quadrat in Figure 75, while Table 31 outlines the implement classes from the excavated area as well as those surface collected from the blow-out by the Smithsonian Institution. The single quartz bipolar core from Area 1 is in the same quadrat as two quartz block cores. The third block core lies close to the concentration of small quartz flakes in 37x52y. All the utilized flakes (exclusively Ramah chert) occur in the eastern extension of the excavation. One of the biface fragments (black chert) is associated with the probable hearth on the west side of the excavation, while the other (slate) lies to the north of the feature. The collection is so small and unrepresentative that little can be inferred from it.

Table 30: Area 1 Flake Raw Materials by Frequency and Weight

	N	(%)	WT	(g)
Quartz	1173	(75.0)	3892	(96.1)
Ramah chert	376	(24.0)	151	(3.7)
Black chert	13	(0.8)	2	(0.0)
Gray Mugford chert	1	(0.1)	1	(0.0)
Gray slate	2	(0.1)	5	(0.1)
TOTAL	1565		4051	

Table 31. Area 1 Tool Class Frequencies.

	Excavation	Surface	N	%
Bifacial points	1	4	5	(11.6)
Flake points		4	4	(9.3)
Bifaces	1	1	2	(4.7)
Endscrapers		3	3	(7.0)
Flake knives		3	3	(7.0)
Utilized flakes	4	18	22	(51.2)
Bipolar cores	1		1	(2.3)
Block cores	3		3	(7.0)
TOTAL	10	33	43	

Area 3

Area 3 lay 38 m west of Area 2, slightly downslope on a narrow, gently sloping terrace at 28 m asl. (Figure 22). In 1979 shovel-testing on the terrace revealed a remarkable red ocher deposit, so an excavation area of 28 m² was opened. Three more features were exposed, two of which had red ocher deposits (Figure 76). Additional shovel tests along the terrace provided negative results except in one area 4.5 m southwest of the main excavation, where a Ramah chert biface base was uncovered. An additional excavation unit 1 by 3 m in size was opened at that spot, but only a few quartz flakes and a small fleck of red ocher were encountered.

The red ocher features were initially believed to be burials, but evaluation of this hypothesis was complicated by the presence of an almost impenetrable indurated soil horizon (cemented "hardpan") that lay beneath the entire surface of Area 3. During the 1980 field season the cemented zone beneath two of the red ocher features was pick-axed down to the underlying bedrock, but no evidence for interments was found. The interpretation of these features remains problematic and is discussed further at the end of this chapter.

This section begins with a discussion of the unique pedological situation at Area 3. A description of the features is then provided, followed by a consideration of their artifact associations. After a discussion of dating, some interpretive possibilities are presented.

Pedology

The soil profile from Area 3 (Figure 77) can be classified within the Ortstein Ferro-Humic Podzol subgroup (Canada Soil Survey Committee, Subcommittee on Soil Classification 1978). The profile has a thin humus horizon underneath a vegetation mat of lichen, crowberry and dwarf birch. A 2 cm thick light gray leaching horizon is underlain by a mottled red-brown horizon containing black-coated, cohering sand grains. In some places this changes abruptly into a platey-textured semi-cemented horizon, which in turn grades into an indurated horizon measuring up to 50 cm thick. The indurated horizon lies directly upon bedrock which, in the center of Area 3, was contacted at 80 cm below the present ground surface. Within the iron-consolidated zone is a considerable amount of semi-decomposed roots. The extremely dark colouration of the sand

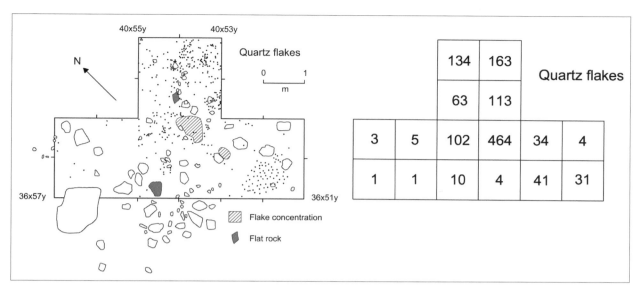

		134	163		
		63	113		
3	5	102	464	34	4
1	1	10	4	41	31

Quartz flakes

Flake concentration

Flat rock

72/ Area 1: distribution of quartz flakes.

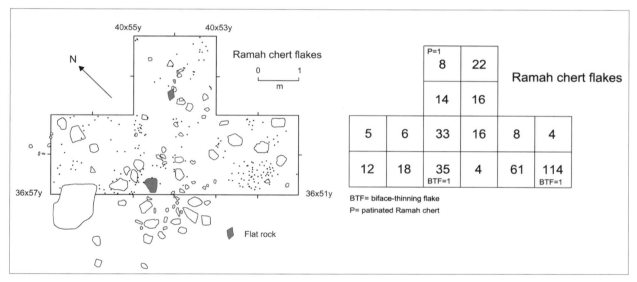

		P=1 8	22		
		14	16		
5	6	33	16	8	4
12	18	35 BTF=1	4	61	114 BTF=1

Ramah chert flakes

BTF= biface-thinning flake
P= patinated Ramah chert

Flat rock

73/ Area 1: distribution of Ramah chert flakes.

makes it very difficult to identify possible feature-related colour shifts.

Field investigations in 1979 determined that this cemented soil horizon was present under most of the western end of Nukasustok-5, from Smithsonian Test Pit C to the entire surface of Area 3. Although the appearance of the podzol profile itself was sufficient evidence to question Fitzhugh's (1978:77) suggestion that this was fat-consolidated sand, the extensive spatial distribution of this pedological feature cast even more doubt on the interpretation. Samples of the Area 3 indurated horizon were analysed in the laboratory for total organic carbon using the Walkley-Black wet oxidation method (Jackson 1958:219-222). The results indicated the cemented horizon did not contain any more organic carbon than samples from the surrounding soil matrix or from Area 2. A sample of the indurated horizon procured by the Smithsonian in 1975 from Test Pit C was subjected to amino acid analysis by David Von Endt of the Smithsonian Institution. No amino acids were identified in this sample (Fitzhugh, personal communication). In addition, the total iron

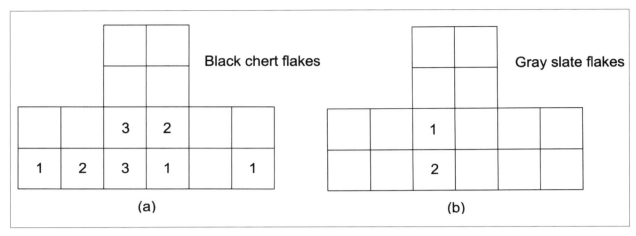

74/ Area 1: distribution of black chert and gray slate flakes.

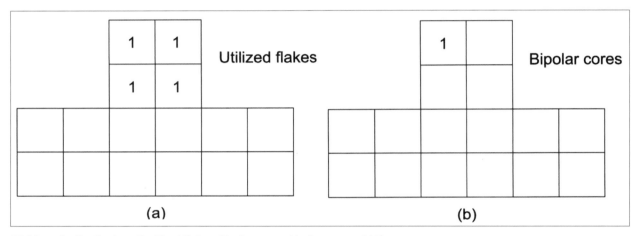

75/ Area 1: distribution of utilized flakes, bipolar cores, block cores and bifaces.

content was determined by atomic absorption spectrophotometry (Hood 1981: Appendix C). The Area 3 profile exhibited an iron-depleted A horizon and iron-enriched B horizon consistent with podzolization. The cemented soil horizon is therefore a natural pedological phenomena, not a cultural deposit.

As the discussion below will demonstrate, Maritime Archaic people engaged in some degree of sub-surface activity at Area 3, so the genesis of the iron pan must have begun subsequent to the occupation, which is suggested to date ca. 5000 B.P.. Precisely when iron pan formation began is impossible to determine without further analysis, but radiocarbon dating the onset of such pedological features is plagued by complex problems related to how organic carbon is incorporated into cemented horizons (Lascelles et al. 2000). An important question is whether iron-pan genesis was a strictly local phenomenon, perhaps a consequence of changes in topography and drainage related to marine shoreline displacement, or whether it was triggered by broader climatic changes such as increased precipitation. Answering this question is problematic because the causes of iron-pan formation are not well understood. Several mechanisms have been proposed: translocation of weathered iron minerals by a fluctuating water table, translocation of iron and aluminum bound up with organic compounds (chelates), or inorganic translocation and precipitation of iron (Anderson et al. 1982; Davidson 1987; Moore 1976).

Features

The four features at Area 3 (Figures 76, 78, 79) were clustered together, evenly spaced about 2-2.5 m distant from each other (center to center). Along the northeast edge of Feature 1 was a sand hummock (Figure 76), which when cross-sectioned revealed an upper leached zone underlain by mottled brown sand, then a charcoal layer overlying red ocher. This sequence indicates that the hummock covers the edge of the feature and thus must postdate it. The hummock is likely a product of aeolian action and downslope movement. Each of the cultural features will be described in turn.

Feature 1: Feature 1 consisted of an oval stain of red ocher, 1.2 m in diameter and 4 cm thick at its center, which was capped by a loose arrangement of small cobbles oriented towards the center of the ocher (Figures 76, 80, 81). A thick linear deposit of charcoal, 1.8 m long and 40 cm wide, lay directly on top of the ocher, crossing the entire feature in a northeast-southwest direction. The subsurface beneath Feature 1 was excavated down to bedrock, which required the assistance of a pick-axe to penetrate the indurated layer. The only subsurface feature identified was a peculiar lens of yellow sand that lay ca. 30 cm beneath the western edge of the red ocher deposit (Figure 82). This lens was 85 cm by 65 cm in size, with

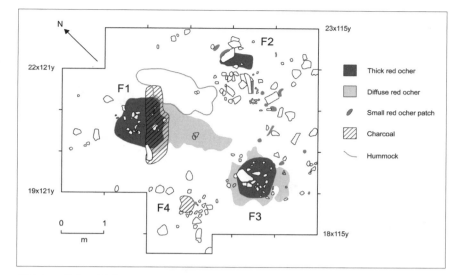

76/ Area 3: level 1 features.

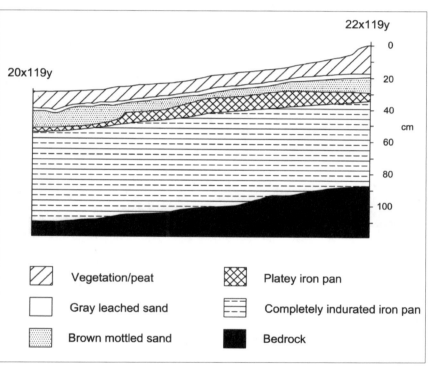

77/ Area 3: soil profile.

an irregular depth ranging from 2.5 to 7 cm. Charcoal was present on top of and within the upper portion of the sand, slightly off-center. A utilized flake of Ramah chert was associated with the sand. It is difficult to account for this lens. Its peculiar form indicates it was not a single decayed rock, although it might have consisted of several rocks of similar composition clustered

78/ Area 3: overview, Feature 1 excavated.

79/ Area 3: vertical bipod photo, Feature 1 excavated.

and two utilized flakes. There were also flakes of quartz, Ramah chert and slate.

Two radiocarbon dates were obtained from Feature 1. The first sample consisted of charcoal from the thick deposit on top of the red ocher and it produced a date of 2845±70 B.P. (UGa-3869). This was unacceptably late, so a second date was run on charcoal from Level 2, beneath the red ocher deposit. The result was closer to expectations: 5090±95 B.P. (SI-5534).

Feature 2: At the center of Feature 2 (Figure 76, 79, 83) was a roughly circular arrangement of small cobbles and flat slabs, 75 cm in diameter. About 30 cm to the northeast were three flat slabs associated with a small red ocher stain that contained a pocket of charcoal. Several other rocks lay scattered to the west and southwest of the circular arrangement. The sub-surface of Feature 2 was pick-axed down to bedrock. Underneath were a number of rocks; two large ones were situated on the southeastern edge of the feature while a series of small rocks was positioned in an arc along its northwestern edge (Figure 82). A patch of red ocher and charcoal lay directly underneath the main surface level concentration. Nearby were two small posthole-like concentrations of yellow sand, similar to that found beneath Feature 1. Together, these features suggest a subsurface activity area 1.6 m by 1.3 m in size.

together. It is unlikely to have been related to organic material since the rapid decay of the latter would have resulted in the lens having been cemented and discolored by the strong iron translocation processes.

Directly associated with the surface of Feature 1 were: a small ground slate celt, a ground slate flake, a fragment of a beveled ground slate tool, a flake knife of Ramah chert, several fragments of a hexagonal cross-sectioned implement of ground slate (possibly a woodworking tool), part of a slate blank, a bipolar core

CHAPTER 7

Four tools were directly associated with the feature: two flake points of Ramah chert, an endscraper of fine-grained beige Mugford chert, and a quartz core. A substantial amount of quartz flakes was also associated with Feature 2 (see below).

Feature 3: Feature 3 (Figures 76, 79, 84) was similar in configuration to Feature 1. It consisted of an oval red ocher stain, 1 m in diameter and 4 cm thick, capped by a flat rock slab and several smaller cobbles. The feature was cross-sectioned and excavated down to the top of the indurated horizon. This procedure revealed a considerable amount of charcoal underneath the ocher, beneath which was a cluster of small cobbles and quartz chunks packed into an area of 80 by 45 cm (Figure 82, 85). Excavation of the indurated zone was not attempted. Tools directly associated with the feature included: a flake point of Ramah chert, a chlorite schist

80/ Area 3: Feature 1.

81/ Area 3: Feature 1 vertical bipod photo.

tablet, a utilized flake, and a bipolar core. There was also a considerable quantity of quartz flakes. Two radiocarbon dates were run on charcoal from Feature 3: 2770±205 B.P. (UGa-3159) and 2805±70 B.P. (UGa-3870). Both were unacceptably recent.

Feature 4

This feature (Figure 76), left mostly unexcavated, consisted of a cluster of small cobbles that may have extended beyond the limit of the excavation. No red

ocher was present, but a charcoal stain lay adjacent to the cobble cluster.

Flake Distribution

Figures 86 to 88 depict the point-plotted and quadrat distributions of flake raw materials. The point-plotted flakes are presented in two levels, the first being the gray leached zone and upper portion of the red-brown sand (ca. 5-10 cm), the second consisting of the lower red-brown sand and the underlying iron-consolidated horizon. The upper level quartz flakes cluster somewhat with Features 2 and 3, but have a much more diffuse spread near Feature 1. Two small clusters of quartz flakes, representing either individual reduction episodes or intentional deposition, lie between Features 1, 2 and 3. Ramah chert flakes in the upper level have a diffuse overall distribution but are clearly associated with Features 1 and 3, which display the most intense red ocher concentrations. Slate flakes from the upper layer are associated only with Feature 1. The lower level quartz flakes are clustered underneath Features 2 and 3. At Feature 2 they form an oval or circular pattern more-or-less coterminous with the buried rock cluster, while at Feature 3 they lie immediately adjacent to (though rarely within) the subsurface rock cluster. Lower level Ramah chert is associated exclusively with Feature 2. Three flakes were measured at ca. 50 cm below the sand surface along the western edge of the feature. Almost all the lower level slate flakes occur in a small concentration adjacent to the cluster of rocks beneath Feature 3.

The lower level flakes, combined with the buried rocks, indicate some degree of deposition below the surfaces of Features 2 and 3. Beneath Feature 2 this deposition appears as a somewhat circular "basin" 1.7 m in diameter and up to 40 cm deep, while beneath Feature 3 there is a basin 1.0 by 0.8 m in size and 15-20 cm deep. Feature 1 lacked indications of subsurface

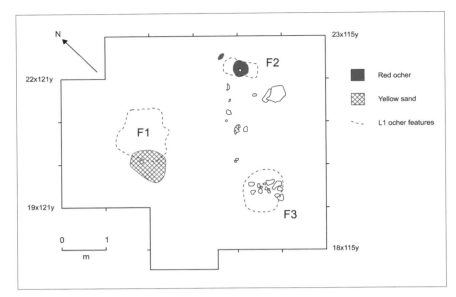

82/ Area 3: level 2 features.

83/ Area 3: Feature 2.

flake deposition, as did the buried yellow sand lens that seemed to be associated with the feature.

Table 32 tabulates the flake raw material variations in relation to the features, based on the quadrat counts. The 1 m quadrats fit reasonably well with the features, with the exception of 20x116/117y, which lie between Features 1, 2 and 3 in an area of seeming overlap. These units have been treated separately. Figure 89 shows the quadrat groupings used in the analysis. The figures for Feature 4 are incomplete,

Table 32: Area 3 Flake Raw Material Frequencies by Feature

	F-1 N (%)	F-2 N (%)	F-3 N (%)	F-4 N (%)	OVERLAP N (%)	OTHER N (%)	TOTAL N (%)
Quartz	120 (57.4)	704 (96.0)	405 (83.9)	18 (66.7)	293 (86.7)	29 (63.0)	1569 (85.5)
Ramah chert	79 (37.8)	28 (3.8)	69 (14.3)	8 (29.6)	42 (12.4)	12 (26.1)	238 (13.0)
Patinated Ramah	1 (0.5)						1 (0.0)
Slate total	9 (4.3)	1 (0.1)	9 (1.9)	1 (3.7)	3 (0.9)	5 (10.9)	28 (1.5)
beige	9		1	1	3	4	17
gray		1	7				1
gray-banded			1				1
red-brown						1	1
TOTAL	209	733	483	27	338	46	1836

Table 33: Area 3 Tool Class Frequencies by Feature

	F-1	F-2	F-3	Overlap	F-4	Other	TOTAL N (%)
Bifaces	1		1		1		3 (4.5)
Biface preforms						1	1 (1.5)
Flake points		2	1				3 (4.5)
Scrapers/knives	1	1					2 (3.0)
Utilized flakes	4	2	4	2		1	13 (19.4)
Celts	1						1 (1.5)
Hexagonal slate tool	0.5*	0.5					1 (1.5)
Slate blanks	0.5	0.5					1 (1.5)
Ground slate flakes	6		3	1	1	3	14 (20.9)
Bipolar cores	1	1	1		1	1	5 (7.5)
Block cores	3	6	5	6			20 (29.9)
Disc cores						1	1 (1.5)
Schist tablets			2				2 (3.0)
TOTAL	18	13	17	9	3	7	67

.5 denotes a conjoining fragment

since it was not excavated fully. All the features exhibit a high proportion of quartz, although Features 1 and 4 also have moderate proportions of Ramah chert. Inspection of the chi-square expected frequencies for this table (treating slate generically) indicates that Feature 1 has a higher than expected frequency of Ramah chert, while Feature 2 has a lower than expected frequency of Ramah. Slate is notable for its paucity, although it is mainly associated with Features 1 and 3. Fine-grained cherts are absent.

Tool Distribution

Figure 90 portrays the plotted tool distribution along with the results of a *k*-means cluster analysis. A four cluster solution seems best: cluster 1 is associated with Feature 3, cluster 3 with Feature 2 and clusters 2 and 4 with Feature 1. There is a strong tendency for tools to be associated with the features. Since Area 3 has some of the same provenience problems as Area 2A (many bipolar cores and utilized flakes only provenienced to 1 m² grids), further analysis was conducted using the quadrat distributions of the tool classes (Figures 91 to 96). Quadrat groupings were the same as used for the flakes (Figure 89). Table 33 presents tool class frequencies broken down by their association with the different features. The tool class frequencies are low, but one might point to the association of flake points with Feature 2, slate tool fragments with Feature 1 (one hexagonal cross-section fragment, possibly of a

84/ Area 3: Feature 3.

85/ Area 3: Feature 3 sectioned, showing rock cluster beneath the red ocher layer.

woodworking implement, and ground slate flakes) and schist tablets and fragments with Feature 3. Variations in tool raw materials (Table 34) are not particularly instructive, except insofar as Feature 1 is associated with quite a few items of Ramah chert (paralleling its higher than expected frequency of Ramah chert flakes) and slate. In contrast to the paucity of slate flakes, slate tools or fragments thereof are fairly common.

The tool distribution can also be considered by depth, which was recorded by depth below surface and

soil profile level. As with the flakes, two levels can be distinguished: the upper level consisting of the gray leached zone and the top portion of the red-brown sand, the second consisting of the lower red-brown sand and the underlying iron-consolidated horizon. At Feature 1, 15 implements were associated with the upper level, while 4 occurred in the lower level. The latter included a bipolar core of Ramah chert, two utilized flakes of Ramah chert (one at ca. 43 cm below the sand surface, directly associated with the yellow sand lens)

CHAPTER 7

Table 34. Area 3 Tool Raw Material Frequencies by Feature.

	F-1	F-2	F-3	Overlap	F-4	Other	TOTAL
Quartz	3	7	5	6		1	22 (32.8)
Ramah chert	7	4	7	1	2	3	24 (35.8)
Slate total	8	1	3	2	1	3	18 (26.9)
beige	5			1	1		7
gray	.5*	.5	3			1	5
green	.5	.5				1	2
gray-banded	1						1
red-brown	1			1		1	3
Mugford chert		1				1	1 (1.5)
Schist			2				2 (3.0)
TOTAL	18	13	17	9	3	7	67

.5 denotes a conjoining fragment

and a flake knife of Ramah chert 10 cm above the yellow sand lens. At Features 2 and 3, all the point-provenienced tools lay within the upper level.

Refits

It was possible to refit pieces of three tools at Area 3 (Figure 90). One refit consisted of a hexagonal cross-sectioned ground slate implement (probable woodworking tool) that was broken into five fragments, four of which refit within Feature 1, while one fragment lay near the northwest edge of Feature 2 (Figure 94). A slate blank fragment associated with Feature 1 was conjoined with a fragment from the east side of Feature 2 (Figure 94). These two refits suggest a behavioral connection between Features 1 and 2. Finally, two pieces of a Ramah chert flake point refit over a short distance at Feature 2.

Consumption of Lithic Raw Materials and Technological Organization

Table 35 summarizes the weights of flake and tool materials at Area 3. Quartz clearly dominates, with only small amounts of other raw materials being represented. Slate occurs primarily as tools; very little

occurs as flakes. Mugford chert is represented by a single tool (endscraper). Table 36 outlines the products of the quartz and Ramah chert reduction systems at Area 3. Quartz is notable for a high frequency of block cores and relatively few bipolar cores. The Ramah chert assemblage is too small to draw any firm conclusions, but it might be noted that 10 of the 17 biface-thinning flakes (BTFs) were classified as "large" (>30 mm), an unusually high proportion. Figure 97 shows the distribution of BTFs by quadrat; three were associated with Feature 1, three with Feature 2 and 11 with Feature 3. Eight of the ten large BTFs were associated with Feature 3.

Dating

Table 37 summarizes the radiocarbon dates for Area 3. Only one of the four dates is reliable. The date of 5090±95 B.P. was run on alder/birch and willow charcoal procured from the subsurface of Feature 1, thus it is contextually more secure than the overlying charcoal deposit from which the 2845±70 B.P. date was derived. The latter sample and all the other later date samples contained coniferous material (Dosia Laeyendecker, personal communication). Given that pollen (Short

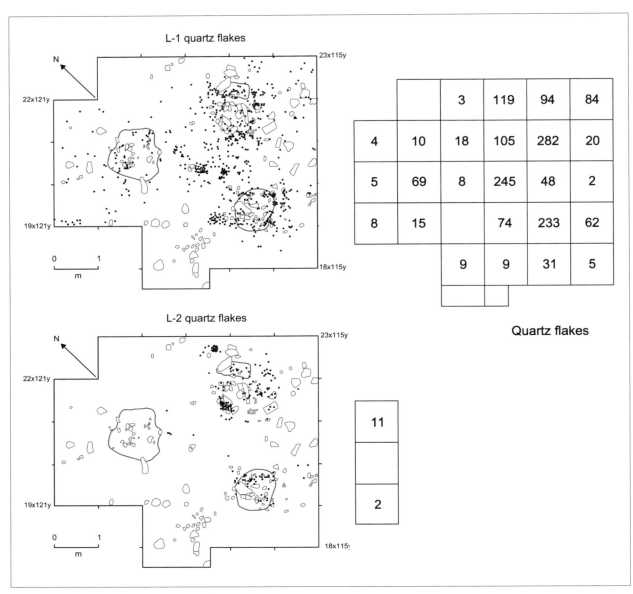

86/ Area 3: distribution of quartz flakes. (a) Level 1. (b) Level 2. (c) Total.

1978:32) and macrofossil data indicate the first coniferous forest did not migrate to the Nain area until 4500-4200 B.P., and that there is no indication of Late Maritime Archaic lithic material at Area 3, the three third millennium B.P. dates likely pertain to a post-occupation burn event. Consequently, the large charcoal concentration overlying Feature 1 was not part of the ritual practice involved in constructing the feature.

Relative sea-level dating is of little help. According to the uplift curve presented in Figure 5, Area 3's elevation of 28 m asl. corresponds to ca. 6800 B.P., but nothing in the lithic material suggests the locality is that old. If we accept the 5000 B.P. radiocarbon date, then Area 3 was positioned far above its contemporary shoreline, ca. 12 m asl.

The paucity of tool material at Area 3 provides only a slim basis for typological dating. A stemmed flake point from Feature 2 is almost identical to one from Area 2A (Figures 113:a and 100:j, respectively). The presence of quartz block cores, flake points, an endscraper of Mugford chert and schist tablets is generally consistent with the Area 2 assemblage and

Table 35. Area 3 Total Lithic Raw Material Weights (Tools and Flakes). In Grams.

	Flakes (g) (%)	Tools (g) (%)	Total (g) (%)
Quartz	6574.3 (95.9)	3886 (87.0)	10460.3 (92.4)
Ramah chert	262.4 (3.8)	205 (4.6)	467 (4.1)
Beige Mugford chert		1 (0.0)	1 (0.0)
Slate total	17.5 (0.3)	104.4 (2.3)	122 (1.1)
Beige	15.3	7.2	22.2
Gray	1.2	7.2	8.4
Gray-banded	0.2		0.2
Red-brown	1	68	69
Green		22	22
Schist		269 (6.1)	269 (2.4)

Table 36. Summary of the Quartz and Ramah Chert Reduction Systems at Area 3.

QUARTZ				
Tools	Block Cores	Bipolar cores	Flakes	Total Weight
24	18	2	1569	10460

RAMAH CHERT								
Tools	Points	Biface Frags.	Preforms	Bipolar Cores	Disc Cores	Biface-Thinning	Flakes	Total Wt
23	—	2	1	3	1	17	238	467

Table 37. Radiocarbon Dates from Area 3. Calibrated with OxCal 3.10 (Bronk-Ramsey 2005).

Provenience	B.P.	Calibrated BC 1δ	Lab.No.	Comment
Feature 1, level 2	5090±95	3980-3770	SI-5534	alder/birch, willow
Feature 1, overlying	2845±70		UGa-3869	coniferous in undated feature sample
Feature 3	2770±205		UGa-3159	birch and conifer in undated feature sample
Feature 3	2805±70		UGa-3870	birch and conifer in undated feature sample

points to a common Middle Maritime Archaic periodization.

Area 3 Conclusions

The Area 3 features, especially 1 and 3, bear at least a superficial resemblance to Maritime Archaic mortuary features. Burials at the Rattlers Bight cemetery (Fitzhugh 1976a:123-125, Fitzhugh 1978a:85, Fitzhugh 2006) consisted of red ocher-lined pits, 0.75-1 m in diameter, that were generally covered by flat slab rocks and layers of sand and rock fill. A similar pattern was documented at the Port au Choix cemetery

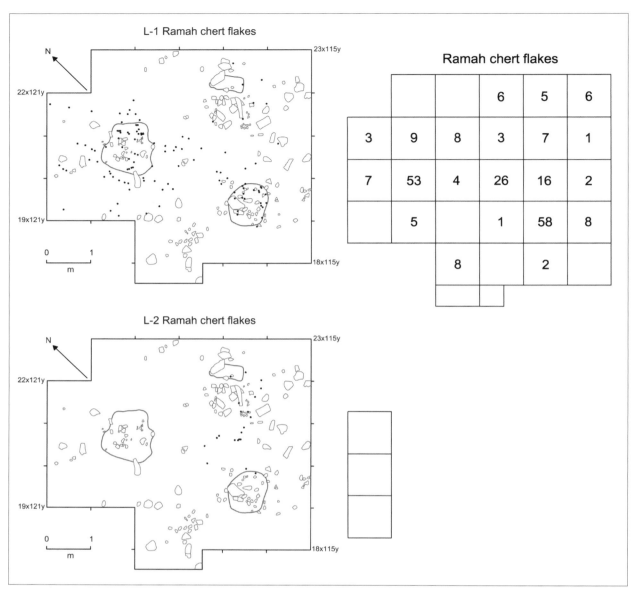

87/ Area 3: distribution of Ramah chert flakes. (a) Level 1. (b) Level 2. (c) Total.

(Tuck 1976:12-13). However, the initial suspicion that the features discovered at Area 3 might be burials could not be confirmed. Extreme post-occupation podzolization processes marked by extensive translocation of iron and humic acids eliminated any possibility of using variation in soil colour to identify sub-surface pits. On the other hand, the clustered distribution of rocks, flakes and a small number of tools beneath the surface of features 1, 2 and 3 indicates deliberate and focused sub-surface deposition. An initial alternative interpretation of the features was that they could be an expression of mortuary ceremonialism without interment: "cenotaphs" for comrades lost at sea without recovery of their bodies (Hood 1981:138).

But accumulating knowledge of the northern Maritime Archaic indicates the culture was marked by such a varied array of ritual expression in material culture that non-mortuary practices should also be considered. For example, red ocher deposits are often associated with hearths, either as flecks adjacent to the features or as distinct deposits within hearth pits. This hearth association may be related to processing

CHAPTER 7

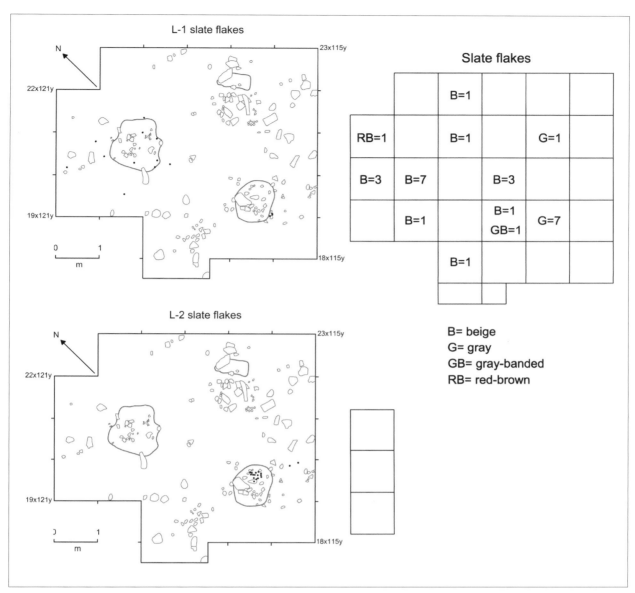

L-1 slate flakes

Slate flakes

	B=1			
RB=1	B=1		G=1	
B=3	B=7		B=3	
	B=1		B=1 GB=1	G=7
	B=1			

B= beige
G= gray
GB= gray-banded
RB= red-brown

L-2 slate flakes

88/ Area 3: distribution of slate flakes. (a) Level 1. (b) Level 2. (c) Total.

hematite by heat alteration and/or it may connect ocher with transformation symbolism (cooking, thermal alteration). Traces of combustion in the form of charcoal were found at all the Area 3 features. The charcoal layer overlying Feature 1 may post-date the feature, but there was also scattered charcoal within and below the red ocher deposit. At Feature 2, a pocket of charcoal occurred within the red ocher deposit, while at Feature 3 charcoal was concentrated beneath the red ocher and above a concentration of small cobbles and quartz chunks. Although the Area 3 features are clearly not conventional hearths, their meaning should be considered in terms of how their constitutive elements might signal metaphorical relations with the domestic features. A more systematic documentation of red ocher's relationship with hearths of different form/function would provide a better context for understanding the varied associations of the material.

One of the interesting aspects of the features is their spatial patterning, which combines an alternating or oppositional sequencing of forms with a possible directional orientation. The two features with thick

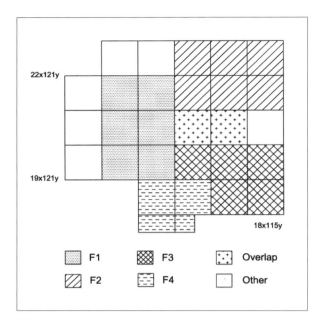

89/ Area 3: quadrat groupings used in the analyses.

F1 F3 Overlap
F2 F4 Other

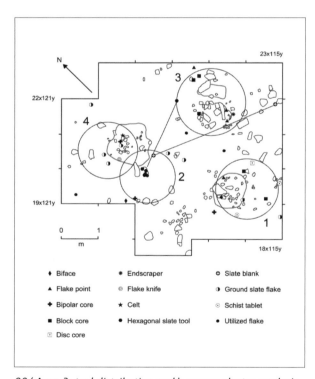

90/ Area 3: tool distribution and k-means cluster analysis.

◆ Biface   ✳ Endscraper   ◉ Slate blank
▲ Flake point   ◎ Flake knife   ◑ Ground slate flake
✚ Bipolar core   ★ Celt   ⊙ Schist tablet
■ Block core   ● Hexagonal slate tool • Utilized flake
▫ Disc core

oval deposits of red ocher (Features 1 and 3) lie opposite each other along an axis that is almost north-
south. The other two features, which either lack red
ocher (Feature 4) or contain only a modest amount
(Feature 2), lie opposite each other along an east-west

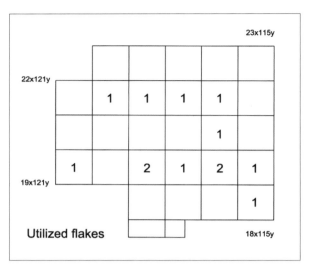

Utilized flakes

91/ Area 3: distribution of utilized flakes.

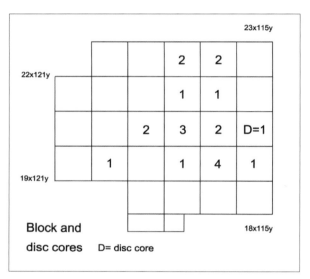

Block and
disc cores   D= disc core

92/ Area 3: distribution of block cores.

axis. This may be merely coincidental and we have no
means of ascertaining contemporaneity between the
features other than a couple of refits possibly connecting Features 1 and 2. Nonetheless, the nearly equidistant spacing of the features relative to each other suggests deliberate placement. The only patterning in lithic materials consonant with this spatial arrangement is
that the major red ocher features (1 and 3) tend to be
more strongly associated with Ramah chert and slate.
Understanding these features and their contextual
relationships will require comparative data from other
Maritime Archaic sites.

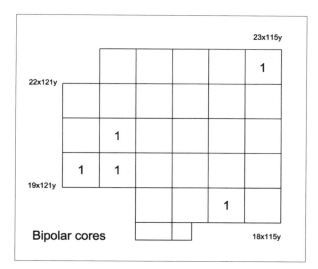

93/ Area 3: distribution of bipolar cores.

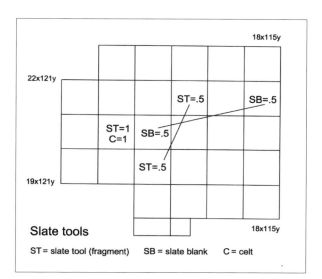

94/ Area 3: distribution of slate tools.

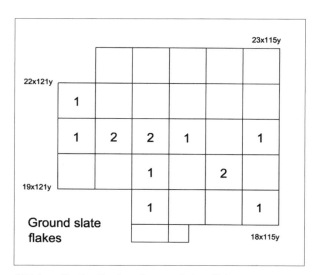

95/ Area 3: distribution of ground slate flakes.

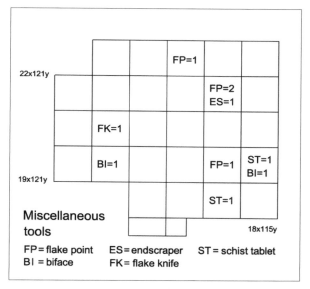

96/ Area 3: distribution of other tool classes.

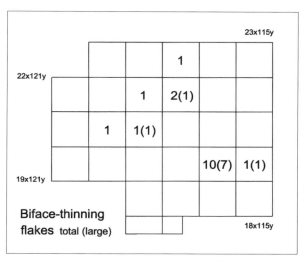

97/ Area 3: distribution of Ramah chert biface-thinning flakes.

98/ Nukasusutok-5: stemmed bifacial points. a: Area 1 surface; b: Area 2A; c: Area 2C1.

CHAPTER 8

Nukasusutok-5: Material Culture

8

The preceding chapters outlined the spatial patterning at Nukasusutok-5 and made general references to the material culture insofar as it was relevant to the spatial patterning. The function of this chapter is to present a descriptive overview of the assemblages from each subarea. Each assemblage is broken down by traditional implement classes and the formal variation in these classes is summarized. A systematic consideration of technological organization at the site is presented in Chapter 9.

DEFINITIONS

For the most part, the categories of lithic implements used here follow the system developed by the Smithsonian Institution during the 1970s. There are deviations, of course, and some categories need more precise definition. Consequently, a series of clarifications is presented prior to describing the assemblages.

Bifacial Points and Flake Points

A bifacial point is retouched over most of its dorsal and ventral surfaces; it may be made on a flake or from a bifacial preform. A flake point is made on a flake and has retouch limited to its margins, either bifacial, unifacial or on alternating edges.

Bifaces and Biface Preforms

Biface denotes implements with bifacial retouch, either a generic form that does not suggest a particular end product or an implement fragment that is not further

identifiable. Biface preform denotes bifacially retouched implements that are assumed to represent the penultimate reduction stage for a specific implement class.

Endscrapers, Flake Knives and Utilized Flakes

Endscrapers are small implements, generally trapezoid or triangular in form, with clearly defined abrupt angle retouch at one end and varying degrees of retouch on their lateral edges. Flake knives are flakes with fairly distinct, continuous and moderate-to-abrupt retouch along a lateral edge; this form might also be termed a backed knife or flake. The term does not exclude a scraper function. Utilized flakes bear traces of intentional retouch or use wear that is less distinct, generally discontinuous and usually, though not always, shallow angled.

Bipolar Cores

This term replaces the problematic *pièce esquillée*. The latter seems to have been introduced into Labrador archaeology by McGhee and Tuck (1975); a contemporary paper (Fitzhugh 1975:122) refers to them as "quartz nuclei or wedges." There has been a long debate in the lithic technology literature regarding bipolar cores and *pièce esquillée;* since these implements constitute such a large part of Early/Middle Maritime Archaic assemblages the main points of the discussion will be summarized here. The heart of the debate is whether *pièce esquillée* are

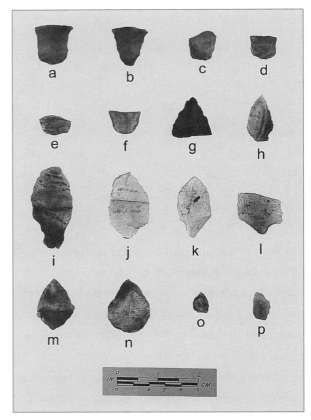

99/ Nukasusutok-5: bifacial points and bifaces. a: stemmed point, Area 2A; b: stemmed point, Area 2B; c: side-notched biface, Area 2A; d: bipoint preform, Area 2C2; e: bipoint, Area 2A; f: biface, Area 2B.

100/ Nukasusutok-5: biface fragments and flake points. a-f: biface stems, all Area 2A; g: biface tip, Area 1; h-p: flake points, all Area 2A.

tools or exhausted bipolar cores. MacDonald's (1968:88) discussion of Paleoindian lithics regards them as tools for wedging or slotting bone, antler or wood. LeBlanc (1992) provides evidence suggesting this may be the case in some contexts. But most commentators have either regarded *pièce esquillée* as bipolar cores or have tried to clarify the distinctions between the two (e.g., Flenniken 1981; Hayden 1980; Kuijt et al. 1995; Lothrop and Gramly 1982; Shott 1989). When cryptocrystalline materials are involved the bipolar technique is seen as a method for reducing small nodules that cannot be handled by direct percussion. In the case of vein quartz, however, the non-isotropic structure and resultant blocky fracture renders attempts at controlled flaking by direct percussion difficult. Consequently, the use of vein quartz is frequently associated with bipolar reduction techniques aimed at producing large quantities of deb-

itage (e.g., Callahan 1987; Callahan et al. 1992; Flenniken 1981; Knutsson 1998). Some of this debitage is selected for further bipolar reduction. A variety of flakes derived from this process can be used expediently for simple processing tasks or specific size/shape variants might be selected for hafting, along the lines of Flenniken's (1981:60-96) discussion of quartz "microliths" hafted in wooden handles and used for processing fish. At any stage in the reduction process bipolar cores could be recycled for use as wedges, scrapers, etc.

The term bipolar core is used here since most of the evidence from Nukasusutok-5 points in the direction of such a reduction system for quartz. It should be noted, however, that Ramah and Mugford cherts sometimes were subjected to bipolar percussion to reduce small fragments, although a wedging function cannot be disregarded.

Block Cores

The term block core is adapted from Hayden et al. (1996) to denote unmodified or partially modified pieces of vein quartz. They are grouped into shape categories, of which tabular blocks and water-rolled cobbles are the best defined. The distinction between quartz core fragments and large flakes is ambiguous; a detailed analysis of the quartz reduction system would be necessary to provide a more nuanced classification.

Ground Slate Flakes and Ground Slate Tool Fragments

Ground slate flakes are pieces of debitage bearing traces of grinding but without identifiable elements of tool edges or surfaces. Ground slate tool fragments exhibit features more clearly indicative of removal from specific tools, such as spalls from slate point lateral edges or adze bits, or lateral edges of an unclassifiable tool.

Slate Plates and Blanks

Slate plates are the unmodified or slightly retouched raw materials used for slate tool production. Slate blanks are moderately retouched items that lack sufficient formal characteristics to be considered preforms for specific tools.

AREA 1

Bifacial Points

Five bifacial points were found in Area 1, of which four are from the Smithsonian surface collection. Two specimens are whole points while three are distal fragments. Both complete points are fabricated from Ramah chert. One is rather long (L=143.1 mm, W=38.4, TH=10.8), made on a large flake, with complete bifacial retouch proximally and distally, but with medial retouch limited to the margins on its ventral side (Figure 98:a). It has rounded shoulders and a slightly contracting stem with a convex base. The sec-

ond example (illustrated in Fitzhugh 1978: Figure 9n) is about half the length of the former and also has a slightly contracting stem with a convex base, but its shoulders are more sharply angled. Of the three distal fragments, two are of Ramah chert and one of black chert (Figure 100:g); only the latter specimen was acquired from the excavation.

Flake Points

All four flake points were surface collected and are made of Ramah chert. Two proximal fragments have slightly tapered stems (one is illustrated in Fitzhugh 1976: Figure 9s) and both are retouched bifacially along their margins. The third specimen is a tip fragment. A very small flake point can be considered a micropoint (illustrated in Fitzhugh 1976: Figure 9q); it has a short stem and is retouched on alternate sides above its shoulders and unifacially on the stem.

Bifaces

Two items are classed as bifaces. One is a medial fragment of black chert while the other is a bifacially worked piece of black slate (Figure 102:f); the latter is from the excavation.

Endscrapers

All three endscrapers were surface collected. One is made of gray Mugford chert, the other two of greenish-yellow Mugford chert. In plan they are trapezoid and each has a differently shaped working edge: concave, straight and convex. The working edge of one specimen originally may have been oriented diagonally. Two specimens exhibit small spurs on one distal corner, in both cases formed by a tiny notch placed on the lateral margin just below the corner. The straight-edged specimen is illustrated by Fitzhugh (1976: Figure 9r).

Flake Knives

The three examples of flake knives from the surface collection are all made from black chert.

Utilized Flakes

Area 1 has a total of 22 utilized flakes, of which 18 were surface collected and four excavated. All but one are made of Ramah chert; the exception is made of black chert.

Bipolar Cores

A single quartz bipolar core was found at Area 1.

Block Cores

Three quartz block cores were recovered from the excavation. One of these is an unmodified squarish block, the second is a split tablet, while the third is a split discoid.

AREA 2A

Bifacial Points

A total of 13 bifacial points or fragments thereof was recovered from Area 2A. Of these, 11 are classified as stemmed points, of which 10 are made of Ramah chert, one of quartz. The single whole example (Figure 98:b) is made of Ramah chert and is completely bifacially flaked, with a slightly contracting stem and a convex base that bears a remnant striking platform (L = 75.6 mm, W =30.5, TH =8.1). An almost identical example was found at Area 2C (Figure 98:c). The quartz specimen (Figure 99:a) lacks most of its stem and exhibits angled rather than indented shoulders, one of which is unifacially retouched while the other is roughly fractured perpendicularly. The remaining nine examples are all proximal stem fragments, perhaps discarded during the rehafting process. Four stem form variants might be identified: large, tongue-shaped with a thinned convex base (one specimen, Figure 100:a); small, almost straight-sided with a straight or slightly convex thinned base (two specimens, Figure 100:c, d); contracting sides with a convex or near-straight base (three specimens, Figure 100:e, f); contracting sides with a pointed base bearing a remnant striking platform (three specimens, Figure 100:b).

Of the remaining two bifacial points, one is a nearly complete side-notched biface made of Ramah chert (Figure 99:c). It has few retouch flakes and one lateral edge is rounded by wear or grinding (L = 54.9 mm, W =21.9, TH =8.3). The other item is a Ramah chert leaf-shaped bipoint (Figure 99:e) with a slightly asymmetric form, abrupt retouch limited to its lateral margins and numerous step fractures (L = 82.1 mm, W =23.0, TH = 9.2). A similar specimen was found in Area 2C (Figure 99:d).

Flake Points

All of the 10 flake points from Area 2A are made from Ramah chert. One is made on a small flake with a striking platform as a base and with abrupt lateral edge retouch (Figure 100:p), while the other has slightly serrated bifacial retouch along its lateral margins and a snapped-off base (Figure 100:o). Five of the others are complete. Two have symmetrically contracting stems with a striking platform at the base (Figure 100:i, j), while two more have asymmetrical stems (Figure 100:h, k). Metrics: $\bar{x}L$ = 39.8 mm, r = 29.9-52.2; $\bar{x}W$ = 22.7 mm, r = 16.4-26.1; $\bar{x}TH$ = 3.8, r =2.7-4.8.

One of the three nearly complete specimens has a snapped-off stem (Figure 100:m), another lacks a stem but has part of a bulb of percussion at its base (Figure 100:n), while a third has a base and lateral edges constituted by snaps and a retouched tip. A proximal fragment has a short asymmetrical stem formed by retouch around a basal striking platform (Figure 100:l). Marginal retouch patterns vary across the specimens; several have alternating retouch, some bifacial, others unifacial. Two tiny specimens measuring under 20 mm in length can be considered micropoints.

Biface Preforms

All six of the implements classed as biface preforms are made of Ramah chert. One is whole (L = 61.2 mm, W = 42.1, W = 9.3), another nearly complete and there

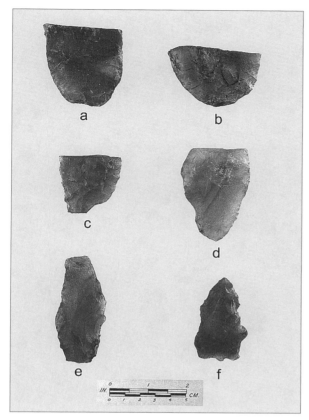

101/ Nukasusutok-5: bifaces and preforms. a: biface, Area 2A; b-d: bifaces, Area 2C; e-f: point preforms, Area 2A.

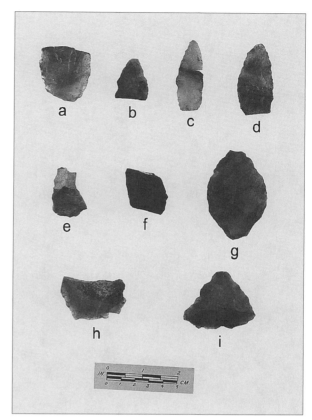

102/ Nukasusutok-5: bifaces and preforms. a: biface, Area 2A; b-c: preforms, Area 2C; d-e: preforms, Area 2A; f: biface fragment, Area 1; g: preform, Area 2A; h: biface, Area 3; i: biface, Area 2C.

are two distal and two proximal fragments. Five of the six are of similar form and dimensions (Figure 101:e, f; Figure 102:a, d, e), representing bifaces ranging from 60-80 mm in length and 25-35 mm in width, with convex bases. They tend to be roughly flaked; one exhibits numerous step fractures and another is only retouched on the margins of its ventral surface. One is thermally altered (Figure 102:e). All appear to be projectile point preforms. The remaining specimen is an oval flake with retouch mostly limited to its margins; a proto-stem is formed by slight notching on alternate sides (Figure 102:g).

Bifaces

Of the 16 bifaces, one is made of quartz while the rest are made of Ramah chert. The quartz implement has a "hand-axe"-like form (Figure 110:a) with alternate edge flaking (L = 120.9 mm, W = 66.8, TH = 21.6). Eight of

the Ramah chert specimens are distal portions of projectile points, two of which exhibit impact fractures. Six items are lateral or proximal edge fragments. The last example is the base of a large asymmetric biface of Ramah chert (Figure 101:a). Made on a large flake, the dorsal surface has large, broad flake scars removed over its entire surface while the ventral retouch is limited to the margins (W = 51.9 mm, TH = 10.0).

Endscrapers

The Area 2A collection includes 16 endscrapers or fragments thereof, of which 11 are made of black chert, four of gray Mugford chert and one of patinated Mugford chert. Of the nine reasonably complete specimens (Figure 103:a-d, f, g, j), seven are trapezoid in form, two triangular. There was a consistent selection of flakes in the 5-7 mm thickness range. Summary statistics are as follows:

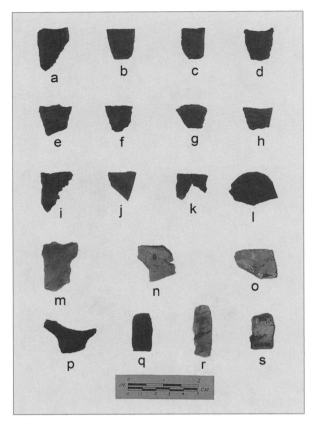

103/ Nukasusutok-5: endscrapers, flake knives, gravers and linear flakes. a-d, f-g, i-l, n: endscrapers, Area 2A; e, m: endscrapers Area 2C; h: endscraper, Area 2B; o: flake knife/scraper, Area 2A; p: graver (?), Area 2A; q-s: linear flakes, Area 2A.

104/ Nukasusutok-5: stemmed flakes and flake knives. a-c: stemmed flakes, Area 2A; d: stemmed flake/flake knife, Area 2C; e-i: flake knives, Area 2A.

Length:	r = 17.9-31.4 mm,	x̄ = 22.8,	sd = 4.3
Width:	r = 16.7-31.8 mm,	x̄ = 22.2,	sd = 4.3
Thickness:	r = 3.2-7.0 mm,	x̄ = 5.5,	sd = 1.4

Working edge shape is relatively straight in five cases, convex in one, concave in one and concavo-convex in two. Edge angles range between 40-65°. The amount of retouch on the lateral margins varies considerably. One example exhibits slight spurring on both its distal corners due to lateral edge notching just below the corners (Figure 103:d) while a second has spurring on one distal corner as a result of similar lateral edge notching (Figure 103:f). The two triangular forms (Figure 103:a, i) are very close in size and both have concavo-convex working edges. One specimen has a slight spur on its right distal corner (Figure 103:i), while the other has a short, straight, retouched

edge with considerable use damage on its right distal corner (Figure 103:a). Two specimens exhibit other forms. One is made on a thin flake and has a relatively long convex working edge terminated by a small notch at one end (Figure 103:l) while the other is a more irregular fragment with a fairly straight working edge (Figure 103:n). The remaining items are lateral and distal edge fragments.

Flake Knives

Of the seven flake knives, four are made of Ramah chert, two of quartz and one of black chert. Three of the Ramah chert specimens are whole or near complete (Figure 104:f-h). They are made on flakes with lengths in the 42-51 mm range and all have convex edges with edge angles ranging from 50-70°. One Ramah chert specimen and the black chert example

CHAPTER 8

105/ Nukasusutok-5: bipolar cores and disc core. a-d, f-h: bipolar cores, Area 2A; e: bipolar core, Area 2C; i: block core with bipolar percussion, Area 2A; j: disc core, Area 2C.

(Figure 104:i) are fragments. Of the two quartz implements, one has fine retouch along a straight edge and ventral step fractures on one corner (Figure 103:o), such that it is unclear whether it should be classed as a flake knife or a scraper. The other quartz specimen is uncertain. An eighth flake knife of Ramah chert is illustrated in Figure 104:e. It is from the northern end of Area 2A, but was eliminated from the analysis because of uncertain provenience.

Utilized Flakes

Of the 97 utilized flakes, 88 (90.7 %) are made of Ramah chert, five (5.2 %) of quartz, three (3.1 %) of black chert and one (1.0 %) of gray Mugford chert.

Bipolar Cores

Area 2A has a total of 57 bipolar cores. Some examples are illustrated in Figure 105:a-c, f-h. Given this relative-

ly large sample size, a detailed attribute analysis was conducted on 56 specimens (one was missing at the time of analysis) to determine if the material could reveal underlying patterning. The approach was modeled after Lothrop and Gramly (1982). Somewhat simplified, the main variables considered were:

1) raw material
2) number of axes of percussion (one, two, indeterminate)
3) length of each axis of percussion
4) thickness
5) edge surfaces (as seen laterally): straight, convex, concave, irregular, flat platform, indeterminate
6) edge shape (as seen vertically, i.e., from above the platform): straight, bowed, wavy, irregular, indeterminate
7) edge damage (combinations thereof): crushing, sharp, faceted, step fractured

Figure 106 provides a graphic depiction of the variables. A major problem in recording and evaluating the results is the absence of any positional criterion (such as proximal/distal) to distinguish consistently between the first and second axes of percussion. Another difficulty is the fragmentary state of many specimens, which prevents complete measurements or hinders the comparison of edge characteristics on opposite sides of an implement. The following summary of the results is based on data derived from an arbitrarily defined first axis and from specimens for which metric variables could be considered as complete measurements. Edge A is the first edge of the axis, Edge B is the opposite edge.

Raw Materials: quartz = 34 (60.7%), Ramah chert = 18 (32.1%), gray Mugford chert = 2 (3.6%), black chert = 2 (3.6%).

Number of Axes of Percussion: 1 = 28 (50.0%), 2 = 18 (32.1%), indeterminate = 10 (17.9).

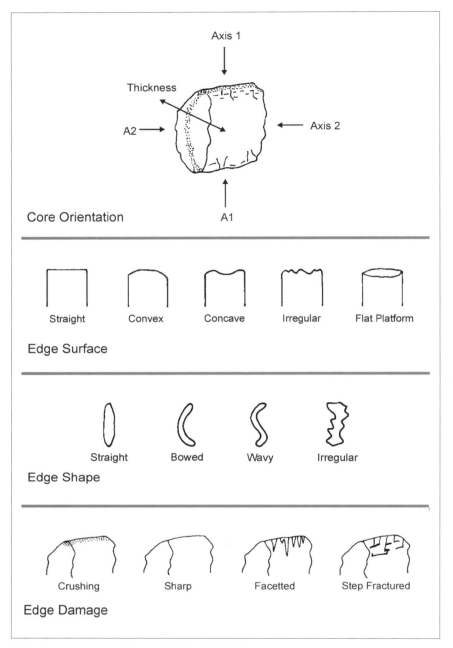

106/ Bipolar core analysis variables and attributes.

Axis 1 Length: n = 32, r = 15.7-38.6 mm, x̄ = 27.21, sd = 5.82

Axis 2 Length: n = 27, r = 9.4-47.2 mm, x̄ = 23.97, sd = 9.08

Thickness: n=47, r = 3.9-23.4 mm, x̄ = 10.93, sd = 4.60

Axis 1, Edge A Surface: straight = 16 (28.6%), convex = 25 (44.6%), concave = 8 (14.3%), irregular = 3 (5.4%), flat platform = 2 (3.6%), indeterminate = 2 (3.6%)

Axis 1, Edge A Shape: straight= 8 (14.3%), bowed = 18 (32.1%), wavy = 23 (41.1%), irregular = 1 (1.8%), indeterminate= 6 (10.7%)

Axis 1, Edge A Damage: (instances of each type in sample; specimens can have combinations of damage types); crushing = 41 (73.2%), sharp = 6 (10.7%), faceted= 27 (48.2%), step fractured = 20 (35.7%)

Axis 1, Edge B (opposite) Surface: straight = 7 (12.5 %), convex = 7 (12.5 %), concave = 3 (5.4%), irregular= 4 (7.1%), flat platform= 1 (1.8%)

Axis 1, Edge B Shape: straight = 7 (12.5 %), bowed = 4 (7.1%), wavy= (9 (16.1%), irregular = 1 (1.8%)

Axis 1, Edge B Damage: (instances of each type in sample; specimens can have combinations of damage types); crushing = 23 (41.1%), sharp = 6 (18.8%), faceted = 12 (37.5%), step fractured = 9 (28.1%)

Cross-tabulations were run between the nominal variables surface, shape and damage for Axis 1, Edge A (the best sample size) to investigate attribute combinations. Only the combination of edge surface and edge shape exhibited interesting patterning, with a slight tendency (when expected values were calculated) for convex edge surfaces to be associated with wavy edge shapes.

Bivariate metric analysis provides more interesting results. Figure 107 is a scatter diagram of Axis 1 length against thickness, coded for different raw material types. There is a slight tendency for three groups in the plot: (1) specimens <20 mm long and <8 mm thick, (2) those from 21-34 mm in length and between 6-14 mm thick, and (3) those >30 mm long and >12 mm thick. Ramah chert specimens cluster in the shorter/thinner area of the plot

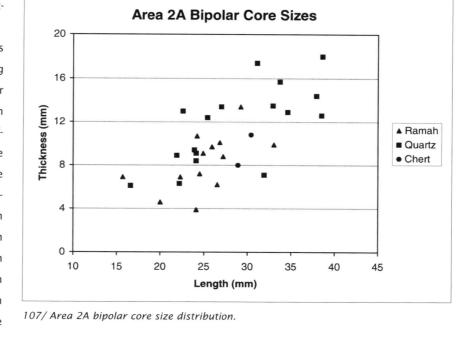

107/ Area 2A bipolar core size distribution.

while quartz is spread out more broadly, although with a clear break between "medium" and "large" groups. The Mugford and black chert specimens lie in the middle. The contrasts between quartz and Ramah chert likely indicate differences in the sizes of the raw materials when bipolar reduction commenced: quartz reduction began with block cores and large flakes while Ramah chert bipolar cores are probably the result of recycling broken tool fragments.

By way of comparison, Flenniken (1981:48) divides his Northwest Coast quartz bipolar cores into three size categories, although he provides no histogram or scatter plot data on the shape of the distributions. Lothrop and Gramly's (1982:16) mostly chert *pièces esquillées* exhibit a unimodal size distribution suggestive of a continuous reduction process. Although the non-unimodal size distribution at Area 2A may simply be an artifact of sample size or reflect stages of core exhaustion (MacDonald 1968:86), it could also be related to purposeful selection of core sizes for the production of different types of flakes. For example, Flenniken (1981:43-46) identifies what he terms "microliths" as deliberate products of the bipolar reduction of quartz. This category may be

more a reflection of the investigator's expectations and sorting procedures than of prehistoric intentionality, but it is clear that careful bipolar reduction can produce at least some fairly regular columnar or linear flakes, although they will likely constitute a small proportion of the total debitage. The quartz debitage from Area 2A (and the other subareas) contains little that resembles deliberately produced linear or columnar flakes. Consequently, it is more likely that discontinuities in the bipolar core size distribution are the result of selectivity in the size of shatter chosen for further bipolar reduction.

It is difficult, however, to see the smallest bipolar core size group as the result of reduction aimed at producing flakes since flakes produced from these cores would be extremely small and cores under 20-25 mm are difficult to hold between the fingers without risking injury during bipolar percussion. If any of the bipolar cores were used for splitting/wedging functions it was perhaps these.

Block Cores

Area 2A produced a total of 37 quartz block cores, which can be divided into five sub-groups. The first

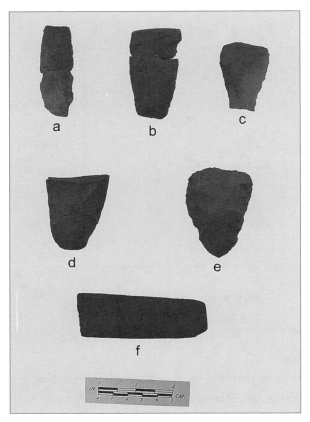

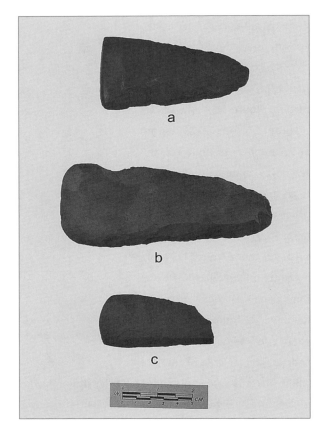

108/ Nukasusutok-5: slate and schist tools. a: ground slate point, Area 2A; b: flake adze, Area 2A; c: reworked flake adze, Area 2A; d: slate blank, Area 2A; e: celt/adze blank, Area 2A; f: schist whetstone, Area 2A.

109/ Nukasusutok-5: ground slate tools. a: adze, Area 2A; b-c: celts, Area 2C.

group consists of 11 tabular or sub-tabular cores, unmodified except for one or two flakes removed (e.g., Figure 110:b). Summary statistics are as follows:

Length: r = 58.3-121.4 mm, $\bar{x}$ = 82.1,   sd = 20.1

Width: r = 41.4-70.3 mm, $\bar{x}$ = 56.6,   sd = 11.6

Thickness: r = 15.7-46.7mm, $\bar{x}$ = 31.7,   sd = 9.06

The second group consists of five quartz beach cobbles marked by various degrees of water-rolling. Four are battered and two of these were split in half. The remaining specimen has only a single flake removed. Their size range is slightly smaller than for tabular cores. Summary statistics are as follows:

Length: r = 29.8-63.5 mm, $\bar{x}$ = 52.2,   sd = 13.4

Width: r = 25.1-52.6 mm, $\bar{x}$ = 43.1,   sd = 12.1

Thickness: r = 22.7-35.2 mm, $\bar{x}$ = 30.3,   sd= 5.8

The third group consists of 13 cores with traces of bipolar percussion. Some of these could be called bipolar cores, but they are distinguished from the latter because of their size and their place at the initial phase of the reduction process. Figure 110:d illustrates an example with crushing on its long sides and on a flat platform at one end; the opposite end has large step fractures. The core is broken across its width, but there was clearly an attempt to split it lengthwise using bipolar percussion. Summary statistics are as follows:

Length: r= 53.1-122.8 mm, $\bar{x}$= 72.4,   sd= 18.9

Width: r= 35.2-70.9 mm, $\bar{x}$= 51.5,   sd= 10.2

Thickness: r= 25.5-43.7 mm, $\bar{x}$= 33.0,   sd= 6.1

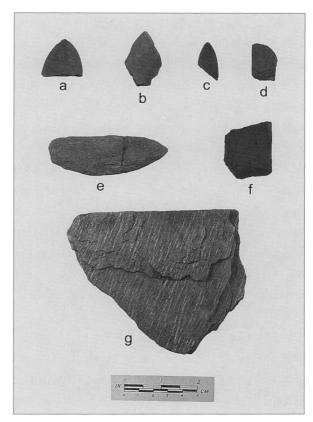

110/ Nukasusutok-5: quartz biface and cores. a: biface, Area 2A; b: tabular block core, Area 2A; c: core/hammerstone, Area 3; d: block core with bipolar percussion, Area 2A.

111/ Nukasusutok-5: slate and schist implements. a-c: ground slate point tips, Area 2A; d: ground slate tool fragment (point stem?), Area 2A; e: schist tablet, Area 3; f: ground slate tool fragment, Area 2A; g: schist tablet, Area 3.

The fourth group consists of two specimens, one discoid the other lenticular in form. The former has three or four flakes removed while it is uncertain whether the latter has been culturally modified. Finally, the fifth group consists of 6 cores with irregular shapes and the following summary statistics:

Length: r = 50.2-82.2 mm, x̄ = 66.2, sd = 13.2
Width: r = 40.2-65.9 mm, x̄ = 52.1, sd = 11.1
Thickness: r = 30.4-48.6 mm, x̄ = 36.6, sd = 6.9

Ground Slate Points

Portions of four ground slate points were found at Area 2A. Three of the four are distal fragments while one is most of a medial portion. Two of the distal fragments have broad flat blades (Figure 111:a-b); one is made of green slate the other of beige slate. The third distal

fragment is narrower with a lenticular cross-section (Figure 111:c) and made of gray slate. The medial specimen is made of green slate and consists of the lower portion of the point's blade and the upper part of its stem (Figure 108:a). Its blade element is very thin and flat (W= 22.6 mm, TH= 3.5); the stem is formed by a slightly rounded constriction.

Ground Slate Adzes

Three examples, all made of green slate, suggest two types of slate adzes. The first (Figure 109:a) is a large triangular form with bifacially retouched margins and a plano-convex cross-section (L= 105.6 mm, W= 53.0, TH= 13.3). Very fine polishing at the bit end extends 40-70 mm back from the working edge. The bit has an edge angle of 60° and exhibits very little evidence of wear. The poll end of the tool has a small surface ground to an angle of 60°; this may be a trace of a second reworked bit or a hafting modification. The second example (Figure 108:b) is a small trapezoid adze made on a flake with a remnant striking platform at its poll end (L = 64.5 mm, W = 33.9, TH = 6.5). The implement has light dorsal retouch on its lateral margins, a bit angle of 35° and polishing limited to within 12-18 mm of the working edge. The third specimen (Figure 108:c) is probably a reworked flake adze similar to the latter type. It consists of a triangular flake with fine abrupt retouch on the distal end, slight retouch on its lateral edges and polishing remnants on one distal corner and one lateral edge. Its maximum width (33 mm) is very similar to that of the previously described flake adze.

Slate Blanks

Three items are classified as slate blanks. One is a triangular celt or adze preform of green slate (Figure 108:e), bifacially flaked over its entire surface, with preliminary grinding of a few facets near the bit end (L = 62.9 mm, W = 42.7, TH = 17.0). The second is a celt or adze preform of gray slate made on a thin slate plate (Figure 112:b). The implement is unifacially retouched on its lateral margins and widest end; two step fractures at the wide end are ground slightly (L = 82.4 mm, W = 49.0, TH = 10.7). The third item is a bifacially flaked fragment of green slate (Figure 112:d).

Slate Plates

Of the nine slate plates or fragments thereof, six are made of green slate, two of red-brown slate and one of beige slate. All but one are thin plates of slate with varying amounts of edge retouch (e.g., Figure 112:a, e, f). The remaining example is a thicker ovoid piece with bifacial retouch on one edge and extensive step fracturing on the opposite edge (Figure 112:c).

Ground Slate Flakes and Tool Fragments

Of the 49 items categorized as ground slate flakes, 24 (49.0 %) are made of gray slate, 16 (32.7 %) of green slate, four (8.2 %) of gray-banded slate, two (4.1 %) of red-brown slate, two (4.1 %) of indeterminate color slate and one (2.0 %) of greenstone. Seven of these specimens are edge-struck flakes from tools; four have medial ridges while three have convex surfaces. Two items are classed as ground slate tool fragments. One is a piece of gray slate with one edge ground perpendicularly and two other edges bifacially flaked (Figure 111:f), apparently a reworked implement fragment. The other is a piece of green slate with rounded lateral edges suggestive of a ground slate point stem (Figure 111:d).

Hammerstones

A single hammerstone was recovered, consisting of a small water-rolled cobble with battering concentrated at one point.

Whetstones

The single whetstone (Figure 108:f) is a thin bar of dense gray schist (L = 87.2 mm, W = 30.7, TH = 5.2). The working edge runs the length of one side of the tool, with wear on both faces but mostly on one. The opposite lateral edge is ground perpendicularly. Several linear incisions made by a pointed tool are visible on one face of the implement as well as on the perpendicular non-working edge. These do not seem to constitute decoration.

Schist Tablets and Ground Schist Fragments

Three schist tablets and two fragments of ground schist were recovered. The three tablets are all made of chlorite schist. Two (Figure 113:a, b) are rectangular with somewhat battered lateral edges suggestive of deliberate shaping (L = 117.4 mm, 100.1 mm; W = 67.1, 56.4; TH = 31.8, 21.2). Both have one smoothed surface, possibly from grinding. The third tablet (Figure 113:d) is a knife-shaped bar with no obvious modification (L = 165.0 mm, W = 44.6, TH = 17.2), so it is uncertain whether the implement is a cultural affordance.

Graver (?)

An unusual tool made of black chert may be a graver (Figure 103:p). It resembles an endscraper with over-size spurs extending from each distal corner (L= 37.4 mm, W= 18.4, TH= 4.9). The left distal spur is shaped like a screwdriver tip while the right spur tapers to a perforator-like point. The concave distal edge exhibits scraper-like wear traces and parts of both spurs also exhibit use-wear. Another possibility is that the specimen is an effigy.

Stemmed Flakes

Three Ramah chert implements are classified as stemmed flakes because they exhibit more systematic retouch than utilized flakes and a tendency towards stem definition, but they do not resemble flake points. One is a roughly triangular flake (L= 55.7 mm, W= 39.2, TH= 4.3) with a short stem formed by alternating unifacial retouch on a slightly indented left shoulder and more sharply defined right shoulder (Figure 104:a). The lateral margins of the "blade" have fine bifacial retouch limited to the margins. The second (Figure 104:b) is a proximal fragment with a stem formed by a single dorsal flake removal on each side; the lateral edge margins above the stem have fine bifacial retouch. The third specimen (Figure 104:c) is a triangular flake with dorsal retouch distally and on one lateral edge (L= 36.0 mm, W= 41.2, TH= 3.5).

Linear Flakes

Two items are classified as linear flakes. One is made of Ramah chert (Figure 103:r) and has a short blade-like form with two medial "arrises," dorsal polishing on its distal end and dorsal utilization wear on its lateral margin (L= 38.7 mm, W= 14.0, TH= 3.4). This specimen may be a product of columnar fracturing during bipolar reduction. The other example is a medial fragment of gray Mugford chert (Figure 103:q); one lateral edge is retouched ventrally along its entire length, the other is retouched dorsally along half its length (L= 28.4 mm, W= 14.6, TH= 2.3). A third linear flake fragment of Ramah chert is illustrated (Figure 103:s), but it was dropped from the analysis because of uncertain provenience.

AREA 2B

Bifacial Points

The single bifacial point from Area 2B is a proximal fragment made of quartz (Figure 99:b). The specimen is crudely flaked bifacially and has a contracting stem. One lateral edge has an angled rather than indented shoulder while the other bears only a slight indentation indicative of a tentative shoulder (W= 26.4 mm, TH= 13.5).

Flake Points

The single Ramah chert flake point is an uncertain specimen bearing limited unifacial retouch, some of which seems designed to taper the flake near its tip and even out one lateral margin.

Bifaces

The only biface (Figure 99:f) is the distal or proximal fragment of a thin, very finely flaked, asymmetric biface of Ramah chert (W = 45.3 mm, TH = 7.6). The quality of flaking suggests the implement is a finished product ("bifacial knife"), but it might be a preform for a lanceolate bipoint such as those illustrated in Figure 99:d, e. Comparison of the biface with the latter two points suggests a reduction process in which the symmetric lateral edge was "keeled" against the hand while the asymmetric edge was reduced towards the bipoint form. This technique might have minimized the risk of breakage when producing the narrow lanceolate forms.

Endscrapers

The single endscraper (Figure 103:h), made of gray Mugford chert, is trapezoid with a slightly concave distal edge and a unifacially retouched lateral edge (L= 15.1 mm, W= 21.1, TH=9.9, edge angle= 60˚).

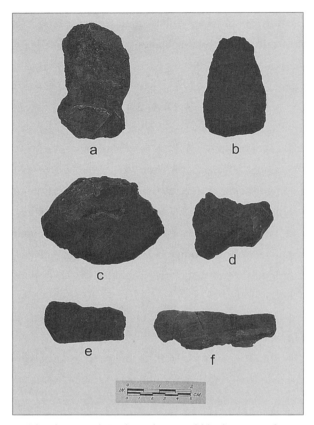

112/ Nukasusutok-5: slate plates and blanks. a, c, e-f: plates, Area 2A; b, d: blanks, Area 2A.

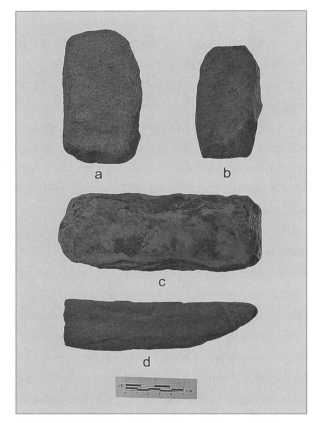

113/ Nukasusutok-5: schist tablets. a-b, d: Area 2A; c: Area 2C.

Flake Knives

Both examples are fragmentary and made of Ramah chert.

Utilized Flakes

Of the 21 utilized flakes, 17 (71.4 %) are made of Ramah chert, four (19.0 %) of black chert, one (4.8 %) of slate and one (4.8 %) of quartz.

Bipolar Cores

Of the six bipolar cores, five are made of quartz, one of Ramah chert. Most of these are fragmentary, so no summary metrics can be presented.

Block Cores

Two quartz block cores were recovered. One is a sub-tabular specimen, unused except for the possible removal of two flakes, the other is unused and prism-

shaped (L= 78.2, 115.8 mm, W= 56.0, 90.6, TH= 39.0, 70.3).

Ground Slate Flakes and Tool Fragments

Of the five ground slate flakes, four are made of green slate and one of gray slate. A sixth flake, made of green slate, is an edge fragment from a celt or adze.

Grindstones (?)

Two conjoining fragments of a sandstone plate were found at Area 2B. It is uncertain whether this was a cultural affordance, but it could have served as a grindstone for slate tools.

Bone Pendants

A small fragment of a bone pendant was recovered from the fine-sieved charcoal sample taken at hearth 11, dated 6040±90 B.P.. Ca. 9 mm in length and 2.4

CHAPTER 8

114/ Nukasusutok-5: fragment of bone pendant, Area 2B.
(Length 9 mm).

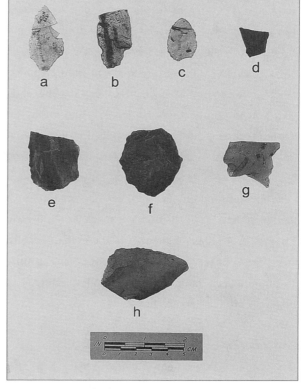

115/ Nukasusutok-5: Area 3 flaked implements. a-c: flake
points; d: endscraper; e: biface preform; f: disc core; g:
biface fragment; h: flake knife.

mm in thickness, the artifact has a gouged hole, flattened and rounded edges, one incised line and two
small notches on one face, and a single incised line on
the other face (Figure 114).

AREA 2C

Bifacial Points

The single bifacial point is from Area 2C1 (Figure 98:c).
Made from Ramah chert, it is nearly complete, finely
flaked, exhibits a contracting stem, rounded shoulders
and has a biconvex cross-section (W= 28.2 mm, TH=
8.5). It is virtually identical to a specimen from Area 2A
(Figure 98:b).

Biface Preforms

The two biface preforms are made of Ramah chert and
are complete. One could perhaps be classed as an

unfinished lanceolate bipoint (Figure 99:d), but here it
is treated as a preform since its asymmetric shape
results from retention of a small portion of unfinished
edge (L= 91.1 mm, W= 28.6, TH= 11.8; biconvex cross-
section). As noted above, it is possible that Figure 99:f-
d-e illustrates a reduction sequence. The other example is made of thermally altered Ramah chert and
exhibits a lanceolate form with a striking platform at
its base (Figure 102:c); it was broken about one third
of the way down from its distal end (L= 48.2 mm, W=
19.1, TH= 7.0; biconvex cross-section). The break
occurred during the final tip-to-base retouch sequence
since the tip is well retouched but the medial and proximal portions are still roughly flaked.

Bifaces

All five biface fragments are made of Ramah chert.
Two large fragments (Figure 101:c, d) are similar in

form: asymmetric with slight stemming or notching and plano-convex cross-sections resulting from extensive retouch on their dorsal surfaces but only marginal retouch on their ventral sides (W = 41.1, 45.5 mm, TH = 10.7, 13.3). Figure 101:d might be a stemmed point preform, but both could conceivably be early stages in the production of bipoints using the asymmetric reduction technique described previously. A third specimen is the proximal fragment of a large biface made on a flake (Figure 101:b), with a remnant striking platform on its proximal end and retouch limited mostly to its lateral edges (W = > 60 mm, TH =10.3). Another implement is the distal end of a large thick biface, possibly a quarry blank (Figure 102:i). The last example is a lateral edge fragment of thermally altered Ramah chert.

Endscrapers

One of the two specimens is made of black chert, the other of Ramah chert. The black chert implement (Figure 103:e) is trapezoid in form, has double concavities on its working edge and abrupt dorsal retouch on its lateral margins (L = 22.4 mm, W = 23.8, TH = 9.0). The Ramah chert specimen (Figure 103:m) is problematic since Maritime Archaic endscrapers are almost never made from this material. The implement has a stem created by unifacial retouch along its lateral margins (dorsally on one edge, ventrally on the other). The distal "ears" produced by the stemming have dorsal retouch and the distal edge itself is broken, with two notch-like flakes removed and the subsequent imposition of slight edge retouch (L = 36.7 mm, W = 31.5, TH = 7.7). Polishing is present on the distal corners.

Utilized Flakes

Of the 31 utilized flakes, 26 (83.9%) are made of Ramah chert, four (12.9%) of quartz and one (3.2%) of black chert.

Bipolar Cores

Only two bipolar cores were found at Area 2C; one is made of quartz, the other of Ramah chert.

Block Cores

Of the 19 block cores, 18 are made of quartz, one of gray quartzite. Of the quartz cores, 11 were tabular in shape. Of these, eight were unused except for minor flaking, four may have been fractured off larger blocks and two have traces of bipolar percussion on their long ends. Four have slightly rounded cortex suggestive of water-rolling. Five cores were prism shaped. Three of the latter are virtually unused while 2 exhibit traces of bipolar percussion. Two cores are simply fragments of blocks. The gray quartzite core is a fragment of a water-rolled cobble split by bipolar percussion. A few flakes removed on one edge might indicate use as an expedient scraper. Summary statistics are as follows:

Length: r = 48.7-97.7 mm, x̄ = 74.9, sd = 15.8
Width: r = 31.9-88.9 mm, x̄ = 56.5, sd = 15.5
Thickness: r = 19.1-70.4 mm, x̄ = 33.5, sd = 12.5

Disc Cores

The single example of a disc core is made of Ramah chert (Figure 105:j). It is a small bifacial disc with sharp edges and no evidence for crushing that might indicate bipolar reduction (L = 40.0 mm, W = 39.6, TH = 27.5).

Ground Slate Celts

Two celts were found at Area 2C, one complete and the other near-complete; both are made of green slate. One is a large sub-triangular specimen (Figure 109:b) with bifacial flaking along its lateral edges and on its poll end (L = 148.3 mm, W = 60.2, TH = 19.7). Polishing is limited to an area 38-48 mm back from the bit edge. The bit has little damage besides some crushing and small flakes removed from near the middle of the working edge. Near the poll end some of the flake facets are polished, presumably hafting-related. Red ocher stains are visible on the celt surface. The second example (Figure 109:c) is a small, presumably sub-triangular, celt with bifacial retouch on both lateral edges, one of which has a thin perpendicularly ground facet (L = >82.0 mm, W = 39.2, TH = 12.4). One face of the tool is mostly polished and flat; the other face is completely polished, but the edge portion has canted grinding that produces a ridge running parallel to the lateral edge.

Ground Slate Celt/Adze

One artifact of greenstone is the proximal (poll) fragment of a celt or adze (Figure 108:d). It is bifacially flaked and the lateral edges have slight perpendicular grinding. The poll edge is slightly ground on one side and one medial flake facet is slightly ground.

Slate Plates

The lone slate plate, of indeterminate slate color (due to weathering), has fine flaking along one edge and an area of possible edge grinding.

Ground Slate Flakes and Tool Fragments

There are 22 ground slate flakes, of which eight (36.4%) are made of green slate, six (27.3%) of beige slate, three (13.6%) of gray slate, three (13.6%) of red-brown slate and two (9.1%) of gray-banded slate. One flake is an edge-struck fragment from a tool.

Hammerstones

The single hammerstone is a small egg-shaped cobble with slight crushing at one end.

Schist Tablets

Two schist tablets were found. One is a large rectangular tablet of chlorite schist (Figure 113:c) with battered edges and one smoothed surface suggestive of use in grinding (L = 171.0 mm, W = 67.7, TH = 27.1). The other is a thin triangular tablet of phyllite schist; it is uncertain whether this was a cultural affordance.

Schist Fragments

Six fragments of schist were collected, of which two display grinding indicative of cultural modification.

Stemmed Flakes

One Ramah chert implement is classified as a stemmed flake (Figure 104:d). Made on a long flake, it has light dorsal retouch on one lateral edge while a slight stem shoulder is formed by ventral retouch (L = 82.9 mm, W = 36.8, TH = 5.3). Perhaps it could also be classified as a flake knife.

Red Ocher Nodules

The vicinity of hearths 14 and 15 produced eight small red ocher nodules, weighing a total of 52 g. Three tiny nodules near hearth 12 weighed 0.4 g.

AREA 3

Flake Points

All three flakes points are made of Ramah chert. One is almost complete with a contracting stem (Figure 115:a); the margins of its lateral edges and stem are retouched unifacially on alternate sides and the blade element is slightly serrated (L = 43.1 mm, W = 22.0, TH = 2.2). Another specimen is a proximal fragment with a stem element formed by a retouched shoulder on one lateral edge and a shallow notch on the opposite edge (Figure 115:b). A striking platform is retained at the base of the stem and the blade margins are retouched on alternate sides (W= 21.4 mm, TH= 2.9). The third example (Figure 115:c) is missing part of its base and has slightly serrated bifacial retouch limited to its margins (L= 28.4 mm, W= 18.7, TH= 3.1).

Biface Preforms

The single example is made of Ramah chert and is a proximal fragment with a convex base (Figure 115:e).

Bifaces

All three biface fragments are made of Ramah chert. Two are edge fragments with deep flake scars, reminiscent of quarry blanks (Figure 102:h, 115:g), while the third is the lateral edge of a smaller biface.

Endscrapers

The single endscraper from Area 3 (Figure 115:d) is made of an unusual extremely fine-grained beige chert, presumably from Cape Mugford. It has a straight distal edge (50° angle) and distinct polishing on its lateral edges (L = 19.0 mm, W = 19.1, TH = 2.8).

Flake Knives

The single flake knife (Figure 115:h) is made of Ramah chert and has two distinct retouch areas, both dorsal; the lateral edge angle is 60° while the proximal edge is 20° (L = 54.8 mm, W = 35.1, TH = 9.2).

Bipolar Cores

A total of five bipolar cores was found at Area 3; two are made of quartz, three of Ramah chert.

Block Cores

Of the 20 quartz cores, seven are tabular in form, six are made from rounded water-rolled cobbles, three are squarish or prism-shaped, two conical, two semi-discoidal and one irregular. Three tabular specimens are unused or exhibit minimal modification; two were probably split with bipolar percussion and two others were fractured. Two of the tabular cores are slightly water-rolled. Of the rounded cobbles, three bear traces of bipolar percussion while a fourth is heavily battered, suggesting use as a hammerstone or resistance to repeated efforts at bipolar reduction (Figure 110:c). One squarish and one conical core show traces of bipolar percussion. Summary statistics are as follows:

Length: r = 38.2-93.9 mm, = 70.8, sd = 12.4
Width: r = 36.9-86.1 mm, = 56.5, sd = 12.2
Thickness: r = 24.0-72.2 mm, = 40.9, sd = 11.2

Disc Cores

The single disc core (Figure 115:f) is a small Ramah chert specimen with bifacial flaking and severe step fractures on both faces (L = 44.7 mm, W = 39.3, TH = 18.8).

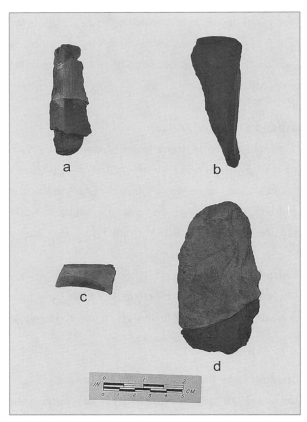

116/ *Nukasusutok-5: Area 3 slate implements. a: ground slate hexagonal shaft; b: celt; c: ground tool fragment; d: blank.*

Ground Slate Celts

The single example is a red-brown slate specimen that was probably sub-triangular in form prior to being broken longitudinally (Figure 116:b). The remaining lateral edge is bifacially flaked. Polishing is concentrated near the bit but also occurs elsewhere on the tool. The poll end has a bevelled ground surface, either a remnant bit or hafting modification (L = 86.2 mm, W = 32.0, TH = 15.7).

Hexagonal Ground Slate Tool Fragment

Figure 116:a illustrates a hexagonal shaft of polished green slate that tapers longitudinally. The tool was broken into several pieces that were spread between Features 1 and 2. Retouch on the ventral surfaces of some fragments indicate the implement was flaked after it was broken. The shape and thickness of the object (W = >26.2 mm, TH = >12.0) suggest it is not a projectile point but possibly the shaft of a more robust tool such as a small gouge.[5]

Slate Blanks

The single slate blank is a conjoined specimen made on a plate of gray slate (Figure 116:d). It is sub-rectangular in form and bifacially retouched along three edges; the fourth edge bears a remnant of the original flat plate edge (L= 99.6 mm, W= 52.2, TH= 8.0).

Ground Slate Flakes and Tool Fragments

Of the 13 ground slate flakes, seven (53.8%) are made of beige slate, four (30.8%) of gray slate and one each (7.7%) of green and red-brown slate. One flake is a tool fragment with a ground, heavily battered bevel (Figure 116:c).

Schist Tablets and Fragments

Two schist tablets were recovered. One is a small knife-shaped bar of chlorite schist (Figure 111:e) that appears worn, although not necessarily by cultural modification (L = 81.9 mm, W= 28.6, TH = 6.7). The other is an unmodified plate of phyllite schist (Figure 111:g); its association with Feature 3 suggests it was a cultural affordance (L = 117.3 mm, W = 101.9, TH = 10.2).

Red Ocher Nodules

Tiny fragments of red ocher were associated with two features. Nearby Feature 2 were nine fragments weighing a total of 3.2 g. Adjacent to Feature 3 were three fragments, weighing 14.2 g.

THE NUKASUSUTOK-5 ASSEMBLAGE IN A COMPARATIVE PERSPECTIVE

As discussed more fully in Chapter 9, significant problems are encountered when comparing Maritime Archaic assemblages. Raised beach sites that have been reoccupied repeatedly, like Nukasusutok-5, have horizontal stratigraphy and potential palimpsest deposits. Consequently, surface collections, test pits and limited excavations that do not define behaviorally relevant units (such as dwelling modules) may produce an unrepresentative material of limited value for inter-assemblage comparisons. Nonetheless, some general observations should be made regarding the position of the Nukasusutok-5 assemblage relative to other material from northern and central Labrador.

Since the radiocarbon dates from Nukasusutok-5 are spread between 6000-5000 B.P. it is hardly surprising that the material shares similarities with both the *Naksak* Complex of northern Labrador (7000-6000 B.P.) and the Sandy Cove Complex (5200-4500 B.P.) of the central coast. Nukasusutok-5 and *Naksak* sites share lanceolate bipoint projectiles, side-notched bifaces, convex-based bifaces, endscrapers, small celts and a high frequency of bipolar cores (cf., Fitzhugh 1978:Figures 6-9). They differ, however, in that Nukasusutok-5 lacks nipple-based points but has a distinct inventory of flake points. Nukasusutok and the Sandy Cove Complex have in common tapered stem points, convex-based bifaces and copious use of quartz reduced by bipolar techniques. They differ in that Nukasusutok has more extensive use of Ramah chert while Sandy Cove lacks endscrapers.

The general stylistic sequence of Maritime Archaic projectile points goes from early triangular and nipple-based types (7500-6000 B.P.) to more sharply shouldered, tapered stem forms (6000-3500 B.P.). Only two projectile points from Nukasusutok-5 are reasonably associated with the 6000 B.P. component. The specimen from near hearth 11 at Area 2B, dated 6040±90, probably has the best context; it is quartz and has a tapered stem angled with the blade rather than clear

---

[5]In contrast, an Early Maritime Archaic gouge from Koliktalik-1 in the Nain area has a relatively cylindrical cross-section (Fitzhugh 1978: Figure 6j) and Late Maritime Archaic gouges have triangular or rectangular cross-sections (Fitzhugh 1978: Figure 5m, Tuck 1976: Plate 33).

shoulders (Figure 99:b). A larger but similar quartz point (Figure 99:a) was associated with the south lobe at Area 2A, which has one radiocarbon date of 5670±175 B.P.. A point from Area 2C1 was found ca. 2 m from hearth 10, dated 6050±80; it is made of Ramah chert and has a tapered stem with rounded shoulders (Figure 98:c). The latter point is virtually identical to one from the southern lobe at Area 2A (Figure 98:b), dated ca. 5600 B.P.. The several stem fragments from the site (Figure 100) provide no information on shoulder form. The rounded shoulder points from Nukasusutok-5 (Figure 98:b, c) are very similar to a point from Karl Oom Island-3 in the Nain area, dated 6080±380 B.P. and 6120±120 B.P. (Fitzhugh 1985:83, 1990:301). Considered as a whole, the Nukasusutok points and stem fragments bear a general resemblance to those from the Gull Arm-1 site in the Nain area, dated 5605±160 B.P. and 3285±80 B.P. (probably multi-component; Fitzhugh 1978:66, 78), as well as slightly later sites in other regions: Okak-2 in Okak Bay (4765±85 B.P., 4905±80 B.P.; Fitzhugh 1978:66, 78) and Sandy Cove-2 at Hamilton Inlet (no radiocarbon dates; Fitzhugh 1972:92, 288).

In conclusion, elements of the lithic assemblages from the various subareas at Nukasusutok-5 resemble those from *Naksak* Complex sites dated ca. 6000 B.P., although there are also similarities with later sites in other regions. Initially, the latter tendencies led Fitzhugh to disregard the ca. 5500 B.P. radiocarbon dates and place Nukasusutok-5 in the 5000-4500 B.P. range, based on "...typological convergence toward Rattlers Bight point styles and greater use of Ramah chert at the expense of quartz and Sandy Cove similarities..." (Fitzhugh 1978:77). This placement has been repeated more recently (Clark and Fitzhugh 1992:196). It should now be clear from the larger excavated assemblage and additional radiocarbon dates that there is no basis for such a dating other than the problematic 4645±65 B.P. assay from Test Pit C at the western end of the site. The excavated assemblage from Nukasusutok-5 can therefore constitute a baseline for defining a late *Naksak* phase in the 6000-5000 B.P. time range.

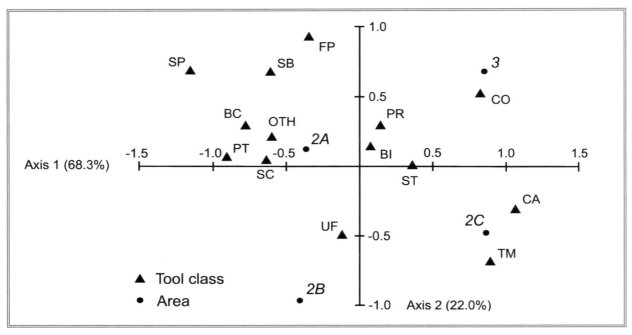

117/ Correspondence analysis plot of tool classes and Nukasusutok-5 subareas.

Nukasusutok-5: Inter-Area Comparisons and Conclusions

The previous chapters have described and interpreted each of the subareas at Nukasusutok-5. While each subarea stands on its own as an analytical unit, they will now be compared to consider the implications of intra-site variation. Evaluation of intra-site variation is based on comparisons of tool assemblages, lithic raw materials, technological organization and behavioral inferences drawn from spatial patterning. Area 1 is omitted, since the scale of investigation was too limited to draw conclusions. Areas 2A and 2B contained spatial configurations that were not completely exposed by excavation, but their assemblages will be considered nonetheless. The chapter ends with some observations on the significance of Nukasusutok-5 for understanding patterns in Early/Middle Maritime Archaic assemblage structure.

INTER-AREA COMPARISONS

Tool Assemblages

The first characteristic to be compared is variation in tool assemblages. Table 38 outlines the tool class percentages at each subarea, showing obvious differences in the proportions of utilized flakes, bipolar cores, block cores and slate tool fragments. Figure 117 displays a correspondence analysis plot based on the frequency data. The first dimension accounts for 68.3% of the variation and distinguishes Areas 2C and 3 on the right, pulled by block cores, from Area 2A on the left, pulled by bipolar cores. The second dimension, which accounts for 22.0% of the variation, contrasts Area 2B on the bottom, pulled by its high percentage of utilized flakes, with assemblages in which block cores are frequent and flake points have a modest significance: Area 3 in particular and Area 2A to a lesser extent. Thus, the subareas are distinguished mainly in terms of lithic reduction and expedient tool variables. The more form-invested tool classes do not occur in high enough frequencies to draw reliable inferences about intra-site patterning.

Tool Raw Materials

Table 39 provides a percentage comparison of tool raw material frequencies between the subareas. Quartz tools occur in similar percentages across the Area 2 subareas while Area 3 has a slightly higher proportion. Ramah chert is also fairly even across the Area 2 subareas, but is slightly less frequent at Area 3. Mugford and black cherts occur in relatively low percentages over most of Area 2, with the exception of Area 2B, which has a high proportion of black chert. Area 3 is notable for containing only a single tool of Mugford chert. Slate varies slightly, with similar proportions in Areas 2A and 2C, a higher proportion in Area 3 and lower percentage in Area 2B. Schist is most frequent at Area 2C. Thus, the differences between the subareas are fairly minor.

Table 38. Inter-Area Percentage Comparison of Tool Classes.

	PT	BI	PR	FP	SC	UF	SP	CA	SB	ST	BC	CO	TM	OTH	TOTAL
2A	3.8	4.7	1.8	2.9	6.5	28.4	1.2	0.9	3.5	15.0	16.7	10.9	2.1	1.8	341
2B	2.4	2.4		2.4	7.2	50.0				14.3	14.3	4.8	2.4		42
2C	1.0	5.2	2.1		2.1	32.0		3.1	1.0	22.7	2.1	20.6	7.2	1.0	97
3		4.5	1.5	4.5	3.0	19.4		1.5	1.5	22.4	7.5	31.4	3.0		67

PT: points (bifacial), BI: bifaces, PR: preforms (biface), FP: flake points, SC: scrapers (endscrapers and flake knives), UF: utilized flakes, SP: slate points, CA: celt/adze, SB: slate blanks (unmodified plates and blanks), ST: slate tool fragments (ground slate flakes and unidentified tool fragments), BC: bipolar cores, CO: block cores (quartz), TM: tool manufacturing (hammerstones, schist tablets, whetstones), and OTH: other (stemmed flakes, linear flakes, graver).

Table 39. Inter-Area Percentage Comparison of Tool Raw Materials.

	Area 2A	Area 2B	Area 2C	Area 3
Quartz	23.5	21.4	23.5	32.8
Ramah chert	46.3	47.6	38.8	35.8
Mugford chert	2.3	2.4		1.5
Black chert	5.3	9.5	2	
Slate	20.5	16.7	24.5	26.9
Schist	1.5		8.2	3.0
Other	0.6	2.4	3.1	
Total	341	42	98	67

Flake Raw Materials

The next comparison is flake raw material percentages, as summarized in Table 40 and visualized in a stacked column graph (Figure 118). There are moderate differences in the proportions of quartz and Ramah chert between the Area 2 subareas, but quartz almost totally dominates at Area 3, associated with a high frequency of block cores. Areas 2B and 2C have more patinated (thermally altered) Ramah chert, Area 2B has a high percentage of black chert, while Area 3 has little slate and entirely lacks Mugford and black chert.

Technological Organization

Organizational studies of lithic technology in "Americanist" archaeology have treated lithic procurement and use as embedded within a regional settlement system (e.g., Andrefsky 1998:189ff.; Bamforth 1991; Binford 1979; Nelson 1991; Odell 1996; Parry and Kelly 1987). Although a regional scale of analysis is impossible here, given the absence of detailed information on other Maritime Archaic lithic assemblages, the discussion is conducted with this broad scale in mind. Another perspective connects social agency theory with

Table 40. Inter-Area Percentage Comparison of Flake Raw Materials.

	Area 2A	Area 2B	Area 2C	Area 3
Quartz	31.4	14.2	40.0	85.5
Ramah chert	60.1	67.7	52.0	13.0
Patinated Ramah	1.7	3.9	3.6	0.0
Mugford chert	0.7	1.4	0.2	
Black chert	0.7	8.8	1.3	
Slate	5.4	3.9	2.9	1.5
Total	**8248**	**2330**	**1809**	**1828**

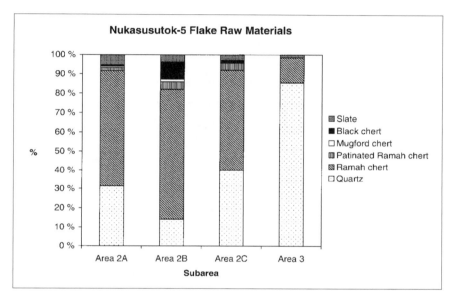

118/ Stacked column graph of Nukasusutok-5 flake raw materials by subarea.

Leroi-Gourhan's concept of *chaîne opératoire* to focus on technology as sequences of choices structured by cultural schemas (e.g., Chilton 1999; Dobres 2000; Gamble 1999; Karlin and Julien 1994; Perlès 1992; Schlanger 1994; Stark 1998). This approach is used implicitly here at the site-specific level, with an assumption of linkages to the regional scale through the settlement system. Chapters 6-7 deployed certain organizational concepts as part of the descriptive framework for the spatial analysis, so the subareas will now be compared more explicitly from this perspective. Each lithic raw material is treated separately since they are used in different kinds of reduction systems.

Quartz

Quartz is ubiquitous in Early/Middle Maritime Archaic assemblages in central and northern Labrador, but largely goes out of use after 4500 B.P.. It is widely dispersed as veins in the Precambrian bedrock, including two outcrops identified on Nukasusutok Island, one on a hill north of Nukasusutok-5. Archaeologically, quartz occurs primarily in the form of unmodified or minimally retouched flakes, block cores and bipolar cores, but it was also used occasionally for crude projectile points. The quartz reduction system began with the collection of small quartz blocks, either tabular pieces derived from the bedrock or water-rolled pebbles from beach deposits; both are in evidence at Nukasusutok-5. The spatial analysis of Area 2A suggested that un- or minimally modified blocks were cached in the middle area between the two behavioral modules, while most reduction occurred within the modules. Reduction was accomplished by both freehand and

Table 41. Variation in Elements of Quartz Technology at Nukasusutok-5.

	No. Tools	Block Cores	Bipolar cores	Flakes
Area 2A	80	37	34	2588
Area 2B	9	2	5	332
Area 2C	22	17		724
Area 3	24	18	2	1569

bipolar percussion, but the lack of partially retouched cores intermediate between the minimally modified blocks and bipolar cores indicates that reduction proceeded rapidly from a raw block to an exhausted bipolar core. The desired product of the reduction process was flakes, since very few visibly retouched implements are found. A wide variety of these flakes could have been used expediently for simple cutting/scraping functions or specific size/shape variants might have been selected for hafting, along the lines of Flenniken's (1981:60-96) discussion of quartz "microliths" hafted in wooden handles being used for processing fish. Flakes might also have been selected for further bipolar reduction to produce even smaller fragments. At any stage in the reduction process bipolar cores could have been recycled for use as scrapers, wedges, etc.

At Nukasusutok-5, quartz reduction characteristics vary slightly between the sub-areas. Table 41 compares aspects of quartz technology at each subarea, with the exception of the small assemblage from Area 1. The subareas at Area 2A are combined, so some of the spatial variation is masked. For all subareas, block and bipolar cores constitute ca. 80% or more of the quartz items classed as tools. Thus, as already noted above for Area 2A, quartz was rarely used to produce recognizable retouched implements; the primary goal was flake production, although the cores could have been put to secondary uses. Areas 2A and 2B have relatively high proportions of bipolar cores relative to block cores and total tools, while Area 3 has few bipolar cores and Area 2C none. While these observations may be affected by incomplete excavation at Areas 2B

and 2C, there is at least a hint that bipolar reduction was less significant at Areas 2C and 3.

If bipolar reduction was less prominent at Areas 2C and 3, these subareas might also exhibit quartz flake size distributions with a better representation of larger sizes than the other subareas since bipolar reduction could lead to more thorough reduction of quartz than the freehand percussion technique. The line graphs of quartz flake size distributions (Figure 119) do not provide much support for this. Area 3 has the lowest percentage of material in the <10 to <20 mm categories (i.e., fewer small flakes) and a slightly higher percentage in the 35-40 mm category. Area 2C has the highest percentage of material in the 10-15mm category (small flakes) and a slightly elevated percentage in the 25-30mm category. Area 2A, which has large numbers of bipolar cores, has the lowest percentage of flakes in the smallest <10mm category, but the highest in the 15-20 mm and 20-25 mm categories. Thus, by themselves, the quartz flake size distributions are not very clear indicators of differences in reduction patterns. More detailed analysis of quartz fracture patterns (cf., Callahan et al. 1992; Knutsson 1998) is necessary to fill out this picture.

Ramah Chert

Ramah chert was derived from its bedrock sources 300 km to the north in the Ramah Bay region (Gramly 1978; Lazenby 1980). The material could be quarried directly from the bedrock or easily picked up as large blocks or plates in stream beds or from loose talus slopes. These blocks were processed at or near the sources into biface blanks of varying sizes, which were then transported south. The blanks were modified as needed by bifacial reduction into the required tool form. Consequently, Ramah chert debitage in the Nain region consists mostly of biface-thinning and other secondary retouch flakes, with little trace of primary reduction flakes bearing cortex. "Stage 1" quarry blanks seem to be rare in the Nain area, but smaller bifacial point preforms are frequent. Ramah chert was used primarily for projectile points throughout the time span of the Maritime Archaic, although flakes from biface reduction were selected for use as expedient tools (utilized flakes, flake knives, flake points). In contrast to Dorset, the Maritime Archaic almost never used Ramah chert for endscrapers. In sum, this is a classic example of a curated biface technology (cf., Kelly 1988; Parry and Kelly 1987).

Table 42 compares elements of Ramah chert technology between the subareas. Area 3 stands out for its general paucity of Ramah chert, yet it also has: a) a relatively high proportion of tools to flakes, and b) a high proportion of large biface-thinning flakes (BTFs), perhaps linked to the presence of possible quarry blank fragments among the bifaces. These variations may be minor,

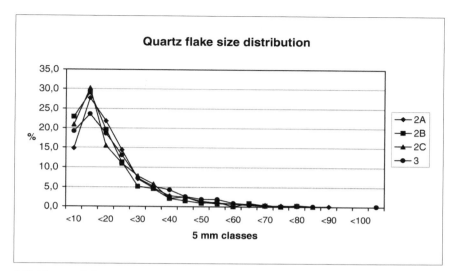

119/ Quartz flake size distribution at Nukasusutok-5.

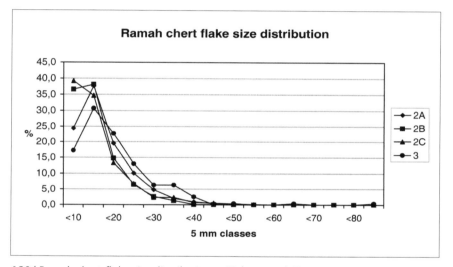

120/ Ramah chert flake size distribution at Nukasusutok-5.

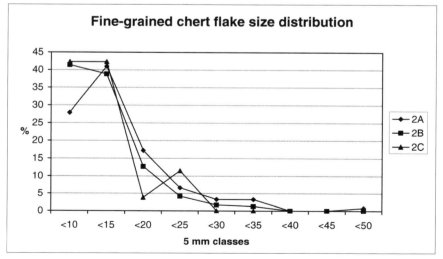

121/ Fine-grained chert flake size distribution at Nukasusutok-5.

Table 42. Variation in Elements of Ramah Chert Technology at Nukasusutok-5.

	Tools	Bifacial Points	Bifaces	Preforms	Retouched Flakes*	Utilized flakes	Bipolar Cores	BTFs (N/large)	Flakes
Area 2A	158	12	15	6	17	88	19	637/88	4957
Area 2B	20		1		2	15	1	149/8	1669
Area 2C	41	1	5	2	1	25	2	114/14	1006
Area 3	23	1		2	4	13	3	17/10	238

*includes flake points, flake knives and stemmed flakes

Table 43. Variation in Elements of Fine-Grained Chert Technology at Nukasusutok-5.

	Tools	Endscrapers	Util./ret. flakes	Bipolar Cores	Flakes
Area 2A	26	16	5	4	122
Area 2B	5	1	4		237
Area 2C	2	1	1		19
Area 3	1	1			

but they parallel other behavioral differences linked to the presence of the red ocher features. Otherwise, the large number of BTFs at Area 2A is clearly associated with the substantial numbers of bifacial points, biface fragments and preforms. The bifacial tool component varies from highs of 21% and 19.5% at Areas 2A and 2C, respectively, to lows of 13% and 5% at Areas 3 and 2B, respectively. The proportion of expedient tools (retouched and utilized flakes) is high in all the assemblages, ranging from 63% to 85% of all Ramah chert implements. It is notable that Ramah chert occasionally was subjected to bipolar reduction, but this was a secondary technique implemented on broken tools or flakes produced by direct percussion. It is unclear whether the purpose was production of small flakes to maximize the use-life of the material or a specific function such as wedging/splitting.

Figure 120 charts the size distribution of Ramah chert flakes at the four subareas. The distributions have generally similar profiles except for the smallest

<10 mm flake size category. For the latter, Areas 3 and 2A have relatively low percentages (17.2% and 24.4%, respectively) while Areas 2C and 2B have higher percentages (39.2% and 36.6%, respectively). All areas were screened with the same mesh size, but the differences could indicate some kind of collection bias since the low-percentage areas were both excavated in 1979 and the high percentage areas in 1992-93. Reviewing the results for quartz (Figure 119), the Area 2A excavation from 1979 also exhibits a slightly lower percentage in the smallest size class than the other subareas, which might support the case for collection bias. Looking more closely at the line graph, Areas 2B and 2C have almost identical profiles from the 15-20 mm class onwards. Area 3, however, has a consistently higher representation of the larger flake sizes from 15-20 mm onwards, while Area 2A is intermediate. If we hypothetically assign a slightly larger number of flakes to the smallest size class to compensate for collection bias it is likely that Area 3 would still have a

relatively low percentage in the smallest size class and the overall profile would remain similar. Although the difference may, therefore, be "real," the small sample size from Area 3 (238 flakes) should also be taken into account.

Fine-Grained Chert

The term fine-grained chert refers to both Mugford cherts of varied colour (gray, green, beige, patinated) as well as black chert, some of which was derived from the Mugford sources (Gramly 1978; Lazenby 1980), some of which might have been from sources in Saglek Bay (Chapter 2). These cherts occur as thin tablets that are transportable without the systematic preliminary reduction used for Ramah chert. Nonetheless, not a single core of the material occurs at Nukasusutok-5. Fine-grained cherts were used almost exclusively for the production of small endscrapers, although one biface fragment is present in the Nukasusutok-5 collection. A few utilized flakes and bipolar cores are also present. As noted in the comparison of flake and tool raw materials (Tables 39, 40), fine-grained cherts occur in rather low percentages. The low frequency of these items is underlined in Table 43, which combines the Mugford and black cherts. Only Area 2A has a substantial number of tools, while Area 2B has twice as many flakes but substantially fewer tools. This might be interpreted as a high rate of tool discard at Area 2A, contrasted with more production or retouch at Area 2B combined with less discard, or curation of finished products to other localities. The almost complete absence of fine-grained cherts at Area 3 reinforces the impression that this subarea differs from the others in function, meaning and chronology. It should be emphasized, however, that low overall frequency of fine-grained chert need not signify minor cultural or organizational significance. Considerable effort was expended to acquire a material that was used mostly for a single purpose: endscrapers.

Figure 121 shows the size distribution for fine-grained chert flakes at Area 2. Again, the portion exca-

vated in 1979 (Area 2A) has a lower percentage of material in the smallest size class. Areas 2A and 2B parallel each other closely, while Area 2A exhibits a slight peak in the 20-25 mm size class. Overall, there is a strong skewing towards small flakes of 10-15 mm or less, which implies emphasis on secondary and tertiary retouch rather than any form of core reduction. In sum, the flake size distribution, the small size of the finished tools (endscrapers) and the lack of cores suggest that fine-grained cherts were curated as finished tools or flake preforms.

Slate

The most likely source for the slates is the Cape Mugford region. Several colour and texture variants were used. In contrast to the fine-grained cherts, it appears that raw plates of slate were often transported "as is" from the sources then reduced as needed. This is suggested by the presence of several minimally worked plates in the Nukasusutok material. These raw materials were then roughed into blanks and preforms by direct percussion. The latter were then ground into finished tools, possibly with schist tablets.

Table 44 outlines elements of the slate technology system at Nukasusutok-5. Area 2A was the obvious center for slate reduction. A considerable number of raw slate plates and tool blanks were present, either cached as raw materials or discarded during the manufacturing process. The frequency of ground slate flakes, in some cases clearly edge-rejuvenation flakes, attests to the reworking of finished or partly finished tools. Attempts to refit these flakes to the tools found in the subarea were unsuccessful, suggesting the "cores" were removed from the site. Combined with the low frequency of finished tools, this could imply maintenance of curated implements. Areas 2C and 3 exhibited only modest indications of tool production and maintenance while Area 2B had the fewest indicators of slate reduction. The flake size distribution for slate is portrayed in Figure 122. The line graph profiles are extremely variable, most likely an expression of ran-

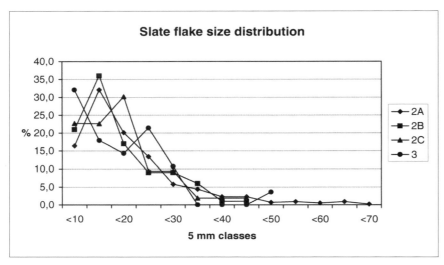

Slate flake size distribution

122/ Slate flake size distribution at Nukasusutok-5.

the social composition of the groups. But the differences could also be the result of "fall-out" from activities positioned at different points on the procurement and reduction cycle; that is, a consequence of raw material availability and contingent organizational constraints rather than a direct reflection of site-function requirements or social variables. Sorting out these alternatives requires situating Nukasusutok-5 within the regional and supra-regional contexts of Maritime Archaic settlement and procurement systems.

dom variations in small samples rather than meaningful patterning.

SUMMARY

The Maritime Archaic inhabitants of Nukasusutok-5 organized their lithic technology into two primary systems: a) a highly expedient component using an abundant local raw material (quartz), and b) a highly curated component involving non-local materials. The latter consisted of different reduction systems for each of the materials involved. The Ramah chert system involved the transport of large bifaces that were: a) reduced along a core-tool trajectory to produce "high performance" form-invested tools (points, bifaces), while b) debitage from core reduction was employed for expedient tools (utilized flakes etc.). Fine-grained cherts were transported as small tablets, flakes or finished tools, with a strong focus on a specific implement— endscrapers— and little expedient flake use. Slate was transported as raw plates, blanks and finished tools; production and maintenance involved a time-consuming grinding process after initial reduction. The subareas at Nukasusutok-5 differ slightly in the emphasis placed on these organizational systems. These differences may signal choices made in response to site-function considerations or variation in

CONCLUSIONS

Nukasusutok-5 is one of the few Early/Middle Maritime Archaic sites that has been excavated sufficiently to provide a reasonably representative sample for understanding spatial patterning and assemblage composition. As such, it is difficult to place the site in a broader systemic context because there are insufficient comparable assemblages to work with. By way of conclusion, a number of points that could be pursued in future research are discussed.

In the last major synthesis of northern Maritime Archaic culture-history, Fitzhugh (1978:72) grouped most of the Early/Middle Maritime Archaic sites in the Nain region into the "*Naksak* Complex," although he recognized that this entity was problematic:

Many of these sites are deflated or partly eroded, with artifacts found on the surface and in buried deposits. Local topographic conditions rendered some sites useful for long periods, while others were occupied briefly. Until these factors can be analyzed it seems better to acknowledge the probable

Table 44. Variation in Elements of Slate Technology at Nukasusutok-5.

	Tools*	Ground flakes/fragments	Plates/blanks	Schist	Flakes
Area 2A	7	51	11	5	443
Area 2B		6			92
Area 2C	3	24	1	6	52
Area 3	2	13	1	3	20

Points, celts/adzes

"lumped" nature of this complex (Fitzhugh 1978:72).

Fitzhugh goes on to refer to "considerable typological variation" at some sites, particularly those situated in topographical locations that could be used over long periods of time, and he mentions sites of different character and dating that may form the basis for defining additional archaeological complexes, such as the Nukasusutok and Gull Arm Groups (Fitzhugh 1978:72-77). This sense of barely ordered variability is understandable since the data base was derived mostly from surface surveys and small test excavations, and radiocarbon dates were scarce. But ordering that variability will be difficult without a better understanding of individual site structure.

Nukasustok-5 illustrates some of these problems. It is located in a protected harbour on a prominent tombolo beach that was a magnet for settlement from 6000 B.P. to 4500 B.P. and perhaps later. Area 2 revealed three or four occupation components representing at least two chronological phases (ca. 6000 B.P. and 5500 B.P.). Components of these two phases overlapped slightly at the junction of Areas 2A and 2B. Within Area 2A two behavioral modules that might represent dwelling features were identified. The modules were similar in spatial organization but varied somewhat in tool and flake raw material contents. Area 2C might have contained a similar dwelling module. Area 2B exhibited a different behavioral pattern consisting of a central pit-hearth complex ringed by deposits of fire-cracked rock. This pattern was interpreted as either an outdoor feature with a concentric drop-toss zone or a dwelling module with fire-cracked rock discarded outside along a tent wall. The Area 2 subareas displayed slight differences in their frequencies of tool types and lithic raw materials and in their technological organization, but the chronological distinctions suggested by the radiocarbon dates were not paralleled by clear differences in tool typology. The probably later occupation at Area 3 (5000 B.P.) was not so much typologically different as it was behaviorally distinct from the Area 2 occupations.

At the *intra-site* level of analysis, the Nukasusutok-5 material underlines: a) the importance of excavating and analysing entire behavioral units so as to provide a meaningful baseline for comparison, and b) the need to acquire several such samples from large, complex and chronologically diverse sites in order to understand both their chronological position and their role in the regional settlement system. At the *inter-site* level, the variability uncovered in the Nukasusutok-5 material raises problems as to what is an adequate unit of inter-assemblage comparison. The subareas cannot simply be lumped together and compared with some other composite of assemblages or with more discrete assemblages. To be meaningful, comparisons and culture-historical integration must be based on behaviorally distinct assemblages, such as the possible dwelling modules at Area 2A.

Another implication of the present analysis is that comparisons based on traditional tool typology may be of limited value for understanding settlement systems and social process. It may be more useful to investigate other dimensions of variation such as patterning in different lithic reduction systems, as discussed in this chapter. The intra-site analysis of Nukasusutok-5 suggests that assemblages could be scaled in relation to which components of lithic reduction systems are present or absent and in relation to the articulation between expedient and more "organized" components of the technologies. Unfortunately, such analyses cannot be undertaken until such a time as a sufficient number of appropriate assemblages become available.

The analysis of Nukasusutok-5 also contributes to the empirical and methodological aspects of Maritime Archaic dwelling structure studies. At Area 2A it was possible to identify two behavioral modules that might be dwelling remains. Two alternative interpretations were suggested: (1) each module represents a small tent structure of 4 by 3 m in size; the spatial organization of activities at each structure was highly symmetrical and the dwellings had a common orientation to a large central rock, and (2) each module was a component of a larger rectangular segmented structure of 4 by 6+ m in size; although the spatial organization of the modules was highly symmetrical the modules were integrated into the rectangular structures in slightly different ways. Both interpretations were problematic, however, since the multiple hearth features could indicate re-occupation events rather than discrete dwellings. Consequently, although the "longhouse model" provided a framework for identifying spatial patterning, the meaning of that patterning remained ambiguous. More detailed investigations of Early/Middle Maritime Archaic sites will be necessary to clarify how the Area 2A patterns fit into the range of variation in Maritime Archaic site structure.

The methodological strategy outlined in Chapter 3 involved playing off a model-based analysis versus model-independent pattern recognition techniques. The model-based analysis focused on hearth-centered distributions that could be viewed within the segmental or modular framework of the longhouse model. Qualitative visual analysis of flake distributions proved to be the crucial element in identifying behavioral modules. Other lines of evidence were then explored within this postulated modular framework, largely through the use of simple cross-tabulation techniques. K-means cluster analysis was used as a model-independent exploratory technique to identify tool groupings by physical proximity rather than by sorting them into preconceived behavioral modules. This proved useful for mapping hearth-centered distributions at the micro-level and for pointing to possible variations in the lithic materials associated with each feature, but the sample sizes in each cluster were too small to have much statistical significance. The cluster analysis could not provide a basis for combining hearth-centered distributions into larger behavioral units; ultimately, this had to be accomplished by qualitative means and within model assumptions. A different model-independent technique, correspondence analysis, was used to explore patterning in flake raw materials at Area 2A. The results were consistent with the model-based analysis.

Overall, the analysis showed that relatively simple qualitative and quantitative methods are capable of detecting meaningful patterning at Maritime Archaic sites lacking in traces of architecture that would facilitate the definition of analytical units. But this patterning would have been difficult to identify if the flake distributions had not been plotted systematically in the field. Consequently, future analyses of Maritime Archaic (and other) sites should point plot debitage distributions so as not to miss patterns that would be indistinct in quadrat summaries. Spatial data should be as high resolution as possible, otherwise it may be difficult to identify behavioral modules such as those that were crucial to the present analysis.

Edward Flowers and Sam Saimat looking for basking seals on the sea ice near Dog Island, April 1994.

123/ Nukasusutok-12: overview towards the southwest.

Nukasusutok-12: Early/ Middle Dorset Axial Structures[6]

Nukasusutok-12 (HcCh-14) was discovered during a 1979 survey when a well preserved axial structure (Structure-1) was observed almost completely exposed in a blow-out. The few tools noted on the surface indicated a Dorset affiliation, but the feature bore a striking resemblance to Pre-Dorset axial structures and it seemed to differ from Middle and Late Dorset tent ring structures recorded in northern Labrador by the Torngat Archaeological Project (e.g., R. Jordan 1980:611). An Early Dorset affiliation was suspected, so the site was investigated further in 1980. It was revisited briefly in 1992.

The site is situated at the head of a shallow bight on the south side of Nukasusutok Island, west of Wyatt Harbour (Figure 16). It lies at an elevation of 6.5-7.5 m asl. at the western end of a narrow east-west trending pass between steep rocky hills. At the time of occupation, higher sea level would have resulted in a well-protected cove extending considerably further inland than at present, providing an excellent location for boat landings. Lithic material occurs sporadically over an area of roughly 1500 m^2, at least half of which is wholly or partially deflated, the rest is covered with lichen and crowberry. Two axial features (Structures 1 and 2) were clearly visible near the middle of the beach, while traces of a third (Structure 3) lay towards

the southern side of the pass, and a fourth (Structure 4) was identified in a test pit on the northern edge of the pass beside a rock-fall (Figures 123 and 124). Three test pits (TP 1-3) in a small area on the south side of the pass revealed a rich tool deposit, but no trace of structural remains. It is possible that additional structures are present at the site, deeply embedded in the gravel. Most of the site is underlain by aeolian sands and gravel, but two large clay boils are located on a low ridge in the center of the main deflated area near Structure 2. The three test pits (TP 1-3) on the south side of the pass exposed a thick basal clay mixed with small cobbles.

The 1980 fieldwork consisted of the complete excavation of two axial features (Structures 1 and 2) and the excavation of seven test pits, two of which revealed the presence of additional structures. The two excavated structures will be presented first, followed by the test units.

STRUCTURE 1

Structure 1 was the lowest feature identified at the site, located at ca. 6.5 m asl. in the middle of the beach pass. When discovered in 1979 the feature was almost completely exposed in a sand-gravel blow-out. A total of 23.25 m^2 was excavated to expose entirely the

---

[6]Nukasusutok-12 was described previously in Hood (1986). This chapter is based on the earlier report, but the material has been reworked, supplemented with tool descriptions and reinterpreted. It should be regarded as the "authoritative" account.

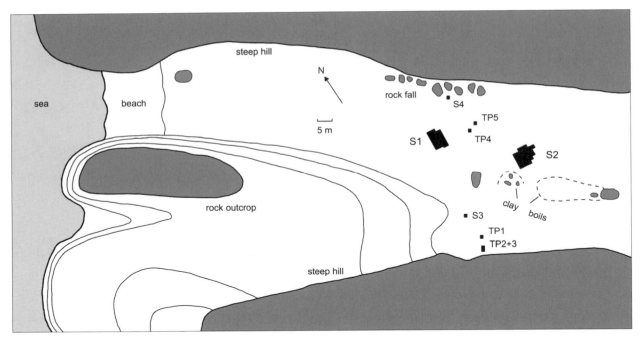

124/ Nukasusutok-12: site map.

structural components and recover any buried lithics. The structure consisted of a ca. 6 m long axial feature aligned NNW-SSE, running obliquely to the beach front (Figures 125 and 126). Excavation at the southern end of the structure required the removal of 25 cm of laminated aeolian sand and thin humus horizons to expose a 2 cm thick black humus zone that appeared to correspond with the floor level of the feature. This humus level was limited to the outer periphery of the excavation, mostly outside what were interpreted as tent anchor rocks. Consequently, the structure took the appearance of an axial feature bisecting a 3.5-4.0 m wide sub-rectangular patch of gravel. Although it is possible this gravel patch is a partial consequence of deflation, its orientation relative to the feature suggests a thin sod layer may have been removed to provide a gravel floor for the dwelling or that it was trampled away during the occupation.

The axial feature was 5.0 m long and 0.75-1.0m wide. It was constructed of parallel rows of thick flat-topped rocks embedded in the gravel end-to-end lengthwise, but was disturbed at its northern end. Several rocks on the eastern edge of the feature were slightly displaced to the west and on the western edge

some of the axial rocks were missing. At both ends of the feature were high large rocks, morphologically unlike those composing the feature itself. These end-rocks lay perpendicular to the feature's long axis and formed the feature terminus, although they were placed slightly back from the feature and did not form a continuous alignment with it. There were no transverse partitions or paving stones inside the axial border rocks, but at each end of the feature were the remains of hearths. Just south of the feature's center lay two thin flat slabs, one of schist. Both slabs were notched on one longitudinal edge and modified to be flat on the other edge. These were presumably soap-stone vessel support rocks. To the north of the feature's center were a broken, blubber-stained, fire-cracked rock and a thin slate slab with a battered and notched edge, probably the remains of additional vessel support rocks.

The only tools associated with the structure were the proximal portions of two Ramah chert microblades (W= 12.4, 12.4 mm, TH= 4.5, 2.8). One of these was surface collected from near the terminus rocks at the north end of the feature, the other was excavated from within the black humus zone at the southern boundary

CHAPTER 10

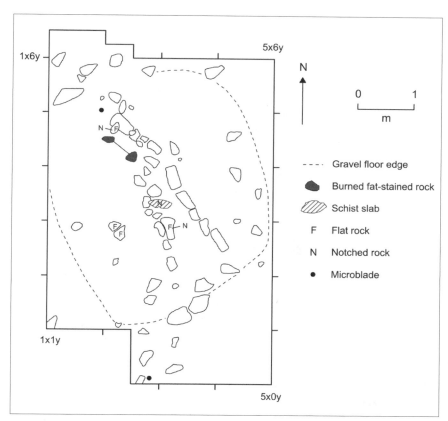

1x6y

5x6y

N

0   1
          m

- - -   Gravel floor edge

◢   Burned fat-stained rock

▨   Schist slab

F   Flat rock

N   Notched rock

•   Microblade

1x1y

5x0y

125/ Nukasusutok-12: Structure 1.

of the excavation. The latter specimen may not be associated with Structure 1 since several rocks at the humus zone level of this end of the excavation may be part of another buried feature. No flakes were found in Structure 1.

126/ Nukasusutok-12: Structure 1, view towards the south.

STRUCTURE 2

Structure 2 (Figure 127 and 128) was located near the center of the beach, about 28 m east of Structure 1 and adjacent to the large clay boils. Its elevation was no more than a meter above Structure 1 and it was oriented at an oblique angle to the beach front, running NE-SW. The structure consisted of an axial feature 4.0 m long and ca. 0.7 m wide, constructed of thick flat slabs embedded in the surface gravel end-to-end lengthwise. The feature boundary rocks were displaced at the cen-

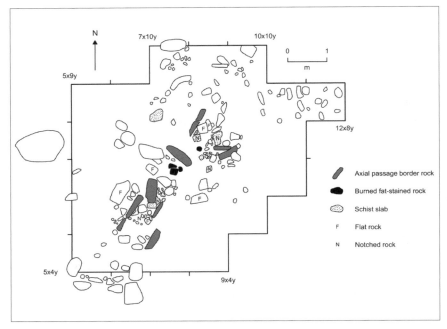

127/ Nukasusutok-12: Structure 2.

ter of the alignment for a distance of 1.5 m and the scatter of rocks at both ends of the feature indicated a greater degree of disturbance than at Structure 1. The southern end of the feature was bounded by two high large terminus rocks, structurally continuous with the feature, but the northern terminus was indistinct.

The axial feature contained at least two and possibly three hearth areas, one at each end of the alignment and perhaps another in the middle. At the southern end of the feature two thin, flat, notched and blubber-encrusted schist slabs lay fallen between the feature boundary rocks near a concentration of crumbled schist fragments. A third notched and burned fat-encrusted schist slab was wedged vertically against a western boundary rock. These notched slabs were probably used as soapstone vessel supports and fragments of a near-complete soapstone vessel were found nearby. Several small horizontally placed flat slabs inside the feature may be the remnants of a floor pavement. At the northern end of the alignment were a pair of fallen notched and burned fat- encrusted schist slabs that lay near a concentration of crumbled schist fragments and a soapstone vessel sherd. Several horizontal flat slabs, one of which was levelled with a shim

rock, may be the remains of an internal floor pavement. In the disturbed center of the feature were three blubber-encrusted rocks, a stray notched schist slab and a soapstone vessel sherd. These may be the remains of a third hearth, but considering the degree of disturbance they could have been thrown there from the other hearth areas.

The overall dimensions of the structure were difficult to determine given the absence of obvious perimeter anchor rocks and the lack of axial terminus rocks at the north end of the passage. But judging from the artifact distribution and the position of possible perimeter rocks the structure may have been about five meters long and four meters wide.

Spatial Patterning

Unlike lithic sterile Structure 1, Structure 2 contained 74 tools. The original spatial analysis of the distribution patterns (Hood 1986) was complicated by artifact provenience problems related to missing records. During re-analysis only 53 of the 74 tools could be point-plotted with certainty; most of the missing items are microblades. Additionally, some of the point-plotted microblades could not be related back to specific

128/ Nukasusutok-12: Structure 2, view towards the southwest.

catalogued implements, which made it difficult to distinguish reliably between utilized and unutilized microblades. Although the missing information could skew the analysis somewhat, it is necessary to work with what is at hand. A nephrite flake and a slate flake

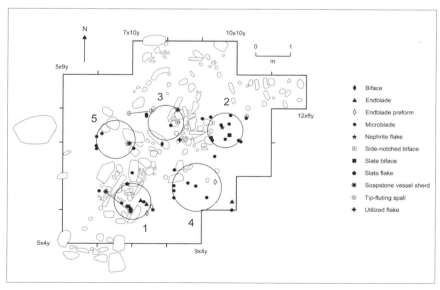

129/ Nukasusutok-12: Structure 2 tool distribution and k-means cluster analysis.

were also included in the analysis, bringing the numbers to 76 total, and 55 plotted items.

The point-plot of tools (Figure 129) indicates that most were concentrated within a 1-1.5 m distance of the axial feature. Following the bilateral organization model, a simple cross-tabulation analysis was presented in the original site description (Hood 1986:64), dividing the provenienced tools into spatial units associated with the feature or lying to the east or west of it. A revised version of this table is presented in Table 45. Most of the tools are located close to the feature or on its eastern flank. There is little clear patterning in tool class distributions besides the limitation of

Table 45. Nukasusutok-12: Structure 2 Tool Classes in Relation to the Bilateral Axial Feature Model.

	Mid	East	West	Prov. N (%)	No Prov.	TOTAL N (%)
Triangular endblades	2	2		4 (7.3)		4 (5.3)
Endblade preforms		3		3 (5.5)		3 (3.9)
Side-notched bifaces	1			1 (1.8)		1 (1.3)
Slate bifaces		1		1 (1.8)		1 (1.3)
Ramah chert bifaces	1			1 (1.8)	4	5 (6.6)
Tip-fluting spalls		1	2	3 (5.5)	3	6 (7.9)
Microblades	13	17	6	36 (65.5)	13	49 (64.5)
Utilized flakes	1			1 (1.8)	1	2 (2.6)
Slate flakes	1			1 (1.8)		1 (1.3)
Nephrite flakes			1	1 (1.8)		1 (1.3)
Soapstone vessels	3			3 (5.5)		3 (3.9)
TOTAL	22	24	9	55	21	76

Table 46. Nukasusutok-12: Structure 2 Tool Classes by Front/Back Divisions.

	Front	Back	Middle	TOTAL N (%)
Triangular endblades	4			4 (7.3)
Endblade preforms	3			3 (5.5)
Side-notched bifaces		1		1 (1.8)
Slate bifaces		1		1 (1.8)
Ramah chert bifaces			1	1 (1.8)
Tip-fluting spalls	1	2		3 (5.5)
Microblades	20	16		36 (65.5)
Utilized flakes		1		1 (1.8)
Slate flakes	1			1 (1.8)
Nephrite flakes		1		1 (1.8)
Soapstone vessels	2	1		3 (5.5)
TOTAL	31	23	1	55

endblade preforms to the eastern flank and soapstone vessels to the axial feature. A division between front (north), back (south) and middle subareas in Table 46 indicates that the only clear difference is the presence of all endblades and endblade preforms in the front subarea. In neither case are there indications of gender-based activity variation.

K-means cluster analysis was used for a model independent analysis of the point plotted tools; a five cluster solution seemed most reasonable (Figure 129). Two of the clusters (1 and 3) have centroids closely associated with the hearths at opposite ends of the axial feature in what might be termed hearth-tending positions. Cluster 2 lies slightly back from

Table 47. Nukasusutok-12: Structure 2 Tool Classes by *K*-Means Cluster.

	C-1	C-2	C-3	C-4	C-5	TOTAL
Endblades	3			1		4
Endblade preforms	2			1		3
Side-notched bifaces			1			1
Ramah chert bifaces			1			1
Slate Bifaces		1				1
Tip-fluting spalls		1			2	3
Microblades	7	12	4	8	5	36
Utilized flakes			1			1
Slate flakes	1					1
Nephrite flakes		1				1
Soapstone vessels	1		1		1	3
TOTAL	14	15	8	10	8	55

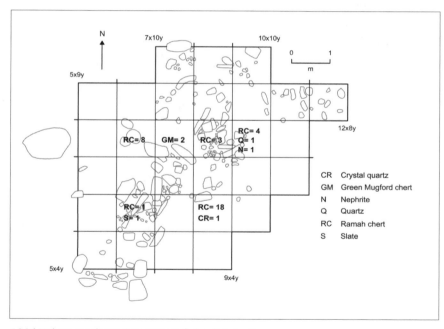

130/ Nukasusutok-12: Structure 2 flake distribution.

CR Crystal quartz
GM Green Mugford chert
N   Nephrite
Q   Quartz
RC Ramah chert
S   Slate

at the ends of the axial alignment. From a different perspective, clusters 3 and 4 could be arm's length discard areas associated with the hearth-tending positions at each end of the axial alignment. Overall, there is a hint of behavioral symmetry at the two hearths.

The tool associations for each cluster are compared in Table 47. Given the low frequencies in each cell the distribution is difficult to evaluate, but there is a slight over-representation of microblades in cluster 2, adjacent to the northern hearth. Inspection of individual tool type distributions provides little to supplement the foregoing observations other than revealing a tendency for endblades and endblade preforms to be located towards the south and tip-fluting spalls towards the north. In other words, deposition of the preforms and finished

the northernmost hearth, but seems positioned in relation to that feature. Clusters 3 and 4 lie in similar positions on opposite sides of the middle of the axial feature where there was uncertain evidence for a third hearth. Each of these clusters is located equidistant from, and thus equally accessible to, the hearths tools is not associated with deposition of the by-products of the manufacturing process. The refits of a tip-fluting spall and a soapstone vessel are spatially proximate, providing little information on material movements at Structure 2.

In contrast to the relatively large tool assemblage, only 55 flakes were found, almost exclusively small secondary retouch flakes of Ramah chert. Their distribution by 1 m^2 units is displayed in Figure 130 (some flakes are missing because of uncertain provenience). The majority of flakes are distributed outside the axial feature, but within a 1 m distance from it. Their concentrations correspond well with the clusters identified in the tool analysis.

Tool and flake raw materials are outlined by frequency in Table 48 and by weight in Table 49. By frequency, Ramah chert dominates both tools and flakes. The weight figures for tools are distorted by soapstone, but if the latter is excluded then Ramah chert constitutes 86% of the flaked tool materials. The weight figures for flakes are misleading; what seems to be a dominance of quartz is mostly the result of a single quartz nodule that is heavier than the 48 small Ramah chert flakes. The single flake of white chert is fossiliferous with a carbonate cortex and is not from the Newfoundland west coast. It appears to be of northern Québec or Eastern Arctic origin.

Table 48. Nukasusutok-12: Structure 2 Tool and Flake Raw Material Frequencies.

	Tools N (%)	Flakes N (%)
Ramah chert	65 (87.8)	48 (87.3)
Gray Mugford chert		1 (1.8)
Crystal quartz	5 (6.8)	1 (1.8)
Quartz		2 (3.6)
Slate	1 (1.4)	1 (1.8)
White chert		1 (1.8)
Nephrite		1 (1.8)
Soapstone	3 (4.1)	

Table 49. Nukasusutok-12: Structure 2 Tool and Flake Raw Material Weights. In Grams.

	Tools g (%)	Flakes g (%)	TOTAL g (%)
Ramah chert	107.9 (23.2)	9.9 (34.1)	117.8 (23.8)
Gray Mugford chert		0.1 (0.3)	0.1 (0.0)
Crystal quartz	2.9 (0.6)	0.03 (0.1)	2.93 (0.6)
Quartz		14.0 (48.2)	14.0 (2.8)
Slate	14.6 (3.1)	0.5 (1.7)	15.1 (3.1)
White chert		n.a.	
Nephrite		4.5 (15.5)	4.5 (0.9)
Soapstone	340.0 (73.1)		340.0 (68.8)

Tool Assemblage

Endblades: All but one of the four Ramah chert endblades are fragments. The single complete specimen (Figure 131:c) is small (L=19.6 mm, W= 14.2, TH= 2.9) with a very slight basal concavity and tiny tip-fluting spalls (L= 2.5, 3.5 mm) on the dorsal surface. A proximal fragment (Figure 131:d) is only slightly larger, with a straight base (W = 17.1 mm, TH = 3.1). The other two specimens are distal fragments of larger endblades (L = >28, >35 mm). One (Figure 131:e) has two tip-fluting spalls (L = 14.0, 16.0 mm) on its dorsal surface while the other broke during removal of the first spall.

Endblade Preforms: The three preforms are made of Ramah chert. One is complete, triangular and straight-based (Figure 131:a), with fine retouch on its ventral side and large flake scars on its dorsal side (L = 35.5 mm, W = 24.9, TH = 5.5). The blunt tip was retouched ventrally to form a platform from which two tip-fluting spalls were removed dorsally (L = 16.8, 19.0 mm). The other two preforms are distal fragments. One (Figure 131:b) has a distal platform from which a single flute was removed down the center of the dorsal side (L= 26.8 mm), probably a production failure, while the other (Figure 131:f) has a convex distal end with faint retouch for platform preparation.

Side-notched bifaces: The single example (Figure 131:h) is the proximal fragment of a Ramah chert biface with broad side-notches positioned towards the

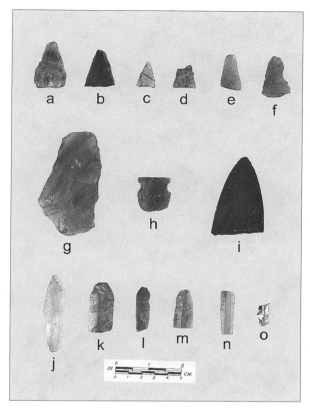

131/ Nukasusutok-12: implements from Structure 2.
a, b, f: endblade preforms; c-e: endblades; g: biface blank;
h: side-notched biface; i: ground slate biface; j-o: microblades.

medial portion of the tool such that the implement resembles a "box-based" biface. The basal edge is bifacially flaked and convex in form. There is slight grinding on the base as well as in one of the notches (W= 24.7 mm, TH= 5.7, notch HT= 12.0, 14.6, notch L= 7.1, 7.5, notch W= 2.2, 2.0).

Slate Bifaces: The distal fragment of a black slate biface is either the tip of a lance or a large knife (Figure 131:i). Each face of the tool has a flat medial surface, but only one face is polished. The lateral edges are bevelled for a width of 6-9 mm on each face, but there is also fine secondary bevelling ca. 0.7 mm wide extending along the immediate working edge.

Bifaces: All five of the bifaces are made of Ramah chert. One (Figure 131:g) is a complete asymmetric blank (L= 82.0 mm, W= 42.6, TH= 16.4). Two are distal fragments, of which one convex-tipped implement might be an endblade preform while the other might

be a tip-fluted endblade fragment. The remaining two specimens are lateral and proximal fragments.

Tip-fluting spalls: All five tip-fluting spalls are made of Ramah chert and all are primary removal spalls. Three of them could be considered relatively large (>25 mm in length). Metrics for the three complete specimens: L = 16.4, 27.1, 27.5 mm, W = 15.6, 11.2, 9.3, TH = 1.3, 3.1, 1.8.

Microblades: The raw materials of the 49 microblades (MNI = 24, based on proximal ends) are overwhelmingly Ramah chert (n = 44, 89.8%), with five examples made of crystal quartz (10.2%). Retouched or utilized microblades constitute 40.4% of the total. Of these, only three items exhibit traces of hafting: one crystal quartz specimen has bilateral notching (Figure 128:o), while another has a constricted stem, and one Ramah chert implement has a bilateral constriction. Two microblades may have been the result of core-trimming. Using only proximal portions and specimens from which reliable measurements could be taken (n=15), the average width of the Ramah chert microblades was 12.3 mm. Platform angles were measured to the nearest 5°, resulting in a range from 75-90° (n=23), with a distribution across the four angle classes as follows: 75° = 4 (17.4%), 80° = 12 (52.2%), 85° = 1 (4.3%), 90° = 6 (26.1%). Of the 22 proximal specimens upon which platform preparation technique could be identified, 17 (77.3%) had plain platforms, four (18.2%) retouched platforms, and one (4.5%) had a crushed platform.

The size of microblade fragments may be the result of random breakage patterns, but in some cases microblades might have been snapped deliberately for use in particular tasks. For the Ramah chert specimens, length measurements of proximal fragments (n=22) cluster into two groups, ca. 11-16 mm and 21-31 mm, while the medial fragments (n=13) exhibit a marked clustering between 14-20 mm. The distal fragments are relatively few (n=7) and exhibit a wide range of values. These groupings may simply result from the mechanics of tool breakage, but they seem consistent enough that deliberate action should also be considered.

Utilized flakes: The two examples are both made of Ramah chert.

Soapstone vessels: Three vessels were identified from a total of 6 sherds. One vessel is ¾ complete (Figure 132), shallow (depth= 31.5 mm), with one long side slightly curved and the other markedly bowed out so as to produce an asymmetric form with a length over 103 mm and a width ca. 66 mm. Wall thickness varies from 2.7 mm at the rim to 7.1 mm near the base. The rim is flattened with slightly rounded edges. The interior bottom exhibits striations and gouge marks indicative of an attempt to thin the vessel, a process that produced a small hole in one corner of the vessel bottom. The vessel weighs 71 g. A second vessel (Figure 133:a) is represented by a wall fragment with a small rim portion (TH= 3.1-5.7 mm). The third specimen is a wall sherd (TH= 3.3-5.7 mm) from a fairly deep vessel (>70 mm) featuring a flattened rim with round edges and an encrustation of burned fat on both the inner and outer surfaces (Figure 133:b).

Discussion

Structure-2 is a double or perhaps triple-hearth axial feature. The distribution of lithic material and rocks indicate the feature was associated with a relatively large tent (ca. 5m long by 5-6 m wide). The lithic materials were concentrated within 1.0-1.5 m of the axial feature, suggesting sleeping areas further out towards the tent walls. Cluster analysis of the tools suggests a degree of behavioral symmetry in the use of space at each end of the axial feature, with hearth-related activities or deposition, although most of the lithics occur on the west side of the feature. A slight front/back distinction noted in the clustering of all endblades and endblade preforms at the front (north end) of the axial feature is the only hint of spatial differentiation by gender, if one invokes the stereotype of male association with harpoon technology. This weak inference need not contradict the possibility that the

132/ Nukasusutok-12: soapstone vessel from Structure 2.

133/ Nukasusutok-12: soapstone vessel fragments from Structure 2.

behavioral symmetry between the hearths, in combination with the assumed size of the dwelling, might indicate the presence of two domestic units within the structure.

Seen in terms of what did and did not "fall out" of the technological organization system, the tool and debitage samples suggest a relatively short duration of occupation and a limited range of activities. Most prominent among what fell out of the system were: (1) a substantial rate of microblade production and (2) a modest deposition of endblades, endblade preforms and tip-fluting spalls. The former may be related to various expedient tasks while the latter indicates

CHAPTER 10

134/ Nukasusutok-12: implements from Structures 3 and 4. a: side-notched biface, Structure 3; b: endblade, Structure 3; c: burin-like-tool preform, Structure 3; d, e: side-notched bifaces, Structure 4; f: endblade preform, Structure 4; g: microblade, Structure 4.

preparation for and/or implementation of sea mammal hunting activities. What did not fall out of the system were flakes and domestic processing tools. The small quantity of Ramah chert debitage and its near-exclusive secondary retouch flake character suggests limited modification of curated implements such as the endblade preforms and the biface blank. The scarcity or absence of domestic processing tools such as bifacial knives, scrapers and burin-like tools indicates that either activities associated with these implements were not undertaken or that such items were less likely to enter into the archaeological record at this locality.

STRUCTURE 3

A 1 m^2 test pit 25 m south of Structure 1 (Figure 124) revealed the probable remains of a third axial feature consisting of cobbles and flat slabs. The test pit and later surface collection in the area produced nine tools:

a tip-fluted endblade, a tip-fluting spall, a side-notched biface, a burin-like tool preform and four microblades. A total of 17 flakes was collected, of which 15 were Ramah chert, one crystal quartz and one schist.

The Ramah chert endblade (Figure 134:b) is complete, with a fairly straight base and some medial basal thinning (L= 42.7 mm, W= 18.2, TH= 5.6). The tip-fluting was placed dorsally and the scars are relatively short (L= 13.0, 16.5 mm). The single side-notched biface of Ramah chert (Figure 134:a) is also complete and displays a slightly asymmetric blade, a biconvex cross-section, a straight bifacially thinned base and slight edge grinding above one of the notches (L= 57.6 mm, W= 30.5, TH= 5.8, notch HT= 9.2, 9.0, notch L= 5.4, 6.6, notch W= 2.2, 2.1).

The burin-like tool preform (Figure 134:c) is complete and made on a long flake of nephrite. One lateral edge has a bifacially flaked wide notch or stem while the opposite edge bears a slight trace of a notch formed by dorsal retouch. The implement has a slight basal concavity and it is unground (L= 48.5 mm, W= 19.8, TH= 5.8, notch L= 13.4, notch W= 1.9).

All four microblades are made of Ramah chert; two are retouched distal fragments while the other two are uncertain proximal fragments.

STRUCTURE 4

Ten meters north of Structure 1, adjacent to a rock-fall beside the north hill-face, a 1.5 by 1.0 m test pit revealed part of a fourth axial feature (Figure 124). Several thick flat-topped rocks and a flat slab were associated with burned sand, charcoal, red ocher patches and a considerable quantity of Ramah chert debitage, some of which was thermally altered. Tools recovered from the test unit include two side-notched biface bases, one primary tip-fluting spall, one tip-fluted endblade preform, three microblades and two utilized flakes. The debitage collection consists of 253 unaltered Ramah chert flakes (78.3 g by weight), 77 thermally altered Ramah chert flakes (29.5 g), one quartz flake (0.6 g), and one schist flake (0.4 g).

Table 50. Nukasusutok-12: Test Pits 1-3 Tool Class Frequencies.

	TP1	TP2	TP3	Surface	TOTAL
Triangular endblades	1		2		3 (4.3)
Side-notched bifaces			3	1	4 (5.8)
Bifaces	1		1		2 (2.9)
Burin-like tools			1		1 (1.4)
Tip-fluting spalls	1	2	8	1	12 (17.4)
Microblades, unutilized	2	7	20		29 (42.0)
Microblades, utilized	2	1	7		10 (14.5)
Microblade cores		1			1 (1.4)
Utilized flakes		1	2		3 (4.3)
Ground schist flakes			2		2 (2.9)
Ground nephrite flakes		2			2 (2.9)
TOTAL	**7**	**14**	**46**	**2**	**69**

Both the side-notched biface bases are made of Ramah chert. One (Figure 134:d) has a single pair of wide notches and a slightly concave base (W= 30.4 mm, TH= 8.2, basal depth= 3.0, notch HT= 6.0, notch L= 13.1, notch W= 3.0). The other (Figure 134:e) has two pairs of notches and a straight base (edge A notch HT= 6.0, 14.6 mm, edge B notch HT= 5.9, 13.1, edge A notch L= 2.9, 4.2, edge B notch L= 3.6, edge A notch W= 1.6, 1.8, edge B notch W= 1.6)

The endblade preform (Figure 134:f) is made on a flake of thermally altered Ramah chert and appears to be a production failure (L= 55.3 mm, W= 22.9, TH= 5.8). It retains a striking platform proximally, has bifacial retouch limited to its margins and a single ventral tip-flute that encompasses the entire tip of the implement and terminates in a step fracture. The margins of the fluting scar were retouched slightly subsequent to spalling.

All three microblades are made of Ramah chert and are medial fragments. One is retouched. A large specimen is illustrated in Figure 134:g. The two utilized flakes are both made of Ramah chert.

Two radiocarbon dates were run from a sample of conifer charcoal associated with the structural rocks. The first assay produced a date of 930±64 B.P. (SI-

5536). Since this result indicated a Late Dorset dating, which seemed inconsistent with the tool collection, the sample was resubmitted and subjected to nitration pre-treatment to remove uncharred cellulose. The second date was 1110±80 B.P. (SI-5822), marginally older than the first and equally inconsistent with the tool collection.

TEST PITS 1-3

Seven meters south of Structure 3 was a vegetated area that was probed with three 1 m^2 test pits (Figure 124). Test Pits 2 and 3 adjoined each other while Test Pit 1 lay 1 m to the northwest. Test Pits 2 and 3 produced a surprisingly dense concentration of Ramah chert debitage and tools in a matrix of brown sand and cobbles superimposed on a soft clay deposit lying 15 cm below ground surface. No features could be discerned in the morass of cobbles and clay. The area might have contained a midden or structure that was badly disturbed by severe clay movement. Table 50 provides an overview of tool frequencies, distributed across the three test pits.

The tool collection from these test units is marked by a large number of microblades (56.5%) and contains a microblade core fragment. Although triangular endblades are only modestly represented, a fairly large number of tip-fluting spalls are present, including eight primary removal spalls. The latter might indicate a focus on endblade production from curated preforms. Tool and flake raw materials are summarized by frequency in Table 51 and by weight in Table 52. Both tool and flake materials are dominated by Ramah chert.

Table 51. Nukasusutok-12: Test Pits 1-3 Tool and Flake Raw Materials by Frequency.

	Tools N (%)	Flakes N (%)
Ramah chert	62 (89.9)	211 (87.2)
Crystal quartz	1 (1.4)	1 (0.4)
Gray Mugford chert		1 (0.4)
Green chert	1 (1.4)	
Nephrite	3 (4.3)	2 (0.8)
Schist	2 (2.9)	27 (11.2)

Table 52. Nukasusutok-12: Test Pits 1-3 Tool and Flake Raw Materials by Weight. In Grams.

	Tools g (%)	Flakes g (%)	TOTAL g(%)
Ramah chert	128.5 (91.3)	107.3 (76.0)	235.8 (83.7)
Crystal quartz	0.6 (0.4)	0.5 (0.4)	1.1 (0.4)
Gray Mugford chert		1.7 (1.2)	1.7 (0.6)
Green chert	2.8 (2.0)		2.8 (1.0)
Nephrite	6.8 (4.8)	11.7 (8.3)	18.5 (6.6)
Schist	2.0 (1.4)	19.9 (14.1)	21.9 (7.8)

Tool Assemblage

Endblades: All three triangular endblades are made of Ramah chert. A complete tip-fluted specimen (Figure 136:a) has a slightly concave base and appears to be fluted on its dorsal side (L= 21.1 mm, W= 14.6, TH= 3.2, basal depth= 1.0, tip-fluting L= 10.6, 14.0). A proximal fragment (Figure 136:b) is bifacially flaked with a slightly asymmetrical concave base; it is impossible to determine if it was tip-fluted (W= 13.1 mm,

135/ Nukasusutok-12: implements from test pits, surface and Structure 1. a: biface, TP-1; b: endblade, TP-1; c: endblade preform, TP-4; d-e: utilized flakes, TP-4, f: ground slate point/knife base, surface; g: microblade, surface; h) microblade, Structure 1.

TH= 2.8, basal depth= 1.0). Another proximal fragment (Figure 135:b) is bifacially flaked (completely on the dorsal side, marginally on the ventral side) and has a straight to slightly convex base with slight basal thinning (W= 22.9 mm, TH= 3.5).

Tip-fluting spalls: All of the 12 tip-fluting spalls are made of Ramah chert. The seven whole or near complete specimens range in length from 12.3-36.4 mm and two size groups are represented: 12.3-13.6 mm and 21.5-36.4 mm. Four of the five fragmentary specimens clearly fall into the larger size class. These large and small classes may indicate the tip-fluting of different sizes of preforms or endblades (cf., Plumet and Lebel 1998). None of the intact finished endblades

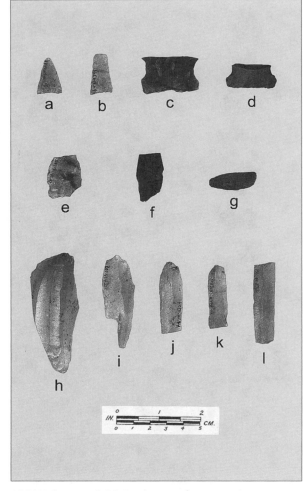

136/ Nukasusutok-12: implements from test pits.
a, b: endblades, TP-3; c-e: side-notched bifaces,
TP-3; f: burin-like-tool, TP-3; g: ground schist, TP-3;
h: microblade core fragment, TP-2; i-l: microblades,
all TP-3.

from Nukasusutok-12 exhibit tip-flutes with a length corresponding to the larger group, although one preform from Structure 2 does. Eight of the spalls are primary, four are secondary.

Side-notched bifaces: All four bifaces are proximal fragments and all exhibit a single set of notches. Three of the four are made from Ramah chert while the fourth is made from a green chert (either Mugford or Newfoundland). One of the Ramah chert implements (Figure 136:c) is from a fairly large biface and displays wide side-notches and a slightly concave bifacially thinned base (W = 33.4 mm, TH = 6.9, notch HT = 5.3, 9.5, notch L = 13.0, 12.6, notch W = 3.0, 3.0, basal

depth = 2.0). A second Ramah chert example (Figure 136:e) lacks one basal corner and has a biconvex cross-section and a slightly concave base with basal thinning (W = 20.3 mm, TH = 4.4, notch HT = 7.3, notch L = 5.4, notch W = 1.2). The third Ramah chert specimen was missing when the collection was re-analysed in the early 1990s but it is illustrated elsewhere (Hood 1986:Figure 5:l). The implement is smaller and narrower than the other bifaces and exhibits predominantly unifacial dorsal retouch and a straight base (base W = 13.8 mm, TH = 2.8, notch HT = 3.2, 3.4). It roughly resembles a Groswater "box-based" endblade, although it has a bifacially thinned base in contrast to the abrupt unifacially retouched bases of the latter. The green chert specimen (Figure 136:d) has a straight bifacially thinned base (base W = 30.0 mm, TH = 6.2, notch HT = 5.4, 5.1).

Bifaces: Both examples are made of Ramah chert. One is the distal portion of a large implement over 78 mm long and at least 37 mm wide, presumably a large knife or lance point (Figure 135:a). The other is a small distal fragment.

Burin-like tools: The single specimen of nephrite is complete but for a portion of its proximal end (Figure 136:f). Polishing traces on the proximal edges suggest a bilateral slightly constricted stem with a unilateral notch just below the bevelled portion of one lateral edge. The distal end is straight and symmetrically bevelled to a cutting edge. The distal lateral edges are ground flat and the dorsal and ventral surfaces are flat and fully ground and polished (L = > 29.0 mm, W max = 16.3, W distal = 12.7, TH = 4.3, notch HT = > 16.0).

Microblades: All but one of the 39 microblades are made of Ramah chert; the single exception is crystal quartz (a few examples are illustrated in Figure 136:i-l). All specimens are fragmentary: 18 proximal, 15 medial and six distal. Traces of utilization or retouch are found on 10 (25.6%). An MNI count of 17 can be formulated for the non-utilized specimens and an MNI of two for the utilized implements. One of the utilized specimens has proximal retouch (unilateral constriction) that may indicate hafting. In another case, a medial fragment has bifacial retouch on one of its snap surfaces that could indicate preliminary retouch for a projectile base. Additionally, a distal fragment is completely retouched on its ventral surface, which may also indicate an intended use as a projectile. The average width of 15 proximal fragments is 12.5 mm.

Platform preparation is primarily plain (n= 6) or retouched (n= 5), while one example each occurs for grinding, crushing and indeterminate. Platform angles were distributed as follows: 60° = 1, 65° = 3, 70° = 1, 75° = 2, 80° = 5, 85° = 1 and 90° =1. A major proportion of the proximal fragments (10 of 17) have lengths in the range of ca. 13-28 mm; the medial fragment lengths exhibit greater spread, but eight of 17 range between ca. 12-25 mm. This is broadly consistent with the pattern observed at Structure 2.

Microblade cores: The single Ramah chert microblade core (Figure 136:h) is a core-face fragment that bears negative scars of five long (ca. 75 mm) microblades. Three of these microblades were struck from a core platform that was broken off when the core face was detached. This detachment occurred when the core was turned over and struck on a flat basal surface used as a platform for the attempted removal of microblades from the opposite direction. Secondary retouch on the edges of the core fragment suggest it may have been re-used as an expedient scraper.

Utilized flakes: All three specimens are made on large (52-62 mm diameter) flakes of Ramah chert. In one case virtually all edges of the flake exhibit fine utilization retouch combined with blunting of exposed facets; the implement may be an expedient scraper.

Ground schist flakes: The two specimens are both small (ca. 17 and 28 mm long); one is illustrated in Figure 136:g. Schist was likely used to grind nephrite burin-like tools and perhaps slate implements.

Ground nephrite flakes: Two of the three flakes are small (L= 15.0, 24.6 mm) with limited areas of distinct grinding. A third specimen is a larger linear flake (L= 72.9 mm) with faint traces of polishing on its facets but no obvious grinding.

Discussion

These three test pits provide little indication as to the function of this part of the site. Any features once present were obliterated by fluctuating movements of the underlying clay deposit. Nonetheless, the large quantity of tools and flakes recovered from these units suggests the presence of a dwelling structure or midden. The most striking aspect of the assemblage is the high frequency of microblades and tip-fluting spalls. The former suggest a high rate of expedient tool production while the latter suggest an emphasis on endblade production— a "gearing-up" for hunting. The lack of scrapers is notable.

TEST PITS 4 AND 5

Two other 1 m² test pits were excavated within *in situ* deposits 10 m east of Structure 1. Test Pit 5 was sterile but the central portion of Test Pit 4 contained part of a shallow depression, measuring 45 by 60 cm, which contained red ocher stains and charcoal. A small notched schist slab with adhering burned fat was recovered from the deposit. A second small charcoal patch lay beside the north wall of the test unit. Charcoal from the central depression was submitted for radiocarbon dating. A first run produced a date of 1000±75 B.P. (SI-5535), which seemed much too late in relation to the tool material from the site. The sample was re-run following nitration pre-treatment, resulting in a date of 1660±90 B.P. (SI-5821).

Test Pit 4 produced 10 tools, all of Ramah chert: an endblade preform, a tip-fluting spall, six microblades, and two utilized flakes. The endblade preform (Figure 135:c) is made on a crudely retouched Ramah chert flake and is only retouched marginally— bifacially at the tip, mostly dorsally on the lateral edges—

while the base is thinned dorsally from a snap edge (L= 36.4 mm, W= 19.3, TH= 4.0). The tip-fluting spall is a large medial fragment (L >30.0 mm) of a primary spall. The six microblades are comprised of four medial and two proximal fragments. Two medial fragments are completely retouched on their ventral surfaces, possibly for use as projectiles. One of the utilized flakes has unifacial dorsal retouch along all its margins and a slight stem at one end (Figure 135:e), while the other has unifacial dorsal retouch along two lateral edges (Figure 135:d). A total of 50 flakes was collected, of which 47 (94.0%) were of Ramah chert, one (2.0%) of crystal quartz, one (2.0%) of black chert, and one (2.0%) of nephrite.

SURFACE COLLECTIONS

Two implements not directly associated with structures were surface collected. A complete retouched microblade (L= 47.9 mm, W= 13.1, TH= 3.7) lay 3 m west of the 1x1y marker at Structure 1 (Figure 135:g). The proximal portion of a ground slate point or knife (Figure 135:f) was found 6 m south of the 5x5y marker at Structure 2. The tool is made of green slate and has a constricted stem formed by a pair of wide side-notches. The base is straight with narrow, symmetrically ground bevelling. Above each notch is a slight trace of edge bevelling with surfaces running in slightly different directions. The medial faces of the implement are largely unground (TH= 4.9 mm, notch HT= 4.5, 3.5, notch L= 14.2, 15.5, notch W= 3.5, 2.5).

OVERALL ASSEMBLAGE CHARACTERISTICS AND TECHNOLOGICAL ORGANIZATION

Consideration of technological organization at Nukasusutok-12 is complicated by rather divergent tool and debitage sample sizes and differences in the representativeness of the samples.

As far as tools are concerned, only Structure 2 and Test Pits 1-3 have sufficient numbers to work with. Although Structure 2 has very little debitage, the com-plete excavation of the feature constitutes a fairly representative sample. The material from Test Pits 1-3 has a reasonable number of tools and flakes, but is a limited area sample from an uncertain context. The test unit at Structure 4 produced a few tools and a modest debitage collection, but the sample cannot be considered representative. Given these limitations the discussion can only hope to point out some tentative dimensions of technological organization at the site.

The most striking characteristic of the Nukasusutok-12 assemblage is the absence of processing tools common in other Dorset sites: endscrapers and sidescrapers. This absence implies that either the activities in which these tools were used (skin scraping and wood working) were not conducted at the site or that the implements were highly curated as part of a hafted tool kit. Instead, microblades are the predominant implement type, suggesting a high frequency of production for use in expedient tasks. The proportion of microblades with traces of utilization varies from 25% at Test Pits 1-3 to 40% at Structure 2. Structure 2 had a modest number of endblades, endblade preforms and tip-fluting spalls, while Test Pits 1-3 had a substantial number of tip-fluting spalls, including several primary removal spalls (but no endblade preforms). In both cases a focus on endblade production is suggested. As far as the debitage is concerned, Structure 2 was notable for a very small amount of flakes (and thus a high tool:flake ratio), while Structure 4 and Test Pits 1-3 had a relatively larger quantity of flakes suggestive of more emphasis on tool production and maintenance.

Considered in isolation these observations are perhaps not that significant, but their relevance is clearer when placed in a comparative context with other Dorset lithic assemblages. The only available material for such a comparison is Nagle's (1984, 1986) analysis of Dorset Ramah chert use. Nagle concluded that distance-decay processes associated with "down-the-line" exchange from the Ramah chert sources had a significant effect on the nature of Dorset lithic assemblages, particularly with regard to tool size and frequency. Preforms for bifaces and endblades are both smaller and less frequent with distance from the source areas and debitage also decreases in size and frequency. But frequency and size may also respond to other variables. Microblade production can generate either a few or many implements in a single production sequence, so the frequency of microblades may be more closely linked to the situational factors behind individual production events than to the raw material supply. The same could be said for the frequency of tip-fluting spalls. Size differences in endblades may have more to do with intended functions— such as seal versus walrus hunting— than with raw material availability (Nagle 1986:98).

One of the questions Nagle (1984:295, 315-316, 434) addressed using Nain Middle Dorset material was whether winter semi-subterranean houses were "gearing-up" sites where tools were produced for use during other periods of the annual round while sites from other seasons were marked by strategies of tool maintenance and conservation (i.e., curation behavior). He concluded that the evidence supported his general line of reasoning, but that inter-assemblage differences were not substantial:

> While sites occupied in the late fall and winter may have been the focus of the majority of flaked stone manufacturing activities in preparation for the ensuing year, it appears that for the most part Dorset knappers were routinely making many new tools throughout their entire seasonal round. Yearly lithic needs were evidently planned carefully, and supplies budgeted reasonably well (Nagle 1984:434).

How does the material from Nukasusutok-12 fit into this picture? Table 53 compares the tool assemblages from Structure 2 and Test Pits 1-3 at Nukasusutok-12 with five of the Nain region Dorset assemblages analysed by Nagle (1984:Appendix A). Koliktalik-1 (highlighted in the table) consists of two semi-subterranean winter houses (Cox 1978:107, 110-111; Fitzhugh 1976:138-140; Nagle 1984:217-228; Spiess 1978), St. John's Island-3, L-4, is an outer island mid-winter hunting camp containing a tent ring with an axial pavement (Nagle 1984:228-230; Spiess 1978:55), Black Island-1A has a possible tent structure (Nagle 1984:230-232), and Dog Bight L-3 lacked a discernable structure but is assumed to be a tent site (Fitzhugh 1976:138; Nagle 1984:209-210). Dog Bight L-3 is Early Dorset, while the rest are Middle Dorset. The proportions of tool types at Nukasusutok-12 are most similar to Dog Bight L-3, with high percentages of microblades and tip-fluting spalls, except that endscrapers and burin-like tools are better represented at Dog Bight. The other two tent-dwelling sites have very different profiles. St John's Island-3 has high proportions of endblades, endscrapers and burin-like tools, but relatively few microblades. This emphasis on sea mammal hunting and processing activities is consistent with the location of the site near the ice-edge and traces of walrus hunting in the small faunal assemblage (Spiess 1978:55). Black Island-1A is dominated by tip-fluting spalls, suggesting final-stage "gearing-up" for hunting. The variation in these tent dwelling assemblages probably reflects differences in the situational variables affecting lithic use in each case. In contrast, the winter house assemblages from Koliktalik are heavily loaded with processing/maintenance tools such as bifaces, endscrapers and burin-like tools. Given the frequency of endblade preform production at Koliktalik and their scarcity at all the tent dwelling sites, it seems likely there was a spatial staging in production, final retouch and use in a *chaîne opératoire* marked by a high degree of curation. But it should be kept in mind that there are significant formational differences between the tent and house assemblages, since the latter are accumulations resulting from multiple occupation phases ("coarse-

Table 53. Comparison of Nain Region Dorset Lithic Assemblages.
Semi-Subterranean Houses Highlighted in Gray.

	Nukasusutok-12 S-2	Nukasusutok-12 TP 1-3	Dog Bight L-3	St. John's Isl.-3 L-4	Black Isl.-1a	Koliktalik-1 H-1	Koliktalik-1 H-2
Bifaces	6 (8.7)	6 (9.8)	11 (3.2)	10 (8.5)	6 (10.2)	334 (22.3)	175 (30.7)
Biface Preforms	1 (1.4)			5 (4.2)		10 (0.7)	
Endblades	4 (5.8)	3 (4.9)	11 (3.2)	25 (21.2)	6 (10.2)	245 (16.4)	85 (14.9)
Endblade Preforms	3 (4.3)		2 (0.6)	2 (1.7)		74 (4.9)	21 (3.7)
Tip-Fluting Spalls	6 (8.7)	12 (19.7)	45 (13.0)	15 (12.7)	33 (55.9)	252 (16.8)	43 (7.5)
Endscrapers			4 (1.2)	11 (9.3)	3 (5.1)	66 (4.4)	46 (8.1)
Microblades	49 (71.0)	39 (63.9)	266 (76.7)	41 (34.7)	11 (18.6)	419 (28.0)	165 (28.9)
Burin-Like Tools		1 (1.6)	8 (2.3)	9 (7.6)		98 (6.5)	35 (6.1)
TOTAL	69	61	347	118	59	1498	570

grained" assemblages in Binford's [1980:17] sense) and the former are probably the result of more discrete events ("fine-grained" assemblages). Organizational dynamics are difficult to infer from coarse-grained assemblages.

Another dimension of variability is debitage characteristics. Table 54 outlines the Ramah chert tool:flake ratio for the Nain area sites (derived from Nagle 1984: Appendix A). Although the Nukasusutok test pits cannot be considered a representative sample, their ratio is consistent with the other Dorset sites, whether tent sites or the semi-subterranean houses at Koliktalik. Structure 2, on the other hand, stands out for its unusually high ratio of tools to flakes. Compared with the other localities, Structure 2 reflects an extremely low rate of lithic reduction combined with a high rate of tool discard. This ratio suggests little emphasis on tool replenishment or "gearing up" strategies, presumably related either to an anticipated ease of tool replacement or the absence of domestic processing and maintenance activities which might place higher demands on raw material use.

The organization of lithic reduction may also be reflected in flake size distributions and the frequency of biface-thinning flakes. Although the Nukasusutok-12 assemblages are not ideal for size analysis given small samples (Structure 2) and samples of uncertain representativeness (test pits), size distribution data for Structure 2 (completely excavated), Structure 4 (test-pitted) and Test Pits 1-3 are presented in Figure 137. Table 55 displays the frequency of biface-thinning flakes. Structure 2, which had only 48 Ramah chert flakes, is distinguished by a high proportion of flakes in the <15 mm and <10 mm categories and low frequencies in the <20 mm and larger categories, suggesting emphasis on late stage retouch rather than multi-stage reduction. The low frequency of biface-thinning flakes suggests limited reduction of preforms. Structure 4 and Test Pits 1-3 have slightly higher percentages of flakes in the <20 to <30 mm range and both have relatively large numbers of biface-thinning flakes, indicating greater reduction of preforms than at Structure 2. Although the sampling problems need to be kept in mind, these data suggest spatial differences in reduction patterns at Nukasusutok-12.

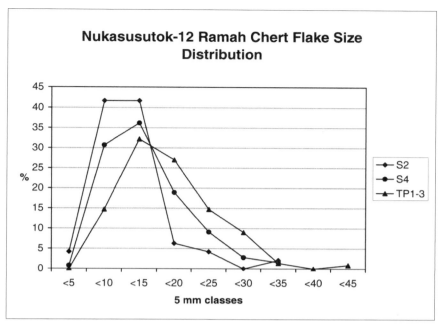

137/ Nukasusutok-12: Ramah chert flake size distribution.

Table 54. Ramah Chert Tool:Flake Ratios for Dorset Sites in the Nain Area.

	Tools	Flakes	Tool:Flake Ratio
Nukasusutok-12 S-2	63	38	1.66
Nukasusutok-12 TP1-3	62	210	0.3
Dog Bight L-3	339	1021	0.33
St. John's Island-3 L-4	127	669	0.19
Black Island 1A	51	479	0.11
Koliktalik-1 H-1	2536	16281	0.16
Koliktalik-1 H-2	1038	7712	0.13

Table 55. Distribution of Biface-Thinning Flakes at Nukasusutok-12.

	Biface-Thinning Flakes
Structure 2	4
Structure 4	30
Test Pits 1-3	53

The Ramah chert debitage size distribution has greater value when compared with other Dorset sites in the Nain region. Comparison necessitated re-sorting the Nukasusutok-12 debitage in accordance with the size category system used by Nagle (1984:261-262): category 4 (>¼ < ½ inch), category 3 (>½ inch, < 1 inch), category 2 (>1 inch, < 2 inches). Nagle eliminated a fifth category (<¼ inch) as unreliable, so the same was done for Nukasusutok-12. Four of the previously discussed Dorset components were used in the comparison: Koliktalik-1 houses 1 and 2, St. John's Island-3, L-4, and Dog Bight L3 (data from Nagle 1984: Appendix B). In the comparison by frequency (Figure 138), Structure 2 at Nukasusutok-12 has a profile similar to all the other Dorset sites, being dominated by category 4 debitage (>¼ inch <½ inch). In contrast, Structure 4 and Test Pits 1-3 are distinctly different from all the other components in their high proportions of larger category 3 flakes (>½ inch, < 1 inch). When the proportions from the three Nukasusutok-12 components are averaged, the site has a deviant profile with a high proportion of class 3 flakes. In the comparison by weight (Figure 139), Structure 2's profile of balanced classes 4 and 3 most closely resembles Koliktalik House 2, while Structure 4 and Test Pits 1-3's profiles with high class 3 proportions are most similar to St. John's Island. The averaged Nukasusutok profile is also very close to St. John's Island. Although the intra-site variation at Nukasusutok-12 should be kept in mind, it is interesting that its greatest similarities are with St. John's Island, since both sites are seasonal hunting camps associated with axial structures.

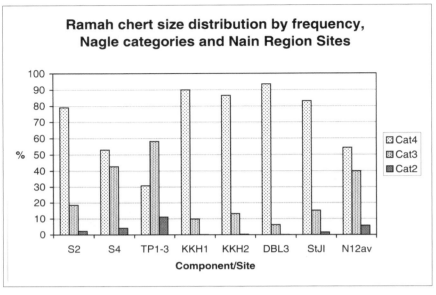

138/ Nain region Dorset site Ramah chert size distributions by frequency, using Nagle's (1984) categories.

The preceding discussion positions Nukasusutok-12 relative to other Nain area Dorset assemblages, drawing out some general similarities and differences, but it is confined by the vagaries of the Nukasusutok sample and by the limited comparative base. Nonetheless, the Nukasusutok-12 assemblage might be characterized as representing a hunting camp marked by a high production of expedient microblades, the final stage reduction of harpoon endblades, as indicated by tip-fluting spalls and endblade preforms, and the reduction of biface preforms, as implied by the biface-thinning flakes. The size/weight distribution of the Ramah chert debitage suggests that Nukasusutok-12 reduction patterns are most similar to another outer island hunting camp, St. John's Island-3, L-4, although the tool assemblages of the two sites differ in that Nukasusutok-12 has a higher rate of microblade production but a lower rate of endblade discard. If, as Nagle (1986:98) observed, variation in microblade frequency is conditioned by highly contingent individual production decisions, then it may be that the contrasts in endblade discard are the only significant differences between the sites.

To conclude, partly following Nagle's (1984, 1986) observations one might say the nature of any individual Dorset assemblage is a product of the articulation of three dimensions: (1) general constraints imposed by the structure of the Ramah chert delivery system on the form and quantity of raw materials circulating within different regions, (2) production decisions linked to specific situations, and (3) social and symbolic context. At this point we have a strong set of inferences concerning the first point, a good start on but still inadequate understanding of the second, and rather little penetration of the third.

CHRONOLOGY

Table 56 outlines the radiocarbon dates from Structure 4 and Test Pit 4. As noted previously, the first run

Table 56. Radiocarbon Dates from Nukasusutok-12.

Location	First Run	Second Run (nitration pre-treatment)	Lab Nos.	1δ Calibration of Second Run (OxCal 3.10)
Structure 4	930±64 B.P.	1110±80 B.P.	SI-5536, 5822	AD 780-1020
Test Pit 4	1000±75 B.P.	1660±90 B.P.	SI-5535, 5821	AD 250-540

(both samples of conifer charcoal)

dates did not correspond with what was expected on the basis of tool typology (2200-2000 B.P.), so the samples were run a second time with nitration pretreatment to remove uncharred cellulose. Although this resulted in a significantly earlier assay for the sample from Test Pit 4, the result for Structure 4 was little different. Regrettably, neither of these samples was associated with clearly diagnostic tools. The material from Structure 4 included two side-notched bifaces (one with a single pair of notches, the other multiple notched), three microblades, a tip-fluted point preform, a tip-fluting spall, and a utilized flake. Typologically, the bifaces seem inconsistent with the 1110±80 B.P. Late Dorset dating. Test Pit 4 contained an endblade preform, a tip-fluting spall, a possible scraper fragment, six microblades (two of which were completely retouched on their ventral surfaces), a utilized flake and a schist fragment with adhering burned fat. The best that can be said is that this material is not inconsistent with a 1660±90 B.P. Middle Dorset dating. Given the ambiguity of the radiocarbon dating the remainder of the chronological discussion must be based on typological comparisons. Since very little Labrador Dorset material has been reported in full, the discussion will be somewhat impressionistic.

Typologically, Nukasusutok-12 appears to be intermediate between Early Dorset material such as Dog Bight L-3 from the Nain region, dated 2455±75 B.P. and 2400±70 B.P. (Cox 1978:99, illustrated in Fitzhugh 1976, Figure 12, m-s), and Iluvektalik-1 from Okak Bay, dated 2845±60 B.P. on charcoal mixed with burned fat (Cox 1977:152-164, illustrated in Cox 1978:108), and Middle Dorset material from Koliktalik-1 in the Nain area (Cox 1978:99; illustrated in Fitzhugh 1976, Figure

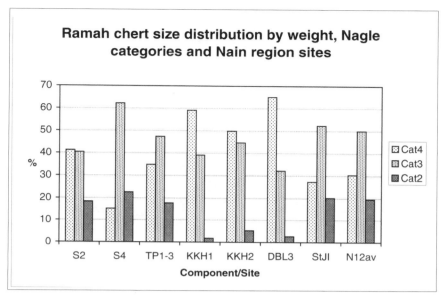

139/ Nain region Dorset site Ramah chert size distributions by weight, using Nagle's (1984) categories.

12 a-l, and Cox 1978:109). The Nukasustok-12 material bears some resemblance to the few tools illustrated from Avayalik-7 in northernmost Labrador, originally believed to date to the Early/Middle Dorset boundary, ca. 2200-1800 B.P. (R. Jordan 1980:609-610), but which produced a later than expected date of 1395±70 B.P. (Morlan 2001-2005).

Several Nukasustok-12 assemblage attributes reflect this Early/Middle Dorset character. First, there is a high frequency of microblades, which is regarded as typical of Early Dorset sites (Cox 1978:107). In a correspondence analysis (not shown here) of Labrador Dorset assemblages based on data from Nagle (1984: Appendix A), Nukasusutok-12 was grouped together with all the Early Dorset sites on the basis of their shared high frequency of microblades. As observed above, however, microblade production was probably situationally conditioned such that one should be wary of using it as a chrono-typological indicator. Second, the triangular endblades are straight-based or only slightly concave and four of them (from Structure 2, Structure 3 and Test Pits 1-3) appear to be tip-fluted on their dorsal surfaces, as are two endblade preforms (Structure 2). Dorsal tip-fluting is thought to be an early Dorset trait. There is no trace of unifacial end-blades or basal thinning on the dorsal surface of end-blades as found in Middle Dorset (Cox 1978:107). Third, a high side-notched or quasi "box-based" biface (Figure 131:h) from Structure 2 and a small unifacial notched biface resembling Groswater style (Hood 1986:Figure 5:l) from Test Pits 1-3 have an Early Dorset stamp, although the latter may simply be an expedient tool (cf., Nagle 1984:347-348). Fourth, a burin-like tool preform from Structure 3 that was destined to be relatively long and have broad side-notching (Figure 134:c) seems more similar to the Early Dorset forms from Iluvektalik-1 (Cox 1978:108) than the narrow-notched Middle Dorset forms from Koliktalik-1 (Cox 1978:109). A fully ground tabular nephrite burin-like tool with a "squared" working end from Test Pit 3, however, exhibits the remnants of a proximal stem and traces of a small notch on a lateral margin, similar to Middle Dorset forms (Figure 136:f). The single and multiple side-notched bifaces from Nukasusutok-12 could be found in either Early or Middle Dorset contexts.

To conclude, on typological grounds we might propose that Structure 2, Test Pits 1-3 and probably Structure 3 are Early/Middle Dorset, perhaps dating 2200-2000 B.P.. On the basis of the radiocarbon dates, unsupported by typological data, Structure 4 and Test Pit 4 may be Middle Dorset or later.

STRUCTURAL COMPARISONS

A major difficulty in providing a broader view of the Nukasusutok-12 structural remains is the lack of published accounts of Dorset structures in Labrador or elsewhere. Three semi-subterranean houses have been given some preliminary documentation: one of the two Middle Dorset houses from Koliktalik-1 in the Nain region (Fitzhugh 1976:130-131; Cox 1978:107-111), Iglusuaktalialuk Island-4 West, a Middle Dorset house in the Okak region (Cox 1977:137-138), and Okak-3, a Late Dorset house in the Okak region (Cox 1977:195-196, 1978:110-111). Koliktalik-1 House 1 lacked an axial feature, but there were a series of central pits associated

with a partial pavement. The other two houses had well-defined stone axial features.

Dorset surface structures are described as consisting of rectangular tent rings with central cobble or slab pavements lacking clear borders, or more ephemeral rock and pavement features (Cox 1978:11). The only published example is a tent ring from Avayalik-2 in northernmost Labrador, typologically dated to the Early/Middle Dorset "transition" (2200-1800 B.P.). This was a rectangular structure with a central boulder alignment but without box hearths, slab pavements or vertical boundary rocks (R. Jordan 1980:612, Figure 4). One of the two radiocarbon dates from the structure is consistent with the typological dating (2000±75 B.P., 1345±70 B.P.;). In the Nain area, tent ring features of broadly similar character are known from an Early Dorset component at the Dog Island West Spur site and the Middle Dorset St. John's Island-3, L-4 site.

The Nukasusutok-12 structures are clearly of a different character than the previously mentioned surface structures in that they consist of long axial features with hearth areas and they lack distinct tent rings. These contrasts may indicate functional or seasonal differences. The lack of ring rocks may indicate the tents were anchored in snow and perhaps used in the early spring or late fall. As discussed in the spatial analysis of Structure 2, the presence of hearth-related pairs of tool clusters at each end of the mid-passage hints at behavioral symmetry, possibly indicative of two domestic units within a large dwelling. This inference can be compared with R. Jordan's (1980:612) preliminary conclusion that the tent ring at Avayalik-2 was used by two family units.

Structures 1 and 2 at Nukasusutok-12 bear a strong resemblance to each other. Although slightly different in size, each had a well defined axial feature, clear evidence for a hearth at each end of the passage, possible traces of a third central hearth, notched schist slabs and traces of large terminus rocks at one or both ends of the passage. These structural and organizational similarities might indicate proximity in time, but the almost total lack of lithics at Structure 1 hinders chronological inferences.

SETTLEMENT PATTERN AND SEASONALITY

Drawing together the discussion so far, the Nukasusutok-12 lithic assemblage gives the impression of a focus on sea mammal hunting with minimal evidence for a wider range of domestic activities. In the case of Structure 2, the high tool:flake ratio indicates a high rate of tool discard with minimal tool production and maintenance, suggesting a social unit arrived with a limited tool kit prepared at another locality, perhaps a winter house, and functioned with low replacement requirements. The latter may not hold for the other features at the site, the sampling of which revealed larger quantities of debitage. The excavated axial features point to the use of large tents (perhaps family pairs?) and the presence of additional structures indicate the site was used repeatedly by small social units, probably around the Early to Middle Dorset "transition," but possibly later as well.

The potential seasonal use of the site can be considered with reference to 18th century Labrador Inuit settlement. According to Taylor (1974:51), Contact Period house sites were typically located with good access to fall harp seal hunting. There is an 18th century communal house complex just west of Nukasusutok-12 (Nukasusutok-8, Chapter 11) and east of Wyatt Harbour the narrow passage between a rocky islet and Nukasusutok Island is said to be a good place for intercepting harp seals. The area between Nukasusutok and Nochalik Island to the southwest has reasonably good open water sealing during the summer. Mid-winter ice-edge sealing is not likely from the site since the usual position of the *sîna* is off Humby's Island, over 20 km to the east (Figure 140). The area to the southeast between Satok Island and Humby's Island can be good for hunting seals basking on the ice in the spring. This area often has thin ice (visible as a darker shading in Figure 4), so open water areas may develop early in the spring. Given these considerations, the optimal periods for site occupation are during the harp seal migrations in the fall or the spring, basking seal hunting in the spring, or open water sealing during the summer.

If we consider the Nain region Dorset site distribution as a whole (Figure 140), it is clear that Dorset activity was concentrated in a 30 km wide band in the mid-outer island zone. Only a handful of sites are situated at inner bay locations. Four of the five Middle Dorset semi-subterranean house sites[7] are located within 7-8 km of the *sîna* (as judged from Figure 4): Koliktalik-1 (Fitzhugh 1976:131, 140; Nagle 1984:217-228; Spiess 1978), Ford Harbour-4 (Fitzhugh 1981:37), Jonathon Island-3 (site files, Cultural Heritage Division) and Drawbucket Tickle-2 (site files, Cultural Heritage Division). Spiess' (1978) interpretation of the faunal remains from the houses at Koliktalik-1 suggests the site was occupied October to December to exploit the southward harp seal migration and from March to June for hunting basking seals and the northward migrating harps. Cox and Spiess (1980:660-661) hypothesize the site was abandoned January through March and postulate movement to camps on more seaward islands near the ice-edge due to a lack of breathing hole sealing techniques. An axial pavement structure at St. John's Island-3, L-4, is proposed as such a camp, oriented towards open water seal and walrus hunting.

A possible variation on this pattern may be inferred from the fifth semi-subterranean house site located 8 km east of Nukasusutok-12: No-Name Island-2 (Sutton et al. 1981). This locality has two houses, with House 1 radiocarbon dated at 1285±75 B.P., 1260±60 B.P. and 915±100 B.P. and House 2 dated 1450±65 B.P. (Fitzhugh, personal communication); in other words late Middle Dorset to Late Dorset.

---

[7]Middle Dorset sod houses have also been registered at Skull Island (Fitzhugh 1981:37), but subsequent investigation led Susan Kaplan to suggest they may actually be Thule houses on top of a Dorset component (site files, Cultural Heritage Division). This locality is located ca. 2-3 km from the *sîna*.

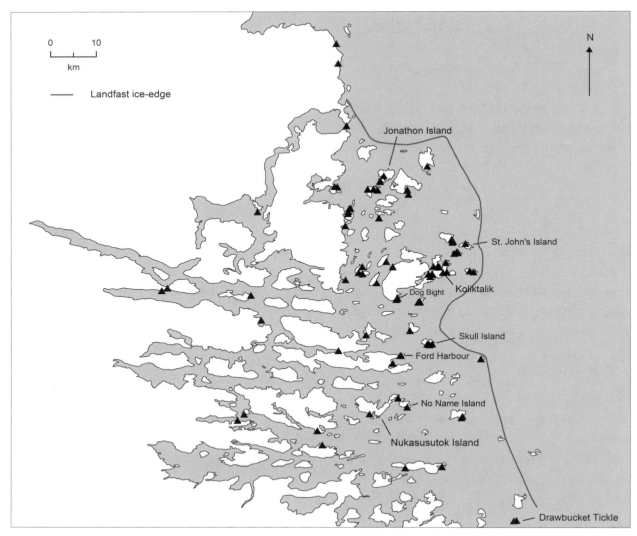

140/ Nain region Dorset site distribution. Original map © 2004 produced under licence from Her Majesty the Queen in Right of Canada, with permission of Natural Resources Canada.

Excavations in a poorly preserved midden revealed the presence of walrus, but mid-winter hunting seems unlikely since the site is located 10-12 km distant from the *sîna*. Given the tendency for thin ice and early open water in the area to the south between Satok and Humby's Island, it is possible walrus were hunted there in the first open leads of the late winter/early spring. They could also have been taken later in the open water period when the eastern end of the small island would serve as an excellent haul-out locale.

With these winter sites as anchor points we could postulate that Dorset settlement patterns involved relatively short distance "lateral" (east-west)

shifts on the scale of 15-30 km between fall-winter-spring semi-subterranean house sites located near the outer coastal fringe and spring-summer-fall tent dwellings at outer and mid-island locations, with similar or longer distance movements also possible on a north-south axis. Periodic shifts between alternative winter house locations may have occurred primarily as "longitudinal" (north-south) movements. However, if the Nukasusutok-12 occupation, or at least part of it, pre-dated the documented Middle Dorset winter houses it could very well have been part of a different settlement pattern configuration than the one outlined here.

CHAPTER 10

Post-Contact Inuit Settlement on Nukasusutok Island

As noted in Chapter 4, there are several localities with traces of Post-Contact Period Inuit activity on Nukasusutok Island. These were not central to the fieldwork conducted in 1979-80 or 1992-93, although the midden at the 18th century communal house site Nukasusutok-8 (HcCh-10) was tested. Subsequent to this testing, the Robert S. Peabody Museum at Phillips Academy, Andover, Massachusetts, was visited in order to inspect collections made on Nukasusutok Island in 1928 by William Duncan Strong, anthropologist with the Rawson-MacMillan Subarctic expedition. Strong's field notes and photographs were consulted at the National Anthropological Archives, Smithsonian Institution, Washington D.C.

Strong excavated some of the house structures at Nukasusutok-8 and collected skeletal material and artifacts from graves at various places on the island. He never published this or other Inuit material he collected between Nain and Hopedale, although the skeletal material was used in a physical anthropological study by T. D. Stewart (1939). The artifact material was first housed at the Field Museum in Chicago, but was eventually transferred through an exchange agreement to the Peabody Museum, Andover. The value of the collection is limited because Strong's cursory field notes lack critical provenience details, but the material is sufficiently interesting to justify an overview here, although the short time available for documentation did not permit a full analysis. Strong's material is supplemented by a small test-pit collection derived from

Nukasusutok-8 in 1992 and a brief survey of Nukasusutok-7 in 2004.

Offsetting the problematic archaeological data is a relatively rich ethnohistoric record for the Nukasusutok-8 settlement. J. Garth Taylor's research on the Moravian missionary diaries uncovered references to the settlement between 1772-1794 and the Moravian Periodical Accounts (abbreviated as P.A.) contain passing references to later settlement on Nukasusutok Island. Some of the documentary information pertains to well-known Inuit individuals, so the usually anonymous archaeological context can be connected with the agency of real people and the social organization of the community can be specified. These ethnohistoric data are marshaled to construct a composite settlement history from the late 18th to early 19th centuries, which is followed by a consideration of the archaeological data. But a brief sketch of post-contact Inuit society and settlement patterns is first presented to set the scene.

POST-CONTACT INUIT SOCIETY AND SETTLEMENT PATTERNS IN LABRADOR

The Thule ancestors of the Labrador Inuit colonized northern Labrador by AD 1250-1300 (Fitzhugh 1994). At the Iglosiatik-1 site in the Nain area, Thule-style sod houses with traces of metal apparently date to the early 16th century (Fitzhugh 1994:258; Kaplan 1983:216, 455-462). During the 16th century Inuit expanded southwards to Hamilton Inlet, the Strait of Belle Isle and the Québec North Shore. Documentary information and archaeological data suggest the Inuit presence in southern Labrador was a year-round occupation that lasted until the mid-1700s, when the increasing scale of European activity may have led to a contraction of Inuit occupancy towards Hamilton Inlet. During the 16th and 17th centuries the southern Inuit were in contact with a variety of Europeans who conducted whaling and fishing in the area: Basques, French, English, Portugese, Spanish and Dutch (Martijn and Clermont 1980; Stopp 2002:75-76). Inuit both traded for and plundered European goods (Stopp 2002:83; Trudel 1980). Although some European wares made their way northwards along the Labrador coast through Inuit social networks, the degree of culture change in the north was limited.

Change accelerated during the 18th century. In 1702 the French Sieur de Courtemanche was granted a concession in southern and central Labrador and he established a base of operations at Bradore on the Québec North Shore. In 1735 the Québec trader Marsal received a concession for sealing and trading at Cape Charles and in 1737 Louis Fornel was one of three partners who acquired a similar concession at Chateau Bay. In 1743 Fornel established a post for trading with the Innu at Northwest River in Hamilton Inlet; after his death in 1745 this post and another at Rigolet were run by his wife until ca. 1755. French relations with the Inuit in southern Labrador were generally marked by considerable conflict (Kennedy 1995:20-23; Stopp 2002:82-83, personal communication; Zimmerly 1975:36-40).

Britain acquired control of the Labrador coast in 1763 after the end of the Seven Years War. British merchants overtook operations at Chateau Bay and a defensive blockhouse called Fort York was constructed there in 1766. In 1770 George Cartwright overtook the trading post at Cape Charles and founded additional posts, including his northernmost establishment at Sandwich Bay in 1775. Cartwright ceased operations in

1786. Other English merchants competed within the same area and by 1784 Québec traders were established in Hamilton Inlet (Kennedy 1995:25-41; Zimmerly 1975:42-44). During the 1760s and early 1770s large numbers of Inuit from the central coast— perhaps mostly from Hamilton Inlet, but also parties from Hopedale and Nain— made trips to the English trading centers at Cape Charles and Chateau Bay. George Cartwright's diary indicates that large groups of Inuit did not appear south of Hamilton Inlet after 1773 (Stopp, personal communication), but major Inuit traders were still making trips to Chateau Bay until ca. 1790 (see below). The establishment of Moravian missions in central and northern Labrador after 1771 provided northern Inuit with closer trading options, which became more advantageous in the late 1780s and 1790s when Moravian trade policies were liberalized.

During the course of the 17th and 18th centuries, Inuit tools traditionally made from stone were replaced by metals and a wide array of European goods was incorporated into Inuit life. Dwelling forms changed from the earlier small single-family sod houses to large multi-family communal houses (Kaplan 1983, 1985). The first Moravian missionary settlement was established at Nain in 1771, followed by Okak (1776), Hopedale (1782) and Hebron in 1830 (and several others later in the 19th century). Eventually, the previously dispersed Inuit settlement became concentrated at the mission stations, where systematic Christianization and incorporation into European material culture systems occurred. But this process did not transpire rapidly. Moravian letters from the late 18th century repeatedly express frustration at the difficulties of acquiring and retaining converts and bemoan the negative influences of "heathens." A poignant note is struck by a comment in the Hopedale diary for 1795 that "...their hearts be as hard as rocks and as cold as the ice of their country" (P.A. 1: 1795:351). Christianity was not consolidated until 1804-1805 when a "revival" spread through the mission settlement areas (Hiller 1971:86). Nonetheless, "heathen" Inuit still dominated northernmost Labrador for many years thereafter (Loring 1998).

Communal Houses and "Big-Men" Traders

Much of the research on Post-Contact Inuit settlement has focused on the so-called "communal house phase" of the 18th century. These semi-subterranean winter houses were rectangular, 7-16 m long and 6 m wide, with long entrance passages and generally three sleeping platforms (Kaplan 1983:238). Taylor's (1974:71) ethnohistorical data indicate the dwellings were occupied by an average of 20 people. The household was generally composed of several closely related families, often fathers and their married sons or brothers (Taylor 1974:74-75) and polygyny was frequent (Taylor 1974:67). Winter settlements consisted of 1-8 houses (average= 2.4; calculated from Taylor 1974:71). Information on the social relationships between households is more limited than for within households, but Taylor (1974:77-78) suggested kinship sometimes played a role, either links between brothers or uxorilocal ties. Certain males had leadership positions within the households by virtue of their kinship positions (father/son or father/son-in-law), but leadership authority at the settlement level was less marked and was tied to personal qualities, shamanist power and success in trading for European goods. There were few mechanisms for solving disputes above the household level and authority conflicts between brothers were common (Taylor 1974:80-84). The latter resonates in the translation of Nukasusutok (NaKasêtjutôk) as "the place where the brothers quarreled" (Wheeler 1953:62) and in a story recounted by Manase Fox (1979) concerning conflict between brothers, one a leader at Nukasusutok.

The shift from single-family to multi-family communal dwellings has been discussed from different perspectives. Schledermann (1976) offered an environmental determinist proposal: climatic cooling and the concomitant decline of whale hunting decreased resource availability, resulting in Inuit co-residential arrangements to facilitate sharing and fuel conservation. An unpublished paper by Taylor (1976) attributed the development to social aggregation around individuals prominent in trading baleen for European goods, a position adopted by R. Jordan (1978) and Kaplan (1983:351-359; also Jordan and Kaplan 1980) and clearly analogous to Sahlins' (1963) "big-man" model and the north Alaskan *umealik,* a man of wealth and boat owner (Spencer 1959). Kaplan went further, suggesting these high profile individuals and their economic and political activities indicate "...that a form of hierarchical organization was in operation in 18th century Neo-Eskimo society" (Kaplan 1983:352). Inuit middlemen from the central coast acquired baleen, whalebone, seal oil and furs from groups in the north and then traveled to southern Labrador trading centers such as Cape Charles and Chateau Bay. There they acquired European goods that later were circulated northwards, either down-the-line along existing social networks or by the traders transporting them northwards themselves (Kaplan 1983:351-353). A well-known trader from the Nain region, Tuglavina, facilitated this activity by acquiring a two-masted sloop (P.A. 1: 1794:251).

Kaplan (1983:355-359) saw these processes in terms of the emergence of new "entrepreneurial" social roles, increased competition for resources and family rivalries. Multi-family households headed by boat owners constituted expanded production units and created social dependencies. Household heads could use these production units to generate the resources needed for participation in regional trade, which in turn provided the economic tools and symbols of status needed to retain followers and recruit multiple wives, who supplemented the household's labour power, served as prestige symbols and extended kinship-based economic networks. Shamanist power could also be used to reinforce social influence.

The Jordan-Kaplan model was challenged by Richling (1993), who drew quite different conclusions from the connection between trade goods and multi-family households. Richling saw the 18th century not as a period of radical shift towards hierarchy, but as a time when Inuit adjusted to changes by intensifying traditional egalitarian social practices. He questioned R. Jordan's (1978:184) assumption that trade goods were regarded as private property and thus not subject to sharing beyond the household. Instead, Richling (1993:74) suggested intensified communalism through sharing was a traditional Inuit means for dealing with economic scarcity and that access to scarce European goods would also have been handled through sharing relationships. Although Richling was probably right in questioning the relevance of private property concepts, his invocation of a blanket communal social ethic as sufficient explanation for the development of multi-family houses leaves much of the dynamics of 18th century Inuit society unaccounted for. It seems more productive to theorize household heads as *active agents* whose strategies drew on traditional internal social resources such as personal characteristics, hunting skill, generosity and shamanist power, and who had varying degrees of ability to exploit the new external resources that became available through engagement with the expanding periphery of the European world system. This leaves open the possibility for varied sets of local outcomes, some marked by a degree of social inequality, others marked by equality maintenance mechanisms.

In order to put human faces on the abstract category of Inuit agents, a short historical narrative derived from Moravian missionary sources is presented in the next section. The late 18th century Moravian accounts provide an interesting glimpse of the prevailing social dynamics, albeit from a Moravian point of view. This story of two well-known Inuit highlights some of the processes outlined above.

An Ethnohistoric Vignette: Tuglavina and Mikak

One individual whose life intersected with the Nukasusutok settlement for a time was the "big-man"

trader Tuglavina, frequently referred to in the late 18th century Moravian accounts. His sometime wife Mikak also has a high profile in the historical records, although there is no indication that she resided on Nukasusutok with Tuglavina. The following is a brief biographical synopsis, culled from J. Garth Taylor's publications and the Moravian Periodical Accounts. It provides a sketch of important aspects of Inuit social and economic life during the late 18th century, but it should be emphasized that neither individual can be taken as representative of a "typical" Inuk of the time.

Mikak was the daughter of the Inuit leader Nerkingoak. After an initial 1765 encounter with Moravian missionaries on an exploratory trip, Mikak was captured in 1767 near Cape Charles in southern Labrador. In 1768 she was taken to England where she resided until her return to Labrador in 1769. She moved within London society and helped promote the Moravian cause; the mission eventually received a land grant in 1769. When the Moravian missionaries returned in 1770 on another exploratory trip to find a location to establish a mission they met Mikak and her new husband Tuglavina near Byron Bay (north of Hamilton Inlet). Mikak clothed herself in a gold-trimmed gown given to her by the Dowager Princess of Wales, and a king's medal. The couple accompanied the Moravians northwards to Nain, Tuglavina serving as guide (Taylor 1979:740, 1984:18-19; Whiteley 1979:536-537). One might speculate as to whether Tuglavina's forming a partnership with a woman who had such close ties with the English was a deliberate strategy on his part to facilitate access to European goods and acquire status.

The Moravians regarded Tuglavina as "...a man of vast authority among his countrymen" (P.A. 3: 1799:435) "...and his word was absolute law" (P.A. 1: 1794:251). His prominence was based partly on hunting success, physical strength and cleverness, but also on the widespread belief that he possessed exceptional powers of sorcery that were given to him by Torngak (a spirit). If, after consulting with Torngak, he stated that someone should be killed, the declaration was implemented. Tuglavina himself allegedly killed several people and his shamanist exhortations resulted in many additional killings by others. During the early years of the mission Tuglavina was a thorn in the side of the Moravians, "seducing" their converts (P.A. 1: 1794:251). He and Mikak did not live at the mission (Whiteley 1979:537); as noted below, we know that he was resident at the Nukasusutok settlement in 1776-77. Despite his activities, Tuglavina maintained a "submissive" tone in the vicinity of the missionaries (P.A. 1: 1794:251) and assisted them in various ways. In 1775 he used a boat constructed for him by the Moravians to transport some missionaries scouting for a new mission site to the Hopedale area. In 1780 a missionary accompanied him into the interior on a caribou hunting trip (Taylor 1969, 1979:740, 1984:21).

Mikak and Tuglavina had a difficult relationship. Prior to Mikak's return from England Tuglavina had been married to Mikak's younger sister. Tuglavina took possession of the sister again in 1772, which alienated the group she had been with and displeased Mikak. Mikak was also displeased when Tuglavina temporarily exchanged her for another man's spouse. A feud was brewing with another group in the Nain region because of complaints that Mikak's family did not share the goods they had accumulated. In 1774-75 Tuglavina and Mikak wintered in the interior, subsisting off stored caribou meat. In the fall of 1775 the couple went to northern Labrador on a trading expedition, collecting baleen at Nachvak, among other places. In the spring of 1776 Tuglavina abandoned Mikak in favour of her two sisters. Mikak then lived with another man who lacked resources and social status (Taylor 1984:21-22). By 1782 Tuglavina had four wives (Taylor 1979:740, 1984:23).

In 1782 Tuglavina went to Chateau Bay in southern Labrador where he traded at European establishments. Mikak and her new husband followed. Tuglavina's southern trading continued until ca. 1790. At the outset he acquired a two masted sloop in the

south (P.A. 1: 1794:251), which was instrumental for his ability to gather baleen from Inuit in northern Labrador. The baleen was exchanged for European goods at Chateau Bay and the goods were then transported to the north. Tuglavina also acquired firearms, which the Moravians had been unwilling to supply, and he solicited Inuit to accompany him on his trading trips, which did not please the missionaries (Taylor 1979:740). On his return to Nain in 1784 he appeared at the mission wearing a European officer's outfit consisting of a coat, wig, laced hat and sword (P.A. 1: 1794:251). In 1783 Tuglavina was baptized in the south and given the Christian name William, but he returned to Nain in 1784 "as sinful as ever," although he assisted the mission in various ways (P.A. 3: 1799:435-437).

Mikak lived mostly in the Hamilton Inlet area until 1795 when she returned to the mission at Nain, where she died about the age of 55 (Whiteley 1979:536-537). Tuglavina's life as a trader ended by 1790 "...when his sloop became unseaworthy and he had only a single dog to pull his sled" (Taylor 1979:740). In 1790 he joined the mission settlement in Nain, now with only one wife. He was not accepted as a full member of the Nain congregation until 1793, since he had difficulty conforming to Moravian expectations. In 1793 the missionaries wrote that Tuglavina and Sikfigak's families departed the mission for other places "...where they spent the winter in many wicked ways...Tuglavina is often very uneasy in his conscience and promises to return, but cannot put his good intentions into execution" (P.A. 1: 1793:215). But by 1795-96 Tuglavina began to "testify" to other Inuit and remained a convert despite "harassment" from "heathen" Inuit (P.A. 1: 1795:354, 2:60). He died of pleurisy in 1798 at ca. 60 years old, a few days after returning from a caribou hunt (P.A. 3: 1799:328, 435).

18th Century Subsistence-Settlement Systems

The 18th century Inuit communal house economy must also be situated in terms of subsistence-settlement systems. The following is a short summary of central points.

Semi-subterranean sod house settlements were occupied during the winter, beginning in mid-October when Inuit moved into their houses prior to the fall hunt for southward migrating harp seals (Taylor 1974:51). According to Taylor (1974:51), all the late 18th century winter house settlements in the Nain-Okak regions were located in areas with access to migrating harp seals. Harps and other seals were hunted by kayak until the formation of sea-ice. Fall sealing was highly productive such that seals were first cached near the hunting sites then transported by sled to the settlements later in the winter (Taylor 1974:35, 51). Bowhead whales were hunted in November by *umiak* crews of 11-15 men (Taylor 1988:123, 125). Moravian records from 1771-1784 indicate the most productive whaling areas (in descending order) were Hebron, Nachvak, Saglek, Okak, and Hopedale, with a total of 63 whales reported taken during this time span. No whales were reported as captured in the Nain area, probably because of the unfavorable bathymetric conditions of the island-studded archipelago (Taylor 1988:125), but stranded drift whales were exploited when available (Taylor 1988:127).

After freeze-up in mid-December, Inuit activities were centered on breathing hole sealing through new thin ice, especially along the *sîna* or at tidal "rattles." This was often undertaken by male hunting parties based in temporary snow-house camps. But January through April was a relatively low productivity period for sealing. Caribou meat taken on fall hunts in the interior might be retrieved from distant inland caches (Taylor 1969:157, 1974:51-55). March and April were marked by sealing and walrus hunting at the *sîna* and rock cod could be jigged through the sea-ice and char through the ice on inland lakes.

The sod house settlements were abandoned in late April when households established tent camps on the outer islands for spring sealing. Both basking seal (*ôttuk*) techniques and open water kayak hunting were employed, with bearded and harbor seals as primary prey. In June the northward migration of the harp seals would be exploited by open water hunting, occasionally walrus and beluga could be had, and sea birds were hunted and their eggs collected (Taylor 1974:55-56). After the ice break-up in mid-June people moved to the inner bays where large regional gatherings occurred at aggregation sites. In the Nain area this was at Amitok (Pardy Island), where 200-300 people participated. Kayak-based sealing was conducted in the bays and char and salmon were fished on their seaward runs (Taylor 1974:18, 56).

In late August and until October, some families went inland to hunt caribou for their skins and to cache meat for the winter. Those remaining on the coast engaged in sealing, fished char and salmon on their landward migrations, caching them for future use, and fished cod (Taylor 1974:57-58).

On the Cusp of Change: Into the Early 19th Century

During the late 18th and early 19th centuries a series of changes occurred as central coast Inuit gradually abandoned their communal houses and resettled at the Moravian mission centers. Although the missions at Nain, Okak and Hopedale were established between 1771 and 1782, it was not until the early 19th century that the majority of Inuit resided in these settlements. In 1793 the Moravians reported four houses with a total of 60 Inuit at Nain (P.A.1:1793:215). In 1795 the Nain mission reported a congregation of 28 plus 40 others who were permitted to live at the settlement (P.A. 1:1795:354). In 1806, after the "revival" episode, there were 42 baptized and 22 unbaptized Inuit (P.A. 4:1806:125). By 1810 there were 91 in the congregation (P.A. 5:1810:55) and in 1819 there were 146 congregants and a total of 175 inhabitants in the Nain settlement (P.A.7:1819:166). The slow recruitment rate well into the early 19th century suggests that Inuit assessed the costs and benefits of affiliating themselves with the missions and initially found few advantages in doing so. Yet by the second decade of the 19th century the dynamics of autonomy/dependence relations had shifted to the extent that autonomy was no longer a viable strategy on the central coast.

The primary attraction of settling at a mission station was close and reliable access to European goods since, as noted above, the Moravians' frustration with a low conversion rate indicates that religious enthusiasm was not a central factor (Kaplan 1983:365). Initially, the Moravians tried to deal with this problem through a strategy of handling economic transactions and religious conversion as separate spheres. Goods and services had to be paid for and food was not dispensed freely except in times of dire need. Since the mission store was accessible to both converts and "heathen," conversion had no direct economic benefits and residence at mission settlements might incur subsistence disadvantages because of the non-optimal placement of the missions relative to game resources (Hiller 1971:84-85). Thus, until the early 1800s Inuit retained their autonomy in the hinterlands of the mission settlements, leaders attempted to lure converts away from the missions and traders continued their travels to southern Labrador.

In the late 1780s and 1790s the Moravian strategy of separating the spiritual realm from utilitarian rewards was undermined by organizational changes involving closer links between mission policy and economic practices, such as providing firearms to compete with southern traders and allowing credit (Hiller 1971:94-95). These practices increased the potential benefits of mission affiliation and subverted the ability of independent Inuit traders to sustain their activities and retain followers. Increased economic engagement with the Moravians impacted social relations and material culture. The availability of guns for caribou hunting eliminated the use of drive systems and large group cooperation, while sealing and fishing with nets provided larger immediate returns with minimal cooperation. In the 19th century, fox trapping drew Inuit into credit/debt relations and greater dependence on European goods since trapping did not generate direct subsistence rewards (Kaplan 1983:361-363).

Those Inuit who settled at the missions not only underwent religious conversion but also significant social transformations. The missionaries abhorred the multi-family houses and their associated "heathen" practices so mission Inuit were required to live in single-family dwellings. The Moravians were concerned about the potential bad influence of "heathens" outside the settlements, so converts were encouraged to hunt and fish close to the missions in order to minimize contacts with "heathens" and to permit Moravian monitoring of the converts' behavior. This tethering was problematic for a traditional economy requiring mobility and opportunism, especially at Nain, where the mission was established at an inner bay location many kilometers distant from the best winter hunting areas on the outer islands. The Moravians therefore had to accept a degree of residential flexibility and seasonal mission occupation on the part of their converts (Hiller 1971:89-9;, Kaplan 1983:365). An important shift in subsistence practices encouraged by the Moravians was an intensification of cod fishing in the fall to lay in a stored food supply to offset frequent winter shortages. But as late as 1814 the Moravians reported difficulties in establishing a storage-oriented cod fishery because Inuit were satisified with 100-200 fish and did not like that type of work (P.A.6:1814:54).

An important aspect of mission-related social transformation concerns women's roles. The status of women in Inuit society in general has been the subject of considerable discussion (e.g., Briggs 1974; Giffen 1930; Guemple 1986). A strong division of labor by gender is evident in the ethnography, but the functional complementarity of roles is generally stressed. At the same time, however, accounts of violence towards women abound, wife-stealing is a recurrent theme and the symmetry or asymmetry of spousal exchange has been debated. The ethnohistorical material from Labrador is no different. Taylor (1974:80) refers to accounts of runaway wives and spousal violence, and the politics of polygyny (Taylor 1974:67-70) were open to abuse as well. From one perspective, multiple wives provided the male household leader with more labor power and higher prestige, while from another perspective co-wives provided each other with labor assistance (Cabak 1991:42). The distribution of these costs and benefits is hard to determine from the published sources and there is no information on the ranking of co-wives within households. Women could also be shamans (Taylor 1974:87, 1989) and thus possess spiritual power. Taylor (1974:87) refers to a joint performance of seal hunting prediction by Sattugana (woman) and Millik (her husband) at Nukasusutok in 1774, commenting: "...it is interesting to consider the indirect control Millik would have over the economic activities in his camp through his wife's reputation as a shaman." But Sattugana seems to have had direct influence over her husband as well, forbidding him to undertake actions on advice from spirits (Taylor 1974:88). The history of Mikak and Tuglavina is a complex mixture of a strong woman as social agent, conflict and spousal abandonment.

Whatever the conflicting evidence, there are strong grounds for assuming that in many cases an Inuit woman's status in 18th century Labrador was not enviable. Perhaps this is an important reason why women were the core converts when the Moravian missions began to attract residents towards the end of the 18th century. In 1799 the Nain mission observed that "...in general, the men do not seem so determined in their resolution to abide faithful as the women" (P.A. 2:1799:328) and it appears that women were important catalysts in the religious revival of 1804-1805 (Brice-Bennett [1981], cited in Cabak 1991:58). Cabak (1991:62-67) suggests that Inuit women affiliated themselves with the missions out of an interest in Christianity as a source of hope and security, a desire to change the unhappy or abusive circumstances of their lives, to take advantage of educational opportunities and childcare possibilities within a larger community, to extract themselves from the marginality of wid-

owhood and old age, and to acquire European goods. As far as the latter is concerned, archaeological materials from 19th century middens at the Nain mission settlement suggest that Inuit women were active in integrating European goods into household contexts and that the use of these goods may have contributed to women's prestige (Cabak 1991:181; Cabak and Loring 2000).

AN ETHNOHISTORIC SKETCH OF THE NUKASUSUTOK SETTLEMENT

References to Nukasusutok in the ethnohistoric sources have been patched together to form a sketchy settlement history. The synopsis is derived primarily from J. Garth Taylor's and Helga Taylor's published research, which draws on the mostly German language Moravian mission diaries and letters. Also consulted were the Moravian Periodical Accounts (P.A.), which are annually published English summaries of mission diary entries and letters. Most of these accounts probably refer to Nukasusutok-8, but it is possible that some of the early 19th century references to Nukasusutok might refer to a dwelling at Nukasusutok-7.

The demographic data pertaining to the Nukasusutok-8 settlement are outlined in Table 57. In the following account the settlement history is broken down according to the years for which relevant information is available. References to other localities are included when the information is relevant to understanding the Nukasusutok settlement.

Table 57. Demographic Data for the Nukasusutok Settlement from Moravian Sources (Taylor 1974:16).

	No. of Houses	Population
1773-74	23	6
1774-75	(3)	(60)
1776-77	4	62
1779-80	2	33
1781-82	2	50

Parentheses indicate estimates

1772-73

The brothers Millik and Pattiguk, who would winter the next year on Nukasusutok, each had a winter house on Niatak Island (7 km northwest of the Nukasusutok settlement). Each household contained 20 people (Taylor 1974:77). Millik's wife Sattugana was an eminent shaman and performed a ceremony during the winter (Taylor 1974:87, 1985:123, 1989:300).

1773-74

The Nukasusutok settlement consisted of two houses containing a total population of 36 people (Taylor 1974:16, 71). Millik (father-in-law) and Okarloak II (son-in-law) shared a household (Taylor 1974:75). Millik's wife Sattugana gave a shamanist performance concerning the weather and seal hunting possibilities (Taylor 1974:87, 1989:301). Taylor (1974:87) suggests that Sattugana's reputation as a shaman may have contributed indirectly to Millik's control over community economic activities. Sikkuliak (father) and Kigluana (son), who would later reside at Nukasusutok, shared a house at Satosoak Island (30 km west of Nukasusutok).

1774-75

Millik ordered his sled and 12 dogs to be prepared for the missionaries when they left the Nukasusutok settlement. He sent his eldest son Aumarak and Akbik with them. Taylor (1974:80) cites this incident as one of the few documented examples of authority assertion by a household head.

1776-77

In December 1776 a stranded whale was towed to the Nukasusutok settlement just before freeze-up (Taylor 1974:76-77, 1988:128, 1990:52). The baleen was described as "marketable," the meat as "spoiled," but the skin was still edible (Taylor 1988:128, 1990:59). Given this bonanza of whale skin, people from all over the Nain region converged on Nukasusutok to feast and celebrate. The community consisted of four sod

houses with a total of 62 people and eight snow houses that probably contained at least 38 visitors, for a total of 100-150 people (Taylor 1974:16, 1990:60). In January 1777 the Inuit built a *kaggik* (festival house) of snow, 5.3 m high and 8.3 m in diameter, with an entrance passage. The *kaggik* activities mostly involved men, and included the *nullutak* game (in which a bone with holes is suspended from the ceiling and participants attempt to skewer the holes with sticks) and boxing (Taylor 1990:53-54). Taylor (1974:78) was able to use the Moravian census data to reconstruct the kinship relations among the sod house inhabitants (Figure 141).

Household 1: Sikkuliak was the head. The unit consisted of 10 people, including Sikkuliak's two wives, six children, and the married son Kigluana (Taylor 1974:75).

Household 2: Millik was the head. The unit consisted of 16 people, including Millik's three wives. Millik's second wife was Sikkuliak's daughter, therefore Millik was Sikkuliak's son-in-law. This provides evidence for an uxorilocal relationship. The household also included five of Millik's children, two of whom were married with their own families.

Household 3: Pattiguk was the head. The unit consisted of six people, including Pattiguk's three wives and two children. Note that the brothers Pattiguk and Millik had lived in the same settlement at Niatak in 1772-73.

Household 4: Tuglavina was the head. The unit consisted of 11 people, including Tuglavina's three wives (not Mikak, who had been abandoned the previous spring) and Tuglavina's brother, with his two wives and three offspring.

Taylor (1974:81) assumes the 1777 Beck census ordered the houses in terms of importance, implying that Sikkuliak (household 1) was most prominent. Taylor goes on to suggest that Sikkuliak's pre-eminence was due to his kinship tie as Tuglavina's brother (possibly elder), as well as being Millik's father-in-law. Additionally, we know that the brothers Sikkuliak

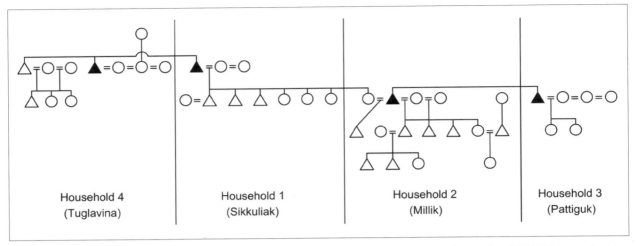

141/ Kinship relations of households at the Nukasusutok settlement, winter 1776-1777. After Taylor (1974:78); reproduced by permission of the Canadian Museum of Civilization.

and Tuglavina quarreled periodically (Taylor 1974:82) and that they probably never shared a *household*, although in this case they were co-resident at the settlement. Parenthetically, this fraternal relationship is interesting in light of the etymology of Nukasusutok given by Wheeler (1953:62-63): "the place where the brothers quarreled."

1777-78

Sikkuliak and his son-in-law Millik began to build a house together at Okak (Taylor 1974:74).

1779-80

This winter the Nukasusutok settlement consisted of two houses and a total of 33 people (Taylor 1974:16). Pattiguk resided here and his nephew Kapik left the mission settlement at Nain to live in Pattiguk's household (Taylor 1974:74). Sikkuliak and his son Kigluana shared the other household (Taylor 1974:75).

1780-81

Sikkuliak and his son Kigluana shared a household at Kheovik, at Voisey's Bay (Taylor 1974:75).

1781-82

Two households with a total of 50 people resided at the Nukasusutok settlement (Taylor 1974:16, 71). A

stranded 18-20 foot minke whale was towed to the settlement (Taylor 1974:32, 1988:128). Three families moved away from Nukasusutok: Millik, his married son Aumarak and Naksuk (Taylor 1974:74). Sikkuliak and Ketornek shared a household at Nain (Sikkuliak was the uncle of Ketornek's wife; Taylor 1974:74). A spring camp was established seaward from Nukasusutok. On May 26 it consisted of three tents (22.5 people estimated) and on May 27 four tents (30 people estimated; Taylor 1974:18).

1783

The Nukasusutok Inuit found "...a hole in the ice with two sled-loads of sea birds," probably dovekies (Taylor 1974:54). In other words, there was an open water area that attracted a large number of birds, which were hunted rather thoroughly.

1784

Millik and his eldest son Aumarak were killed by Tuglavina and others while trading at Cape Charles in southern Labrador (Taylor 1974:92).

1794

Apkajunna, his family and two others visited Okak in February from Nukasusutok. He was instrumental in organizing the construction of a festival house at

CHAPTER 11

Okak. A 1783 Moravian account states that Apkajunna was originally from Saglek and a 1784 account mentions him as a whale harpooner at Okak. According to accounts from 1787 and 1794, he later became a middleman in the trade with Europeans, acquiring a wooden boat and wintering in the Hamilton Inlet region (Taylor 1990:62).

1800

Only a few "heathen" families remained in the Nain area. It appeared that the "heathen" were: "...more than ever convinced of the necessity for conversion" (P.A. 2: 1800:472). In December the *angakok* (shaman) Sigsikak went from Nukasusutok to Nain with his "whole numerous family" (P.A. 3: 1801:12). Two Englishmen arrived unexpectedly and came to the Nukasusutok settlement to catch seals in nets and winter there, but the Inuit "...didn't seek the company of the strangers." (P.A. 2: 1800:472)

1805-6

A group of "heathen" were reported at Nukasusutok. They maintained relations with traders and settlers in Hamilton Inlet (P.A. 3: 1805:489). At Hopedale in 1806, Siksigak was baptized and re-named Mark, which the Moravians regarded as a "striking conversion" (P.A. 4: 1806:87).

1809

The missionaries in Nain reported: "We have heard with much concern, that a man, who had lived two winters on our land, and even last winter gave good hopes that he would be converted, has been seduced by the heathens at Nokkasusuktok to change his mind, and no more intend[s] to live on our land" (P.A. 4: 1809:453).

1811

During the winter Inuit from Nukasusutok came frequently to the mission at Nain to trade. Their "principle leader" moved to Nain in February, seemingly ready for conversion (P.A. 5:1811:130).

Discussion

One of the major points emerging from this short settlement history is that Nukasusutok-8 represents repeated occupations by many different household units. These households circulated among several settlement locations over the years, some close by in the Nain area, others further afield in Okak, Saglek and Hamilton Inlet. Nonetheless, there appears to have been a degree of consistency in the social composition of the settlement during the 10 year period of 1772-82, with the families of Sikkuliak, Millik and Pattiguk being mentioned frequently. This is probably a consequence of the fraternal relationship between Millik and Pattiguk and Millik's marriage to one of Sikkuliak's daughters (see Figure 138). But although some settlements may have been associated with specific families or kin units for a time, residential mobility was high and structured by both kinship and opportunistic factors.

Another point is that despite considerable contact with the Moravians in the early years after the establishment of the Nain mission in 1771, the inhabitants of the Nukasusutok settlement remained unconverted. By the early 1800s Nukasusutok was regarded by the missionaries as an outpost of recalcitrant "heathens." Not only did they still resist conversion, but they encouraged converts residing at the Nain mission to abandon their new beliefs. Furthermore, the Nukasusutok Inuit maintained contacts with traders and European settlers in Hamilton Inlet, an undesirable link in Moravian eyes, since it undercut Moravian influence and control. This, along with the residence of several prominent traders and shamans at the settlement, suggests that Nukasusutok was a prominent site of resistance to European domination.

There are two obvious archaeological consequences of this settlement history. First, the sod houses at Nukasusutok-8 were probably cleaned out or renovated periodically, thus it is unlikely that the house and midden contents can be related to any of the documented individuals and the house floor contents will mostly represent the last occupation phase. Second, we might expect that a settlement composed of Inuit resisting control by the Moravians might contain a combination of traditional Inuit and European goods, but unusual quantities of European goods might be present, particularly if prominent traders such as Tuglavina and the nascent middleman Apkajunna were resident there for extended periods. Another possibility might be the presence of artifacts related to shamanist practices, since Sattugana, Tuglavina and Sigsikak all were believed to possess special powers.

THE ARCHAEOLOGY OF NUKASUSUTOK-7 (HcCl-8)

Nukasusutok-7 is a Contact to post-Contact Period site located on Pumialuk Point on the southwestern portion of Nukasusutok Island (Figure 16). The area was traversed by a Smithsonian associate in 1973 but was not revisited until contract and provincial government archaeologists passed by on a mineral exploration-related survey in 1997 (Penney 1997; K. Reynolds, personal communication). The author conducted a brief reconnaissance in 2004. The site designation lumps together five separate localities that are distributed along a 700 m stretch of the point. Each locality is described separately, proceeding westwards.

L-1

On an extensive flat area near the base of the point were a large oval tent ring (5 by 5 m) and a small stone grave or fox trap.

L-2

A large stone grave was located in a narrow beach pass. Constructed of boulders, the grave was 3.5 by 1.5 m in size and was oriented east-west. A gift cache (1 by 1 m) directly adjoined its western end. This feature might be Strong's Grave 3 (see below), which had a gift cache and skeletal remains oriented with the head towards the east, but his description is so sketchy it is impossible to be sure. Strong mentioned that the chamber of Grave 3 contained broken brass

and iron objects and the cache had broken metal objects.

L-3

Two oval tent rings (both 4 m in diameter) and one square tent ring (4 by 4 m).

L-4

Four square tent rings (two 5 by 5 m, one 5 by 4 m, one 4 by 4 m); one contained a probable internal hearth. A clay pipestem was noted on the surface of the beach crest. At the western side of the beach pass was a wood cache positioned under a bedrock overhang.

L-5

A broad beach pass contained four features. On the western side of the pass was a semi-subterranean house. Ten meters east of the house was a small rectangular stone "frame" and 20 m east of this were two more such frames.

Semi-Subterranean House

This feature was square, 5 by 4.5 m in size. Its well-preserved back and side walls (30-50 cm wide) were built up with sod to a height of 25 cm above the external ground surface and 50 cm above the internal floor level. The front of the house lacked a distinct above-surface wall; it was simply dug down ca. 20 cm from the turf surface. There was no clear entrance passage, only a shallow depression 1.5 m wide by 2.5 m long that extended from the center of the front wall. The entrance faced south. There was a single rear sleeping platform that encompassed the entire rear wall and was 1.3 m wide.

Three small shovel tests were excavated in an attempt to find diagnostic materials to date the structure. Test Pit 1 was placed 1.4 m from the front wall of the house, just east of the entrance depression. It revealed a 20 cm thick and extremely compact peat layer on top of beach gravel. About 10 cm below the peat surface was a charcoal layer that contained two well preserved seal bones. Test Pit 2 was excavated in the center of the house floor, 1 m from the front wall. Here there was a 10 cm deep peat layer on top of beach gravel. Towards the bottom of the peat were two small iron fragments, a poorly preserved seal bone and a piece of wood embedded vertically into the floor. Little charcoal was encountered. Test Pit 3 was placed 2 m from the front wall, on the western side of the entrance depression. It contained 25 cm of peat on top of beach gravel; no cultural material was observed.

This semi-subterranean structure is notable for its "light" construction, exhibiting a form more similar to a transitional season *qarmat* than a winter house. The relatively small size of the dwelling, plus its lack of a well-defined entrance passage, is suggestive of a 19th century structure. Unfortunately, no datable finds were recovered. The paucity of cultural material suggests the dwelling was occupied for only a short period of time.

Stone "frames"

The three stone "frames" were rectangular alignments of small rocks, similar in size (1.3 by 0.80 m) and oriented approximately north-south. They may mark early Christian graves.

THE ARCHAEOLOGY OF NUKASUSUTOK-8 AND W. D. STRONG'S GRAVE COLLECTION

The sod-house village Nukasusutok-8 (HcCh-10) is located towards the southwest portion of the island at the base of a steep spruce-clad valley (Figures 16, 142, 143). W. D. Strong was informed about the Nukasusutok house structures by an Inuk from Nain. In 1928 Strong and an expedition companion spent the period of August 1-7 on the island investigating Nukasusutok-8 and several Inuit graves. This occurred at the tail-end of the Rawson-MacMillan expedition and

it is evident from Strong's diary entries that he was fed-up and looking forward to heading home. Kaplan's (1983:469) visit in 1980 identified five sod houses, but Strong's field notes indicate seven dwellings, two of which may be tentative. Since the two "missing" structures could be obscured beneath today's heavy vegetation cover, Strong's sketch map is used as the basis for Figure 142 and his numbering sequence for the houses[8] is retained. Also present at the site are a tent ring and the remains of a kayak stand or cache. A grave lies near the shore ca. 200 m west of the site. Besides Kaplan's brief visit in 1980, more recent investigations of the site include the author's 1992 test-pitting of the midden in front of House 5 and a reconnaissance by J. Garth Taylor in 1966 (Taylor 1966).

Strong excavated much of House 1, part of House 5, and tested Houses 4, 6 and 7. He found relatively little artifact material within the houses. Much of his interest seems to have been directed towards graves located in several places on the island, some of which contained considerable quantities of artifacts. Unfortunately, the Peabody Museum collection is simply registered as from "Nukasujuktok Island," with no indication as to which parts of the material derive from the house excavations versus the graves, or to which graves the material belongs. Strong's fieldnotes and photographs can be used to associate a very few artifacts with specific graves, but over 90% of the material must be regarded as of uncertain provenience. Nonetheless, given his comments on the paucity of artifacts within the excavated houses it is likely that much of the museum collection is derived from the graves. Strong's fieldnotes suggest some items excavated by him are either not present in the Peabody Museum material or were never collected and brought south, possibly because they were regarded as too "modern" (e.g., European ceramics and an iron shovel). The seven sod houses at Nukasusutok-8 are

[8]Strong's and Kaplan's (1983:470) house numbering is identical for Houses 1 and 2, but Kaplan's Houses 3, 4, and 5 correspond to Strong's Houses 5, 6, and 7, respectively.

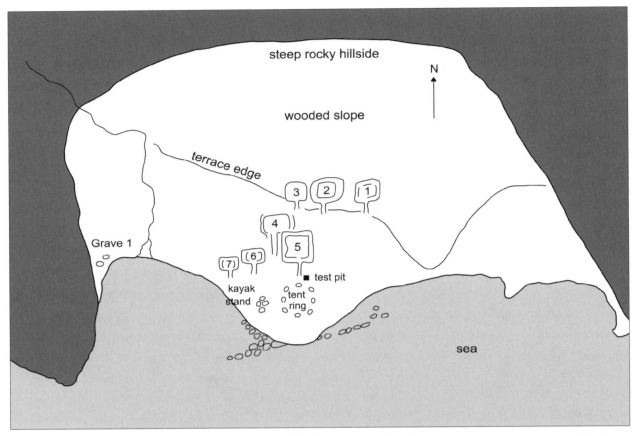

142/ Nukasusutok-8 site map. Based on W. D. Strong's 1928 field notes, with modifications. Used by permission, National Anthropological Archives, Smithsonian Institution.

arranged in two different groups (Figure 142). Houses 1, 2 and 3 lie furthest from the modern shoreline and are built into the side of a steep slope, while Houses 4, 5, 6 and 7 are excavated into a relatively flat beach surface closer to the contemporary shoreline. Two house types are present. Houses 1, 2 and 5 are large rectangular communal houses with long straight entrance passages; this form was common in the 18th century. They measure about 8 m along their rear walls and 7 m along their side walls. Houses 1 and 5 have prominent midden deposits. Houses 6 and 7 are smaller. House 6 measures 5 m along its side, while House 7 measures 6 m along its rear wall and 5 m along its side walls; both have short entrances rather than long entrance passages. Kaplan (1983:469) dates these structures to the 19th century and Strong's field notes confirm this in referring to them as "regular board houses," in which were found

an iron shovel and "pink plates." No size data are available for the currently "invisible" Houses 3 and 4. Strong's sketch map and his field note comments that iron and porcelain from House 4 indicate it is the same age as House 5 suggest that the former may have had communal house dimensions. This would increase the total of communal houses to at least four, which would be consistent with Moravian observations of four occupied sod houses in the winter of 1776-77. House 3 was not tested by Strong so there are no chronological indicators.

House 1

Strong began the excavation of House 1 by digging a trench up the long entrance passage towards the front of the house. He refers to a thin and scattered midden deposit full of iron, brick, china, porcelain and chamber pot handles. These European objects were domi-

143/ Nukasusutok-8: overview towards the southwest, August 1928. W. D. Strong Collection, © Smithsonian Institution, National Anthropological Archives, Negative No. 99-10590.

144/ Nukasusutok-8: House 5 overview towards the southwest, August 1928. W. D. Strong collection, © Smithsonian Institution, National Anthropological Archives, Negative No. 99-10591.

stones that Strong regarded as part of the roof support system. There was a stone sleeping platform on the rear-left side of the house (1.68 m wide, 15 cm high) and another platform of wood (1.2 m wide) on the rear-right side; between the two was a wooden flooring. The well-preserved wooden superstructure (mostly spruce) collapsed onto the floor such that Strong reconstructs the roof supports as consisting of a hewed beam (15 by 15 cm) laid from back to front across the center of the house that provided support for smaller beams extending in from the wall tops. He also hints at traces of wooden walls.

Strong provides only minimal descriptions of the artifacts found in the house. Half of a large soapstone lamp lay upside-down on the right hand platform. He notes a possible hammerstone ca. 30 cm deep in the midden near the end of the entrance passage, although his sketch maps do not indicate any excavation units there. From uncertain locations were: a few pieces of cut whalebone, at least three fragments of soapstone vessels, an ivory harpoon socket, a bone knife handle, a stone "chisel," chinaware fragments, nails, an iron axe and a gun butt-plate. Strong refers to the layers as "quite modern," noting there were more European goods here than at Hopedale, suggesting the Nukasusutok material was more recent. The hammerstone, stone chisel, most of the ceramics and nails, the axe and the gun butt-plate are all missing from the Peabody Museum collection.

nant to a depth of two or three feet (60-90 cm), at which point a frozen layer containing bone fragments was encountered. Strong's rough sketches and description suggest he exposed most of the house, but it is unclear if the back wall was completely excavated. The inside measurements of the long walls were 6.2 m and 6.6 m while the inside lengths of the short walls were 3.1 m and 3.8 m. The height of the stone walls was 60 cm while the depth of the house from the center of floor to the top of the wall mound was 1.2 m. The entrance passage was 5.8 m long and up to 1.0 m deep. Near the center of the floor was a "pillar" of

House 5

House 5 is the largest and most prominent house at the site (Figures 144 and 145). The structure was hastily and only partially excavated over a two day period. Strong records wall measurements of 8.2 m for the south wall, 8.0 m for the west, 7.1 m for the north and 7.0 m for the east, and he measured the house depth at center as 1.5 m. The entrance passage is ca. 7 m long. A raised wall mound up to 1.2 m wide surrounds the structure. Sleeping platforms are visible along the back and

145/ Nukasusutok-8: House 5 excavation towards the west, August 1928. W. D. Strong collection, © Smithsonian Institution, National Anthropological Archives, Negative No. 99-10593.

one side wall. As in House 1 there is a central rock cluster. Strong reports very few finds in the front portion of the house.

In 1992 a 70 by 70 cm test pit was placed in the midden near the end of the entrance passage. The test pit was excavated to a depth of ca. 50 cm below ground surface, using three naturally defined collection levels. Level 1 (0-23 cm) was a highly humified soil zone with poorly preserved bone. Level 2 (23-36 cm) began where the deposit took on a more sandy/gravelly texture, which coincided with better bone preservation and included mussel shell remains and wood fragments. Level 3 (36-50 cm) commenced with a clear stratigraphic break in the form of a thin (1 cm) continuous layer of fibrous peat. Beneath the peat was 3 cm of dark-stained beach gravel and sand with poorly preserved bone, mussel shells and wood fragments. The excavation terminated at 50 cm within the basal yellow sand/gravel.

The total thickness of the well-defined bone-bearing deposit was only 25 cm (somewhat thicker if the poorly preserved material in the humus-root zone is included). This relatively thin deposit suggests an intensive but short-lived occupation.

Artifacts recovered from the midden test pit consisted of:

Level 1: · one hand wrought nail

Level 2: · 26 fragments of earthenware ceramic
· two hand wrought nails
· one round iron shaft
· one iron knife tip with adhering baleen

Level 3: · one soapstone vessel sherd

The fragments of earthenware ceramic are difficult to identify, but small remnants of green glaze and microscopic examination of the paste indicated similarities to French St. Onge earthenware, as classified in the Parks Canada comparative collection housed at the Archaeology Unit, Memorial University. According to Auger (1991:40), St. Onge earthenware was manufactured between 1700 and 1750. The three hand wrought nails, round iron shaft and iron knife tip are illustrated in Figure 146. These few finds suggest an 18th century dating, but there is not much to go on. The thin Level 3 deposit under the peat raises the possibility of an earlier component.

Faunal material from the midden test pit was identified by Ann Rick of the National Museum of Nature, Ottawa. Table 58 lists the number of identified speci-

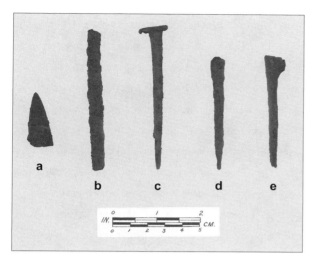

146/ *Nukasusutok-8: House 5, 1992 midden test pit collection. a: iron knife tip; b: round iron shaft; c-e: nails.*

Table 58. Fauna from the House 5 Midden at Nukasusutok-8.

TAXON	NISP	MNI
Seal	144	9
Phoca sp.	4	2
harp seal (*Phoca groenlandica*)	1	1
ringed seal (*Phoca hispida*)	9	2
harp/ringed seal	1	1
harbor (*Phoca vitulina*)/ringed seal	11	5
Artiodactyl	1	1
Caribou (*Rangifer tarandus*)	1	1
Canis sp.	3	1
Dog (*Canis familiaris*)	1	1
Wolf (*Canis lupus*)	1	1
Red Fox	3	1
Arctic fox/red fox	1	1
Unidentified mammal	49	
Unidentified mammal fragments	114	
Bird		
Murre/Razorbill (*Uria sp./Alca sp.*)	1	1
Unidentified bird	1	
Unidentified bird/mammal	4	
Unknown (possibly baleen)	4	
TOTAL	**354**	

mens (NISP) and minimum numbers of individuals (MNI) for each taxon. These data cannot be considered to be particularly representative given the limited scope of the testing and the hand-picking collection technique, but they are broadly consistent with Strong's observation that there were considerable amounts of seal bone at Nukasusutok-8. Relatively few of the seal bones were identifiable as to species, but harp seal is represented less than one might expect, considering Taylor's (1974:51) observation that communal houses were generally situated near fall harp sealing locations. The inability to distinguish clearly between harbor and ringed seal is a problem, but the frequency of possible harbor seals is interesting in relation to Wollett's (1999:380) observation that the 18th century communal houses in Hamilton Inlet have high harbor seal to ringed seal ratios, which he attributes to more moderate sea ice conditions. The relative lack of caribou is not surprising, given the distance to inner bay and interior caribou wintering areas. One might have expected more bird material given the abundance of wildfowl among the small islands east/southeast of Nukasusutok during the spring and fall, but birds may have been exploited mostly from spring to fall tent camps. The occurrence of fox is consistent with the presence of several large stone fox traps elsewhere on the island.

Strong's Grave Collections

Strong investigated six graves on Nukasusutok Island. Of these, only one is located relatively close to the sod house village at Nukasusutok-8. Some of the others can be located approximately using Strong's descriptions and photographs.

Grave 1 Strong reports this as a rock cairn near the shore, 200 m west of Nukasusutok-8. The individual was an adult whose head was positioned towards the north, but the bones were too decayed to save. The only other grave contents were a few boards.

Grave 2 Grave 2 was situated on a high ridge 800 m north of Nukasusutok-8; Figure 147 probably illustrates this feature. The cairn was almost round and was well-constructed of slabs placed over the grave chamber with counterbalanced boulders on top. The chamber was 2 m long, 25-50 cm wide, with the head positioned towards the northwest. The skeletal material consisted of a broken skull and mandible, which Strong assumed to be female. Two meters to the southeast lay a gift cache covering a decayed round wooden box containing "many" glass beads and a small (32 mm long) perforated soapstone model of a polar bear.

Grave 3 Strong specifies the location of this grave as lying on a narrow neck between two small bays on the northwest end of Nukasusutok Island. This may be L-2 at Nukasusutok-7 on Pumialuk Point (Figure 16). The grave chamber was 1.6 m long and the head of the individual was oriented to the east. The human remains consisted of a broken skull and long bones. Broken brass and iron objects lay in the chamber. A gift cache connected with the foot of the grave contained only broken metal objects.

Grave 4 This feature was situated on a ridge 200 m north of Grave 3, the location providing a good view up

The Bridges Passage and towards Paul Island. The grave consisted of boulders piled alongside an even larger boulder. The head was oriented towards the north or northwest. The skull was large and accompanied by a mandible and unusually massive long bones; Strong assumes the individual was male. Grave goods were piled at the foot of the cairn and along its east side. They included the remains of a kayak, a complete wooden kayak paddle with one bone paddle tip, a wooden harpoon shaft with an ivory socket, bone foreshafts, many iron points and bird darts, a crooked iron knife, a metal jigger, two sheet iron pieces, a box, a kettle and a whetstone.

Grave 5 Grave 5 was located on a ridge parallel with that upon which Grave 4 was placed. It was a small stone cairn with an inner chamber 1.6 m long, 45-80 cm wide, with the head positioned towards the south-southeast. Skeletal remains consisted of a fragmented skull, mandible and long bones; Strong considered this to be a woman's grave. A gift cache near the head contained a "considerable" amount of metal, including an ulu and "many" glass beads. If the cataloging sequence can be taken to indicate things found together, as

147/ Nukasusutok Island: probably Grave 2, August 1928. W. D. Strong collection, © Smithsonian Institution, National Anthropological Archives, Negative No. 99-10592.

seems to be the case for Grave 4, then many or all of the brass headbands and pendants as well as the perforated and unperforated pewter spoons may have been derived from Grave 5.

Grave 6 There is little locational information for this grave other than it lay up the hill behind Nukasusutok-8 and near two sliding door fox traps. The grave consisted of a large, well-built cairn with an inner chamber 2 m long, 30-60 cm wide. The skeleton was badly decayed except for the skull and a fragmentary mandible; the head was oriented towards the north. A gift cache positioned 2 m to the south contained the rim of a kayak, a board, an iron ulu and iron pyrites. One meter west of the grave were three small rocks in a line, beyond which was a small cache containing a beaten iron spearhead.

Description of the Artifact Material

Given the uncertainties regarding the find-contexts of Strong's artifact collection, a general description of the material in terms of activity categories will be presented. Assessment of the Peabody Museum catalog in relation to the Grave 4 goods photographed in the field by Strong suggests that at least some of the items associated with an individual grave feature were cataloged sequentially. Although it is impossible to draw reliable boundaries within the catalog sequence, this hint will be used to suggest some possible contextual associations.

Hunting-Fishing Tools Table 59 outlines the range of hunting-fishing tools in the collection. Many of the implements associated with hunting-fishing activity were probably derived from Grave 4, apparently a male interment. Only a short fragment of the harpoon shaft

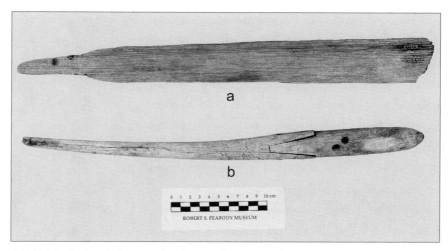

148/ W. D. Strong Nukasusutok collection: hunting and transportation implements. a: kayak paddle tip (Grave 4); b: harpoon foreshaft. © R. S. Peabody Museum of Archaeology, Phillips Academy, Andover, Massachusetts. All Rights Reserved.

remains, consisting of the distal end of the wooden shaft to which is affixed a weathered ivory socket piece. Three bone foreshafts might be among those attributed to Grave 4 by Strong. One of the them (Figure 148:b) is a composite harpoon foreshaft made on a walrus rib that has been sawed in two to create a tongue and groove flange; the two components were then fastened with iron rivets. Another is a lance foreshaft made on a walrus rib (Figure 149:b) that has a distal slot for an endblade and a conical base with two drill holes for lashing to a wooden shaft. The third example is also a lance foreshaft made on a walrus rib (Figure 150:a); it retains a fragment of an iron endblade riveted into its distal slot.

Table 59. Hunting-Fishing Tools from the Strong Collection.

Harpoon foreshafts	1
Lance foreshafts	2
Harpoon sockets	3
Iron arrow points	4
Iron bird dart points	7
Iron lance points	1
Wound pins	1
Spools (bladder inflation?)	1
Jiggers	1
Gunflints	1

Almost certainly from Grave 4 are seven iron bird-dart points (Figure 151:b-h). These are thin (5 mm) hammered square iron shafts, some of which have a single small barb. The points are similar to those illustrated in the well-known 1724 painting of Greenlandic Inuit Pooq and Qiperoq (Gulløv 1997:356). Probably from Grave 4 are four iron arrow points (Figure 152:a-d), all with flat blades, a squarish hammered shaft and pointed proximal ends. R. Jordan (1978:182) illustrates a similar arrow point, but with a longer stem, from an 18th century context at Eskimo Island in Hamilton Inlet. A long (40 cm) lance point made on a hammered square iron bar (8 mm thick) may also

150/ W. D. Strong Nukasusutok collection: hunting, transportation and household implements. a: bone lance foreshaft with iron point fragment; b: bone paddle tip; c: ivory harpoon socket; d: wooden wound pin; e: wood and bone ulu handle; f: whalebone sled shoe. © R. S. Peabody Museum of Archaeology, Phillips Academy, Andover, Massachusetts. All Rights Reserved.

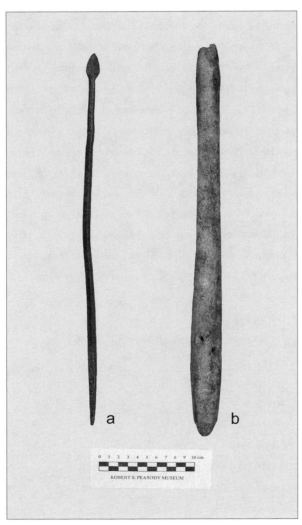

149/ W. D. Strong Nukasusutok collection: hunting implements. a: iron lance point; b: bone lance foreshaft. © R. S. Peabody Museum of Archaeology, Phillips Academy, Andover, Massachusetts. All Rights Reserved.

belong to this grave (Figure 149:a). Definitely from Grave 4 is a jigger consisting of three iron hooks weighted with lead (Figure 153:b).

Among the remainder of the material for which find-context is uncertain there are two harpoon shaft sockets. One (Figure 150:c) is made of heavily weathered ivory, while the other is a composite implement of bone, consisting of two halves fastened with four iron rivets. One of these could be from Strong's excavation at House 1. The wound pin (Figure 150:d) is made of wood. An iron triangular point with a central rivet (Figure 152:e) is probably a lance tip intended to be mounted in foreshafts such as those illustrated in Figures 149:b and 150:a. A wooden spool (Figure 154:a) may be of European origin, but perhaps it could have been used as a bladder inflation nozzle, since it is pierced through the middle. The single gunflint is a dark gray specimen made on a blade (Figure 161:a). Its square shape and trapezoidal cross-section suggest it is of English manufacture, from the late 1700s onwards (Luedtke 1999:37-39). Since the gunflint is

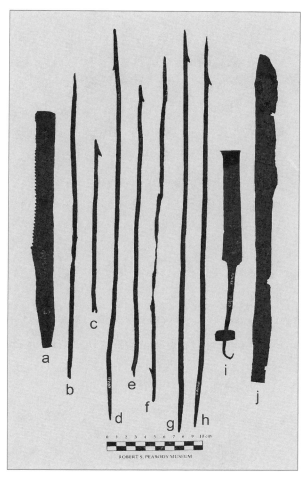

151/ W. D. Strong Nukasusutok collection: hunting and household implements. a: iron saw; b-h: iron bird dart points (probably Grave 4); i: iron curved knife (Grave 4); j: iron knife blade. © R. S. Peabody Museum of Archaeology, Phillips Academy, Andover, Massachusetts. All Rights Reserved.

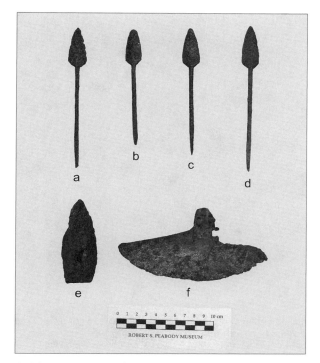

152/ W. D. Strong Nukasusutok collection: hunting and household implements. a-d: arrow points (probably Grave 4); e: iron lance point with rivet; f: iron ulu blade. © R. S. Peabody Museum of Archaeology, Phillips Academy, Andover, Massachusetts. All Rights Reserved.

cataloged in the middle of a sequence running from soapstone vessel sherds to cut whalebone fragments it may be from one of the houses.

Household Tools The category household tools includes a mix of traditional Inuit and European forms, listed in Table 60. Among the traditional implements are a probable snow-beater made on a walrus rib. Of the four iron knives, two consist of bone handles with fragments of inset iron blades (one is illustrated in Figure 153:a); one of these could be from House 1. The third is a 35 cm long, 2 cm wide blade (Figure 151:j). The fourth is the blade of a curved knife together with an iron ring for fastening it to a European-style handle (Figure 151:i); this specimen is definitely from Grave 4. There are three ulu handles in the collection. One of these (Figure 151:e) has a wooden palm element and a bone stem, another consists of a bone stem element with iron rivets and an iron blade fragment, while the third is made of wood. Three items might be considered to be wood and bone-working tools: an iron saw blade (Figure 151:a), an iron drill bit and a small iron wedge. An iron hook (Figure 153:c) could be kettle hook. Eight pieces of pyrite are present; although Strong mentions their occurrence in Grave 6 it is uncertain whether all were associated with the burial. Presumably, they were used as strike-a-lights. At least one of the three schist whetstones was associated with a grave. A small brass ring with a knurled outer surface is probably a tailor's ring thimble. A single unmodified pewter spoon is included in the domestic tool category; the modified spoons are discussed below in the decorative category.

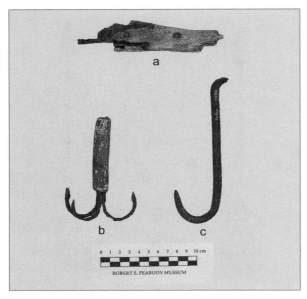

153/ W. D. Strong Nukasusutok collection: fishing and household implements. a: bone knife handle with iron blade fragment; b: iron and lead jigger (Grave 4); c: iron kettle hook. © R. S. Peabody Museum of Archaeology, Phillips Academy, Andover, Massachusetts. All Rights Reserved.

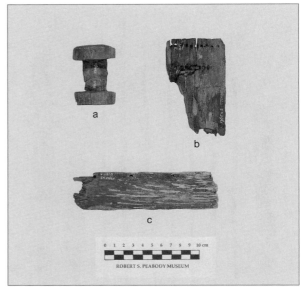

154/ W. D. Strong Nukasusutok collection: wooden implements. a: wooden spool; b: drilled wood with baleen lashing; c: curved wooden slat. © R. S. Peabody Museum of Archaeology, Phillips Academy, Andover, Massachusetts. All Rights Reserved.

Table 60. Household Tools from the Strong Collection.

Snow beaters	1
Iron knives	4
Ulu handles	3
Iron ulu blades	1
Iron saw blades	1
Iron drill bits	1
Iron wedges	1
Iron hooks	1
Pyrites	8
Whetstones	3
Brass thimble	1
Pewter spoons (unmodified)	1
Wooden platters	1
Soapstone vessels	12
European ceramics	7

Different types of containers are represented. A large, partially preserved, oval wooden platter (Figure 155) bears a scarf-joint with small nail holes around its outer edge, indicating the platter was the top or bot-

155/ W. D. Strong Nukasusutok collection: wooden box component. © R. S. Peabody Museum of Archaeology, Phillips Academy, Andover, Massachusetts. All Rights Reserved.

CHAPTER 11

tom of a wooden box. Quite speculatively, it might be a remnant of the wooden box containing glass beads and the small soapstone polar bear found in the gift cache associated with Grave 2. On the other hand, it could have served a more mundane function as a meat platter. There are 12 fragments of soapstone vessels. Since Strong does not refer to any in the Nukasusutok grave material while he does so for graves elsewhere in the Nain area, it is likely that all of them were derived from the house excavations. As noted previously, half of a large lamp was found on the platform of House 1; this is probably the specimen illustrated in Figure 156:b. The latter has a rim up to 25 mm thick and a drilled repair hole on the bottom/middle of the vessel. There is also most of a small oval lamp, at least 13 cm in diameter (Figure 156:a). Neither of the lamp fragments has a wick stand. The rest of the vessel fragments range from 11-20 mm thick; two are illustrated in Figure 157.

Given Strong's field note comments on the frequency of European ceramics in his house excavations, it is strange that only seven fragments of European ceramics are present in the collection. Six of these are coarse reddish earthenware with white carbonate inclusions, some pieces with a curved surface bearing convolutions. The remaining specimen is a lump of brick-like material.

Transportation-Related Items Transportation related items consist of one kayak paddle blade fragment, two kayak paddle tips and seven sled runners. All that remains of the Grave 4 kayak paddle is the broken wooden paddle blade illustrated in Figure 148:a. The two kayak paddle tips are made of bone; one is shown in Figure 150:b. One of these two implements must be from Grave 4. The seven sled runners (one illustrated in Figure 150:f) are all made of whalebone, are mostly 39-56 mm wide and display varying numbers of drill holes; two were curved for use at the front of a sled. It is possible the runners are from one or more of the houses or middens.

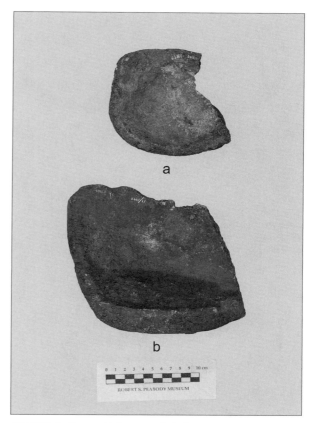

156/ W. D. Strong Nukasusutok Collection: soapstone lamps. © R. S. Peabody Museum of Archaeology, Phillips Academy, Andover, Massachusetts. All Rights Reserved.

157/ W. D. Strong Nukasusutok collection: soapstone vessel rim fragments. © R. S. Peabody Museum of Archaeology, Phillips Academy, Andover, Massachusetts. All Rights Reserved.

Decorative Items A significant number of items in the collection could be considered decorative; these are listed in Table 61. It is unclear from Strong's field-notes, but the copper/brass head bands and pendants

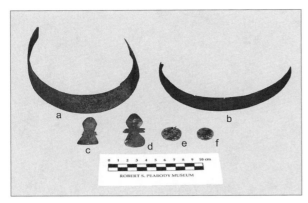

158/ W. D. Strong Nukasusutok collection: copper/brass decorative items. a-b: headbands; c-f: pendants. © R. S. Peabody Museum of Archaeology, Phillips Academy, Andover, Massachusetts. All Rights Reserved.

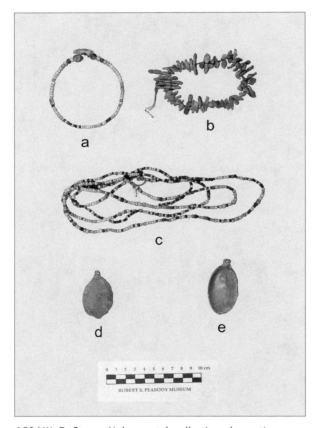

159/ W. D. Strong Nukasusutok collection: decorative items. a: 86 glass beads and soapstone polar bear sculpture; b: 58 lead pendants, c: 672 glass beads (probably Grave 5); d-e: perforated pewter spoons. © R. S. Peabody Museum of Archaeology, Phillips Academy, Andover, Massachusetts. All Rights Reserved.

may have been derived from Grave 3 and/or Grave 5. The collection contains what are probably two complete headbands (Figure 158:a,b) as well as three large

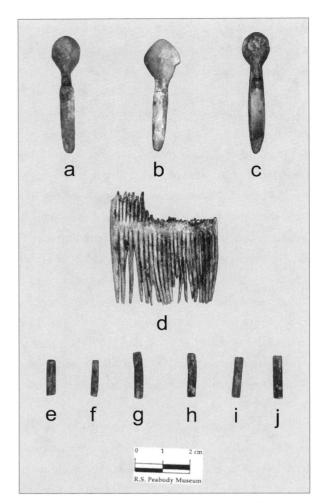

160/ W. D. Strong Nukasusutok collection: bone decorative items. a: ivory pins; b: bone comb; c: bird bone beads. © R. S. Peabody Museum of Archaeology, Phillips Academy, Andover, Massachusetts. All Rights Reserved.

portions thereof and two probable fragments. The headbands range between 20-29 mm wide; one has four small perforations along one edge while another has two perforations. The pendants are made on very thin copper/brass sheets; two of these are circular with perforations (a trace of baleen twine is present on one), while two others are fish-shaped (Figure 158:c-f). The headbands and pendants, together with glass beads, formed a decorative headdress for Inuit women. A perfect illustration of this arrangement is provided in a 1773 drawing by English artist Nathaniel Dance of a Labrador Inuit woman, Caubvick (Figure 162), made during her stay in England (Lysaght 1971:83). Caubvick is portrayed wearing a headband

and fish-shaped pendants are attached to her hair near her ears, with strings of beads extending down from the pendants.

Table 61. Decorative Items from the Strong Collection.

Copper/brass headbands	5
Copper/brass band fragment	2
Copper/brass pendants	6
Glass trade beads	767
Polar bear bead	1
Lead pendants	80
Pewter spoons, modified	12
Bone beads	49
Combs	2
Bone pins	4

Strong's collection also contains 80 small cast lead pendants, 58 of which are strung as a "bracelet" in the Peabody collection (Figure 159:b). Most of these exhibit either two or three globular segments, some have two perforations, others only one, others none. In the 1880s these items were used by Ungava Inuit as part of the front fringe on parkas (Turner 1894:211), but combined with glass beads they were also used as components of amulets attached to shaman dolls (Turner 1894:196-198; see also Karklins 1992:195-199). According to Hawkes (1916:39) these ornaments were made by melting down pewter spoons and pouring the molten material into steatite moulds. But pewter spoons were themselves used as ornaments for parkas. Their handles were removed and the remaining handle stub was perforated such that the spoons could be sewn onto the front of coats (Turner 1894:211, Karklins 1992:195-198). Twelve modified spoons are found in the Strong collection; two are illustrated in Figure 159:d, e.

The glass trade beads in Strong's collection were derived from Graves 2 and 5, both of which Strong considered to be women's graves. Besides their use in decorative headdresses and amulets, beads were also

161/ W. D. Strong Nukasusutok collection: lithic implements. a: English gun flint; b: Ramah chert stemmed point. © R. S. Peabody Museum of Archaeology, Phillips Academy, Andover, Massachusetts. All Rights Reserved.

used extensively to decorate skin coats (Karklins 1992:195-199, Turner 1894:211; see Caubvick in Figure 162). The beads were described following the typology developed by Kidd and Kidd (1970), but lacking their color diagrams and a formal color code chart, the color designations provided here are "best guess" matches with their system. Where relevant the type designations below include reference to Brain's (1979) modification of the Kidd typology (e.g., IIa14/IIA1, Kidd/Brain). Of the total 873 beads, only 4 or 5 are wire wound, the rest are drawn.

It seems likely that the 672 beads cataloged as 17.1514 (Figure 159:c) are derived from Grave 5. They are all circular tube beads (class IIa) and several colors are represented:

· opaque white (IIa14/IIA1): small= 395, medium= 22
· clear brite navy (IIa56/IIA6): small= 78
· clear light blue (IIa41?/IIA7?): small= 83
· opaque black (IIa7/IIA5): small= 35
· opaque red (IIa2?): small= 26
· clear emerald green (IIa27/IIA15): small=15
· translucent sea green (IIa): small= 9
· opaque amber (IIa19): small= 6, medium= 1
· opaque dark burgundy red (IIa): small= 1
· clear rose red (IIa): small= 1

162/ A 1773 drawing of Caubvick by Nathaniel Dance. Note headband, fish-shaped pendants and glass beads on pendants. From the Knatchbull Portrait Collection. Photograph © Photographic Survey, Courtauld Institute of Art, London.

Catalog number 17.1513, from either Grave 2 or 5, consists of 52 beads, some of which are found on their original strings in blue/white bead groups. All are small, circular, monochrome tube beads (class IIa): opaque white (IIa14/IIA1) = 25, translucent brite navy blue = 16, uncertain colour (probably white) = 8, clear emerald green (IIa27/IIA15) = 2, and opaque red = 1. Catalog number 17.1531, from either Grave 2 or 5, includes four groups of beads on their original string, also ordered in blue and white groups (suggesting they are from the same context as 17.1513) as well as loose beads. There are 60 small, circular, monochrome tube beads (class IIa), of which 26 are opaque white (IIa14/IIA1)and 34 clear Brite navy (IIa56/IIA6). There is also one large, round, monochrome, opaque black tube bead (IIa6/W1A6), as well as two large mono-

chrome ground beads. Of the latter, one is clear amber (resembles WIIc5/WIIA4) and the other opaque black (resembles WIIc1/WIIA7).

The small (32 mm long) soapstone model of a polar bear is perforated and strung on a museum fabricated bracelet consisting of 86 glass beads (Figure 159:a). Strong makes no mention of a bracelet in his fieldnotes, so it is unclear whether this was their original arrangement or a *post-facto* museum interpretation. The beads consist of two large-sized round tube beads, one black opaque (IIa6/W1A6), one amber translucent, two medium-sized circular tube beads (class IIa), both light blue, and 82 small-to-medium-sized circular tube beads (class IIa), of which 76 are white (IIa14/IIA1), six dark blue and two light blue.

Dating these beads is difficult because they are virtually all common "seed beads" that were in use for extended periods of time. Brain's (1979) dating of the bead types mentioned above ranges from 1600-1890, with slightly more restricted dates for types WIIc5/WIIA4 (1680-1833), IIa41/IIA7 (1600-1836), IIa14/IIA1 (1600-1836) and IIa6/W1A6 (1700-1890). Some of these bead types were present in 18th century Inuit houses in west Greenland (Gulløv 1997:278-291), but the Nukasusutok material is more restricted in its representation of types, completely lacking polychrome specimens and with only 0.4-0.5% wire wound types.

The collection also contains decorative items of bone. There are 49 beads made of small bird bones, mostly in the range of 1.8-2.0 cm long (Figure 160:e-j). There are two combs, one a near complete specimen of bone with two opposed tooth rows (Figure 160:d), the other a fragment made of wood. Finally, the collection contains four small (4.5 cm) spoon-shaped ivory pins of uncertain function (Figure 160:a-c), possibly amulets to be attached to clothing.

Miscellaneous Metal The collection contains metal fragments not identifiable to specific implement types. These include 14 iron fragments, an iron bar, two lead fragments, a pewter fragment and a copper/brass sheet.

Miscellaneous Organic Materials Table 62 outlines the miscellaneous organic materials in the collection. Most of the bone is modified whalebone. Modification consists of cutting, sawing and drilling; a major desired end product was sled runners. Most of this material was probably derived from the house or midden excavations. The five fragments of animal skin are not identifiable as to their functional origin as clothing or equipment. One piece exhibits hair on one side and has stitching perforations.

Table 62. Miscellaneous Organic Materials from the Strong Collection.

Bone	
Modified bone	2
Unmodified bone	1
Modified antler	3
Modified whale bone	19
Unmodified whale bone	1
Unmodified baleen	4
Animal skin fragments	5
Wood	
Modified wood	13
Modified birch bark	6
Unmodified birch bark	1

There are two main types of modified wood. One consists of flat pieces with drill holes, sometimes countersunk in grooves. Figure 154:b shows two connected pieces of flat wood; the upper portion has a line of ten drill holes, the middle portion has eight drill holes through which run remnants of baleen twine. The other type consists of curved slats (ca. 4 cm wide) with nail holes, resembling barrel hoops (Figure 154:c). Of the six pieces of modified birchbark, four are perforated and sewn together with thin (3.5 mm) birchbark strips. Another piece has been cut into a curious "wrench" shape with a circular hole at each end.

162/ Detail.

Other Items Not included within the previous categories are three flakes of quartz and one of Ramah chert. There is also a Ramah chert projectile point of stemmed or wide side-notched form with a completely flaked dorsal surface, but ventral retouch limited to the margins (Figure 161:b). It bears a general resemblance to Late Dorset forms, but the Point Revenge component at Koliktalik-5, north of Nukasusutok Island, has a somewhat similar specimen (Fitzhugh 1978b:161, Figure 10c). There are also two natural stones, including an iron-rich concretion and a water-rolled pebble, as well as two scallop shells.

Dating Nukasusutok-8 and the Strong Grave Collection

Taylor's documentary sources indicate the Nukasusutok-8 village was occupied from 1772-1782 and passing references in the Moravian Periodical Accounts to "heathen" Inuit residing on the island continue until 1811. The two smaller structures at Nukasusutok-8, houses 6 and 7, might pertain to the early 19th century occupation, but the later written sources could also refer to the small sod house at Nukasusutok-7. Archaeological confirmation of such dating is difficult given an inability to specify find-contexts for much of the Strong collection and Strong's apparent neglect in collecting European ceramics and other "recent" artifacts from the houses. If the fragmentary earthenware ceramics from a test pit in the House 5 midden actually are French St. Onge ware, this would imply a production date from 1700-1750 (Auger 1991:40). Strong's field notes mention that a gun butt-plate was found in House-1, but it is missing from the collection. If this item represents the presence of firearms, as opposed to a purloined piece of metal, it may indicate a date later than 1782, since it was at that time that guns were first purchased from a trader at Chateau Bay in southern Labrador and then distributed northwards (Hiller 1971:93). The presence of a gun flint might support this. If the House 5 midden test pit stratigraphy is considered, the thin Level 3 deposit underneath a peat layer raises the possibility of a component that considerably pre-dates the mission period (i.e., pre-1771).

The contextual information from the graves is marginally better, at least for Graves 4 and 5. The glass beads from Graves 2 and 5 are generally consistent with 18th century types, but a more precise chronological reckoning is problematic. It is possible that some of the Nukasusutok graves pre-date the historically documented communal houses. The head bands and pendants of copper/brass and the lead pendants are similar to those reported by Bird (1945:175-177) from a grave at Iglosoataligarsuk near Hopedale, which also contained a French copper coin dated 1643. The coin provides a *terminus post quem* date for the grave. Grave 4 at Nukasusutok was associated with kayak remains and a large quantity of metal items was placed alongside the grave. A kayak burial found at Kikkertavak-1, ca. 25 km west of Nukasusutok Island, included a wooden tool box containing 150 items, among them harpoons and knives with iron blades. Kaplan (1983:235) dated Kikkertavak to the 17th century. At Rose Island in Saglek Bay, graves containing copper/brass headbands and pendants, glass trade beads, European iron and other goods, as

well as kayak parts, were dated to the 18th and early 19th centuries (Way 1978:134). With these slim comparative data and the poor contextual information for Strong's collection, the Nukasusutok graves might simply be time-bracketed between ca. 1650 and 1810.

Graves and Society

Given the paucity of contextual information for the Nukasusutok graves the possibilities of assemblage analysis are minimal, either for comparisons between the Nukasusutok graves themselves or for comparisons with graves from elsewhere in Labrador. Be that as it may, the question of the social context must still be addressed, if only in a rudimentary fashion.

The male kayak burial at Grave 4 with its substantial quantity of metal goods suggests either a relatively high status individual involved in the circulation system for European goods or a prominent hunter with easy access to a metal tool kit. Nearby was Grave 5, a woman's burial with a substantial amount of decorative metal and glass trade beads. This grave signals a woman with access to quantities of European goods and a status broadly equivalent to the male grave. Grave 2, also a woman's burial, was situated in a prominent location on the hill north of the communal house settlement at Nukasusutok-8 and had a gift cache containing many glass trade beads and a small perforated soapstone polar bear sculpture. The grave goods, as well as the prominent positioning of the burial and its independence from a male grave, suggest a form of social recognition.

Information on grave associations from other parts of Labrador is limited, but it underlines the impression that certain individuals were marked by special treatment involving the deposition of unusual amounts of European goods. As noted previously, Junius Bird (1945:175-177) reported a grave at Iglosoataligarsuk near Hopedale that contained a copper/brass head band fragment along with a lance foreshaft and socket, 27 flat lead pendants, 75 globular lead pendants, glass beads, a pipe stem fragment, pyrites and a French copper coin dated 1643. A grave collection purchased by Bird in Hopedale contained three or four copper/brass headbands (the most complete specimen virtually identical to those from Nukasusutok), six copper/brass pendants, a harpoon or lance foreshaft, bone handles, seal teeth, a beaver incisor, a wooden dish fragment, worked ivory pieces, part of an ivory needle case, an iron harpoon point, pyrites and a quartz fragment. Also noted earlier was the presumed 17th century kayak burial at Kikkertavak-1, west of Nukasusutok Island, that included a wooden tool box containing 150 items, among them harpoons and knives with iron blades (Kaplan 1983:235).

The largest sample of Inuit grave material from Labrador comes from Saglek Bay. A total of 78 graves was investigated on Rose Island and another two on Upernavik Island (Way 1978). Of these, 78 were pre-modern, presumably dating ca. 1725-1850 (Way 1978:134). They consisted of 29 female graves, 22 male graves, 7 with both sexes and 19 of indeterminate sex. A total of 21 graves had no burial goods; there is no particular sex/age association to this and looting cannot be discounted. For the purposes of the present discussion, single male and female graves were coded for the presence/absence of individual grave good types and subjected to quantitative analyses, but no clear patterns were apparent. This was partly attributable to the high diversity of items deposited in the graves (60 types were coded) and the resulting infrequent occurrence of individual item types, but it was also a consequence of item types being associated with both sexes. Male exclusive associations included: kayak parts, bow drill parts and wooden dolls (four male figures, one female). Female exclusive items included ulus, copper/brass headbands and copper/brass pendants. Female graves also contained most of the glass trade beads and tended to have most of the animal bone deposits.

Overall, 18 of the Saglek graves contained European metal objects or traces thereof, totaling 51 pieces and ranging from 1-10 items per grave. Glass trade beads were present in seven graves, totaling 178 items, but 118 of these were from a single grave. Of the other graves, one had 44 beads, another 12, while the remaining four had only one each (summarized from Way 1978:322-327). These figures suggest the frequency of European items deposited in the graves was not particularly high overall and that they were concentrated with a small number of individuals. Schledermann's (1976:28-29) excavation of 18th to 19th century communal houses at the nearby Ikkusik site produced a range of European goods, but also not in great quantity.

If the Saglek graves are ranked in terms of total numbers of grave goods and the amount of European items present, one burial stands out clearly. Grave 24 was a woman's burial containing a whalebone comb, four copper/brass head bands, a copper/brass pendant, two copper/brass disks, a copper/brass ring, a copper/brass strip, 3 ivory pendants, 29 lead pendants, 118 glass beads, 49 shell beads, 9 wooden beads and 11 stone beads (Way 1978:85-86, 323-324). Assuming the large sample of graves is fairly representative (though it may not be), Grave 24 suggests that certain women had roles that enabled them to access significant quantities of European goods and that this access was associated with some form of status distinction.

These comparative data indicate the Nukasusutok graves are similar in pattern to others in central and northern Labrador, but that Graves 4 and 5, and to a lesser extent Grave 2, are particularly rich in their deposits of European goods. The inhabitants of Nukasusutok Island seem to have had better access to European materials than was the case in Saglek Bay. Both Graves 2 and 5 at Nukasusutok and Grave 24 at Rose Island suggest that the contact period was not just a story of big-*man* traders; as illustrated in the narrative of Tuglavina and Mikak, Inuit women may also have attained distinctive social identities and statuses.

Conclusion: Big-Men, Big-Women and Negotiating the 18th Century European World System

The ethnohistoric information presented at the beginning of this chapter provides a narrative of Inuit life in 18th century Labrador. Households were organized as multi-family units and in some cases settlements were composed of several households. Certain males had authority within households, but in multi-house settlements there was conflict between household leaders concerning lines of authority. The most prominent of these household leaders were involved in the baleen trade with Europeans, which involved long-distance travel between baleen supply areas in the north and the trade centers in southern Labrador. Some of these leaders, such as Tuglavina, were able to amass a degree of personal wealth and influence. It is unclear to what extent the social networks in which the Inuit leaders were embedded had effective mechanisms to redistribute that wealth and limit authority. After the establishment of the Moravian missions along the central coast of Labrador these leaders were prominent in resisting Christianization and Moravian attempts to draw the Inuit into church-controlled settlements and economic transactions. Inuit "big-men" continued to travel south to trade and local leaders attempted to lure converts away from the missions. In the Nain region the inhabitants of the Nukasusutok settlement were prominent among these recalcitrant "heathens" and they remained a thorn in the side of the Moravians until about 1810. But beginning in the late 1780s changes in the mission economy that linked mission policy more closely with economic affairs, such as supplying firearms to compete with southern traders and allowing credit, may have undercut the ability of independent Inuit traders to sustain their activities and maintain followers.

Inuit women have a more ambiguous role in this narrative. They were frequently drawn into polygynous households where their labor could be exploited by the household leader and their presence as co-wives could symbolize the leader's status. Co-wives constituted cooperative labour sharing units, with potential for both household solidarity and schisms. Frequent references to wife stealing and abuse suggest that women's roles were often unenviable. On the other hand, some women were able to exert significant influence through shamanist power. The story of Mikak reveals both the strengths and limitations of Inuit women as agents as she careened from being the daughter of a prominent leader, to experiencing English high society, to accompanying Tuglavina on trading journeys, to being abandoned and ending up as the partner of a low status man. During the early 19th century it appears that Inuit women were catalysts in the Christianization process and played important roles in incorporating European goods into domestic contexts.

What little information can be gleaned from Strong's excavations of the 18th and early 19th century houses at Nukasusutok-8 indicates households engaged in the traditional hunting economy, but with a material culture strongly marked by the use of iron and other European goods. The graves provide a different perspective on these processes. The male kayak burial at Grave 4, with its substantial quantity of metal goods, suggests a relatively high status individual involved in the circulation system for European goods. Nearby Grave 5, a female burial with a substantial amount of decorative metal and glass trade beads, suggests a woman with access to quantities of European goods and a status broadly equivalent to the male grave. Grave 2, a woman's burial associated with many trade beads and situated prominently on a hill, implies a form of social recognition. In each case many European goods with both high use and symbolic values were removed from circulation.

Although Strong's archaeological investigations of 1928 do not provide a strong source of inferences concerning the nature of 18th century Inuit society, the grave material at least supplements the ethnohistory by hinting at how the agency of Inuit men and women was valued and represented when individuals passed beyond active involvement in the life of their households.

At a more general level, the Nukasusutok material points to several dimensions of change experienced by Labrador Inuit people during their incorporation into the late 18th century European world system. Most obvious in the archaeological finds is the marked shift in their material culture towards greater reliance on European goods, a reliance that over time undermined household self-sufficiency, at least in the more southerly regions of Inuit settlement. Equipping households with these goods entailed either direct dependence on an influential middle-man, indirect acquisition through kin-ties, or long-distance movements to southern Labrador for direct access to the European suppliers. Although inter-regional mobility was probably a normal practice during the Pre-Contact Period, the wide scale of the movements documented during the late 18th century "stretched" Inuit social relations over space and involved Inuit in transactions that opened up a series of new social strategies. These strategies had important spatial dimensions. Middlemen were highly dependent upon an ability to extend and maintain their spatial range: goods such as baleen had to be collected in the north and transported south to the trading locales and European wares had to be transported northwards and distributed to those who had invested baleen. Consequently, differences in geographical location and access to transport resources generated spatial inequalities that contributed to social differentiation. The establishment of the Moravian missions eventually transformed these spatial relations by creating seasonal population centers and by bringing supply points closer to the Inuit, thereby subverting the middlemen strategies that were based on exploiting spatial inequalities in access to European goods.

The growth of the missions during the late 18th and early 19th centuries also resulted in more localized changes in landscape use and understanding. The Moravians attempted to keep converted Inuit tethered to the mission centers to prevent undesirable contact with "heathens" living in traditional settlements spread over the landscape. This proved difficult at Nain, where the inner bay location of the mission was not well-suited for year-round settlement; Inuit had to maintain a seasonal dispersal to hunting and fishing areas considerably distant from the mission. As long as the Moravians refused to tie economic rewards to conversion there would be a strong incentive for Inuit to maintain their autonomy by opting for traditional settlements such as Nukasusutok-8 and by aligning themselves with "big-man" traders who could supply goods without the subsistence inconvenience and the ideological pressure of living at a mission center. But the late 18th century Moravian shift towards combining economic rewards with conversion increased the attractiveness of mission affiliation and undermined the ability of autonomous Inuit traders to retain followers.

The settlement history of Nukasusutok-8 provides a partial illustration of these changes in landscape organization and the meaning of places. Prior and subsequent to the establishment of the Nain mission in 1771, the Nukasusutok settlement was a fall-spring residence for prominent "big-man" traders and their kin. The settlement was just one in a network of places through which Inuit circulated within the Nain region. It was a place where brothers had quarreled. Although the recruitment of converts to the mission center initially was slow, by 1800 relatively few "heathen" families remained in the Nain region. The Nukasusutok settlement was no longer one winter residence within a network of settlement options, but an isolated "heathen" outpost on a landscape that increasingly was defined in relation to the mission center. Nukasusutok's meaning in this landscape was now as a symbol of "heathen" resistance to Moravian hegemony, a resistance that continued until about 1811, when the last "heathen" Inuit may have abandoned the island and settled at the Nain mission. Today, settlements such as Nukasusutok are simply "old cabins" in the collective memory of oral history, or merely sites on a heritage management inventory.

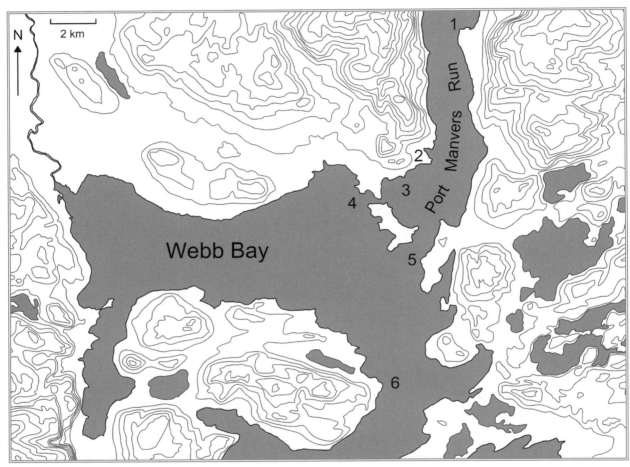

163/ Webb Bay and inner Port Manvers Run with sites mentioned in the text. (1= Port Manvers Run-1, 2= Double Island Cove L-1, 3= Attu's Bight, 4= Attu's Point, 5= Sunset Point, 6= Webb Point). Precise locations withheld by request. Original map © 2004 produced under licence from Her Majesty the Queen in Right of Canada, with permission of Natural Resources Canada.

Webb Bay-Port Manvers Run: Small Scale Investigations

12

As outlined in Chapter 2, Port Manvers Run is a fjord-like inner passage that provides a protected travel route from its seaward outlet at Thalia Point inland to Webb Bay (Figure 3). Smithsonian Institution fieldwork in the 1970s and early 1980s identified a considerable number of archaeological sites along the Run. Pre-Dorset localities were particularly well-represented and an extensive Late Maritime Archaic site was identified on Webb Bay, just west of the southern entrance to the Run. Additional portions of Webb Bay were surveyed by the author in 1992 and 1993, focusing on the Pre-Dorset/Maritime Archaic boundary problem. The surveys included parts of the northern shoreline of Webb Bay, up to ca. 10 km west of the entrance to the Run, Webb Point on the southern side of the bay, as well as selected areas on South Aulatsivik Island between Red Point and Cleat Point (Figure 163). The portion of the north shore around Attu's Brook (5 km west of the Run) contains raised beaches, but extensive foreshore flats prevented access. The innermost portion of Webb Bay and most of its southern shore have not been surveyed.

This chapter summarizes the small scale investigations undertaken at Maritime Archaic and Pre-Dorset sites between 1992 and 1994. A detailed analysis of Attu's Point-1 (HeCk-5), a major Pre-Dorset locality, is presented separately in Chapter 13. Background information on the environmental aspects of the area were discussed in Chapter 2. Chapter 14 ties together the information on Pre-Dorset and Late Maritime Archaic localities and presents a broader discussion of settle-ment patterns and the social boundary relations between the two cultures.

PORT MANVERS RUN-1 (HfCj-5)

Port Manvers Run-1 is a Pre-Dorset locality situated roughly 10 km north of the Webb Bay entrance to the Run (Figure 163). The site lies on top of a windy, exposed anorthosite knoll, 10-12.5 m asl. Discovered by the Smithsonian Institution in 1980, the site was re-investigated in 1993. Pre-Dorset material was associated with gravel pockets in bedrock clefts and there were also caches and cairns of uncertain cultural affiliation. A large quartz vein cut across the north end of the site; a considerable amount of shattered material was present, but it was probably frost-cracked. L-1 was located centrally on the knoll; the Smithsonian survey identified what seemed to be four structures. S-1 was a vague cobble feature within a gravel pocket. Measuring 3.0-3.5 m long and 1.25 m wide, the feature was associated with flakes of Mugford chert and slate. In a nearby linear gravel pocket were what the Smithsonian survey recorded as two rock structures, S-2 and S-3. This area was excavated in 1993, revealing a linear alignment of hearths rather than two structures (described below). S-4 was also located in a gravel pocket; the 1993 observations suggested it was a 6 m long alignment of four hearth-like cobble clusters, each associated with flakes of Mugford chert and slate.

L-2 was located at the northern edge of the rock outcrop. It consisted of the remnants of a small cache

164/ Port Manvers Run-1, S-2/3: view towards the northwest.

or shelter, 1.25 by 1.0 m, constructed against the north side of a boulder. Slightly to the west was L-3, a gravel pocket containing naturally shattered vein quartz and flakes of slate and crystal quartz. A burin made of dark gray Mugford chert was surface-collected here (Figure 169:n). It retains a striking platform at its proximal end and its left lateral edge is lightly retouched and bears a notch that served as a spall terminator. The right lateral margin is minimally retouched. The distal end is spalled dihedrally with a total of eight spall removals; one of the last transverse spalls crosscuts an earlier spall removed parallel to the right lateral margin. There is no hafting modification or facial grinding (L=30.0 mm, W= 21.9, TH= 3.9).

Feature S-2/3

The rock features identified by the Smithsonian survey as S-2 and S-3 were located in a long, narrow, north-south oriented gravel pocket in a bedrock cleft (Figures

164 and 165). Surface inspection did not reveal obvious hearths or structural alignments. A small excavation was conducted because the features seemed unusual and were associated with a moderate amount of flakes and some tools. Given the linear distribution of rocks, the grid was aligned with a baseline running up the middle of the gravel pocket. A total of 14 m^2 was excavated, in the form of a 7 by 2 m field. Tools and flakes were point-plotted, while the flakes were collected in 1 m^2 units.

At first glance the feature appeared to be a continuous 7 m long distribution of rocks, but closer inspection suggested there were actually four cobble concentrations (here considered from south to north). The centers of the first three concentrations were spaced at 1.5 m intervals while the centers of the third and fourth were spaced 2 m apart. Three of the concentrations are fairly nondescript, but the second seemed slightly larger and contained two flat slabs

CHAPTER 12

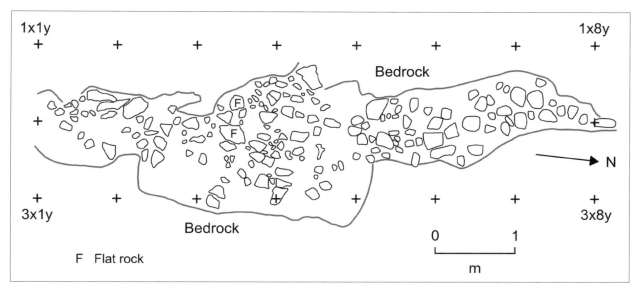

165/ Port Manvers Run 1, S-2/3: rock features.

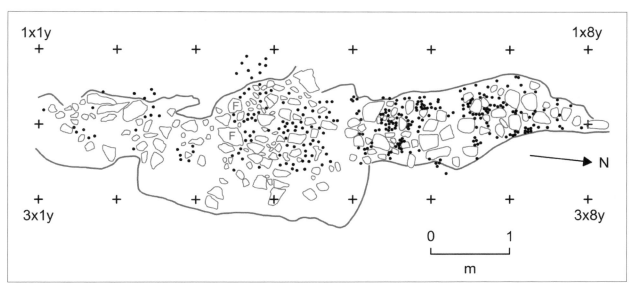

166/ Port Manvers Run-1, S-2/3: total flake distribution.

positioned near each other and adjacent to other rocks in a manner vaguely suggestive of a disturbed hearth. No charcoal was observed. Figure 166 plots the distribution of all flakes and clearly indicates four discrete clusters, each associated with one of the cobble concentrations. The tool distribution (Figures 167 and 168) is broadly consistent with the flake and rock concentrations. *K*-means cluster analysis distinguishes five tiny clusters, two on opposite sides of the second hearth-like rock feature, one at the center of rock

concentration three and two small clusters are associated with concentration four. Rock concentration one entirely lacks tools. Since virtually all the lithic material was confined to the narrow gravel pocket the possibility that it accumulated there after having been washed in from the surrounding bedrock might be considered as a formational factor. The discrete spatial clustering of the flakes is so distinct, however, that it seems unlikely to have been a result of geological processes.

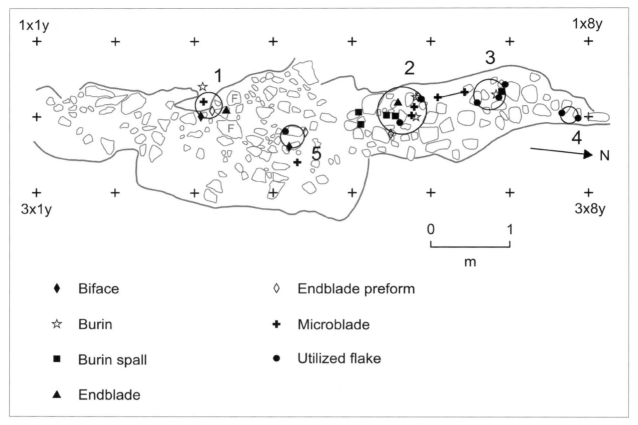

167/ Port Manvers Run-1, S-2/3: tool distribution and k-means clusters.

		EB= 2 EBP= 1 BI= 2 BU= 1 M= 1	BI= 1 BS= 1 M= 3	EB= 1 EBP= 1 BU= 2 BS= 2 M= 2 UF= 1	BU= 1 BS= 1 M= 1 UF= 3	UF= 1
		EB= 1	EBP= 1 BI= 1 M= 1 UF= 1	EBP= 1 BS= 3 UF= 1		UF= 1

3x1y

EB	Endblade	BS	Burin spall	
EBP	Endblade preform	M	Microblade	
BI	Biface	UF	Utilized flake	
BU	Burin			3x8y

168/ Port Manvers Run-1, S-2/3: tool distribution by quadrat.

Table 63 summarizes the distribution of tool classes across the five k-means clusters and includes several non-point provenienced implements that can probably be assigned to the clusters. Given the small sample size little can be said about the distribution except for the concentration of four burin spalls and

CHAPTER 12

Table 63. Port Manvers Run-1 Tool Classes by *K*-Means Cluster.

	C-1	C-2	C-3	C-4	C-5	Quadrat Provenience	TOTAL N (%)
Endblades	1 (1)	1				1	4 (10.3)
Endblade preforms	1	2			1		4 (10.3)
Bifaces	1 (1)				1	1	4 (10.3)
Burins	1	2	1				4 (10.3)
Burin spalls		4 (1)	1			1	7 (17.9)
Microblades	1	2.5	0.5		1	3	8 (20.5)
Utilized flakes		2	3	2	1		8 (20.5)
TOTAL	**5 (2)**	**13.5 (1)**	**5.5**	**2**	**4**		**639**

Parentheses indicate items lacking point provenience, but are probably cluster-related.

two burins in cluster 2, associated with the third rock concentration. On the other hand, the distribution of flake raw materials (see below) exhibits some differences between the rock concentrations associated with clusters 1 and 5 versus clusters 2, 3 and 4. If we attribute possible behavioral significance to the flake raw material distinctions and group the tool clusters accordingly— dividing the linear rock feature in the middle near the 5y line— then differences are apparent between the northern and southern halves of the feature. The southern half (clusters 1 and 5) has slightly more bifaces (three versus one) whereas the northern half (clusters 2, 3 and 4) has slightly more burins (three versus one), contains all the burin spalls and the majority of the utilized flakes (seven versus one). The distribution of microblades is ambiguous given the uncertain cluster association of several non-provenienced implements. Overall, the assemblage is dominated by microblades, utilized flakes, endblades and endblade preforms, as well as burin spalls. Scrapers and axes/adzes are absent.

Table 64. Port Manvers Run-1 Tool Raw Material Frequencies by *K*-Means Cluster.

	C-1	C-2	C-3	C-4	C-5	Quadrat Provenience	TOTAL N (%)
Gray Mugford chert	1	7.5 (1)	2.5	2	2	3	19 (48.7)
Dark gray Mugford	2	2			1	1	6 (15.4)
Gray-speckled Mugford	1 (1)	1	1		1		5 (12.8)
Gray-banded Mugford		2	1				3 (7.7)
Black chert					1		1 (2.6)
Crystal quartz	1	1	1			1	4 (10.3)
Ramah chert	(1)						1 (2.6)
TOTAL	**5 (2)**	**13.5 (1)**	**5.5**	**2**	**4**	**6**	**39**

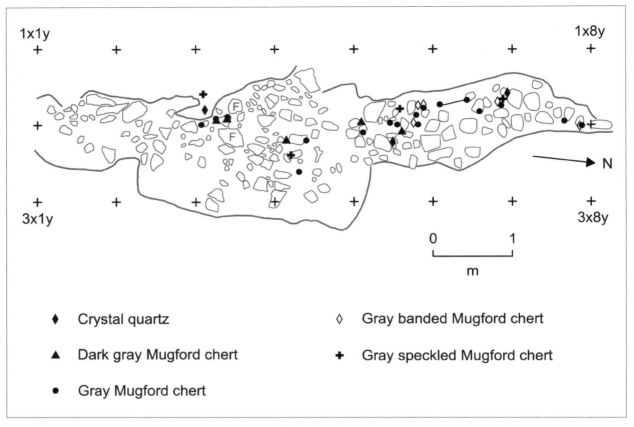

169/ Port Manvers Run-1, S-2/3: tool raw material distributions.

The spatial distribution of tool raw materials is presented in Table 64 and Figure 169. There is little meaningful variation besides a considerable number of gray Mugford chert implements associated with cluster 2. The absence of slate tools should be noted, however, particularly in contrast with the abundance of slate debitage (see below).

As noted earlier, the total distribution of flakes shows a marked tendency for clusters associated with each of the four rock concentrations (Figure 166). Unfortunately, the field plots of individual flake raw materials proved to be unreliable because of the tendency of slate to grade into a silicified material resembling Mugford chert, thus exacerbating the problems of distinguishing raw material types in the field. Consequently, only quadrat distribution diagrams based on lab identifications are presented here (Figure 170). Overall, the various Mugford cherts comprise 56% of the total, while slate constitutes 40%. Black

chert, Ramah chert and crystal quartz are only represented by a few flakes each. The quadrat counts suggest that the distribution of some raw materials varies relative to the northern and southern sides of the linear rock feature, roughly corresponding to the 5y grid line. Table 65 outlines the frequency of flake raw material types structured by this north-south distinction. The vast majority of gray-banded Mugford chert lies on the north side of the feature, while there is a slight tendency for gray-speckled Mugford chert to lie on the south side. Additionally, patinated chert, black chert, Ramah chert and crystal quartz mostly occur on the south side. Slate is evenly distributed. If the table is collapsed to combine low frequency cells (dark gray Mugford with gray Mugford, patinated, black and Ramah cherts plus crystal quartz in an "other" category), a chi-square test is significant at the .05 level ($\chi^2 = 56.45$), indicating these contrasting north-south distributions are unlikely to be fortuitous.

CHAPTER 12

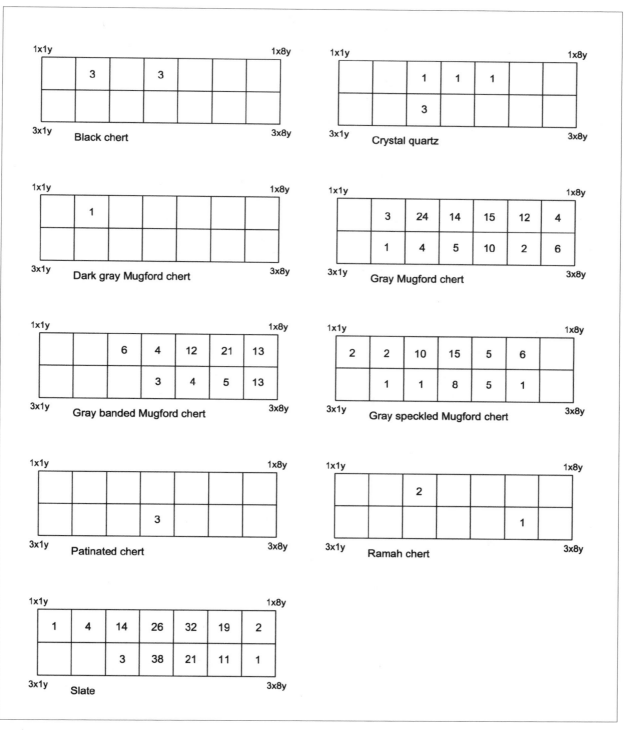

170/ Port Manvers Run-1, S-2/3: flake raw material distributions.

Table 65. Port Manvers Run-1 Flake Raw Material Frequencies.

	North	South	TOTAL N (%)
Gray Mugford chert	49	51	100 (23.4)
Dark gray Mugford		1	1 (0.2)
Gray-banded Mugford	68	13	81 (18.9)
Gray-speckled Mugford	17	39	56 (13.1)
Patinated chert		3	3 (0.7)
Black chert		6	6 (1.4)
Ramah chert	1	2	3 (0.7)
Crystal quartz	1	5	6 (1.4)
Slate	86	86	172 (40.2)
TOTAL	**222**	**206**	**428**

Table 66 portrays the total weights of the lithic raw material types present, combining tools and flakes. There are some major differences in the tool versus flake weight proportions for some of the raw materials, but Mugford cherts and slate dominate overall. As noted above, though, slate is represented only as flakes.

The size distribution (maximum length) of Mugford chert (generic) and slate flakes is graphed in Figure 171. The materials exhibit similar size profiles, although a greater proportion of Mugford chert is found in the <10 mm class while slate is slightly more abundant in the larger size classes. The Mugford chert size profile is similar to those from other Pre-Dorset localities at Attu's Point (Chapter 13, Figure 226), but the slate proportions are low in the <30 to <35 mm classes that are better represented at Attu's Point (Chapter 13, Figure 227). This might indicate a lesser significance for the earlier rough-out reduction stages at Port Manvers Run-1, but a more detailed study of slate reduction systems is necessary to clarify this point.

Only one tool refit was identified: two fragments of a microblade that conjoined over a short distance of 34 cm (Figure 167). None of the burin spalls could be refitted with the burins, but both items were discarded close to each other, mostly in a tight cluster at the third rock concentration (Figure 167). Two burin spalls of dark gray Mugford chert could not have been produced from any of the four burins recovered from the locality, suggesting the operation of curation processes.

Discussion

The distribution of tools and flakes at S-2/3 gives the impression that each rock concentration was the focus of somewhat discrete activity. Spatial variations in the flake raw materials and tool types, however, suggest behavioral differences between the northern and

Table 66. Port Manvers Run-1 Total Lithic Raw Material Weights (Tools and Flakes). In Grams.

	Tools g (%)	Flakes g (%)	TOTAL g (%)
Gray Mugford chert	12.5 (43.1)	56.1 (17.1)	68.6 (19.2)
Dark gray Mugford	4.8 (16.6)	2.6 (0.8)	7.4 (2.1)
Gray-banded Mugford	3.9 (13.4)	74.3 (22.7)	78.2 (21.9)
Gray-speckled Mugford	4.6 (15.9)	37.9 (11.6)	42.5 (11.9)
Patinated chert		4.4 (1.3)	4.4 (1.2)
Black chert	0.4 (1.4)	12.1 (3.7)	12.5 (3.5)
Ramah chert	0.6 (2.1)	0.5 (0.2)	1.1 (0.3)
Crystal quartz	2.2 (7.6)	3.1 (0.9)	5.3 (1.5)
Slate		137.0 (41.8)	137.0 (38.4)

CHAPTER 12

southern halves of the linear feature, each half centered on a linked pair of rock concentrations. The southern half has slightly more bifaces whereas the northern half has slightly more burins as well as containing all the burin spalls and the majority of the utilized flakes. Most of the gray-banded Mugford chert flakes lie on the north side of the feature while there is a tendency for gray-speckled Mugford chert to lie on the south side. Although no charcoal was observed during

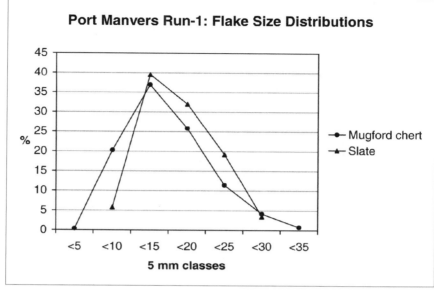

171/ Port Manvers Run-1, S-2/3: flake size distributions.

the excavation, a single flake of gray-speckled Mugford chert from unit 1x6y (associated with the third rock concentration) exhibited a pot-lid fracture characteristic of thermal stress and a small biface fragment of Ramah chert from unit 1x3y (associated with the second rock concentration with more evident hearth features) bore traces of heat patination.

This linear arrangement of rocks does not represent a known form of Labrador Pre-Dorset dwelling. At this point it seems most credible to interpret the feature as a line of external hearths, each associated with a discrete lithic deposit. A similar linear rock cluster feature was found nearby at the same site (S-4). The pattern of possible hearths spaced 1.5-2.0 m apart might also be present at L-5 at the Attu's Point Pre-Dorset site (Chapter 13), although in that case a disturbed axial feature seems a more likely interpretation. On the other hand, the feature could be the remains of an as-yet undocumented dwelling form, such as a 7 m long tent structure with a central line of hearths. Unconventional models should be considered given the shifting interpretations of Maritime Archaic site structure (Chapter 3) and reports of a Pre-Dorset "longhouse" on the Melville Peninsula in the central arctic (S.

Rowley, cited in Ramsden and Murray 1995:106; Rowley and Rowley 1997:274).

Dating

No charcoal was recovered from the excavation, so the site can only be dated by relative means. Height above sea level (10-12.5 m) corresponds to that of other Pre-Dorset sites in the area, but does not help much otherwise. The small tool collection does not provide much typological basis for dating besides exhibiting a general Early Pre-Dorset stamp.

Tool Assemblage

Endblades All four of the endblades (Figure 172:d-f) are fragmentary: three medial portions, one proximal. Two implements are made of gray-speckled Mugford chert, one of dark gray Mugford chert, and one of crystal quartz. The proximal specimen (Figure 172:f) is made of gray-speckled Mugford chert and has a straight base, a biconvex cross-section and slightly serrated edges (W= 9.5 mm, TH= 2.0). The three medial fragments have very fine flaking; a tiny dark gray Mugford chert example (not illustrated) has medial polish on one face.

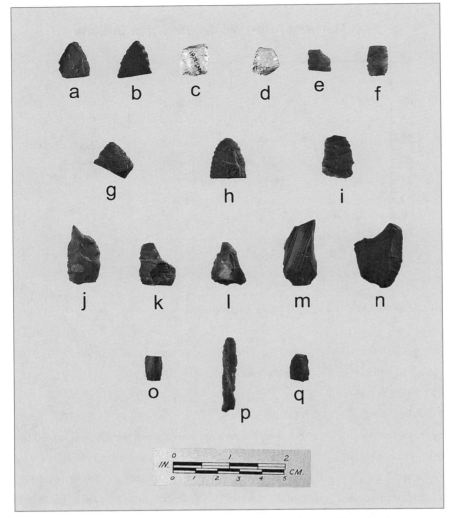

172/ *Port Manvers Run-1, S-2/3: tools. a, b: endblade preforms; c-f: endblades; g, h: bifaces; i: endblade preform; j-n: burins; o-q: microblades.*

began at the distal end but did not go very far before the tip broke off and the implement was discarded.

Bifaces All four of the bifaces are small fragments, two made of gray Mugford chert, one of gray-speckled Mugford, one of Ramah chert and one of black chert. Three of them are probably fragments of bifacial points or knives rather than endblades; two of these are illustrated in Figure 172:g, h. Their widths are probably in the 16-19 mm range.

Burins Three of the four burins are whole, while one is a distal fragment. Two are made from gray-banded Mugford chert and one each from gray-speckled and gray Mugford chert. None exhibit facial grinding or side-notching, although all bear traces of lateral edge grinding. The specimen illustrated in Figure 172:j has unifacial dorsal retouch on one lateral edge, mostly ventral and relatively rough retouch on the other lateral edge, and minimal bifacial retouch on its base (L= 27.4 mm, W= 15.3, TH= 5.4). The distal end is spalled dihedrally with the shorter left-side spall terminated by a distinct notch just below the tip; a total of seven spalls were removed. Figure 172:k shows a burin made on a minimally retouched flake with slight unifacial distal notching from which a single spall was removed (L= 19.2 mm, W= 16.3, TH= 7.4). The item shown in Figure 172:l is a distal fragment with a right lateral edge retouched mostly on the ventral side from the surface of an earlier spall (W=14.0 mm, TH=4.8). The distal

Endblade Preforms Of the four endblade preforms, two are distal fragments and two are proximal fragments. The two distal fragments, one made of gray Mugford chert, the other of dark gray Mugford chert, were made on flakes of roughly triangular form that were modified with fine bifacial retouch around their margins (Figure 172:a, b). One of the proximal fragments is made of crystal quartz (Figure 172:c) and has a plano-convex cross-section, two long basal thinning flakes on its ventral side and a slight shoulder formed by incomplete bifacial retouch on one edge (W= 13.2 mm, TH= 2.7). The other is made of gray Mugford chert (Figure 172:i) and has a straight base as well as fine flaking primarily on one face. Final edge retouch

CHAPTER 12

end is spalled dihedrally with two additional spalls. Figure 172:m has very minimal dorsal retouch on its lateral edges, a remnant striking platform at its base, and slight ventral thinning of the bulb of percussion (L= 30.1 mm, W= 15.3, TH= 6.2). The distal end is spalled dihedrally with two spall removals, one of which removed most of one lateral edge of the flake.

Burin Spalls Of the seven burin spalls, three are made of dark gray Mugford chert, three of gray Mugford chert and one of gray-speckled Mugford chert. One is complete, three are proximal fragments, and one each are medial and distal fragments. All are secondary spalls and none exhibit evidence for facial grinding.

Microblades Of the eight microblades (MNI= 3), six are fashioned from gray Mugford chert, one from gray-banded Mugford chert and one from crystal quartz. One is nearly complete while five are medial fragments, one a distal fragment and one a proximal portion. Seven of the eight exhibit use-wear, the only exception being the nearly complete specimen (L = 35.1 mm, W = 6.6, TH = 2.7). The widths of the proximal and medial fragments range between 5.3-8.7 mm. Examples are shown in Figure 172:o-q.

Utilized Flakes Five of the eight utilized flakes are made of gray Mugford chert, two of dark gray Mugford chert and one of crystal quartz.

Conclusions

Port Manvers Run-1, L-1, is most likely a small hunting stand (cf., Binford's [1978] Mask site). The site location provides an excellent look-out for spotting sea mam-

173/ Double Island Cove-1, Structure 1. Approximate pit boundaries indicated. View towards the southwest.

mals moving through the Run. The inferred linear hearth feature at S-2/3, as well as the similar but unexcavated S-4 area, suggest hearth complexes used by small groups while staging hunting activities. The tool assemblage is small and functionally limited, mostly to endblades and endblade preforms, burin spalls, microblades and utilized flakes. Scrapers are conspicuous by their absence. Although slate flakes indicative of tool reduction were present, there were no axes or adzes. There is little basis to determine site seasonality, but an open water season seems most likely given the site's look-out character and its location ca. 6 km south of the modern polynya at the "Second Rattle," which was probably the most optimal winter hunting location in the area.

DOUBLE ISLAND COVE-1, L-1 (HeCj-1)

Double Island Cove lies on the western side of the southern entrance to Port Manvers Run (Figure 163). L-1, a Pre-Dorset occupation, was registered in 1985 by the Smithsonian Institution and revisited in 1992 and 1993 since it lay near our field camp. The site is situated on a small sloping terrace on the south side of the cove, directly backed by a rocky knoll. Two possible structures were exposed in small blow-outs. The clear-

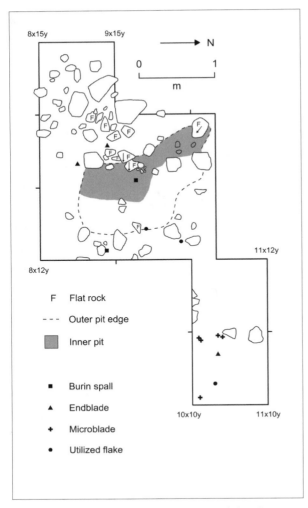

F   Flat rock

- - -   Outer pit edge

    Inner pit

■   Burin spall

▲   Endblade

＋   Microblade

●   Utilized flake

174/ Double Island Cove-1, Structure 1: tool distribution.

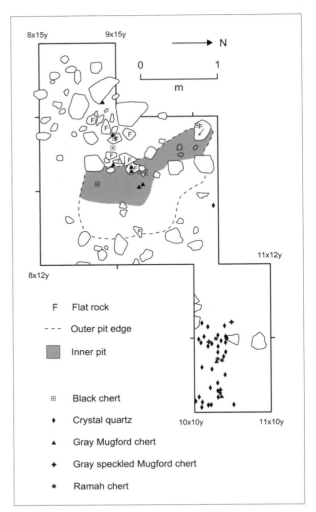

F   Flat rock

- - -   Outer pit edge

    Inner pit

⊡   Black chert

◆   Crystal quartz

▲   Gray Mugford chert

＋   Gray speckled Mugford chert

＊   Ramah chert

175/ Double Island Cove-1, Structure 1: flake distribution.

est of these, Structure 1, was partially excavated in 1992. Structure 2 was located 10.4 m northeast of S-1 and 0.5-1.0 m lower in elevation. A small excavation was begun at S-2 in 1993 but was not completed because of a hasty departure necessitated by strong winds and boat problems.

Structure 1

At first glance Structure 1 consisted of a small rock alignment and a minimal amount of lithic material exposed on the surface, altogether covering an area of 15 m². A total of 7.5 m² was excavated (Figures 173 and 174), exposing a central feature but incompletely documenting its periphery. The excavation indicated that this was not an axial structure. The most promi-

nent feature was a roughly oval depression, the outer limits of which measured 2.0 by 1.0 m, with a long axis running NE-SW. The depression was bordered on the north by a cluster of large seemingly "structural" rocks embedded in the surrounding sand/gravel and on the south by a smaller cluster of rocks. The base of the depression was 15-20 cm below ground surface on the north side, 35 cm below the surface of the higher south side. The entire depression was filled with black humus-rich soil and charcoal flecks. It was partially covered by a thin layer of yellow sand/gravel, possibly slope wash.

The lower portion of the southern and western sides of the depression contained a smaller pit, 2.0 by 0.5 m. This second pit was bordered by flat rock slabs

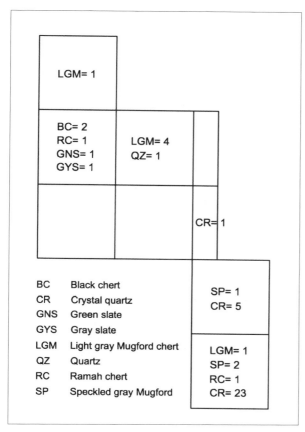

LGM= 1	
BC= 2 RC= 1 GNS= 1 GYS= 1	LGM= 4 QZ= 1
	CR= 1

BC Black chert	SP= 1
CR Crystal quartz	CR= 5
GNS Green slate	
GYS Gray slate	
LGM Light gray Mugford chert	LGM= 1
QZ Quartz	SP= 2
RC Ramah chert	RC= 1
SP Speckled gray Mugford	CR= 23

176/ Double Island Cove-1, Structure 1: flake distribution by quadrat.

that extended towards the cluster of "structural" rocks. Perhaps these slabs once lined the depression and were thrown out after use, but some of them seem to be arranged deliberately between the large "structural" rocks. Alternatively, the "structural" rocks may have been removed when the depression was constructed. At the center of the secondary pit was a small inclined flat slab and three or four small fire-cracked rocks. Directly associated with this inclined slab was charcoal, a few tiny retouch flakes of Mugford chert and a large burin spall. Another inclined flat slab was positioned at the extreme eastern end of the depression.

Very little lithic material was recovered. Thirteen tools were collected: a triangular endblade fragment, two burin spalls, two biface fragments, five possible microblade fragments and three utilized flakes. With the exception of the burin spall from the base of the pit, all the tools were found either around the rim of

the depression or in a small cluster 1.4 m to the east. In contrast, most of the flakes were clustered in the latter area, 1.4 m east of the pit (Figures 175 and 176). Flake raw material frequencies are listed in Table 67. The modest total of 59 flakes is dominated by crystal quartz and gray Mugford chert. All but one of the crystal quartz flakes were found in the cluster east of the depression while gray Mugford and black cherts seem to have a stronger association with the pit. The concentration of flakes and tools associated with several rocks in the excavation area east of the depression might indicate the presence of another structure.

Table 67. Double Island Cove-1, L-1, S-1: Flake Raw Material Frequencies.

	N	%
Crystal quartz	29	(64.4)
Light gray Mugford chert	6	(13.3)
Black chert	2	(4.4)
Gray-speckled chert	3	(6.7)
Ramah chert	2	(4.4)
Quartz	1	(2.2)
Green slate	1	(2.2)
Gray slate	1	(2.2)
TOTAL	**45**	

The tool assemblage contains little chronologically diagnostic material. The small triangular endblade is a proximal fragment made of gray Mugford chert (Figure 179:b). It is extremely thin, slightly serrated and has a straight base modified by basal thinning flakes on both faces (W= 10.0 mm, TH= 1.8). The two biface fragments are made of gray Mugford chert and gray-speckled Mugford chert; one is a proximal portion, the other a lateral edge fragment (Figure 179:a,c). Both have nearly plano-convex cross-sections, fine parallel flaking and slightly serrated edges. The two burin spalls are both made of gray Mugford chert; one is complete, the other is a proximal fragment, and both are secondary spalls. Of the five possible microblades,

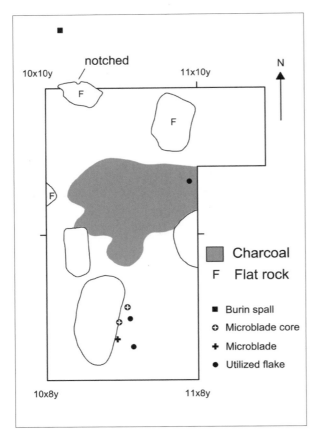

177/ Double Island Cove-1, Structure 2: tool distribution.

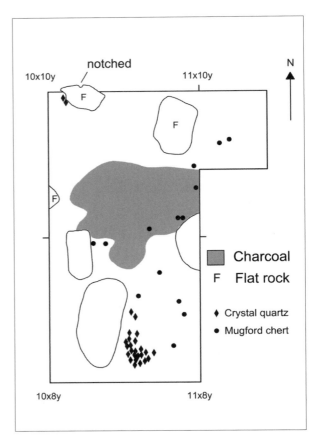

178/ Double Island Cove-1, Structure 2: flake distribution.

four are made of crystal quartz, one of gray-white sili-cified siltstone. The single complete specimen is made of crystal quartz, although it is poorly formed (L= 18.8 mm, W= 8.3, TH= 3.1), while three are small proximal fragments and one is a medial portion. Two of the three utilized flakes are made of gray Mugford chert, the other of patinated chert.

A sample of charcoal from the depression was radiocarbon dated to 3640±70 B.P. (Beta-57125). The tool collection provides minimal basis for evaluating this result. The endblade basal form and slight serra-tion, the serrated bifaces, and the unground burin spalls, are all attributes that are at least consistent with the Early Pre-Dorset radiocarbon date.

Several seeds and tiny bone fragments were retrieved when soil samples from the depression were wet-sieved. The seeds were identified by Michael Deal (Archaeology Unit, Memorial University). All identifi-able elements were of crowberry (*Empetrum nigrum*)

and they consisted of: 15 single seeds, another in two sections, 2 seeds with partial coats, two complete clus-ters (9 seeds each) and 2 partial clusters (3 and 6 seeds respectively). Given the presence of seed clus-ters, Deal suggests that the seeds may have been green when burned, otherwise they might not have stuck together. If so, that might suggest they were burned during the summer. This need not indicate human consumption of the berries, though, since the plant as a whole could have been burned in a smudge pit to discourage flies or to smoke fish. Additionally, since crowberries survive intact over the winter when covered with snow, their use in other seasons cannot be eliminated.

Structure 2

Structure 2 was visible on the surface as a cluster of flat rock slabs and Mugford chert flakes. Given the interesting results from the Structure 1 investigation, a test excavation was begun in 1993. Unfortunately, the work was terminated early by a hasty departure, at which point only 2.5 m^2 had been excavated (Figure 177). Several possible "structural" rocks were uncovered, as well as some flat slabs, one with a trace of notching. A patch of charcoal was present in the center of the excavation, but there was no clear indication of a hearth structure. Charcoal from this concentration was radiocarbon dated to 3320±70 B.P. (Beta-71476).

Minimal lithic material was recovered. Only seven tools were collected, mostly from a tight cluster beside a large rock (Figure 177): a burin spall of gray Mugford chert, two microblade core fragments of crystal quartz (Figure 179:e, f), a microblade fragment of crystal quartz (Figure 179:d) and three utilized flakes (two of crystal quartz, one of gray Mugford chert). Flake material consisted of crystal quartz (n=31), gray Mugford chert (n=10), patinated chert (n=2) and slate (n=1). The crystal quartz flakes were tightly concentrated beside the same large rock where most of the tools were found (Figure 178).

Discussion

The material from Double Island Cove-1 is so limited it is difficult to draw substantive conclusions. The slightly lower elevation of Structure 2 might fit with its radiocarbon dating 300 years later than Structure 1, but nothing in the scanty lithic assemblage from Structure 2 points to a Late Pre-Dorset dating. The raw material patterns of the two structures are similar: a predominance of crystal quartz, which seems to be spatially concentrated. Consequently, there are no grounds to support or reject the radiocarbon datings. If the 3300 B.P. date is reasonable, however, it is one of relatively few indications of a Late Pre-Dorset presence in the Nain area. The other is Nukasusutok-2, discussed briefly in Chapter 4 and presented in detail by Fitzhugh (2002).

Double Island Cove-1 seems to be a minor camp, possibly used on a couple of occasions widely separated in time. Its main value, apart from yielding some

179/ Tools from Double Island Cove, Sunset Point and Webb Point. a-c: biface, endblade, biface (Double Island Cove S-1); d-f: microblade, core fragment, core fragment (Double Island Cove S-2); g, h: burin, microblade (Sunset Point); i-n: microblade, endblade (Pre-Dorset), biface stem, biface (Maritime Archaic), stemmed point (Maritime Archaic), flake point (Maritime Archaic) (all Webb Point).

additional radiocarbon dates, is that Structure 1 provides evidence for a feature type unknown from elsewhere in Labrador. The depression and its association with burned crowberry seeds and bone fragments indicates a function different from that of documented Pre-Dorset axial structures and tent rings. If the crowberry seeds imply use during the summer, this would be the first direct evidence for seasonality at a Pre-Dorset site in Labrador. Today, summer is not a period of optimum resource availability in the Webb Bay/Port Manvers Run area, although the cove sometimes offers

180/ Attu's Bight overview towards the southwest.

SUNSET POINT (HeCj-8)

Sunset Point is a neo-toponym for a small rocky crag between Red Point and Cleat Point on South Aulatsivik Island (Figure 163). The site consists of two lithic scatters in gravel deposits on top of an exposed bedrock knoll, a form and placement typical of several small Pre-Dorset sites in the Port Manvers Run area. Two implements were surface-collected: a burin and a microblade. The burin (Figure 179:g) is made on a large flake of gray-speckled Mugford chert (L= 38.4 mm, W= 20.0, TH= 6.3). The implement bears a remnant striking platform on its base. The distal and medial margins of the left lateral edge are bifacially retouched while the proximal edge margin is unifacially retouched ventrally. The right lateral margin bears a bifacial notch, possibly for spall termination. The flake facets and lateral edges of the basal area are slightly polished. The distal burination

good char fishing. With a higher sea level at the time of Pre-Dorset occupation, however, Double Island Cove would have been a much larger embayment, perhaps with a slightly different mix of resources than today. A minor Pre-Dorset locality on the north side of the cove (Double Island Point-2, HeCj-4) indicates additional Pre-Dorset activity in the area, but overall the use of the cove was more limited than at Port Manvers-Run-1 or certainly Attu's Point (Chapter 13).

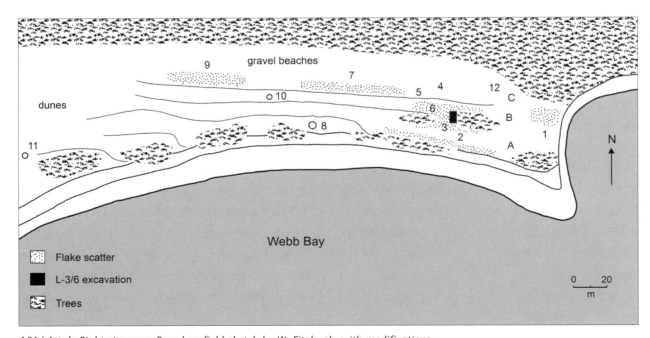

181/ Attu's Bight site map. Based on field sketch by W. Fitzhugh, with modifications.

is transverse with five spall removals and the distal tip is heavily rounded by wear. The microblade (Figure 179:h) is made of gray-speckled Mugford chert and is relatively large (L= > 40.0 mm, W= 11.0, TH= 2.7), with fine use retouch along part of one edge.

ATTU'S BIGHT-1 (HeCk-4)

Attu's Bight-1 is a large Rattler's Bight Phase (4200-3500 B.P.) Maritime Archaic site, located on the north side of Webb Bay, just west of the entrance to Port Manvers Run (Figure 163). It was discovered and surface collected by the Smithsonian Institution in 1985 (Fitzhugh 1986:57) and revisited by the author in 1992 and 1993. The site consists of cultural remains extending for about 350 m along a set of sand and gravel terraces 19-21 m asl. (Figure 180, 181). Smithsonian field notes identify three different beach levels (A, B, C); that were suggested to be indicative of chronological differences within the site. However, the vertical distance between these terraces is minimal (0.5-1.0 m) and the slope is very gradual, so the levels may have little relevance for relative dating the site contents. Indeed, according to the general uplift regime for the Nain inner bay area (Figure 5) the 19 m terrace emerged 6000-5500 B.P., well prior to the Rattlers Bight phase. Since the terrace front is an erosion face that plunges steeply from 19 m to the modern shoreline, during the Rattlers Bight Phase there were probably no lower beaches suitable for habitation. In any event, the large horizontal extent of the 19-21 m surface was ideal for longhouse placement and it provided a broad field of view over Webb Bay.

Most of the site is completely deflated by wind erosion. The little surface vegetation present consists of moss-lichen and isolated stands of spruce trees. Thicker spruce growth is found immediately north of the site, downslope to the south, and to the west. Flakes and implements of Ramah chert and other materials lie exposed on the sand/gravel surface, distributed in linear patterns parallel to the beach levels. The 1985 Smithsonian survey identified nine separate

loci and the 1992-93 investigations added three more. These 12 loci (Figure 181) are described briefly below, based on Smithsonian field notes and later observations. Test excavations conducted at L-3/6 in 1992-93 are described thereafter.

Overview of Localities

L-1: At the extreme eastern end of the terrace was a Ramah chert scatter. The 1992 surface collection included three biface fragments of thermally altered Ramah chert, of which two are probably point preforms (Figure 190:j, k), while the third is an edge fragment from a larger bifacial implement (Figure 190:i). Also recovered was a large green slate flake (Figure 191:a) with a slightly polished medial surface and scraper-like retouch along one edge (L= 79.6 mm, W= 64.4, TH= 7.7).

L-2: Parallel to the southeastern terrace front was a scatter of Ramah chert flakes, 60 m long, 6 m wide. Just north of this was a packed cobble feature, sub-rectangular in shape and 2.5 by 1.0 m in size. The Smithsonian surface collection consisted of two Ramah chert micropoints, a ground slate preform and two utilized flakes (one of Ramah chert the other of "chert").

L-3 and L-6: Located on the middle beach level near the eastern end of the terrace, these loci contained the only *in situ* portion of the site. The Smithsonian registered two separate loci here, but they probably constitute a single occupation area, of which perhaps two-thirds is deflated. L-3/6 was marked by a scatter of Ramah chert flakes 40 m long and at least 5-6 m wide, the easternmost portion of which extended into the *in situ* deposit. At L-3 the Smithsonian collected a Ramah chert stemmed point, three flake points (two of Ramah chert, one of unspecified material), four Ramah chert biface fragments and a slate celt fragment, while at L-6 they collected two Ramah chert biface fragments and a slate celt fragment. The 1992-93 test excavations are described below.

182/ Attu's Bight L-3/6: view towards the east.

L-4: Positioned on the highest beach level, L-4 consisted of a small scatter of quartz flakes, from which the Smithsonian collected two quartz biface fragments and a Ramah chert flake knife. In 1992 a Ramah chert biface preform (Figure 190:c) was collected 7 m north of L-4. The implement is fully flaked dorsally but only partially flaked ventrally, and it bears a striking platform distally (L= 43.5 mm, W= 21.9, TH= 9.2).

L-5: Situated on the upper portion of the middle beach level and adjacent to L-3/6, L-5 was a lithic scatter containing flakes of Ramah chert, Mugford chert and slate. The Smithsonian collected two stemmed points, a single-shouldered biface and a biface fragment, all of Ramah chert.

L-7: Located on the central portion of the highest beach level, L-7 was a 120 m long scatter of Ramah chert flakes. The Smithsonian surface collected four flake points, three of Ramah chert, one of quartz. In 1992 a complete Ramah chert stemmed point was recovered (Figure 190:a). The implement is "typical" of the Rattlers Bight phase, with bifacial flaking, a biconvex cross-section, a slightly tapering stem and a slightly convex base (L= 47.0 mm, W= 21.2, TH= 6.2, stem L= 16.4, stem W[shoulder/base] = 14.1/11.3).

L-8: Near the center of the site, slightly back from the eroded terrace front, was an oval ring of cobbles, 4 m in diameter. The feature was associated with large chunks of Ramah chert, banded slate and quartz flakes. The Smithsonian surface collected a stemmed point preform, two biface preforms and a sidescraper, all of Ramah chert.

L-9: Near the western end of the site, on the highest beach level, was a 50 m linear scatter of Ramah chert flakes. Smithsonian field notes mention the presence of a stemmed point resembling Sandy Cove Complex form.

L-10: Lying between L-7 and L-9, but slightly lower, was a 1 m diameter cluster of about 10 head-sized rocks associated with smaller cobbles. A couple of Ramah chert flakes lay on top of the feature, which may be a burial cairn. West of the feature was a 10 by 10 m scatter of Ramah chert flakes.

L-11: This was the westernmost cultural feature observed at the site, lying in an isolated area 40 m south of some sand dunes. It consisted of a cluster of about 10 head-sized or smaller rocks, 1 m in diameter, without associated lithic material. The feature may be a burial cairn.

L-12: Located on the highest beach level and towards the northeast corner of the site, L-12 was a small scatter of Ramah chert flakes. A Ramah chert flake point was surface collected (Figure 190:b); it has bifacial retouch limited to the edge margins, a slight shoulder on one lateral edge, and slight basal thinning (L= 23.9 mm, W= 11.6, TH= 3.7, shoulder HT= 9.3).

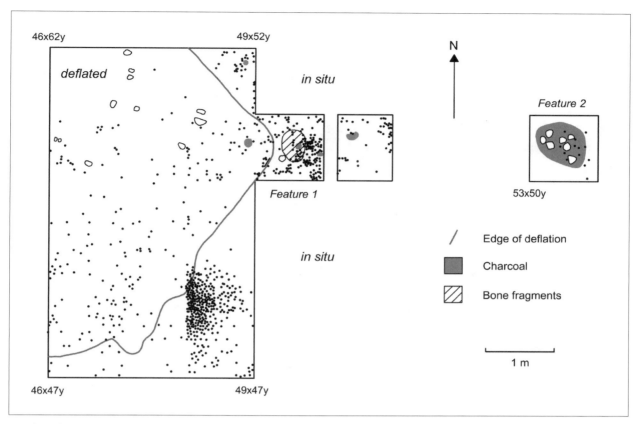

183/ Attu's Bight L-3/6: excavation with flake distribution.

Test Excavations at L-3/6

In 1992 and 1993 small scale test excavations were undertaken in the *in situ* deposits at L-3/6 (Figure 182) to acquire material for radiocarbon dating and to determine if there was much likelihood of identifying traces of dwelling structures or other features. In 1992 a small grid system was set up on the western edge of the *in situ* deposit, including part of the deflated area. A total of 17.8 m² was investigated, of which only 3 m² was excavated *in situ,* the rest was simply a trowel-through of the exposed sand and gravel. Tools and flakes were point-plotted, while flakes were collected in 1 m² units. A profile from the *in situ* deposit indicated possible traces of two occupation layers, so in 1993 two 1 m² test pits were excavated further eastward in the *in situ* deposit to provide additional stratigraphic information (Figure 183).

The sediments in the vicinity of L-3/6 consisted of coarse sand and pea-size gravel. The depth of deflation varied from 10-40 cm. A stratigraphic profile

(50x51y/50x50y) taken from the edge of the *in situ* deposit exhibited some interesting details (Figures 184 and 185). A total of 11 separate stratigraphic units were identified, including at least four buried humus layers that indicate a repetitive cycle of temporarily stable vegetation surfaces followed by eolian deposition. The main cultural level was unit 9, 35 cm below the surface, a sand layer that exhibited a shallow basin-like feature excavated slightly into the underlying sand/gravel. Unit 9 contained flakes, tools, red ocher and oxidized sand, and charcoal flecks. Immediately above unit 9 was unit 8, a humus layer containing charcoal flecks. The other stratigraphic units were culturally sterile, except for unit 2, a faint buried humus layer 15 cm below the surface that contained two Ramah chert flakes. In other parts of the *in situ* deposit Ramah chert flakes were exposed in a shallow deflated area 10-12 cm below the surface, suggesting there may have been an occupation at roughly that depth. But given the instability of sand surfaces,

184/ Attu's Bight L-3/6: excavation at the edge of the in situ deposit.

greenstone and a split cobble with a faint trace of red ocher on its surface. An extremely faint spot of red ocher was observed in the sand. Given the paucity of material it is difficult to conclude there was a distinct occupation floor at this level, but the split cobble and red ocher might counter the redeposition argument, since the former would be resistant to wind action and the latter would have been erased by it. No flakes were observed at a corresponding level in test pit 53x50y, further to the east. In both 1993 test pits, however, a distinct occupation floor was found corresponding to the lower unit 9 level in the 1992 test, although this floor lay somewhat deeper (45 cm) than in the 1992 units (35 cm).

redeposition by deflation and eolian processes cannot be ruled out.

In 1993, test pit 50x50y was excavated adjacent to the 1992 profile. At the 10 cm level, seven Ramah chert flakes were encountered, as well as one flake of

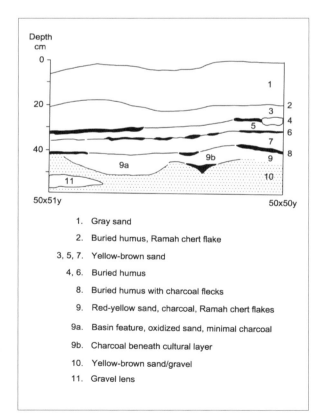

185/ Attu's Bight L-3/6: profile.

Depth cm

1. Gray sand
2. Buried humus, Ramah chert flake
3, 5, 7. Yellow-brown sand
4, 6. Buried humus
8. Buried humus with charcoal flecks
9. Red-yellow sand, charcoal, Ramah chert flakes
9a. Basin feature, oxidized sand, minimal charcoal
9b. Charcoal beneath cultural layer
10. Yellow-brown sand/gravel
11. Gravel lens

Two features were identified in the basal unit 9 deposits, both of which appeared to be small hearths (Figure 183). Feature 1 was located near the edge of the deflated area. It was a 60-70 cm in diameter oval patch of red-yellow oxidized sand mixed with charcoal and faint red ocher stains, accompanied by a 55 by 35 cm oval concentration of 38 small burned bone fragments. None of the bone fragments were identifiable, although one might be a rib fragment. There were no distinct hearth border or other "functional" rocks associated with the feature. The slightly basin-shaped profile of the feature suggests a fire was simply kindled in the upper portion of the ground surface. A sample of charcoal from this concentration was radiocarbon dated to 4080±100 B.P. (Beta-57126). Within and adjacent to the feature were small Ramah chert retouch flakes and a few tools: a slate celt fragment, a utilized flake of Ramah chert, a ground slate flake and a small mica fragment. Feature 2 was found at the bottom of test pit 53x50y,

CHAPTER 12

3.5 m east of Feature 1. It consisted of a 60 cm in diameter oval cluster of fist-sized cobbles associated with a considerable amount of charcoal and a few Ramah chert flakes. Two small red ocher stains occurred nearby. Charcoal from this feature was radiocarbon dated to 4080±90 B.P. (Beta-71477).

Figure 186 depicts the spatial distribution of tools while the tool classes are listed by frequency in Table 68. The implements lay in two elongated east/west distributions separated by 1.0-1.5 m, one extending out from the Feature 1 hearth, the other along the southern edge of the excavation. These distributions parallel that of the flakes (see below). The small collection is dominated by utilized flakes of Ramah chert. Also collected were two small mica fragments and 11 schist fragments.

**Table 68. Attu's Bight L-3/6
Tool Class Frequencies.**

	N (%)
Stemmed points	3 (15.0)
Bifaces	2 (10.0)
Flake points	1 (5.0)
Stemmed flakes	1 (5.0)
Utilized flakes	10 (50.0)
Celts	1 (5.0)
Ground slate flakes	1 (5.0)
Split cobbles	1 (5.0)
TOTAL	**20**

The flake distribution is shown in Figure 187. The plotted distribution of flakes in the deflated areas is probably misleading since eolian processes have doubtless smeared the spatial distributions and the material could represent a palimpsest of different occupation levels. Nonetheless, the frequencies of Ramah chert flakes indicate a distribution about 4-5 m wide (north/south) with two dense concentrations: one associated with the Feature 1 hearth area near the center and another ca. 1.0-1.5 m to the south. Thermally altered patinated Ramah chert is found in most of the excavation units, but is most frequent in the hearth area. Table 69 indicates the flake raw material frequencies are almost totally dominated by Ramah chert, typical of Rattlers Bight Phase localities. A fairly high percentage of the Ramah chert is patinated. Figure 188 portrays the size distribution of Ramah chert flakes. A total of 78.4% of the flakes measure < 20 mm and 61.7% < 15 mm, suggestive of an emphasis on secondary retouch. Additionally, a total of 134 biface-thinning flakes (BTFs) was identified (Figure 189). BTFs were distributed over most of the excavated area, although units with the largest quantities tended to be those with the most flakes overall. Additionally, 42 (31.3%) of the BTFs were >30 mm in size, suggestive of the reduction of large quarry blanks or preforms. This percentage is much higher than those recorded for the Middle Maritime Archaic site Nukasusutok 5 (Area 2A = 13.5%, 2B = 5.4% and 2C = 12.3%). The large BTFs were also distributed fairly evenly across the units.

**Table 69. Attu's Bight L-3/6 Flake
Raw Material Frequencies.**

	Excavation	Surface	TOTAL N (%)
Ramah chert	674	311	985 (88.2)
Patinated Ramah	76	48	124 (11.1)
Gray slate	2	1	3 (0.3)
Greenstone	2	1	3 (0.3)
Gray Mugford chert		1	1 (0.1)
Quartz		1	1 (0.1)
TOTAL	**754**	**363**	**1117**

The total weights of the lithic raw materials (tools and flakes) are given in Table 70. Ramah chert is clearly dominant; together, patinated and unpatinated Ramah account for 89.2% of the material. Patinated Ramah chert constitutes a larger proportion of the Ramah chert flakes by weight (21.7%) than by frequency (10.1%).

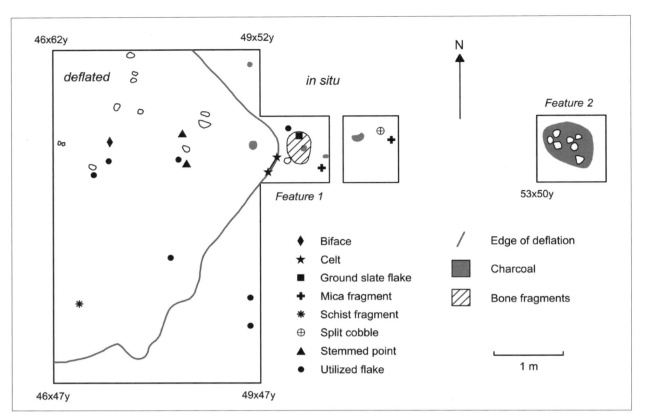

186/ Attu's Bight L-3/6: tool distribution.

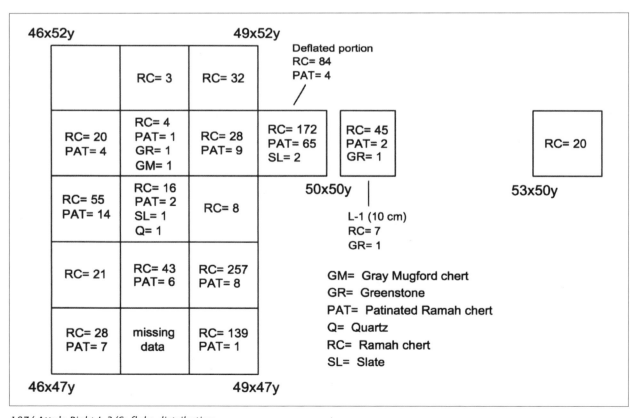

187/ Attu's Bight L-3/6: flake distribution.

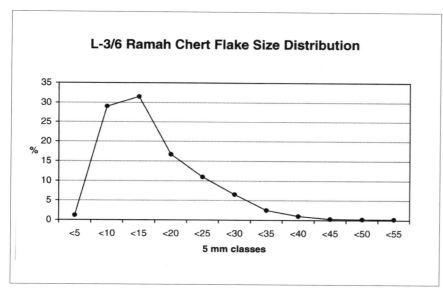

L-3/6 Ramah Chert Flake Size Distribution

188/ Attu's Bight L-3/6: Ramah chert flake size distribution.

Table 70. Attu's Bight L-3/6 Total Lithic Raw Material Weights (Flakes and Tools). In Grams.

	Flakes g	Tools g	TOTAL g (%)
Ramah chert	434.0	66.2	500.2 (71.6)
Patinated Ramah	120.0	3.0	123.0 (17.6)
Gray slate	0.8		0.8 (0.1)
Green slate	3.0	3.0	(0.4)
Red slate	68.0	68.0	(9.7)
Greenstone	2.4	2.4	(0.3)
Gray Mugford chert	0.5	0.5	(0.1)
Quartz	0.5	0.5	(0.1)
TOTAL	**629.2**	**143.6**	**624.0**

Tool Assemblage

Stemmed points: The three stemmed points are all made of Ramah chert. Two are stem fragments of similar dimensions that retain striking platforms on their bases (Figure 190:e, f). The third is a marginally retouched flake fragment with a striking platform or break at the base of a slight stem (Figure 190:l); it is unclear if this is a finished product or a preform.

Bifaces: Two Ramah chert biface fragments were recovered, one a medial portion the other a distal element bearing an impact fracture (Figure 190:d, h). Both are probably from stemmed points.

Flake points: The single example, made of Ramah chert, is a medial fragment with dorsal marginal retouch on opposite lateral edges (Figure 190:g).

Stemmed flakes: This Ramah chert implement (Figure 190:m) exhibits limited marginal retouch on opposite edges that creates a stem-like constriction; the stem base was thinned to remove the striking platform. It could be a point preform or simply a utilized flake.

Utilized flakes: All of the 10 utilized flakes are made of Ramah chert. One fragment has fine bifacial marginal retouch on opposite edges, possibly indicative of intended use as a flake point. Two implements are made on large biface-thinning flakes, probably derived from quarry blanks.

Celts: The implement identified as a celt is a medial fragment made on a plate of red slate (Figure 191:b). The only grinding occurs on two opposite edges that are ground perpendicular to the plate surface (W= 70.0 mm, TH= 14.7).

Ground slate flakes: The single example is made of green slate.

Split cobbles: A water-rolled flat cobble is split transversely and bears a faint trace of red ocher on its edge. It may have functioned as a hammerstone, red ocher crusher, or both.

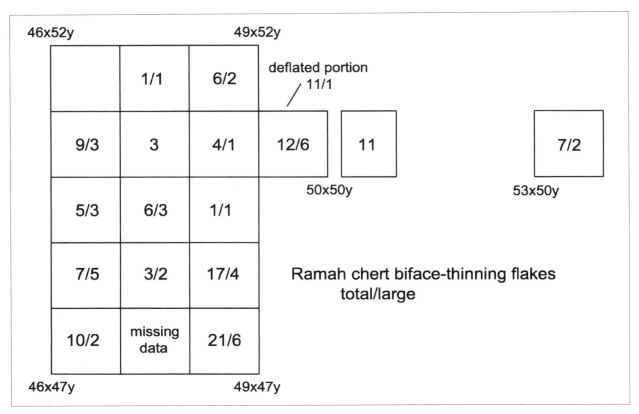

46x52y   49x52y

| | 1/1 | 6/2 | deflated portion |
| | | | / 11/1 |

| 9/3 | 3 | 4/1 | 12/6 | 11 | | 7/2 |

50x50y   53x50y

| 5/3 | 6/3 | 1/1 |

| 7/5 | 3/2 | 17/4 |

Ramah chert biface-thinning flakes
total/large

| 10/2 | missing data | 21/6 |

46x47y   49x47y

189/ Attu's Bight L-3/6: distribution of Ramah chert biface-thinning flakes.

Discussion

The excavation of L-3/6 suggests that two components may be present. The earlier component is the floor buried 35-45 cm below the modern surface. It contains two hearth features with virtually identical radiocarbon dates (4080±100 B.P. and 4080±90 B.P.). The charcoal comprising these samples was not identified to wood species, so it is possible that if spruce trees were used the dates could be somewhat older than the occupation. The later component is a trace layer 10 cm below the modern surface, inferred from a few *in situ* flakes, a split cobble, a small red ochre stain and deflated Ramah chert flakes lying near the same level. There are no clear chronological indicators for the later component, but enough time elapsed for at least two humus layers to have developed and been covered by drifting sand. This two component interpretation falls if the upper layer is composed of redeposited material. Smithsonian field notes suggested a Sandy Cove-like point from L-9 could indicate occupations pre-dating

4500 B.P.. However, nothing else in the artifactual material suggests anything other than a Rattler's Bight Phase dating and the slight differences in beach terrace elevation do not provide much basis for relative dating within the site. Consequently, the vast majority of the material probably pertains to repeated occupation during the Rattler's Bight Phase.

Linear scatters of Ramah chert such as those found at Attu's Bight have been interpreted as traces of Maritime Archaic longhouse structures (Fitzhugh 1981, 1984). While this may have been the case here, we should not assume that flake scatters ranging from 40-120 m long necessarily represent single continuous structures. Besides the possibility of non-contemporaneous overlap, the stratigraphic situation at L-3/6 raises the possibility that some of the flake scatters in deflated parts of the site could be palimpsests of more than one occupation.

Two aspects of Attu's Bight seem significant in comparison with some other Rattler's Bight Phase

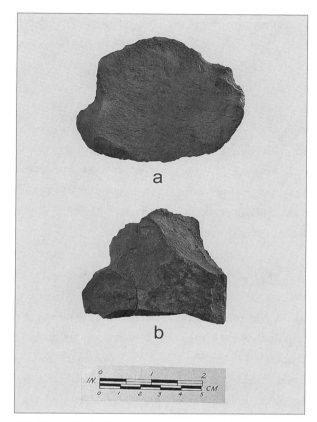

190/ Attu's Bight Tools. a: stemmed point, L-7; b: flake point, L-12; c: biface preform, north of L-4; d: biface mid-section, L-3/6; e, f: point stems, L-3/6; g: flake point fragment, L-3/6; h: biface tip, L-3/6; i: biface edge, L-1; j: biface tip, L-1; k: biface base, L-1; l: stemmed point preform, L-3/6; m: stemmed flake (point preform), L-3/6.

191/ Attu's Bight Tools. a: polished slate flake, L-1; b: celt fragment, L-3/6.

sites. First, considering how much of the site has been exposed on the surface there are very few visible features, such as stone-lined hearths. This may reflect either the lack of readily available rocks in the sand-gravel deposits, or a lack of investment in hearth construction. Excavation of the *in situ* deposit at L-3/6 indicates that hearths there were kindled on the ground surface or merely consisted of a cluster of small cobbles. There are, however, two possible burial cairns (L-10, L-11), an oval cobble ring (L-8) and a sub-rectangular rock feature of uncertain function (L-2). The lack of investment in features is paralleled by the

second significant aspect of the site: a low rate of tool discard. Although a considerable amount of debitage is present, there are relatively few tools on the surface. Such a pattern suggests time spent "gearing up" (Binford 1979:268), producing or repairing tools to be used and discarded elsewhere. This inference is supported by the presence of many biface-thinning flakes and especially the high frequency of large flakes likely derived from the reduction of quarry blanks. Thus, in terms of these depositional patterns and their implied curation processes, Attu's Bight seems to be a short-term aggregation site.

In light of the foregoing, Attu's Bight is not a good candidate for the elusive Maritime Archaic fall/winter sites, postulated to lie in the inner bays (Fitzhugh 1978:83-84). In terms of (contemporary) resource availability, the most likely seasons for the occupation of Attu's Bight would be late spring and early fall, when seals, waterfowl and caribou could be hunted and char and salmon caught. The site is positioned almost equidistant between the entrance to Port Manvers Run and the narrow passage between Igloo Island and the mainland, both of which are constrictions where it might have been easier to exploit herds of migrating harp seals in the spring or fall. One might also suggest the area could have been used for "gearing up" with wood products prior to moving further north, but the paucity of slate woodworking tools and slate debitage might argue against that.

On the other hand, it may not be the exploitation of local resources so much as the *location* of the site that is most relevant to its interpretation. Attu's Bight is situated 1.5 km west of the entrance to Port Manvers Run and its broad beach terrace was probably the best location for a large group gathering that could be found in the region between Webb Bay and Thalia Point on the coast. In this respect Attu's Bight is physically and topographically similar to large aggregation sites like Nulliak Cove-1, north of Hebron (Fitzhugh 1981, 1984, 1985a). Since it is likely that the Run was used as a travel corridor to avoid rough weather on the outer coast, it is reasonable to suggest that the main function of the site was as a temporary staging area for travel towards the north or south. Although these topographic or physical attractors may have been the main variables for site location, positioning of the site a short distance west of the Run could also have been a response to inter-cultural relations. Given the indications of a strong Pre-Dorset presence in the Run, placement of the site slightly back from the entrance to the Run could be seen as spatial distanciation from an area of frequent Pre-Dorset activity. Alternatively, Attu's Bight might have been selected on the grounds of relative proximity to the Pre-Dorset "central place" at the Attu's Point site, merely 1.8 km to the west, if a more interactive relationship with Pre-Dorset is postulated. On the other hand, it is also possible that Attu's Bight was no longer used after Pre-Dorset colonized the Nain area. The implications of these points will be discussed further in Chapter 14.

WEBB POINT (HeCk-6)

At the southern entrance to Webb Bay is a prominent tombolo beach that forms the spine of Webb Point. The beach runs roughly north-south, is bounded at each end by a rock outcrop, and has steep eastern and western edges. Its surface is almost entirely deflated. Since this seemed like an ideal location for a Maritime Archaic site the point was surveyed briefly in 1993, with another short follow-up visit in 1994. No elevation was recorded for the Webb Point terrace, but it seems higher than Attu's Bight (i.e., >19-21 m). Five small localities (L-1 to L-5) were identified on the primary beach surface, two more (L-6 and L-7) were recorded slightly down-slope of the northwestern corner of the beach, while one (L-8) was observed down-slope to the northeast.

L-1 was located near the rock outcrop at the northern end of the main beach terrace and consisted of a few Ramah chert flakes and tools. A stemmed point and a flake point of Ramah chert were surface-collected. The stemmed point is similar to Rattlers Bight styles (Figure 179:m). The dorsal side of the implement is completely flaked but the ventral side is retouched only on the lateral margins. A remnant striking platform runs oblique to the stem base and although the shoulders and upper stem are retouched the basal portion is unmodified, presumably unfinished (L = 47.9 mm, W = 26.4, TH = 6.1). The flake point (Figure 179:n) is formed by unifacial dorsal retouch limited to the edge margins (L = 33.1 mm, W = 13.8, TH = 2.7, stem L = 10.6, stem W [shoulder] = 9.2, stem W (base) = 7.7).

L-2 was situated near the southeastern corner of the terrace and consisted of a small rock mound, 1 m in diameter, with no visible lithic association. It resembled the cobble features at Attu's Bight (L-10 and L-11) and may be a burial cairn. L-3, L-4 and L-5 were all located towards the southern end of the terrace and all consisted of small scatters of Ramah chert flakes. L-6 was a gently sloping beach surface situated 40-50 m northwest of, and several meters below, the rock outcrop at the northwest end of the beach. L-6 contained a blow-out with exposed flakes of Ramah and Mugford chert and a Ramah chert biface stem, possibly Maritime Archaic (Figure 179:k). Small cobbles and charcoal flecks were also visible on the surface. A 50 by 50 cm test pit adjacent to the blow-out produced some charcoal, but no associated cultural material. Systematic shovel tests were conducted up and down the L-6 beach, but they did not reveal additional traces of occupation.

L-7 was a lithic scatter in a deflated sandy cleft beside the bedrock knoll at the north end of the main terrace and up-slope from L-6. Flake material exposed on the surface consisted of Mugford chert, crystal quartz and slate. A surface collection produced a few Pre-Dorset tools and a biface of either Pre-Dorset or Maritime Archaic origin. The Pre-Dorset implements include a medial fragment of a Pre-Dorset crystal quartz biface with fine parallel pressure flaking (Figure 179:j), two small microblade fragments of dark gray Mugford chert, a complete burin spall of gray Mugford chert and a utilized flake of patinated Mugford chert. The medial portion of a burned Ramah chert biface (Figure 179:l) might be Maritime Archaic, but a Ramah chert biface of similar width (ca. 40 mm) was found in a Pre-Dorset context at Attu's Point (Figure 201:a, Chapter 13). A blow-out 15 m north of L-7 contained a dark gray Mugford chert microblade fragment. A test pit excavated beside the blow-out did not reveal additional cultural material. Finally, L-8 was located downslope from the northeast corner of the main beach terrace. Yellowish-green slate flakes similar to those found in Pre-Dorset sites in the area were observed on the surface.

Discussion

Webb Point provides evidence for limited Maritime Archaic and Pre-Dorset activity. The most definite traces of Maritime Archaic presence were found on the prominent terrace, where evidence for Pre-Dorset was lacking. The stemmed point and flake point found at L-1 might indicate a Rattlers Bight phase or slightly earlier occupation. Pre-Dorset appears restricted to the lower beach levels, although possible Maritime Archaic implements were found at L-6 and L-7. The varying beach elevations may indicate chronological differences in occupation period, but the material is so scanty that no reliable conclusions can be drawn. The minimal occupation of the main beach terrace was surprising given its topographic prominence and its physical similarities with the beach terrace at Attu's Bight. Indeed, the limited use of Webb Point contrasts strongly with the amount of Maritime Archaic and Pre-Dorset activity on the north shore of Webb Bay.

The next chapter (13) describes Attu's Point, a major Pre-Dorset locality on the north shore of Webb Bay. Following that, Chapter 14 integrates the material presented in Chapters 12 and 13 and welds it into a more comprehensive discussion of Maritime Archaic/Pre-Dorset social relations in northern Labrador.

Northern entrance to Port Manvers Run, Thalia Point on right. July 1997. (Photo: B. Hood)

CHAPTER 13

Attu's Point: A Pre-Dorset "Central Place" on Webb Bay

13

In 1993 surveys were undertaken west of the entrance to Port Manvers Run along the north shore of Webb Bay. A Pre-Dorset locality dubbed Attu's Point (HeCk-5) was discovered near a rocky point overlooking the narrow tickle between Igloo Island and the mainland (Figure 163). In the middle of a raised beach was an extremely well-preserved axial structure containing a box-hearth filled with thermoliths.[8]

The initial survey identified at least a dozen loci of Pre-Dorset activity, of which five had traces of dwelling structures, as well as a locus with Maritime Archaic material. Since Attu's Point lay only 1.8 km west of the Late Maritime Archaic occupation at Attu's Bight, and since Attu's Point is the only major Pre-Dorset inner bay locality in the Nain region, the site was deemed high priority and was investigated further in 1994. The 1994 work identified several additional loci, for a total of 21 find spots. These substantial traces of occupation suggest that Attu's Point was a "central place" in the Nain region Pre-Dorset settlement system: a repeatedly used seasonal site that contrasts with the scattered and ephemeral small localities that otherwise characterize Pre-Dorset landscape use.

OVERVIEW

The Attu's Point site is spread out along two west-facing raised beach terraces ranging between 10-12 m asl. (Figures 192 and 193). The beach deposits consist of medium-sized gravel and they are bordered on the southeast and west by eroded outcrops of anorthosite bedrock. Some portions of the beaches are deflated while other parts are covered with a thin layer of crowberry or moss. Open spruce forest begins immediately east of the site.

The 21 loci were arranged in three linear distributions on different beach levels. L-1 to L-5, L-20 and L-21 lay near the edge of the 10 m beach terrace, L-6 to L-8 and L-17 were in a line slightly higher up and L-9 to L-16, L-18 and L-19 lay on the uppermost terrace between 11-12 m. At least one structure from each of these three levels was excavated or tested (L-1, L-5, L-7 and L-9) and surface collections were made at some of the other loci. All but one locus exhibited evidence of Pre-Dorset material; L-12 produced traces of Late Maritime Archaic.

Each of the excavated features will be described in turn, along with a spatial analysis and descriptive summary of the tools. The surface collected loci will then be described briefly. A summary of the significant spatial patterns and a general culture-historical conclusion is presented at the end of the chapter.

---

[8]Thermolith is a generic descriptor for rocks heated within a box-hearth for uncertain intended function (heating, cooking or other practices); it denotes both fire-cracked and non-thermally altered specimens.

192/ Attu's Point overview towards the northeast.

EXCAVATION AND COLLECTION METHODS

Excavation of the structures involved removal of the thin crowberry vegetation mat and troweling through the upper few centimeters of the beach gravel. Given time constraints, the size of the excavation areas at each structure was relatively small. Although *most* of the structurally relevant space was excavated at L-1, L-5 and L-7, a better picture would be available if a larger area around the periphery of the features had been exposed. All tools were point-plotted. Flakes were point-plotted by raw material types, then bagged by 1m^2 units. The gravel was not screened, so small implements such as burin spalls and retouch flakes may be somewhat under-represented.

L-1 Excavation

L-1 was located on the lowest beach ridge, 10 m asl. (Figure 193). Because the 1993 survey produced an interesting surface collection and suggested the presence of structural remains, a 14 m^2 area was excavated in 1994, revealing a cluster of rocks associated with hearth remnants (Figures 194 and 195). The presumed structural feature consisted of a north-south oriented concentration of rocks covering an area of 3.5 by 2.0 m. A hearth area composed of three flat slabs and a charcoal concentration was identifiable at the northern end of the concentration. A small charcoal sample from the hearth was radiocarbon dated to 3750±60 B.P. (Beta-77611; $^{13}C/^{12}C$ ratio -26.1). A line of three rocks extending northwest from the hearth to a small boulder gave the impression of perimeter delineation, but it was otherwise difficult to discern an internal order in the associated scatter of rocks. The feature may have been disturbed, but it is possible that it was oriented differently from our expectations, or that it is not of the anticipated axial form.

CHAPTER 13

Tool Distribution

A total of 49 tools was recovered. Figure 196 shows the tool distribution and the results of a *k*-means cluster analysis. A five cluster solution seemed best, defining a hearth-centered group (cluster 5), another immediately west of the hearth (cluster 3), a small cluster near the western boundary of the excavation (cluster 1), and two diffuse clusters on the southern side of the excavation (clusters 2 and 4). Table 71 compares the tool contents of these clusters. Although it is difficult to draw inferences from such low frequencies there is a contrast between the prevalence of burin spalls, microblades and utilized flakes in cluster 3 adjacent to the hearth, and the concentration of endblades in cluster 1, 2 m west of the hearth.

**Table 71. Attu's Point L-1:
Tool Classes by *K*-Means Cluster.**

	C-1	C-2	C-3	C-4	C-5	TOTAL N (%)
Endblades	4					4 (8.2)
Endblade preforms	1		1	2		4 (8.2)
Bifaces		1		1		2 (4.1)
Burin spalls	1	1	5		4	11 (22.5)
Microblades	3	2	4	1	3	13 (26.4)
Scrapers	1			1		2 (4.1)
Scraper/burins	1					1 (2.0)
Utilized flakes	2	1	6		1	10 (20.4)
Adzes/celts			1	1		2 (4.1)
TOTAL	**13**	**5**	**17**	**5**	**9**	**49**

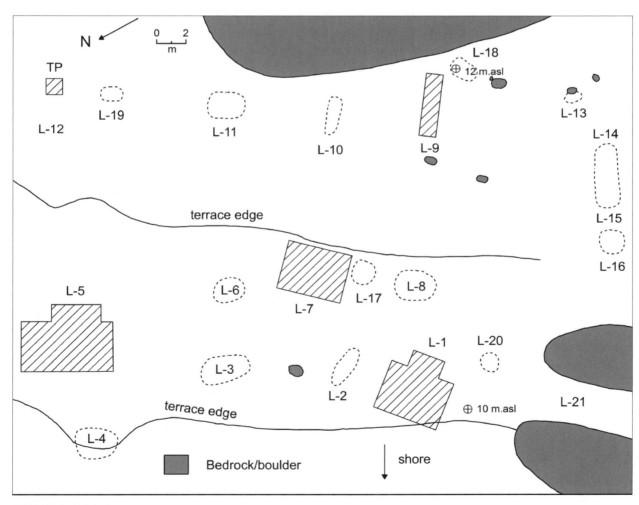

193/ Attu's Point site map.

In the absence of a clearly defined axial feature, the spatial divisions used for the bilateral model-based tool distribution analysis are association with the central rock feature, or placement on its east or west flanks (Table 72). The majority of tools (55.1%) lie in the vicinity of the rock feature. Although the frequencies are rather low, there are slight differences in where the tool types were discarded. Most of the endblades and preforms occur on the flanks of the rock feature, including a cluster of five implements deposited together on the west side (possibly a cache), while the majority of the burin spalls, microblades and utilized flakes are closely associated with the feature. Table 73 breaks down the tool distribution along a north-south division (front/back) running along the 6y grid line. In this case, nearly 80% of the tools lie on the northern (seaward) end of the rock feature, with endblades, burin spalls, microblades and utilized flakes being particularly well represented.

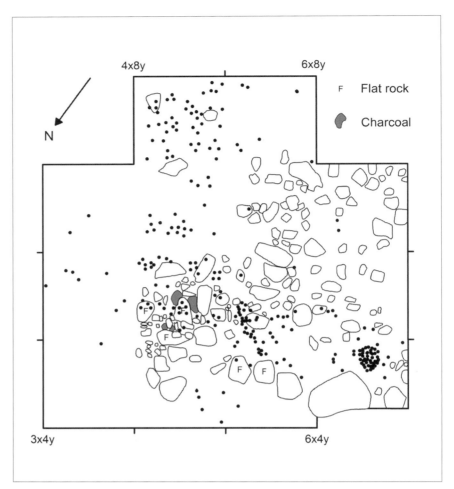

194/ Attu's Point L-1: rock feature and total flake distribution.

195/ Attu's Point L-1: overview towards the east.

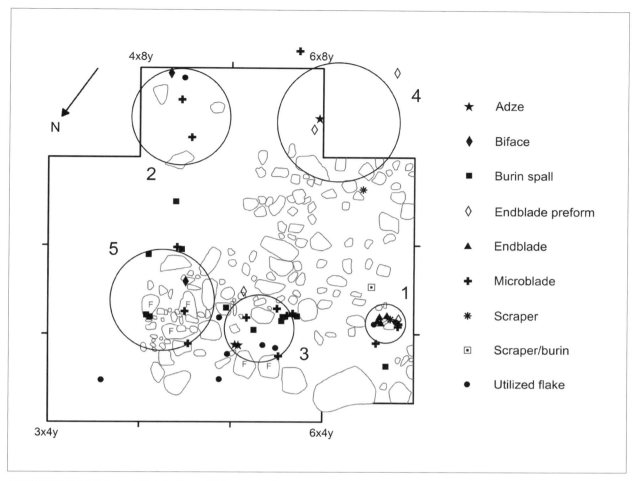

196/ Attu's Point L-1: tool distribution with k-means clusters.

Legend:
★ Adze
♦ Biface
■ Burin spall
◇ Endblade preform
▲ Endblade
✚ Microblade
✳ Scraper
⊡ Scraper/burin
● Utilized flake

Table 72. Attu's Point L-1:
Tool Classes by Bilateral Position.

	Central (Axial)	East	West	TOTAL N	(%)
Endblades			4	4	(8.2)
Endblade preforms	1	2	1	4	(8.2)
Bifaces	1	2		2	(4.1)
Burin spalls	9	1	1	11	(22.5)
Microblades	7	3	3	13	(26.4)
Scrapers	1		1	2	(4.1)
Scraper/burins			1	1	(2.0)
Utilized flakes	7	1	2	10	(20.4)
Celts/adzes	1	1		2	(4.1)
TOTAL	**27**	**9**	**13**	**49**	

Table 73. Attu's Point L-1: Tool Classes by
North-South (Front/Back) Position.

	North (Front)	South (Back)	TOTAL N	(%)
Endblades	4		4	(8.2)
Endblade preforms	2	2	4	(8.2)
Bifaces	1	1	2	(4.1)
Burin spalls	10	1	11	(22.4)
Microblades	10	3	13	(26.5)
Scrapers	1	1	2	(4.1)
Scraper/burins	1		1	(2.0)
Utilized flakes	9	1	10	(20.4)
Celts/adzes	1	1	2	(4.1)
TOTAL	**39**	**10**	**49**	

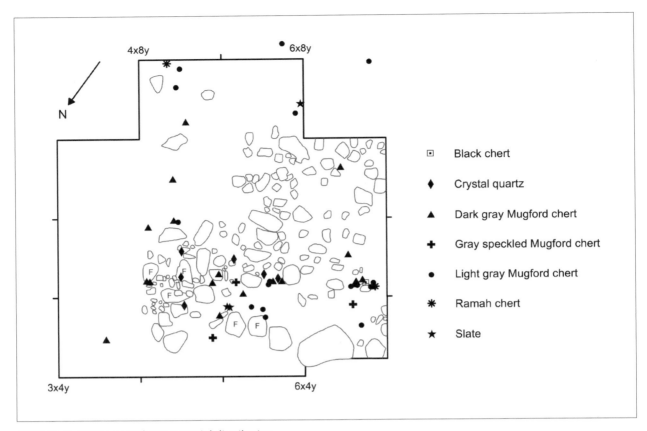

197/ Attu's Point L-1: tool raw material distribution.

Tool raw material distribution patterns can be evaluated visually in Figure 197. Mugford chert tools tend to lie near the central rock feature, although they are also found on its flanks. Crystal quartz tools are clustered near the hearth (similar to the flake distribution, see below). The other materials are too few to indicate a pattern, but the two implements of Ramah chert are located some distance away from the central rock feature. Quantitatively, the distributions can first be evaluated by their location relative to east-west bilaterality (Table 74). The only clear pattern is the exclusive association of crystal quartz with the rock feature. When broken down by the north-south (front/back) division (Table 75) there is little clear patterning other than the exclusive association of crystal quartz and gray-speckled chert with the northern (hearth-related) division. Tool raw materials can also be seen in relation to the k-means clusters (Table 76),

but the numbers are too low for the comparison to be worth much.

Table 74. Attu's Point L-1: Tool Raw Material Frequencies by Bilateral Position.

	Central (Axial)	East	West	TOTAL N (%)
Dark gray Mugford chert	12	2	4	18 (36.7)
Light gray Mugford chert	6	4	6	16 (32.7)
Gray-speckled chert	2		1	3 (6.1)
Black chert			1	1 (2.0)
Ramah chert		1	1	2 (4.1)
Crystal quartz	6			6 (12.3)
Gray silicified slate		1		1 (2.0)
Slate	1	1		2 (4.1)
TOTAL	**27**	**9**	**13**	**49**

CHAPTER 13

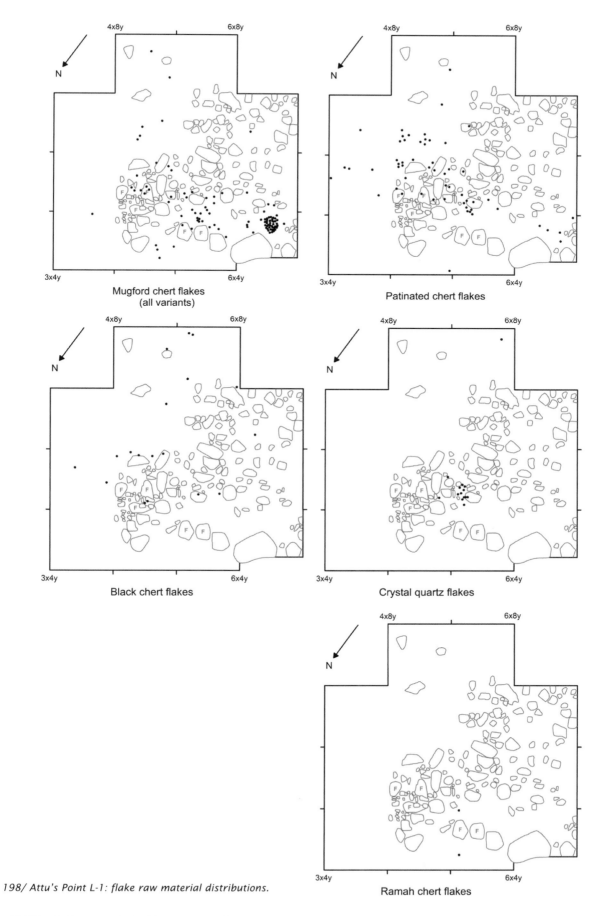

198/ *Attu's Point L-1: flake raw material distributions.*

Mugford chert flakes
(all variants)

Patinated chert flakes

Black chert flakes

Crystal quartz flakes

Ramah chert flakes

ATTU'S POINT: A PRE-DORSET "CENTRAL PLACE" ON WEBB BAY

Table 75. Attu's Point L-1: Tool Raw Materials by North-South (Front-Back) Position.

	North	South	TOTAL N (%)
Dark gray Mugford chert	15	3	18 (36.7)
Light gray Mugford chert	12	4	16 (32.7)
Gray-speckled chert	3		3 (6.1)
Black chert	1		1 (2.0)
Ramah chert	1	1	2 (4.1)
Crystal quartz	6		6 (12.3)
Gray silicified slate		1	1 (2.0)
Slate	1	1	2 (4.1)
TOTAL	**39**	**10**	**49**

Flake Distribution

The total flake distribution (Figure 194) parallels the tool groupings identified by the cluster analysis (Figure 196). There are concentrations on either side of the hearth (similar to tool clusters 3 and 5), a tight concentration west of the hearth (cluster 1) and a diffuse concentration in the southeast corner of the excavation (cluster 2). Figure 198 presents point-plots for each flake raw material type while Figure 199 displays quadrat counts. The Mugford and patinated chert distributions are very similar, which is not surprising since the latter is probably a weathered version of Mugford chert. They are spread in a roughly linear east-west distribution centered on the hearth area at the northern end of the rock feature. The marked concentration of Mugford chert on the western side of the excavation lies only a few centimeters distant from the tight tool concentration of cluster 1, which included a cache of four endblades and an endblade preform (all of Mugford chert), two microblades, a scraper and two utilized flakes. In the absence of refitting data, one might speculate as to the relation between the Mugford flake concentration and production of the endblades.

The distributions of slate and Mugford chert are almost mutually exclusive. Slate clusters in the southeast corner of the excavation (with over 70% in a single unit), although a few flakes are present near the cen-

ter. A slate adze bit was found 1 m west of the slate concentration. Mugford cherts have a more diffuse distribution, but are mostly associated with the hearth area and the northwestern portion of the excavation. This placement broadly parallels the tool distribution. Crystal quartz occurs in a small cluster immediately west of the hearth, virtually in the center of the crystal quartz tool distribution, which was also hearth related (Figure 197). Black chert has a diffuse distribution, but occurs almost exclusively west of the rock feature; the single tool of this material lay west of the rock feature (Figure 197). The two Ramah chert flakes are found towards the north end of the rock feature.

Table 77 outlines the distribution of flake raw materials according to their east-west bilateral position, tabulated by $1m^2$ quadrats (unit 6x5y missing). Overall, the flakes are dominated by Mugford chert and slate; 61.1% of the debitage was deposited on the west side of the structure, consistent with, though not as marked, as the tool distribution. A chi-square test ($x^2 = 85.80$) indicates a statistically significant difference between the two areas at the .05 level of significance. This difference is based on a marked tendency for light gray Mugford chert and crystal quartz to be found on the west side, while slate is associated primarily with the east side. Variation can also be seen in the north-south (front/back) direction, with a not entirely artificial division imposed along the 6y line. Table 78 indicates that 64.6% of the debitage is found on the north side of the rock feature. A chi-square test ($x^2 = 103.59$) indicates a statistically significant difference between the two areas. The pattern is linked to the high frequency of light gray Mugford chert (and to a much lesser extent, patinated chert and crystal quartz) on the north side versus a preponderance of slate on the south.

Integration

The distribution of Mugford chert and crystal quartz tools and flakes is largely coterminus, while the slate, black chert and Ramah chert implements are found

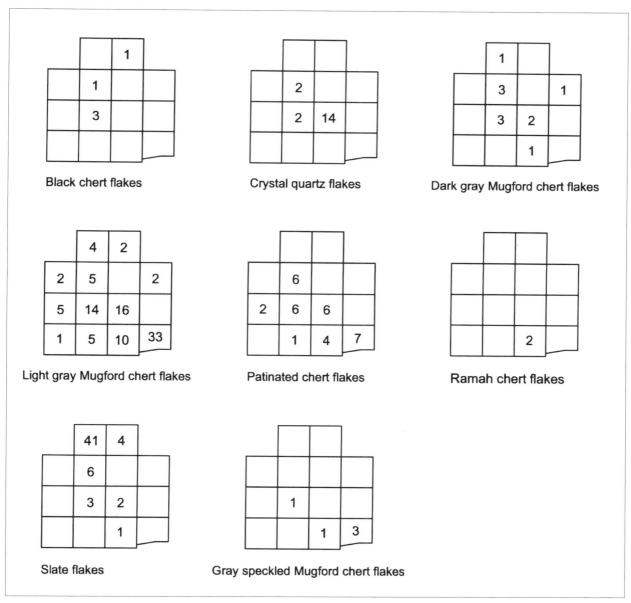

199/ Attu's Point L-1: flake raw materials by quadrat.

outside the distributions of their debitage. An attempt to refit burin spalls to the single scraper/burin was unsuccessful. While the spalls mostly cluster towards the north end of the rock feature, generally associated with the hearth, the burinated implement lies on the western periphery of the excavation.

Table 79 tabulates tool and flake raw materials by weight for L-1 as a whole. Slate is the dominant material (54.2%), with gray Mugford cherts ranked second (22.6%). Several observations can be made if Table 79 is used in conjunction with Tables 74 and 77 (tool and flake frequencies). The high proportion of dark gray Mugford chert among the tools by both weight and frequency is not parallelled by a high proportion of such flakes; in fact, light Mugford chert dominates the debitage. This suggests most of the tools made of dark gray Mugford were manufactured elsewhere (either at Attu's Point or another site) and curated into the locus. The opposite pattern is seen with patinated chert; no tools were present but a modest amount of debitage was, indicating the

Table 76. Attu's Point L-1: Tool Raw Material Frequencies by *K*-Means Cluster.

	C-1	C-2	C-3	C-4	C-5	TOTAL
Dark gray Mugford chert	4	2	6	1	5	18
Light gray Mugford chert	6	2	5	2	1	16
Gray-speckled chert	1		2			3
Black chert	1					1
Ramah chert	1	1				2
Crystal quartz			3		3	6
Gray silicified slate				1		1
Slate			1	1		2
TOTAL	13	5	17	5	9	49

Table 77. Attu's Point L-1: Flake Raw Material Frequencies by East-West Bilateral Position.

	East	West	TOTAL N	(%)
Dark gray Mugford chert	7 (5.9)	4 (3.6)	11	(4.8)
Light gray Mugford chert	33 (27.9)	66 (59.5)	99	(43.2)
Gray-speckled chert	1 (0.8)	4 (3.6)	5	(2.2)
Patinated chert	14 (11.9)	18 (16.2)	32	(13.9)
Black chert	5 (4.3)		5	(2.2)
Ramah chert		2 (1.8)	2	(0.9)
Crystal quartz	4 (3.4)	14 (12.6)	18	(6.8)
Slate	54 (45.8)	3 (2.7)	57	(25.6)
TOTAL	94	140	229	

removal of tools from the locus. Ramah chert is better represented by tools than by flakes.

Having presented the lithic distribution patterns along several dimensions, the overall spatial configuration at L-1 can be evaluated. The initial assumption was that the central rock feature could indicate a disturbed axial structure running roughly north-south, oblique to the beach front. Inspection of the individual distributions in relation to the feature suggests an alternative interpretation. If the more numerous item classes are considered (e.g., microblades, utilized flakes, Mugford chert tools, crystal quartz tools and flakes), there is a strong tendency for them to display a roughly northeast-west linear distribution ranging from the hearth to the edge of the excavation on the 7x line. The clustering of slate flakes and some microblades in the southeast corner of the excavation is the primary deviation from this pattern. In light of these tendencies one can postulate an axial feature running parallel with the beach front and consisting of a hearth at its northeastern end and a small, roughly rectangular feature 1 by 2 m in size that extends westwards. The presence of a similar configuration at L-5 (see below) might support this interpretation. It is also instructive to compare the small concentration of Mugford chert flakes in the northwest corner of the L-

Table 78. Attu's Point L-1: Flake Raw Material Frequencies by North-South (Front-Back) Position

	North (Front)	South (Back)	TOTAL N (%)
Dark gray Mugford chert	6 (4.0)	5 (6.2)	11 (4.8)
Light gray Mugford chert	84 (56.8)	15 (18.5)	99 (43.2)
Gray-speckled chert	5 (3.4)		5 (2.2)
Patinated chert	26 (17.5)	6 (7.4)	32 (13.9)
Black chert	3 (2.0)	2 (2.5)	5 (2.2)
Ramah chert	2 (1.3)		2 (0.9)
Crystal quartz	16 (10.8)	2 (2.5)	18 (6.8)
Slate	6 (4.1)	51 (62.9)	57 (25.6)
TOTAL	148	81	229

Table 79. Attu's Point L-1: Total Lithic Raw Material Weights (Tools and Flakes). In Grams.

	Tools g (%)	Flakes g (%)	TOTAL g (%)
Dark gray Mugford chert	32.5 (10.8)	16.1 (9.0)	48.6 (10.1)
Light gray Mugford chert	21.3 (7.1)	38.6 (21.6)	59.9 (12.5)
Gray-speckled chert	19.1 (6.4)	4.9 (2.7)	24.0 (5.0)
Patinated chert		13.2 (7.4)	13.2 (2.8)
Black chert	1.0 (0.3)	2.1 (1.2)	3.1 (0.6)
Ramah chert	41.7 (13.9)	0.8 (0.4)	42.5 (8.9)
Crystal quartz	11.7 (3.9)	16.6 (9.3)	28.3 (5.9)
Slate	**173.0 (57.6)**	**86.8 (48.5)**	**259.8 (54.2)**

1 excavation— which would lie at the western end of a beach-parallel axial feature— with the concentration of Mugford chert flakes at the foot of the axial structure at L-7 (see below). In any event, it appears that the L-1 hearth is located at the terminal end of a feature rather than in the middle, as expected from a classic axial structure. Another possibility is that the scatter of rocks in the southwestern portion of the excavation may represent a second overlapping feature.

L-1 Tool Assemblage

Endblades: Three of the four endblades are complete, one is a distal fragment (Figure 200:a-d). Three are made of dark gray Mugford chert, one of light gray

Mugford chert. The complete specimens are triangular and two have straight bases and biconvex cross-sections (L= 25.1, 16.1, 21.4 mm, W= 9.5, 7.7, 9.2, TH= 2.2, 1.5, 1.9). One implement has a plano-convex cross-section and a concave base (depth= 1.3 mm); its dorsal face is completely retouched, but ventrally only the edge margins are retouched (Figure 200:d). The lateral edges of the latter specimen are distinctly serrated; the other three endblades also have slightly serrated edges.

Endblade preforms: Of the four endblade preforms (Figure 200:e-h), one is complete, two are proximal fragments and one a distal fragment. Two are made of light gray Mugford chert, one of dark gray

200/ Attu's Point L-1 tools. a-d: endblades; e-h: endblade preforms.

201/ Attu's Point L-1 tools. a: biface; b: sidescraper; c: burin/sidescraper ; d-e: microblades.

202/ Attu's Point L-1 tools. a: adze; b: celt/adze preform or proximal fragment.

Mugford chert and one of crystal quartz. Two of the three specimens with a proximal portion exhibit straight bases while the third is straight-based with an eared basal corner (Figure 200:f). The complete implement of crystal quartz (Figure 200:e) has near-final retouch completed from its tip to its medial region and an unfinished basal portion, indicating a distal to proximal flaking sequence (L= 23.8 mm, W= 16.1, TH= 8.6). The two proximal fragments differ somewhat in width (W= 13.4, 19.9 mm, TH= 2.8, 3.4). One of these fragments (Figure 200:g) is flaked mostly on its dorsal face, upon which two long parallel basal-thinning flakes were removed medially.

Bifaces: Two biface fragments were recovered, one made of Ramah chert, one of crystal quartz. The Ramah chert specimen (Figure 201:a) is the proximal end of a biface that originally must have been ca. 10 cm long (W= 39.3 mm, TH= 6.9). There is a remnant striking platform near the base, which seems less finished than the rest of the implement. The crystal quartz specimen is a small lateral edge fragment.

Combination scraper/burins: The single specimen of a combination scraper/burin (Figure 201:c) is made on a blade-like flake of dark gray Mugford chert (L= 70.5 mm, W= 20.6, TH= 8.1). It consists of a con-

cave scraper running distally-medially on one lateral edge and a burination plane along the other lateral edge, with removals from a platform on the slightly convex, unifacially retouched distal end. The scraper

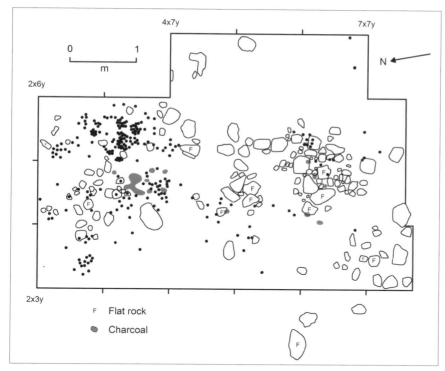

203/ Attu's Point L-5: features and total flake distribution.

Legend:
F Flat rock
● Charcoal

Map labels: 4x7y, 7x7y, 2x6y, 2x3y, N
Scale: 0 — 1 m

edge angle is 50° and there are three burin spall removals. Slightly below the mid-portion of each lateral edge there is a faint shoulder, which creates a slight stem effect proximally. A striking platform is present proximally and both the platform and bulb of percussion are highly polished, presumably by hafting wear. There is no facial grinding. The middle of the scraper

204/ Attu's Point L-5: possible axial structure, view towards the southwest.

edge and the distal end of the tool exhibit wear polish; the first burination scar has polished edges and small fractures while the third burination scar has clear striations on the adjacent ventral surface, perpendicular to the scar edge.

Scrapers: Two implements were collected. A complete sidescraper (Figure 201:b) is made of dark gray Mugford chert and has a slightly concave working edge (L= 43.8 mm, W= 23.9, TH= 8.2). The tool is dorsally retouched on all lateral edges while on the ventral side the proximal end has been flaked to thin out the bulb of percussion, although the striking platform remains at the base. The concave working edge and distal end are distinctly polished by wear. Seen alongside the combination scraper/burin (Figure 201:c), it is likely that the sidescraper is a reworked and perhaps exhausted version of the latter, since both have very similar basal forms and dimensions. Rather than representing different "types," they may indicate start and end points in a reduction sequence. The second implement is an edge fragment made of black chert.

Burin spalls: Of the 11 burin spalls (MNI=10), seven were complete, three were proximal fragments and one a distal fragment. All were made of gray Mugford chert variants. None bore traces of grinding and all were secondary spalls. Their metrics can be summarized as follows:

$\bar{x}L$ = 15.9, r = 9.2-21.8, $\bar{x}W$ = 3.3, r= 2.2-4.3, $\bar{x}TH$ = 1.7, r = 1.1-2.4.

Microblades: Of the 13 microblades, three are complete, six are medial fragments, three are proximal fragments and one is a distal portion. Based on proximal elements, MNI=10. Nine are made of gray Mugford cherts and four of crystal quartz. Two specimens (Figure 201:d,f) are large enough to be considered "macroblades" (L = 61.0, 56.7 mm, W = 17.7, 20.9, TH = 5.6, 4.8). Metrics for the others are as follows: $\bar{x}W$ = 9.4 mm, r = 6.1-15.0, $\bar{x}TH$ = 2.1, r = 1.4-2.9. Platform angles: 80° = 3, 75° = 1, 70° = 1. Platform preparation: retouched= 2, retouched/ground = 1, plain = 2. Eight specimens exhibit use-wear or light retouch.

Adzes/Celts: The two specimens are fragmentary and both are made of green slate. The first is the distal portion of an adze (Figure 202:a); one lateral edge is bifacially retouched while the other is retouched abruptly from the dorsal (top) side of the implement, resulting in an asymmetrical cross-section. A considerable amount of cortex is still present on the dorsal surface. The dorsal edge of the bit is only polished 1-3 mm back from the edge, while the ventral polishing is mostly limited to an area within 7.5 mm of the bit edge, although a few facets further back are also polished. Use-wear consists of a slight rounding of the bit edge, although some rather large step fractures on one ventral corner may indicate heavier work pressure or retouch. L = >64 mm, W = 41.8, TH = 16.2, Edge Angle = 70°.

The second specimen (Figure 202: b) is the proximal end of an adze or celt. It is made on a rectangular slate tablet, the lateral edges of which are retouched with small flakes removed at 90° from both the dorsal and ventral surfaces of the tablet such that the squared edge and rectangular cross-section is maintained. The flake facets on what appears to be

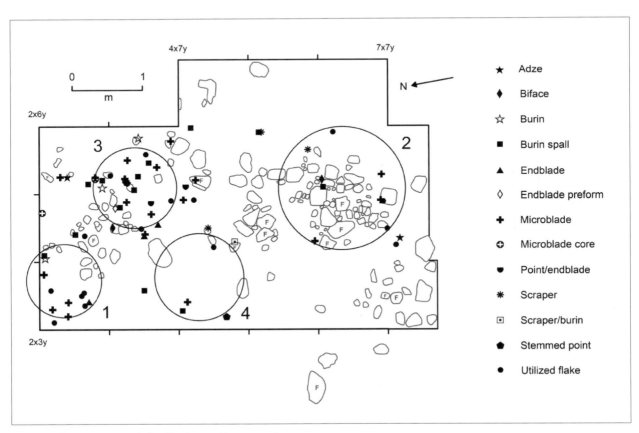

205/ *Attu's Point L-5: tool distribution and k-means clusters.*

Table 80. Attu's Point L-5: Tool Classes by K-Means Cluster[10]

	C-1 N (%)	C-2 N (%)	C-3 N (%)	C-4 N (%)	TOTAL N (%)
Endblades	1 (6.7)		3 (8.4)		4 (5.6)
Endblade preforms			1 (2.8)		1 (1.4)
Stemmed points				1 (14.3)	1 (1.4)
Biface fragments		1 (7.7)	3 (8.4)		4 (5.6)
Burins	1 (6.7)		2 (5.6)		3 (4.2)
Burin spalls	2 (13.3)	2 (15.4)	9 (25.0)	2 (28.5)	15 (21.1)
Microblades	4 (26.6)	3 (23.1)	12 (33.3)	1 (14.3)	20 (28.1)
Microblade cores	1 (6.7)		1 (2.8)		2 (2.8)
Scrapers		2 (15.4)		1 (14.3)	3 (4.2)
Scraper/burins				1 (14.3)	1 (1.4)
Utilized flakes	6 (40.0)	4 (30.7)	5 (13.9)	1 (14.3)	16 (22.4)
Celts/adzes		1 (7.7)	1 (2.8)		2 (2.8)
TOTAL	15	13	36	7	71

the dorsal surface are polished slightly and one lateral edge is slightly rounded. L = > 62 mm, W = 33.7, TH = 16.7.

Utilized Flakes: Eight of the ten utilized flakes are made of gray Mugford chert, one of black chert and one of gray-speckled chert.

L-5 EXCAVATION

L-5 was located on the lowest beach ridge at 10 m asl. (Figure 193). Initially, L-5 appeared to contain the remains of a well-preserved axial structure, so an excavation of 21.5 m^2 was opened up. Unfortunately, the structure turned out to be less distinct than anticipated (Figures 203 and 204). Towards the southern end of the excavation was a hearth composed of a few flat slabs, a small scatter of charcoal and a number of small rocks that may have been thermoliths. What appeared to be the remnants of an axial structure extended out from the hearth, suggesting a feature 2 m long, 0.75-1.0 m wide, oriented N-S, parallel with

the shoreline, but with the hearth placed at one end of the axial structure rather than in the middle (cf., L-1). A small charcoal sample procured from the hearth area was radiocarbon dated to 3790±70 B.P. (Beta-77612; $^{13}C/^{12}C$ ratio -24.7). To the north of the axial structure was a cluster of rocks associated with a charcoal concentration and a substantial quantity of tools and debitage. This area may represent an outdoor dump or activity area at the entrance to the axial structure or it could be the remains of a second, badly disturbed axial structure with a NW-SE orientation. Finally, in the southwest corner of the excavation and just outside the excavation limits was another cluster of rocks, including a few flat slabs. Although there were no associated lithics, the rock cluster might indicate the presence of another feature.

Tool Distribution

A total of 82 tools was recovered; some were scattered around the postulated axial feature, but most (68.7%)

[10] Items excluded from the analysis due to lack of point provenience are displayed by quadrats in Figure 206.

Table 81. Attu's Point L-5: Tool Classes by General Spatial Position.

	Axial N	(%)	North N	(%)	TOTAL N	(%)
Endblades			4	(6.1)	4	(4.9)
Endblade preforms			1	(1.5)	1	(1.2)
Endblades/points			2	(3.0)	2	(2.4)
Stemmed points			1	(1.5)	1	(1.2)
Biface fragments			3	(4.5)	3	(3.7)
Burins			3	(4.5)	3	(3.7)
Burin spalls	2	(12.5)	15	(22.8)	17	(20.7)
Microblades	3	(18.8)	16	(24.3)	19	(23.2)
Microblade cores			2	(3.0)	2	(2.4)
Scrapers	3	(18.8)			3	(3.7)
Scraper/burins	1	(6.2)			1	(1.2)
Utilized flakes	6	(37.5)	18	(27.3)	24	(29.3)
Celts/adzes	1	(6.2)	1	(1.5)	2	(2.4)
TOTAL	**16**		**66**		**82**	

Table 82. Attu's Point L-5: Tool Raw Material Frequencies by General Spatial Position.

	Axial N	(%)	North	N	(%)TOTAL N	(%)
Dark gray Mugford chert	6	(37.6)	30	(45.5)	36	(43.9)
Light gray Mugford chert			3	(4.5)	3	(3.7)
Light gray silicified slate	2	(12.5)	6	(9.2)	8	(9.8)
Patinated chert			2	(3.0)	2	(2.4)
Gray-speckled chert	1	(6.2)	5	(7.6)	6	(7.3)
Crystal Quartz	2	(12.5)	8	(12.1)	10	(12.2)
Ramah chert	3	(18.8)	8	(12.1)	11	(13.4)
Black chert	1	(6.2)	3	(4.5)	4	(4.9)
Slate	1	(6.2)	1	(1.5)	2	(2.4)
TOTAL	**16**		**66**		**82**	

were located to the north in the possible dump/activity area. A bilateral analysis could not be undertaken given the paucity of tools associated with the axial feature. Instead, *k*-means cluster analysis was used to define groupings based on proximity rather than model-derived spatial categories. The analysis used a total of 71 tools for which precise point provenience was available; a four cluster solution seemed most appropriate (Figure 205). One of these clusters (cluster 2) is centered on the hearth area of the axial structure while two others (clusters 1 and 3) partition the dump/activity area into two groups. Cluster 4 is a dif-

Table 83. Attu's Point L-5: Tool Raw Material Frequencies by *K*-Means Cluster.

	C-1 N (%)	C-2 N (%)	C-3 N (%)	C-4 N (%)	TOTAL N (%)
Dark gray Mugford chert	6 (40.0)	3 (23.1)	24 (67.7)	2 (28.6)	35 (49.3)
Light gray Mugford chert	1 (6.7)		2 (5.5)		3 (4.2)
Light gray silicified slate	2 (13.3)	2 (15.4)			4 (5.6)
Patinated chert			1 (2.8)	1 (14.3)	2 (2.8)
Gray-speckled	3 (20.0)	1 (7.7)	1 (2.8)	1 (14.3)	6 (8.5)
Crystal quartz	2 (13.3)	2 (15.4)		3 (42.8)	7 (9.9)
Ramah chert	1 (6.7)	3 (23.1)	5 (13.9)		9 (12.7)
Black chert		1 (7.7)	2 (5.5)		3 (4.2)
Slate		1 (7.7)	1 (2.8)		2 (2.8)
TOTAL	15	13	36	7	71

fuse distribution of questionable significance immediately northwest of the axial feature. Table 80 displays the variation in tool classes between the clusters. Cluster 3, immediately north of the presumed axial feature, has by far the largest proportion of the tool collection (N = 37, 51.4%). It also has a tendency towards more endblades, perhaps burins and burin spalls, as well as microblades and microblade cores. Cluster 2

(associated with the hearth) and cluster 1 exhibit somewhat higher proportions of utilized flakes.

A broader spatial comparison can be made between the frequency of tool types associated with the presumed axial feature and the concentration to the north of the feature using a dividing line running along 4.30x. Table 81 shows clear differences between the two subareas. Endblades, points, bifaces, burins and microblade cores are exclusively associated with the northern subarea, while burin spalls and microblades are predominantly to the north. Scrapers and the combination scraper/burin are exclusive to the southern area associated with the axial feature. The relationship is statistically significant at the .05 level ($\chi^2 = 22.49$).

The first step in evaluating variation in tool raw materials is to consider their distribution relative to the axial feature/northern subarea division used in the tool type analysis (Table 82). There is no significant difference between the two areas ($\chi^2 = 3.26$). The distribution of tool raw materials can also be compared across the cluster groups (Table 83). It is difficult to evaluate the low frequencies, but higher proportions of dark gray chert occur in clusters 1 and 3 and crystal quartz is absent from cluster 1. Point distributions of tool raw materials are shown in Figure 207.

Utilized flakes (UF)
Endblades (EB)
Bifaces (BI)
Burin spalls (BS)

206/ Attu's Point L-5: no provenience tools by quadrat.

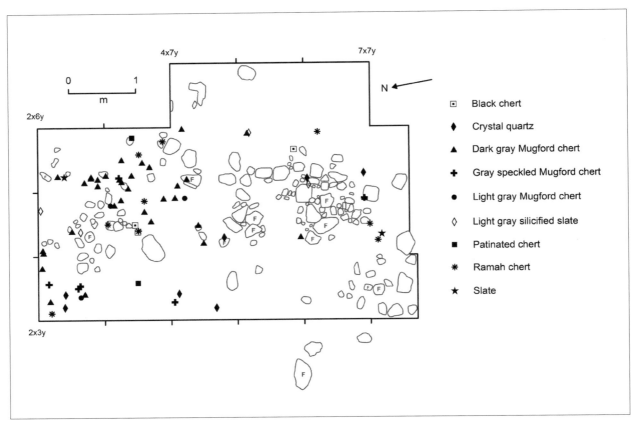

207/ Attu's Point L-5: tool raw material distribution.

Table 84. Attu's Point L-5: Flake Raw Material Frequencies by Analytical Quadrant.

	NW N (%)	NE N (%)	SW N (%)	SE N (%)	TOTAL N (%)
Dark gray Mugford	9 (10.7)	21 (12.0)	4 (13.8)	3 (10.7)	37 (11.7)
Light gray Mugford	1 (1.2)	5 (2.9)	2 (6.9)	2 (7.1)	10 (3.2)
Gray-speckled chert		10 (5.7)		1 (3.6)	11 (3.5)
Black chert		2 (1.1)	1 (3.4)	1 (3.6)	4 (1.3)
Ramah chert	5 (6.0)	30 (17.1)	2 (6.9)	7 (25.0)	44 (13.9)
Patinated chert	1 (1.2)	12 (6.9)	1 (3.4)		14 (4.4)
Biostrome chert[11]	1 (1.2)				1 (0.3)
Crystal quartz			1 (3.4)	3 (10.7)	4 (1.3)
Slate	17 (20.2)	78 (44.6)	6 (20.7)	8 (28.6)	109 (34.5)
Clastic slate[12]	43 (51.2)	17 (9.7)	8 (27.6)	2 (7.1)	70 (22.2)
Light gray silicified slate	7 (8.3)		4 (13.8)	1 (3.6)	12 (3.8)
TOTAL	84	175	29	28	316

[11] Biostrome chert denotes possible stromatolite structure.
[12] Clastic slate denotes a material containing small rounded clast inclusions.

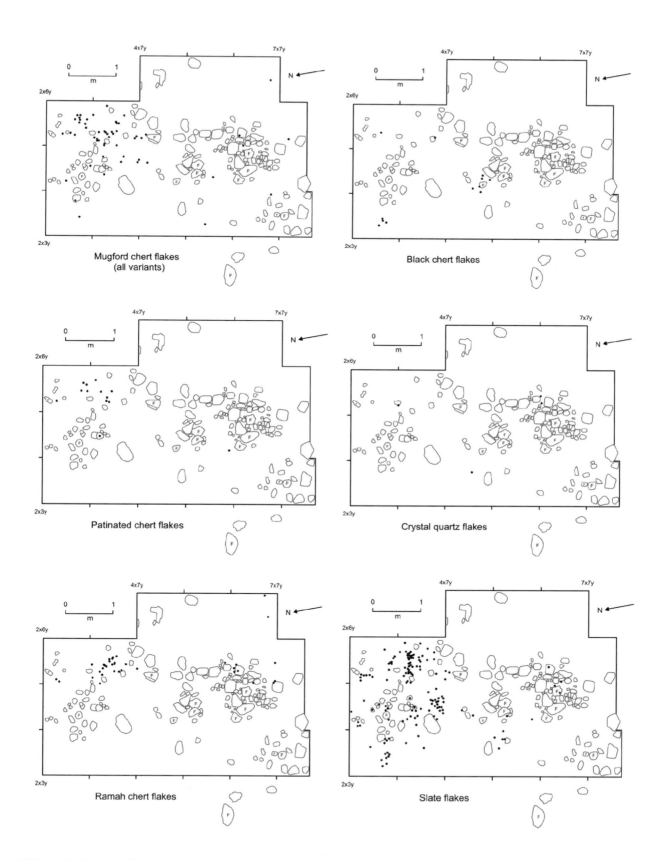

208/ Attu's Point L-5: flake raw material distributions.

Table 85. Attu's Point L-5: Total Lithic Raw Material Weights (Tools and Flakes). In Grams.

	TOOLS g (%)	FLAKES g (%)	TOTAL g (%)
Dark gray Mugford	69.8 (26.8)	19.9 (7.8)	89.7 (17.4)
Light gray Mugford	8.0 (3.1)	8.5 (3.3)	16.5 (3.2)
Gray-speckled chert	2.3 (0.9)	5.5 (2.2)	7.8 (1.5)
Black chert	5.5 (2.1)	1.5 (0.6)	7.0 (1.4)
Ramah chert	13.1 (5.0)	17.7 (7.0)	30.8 (6.0)
Patinated chert	0.9 (0.3)	8.5 (3.3)	9.4 (1.8)
Biostrome chert		0.4 (0.2)	0.4 (0.1)
Crystal quartz	7.2 (2.8)	1.1 (0.4)	8.3 (1.6)
Slate	110.0 (42.2)	112.5 (44.2)	222.5 (43.2)
Clastic slate		72.5 (28.5)	72.5 (14.1)
Light gray silicified slate	43.9 (16.8)	6.2 (2.4)	50.1 (9.7)

No refits of broken tools were identified and attempts to refit burin spalls with the three burins were unsuccessful. The majority of burins and burin spalls lie clustered together on the north side of the excavation (Figure 205). Two of the three burins are made of dark gray Mugford chert, as are 13 of the 16 spalls, while one burin is made of patinated chert, as is one spall. A single spall of gray-speckled chert lacks a burin of the same material.

Flake Distribution

The total flake distribution is shown in Figure 203. The vast majority of flakes (81%) are concentrated on the northern side of the excavation. This concentration actually consists of two smaller elongated clusters, one associated with a small charcoal concentration, the other running parallel ca. 50 cm to the east. The axial feature has relatively few flakes, but these seem to be concentrated in two clusters: one on the southeast edge of the hearth, the other at the northwest corner of the axial alignment in the vicinity of three flat slabs. In sum, the overall debitage distribution tends to parallel the k-means clusters of tools. The individual flake raw material distributions are shown as point plots and quadrat counts in Figures 208 and 209, respectively.

Generic Mugford chert, patinated chert and Ramah chert tend to be found on the east side of the northern concentration, while generic slate is found on both sides. Black chert occurs mostly in two small concentrations, one at the northwest corner of the excavation, the other at the northwest corner of the axial feature. There are few crystal quartz flakes, but two are located close to the hearth associated with the presumed axial feature (cf., the hearth-related crystal quartz distribution at L-1). Ramah chert occurs in two clusters, one on the east side of the northern concentration, the other adjacent to the axial feature hearth.

Given the strong spatial clustering, a quantitative analysis of the debitage was conducted using four quadrants, distinguished along an east-west axis by the 5y line and along the north-south axis by the 4x line (Table 84). These quadrants separate the two clusters of the northern concentration and distinguish the latter from the axial feature, and they are generally consistent with the results of the k-means analysis of the tool assemblage. There are several clear tendencies. Most of the Ramah chert is found on the east side of the excavation, particularly in the northeast quadrant. Slate is mostly distributed on the north side, also primarily in the northeast quadrant. Gray-speck-

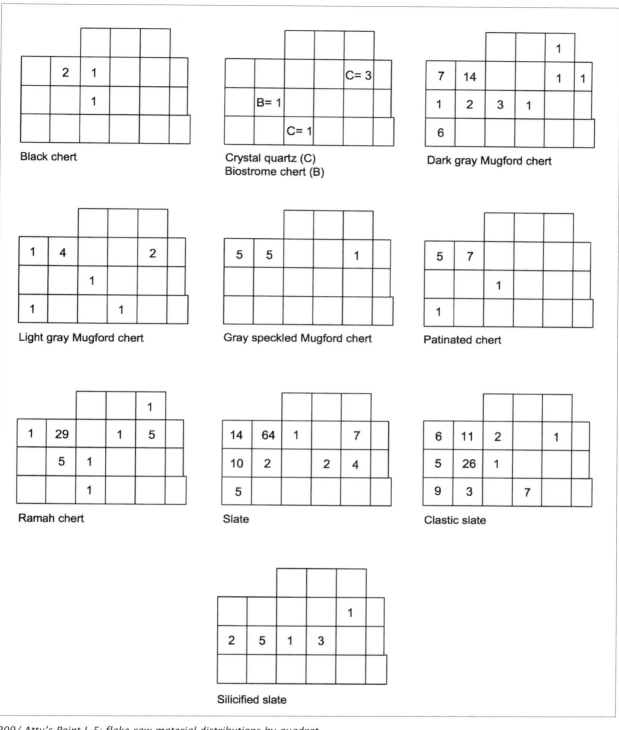

209/ Attu's Point L-5: flake raw material distributions by quadrat.

led Mugford chert and patinated chert are exclusively and primarily (respectively) associated with the northeast quadrant. Another noticeable pattern is the tendency for "plain" slates to cluster in the northeast quadrant, while "clastic" slate is mostly found in the northwest quadrant. The latter pattern suggests *in situ* distributions resulting from two separate knapping episodes using slightly different raw materials rather than dumping behavior resulting from floor

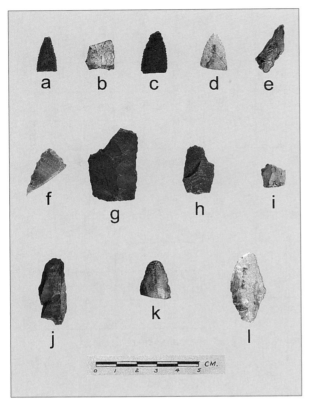

210/ Attu's Point L-5 tools. a-d: endblades; e: stemmed point; f: endblade preform; g-i: burins; j, k: endscrapers; l: burin/endscraper.

cleaning, which would probably mix the two slate types more thoroughly.

Integration

Comparison of the tool and flake raw material plots (Figures 207 and 208) indicates the distribution of Mugford chert flakes and tools largely coincides, except for a small concentration of tools in the extreme northwest corner of the excavation. Ramah chert tools and debitage tend to be spatially associated and are fairly tightly clustered around the hearth area and the northeast portion of the external dump/activity area. Both black chert and crystal quartz have a somewhat different distribution pattern than the other materials, tending to be found towards the more westerly portion of the excavation on the periphery of the other materials' main distributions.

If we compare the frequencies of raw materials present in the tool assemblage to those among the flakes (Tables 82 and 84) there are some marked differences. The high percentage of dark gray Mugford chert tools contrasts with a relatively low percentage of flakes, suggesting that some of the tools entered the locus in finished form. The frequency of crystal quartz debitage also seems low relative to the quantity of tools, suggesting the same pattern. The frequency of slate debitage is high compared to the few tools, which might indicate that some of the finished products or preforms were removed from the locus. This is underscored by the presence of clastic slate debitage, but the absence of tools of this material.

Table 85 tabulates tool and flake raw materials by weight for L-5 as a whole. All materials occur in low weights, but slates dominate, followed by dark gray Mugford chert. The most striking variations are that dark gray Mugford chert and light gray silicified slate are more significant as tools than as flakes; the former is consistent with the frequency data.

The initial assessment of L-5 suggested the locality consisted of an axial feature with a hearth at one end and an activity area to the north, or that perhaps the latter was a disturbed structure. Support for the disturbed structure alternative might be seen in the clustering of the flake distributions, one concentration related to a charcoal deposit and rocks, the other concentration lying 50 cm to the east (Figure 203), hinting at the bilaterality sometimes associated with axial features. On the other hand, a similar pattern could also be associated with an isolated hearth without an accompanying mid-passage structure. But there may be a third alternative. We might deconstruct the axial structure interpretation by pointing out that the feature consists of a hearth on the south side connected by a single line of rocks to a cluster of rocks and flat slabs on the north side. These two components could be separate features, with the small charcoal patch at the northern cluster of flat slabs representing a second disturbed hearth. Seen in conjunction with the northern activity area, we might then have a linear series of three hearths spaced at 1.5 m intervals. Such a linear feature, possibly consisting of four hearths, was excavated at Port Manvers Run-1 (Chapter 12).

L-5 Tool Assemblage

Endblades: Of the four endblades from L-5 (Figure 210:a-d), one is nearly complete and the others are proximal, medial and distal fragments. One is made of dark gray Mugford chert, one of light gray Mugford chert, one of light gray silicified slate and one of black chert. The nearly complete example (Figure 210:a) is triangular with a biconvex cross-section and a straight base that is thinned on both sides by two parallel flakes placed medially. It is finely flaked with distinctly serrated lateral edges and there is a small area of medial grinding on one face (L= >17.7 mm, W= 10.2, TH= 1.4). The proximal example (Figure 210:b) has a slightly concave base (depth= 0.6 mm) with two parallel basal-thinning flakes on one side and one central basal-thinning flake on the other side. A striking platform remains on one lateral edge. The implement may be unfinished (W= 14.6 mm, TH= 2.7). The other two examples are small fragments deemed to be endblades by virtue of their size and flaking patterns.

Points/endblades: Two distal fragments are difficult to classify as points or endblades. One is made of Ramah chert (Figure 210:d) and has distinct edge serration and a plano-convex cross-section resulting from near-complete dorsal flaking combined with ventral retouch limited to the edge margins. The other is made of dark gray Mugford chert and has fine edge serration, slight medial grinding, a biconvex cross-section and a slight hint of a shoulder (Figure 210:c). Combined with its slightly greater thickness, these attributes suggest this specimen may represent a point rather than an endblade.

Endblade preforms: The single example is a distal fragment made of gray-speckled Mugford chert (Figure 210:f). It bears minimal lateral retouch limited to within 2.5 mm of the edge.

Points: The single definite specimen (Figure 210:e) is the proximal/lateral portion of a crystal

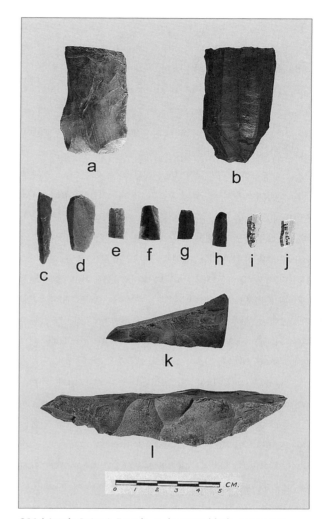

211/ Attu's Point L-5 tools. a, b: microblade cores; c-j: microblades; k: adze; l: celt/adze preform.

quartz point with a contracting stem and a biconvex cross-section (TH= 5.7 mm, stem L= 11.4).

Bifaces: Three small biface fragments were found, all lateral edge fragments, two are made of crystal quartz, one of Ramah chert. The latter has a very slight hint of a shoulder, suggesting it was a lanceolate biface.

Burins: Two of the three burins are fashioned from flakes, one is made on a microblade. Both of the flake burins are made of gray Mugford chert while the microblade burin is made of patinated chert. None of the implements are ground. One of the flake burins is relatively large (Figure 210:g) with fine retouch on both lateral edges, dorsal on the left, ventral on the right (L = 37.6 mm, W = 24.1, TH = 4.8). There is a faint shoulder on each side and a slight notch-like indentation on the right side, where the retouch is bifacial. The proximal end is thinned bifacially but two long parallel flakes were used to remove the bulb of percussion on the ventral side (similar to the technique used on some endblades). The right distal corner is bifacially retouched, providing a platform for the oblique removal of four burin spalls. The other flake burin (Figure 210:h) exhibits minimal unifacial retouch on its lateral edges (L= 25.4 mm, W=14.9, TH=6.7). A single spall removal runs obliquely from a slightly retouched area on the distal end to a terminus marked by a steeply retouched notch (65˚) on the opposite lateral edge. The notch might be either a remnant concave scraper edge or a termination control feature. The retouched edge is wear-polished.

The third burin (Figure 210:i) is a very small implement made on the proximal fragment of a microblade (L= 12.6 mm, W= 11.8, TH= 2.8). The left distal corner has a small notch that may have been made for a controlled snap of the microblade, but the notch also served as a platform for the oblique removal of four tiny burin spalls. No other retouch is present.

Combination scraper/burins: The single implement (Figure 210:l) is made on a lozenge-shaped flake of crystal quartz (L= 35.6, W= 22.4, TH= 6.5). The medial-distal portion of one lateral edge has abrupt scraper-like retouch on the dorsal side while on the other lateral edge the medial-proximal portion is retouched similarly on the dorsal side. Burinations are present at both ends of the implement; one end has two spall removals— the first an angle burination, the second oblique across the tip of the implement— while the other end has a single angle burination.

Burin spalls: Of the 17 burin spalls (MNI = 13), eight are complete, five are proximal fragments, three are distal fragments and one is a medial portion. Eight are made from dark gray Mugford chert, five from gray Mugford chert, one from light gray Mugford chert, two from light gray silicified slate and one from Ramah

chert (the latter is an uncertain spall). Two spalls are primary, the rest are secondary. None are ground. Metrics are as follows: $\bar{x}$ L = 16.0 mm, r = 9.6-20.5, $\bar{x}$ W = 3.8, r = 2.4-5.2, $\bar{x}$ TH = 1.9, r = 1.1-3.2.

Scrapers: Three scrapers were recovered. One is the distal fragment of an endscraper (Figure 210:k) made on a blade of light gray silicified slate, with a relatively narrow convex "nose" (W = 14.9 mm, TH = 3.8, edge angle = 40˚). Another is an end/sidescraper (Figure 210:j) made on an irregular linear flake of dark gray Mugford chert. The partially retouched distal end is convex and half of one lateral margin is also retouched (L = 33.7 mm, W = 13.5, TH = 9.1, edge angle = 65˚). The third specimen is a possible medial fragment of black chert that has shallow dorsal retouch on opposite edges.

Microblades: Of the 20 microblades (MNI=12), fourteen are made of Mugford chert, four of crystal quartz and two of Ramah chert (Figure 211: c-j). Only one is complete; 11 are proximal fragments, six are medial fragments and two are distal fragments. Metrics are as follows: $\bar{x}$ W = 8.08 mm, r = 5.1-14.6, $\bar{x}$ TH = 2.1, r = 1.1-4.4. Platform angles: 85˚ = 1, 80˚ = 7, 75˚ = 1, 70˚ = 3. Platform preparation: plain = 1, ground = 1, plain/ground = 1, retouch = 2, retouch/ground = 3. Four specimens have traces of deliberate retouch while eight exhibit minor notching and use-wear.

Microblade cores: The first of the two cores (Figure 211:b) is made on a sub-rectangular to triangular block of dark gray Mugford chert (L =56.4 mm, W =33.4, TH = 20.59). A triangular platform is positioned at one of the long ends of the chert block. The platform surface is fully retouched by shallow flakes and has a platform angle of 80˚. Flake scars from six blade removals run the length of the front and sides of the core. The blades ranged in size from 37-55 mm long and 5.5-10 mm in width. The back of the block is not retouched. The second example (Figure 211:a) is a tabular-shaped core of light gray silicified slate (L = 51.6 mm, W = 32.7, TH = 14.3). The platform is located on one of the long ends of the core. The edges of the core are retouched slightly, including some thinning on the long end opposite the platform. The platform is long, narrow and flat, without preparation; a well defined point of impact indentation is found on the platform edge. The platform angle is 80°. One microblade ca. 29.5 mm long and 10.1 mm wide was removed from the narrow longtitudinal edge of the core.

Celts/adzes: Both specimens are made of green slate. A definite adze (Figure 211:k) is made on a slate tablet and is broken longtitudinally (L = >56.7 mm, W = >27.2, TH = 12.7). The implement has a rectangular cross-section with lateral edges flaked perpendicular to the tool faces. On the dorsal side of the tool polish is mostly limited to within 4.5 mm of the tool edge, although it extends up to 16 mm back. The ventral side is almost completely polished while the lateral edges are unpolished. There is little indication of use wear on the bit apart from three small fractures on the ventral side and a slight rounding of the edge. The second implement is a complete unground preform for a celt or adze (Figure 211:l). Its overall form is "pick-like," with a square cross-section resulting

212/ Attu's Point L-7: axial structure, view towards the northeast.

213/ Attu's Point L-7: box-hearth with thermoliths. View towards the southeast.

214/ Attu's Point L-7: box-hearth, thermoliths removed. View towards the northeast.

Table 86. Attu's Point L-7: Tool Classes by *K*-Means Cluster.

	Cluster 1	Cluster 2	Other	TOTAL N (%)
Endblades	4.5*	1.5		6 (25.0)
Endblade preforms	1			1 (4.2)
Biface fragments	2			2 (8.3)
Burins	2			2 (8.3)
Burin spalls	6			6 (25.0)
Microblades	3	1		4 (16.7)
Utilized flakes	2		1	3 (12.5)
TOTAL	20.5	2.5	1	24

* half numbers denote refits across units

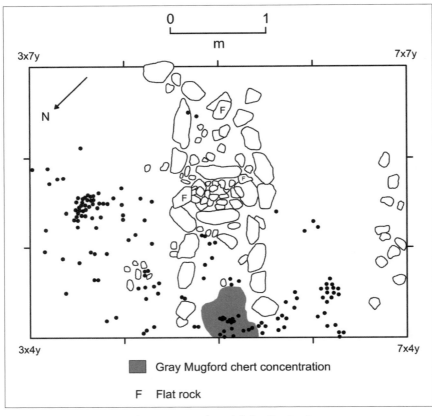

215/ *Attu's Point L-7: axial structure and total flake distribution.*

Key:
- Gray Mugford chert concentration
- F Flat rock

silicified slate, one of crystal quartz, six of Ramah chert and one of slate. The relatively high frequency of Ramah chert specimens is noteworthy.

L-7 EXCAVATION

L-7 was located in the middle of the site, just below the edge of the second beach ridge at 11 m asl (Figure 193). The locality consisted of a small but perfectly preserved axial feature, around which a total of 12 m^2 was excavated (Figures 212 to 215). A debitage concentration at the foot of the feature extended slightly outside the limits of the excavation, so it is possible that an external midden area remains uninvestigated.

The axial feature was just under 3 m long, 1 m wide and was oriented northwest-southeast, perpendicular to the shoreline (Figures 212 and 215). A beautifully preserved box-hearth lay at the center of the feature (Figures 213 and 214). It was comprised of four thick inclined rock slabs that created a

from perpendicular retouch on all sides (L = 115.4 mm, W = 24.9, TH = 24.3).

Utilized flakes: The 24 utilized flakes are made of a variety of materials: seven of dark gray Mugford chert, five of light gray Mugford chert, one of light gray

Table 87. Attu's Point L-7: Tool Classes by Structural Position.

	East	Axial	West	Ax/E	Ax/W	TOTAL	N (%)
Endblades	1.5	3.5	1			6	(25.0)
Endblade preforms		1				1	(4.2)
Biface fragments		2				2	(8.3)
Burins			1		1	2	(8.3)
Burin spalls		1			5	6	(25.0)
Microblades	1	1	2			4	(16.7)
Utilized flakes		2		1		3	(12.5)
TOTAL	**2.5**	**10.5**	**4**	**1**	**6**	**24**	

compartment of 60 by 40 cm. The compartment was filled with tightly packed fist-sized thermoliths (some fire-cracked) that overlay three small horizontal flat stone slabs at the base of the feature. The gravel at the bottom of the hearth contained a few flecks of solid charcoal as well as a faint stain of powdered charcoal.

Two small clusters of probable thermoliths were found outside the hearth, one immediately to the east of the hearth within the axial feature, another outside the feature 1 m north of the center of the hearth. There was also a 1.7 m long scatter of small rocks 1.3 m west of the axial feature that likely represents thermoliths

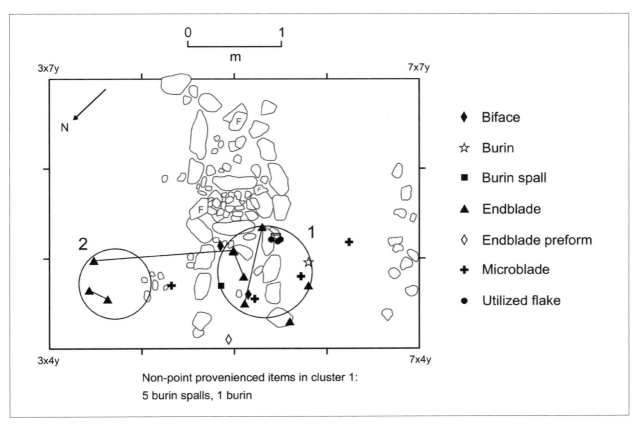

216/ Attu's Point L-7: tool distribution and k-means clusters.

Table 88. Attu's Point L-7: Tool Raw Material Frequencies by Structural Position.

	East	Axial	West	Ax/E	Ax/W	TOTAL N (%)
Dark gray Mugford chert	2.5	3.5	2		6	14 (58.3)
Light gray Mugford chert		3				3 (12.5)
Gray-speckled chert			1			1 (4.2)
Crystal quartz		1	1	1		3 (12.5)
Ramah chert		3				3 (12.5)
TOTAL	2.5	10.5	4	1	6	24

cached or discarded against the wall of a tent. There was no trace of tent anchor rocks.

A tiny charcoal sample collected from beneath the flat rocks at the bottom of the hearth was submitted to Isotrace Laboratory, University of Toronto, for AMS dating. The result was very surprising: 50±50 B.P. (TO-4793). Of all the charcoal samples from Attu's Point, this one seemed to have the strongest contextual asso-ciation, virtually sealed underneath an undisturbed hearth feature. The anomalous result might be attrib-utable to recent burning of roots that had penetrated beneath the hearth or post-excavation contamination.

Tool Distribution

The L-7 tool distribution is plotted in relation to a *k*-means cluster analysis in Figure 216. Cluster 1 is

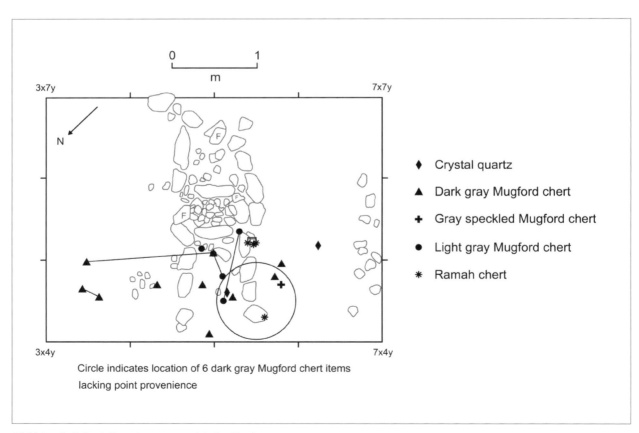

217/ *Attu's Point L-7: tool raw material distribution.*

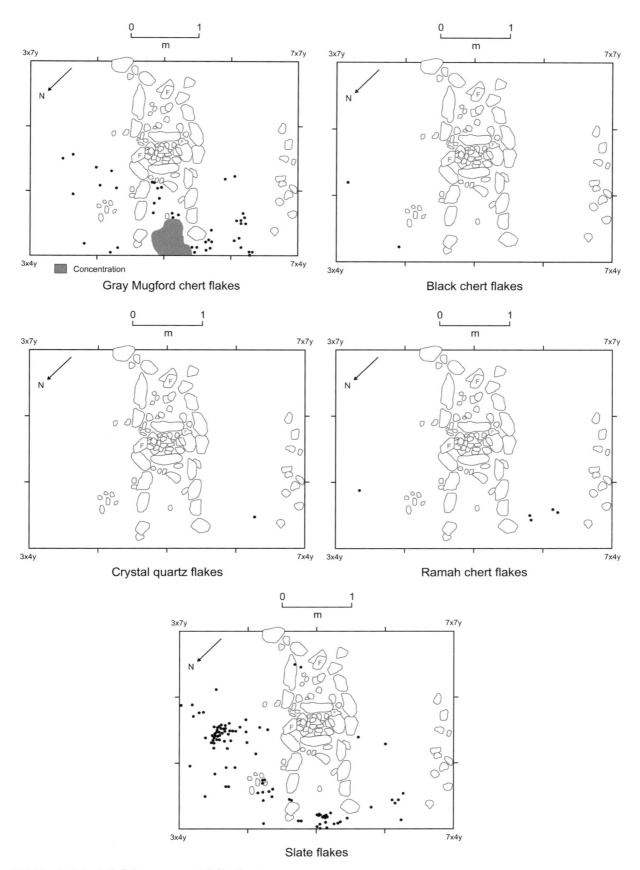

218/ Attu's Point L-7: flake raw material distributions.

Table 89. Attu's Point L-7: Flake Raw Material Frequencies by Structural Position.

	East N (%)	West N (%)	TOTAL N (%)
Dark gray Mugford chert	18 (12.8)	157 (54.5)	175 (40.8)
Gray-speckled chert	19 (13.5)	54 (18.8)	73 (17.0)
Patinated chert		14 (4.9)	14 (3.3)
Black chert	3 (2.1)	1 (0.3)	4 (0.9)
Ramah chert	4 (2.8)	19 (6.6)	23 (5.4)
Crystal quartz	6 (4.3)	1 (0.3)	7 (1.6)
Slate	91 (64.5)	42 (14.6)	133 (31.0)
TOTAL	141	288	429

positioned on the northwestern arm of the structure while Cluster 2 flanks the feature. Six of the seven quadrat provenienced items (five burin spalls and a burin) can be associated with Cluster 1, while one item (utilized flake) lay somewhere between the two clusters. A refitted endblade connects the two clusters. All the implements are found on the northern (seaward) side of the excavation and Table 86 indicates almost all the tools belonged to Cluster 1 at the northwest corner of the axial feature. Although the distinct structure could facilitate a model-based bilateral analysis, the paucity of tools limits the value of such an approach. Nonetheless, Table 87 outlines the distribution of the tool classes partitioned by spatial position relative to the feature. Little can be

concluded except that the majority of tools were associated with the feature and that biface fragments and burin spalls tend to be associated with the feature.

Spatial distributions of the tool raw materials are shown in Figure 217 and summarized in Table 88. Given the low frequencies little can be said except that light gray Mugford chert and Ramah chert tend to be more closely associated with the axial feature than are the other raw materials.

The total flake distribution (Figure 215) indicates deposition restricted to the north side of the structure, the same pattern as the tool distribution. Looking at the distribution of individual flake raw materials (Figure 218), a major concentration of Mugford chert

Table 90. Attu's Point L-7: Total Lithic Raw Material Weights (Tools and Flakes). In Grams.

	Tools g	Flakes g	TOTAL g (%)
Dark gray Mugford chert	5.9	52.1	58.0 (25.0)
Gray-speckled chert	0.4	10.7	11.1 (4.8)
Patinated chert		7	7.0 (3.0)
Black chert		2.6	2.6 (1.1)
Ramah chert	4.3	2.6	6.9 (3.0)
Crystal quartz	3.4	3.3	6.7 (2.9)
Slate	139.3		139.3 (60.1)

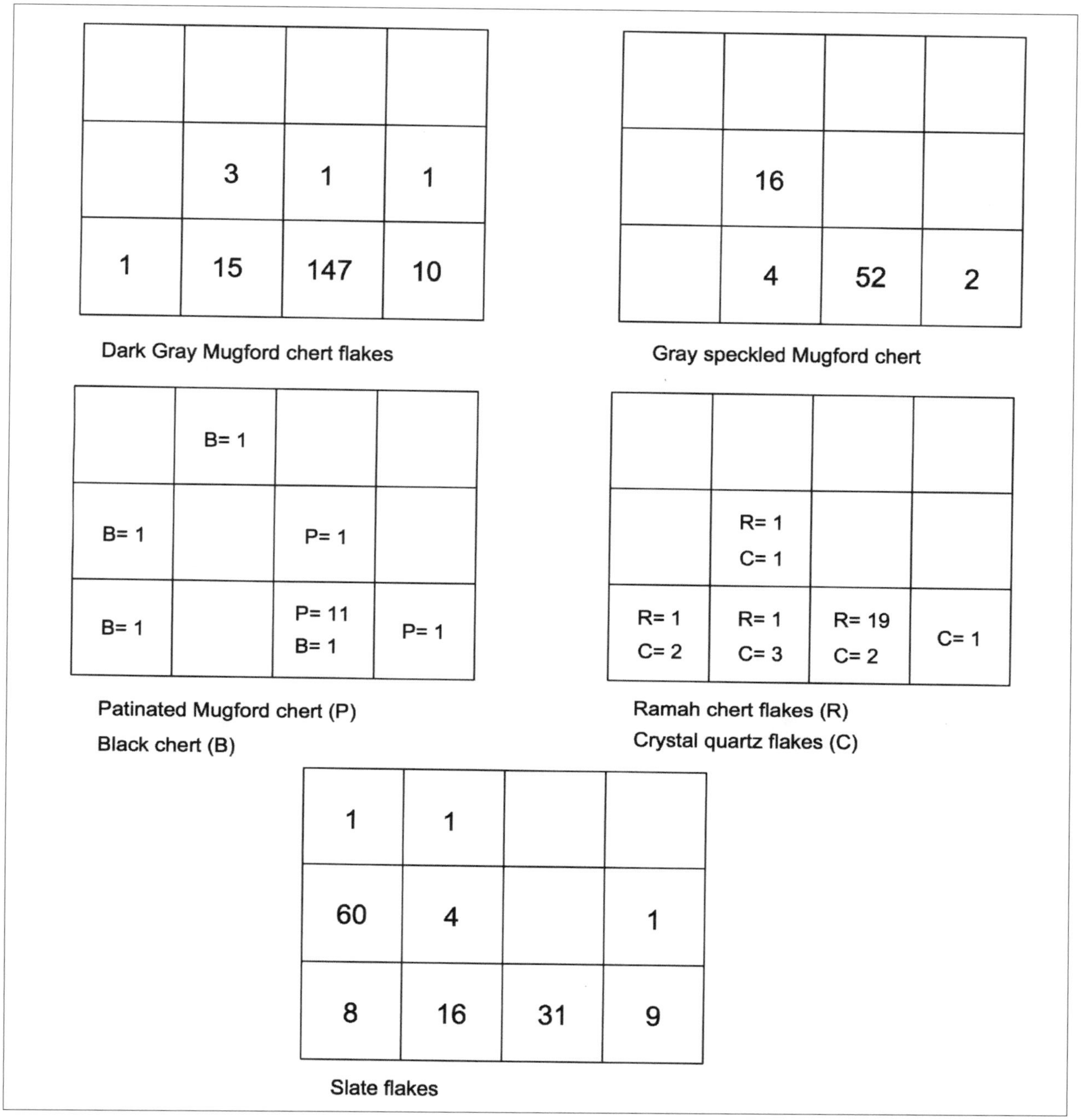

Dark Gray Mugford chert flakes

	3	1	1
1	15	147	10

Gray speckled Mugford chert

	16		
	4	52	2

Patinated Mugford chert (P)
Black chert (B)

	B= 1		
B= 1		P= 1	
B= 1		P= 11 B= 1	P= 1

Ramah chert flakes (R)
Crystal quartz flakes (C)

	R= 1 C= 1		
R= 1 C= 2	R= 1 C= 3	R= 19 C= 2	C= 1

Slate flakes

1	1		
60	4		1
8	16	31	9

219/ Attu's Point L-7: flake raw material distributions by quadrat.

flakes (generic) is found at the northern terminus of the axial feature. This concentration is strongly suggestive of a restricted knapping or dumping locale. In contrast, although some of the slate flakes also occur at the northern end of the feature, they are clearly concentrated in a small area east of the hearth. For quantitative analysis the debitage was divided into two subunits— east and west of the axial feature— based on the 5x grid line that ran through the center of the feature (see Figure 219). This is a somewhat inconvenient and arbitrary division, but in combination with the point-plotted debitage, the results are acceptable. As outlined in Table 89, Mugford cherts clearly dominate on the west side of the axial feature (mostly in the concentration at the end of the feature), patinated chert occurs exclusively on the west side and Ramah chert is mostly on the west. Slate and crystal quartz are associated mainly with the east side. A chi-square test indicates there is a statistically significant difference in the distribution of raw materials between the two sides of the feature (x^2 = 139.65).

Integration

Comparison of the tool and flake raw material distributions (Figures 217 and 218) indicates Mugford chert tools have a distribution broadly similar to the flakes, although most of the tools (with the exception of the non-provenienced burin spalls) were deposited slightly outside the dense concentration of flakes at the end of the axial feature. Despite the high frequency of slate flakes, no slate tools were recovered. Unless some slate implements are present in the unexcavated area at the foot of the axial feature, they were either disposed of elsewhere on the site or curated to other localities. The low frequency of the other raw materials makes their distributions hard to evaluate. Neither the crystal quartz nor the Ramah chert flakes and tools are precisely associated with each other and there are no black chert tools to plot against the three flakes. The total raw material weights (Table 90) are extremely low. Slate and dark gray Mugford chert are the most abundant materials by weight, although for slate this is exclusively flake material and for dark gray Mugford chert it is primarily flakes. Overall, the paucity of lithic material suggests a relatively short occupation.

The spatial organization of lithic-related activities at L-7 is strongly oriented towards the seaward side of the axial feature, leaving the "back" area almost totally free of lithic material. Within this general tendency is a marked differentiation between a Mugford chert deposit at the "front" of the feature and a slate concentration in the lateral area east of the hearth, suggesting spatial separation of reduction activities linked to the two materials. On the other hand, refits between endblade fragments provide a behavioral link between the front of the feature and the lateral area to the east (Figure 216).

L-7 Tool Assemblage

Endblades: Of the six endblades, five are complete and one is a proximal fragment (Figure 220:a-e); four of the five complete specimens are refits of broken portions. Two are made of gray Mugford chert, two of light gray Mugford chert, one of gray-speckled Mugford chert and one of Ramah chert. All are triangular, but two size classes are represented. Five of the six are "medium-sized," with lengths ranging between 21.2-28.3 mm and widths between 11.9-15.4 mm. Figure 220:b has a straight base and a sinusoid cross-section; it was broken medially (L = 26.2 mm, W = 14.1, TH = 2.2). Figure 220:c has a straight base, a biconvex cross-section, slight edge serration and faint polishing on one basal corner (L = 26.7 mm, W = 12.7, TH = 1.9). It was broken at about 1/4 of the distance up from its base. Figure 220:d has a straight base and a biconvex cross-section; one lateral edge is not completely retouched (L = 28.3 mm, W = 15.4, TH = 2.9). It was broken at about 2/3 of the distance up from its base. Figure 220:e has a straight base, a sinusoid cross-section and slightly serrated edges (L = 21.2, W = 11.9, TH = 1.8); it was broken medially. The

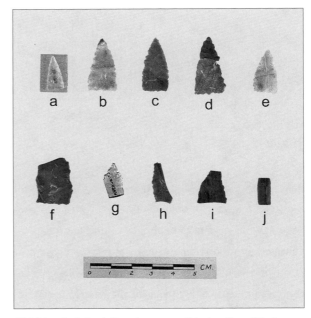

220/ Attu's Point L-7 tools. a-e: endblades; f: endblade preform; g: biface tip; h-i: burins; j: microblade.

CHAPTER 13

proximal fragment (not illustrated) has a thinned base (W = >14.1 mm, TH = 2.3).

The sixth specimen is a very small complete endblade made of Ramah chert (Figure 220:a). It has a biconvex cross-section, a slightly concave base (depth= 0.5 mm) and faint edge serration (L= 16.3 mm, W= 8.5, TH=1.7). There is also slight medial grinding on both faces.

Endblade preforms: The single endblade pre-form (Figure 220: f) is a proximal fragment made of gray Mugford chert. It has a straight base and rough bifacial flaking (W= 16.8 mm, TH= 2.9).

Points/endblades: The two fragments are so small it is impossible to determine which tool class is represented. One of them is a distal element made of crystal quartz (Figure 220:g) with a biconvex cross-section and slight edge serration. The other is a medial fragment made of light gray Mugford chert with a biconvex cross-section.

Burins: The two burins are both made of gray Mugford chert. One is a small specimen that initially was classed as an endblade fragment (Figure 220: h). The implement is made on a very thin flake with a remnant basal striking platform. It is completely bifacially flaked and a burination platform was pre-pared using a small bifacial distal notch. Two spalls were removed obliquely from the notch; the first sheared off most of one lateral edge of the flake while the second is very short and runs parallel to the first. Much of the medial portion of one face is ground while the other face has slight grinding dis-tally (L = 20.6 mm, W = 9.3, TH = 1.6). The second example is a distal fragment, also made on a small thin flake (Figure 220:i). Fine retouch towards the distal end of one lateral edge was used as a platform to remove a transverse spall. This spall surface was then employed as a platform to remove two small spalls from the other lateral edge of the flake. Near the distal end on both faces there are numerous stri-ations that run 70-80° to the burin spalls; this appears to be incipient grinding.

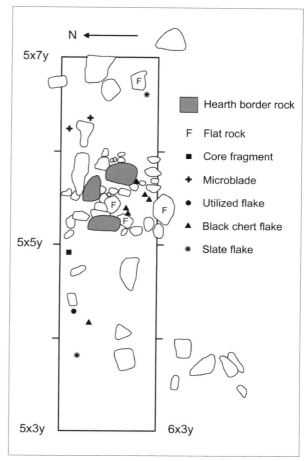

221/ Attu's Point L-9: axial structure.

Burin Spalls: Of the six burin spalls, three are complete, two are proximal fragments and one is a medial fragment. All are made of gray Mugford chert. One is a primary spall, the rest secondary. The pri-mary spall is long (24.7 mm) while the two complete secondary spalls are half its length (11.7, 13.6 mm). Additional metrics: $\bar{x}$W = 3.5 mm, r = 2.0-4.4, $\bar{x}$TH = 2.1, r = 1.2-3.3.

Microblades: All four of the microblades (MNI = 2) are medial fragments. Three are made of gray Mugford chert, one of crystal quartz (Figure 220: j, illustrates a Mugford chert example). Reliable widths vary between 6.5-8.6 mm. One has retouch on both lateral edges while two others exhibit slight use-wear on their margins.

Utilized Flakes: Two of the three utilized flakes are made of Ramah chert, one of crystal quartz.

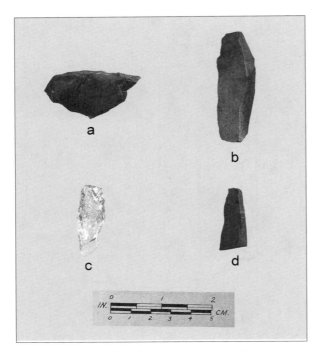

222/ Attu's Point L-9 tools. a: core fragment; b: macroblade; c: utilized flake; d: macroblade.

L-9 TEST EXCAVATION

L-9 was located on the uppermost beach ridge at 12 m asl. (Figure 193). At first glance it appeared to consist of a well-preserved axial structure, so a 1 m by 4 m excavation unit was placed along the length of the feature (Figure 221). After exposure, a hearth was clearly identifiable but other structural elements were less distinct. The axial feature was 3.5 m long, 0.80-1.0 m wide and was oriented east-west, perpendicular to the beach front. The slightly disturbed hearth was composed of three thick border rocks and a fourth large flat rock that surrounded a pair of small horizontal flat slabs, creating a compartment of 60 by 40 cm. Some of the fist-sized stones within the hearth area were likely thermoliths and small fire-cracked rocks were noted on the eastern edge of the hearth. Small flecks of charcoal were found in the gravel on the outer perimeter of the hearth and beneath some of the hearth and central axial feature rocks. Just outside the excavation at the western end of the feature was a small rock cluster that might be part of the L-9 feature, but it could also represent a separate structure. A

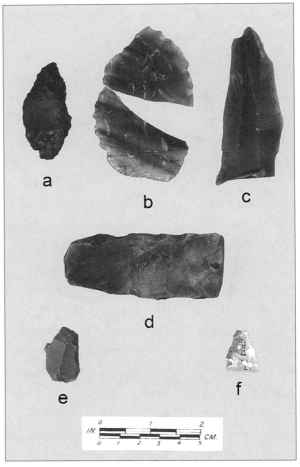

223/ Attu's Point surface collected tools. a, b: bifaces (L-4); c: large Ramah chert flake (L-4); d: adze (L-3); e-f: burin, endblade preform (L-15).

small charcoal sample procured from the gravel immediately adjacent to the hearth rocks was submitted to the Isotrace Laboratory, University of Toronto, for AMS dating. The result was an unacceptably recent date of 690 ± 60 B.P. (TO-4794). The sample was not from a sealed context and could conceivably be related to a post-occupation vegetation burn.

Very little lithic material was found in the L-9 excavation: two "macroblades," one core fragment, a biface fragment and two utilized flakes. Both macroblades (Figure 222:b, d) are made of gray Mugford chert; one is complete (L = 56.8 mm, W = 18.9, TH = 8.9), the other a proximal fragment. Both have a platform angle of 80°; one has a unprepared plain platform the other platform is retouched. Both have slight use-wear on their edges. The core fragment (Figure 222:a) is made

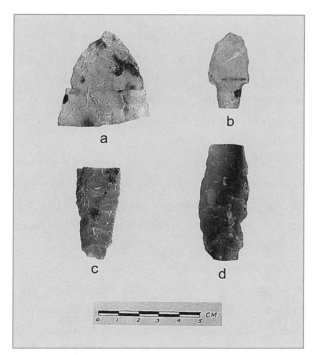

224/ Attu's Point surface collected tools. a-b: Maritime Archaic biface, Maritime Archaic stemmed point (L-12); c: lanceolate biface (L-6); d: lanceolate biface (east of L-5).

of gray Mugford chert. The biface fragment is a tiny, finely flaked lateral edge element of black chert. One of the utilized flakes is made of gray Mugford chert, the other of crystal quartz (Figure 222:c). Eight flakes were collected, five of which are made of black chert, two of slate and one of dark gray Mugford chert.

OTHER LOCI

Throughout the course of the work at Attu's Point the site surface was scanned for traces of additional structures and artifact concentrations. Surface collections were made at some of these localities. Each is described briefly below (see Figure 193 for locations).

L-2: Located on the first beach terrace at 10 m asl., there was a possible axial structure, 3.5 m long, oriented northwest-southeast. Visible on the surface was a microblade and flakes of Mugford chert, Ramah chert and slate.

L-3: Situated on the first beach terrace at 10 m asl., a few rocks and flat slabs were observed, but no clear structure. A flake scatter measuring 4.5 m north-

south and 2.5 m east-west contained Mugford chert and abundant slate. A complete adze of green slate (Figure 223: d) was surface collected. The implement is sub-rectangular in form, with abrupt perpendicular flaking on one lateral edge and more irregular retouch on the other lateral edge (L = 78.6 mm, W = 33.2, TH = 21.6). The dorsal side of the adze bit was formed by flaking out a concavity, then polishing no more than 4.5 mm back from the edge (edge angle = 75°). On the ventral side the bit is mostly polished within 6.0 mm of the edge, although it extends back to 21.5 mm. Edge wear consists of a few small fractures and a slight rounding of the edge.

L-4: This locality was situated on the edge of the lowest beach terrace, just under 10 m asl., so it could be the youngest locus at the site. Various rocks were present, but no clear structure. A lithic scatter measuring 4.5 m north-south and 2.5 m east-west contained Mugford chert, slate and large Ramah chert flakes. A Ramah chert biface fragment, a biface preform of black chert and a large Ramah chert flake were surface collected. The Ramah chert biface (Figure 223:b) is broken in the middle and is missing part of its mid-section. It is unfinished, with a slightly convex base bearing traces of grinding and there are three slight notches near the proximal end of one lateral edge (L = ca. 76.5 mm, W = 32.1, TH = 13.7). The black chert biface preform (Figure 223:a) is leaf-shaped; one face of the distal end is fairly well flaked but the rest of the implement is only retouched marginally (L = 49.8 mm, W = 26.0, TH = 7.7). The large Ramah chert flake (Figure 223:c) is the largest piece of that material observed at the site (L = 82.9 mm, W = 32.1, TH = 13.7).

East of L-5: About 4.75 m east of the L-5 excavation the mid-section of a lanceolate biface made of Ramah chert (Figure 224:d) was surface collected. It is completely retouched bifacially, with a biconvex cross-section. Weak shoulders occur just below the mid-section on both lateral edges, but there is more distinct stemming near the base (L = > 49 mm, W = 23.9, TH = 8.1).

225/ Attu's Point surface collected tools. a: stemmed point (L-14); b-c: biface tip, burin (L-15); d: burin (L-16), e-f: biface base, sidescraper (L-14).

L-6: Positioned on the upper portion of the first beach level at 10.5-11 m asl., this locality consisted of an indistinct rock structure, flakes of slate, crystal quartz and black chert, as well as a lanceolate biface fragment and a core tablet. The biface fragment (Figure 224:c) is a proximal specimen made of gray Mugford chert, with a biconvex cross-section and a slight contraction towards the base (W= 21.4 mm, TH= 5.6). The core tablet is made of black chert; three linear flakes removed from one end of a flat-flaked platform suggest it was a test piece for a microblade core (L = 76.4 mm, W = 62.3, TH = 22.6).

L-8: Located on the upper portion of the first beach level at 11 m asl., an axial structure may be present in a moss-covered area 3.8 by 3.0 m in size. Flakes of Mugford and Ramah chert were noted, along with a large microblade of Mugford chert.

L-10: This locality was situated in the middle of the second beach terrace, just under 12 m asl. There appeared to be a small axial structure, 2.4 m long, 70 cm wide, oriented northwest-southeast. A bifacial implement of Ramah chert was noted nearby.

L-11: Near the middle of the second beach terrace, at just under 12 m asl., was an indistinct rock structure associated with flakes of Ramah chert, slate and crystal quartz, as well as a large black chert microblade.

L-12: This find spot was situated at the extreme eastern edge of the site, on the uppermost beach level at 12 m asl. It consisted of a Ramah chert stemmed point of Late Maritime Archaic Rattler's Bight form and a Ramah chert biface fragment that might also be of Maritime Archaic origin. A 1 m² test pit was excavated in a mossy area 2 m southeast of these surface finds, since a few rocks suggested the possibility of a feature, but no cultural material was encountered. The stemmed point is complete except for its tip (Figure 224:b). It has well-defined shoulders and a striking platform at the base of its stem. The dorsal side of the stem is completely retouched, but the ventral side is only partially retouched. Only the margins of the blade element are retouched (L = >40 mm, W = 20.2, TH = 4.9, Stem L = 12.5 Stem W[shoulder]= 11.8, Stem W[base] = 9.5). The Ramah chert biface is a distal fragment (Figure 224:a). Its dorsal face is almost completely flaked while the ventral retouch is limited to the margins (W = >45 mm, TH = 6.3).

L-13: This small locality was situated on the uppermost terrace of the beach, near the southwestern edge of the site at just under 12 m asl. It consisted of a dense concentration of green slate flakes in front of a boulder, suggestive of a reduction locale for adze/axe production.

L-14 & 15: These two localities seemed continuous with each other and were located on the uppermost beach terrace at the western extremity of the site, about 11 m asl. L-14 contained possible structural rocks and a surface collection procured there consisted of a stemmed point, a biface base, and a large sidescraper. Slate flakes were also observed. The stemmed point (Figure 225:a) is a distal fragment made of Ramah chert with a biconvex cross-section and slightly serrated lateral edges (W= 11.2 mm, TH= 2.5). The biface base (Figure 225:e), also made of Ramah chert, exhibits a faint trace of a shoulder 17.5 mm above the base; it is probably part of a shouldered lanceolate implement (cf., Figure 224:c, d). The complete sidescraper (Figure 225:f) is made on a blade-like flake of dark gray Mugford chert (L = 57.0 mm, W =21.6, TH =6.3). The working edge is slightly concave, with a 65° angle. Both lateral edges are retouched and ground slightly, while the ventral side of the proximal end exhibits some thinning retouch. Use-wear in the form of edge rounding and a few small ventral fractures is present on the screwdriver-like distal tip and the distal portion of the working edge. The implement is almost identical to the combination burin/scraper from L-1 (Figure 201:c), minus the burination.

At L-15, 2 m northwest of L-14, flakes of Mugford chert and slate were observed and an endblade preform, biface tip and two burins were surface collected. The endblade preform (Figure 223: f) is triangular, although missing its tip, and made from crystal quartz. It has a slightly concave base, which has been thinned bifacially, and a roughly biconvex cross-section (W = 16.2 mm, TH = 4.0). The biface tip (Figure 225:b) of patinated chert has a biconvex cross-section. Both burins are made of gray Mugford chert and are unground. The first specimen (Figure 225:c) is made on a large flake with a striking platform at the base (L = 33.4 mm, W =21.6, TH =6.2). On its dorsal side the proximal end is retouched with long flakes extending over the entire surface, while on the ventral side retouch is limited to the edge margins. One lateral edge has a slight shoulder while the other exhibits a small notch below the termination of a burin scar. The distal end platform has unifacial dorsal retouch, from which eight burin spalls have been removed obliquely. The second burin (Figure 223:e) is also made on a flake with a striking platform at its base (L =28.5 mm, W =17.5, TH = 4.3). The proximal portion of one later-

al edge has a faint shoulder created by fine ventral retouch and slight grinding. The other lateral edge exhibits ventral retouch that thinned the bulb of percussion. The distal end is "beaked" with three burination planes that involved 10 visible spall removals.

L-16: This small locality was located downslope from L-14/15 at 11 m asl. It consisted of a lithic scatter of Mugford chert flakes, a burin and an endblade; only the burin was collected.

The burin (Figure 225:d) is made on a flake of gray Mugford chert with a striking platform at the base (L = 28.9 mm, W = 20.9, TH = 6.2). Its lateral edges are slightly retouched dorsally, producing faint constrictions on each edge. The distal end has oblique dorsal retouch, including a small notch. Two burin spalls were removed, slightly obliquely. There is no facial grinding.

L-17: This locality lay between L-7 and L-8 at 11 m asl. Possible structural cobbles were associated with flakes of Mugford chert and slate.

L-18: About 1 m south of L-9, on the uppermost beach terrace at 12 m asl., was a rock structure 2 m in diameter that was associated with Mugford chert, Ramah chert and slate flakes.

L-19: Positioned near the eastern edge of the site between L-11 and L-12, at 12 m asl., this find spot contained a few Mugford chert flakes.

L-20: Located between L-1 and a bare rock outcrop to the southwest, at 10 m asl., L-20 consisted of possible structural remains associated with a Ramah chert biface base and crystal quartz flakes.

L-21: Southeast of L-1 was a vegetated area between two rock outcrops. A few flakes of Mugford chert and slate were observed and there is potential for structural remains beneath the vegetation.

INTER-LOCUS COMPARISONS

The preceding sections explored spatial variation within each locus. Before providing an overall assessment of the site a comparison between the excavated loci will be presented, considering variation in tool types, lithic raw materials and spatial organization. Table 91

Table 91. Attu's Point: Comparison of Tool Classes by Excavated Loci and Other Collections.

	L-1 N (%)	L-5 N (%)	L-7 N (%)	Surface, L-9 N (%)
Endblades	4 (8.2)	4 (4.9)	6 (25.0)	
Endblade preforms	4 (8.2)	1 (1.2)	1 (4.2)	1 (5.0)
Endblades/points		2 (2.4)	2 (8.3)	
Stemmed points		1 (1.2)		1 (5.0)
Lanceolate bifaces				2 (10.0)
Bifaces	2 (4.1)	3 (3.7)		5 (25.0)
Burins		3 (3.7)	2 (8.3)	3 (15.0)
Burin spalls	11 (22.4)	17 (20.7)	6 (25.0)	
Microblades	13 (26.5)	19 (23.2)	4 (16.7)	2 (10.0)
Microblade cores		2 (2.4)		
Other cores				2 (10.0)
Scrapers	2 (4.1)	3 (3.7)		1 (5.0)
Scraper/burins	1 (2.0)	1 (1.2)		
Utilized flakes	10 (20.4)	24 (29.3)	3 (12.5)	2 (10.0)
Celts/adzes	2 (4.1)	2 (2.4)		1 (5.0)
TOTAL	**49**	**82**	**24**	**20**

Table 92. Attu's Point: Comparison of Tool Raw Material Frequencies by Excavated Loci and Other Collections.

	L-1 N (%)	L-5 N (%)	L-7 N (%)	Surface, L-9 N (%)
Dark gray Mugford	18 (36.7)	36 (43.9)	14 (58.3)	9 (45.0)
Light gray Mugford	16 (32.7)	3 (3.7)	3 (12.5)	
Gray-speckled chert	3 (6.1)	6 (7.3)	1 (4.2)	
Patinated chert		2 (2.4)		1 (5.0)
Black chert	1 (2.0)	4 (4.9)		3 (15.0)
Ramah chert	2 (4.1)	11 (13.4)	3 (12.5)	4 (20.0)
Crystal quartz	6 (12.3)	10 (12.2)	3 (12.5)	2 (10.0)
Slate	2 (4.1)	2 (2.4)		1 (5.0)
Gray silicified slate	1 (2.0)	8 (9.8)		
TOTAL	**49**	**82**	**24**	**20**

outlines the variation in Pre-Dorset tool types between the three excavated loci and the other localities at the site. Most notable is the relatively high proportion of endblades and preforms at L-7 (the smallest sample) versus their low proportion at L-5 (the largest sample),

a trend supported by the expected frequencies calculated for the table. The proportion of burin spalls is consistent across the loci, although burins themselves are absent at L-1, aside from a single combination scraper-burin. L-7 is relatively lacking in implement

Table 93. Attu's Point: Comparison of Flake Raw Material Frequencies by Excavated Loci.

	L-1 N (%)	L-5 N (%)	L-7 N (%)
Dark gray Mugford	11 (4.8)	38 (11.9)	175 (40.8)
Light gray Mugford	99 (43.2)	9 (2.8)	
Gray-speckled chert	5 (2.2)	11 (3.5)	73 (17.0)
Patinated chert	32 (13.9)	16 (5.0)	14 (3.3)
Black chert	5 (2.2)	4 (1.3)	4 (0.9)
Ramah chert	2 (0.9)	44 (13.9)	23 (5.4)
Biostrome chert		1 (0.3)	
Crystal quartz	18 (6.8)	4 (1.3)	7 (1.6)
Slate	57 (25.6)	115 (36.3)	133 (31.0)
Clastic slate		62 (19.6)	
Light gray silicified slate		13 (4.1)	
TOTAL	229	317	429

Table 94. Attu's Point: Comparison of Total Lithic Raw Material Weights by Excavated Loci. In Grams.

	L-1 g (%)	L-5 g (%)	L-7 g (%)
Dark gray Mugford	48.6 (10.1)	89.7 (17.4)	58.0 (25.0)
Light gray Mugford	59.9 (12.5)	16.5 (3.2)	
Gray-speckled chert	24.0 (5.0)	7.8 (1.5)	11.1 (4.8)
Patinated chert	13.2 (2.8)	9.4 (1.8)	7.0 (3.0)
Black chert	3.1 (0.6)	7.0 (1.4)	2.6 (1.1)
Ramah chert	42.5 (8.9)	30.8 (6.0)	6.9 (3.0)
Biostromatic chert		0.4 (0.1)	
Crystal quartz	28.3 (5.9)	8.3 (1.6)	6.7 (2.9)
Slate	259.8 (54.2)	222.5 (43.2)	139.3 (60.1)
Clastic slate		72.5 (14.1)	
Light gray silicified slate		50.1 (9.7)	

classes that might be considered "maintenance" tools: microblades, scrapers, and utilized flakes. Celts/adzes were also absent at L-7, despite the presence of considerable slate debitage. Lanceolate bifaces ("knives") are lacking from all three loci, with the possible exception of a biface edge fragment from L-5, although they were surface collected elsewhere at the site. The limited excavation areas may contribute to sampling error, but there seem to be functional or depositional differences here.

The overall trend in the excavated and surface collected material is towards a high proportion of harpoon endblades and preforms, relatively few stemmed points or small bipointed bifaces that might be arrow points, relatively few burins, scrapers and bifacial knives. There is a fairly high proportion of burin spalls relative to burins and a low proportion of microblade cores relative to microblades, both of which point to curation processes. The functional significance of this pattern for the site as a whole will be taken up below.

Table 92 displays the frequency of tool raw materials across the excavated and surface collected loci. Dark gray Mugford chert dominates overall. The most notable differences are that tools of light gray Mugford chert are found primarily at L-1, less Ramah chert is present at L-1 and most of the gray silicified slate occurs at L-5. When expected frequencies are considered it is clear that the high proportion of light gray Mugford chert at L-1 is the strongest pattern. Table 93 compares the flake raw material frequencies across the three excavated loci. The clearest patterns are the predominance of dark gray Mugford chert at L-7, light gray Mugford chert at L-1, a slightly higher proportion of gray-speckled chert at L-7, a higher proportion of patinated chert at L-1, a higher proportion of Ramah chert at L-5 and the limitation of clastic slate to L-5. These trends are confirmed when expected frequencies are considered. Slate occurs in high proportions across the board.

If we compare the proportions of tool and flake raw materials there are several examples of inconsistencies between the two. Both L-1 and L-5 seem to be somewhat low in debitage of dark gray Mugford chert compared with their abundance of tools made of this material. Conversely, L-1 and L-7 are completely lacking in tools made of patinated chert, while each has at least a modest number of flakes of the material, and L-7 lacks tools of black chert but contains a few flakes of the material. L-7 also lacks tools made of slate, while it has the highest frequency of slate flakes of the three localities. These inconsistencies point to a technological organization involving asynchronous tool production/retouch and discard; in other words, curation processes and locational staging of reduction. Variations in the quan-

tities of raw materials can result from the differential access of social units to point sources, personal preference, or from households being at different positions on the supply/consumption cycle. Table 94 compares total lithic raw material weights across the loci. Generic slate is clearly dominant in all cases, followed by dark gray Mugford chert, but the other materials vary somewhat in their proportions.

Organizational differences in lithic reduction between the loci might also be seen in flake size distributions. Figure 226 shows the size distributions of Mugford chert flakes (all variants lumped together) at each locality.[13] L-1 and L-5 have similar profiles, but L-7 has a much higher percentage of material in the <10 mm category and lower percentages in the categories from <20 mm and larger. While sample size may be a factor, the L-7 material suggests more intensive secondary/tertiary reduction. In contrast, the flake size profiles for slate are very similar for all three loci (Figure 227). Furthermore, slate flake sizes are significantly larger than Mugford chert flakes, the former with modes ranging from <20 mm to <25 mm, the latter with modes at <10 mm and <15 mm. Thus, not only is slate the most abundant material by weight at all loci, it is also reduced with less secondary/tertiary retouch than is the case for Mugford chert. This tendency may result from larger sized slate raw materials, the role of grinding rather than fine retouch in creating the final working edge, or lack of concern for material conservation.

The ambiguous nature of the structural remains at L-1 and L-5 render comparisons of spatial organization somewhat difficult. Nonetheless, a set of similarities and differences can be formulated. At both L-1 and L-7 the majority of lithic materials were deposited on the seaward ("front") side of the features. At L-7 this might be a consequence of the feature's orientation perpendicular to the beach front, with most activity being cen-

---

[13] Given the lack of screening the smaller size categories may be underrepresented.

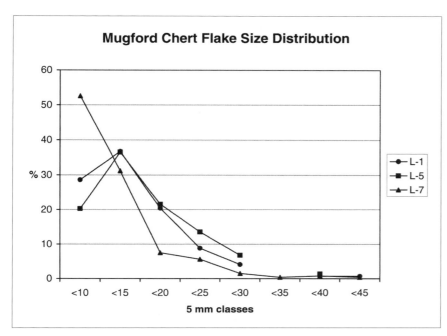

226/ Attu's Point: Mugford chert flake size distribution.

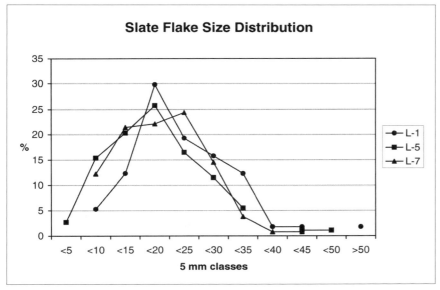

227/ Attu's Point: slate flake size distribution.

both L-1 and L-5, a hearth would be positioned at the terminal end of the feature rather than in the middle. An alternative reading of L-5 as a linear series of three hearths would represent a quite different organization of space than the other two loci.

At all three localities a high proportion of the tools tend to be associated with the axial features (or in the case of L-5 possibly an isolated hearth), although a few implements occur on the flanks of the features. Tool frequencies are too low to identify statistically significant patterns in the spatial distribution of types, but a few observations are pertinent. At L-7 endblades and preforms lay close to the axial structure with a refit leading to a small group on one flank of the feature. At L-1 endblades and preforms were concentrated in a cache-like deposit, although this lay some distance from the hearth. However, if the L-1 feature was oriented parallel to the beach front, then the endblade/preform concentration would lie at

tered on a dwelling entrance. L-1 is problematic since the orientation of the apparent structure is uncertain, possibly oblique to the beach but conceivably parallel. Also, there may be more than one feature represented. One interpretation of the L-5 pattern was of an axial feature oriented parallel to the beach front with a possible "external" activity area positioned along that parallel axis. In the parallel to the beach interpretation of

the foot of the structure, a placement similar to L-7. At both L-1 and L-7 burin spalls were concentrated near the hearth/axial feature areas.

One reason for the limited spatial patterning in tool types, which has also been observed elsewhere in the eastern Arctic (e.g., Dekin 1976; McGhee 1979:52-55; Jensen 1996:157; Mikalsen 2001:86), may simply be the narrow range of types represented at the Attu's

Point localities. The paucity of burins, bifaces and scrapers is probably related to functional or social aspects of site use (see below). Another variable is preferential deposition of tools in the vicinity of axial features after use or rehafting, rather than in the places they were used— an axial feature "attraction effect" (Jensen 1996:156-158).

Jensen's (1996) analysis of the spatial sorting of raw material types at Paleoeskimo sites in east Greenland observed that: "...each raw material must therefore have had its own individual depositional history" (Jensen 1996:156; see also Mikalsen 2001). There are hints of similar patterning at Attu's Point. At both L-1 and L-7 Mugford chert flakes are generally associated with the axial features while slate flakes are concentrated in separate clusters on the flanks, suggesting the reduction activities for these materials were deliberately separated. This does not seem to be the case at L-5, but there it is possible to discern spatial distinctions in the deposition of "normal" versus "clastic" slate debitage. At L-1 there is a clear pattern of crystal quartz tool and flake deposition centered on the hearth/rock feature, but this does not seem to be the case at either L-5 or L-7. The frequencies of other raw materials are either too low or too variable from locus to locus to draw any conclusions. Nonetheless, it does seem that some of the more useful behavioral inferences from Paleoeskimo dwellings will be derived from raw material distributions, combined with detailed refitting studies.

Chronology

The 21 loci at the site occur as three separate linear distributions on two main beach terraces, suggesting that Attu's Point was repeatedly occupied over some length of time. All loci lie between 10-12 m asl., a typical elevation for Pre-Dorset sites in the Nain region. The two excavated localities at 10 m asl. on the lowermost beach terrace, L-1 and L-5, were radiocarbon dated 3750±60 B.P. and 3790±70 B.P., respectively. These assays provide a fairly good maximum date for the low-

est beach level. As noted previously, attempts to acquire reliable radiocarbon dates from the higher beach levels were unsuccessful. Although the Pre-Dorset (and Maritime Archaic) material on the uppermost beach level near 12 m asl. could date ca. 4000-3900 B.P., it is also possible that some of it could date ca. 3700 B.P. or later. Although the linear distribution of the Pre-Dorset occupation on three different levels might indicate three periods with several contemporaneous social units, there is no reason to believe that settlement of the gently sloping beach was so closely bound to the shoreline that the different levels were not used simultaneously. One might even argue that the undisturbed condition of the axial feature at L-7, on the middle beach level at 11 m asl., could indicate that it was the last occupation at the site, post-dating the localities on the 10 m level. Consequently, without further radiocarbon dating, shoreline relations provide little help in developing an internal chronology for the site.

In the absence of sufficient radiocarbon dates we are left with tool typology. Unfortunately, it has proved difficult to seriate Labrador Pre-Dorset sites beyond Early (4000-3600 B.P.), Middle (3500-3000 B.P.) and Late (3000-2800 B.P.) phases (Cox 1978); indeed, it has been particularly difficult to identify sites pertaining to the Middle phase. Cox (n.d.:8) concludes that, typologically speaking, Pre-Dorset was fairly static until 3000 B.P., when a series of changes led to the emergence of Groswater. He suggests that "subtle" differences may signal Middle phase material: concave vs straight based triangular endblades, thicker and less well-flaked triangular endblades, lack of edge serration on scrapers and burins, less edge serration on bifaces, predominantly straight vs tapered stems on bifaces and the presence of very small burins. One might add to this an increase in facial grinding on burins.

It is difficult to identify any substantial evidence for such "later" attributes in the Attu's Point collection. Typologically, the two loci radiocarbon dated ca. 3800-3700 B.P. exhibit typical Early Pre-Dorset features such as straight-based triangular endblades with slight edge serration. The only unusual item is a tiny burin on a microblade at L-5 (Figure 210:i). L-7, however, has a few implements with a possible later stamp. The two burins from this locus were both unusual types made on small flakes, one a very thin bifacially retouched specimen with partial grinding on both faces, the other with striations indicative of proto- or incomplete grinding (Figure 220:h, i). Additionally, a small triangular endblade was slightly ground on both faces and another triangular endblade had slight grinding on one basal corner (Figure 220: a, e). These features are the only support for the suggestion that the undisturbed nature of the axial structure at this locus may indicate a late phase in the site occupation. In conclusion, without further excavation and dating of other loci at the site there are no grounds for supposing that the occupation of Attu's Point extends beyond the 4000-3600 B.P. period.

Structural Comparisons

The well-preserved axial structure at L-7 bears some resemblance to the partially excavated structure at L-9. L-7 is also broadly similar in form to Pre-Dorset features excavated at Dog Bight L-5, east of Nain (Fitzhugh 1976a:130-133; Cox 1978:101). The latter site contained three structures, two of which consisted of well defined axial features measuring 3 m by 1 m in size, with central box-hearths constructed of thick rocks and partial rings of tent anchor rocks. One of these structures had a number of small thermoliths concentrated within the bounds of the axial feature, although there were few within the box-hearth itself (Fitzhugh 1976a:133). A third structure, possibly disturbed, had an axial feature 2 by 1 m in size. The main difference between these structures and L-7 is the total lack of perimeter anchor rocks at L-7. Looking further afield, L-7 bears a striking resemblance to an axial structure at Tuapagssuit (64V1-I,10) near Nuuk, west Greenland (Gulløv 1983:51; Gulløv and Kapel 1988:47). Otherwise, L-7 clearly lies within the broad tradition of Paleoeskimo

axial features with box-hearths and thermoliths that is well documented from Independence I and Saqqaq contexts (e.g., Grønnow and Jensen 2003; Grønnow and Meldgaard 1991; Knuth 1967; Kramer 1996; McGhee 1979; Mikalsen 2001; Møbjerg 1998, 1999; Olsen 1998; Schlederman 1990).

The features at L-1 and L-5 are more difficult to evaluate given the likelihood of disturbance, but in both cases a hearth is positioned at the terminal end of a rock alignment rather than in the middle. Whether this signals a functional difference from the more standard axial model at L-7 or individual choice in hearth placement cannot be determined from the present data. It is also conceivable that the spatial pattern at L-5 should not be interpreted within the expectations of the axial model, but instead as a linear series of hearths such as at Port Manvers Run-1 (Chapter 12). Not only might a linear hearth arrangement signal a functional difference from axial features, it could also be associated with different socio-spatial practices.

Functional Variability

The term functional variability denotes activity-related variability attributable to resource extraction practices, the latter being subject to seasonal differences. As such, functional variability at Attu's Point is considered along two dimensions: dwelling structures and lithic assemblages.

Arctic archaeologists have increasingly recognized formal variability in Early Paleoeskimo structures, some of which is probably seasonal in nature. Yet there are no solid criteria for identifying structures of different seasonality. The most common assumption is that cold weather structures were of more substantial construction and should exhibit considerable attention to heating facilities, resulting in emphasis on the hearth/axial feature arrangement and possibly larger accumulations of charcoal and fire-cracked rock (e.g., Cox 1978:98; Knuth 1967:45-51; Maxwell 1985:96-98; Odgaard 2003; Olsen 1998:111-116; Renouf

1993:191-197). It is also expected that there may be larger accumulations of tools than at warm-weather sites, and that these accumulations will occur primarily inside the structures, whereas warm-weather dwellings may be associated with external activity areas.

On the other hand, Maxwell (1985:98) suggested that sites lacking structural remains may be traces of snow house camps. Ramsden and Murray (1995) provide tentative support for this from faunal associations that suggest "substantial" structures represent warm weather tent structures, while features consisting only of small vegetation patches with rocks indicate snow-walled winter dwellings. They also note, however, that structural variability can be expected in "transitional" seasons with variable weather and variable demands on construction techniques (Ramsden and Murray 1995:115-116). Although the safest conclusion to draw is that correlating structures and seasonality is highly problematic in the absence of faunal remains, it is by no means the case that the presence of faunal material will be decisive for interpretation. Grønnow and Jensen (2003: 337) note significant contradictions between faunal data and structural and lithic evidence from Independence I sites in northernmost Greenland.

None of the excavated localities at Attu's Point exhibit structural remains that might be considered substantial constructions. There is little besides a hearth and the remains of a small axial feature or rock alignment. None of the features display a clear perimeter of anchor rocks. L-7 is unusual in its degree of preservation; its classic box-hearth illustrates the use of thermoliths, but there was minimal accumulation of fire-cracked rock and very few tools. At L-5 there were few tools or flakes associated with the possible axial feature, but larger quantities of lithics were found a short distance away in a context that could be interpreted either as a disturbed structure or as an external dump/activity area.

The lack of perimeter rocks might be explained either by warm season use of wooden pegs to hold down tent skins or cold season use of snow. The lack of lithic accumulation has dubious relevance to the seasonality issue, since it is linked to longevity of occupation, group size and staging behavior in technological organization. The location of the Attu's Point features on beaches highly exposed to westerly winds is advantageous for mitigating insect torment during warmer seasons, but disadvantageous for cold seasons. In sum, the structural information is, by itself, of little value for the interpretation of site seasonality.

As far as lithic assemblage variability is concerned, given the lack of fully published Pre-Dorset collections from other parts of Labrador it is difficult to provide a concrete assessment of how the Attu's Point assemblage fits into the overall range of functional variation in Pre-Dorset material. The few existing accounts either provide no information on tool frequencies or lump together material from what are probably different loci, such that intra-site variation is masked (Cox 1977, n.d.; Fitzhugh 1976; Tuck 1976). Inter-site comparisons are of limited value without control over intra-site variation. That said, Attu's Point seems to exhibit a lower proportion of burins and perhaps scrapers than elsewhere. Lanceolate bifaces, probably hafted as knives (Grønnow 1994:206-207), are absent from the excavated loci (except for a possible fragment at L-5), although two were surface collected. There is a paucity of small stemmed or bipointed bifaces, which elsewhere have been identified as arrow points (Grønnow 1994:224; Grønnow and Meldgaard 1991:135), presumably for hunting terrestrial mammals.

On the other hand, Attu's Point exhibits a fairly high proportion of triangular endblades, which were used as harpoon tips. Consequently, the excavated assemblages give the impression of being weighted towards "procurement" rather than "maintenance" activities and possibly towards the exploitation of seals rather than land mammals. This contrasts with the situation further north at Okak, where inner bay sites have relatively few triangular endblades, which Cox (1978:102) interprets as indicating summer occupation with less emphasis on sea mammal hunting. However, endblade equipped harpoons could also be used for hunting caribou, which seems likely at Pre-Dorset inland sites from the Barrenlands of the Northwest Territories (B. Gordon 1996:155-159). Finally, the presence of three slate adzes and two celt/adze preforms indicates that procurement and processing of wood products, and/or butchering of frozen meat, may have been an important activity at this inner bay settlement.

The emphasis in the foregoing was on tool assemblages reflecting different activities. A related dimension is the articulation of activities with social group composition.

Some of the observed variation in assemblages could be related to differences in the gender composition of the social units responsible for each occupation. For example, the high proportion of endblades and lack of maintenance tools (e.g., L-7) might indicate a predominantly male hunting party. On the other hand, there are no compelling grounds to assume strongly gender-specific tools, and the absence of such tools would not necessarily imply the absence of a gender.

The quantity of Mugford cherts used at Attu's Point is fairly typical of Labrador Pre-Dorset. Black chert, on the other hand, seems unusually low in frequency for the Nain region. The high frequency of slate debitage also seems unusual for the Nain area, but a geographically comparable site from deep within the inner bay zone of the Okak region, Sipukat Bay-1 (HjCn-1), also has a high frequency of celts/adzes (n=6) and slate is the dominant raw material (Cox 1977:230-237).[14] The use of large quantities of slate for celts/adzes in the inner bay zones of Nain and Okak presumably is related to wood procurement and processing in forested areas. The quantity of Ramah

chert found at Attu's Point appears to be somewhat greater than that noted at other Pre-Dorset sites in the Port Manvers Run area, but it is well below that reported for sites closer to the Ramah chert sources, such as Tuck's (1975:135) localities at Saglek Bay (5.4-37.2% of the tools). It is possible that Pre-Dorset people at Attu's Point procured some of their Ramah chert from their Maritime Archaic neighbours in the Nain region, or that they scavenged chert from abandoned Maritime Archaic sites such as Attu's Bight (see Chapter 12).

These superficial observations on functional variation in Pre-Dorset lithic assemblages underline the importance of more detailed studies of Pre-Dorset technological organization. More information is needed concerning how Pre-Dorset lithic assemblages were formed and how variability relates to seasonal and situational factors as well as raw material availability.

CONCLUSIONS

Attu's Point was used repeatedly for short seasonal occupations, presumably over a few hundred years. These occupations were directed towards a relatively limited range of functions and in some cases might have involved social units of restricted composition. But despite the ephemeral nature of individual loci, the repeated use of the site suggests it played a significant role in the regional settlement pattern, serving as a seasonal "central place." Few other Pre-Dorset sites in the Nain area exhibit such repetitive use.

The functional signature of the Attu's Point lithic assemblage points to two main activities: sea mammal hunting and wood procurement and processing. Contemporary fauna availability patterns suggest it is most likely Attu's Point was occupied either in the early spring or the fall. At both these times a variety of seal species (but especially harps) may be plentiful in Webb Bay and could have been harpooned close to the site as they moved through the narrow passage between Igloo

---

14 Sipukat Bay-1 was surface collected for tools, so no quantitative information on debitage frequencies is available.

Island and the mainland (Figure 163). Today the passage sometimes may not freeze over until February; if this was the case in the past, open water sealing might have been possible during the early winter. Caribou have wintering areas in the mountains to the north and west of Webb Bay (Brice-Bennett 1977:158-159), but in some years herds may winter on the coast, including in the valleys of neighboring South Aulatsivik Island. Their early spring and early winter movements over the ice between the mainland and South Aulatsivik Island[15] might be ideal periods to intercept major herd concentrations. However, the low frequency of stemmed points and lanceolate bifaces could indicate this was not a major activity at Attu's Point.

Our own experience in early-middle July was that relatively little game is available at that time, or at least it is difficult to find. A shift to coastal settlements would be more advantageous during this period when seals, fish and sea birds are concentrated in the outer island fringe. The situation changes in late summer and early fall when char and salmon re-enter the inner bays, geese and ducks are plentiful and black bears come down to the shores and stream mouths. Later in the fall harp seals move through Port Manvers Run. Consequently, late summer and fall might provide a mix of resources to draw Pre-Dorset people from the outer coast. Additionally, given the prominence of slate tools and debitage at Attu's Point, it is likely that fall occupations were used to stock up on needed wood supplies and to prepare wooden implements for the winter, while spring occupations could have replenished supplies exhausted during the winter. How this interpretation of Attu's Point fits into the broader view of Pre-Dorset settlement patterns in the Nain area and Labrador as a whole is taken up in Chapter 14.

A nefarious crew at Immilikulik Island. Left to right: Eric Loring, Dosia Laeyendecker, Susan Rowley, Ben Fitzhugh, Joshua Fitzhugh. (Photo: W. Fitzhugh 1985)

[15] Such a situation was observed in late April 1994, with westward moving animals crossing the ice over the southern entrance to Port Manvers Run near Double Island Cove.

CHAPTER 13

The Structuration of Maritime Archaic/Pre-Dorset Social Boundaries in Labrador[16]

14

One of the recurring themes in Labrador prehistory and history has been the shifting social boundaries between Inuit/Pre-Inuit and Innu/Pre-Innu peoples (e.g., Fitzhugh 1972, 1977, 1987; Taylor 1979).With that in mind, it is now time to draw together several threads that were developed in the previous two chapters and address the question of social boundary relations between the Maritime Archaic and Pre-Dorset peoples. Evidence accumulated since the early 1970s demonstrates that these two cultures overlapped in time between 4000-3500 B.P., corresponding to 2500-1800 BC (calibrated). Despite this lengthy period of coexistence, the archaeological assemblages of the two cultures exhibit virtually no unambiguous indications of interaction.

Up to this point, the Maritime Archaic/Pre-Dorset boundary problem has been discussed largely as a culture-historical problem, using the traditional concepts of contact situations with a cultural-ecology overlay. This has been useful, certainly, but the importance of this unique situation for understanding the developmental trajectories of each culture necessitates linking the specific historical context to broader theoretical issues. This chapter considers frameworks for doing so, although some new data will also be presented. These frameworks are drawn from different paradigmatic sources, one emphasizing ecological causality, the other focusing on culturally constructed landscapes. Crudely put, they correspond to the theoretical boxes termed, respectively, processual and post-processual archaeology. The boundaries constructed around these viewpoints originate from major ontological differences, but their architecture is also derived partly from the polemics of territorial defense within theoretical identity politics. Although the pragmatic approach is to regard the opposed arguments as representing alternative entry points to a common problem and work towards some form of integration, it is difficult to reconcile conceptual structures emanating from divergent ontological first principles. Consequently, one function of this chapter is to reflect upon the dilemma of working with the conceptual tensions found at the boundaries between different archaeologies. When all is said and done, it is hoped that the chapter can show how a specific problem in Subarctic culture-history can, in a modest way, illuminate central issues in archaeological knowledge construction.

CULTURE-HISTORICAL BACKGROUND

The potential for interaction between the Maritime Archaic and Pre-Dorset in Labrador was first identified during James Tuck's 1969-1971 research at Saglek Bay (Tuck 1975, 1976). Given virtually contemporaneous radiocarbon dates for the cultures from superimposed strata at Rose Island Site Q, Tuck (1975:195-

[16] A shorter preliminary version of this chapter was published in Hood (2000).

196) speculated about possible cultural transfers: toggling harpoons from the Maritime Archaic to the Pre-Dorset and the bow and arrow from the Pre-Dorset to the Maritime Archaic, as suggested by the initial appearance of small projectile points in the Late Maritime Archaic. More recent research indicates these proposals are problematic. Toggling harpoons have been found in early Saqqaq contexts such as Qeqertassusuk, Greenland (Grønnow 1994) and small "flake points" have been found in Maritime Archaic sites dated as early as ca. 6000-5500 B.P. (e.g., Nukasusutok-5), although these need not indicate the presence of bows and arrows.

During the 1970s and 1980s, William Fitzhugh and his colleagues' fieldwork on the north coast of Labrador expanded the data base for both cultures and radiocarbon dates confirmed the overlap of the Late Maritime Archaic Rattlers Bight Phase and Early Pre-Dorset between 3900-3500 B.P. (Cox 1978, 1988; Fitzhugh 1975, 1976, 1978, 1980, 1984; Thomson 1982, 1983, 1985). Although the two cultures sometimes occupied the same or nearby sites, little indication of contact was seen in their tool assemblages. Fitzhugh (1978:91, 1984:22) referred to a possible Maritime Archaic copy of a Pre-Dorset burin, Cox (1977:235) pointed to a Maritime Archaic gouge reworked by the Pre-Dorset and the presence of a Maritime Archaic sandstone plummet at a Pre-Dorset site (Cox 1988:3), and Chapter 13 in the present volume reported a Late Maritime Archaic stemmed point and possible biface on the upper terrace of the Attu's Point Pre-Dorset site. Each culture used a distinct set of lithic raw materials. The Maritime Archaic focussed almost exclusively on translucent Ramah chert for their flaked stone tools; this had to be procured from the Ramah Bay region at the northernmost periphery of the Maritime Archaic world (Gramly 1978; Lazenby 1980). The Pre-Dorset used a varied set of colored cherts, most of which were obtained in the Cape Mugford area, north of Okak (Gramly 1978; Lazenby 1980), although varying amounts of Ramah chert also appear

in their assemblages. The organization of their lithic technologies was therefore anchored at different points in the landscape.

Much of the 1980s' fieldwork focussed on interpreting Maritime Archaic social organization and community structure. Late Maritime Archaic people used longhouse structures— presumably interconnected tent dwellings— ranging in size from 15 to 100 m long. The individual segments of the longhouses were interpreted as the floor spaces of individual families, which suggested co-residential group sizes ranging from 50 to 100 people. The northern Labrador site of Nulliak Cove, situated between Hebron and Saglek Bay, contained up to 27 longhouses and was interpreted as a short-term seasonal staging camp for accessing the Ramah chert sources, 50 km to the north (Fitzhugh 1980, 1984, 1985a,b). Maritime Archaic longhouse community organization, combined with mortuary ceremonialism and exchange systems, suggested some degree of social elaboration or "complexity" (Fitzhugh 1981, 1984; Hood 1993, 1995).

In contrast, Pre-Dorset usually maintained small group sizes of perhaps one to three co-residential families housed in independent tent dwellings. There are, however, a number of Pre-Dorset sites with multiple occupation locales indicating either seasonal aggregation or regular re-occupation. In contrast to the Maritime Archaic, Pre-Dorset exhibits no evidence for social "complexity," at least if one considers the most frequently used indicator variables.

The spatial distribution of Maritime Archaic and Pre-Dorset sites from Nain to the Torngat Mountains suggested that the two cultures partitioned their settlement space. Fitzhugh (1984:21-23) proposed an "enclave model" that consisted of a Maritime Archaic "core area" along the central coast south of Nain and a Pre-Dorset core area in the northern Torngat mountains and the Nain-Okak regions. The Pre-Dorset core areas encompassed both the sources of their preferred cherts near Cape Mugford as well as the Ramah chert sources preferred by the Maritime Archaic (Figure

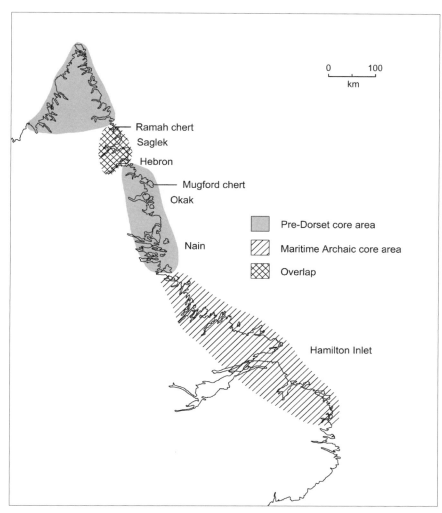

228/ *Distribution of Late Maritime Archaic and Pre-Dorset settlement in Labrador: the macro-territorial model (after Fitzhugh 1984).*

northern Labrador in order to acquire Ramah chert, the stress of maintaining a long distance chert delivery system, and territorial behavior in the overlap zone, may all have contributed to the cultural elaboration seen during the Rattlers Bight Phase (Fitzhugh 1984:23-24). Ultimately, however, these features may have overloaded Maritime Archaic organizational capacities and contributed to the apparent disappearance of the culture as a recognizable entity in the archaeological record after 3500 B.P. (Hood 1993:179). Although the situation is usually seen from the perspective of the Maritime Archaic (given fascination with the puzzling disappearance of "complexity"), Pre-Dorset was also affected by the inter-cultural dynamic. The visibility of Pre-Dorset sites also diminishes markedly after 3500 B.P., although to some extent this might be attributable to few radiocarbon dates and limited typological change that masks the presence of sites post-dating 3500 B.P. (Cox 1988).

With this basic culture-historical framework in mind we can consider the issues involved in theorizing Maritime Archaic/Pre-Dorset social boundary relations using Fitzhugh's (1984) preliminary model as a point of departure. On the one hand, the model postulates cultural macro-territoriality: the Maritime Archaic dominating the central coast, Pre-Dorset the Torngats and the Nain-Okak regions. On the other hand, the model also postulates micro-territoriality occurring within a zone of seasonal overlap (Hebron-Ramah) in which the

228). The Hebron-Saglek area was an overlap zone since it contained Maritime Archaic seasonal staging camps for accessing the Ramah chert sources. Fitzhugh (1984:21-23) identified a local Maritime Archaic enclave at Nulliak Cove, situated between Hebron and Saglek, and a local Pre-Dorset enclave at Harp Isthmus on the south side of the entrance to Hebron Fjord. In later years, the find of a substantial Late Maritime Archaic Rattlers Bight Phase site at Attu's Bight in the Nain region (see Chapter 12) led Fitzhugh (1986:57) to suggest the enclave model might have to be modified.

One implication of the enclave model is that the Maritime Archaic need to maintain seasonal bases in

Maritime Archaic maintained "enclaves," staging camps for Ramah chert acquisition expeditions. While useful as an initial discussion, this image is somewhat static, implying a degree of boundary equilibrium over several centuries. Additionally, territoriality is a complex concept that has often been formulated in ecological terms, but which has intertwined ecological and social components that need to be drawn out. The following pages will attempt gradually to re-work this preliminary image into something potentially more dynamic.

One issue that needs to be addressed is whether this "contact" relationship might be formulated in terms of ethnicity. Over 30 years later, it is still the case that Barth's (1969) conceptualization of ethnicity remains fundamental. Summarized briefly, it postulates that ethnicity is a self-ascribed category and a form of social organization used to structure interaction. Ethnicity arises through engagement rather than isolation, such that "...boundaries persist despite a flow of personnel across them" (Barth 1969:9). Inter-ethnic relations are ordered by rules that define potential roles and statuses and boundaries are signaled by a selected range of features, behaviors or values that agents regard as significant. Fundamental as this definition may be, the conceptualization is inconvenient for prehistoric archaeologists in that self-ascription and the persistence of boundaries despite social mobility render recognition of ethnic boundary processes highly problematic in the absence of supplemental textual information. Variations in material culture can be related to the formation of social identity groups at different scales (e.g., clans, gender, regional bands, dialect groups, etc.) and it is difficult to untangle the various threads in archaeological situations. For example, contrasts between the northern and southern branch Maritime Archaic, as exemplified by the intrusive Black Island Complex (4500-4100 B.P.) at Hamilton Inlet (Fitzhugh 1975), suggest the existence of different social identity groups in southern and central Labrador prior to the Pre-Dorset colonization, but to what extent can those differences be viewed as "ethnic"? Most archaeologists would agree that the material culture and behavioral differences between the Pre-Dorset and the Maritime Archaic are so marked that they were distinct social identity groups, but it is debatable whether understanding of their interaction can be enhanced by invoking ethnicity theory. In any event, one could say that pronounced ethnic differences may not have existed in northern Labrador prior to the Pre-Dorset colonization ca. 4000 B.P.. Ethnicity only became an emergent relation in a culture contact situation structured by marked differences in language and behavior, and potentially competitive land-use relations.

Whether or not ethnicity concepts are involved, the interaction situation must be understood in terms of two main dimensions. First, there must be ecological parameters focusing on the energetics of boundary maintenance. Population interaction models from evolutionary ecology may direct us towards alternative modes of resource partitioning with different outcomes for inter-cultural relations. Second, there must be social parameters involving the different organizational and cultural practices used by the two societies to structure boundary maintenance strategies. Overall, how did the cultural construction and use of the landscape articulate with these two dimensions of human action? Here we have a set of seemingly incompatible or incongruent themes— one ecological and materialist, the other social and constructionist— that network themselves around a common problem. How do we go about constructing interpretive narratives or theory in this or similar situations? The next section lays out some of the issues that draw our local problem into the heart of recent debates in archaeological theory.

WORKING AT THEORETICAL BOUNDARIES: "LANDSCAPE" AS A PLATFORM FOR DIALOGUE?

After over 15 years of often heated debate and mutual dismissal tactics between what we have come to call processual and post-processual archaeologies, a series of statements have appeared that call for some degree of convergence, reconciliation, or *modus vivendi*. Schiffer (2000) for example, advocates "building bridges" between different conceptual structures. Following Galison (1996), Wylie (2000) refers to inter-field "trading zones." Hodder (2001) and Preucel and Hodder (1996) argue for a multi-perspectival pluralism, while Schiffer (2000) sees this as resulting in potentially dangerous fragmentation and eclecticism. Despite the proliferation of various archaeological sects since the 1980s and the groping towards some fusion of interpretive horizons, much of the discipline's discourse still seems to migrate towards poles defined by "processual" or "post-processual," which have now become firmly entrenched categories of research history as well as axes of social organization within archaeology.

Tendencies towards polarization have been aided and abetted by clinging to resistant first principles that are played out as a series of explicit or implicit conceptual dualisms which, when assembled, constitute two competing ontologies of archaeology. One ontology privileges the view of humans as biological beings and is founded on adaptation as its central metaphor, from which a series of more specific causal theories is derived. The other ontology privileges the view of humans as thoroughly cultural beings, suspended in webs of significance they themselves have constructed. Language is the dominant metaphor, from which subsidiary interpretive theories of meaning are drawn. Thus, the Nature/Culture opposition is the *éminence gris* lurking behind much of the debate.

Attempts to move beyond the sterile processual/ post-processual debates require working at overcoming the troublesome Nature/Culture dualism. A recent review article by Anschuetz et al. (2001), who write from an American "liberal processual" perspective, suggests that a "landscape paradigm" can bridge the great divide between processual and post-processual views. The authors are careful to define this approach as a "methodological paradigm": a set of tools that can be used in solving common puzzles (as *per* Masterman 1970:70), thereby leading to accommodation or integration between different theoretical frameworks (Anschuetz et al. 2001:160-164, 191). Besides the residual odor of "unified science" views (cf., Wylie 2000), which are highly problematic, this "integrative" methodological approach attempts to insulate practical action from ontological issues and deliberately skirts the difficulties of bridging radically different conceptual structures. Research in cognitive history of science and on conceptual change in general suggests these issues cannot be ducked so easily (e.g., Chi 1992; Giere 1994; Kuhn 2000; Latour 1993; Nersessian and Andersen 1997; Thagard 1992).

Writing from a different perspective, Tilley's (1994) landscape phenomenology has also argued for overcoming the Nature/Culture opposition. It is difficult to quarrel with Tilley's statement that: "...the relationship between people and it [landscape] is a constant dialectic and process of structuration: the landscape is both medium *for* and outcome *of* action and previous histories of action. Landscapes are experienced in practice, in life activities" (Tilley 1994:23). But Tilley's landscape phenomenology is positioned in strategic opposition to adaptationism, so he takes a thoroughly constructionist view of landscape structuration: "Landscape is a signifying system through which the social is reproduced and transformed, explored and structured — process organized. Landscape, above all, represents a means of conceptual ordering that stresses relations" (Tilley 1994:34). With Tilley it is the meaningful and symbolic that is privileged, with practice and life activities exemplified by Australian hunter-gatherers moving through a landscape of sacred places encoded by Dreamtime mythology, but completely without reference to practices and environmental knowledge that facilitate subsistence. To adapt a phrase from Tim Ingold, Tilley treats Nature primarily as "...raw material for imaginative acts of world-making" (Ingold 1996:150). The landscape is so good to think we don't need to worry about eating.

Ingold's (1996:150) critique of constructionist thinking argues that constructionism reinforces rather than challenges the ecological determinist models because its logic creates separate domains in which such models can be used. With a slice of the intellectual knife, two conceptual planes are created: (1) Nature, a space inhabited by biological organisms (animals) that forage to extract resources, and (2) Society, consisting of persons (thinking subjects) living in a culturally constructed landscape and engaged in the production and distribution of resources (Ingold 1996:127, 149). Ingold rejects the cultural constructionist argument that social relations serve as a model for ecological relations because it requires a disembedding of practical engagement with the environment from the social relations that constitute humans as social actors, a separation of Mind from World, Nature from Society, Organism from Person and Biological relations from Social relations (Ingold 1996:126-128). Ingold suggests hunter-gatherers do not make such conceptual separations; instead, they have similar kinds of relations with both the human and non-human constituents of the environment. In hunter-gatherer worlds, animals can be persons and humans have social relations both with other humans and with animals, such that harvesting animal resources is not just a technical relation (Ingold 1996:127-131). Consequently, landscapes are not simply "socially constructed" by imposing a conceptual schema over Nature. Movement through the landscape involves engagement and learning, discovery rather than imposition of a predefined mental grid; practice in the environment constitutes persons and persons constitute their environments (Ingold 1996:138-146). There is no radical break between ecological and social relations and "environments are constituted in life, not just in thought, and it is only because we live in an environment that we can think at all" (Ingold 1996:150-151).

While Ingold's argument is attractive, it is far from clear how such ontological reflection can be translated into research practice. The analysis of concrete archaeological/anthropological problems may be difficult without some sort of fundamental Nature/Culture conceptual categorizations (Ellen 1996:29-30). Analytical arguments, as opposed to abstract ontological reflections, require a choice of entry points, each of which commit the entrant to navigate certain directions along conceptual networks rather than others. The alternative is eclectic incoherence or a discussion conducted at such a high level of abstraction that it would lose the very connection with human practice that Ingold views as the key issue. One of the hallmarks of "paradigm" shifts is the emergence of new concepts, changes in the meaning of old concepts and the shifting of old concepts into new systems of relations, sometimes by analogical extension, which involves major changes in lexical systems and results in incommensurability problems (e.g., Chi 1992; Kuhn 2000; Nersessian and Andersen 1997; Thagard 1992). For Ingold's (2000) perspective to become a viable alternative research program it is necessary to build up a new conceptual system that embeds his terms— such as "enskillment," "affordances" and "taskscapes"— within a semantic network of greater depth and precision that includes archaeologically relevant categories. Gamble (1999) has made a valiant effort in that direction, but the conceptual affordances for steering concrete research problems remain very limited.

All things considered, during the current period of stalemate between competing ontologies of archaeology there is something to be said for Anschuetz et al.'s (2001) advocacy of a landscape perspective. Although their view of landscape as an integrative methodological paradigm should be rejected, there is no reason why "landscape" cannot serve as a platform for dialogue, a point of departure for debating the problems and commitments that separate contemporary archaeologies.

PARTIAL READINGS: NAVIGATING THE BOUNDARIES

...tension in theories, as in politics, is a creative force...we may see theories...as articulated within an intertextual field wherein they derive much of their meaning from what they oppose and thus, in a sense, confirm the importance of what they deny...Let us call this dissonance, facetiously, 'hypertension'... (Edwards 1994:261-262).

If there are incommensurable frameworks or conceptual schemes, as Collingwood, Kuhn and others affirm, there could be no neutral overarching standards in virtue of which a rational adjudication between them could be made. Yet the mutual non-translatability of such schemes does not prohibit one from pursuing each in turn— much as a bilingual uses one language and then another— all the while constrained by such practical matters as the seemingly obvious requirement that one must speak one language at a time or by the different aims inherent in each framework (Harré and Krausz 1996:217).

Arguments that today's competing archaeologies are irrevocably incommensurate are exaggerated and serve mostly as a boundary maintenance strategy in theoretical identity politics. Despite significant conceptual differences, competing "paradigms" must overlap to some extent, otherwise discussion between their respective proponents would be impossible (Bernstein 1983:85-93). Paradigms may be compared in various ways by moving back and forth between them in order to draw out elements of overlap and contrast (Bernstein 1983:86, 90); Wylie (1989) uses C.S. Pierce's "cables and tacking" metaphor to characterize these interpretive strategies at the boundaries of different frameworks. Working at these points of contact and contrast may help expose the processes through which intellectual boundaries are constructed. The oppositional tone between processual and post-processual archaeologies was understandable and perhaps inevitable, but such "hypertensional" rhetoric may serve as a cloaking device, disguising the process whereby each side "...derive[s] much of their meaning from what they oppose and thus, in a sense, confirm the importance of what they deny" (Edwards 1994:261). Also cloaked is how these conceptual boxes create artificial closures around what are best described (metaphorically) as idea *networks*. Such polemical closures are ironic for post-processualists who otherwise write of *intertextuality;* they ignore the consequences of their own constructionism.

Intertextuality notwithstanding, navigating conceptual structures cannot be a random walk through a network. Choices of entry point are required and these choices have consequences for the direction of the entrants' navigation route. One cognitive-philosophical approach sees knowledge as structured in type hierarchies, with different type hierarchies implying different ontologies about how the world is organized (e.g., different type hierarchies for the adaptationist vs cultural constructionist ontologies). Since concepts at lower portions of a hierarchy inherit properties from supertypes positioned higher in the hierarchy, activating concepts at any level of the hierarchy implicitly downloads other properties of the ontological system (Aronson et al. 1995:27-54). This is not to say that such structures are governed by rigid necessity; if they are to function in practice and develop further they must be marked by an "open texture" that permits some flexibility in ordering (Harré 2002:264). But it does suggest that working at the boundaries of ontologies and attempting to develop new "conceptual blends" (Fauconnier and Turner 2002) cannot escape the dilemma of conceptual inheritance that is an automatic consequence of choosing a starting position.

Considering the multitude of problems attendant with attempts to build new theory at the boundaries between current archaeological ontologies, the following discussion of theoretical models is presented in two parts: ecological space and culturally constructed social and ideological landscapes. Selected aspects of these models are used to frame the subsequent culture-historical narratives. Although this mode of presentation remains trapped in the Nature/Culture dualism, each model and narrative is considered a partial reading, using one language at a time, launched from entry points that activate different conceptual domains relevant to human practices in the landscape.

ECOLOGICAL SPACE

From the perspective of the humans as adaptive beings ontology, the landscape is an ecological space with varying distributions of resources from which foragers must make rational selections in order to reproduce or meet social obligations. Interaction between populations of organisms inhabiting the same ecological community and engaged in foraging for similar resources (niche overlap) leads ecologists towards competition theory. Two main types of competition have been identified: exploitation and interference competition. In exploitation competition, foraging by one organism reduces the quantity of a resource needed by another organism. In interference competition, one organism reduces the ability of another to make use of a common resource, through mechanisms such as territoriality (Carothers and Jaksić 1984; Keddy 1989). Although the first type is the most traditional view of competition, the second has become increasingly significant to researchers and seems more relevant for discussing human practice in the environment, so interference competition will be the focus here. Another approach to niche overlap— mutualism— has

been less theorized in ecology (perhaps for ideological reasons,[17] Keddy 1989), but may have considerable relevance for human practice (Spielmann 1986). Competition theory has been marked by the extensive use of mathematical models. Most of these are concerned with the relationship between resource availability and population dynamics in situations of niche overlap. The following discussion will not be concerned with this quantitative dimension and population dynamics will play little role in the discussion. Much of the focus will be on spatial dynamics, since this has the most visible archaeological consequences.

The central element in competitive or mutual relations concerns how organisms *partition* resources and habitats. Partitioning can be accomplished by scheduling the use of foraging sites at different points in time, by dispersing foraging sites in space, or by shifts in foraging behavior towards specialization on different resources. Preventing temporal overlap at foraging sites can minimize the potential for direct conflict in interference competition, such as fighting over the best fishing or sealing locations, stealing food etc. Temporal partitioning of the same foraging sites may be accomplished by the potential competitors selecting resource types that are available at different times, or by exploiting continually renewing resources at different times. An effective temporal partitioning of activity may not require or result in the partitioning of other variables, such as habitat space or particular food resources (Carothers and Jaksić 1984:405-406). Some highly desirable resources, however, may be available only for short time frames (e.g., seasonally), decreasing the likelihood that temporal partitioning would be an effective means of limiting competition.

Partitioning of space is perhaps the most frequent means of preventing direct competition. In patchy

---

[17] "Competition" is a category in need of deconstruction. Its conceptual privileging relative to other relational possibilities— such as mutualism— may reflect its metaphorical role in the intertextual relations between biological and sociopolitical discourse (Keddy 1989:160-162). Keene (1983) discusses the sociopolitical baggage of evolutionary ecology in archaeology.

CHAPTER 14

environments where resources are dispersed, dispersal of foraging sites in space minimizes competition. Of course, patches may differ markedly in their quality of resources such that competition may arise from foraging decisions to prioritize high quality patches. The likelihood of competition increases if such resources are also temporally limited in availability. For example, seasonally migrating harp seals have, in a general sense, a patchy distribution. But they may have higher accessibility to human foragers in certain predictable places, such as narrow inlets and passages that restrict and funnel herd movements. Such places may become the focus of competition.

One of the central (and traditional) issues in spatial partitioning is territoriality. As humans use such a wide range of interaction mechanisms it is very simplistic to categorize behavior as either territorial or non-territorial (Dyson-Hudson and Smith 1978). One might say there is a continuum of territorial behaviour from highly territorial competitive exclusion, to cooperative interaction as non-territorial behaviour. Dyson-Hudson and Smith (1978) regard territoriality as a response to interaction situations in which resources are dense and predictable. The articulation of these two properties promote territoriality by setting conditions of economic defendability. Kelly's (1995) discussion of territoriality among foragers builds largely upon their observations. Although he gives lengthy consideration to the social mechanisms involved a group's extending permission to others to use their territories (Kelly 1995:181-189), his arguments turn on the centrality of resources and demography, seen in terms of cost-benefit analysis: "...for any given case we should be able to translate the interplay between environmental and population variables into their significance in terms of intragroup variance and intergroup correlation, and from these predict the specific form of

land tenure" (Kelly 1994:201). Although Kelly is sensitive to the social mechanisms involved in regulating access to the landscape, his view of "land tenure" is premised on a reductionist attempt to predict social relations from ecological relations (Ingold [1986:130-133] provides an alternative conceptualization of these terms, see below). It should be noted, however, that most of Kelly's ethnographic examples pertain to boundary processes between social units *within* single ethnic/linguistic units, rather than across such units.

To this point the discussion has focused on the properties of available resources, but variations in the behavioral properties of the competitors must also be considered. Competitors may exhibit varying technological capacities for resource extraction or differences in organizational characteristics, such as labor mobilization or social differentiation. These abilities may change over time, resulting in either shifts of competitive advantages/disadvantages, or the development of coexistence. In the ecological literature, the relative degree of specialization/generalization in resource exploitation (niche breadth) is a frequently used dimension of variation.[18] In some situations both competitors may specialize, thereby minimizing niche overlap and potential competition. If two populations specialize on different resources we might expect the development of relatively weak territoriality, or perhaps even reciprocal resource exchange in a mutualistic relation between the two populations (cf., Spielmann 1986). In other situations one competitor may shift to more generalist strategies, exploiting the resource patches not used by the specialist. Depending on the degree of niche overlap, this could be an unstable coexistence marked by some degree of territoriality. The specialists might be expected to invest in defending their resources since they have less alternative resource flexibility than generalists and

---

[18] How such a distinction could actually be measured empirically among human foragers is a serious problem, particularly in archaeological cases for which we lack zooarchaeological data, and draw subsistence inferences primarily from site location, such as in the Pre-Dorset/Maritime Archaic context.

thus much to lose. The generalists would be unlikely to incur defence costs for gaining only a small increase in resource variety unless the niche overlap with the specialist included resources that were seasonally critical for the generalist. In all these cases, as long as the interaction effects are fairly equal for both parties, the competition could be termed symmetric (Keddy 1989:15-16).

But an inability to shift niche breadth or foraging characteristics may militate against coexistence, leading to exclusion of one of the competitors. Marked organizational differences between populations raise the possibility of competitive dominance, or asymmetric competition (Keddy 1989:16). Asymmetric relations might involve avoidance strategies on the part of subordinate populations, such as: a) refuging behavior, with movement to poorer quality habitats or favored retreat sites, perhaps linked with an increase in specialization, b) a "floating-nomadic" existence, moving through the interstices between the favoured locations of the dominant population, perhaps involving a shift to more generalist strategies, or c) shifts in activity times, such as the subordinate exploiting a dominant's favoured resource during a non-optimal period (Carothers and Jaksić 1984:405; Schoener 1974b; Smith 1978; the latter two cited in Carothers and Jaksić 1984:405).

Dominance patterns may also be related to the temporal dimension of niche relations. Yodzis (1978:25) discusses spatial pre-emption resulting from the history of colonization sequences. It is generally assumed that already established organisms have a competitive advantage over new colonizers, resulting in what Yodzis (1978:26) calls founder-controlled communities. In such communities, colonization by new organisms may involve a "reshuffling" of species among patches, a rearrangement structured by founder-dominance, which results in re-equilibration. In some cases, however, repeated colonization events may produce what Yodzis (1978:49) terms "quasi-cycles": a series of colonizations *without* equilibrium.

This discussion is important in that it draws attention to the problem of historical contingency in competitive relations and highlights the static nature of the standard equilibrium models.

Another dimension that may lead away from simple equilibrium models is temporal variation in the environment, which may be linked to variable competition over time (Wiens 1977). In general, there should be limited competition when resources are abundant and maximal competition at resource lows. In environments marked by strong spatial variations in resource availability, periodic resource minimums will lead to greater competition for the limited high quality resource patches or extraction locales. Although for modelling purposes temporal variation in resource availability has often been depicted using shifting equilibrium models, cycling between high and low abundance, more recent non-linear systems ecology draws in the abrupt and chaotic aspects of environmental change. This puts a premium on the historically contingent in Nature/Culture relations.

For the purposes of further discussion related to the specifics of the Maritime Archaic/Pre-Dorset social boundary issue, three aspects of spatial partitioning are extracted for particular attention. First, "territoriality," involving either: a) symmetric relations or mutualism, or b) asymmetric relations marked by the relegation of one group to less favored patches or refuging behaviour. Second, "floating" strategies, involving inter-patch mobility through cultural interstices to avoid contact. Third, "cycling," involving repeated colonization events on varying time scales within regions, either as a partial avoidance strategy or simply failure to colonize permanently.

CONSTRUCTED SOCIAL AND IDEOLOGICAL LANDSCAPES

From the perspective of the humans as intrinsically cultural beings ontology, space is not a neutral resource foraging arena, but a culturally constructed landscape imbued with social and ideological meanings. Instead of locations or sites that are the settings or physical frames for activities— simply utilized spaces— landscapes are actively constructed and experienced by minds and bodies. Natural spaces become cultural landscapes by being enveloped in conceptual grids and a history of practices as well as through the construction of built environments that physically and conceptually act back upon the humans who experience these places. The central point is that in the course of social practice, agents "draw on their settings" as resources for action and, in turn, that places constitute agents as social actors (Giddens 1979:206; Tilley 1994: 16,19-20, 23). The "existential spaces" in which agents act are not static, but are continually produced and reproduced through practices involving movement through the landscape (Tilley 1994:16-17). Thus, the biographies and identities of individuals and groups are constructed in relation to places and in the course of movement along the paths that tie places into meaningful networks, and these relations between place, people and movement are central to the construction of cultural memory (Tilley 1994:27-28). The mutual structuration of practices and networks of places gives a spatial dimension to cultural knowledge and power relations (Hood 1988).

Some of the best examples of this approach applied to the study of hunter-gatherers come from Australia (for other examples see Bender 1993; Hirsch and O'Hanlon 1995; P. Jordan 2003; Tilley 1994; Ucko and Layton 1999). Morphy's (1995) discussion of the Yolngu makes clear the relationship between landscape, the ancestral past and social reproduction. All parts of the Yolngu landscape are imbued with the actions of ancestral beings such that the landscape consists of ancestral tracks and mythological coordinates anchored to specific places. The ancestral past becomes part of subjective experience as the individual moves through and experiences the totemically coded landscape. Kinship relations (moieties and clans) are mapped onto the landscape and thus integrated with the ancestral grid, and rituals relate

groups and places in relation to ancestral tracks. Thus, a set of long-term structures encoded in the landscape constitute a framework for active social structuration processes:

> The ancestral past is continuously re-created by the sedimenting of past and present experiences and political outcomes on pre-existing loci...In reality places are continually being reformed into new sets. New divisions of the landscape are made as clans die out and new ones emerge...Thus the articulation of social groups with the landscape is always changing, but the mythic screen that covers the landscape makes the relationship appear unchanging...The acting out of individual lives ultimately produces the cumulative changes which force the ancestral screen to adjust in order to mirror present circumstances...The ancestral past, though changed and reproduced through present human action, is absorbed as a precedent for future action (Morphy 1995:204-205).

The aforementioned perspectives provide important analogies for thinking about hunter-gatherer action in the landscape. Yet, as discussed previously, they present a rather one-sided cultural constructionist view that generally ignores resource extraction practices or treats them as epiphenomenal to meaning. The consequence is an extremely idealist view of human relationships with the landscape in which Nature is viewed primarily as a source of raw materials for cultural acts of imagination (Ingold 1996:150). But the landscape needs to be both good to think and a source of raw materials for cultural acts of survival.

If we take more seriously the mix of constraints and opportunities afforded by the natural world and different types of mobility systems, then we might identify some general patterns or at least some general consequences for cultural construction of the landscape. For example, there is surely a difference in landscape construction practices between populations that have been established in an area for many generations and those which are initially colonizing an area. As in the Yolgnu example, established populations operate within a pre-existing network of places and paths that are implicated deeply in the reproduction of social relations and cultural memory. The landscape is a long-term structure that is both the product and precedent of action. Colonizers enter new landscapes for which there is no pre-existing cognitive map, no precise knowledge of resource distributions, no coded network of known places or paths to relate to. They must act without structural precedents, except insofar as they can extend analogies from previous experiences elsewhere. Consequently, besides engaging in flexible resource-searching and knowledge-gathering practices, colonists must actively construct a landscape by building up an archive of experiences with places and paths. These differing implications for social action in landscapes have obvious relevance for the Maritime Archaic/Pre-Dorset situation.

Another argument relevant to a critique of the constructionist privileging of Culture is Ingold's (1986:130ff.) discussion of the concepts of *tenure* and *territoriality,* which stand in a dialectical relation that illustrates what is involved in working with the Nature/Culture dualism. Ingold (1986:131, 136-137) considers *tenure* to be the schema and practices through which the landscape is appropriated, claims are made on resources and individuals are constituted as agents. Tenure binds groups into historical relationships with landscapes, which are reproduced as long-term structures. Hunter-gatherer tenure is a relationship with *places* and *paths* through the landscape— a dispersed network— not a partitioning of space into two-dimensionally bounded patches, which is the usual thinking with "territoriality." For Ingold (1986: 130-131, 136, 141-145, 156-157), *territoriality* is the schema and practices used in appropriating *resources* and for communicating about the locations of persons and resources. Although it does involve divisions of the landscape, it is not about maintaining exclusive access to resources, but is a set of practices aimed at minimizing interference in resource extraction or the disturbance of sacred sites. Unlike the structural continuity of tenure over time, however, territoriality is situationally contingent since different modes of territoriality are implemented in response to changes in environmental (and social) contexts. To summarize: "...tenure engages nature in a system of social relations, territoriality engages society in a system of natural relations" (Ingold 1986:136).

Such a brief summary does not do complete justice to Ingold's ideas, but in conjunction with the previous discussion it outlines a framework that can be used to stimulate thinking regarding questions of landscape and social boundaries in Labrador. Details of the archaeological context for Maritime Archaic/Pre-Dorset relations are presented in the next section, which is followed by an interpretative integration of the archaeological context with the threads cast out in the theoretical sections.

BACK TO THE ARCHAEOLOGICAL CONTEXT

We know that the Maritime Archaic and Pre-Dorset shared the north-central Labrador coast for several hundred years and preliminary interpretations have pointed to spatial partitioning as one of the mechanisms by which that coexistence was sustained. The preceding theoretical discussion established frameworks for understanding that coexistence from different entry points to human use of the landscape. Now, the empirical aspects of Maritime Archaic and Pre-Dorset settlement need to be considered in greater depth. The foraging characteristics of the two cultures are difficult to ascertain, since we completely lack archaeozoological material from Pre-Dorset sites and that from the Maritime Archaic consists mostly of calcined bone fragments. Subsistence-settlement inferences are therefore drawn primarily from site locations, structural information and lithic assemblage variation.

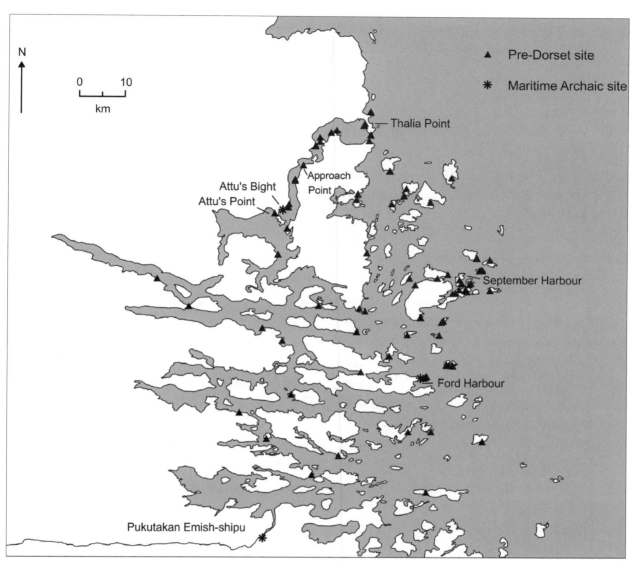

229/ *Distribution of Late Maritime Archaic and Pre-Dorset Settlement in the Nain Region. Original map © 2004 produced under licence from Her Majesty the Queen in Right of Canada, with permission of Natural Resources Canada.*

Broad similarities in site location have led to both cultures being characterized as having "interior-maritime" settlement systems, which involved spring to fall land-use ranging across the inner and outer coastal islands and inner bays for sea mammal hunting, fishing and caribou hunting, and winter occupation of the inner bays or near-interior based on caribou hunting and fishing (Cox 1978:102; Fitzhugh 1978:83-84). As of yet, however, none of the inner bay sites known for either culture provide convincing evidence for winter occupation. The discussions of the Late Maritime Archaic site Attu's Bight in Chapter 12 and the Pre-

Dorset site Attu's Point in Chapter 13, both inner bay localities, highlighted the difficulties of drawing seasonal inferences. Nonetheless, the settlement data are sufficient to make the case that there was potential for resource competition between the two cultures. On the other hand, the settlement typology is static and insensitive to possible organizational changes over time. As will be discussed further below, Early/Middle Maritime Archaic settlement patterns may have differed from those of the Late Maritime Archaic. For Pre-Dorset, the paucity of radiocarbon dates makes it impossible to track temporal shifts in the configuration of their settlement patterns, although regional variations can be considered. The following pages outline the settlement pattern data on a region-by-region basis.

The Nain Region

Figure 229 depicts the distribution of Late Maritime Archaic and Pre-Dorset sites in the Nain region.[19] One concentration of Pre-Dorset sites is found in the outer island area. Most of these outer coast sites are small, consisting of lithic scatters with and without traces of dwelling structures. On Natsutuk Island, in the outer island fringe, the September Harbour-1 site is a relatively large locality with repeated occupations, although few clear structures (Fitzhugh 1976a:136; Fitzhugh, personal communication). On Dog Island, Dog-Bight L-5, dated 3810±75 B.P., contains three closely spaced axial structures, but very few lithics (Cox 1978:99, 101; Fitzhugh 1976:130-133). Finally, one of the few late Pre-Dorset sites in the Nain region is Nukasusutok-2 (Chapter 4), which consists of two substantially built axial structures, one of which is dated 3315±85 B.P. (3055±85 with $^{12}C/^{13}C$ correction; Cox 1978:99, 101; Fitzhugh 2002).

The other concentration of Pre-Dorset sites is found along Port Manvers Run, the long passage west of South Aulatsivik Island. The Run can be used as a protected "inside" travel route to avoid rougher outer coast waters. In spring and fall, migrating harp seal herds may be funnelled through the Run and during the winter strong tidal currents maintain a polynya at the "Second Rattle" that can be used for open water sealing. Caribou of the Kingurutik and Kiglapait Mountain herds may be accessed from the Run and small herds may move across the Run onto South

Aulatsivik Island during the winter. Three large Pre-Dorset sites with multiple localities indicative of frequent re-occupation are found on or near the Run. At the seaward end of the Run, Thalia Point contains several localities, one dated 3660±140 B.P., which are marked by a high frequency of burins and burin spalls (Fitzhugh 1976b:106-107). About one third of the way southward along the Run is Approach Point-2, located adjacent to the polynya. The site consists of at least a dozen localities, some with ambiguous structural remains, two of which have fairly substantial accumulations of tools. The location is favorable for spring and fall sealing as well as winter open water sealing in the polynya. Oddly enough, harpoon endblades are rare in the surface material; a considerable amount of slate debitage is present (Smithsonian field notes, 1980). The third site is Attu's Point on Webb Bay, slightly west of the entrance to Port Manvers Run. As outlined in Chapter 13, Attu's Point contains over 20 small localities, including several dwelling structures, two of which are dated 3750±60 B.P. and 3790±70 B.P.. The lithic assemblage is marked by a fairly high frequency of endblades, abundant slate materials and a paucity of scrapers. Its location and assemblage characteristics suggest a focus on spring and fall seal hunting at a nearby narrow channel. Most of the other sites along the Run are small, with single or two or three localities. Two of these, Port Manvers Run-1 and Double Island Cove-1 (the latter with dates of 3640±70 B.P. and 3320±70 B.P.), were described in Chapter 12.

To summarize, there are two frequently re-used "central places" on the outer coast, at September Harbour and Thalia Point. A third central place is found at an inner bay location, Attu's Point, while a fourth,

---

[19] The site distribution information is derived from the files of the Cultural Heritage Division, Government of Newfoundland and Labrador. Several caveats must be noted regarding these data. (1) The distribution data are most reliable for the Nain and Saglek Bay regions, since these areas have been subjected to the most intensive and long-term survey programs. (2) Generally speaking, the inner bay areas have not been surveyed as extensively as the outer coastal regions. (3) There are problems in separating Late Maritime Archaic sites from Early and Middle period sites, since chronological information has not been entered systematically in the site files. Site selection was based on preliminary reports, personal experience, archaeological oral history, and elevation above sea level.

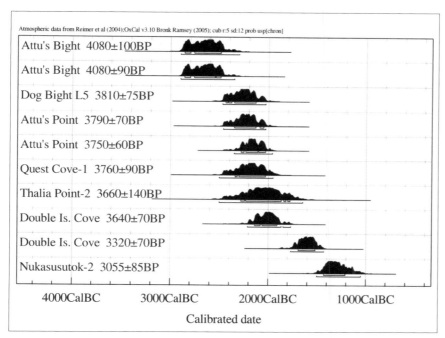

Atmospheric data from Reimer et al (2004);OxCal v3.10 Bronk Ramsey (2005); cub r:5 sd:12 prob usp[chron]

Attu's Bight 4080±100BP

Attu's Bight 4080±90BP

Dog Bight L5 3810±75BP

Attu's Point 3790±70BP

Attu's Point 3750±60BP

Quest Cove-1 3760±90BP

Thalia Point-2 3660±140BP

Double Is. Cove 3640±70BP

Double Is. Cove 3320±70BP

Nukasusutok-2 3055±85BP

4000CalBC   3000CalBC   2000CalBC   1000CalBC

Calibrated date

230/ Calibrated radiocarbon date probability distributions for Late Maritime Archaic and Pre-Dorset sites in the Nain region. From OxCal 3.10.

Approach Point, lies in an intermediate position on Port Manvers Run. As a tentative proposal for a "local" settlement pattern within the Nain region, one might treat the Thalia Point, Port Manvers Run, Webb Bay area as a north-south linear settlement system. The abundance of Pre-Dorset sites along this stretch suggests the Run was an important "highway" between the outer coast and the inner bay zone. Winter settlement might be suggested at the northern seaward end near Thalia Point, which is close to the *sîna,* and at Approach Point, near the Second Rattle polynya. In spring, Pre-Dorset people may have shifted to the southern anchor of the system at Attu's Point, exploiting seals during and after breakup, hunting caribou moving back to the mainland from South Aulatsivik Island and replenishing wood supplies. Summer might see a shift back to the outer coast, then another return to Webb Bay in the fall for wildfowl, seals, fish, caribou and wood supplies. The concentration of Pre-Dorset sites in the outer islands might be linked to a similar outer coast/inner bay movement, perhaps through the area south of South Aulatsivik Island and west towards Nain

Bay, but multi-season occupation of the outer island region is also a possibility.

Although Early and Middle Maritime Archaic sites are abundant in the Nain region, Late period Rattler's Bight Phase sites are extremely rare. The only substantial locality is the Attu's Bight site on Webb Bay near the entrance to Port Manvers Run, only 1.8 km east of the Pre-Dorset central place at Attu's Point (Chapter 12). Although the Maritime Archaic site is extensive, the low frequency of tools and paucity of features suggest it was used as a short term transit camp for movements north and south along Port Manvers Run. A small Rattlers Bight locality is located on the outer coast at Ford Harbour (Paul Island), where there is also a trace of Pre-Dorset activity. The other late Maritime Archaic site relevant to the discussion is located south of the Nain region, slightly inland up the Kogaluk River, which empties into Voisey's Bay. This locality, Pukutakan Emishshipu-2, has not been investigated in detail, but appears to be a camp on a portage route into the interior (Labrèche et al 1997:135). This site suggests that in addition to the documented Maritime Archaic movements south-north along the coast related to Ramah chert procurement there was also an east-west coast-interior axis. Recent research in the interior at Lake Kamistastin indicates that Maritime Archaic activity in the interior may have begun as early as 7000 B.P., with possible traces of activity ca. 5000 B.P. (Loring 1999); this parallels finds from Lake Mushuau Nipi (Indian House Lake, Samson 1978)

Table 95 summarizes the radiocarbon dates for Pre-Dorset and Maritime Archaic sites in the Nain region and Figure 230 presents their calibrated BC

Table 95. Radiocarbon Dates for Pre-Dorset and Late Maritime Archaic Sites in the Nain Region.

SITE (CULTURE)	DATE (B.P.)	LAB NO.	1δ Calibrated BC OxCal 3.10	REFERENCE
Attu's Bight L-3/6 (MA)	4080±100	Beta-57126	2860-2490	Chapter 12
Attu's Bight L-3/6 (MA)	4080±90*	Beta-71477	2860-2490	Chapter 12
Attu's Point L-1 (PD)	3750±60*	Beta-77611	2280-2030	Chapter 13
Attu's Point L-5 (PD)	3790±70*	Beta-77612	2350-2050	Chapter 13
Structure 1 (PD) Double Island Cove L-1	3640±70	Beta-57125	2140-1910	Chapter 12
Structure 2 (PD) Double Island Cove L-1	3320±70*	Beta-71476	1690-1520	Chapter 12
Dog Bight L-5 (PD)	3810±75	SI-2521	2440-2130	Fitzhugh 1976a:130-133; Cox 1978:99
Quest Cove-1 (PD)	3760±90	SI-4826	2340-2030	Clark and Fitzhugh 1990:301
Thalia Point-2-A19 (PD)	3660±140	GSC-1264	2280-1780	Fitzhugh 1976b:107; Cox 1978:99
Nukasusutok-2 (PD)	3055±85(F)	SI-2988	1430-1210	Cox 1978:99

* ^{13}C corrected
(F) burned fat sample; 3315±85 prior to ^{13}C correction

probability distributions. At one sigma there is no overlap between the Maritime Archaic dates from Attu's Bight and the Pre-Dorset sites. A closer look at the archaeological contexts of the Attu's Bight and Attu's Point dates at least opens up the possibility of chronological overlap, although it is important not to fall prey to wishful thinking. At L3/6 of the Attu's Bight Maritime Archaic site there was a faint trace of an occupation layer 20 cm above, and therefore possibly later than, the dated 4000 B.P. component, although deflation and redeposition processes in the sand matrix have to be taken into account. At the Pre-Dorset site Attu's Point, the two 3700 B.P. dates are both from structures on the lowest 10 m beach level, while additional features are found up to and including the uppermost 12 m beach, suggesting that some of these features could be earlier than the radiocarbon dated loci. Additionally, the uppermost 12 m beach of the Pre-Dorset site had surface finds of a Late Maritime Archaic stemmed point and a possible Maritime Archaic biface. Although these implements might hint at some form of cultural contacts, they could also be traces of an earlier Maritime Archaic occupation or items Pre-Dorset people scavenged from a nearby Maritime Archaic site. In any event, the stratigraphic factors suggest that chronological overlap between the two sites cannot be ruled out. If so, we would have two "central places" within a 1.8 km distance of each other. Overall, however, the evidence for contemporaneity is thin.

Although the discussion of Pre-Dorset settlement patterns assumed a year-round presence in the Nain region, there is no reason to suggest that the sparse evidence for Late Maritime Archaic occupation should be interpreted similarly. It is quite conceivable that the Maritime Archaic sites Attu's Bight and Ford Harbour may represent only seasonal forays into the Nain area

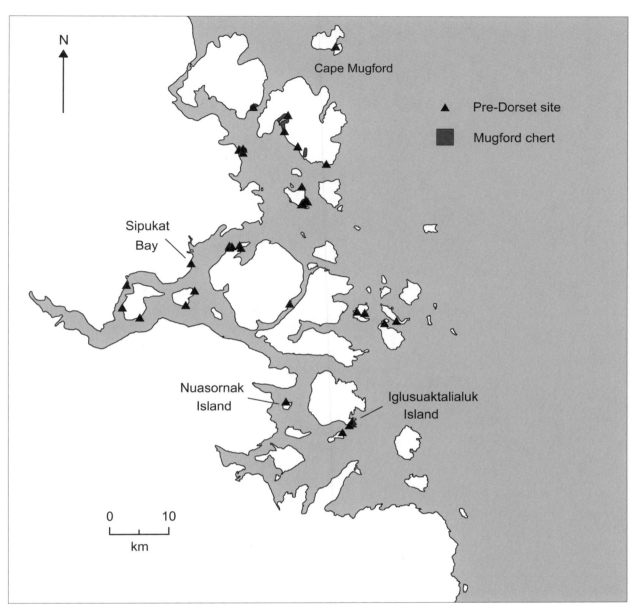

231/ *Distribution of Pre-Dorset sites in the Okak region. Original map © 2004 produced under licence from Her Majesty the Queen in Right of Canada, with permission of Natural Resources Canada.*

from Maritime Archaic bases further south. Indeed, the overall distribution of sites in Figure 229 is curious, with the density of Pre-Dorset locales dropping off markedly south of Ford Harbour. The pattern is suggestive of a boundary effect, with an area of limited settlement between the Pre-Dorset "core area" in the northern part of the Nain district and a possible area of Maritime Archaic dominance in Voisey's Bay and points south. Furthermore, given the currently limited evidence for Maritime Archaic activity in the Nain

region during the period 5000-4000 B.P., it is possible the region might have been abandoned by the Maritime Archaic as a year-round settlement area centuries prior to the Pre-Dorset colonization (see below).

The Okak Region

The Okak region has not been surveyed as intensively as the Nain area, but the site distribution (Figure 231) shows a broadly similar pattern. Pre-Dorset sites are rare on the outermost islands, but are frequent on the

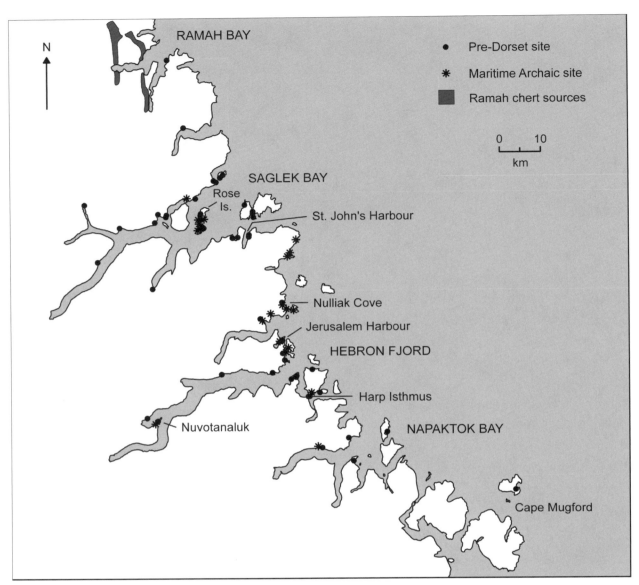

232/ Distribution of Late Maritime Archaic and Pre-Dorset sites in the Hebron Fjord, Saglek Bay and Ramah Bay regions. Original map © 2004 produced under licence from Her Majesty the Queen in Right of Canada, with permission of Natural Resources Canada.

inner islands and well represented at inner Okak Bay (Cox 1976, 1978). Frequently re-occupied "central places" are found on the inner islands at Iglusuaktalialuk (Cox 1977:130) and Nuasornak-2 (Cox 1988, 2003). At Nuasornak there are up to 40 structures that chronologically span most of the Pre-Dorset to Groswater sequence. A small inner island Pre-Dorset component at Okak-6 was dated 3475±75 B.P. (Cox 1977:223, 1978:99).

Another relatively large and repeatedly used locality is situated in the inner bay region at Sipukat Bay-1

(Cox 1976:229-237). In contrast to the outer coast sites, Sipukat Bay contained few triangular endblades but had a substantial slate component, including adzes and celts; one of the adzes appears to be a reworked Maritime Archaic gouge (Cox 1977:235). As at Attu's Point in the Nain region, the frequency of ground slate tools suggest this inner bay location was used to replenish wood supplies or butcher frozen meat. The lack of endblades, however, contrasts strongly with the Attu's Point assemblages. Overall, like the Nain region, there is a hint of functional differ-

CHAPTER 14

ences between inner bay and coastal localities. Also similar to the Nain region is a possible pattern of repeatedly used central places at both coastal and inner bay locations, which may have been linked by seasonal settlement mobility. Another important variable in the geographical positioning and assemblage content of Pre-Dorset sites in the Okak area is the presence of their preferred chert sources in the Cape Mugford area at the northern edge of the Okak region (Gramly 1978; Lazenby 1980).

Like the Nain region, there is evidence for Early and Middle Maritime Archaic sites at Okak (Cox 1977; Fitzhugh 1978), but few signs of Late Maritime Archaic activity. There are no definitive sites, but a diagnostic Maritime Archaic incised sandstone plummet was found on an upper beach terrace at the Pre-Dorset site Nuasornak-2, an occurrence that Cox (1988:3) interprets as evidence for culture contact. Otherwise, Pre-Dorset material is superimposed upon Maritime Archaic material at the inner island Okak-2 site (Cox 1977:184-195; Fitzhugh 1978:77), but the Maritime Archaic component is dated 4765±85 B.P. and 4905±80 B.P., a millennium earlier than the Pre-Dorset colonization. Consequently, as with the Nain region, the Maritime Archaic may have abandoned year round settlement of the Okak area prior to Pre-Dorset colonization.

The Hebron Fjord Region

Moving north of the tree line (Napaktok Bay) to the Hebron region, we encounter a key area for the formulation of Fitzhugh's enclave model. But it is also an area in which Smithsonian field surveys have mostly been limited to the outer fjord. Although the author conducted a brief reconnaissance deep inside Hebron Fjord in 1997 (Hood 1998a), most of the mid-inner fjord area must be regarded as archaeologically unknown and the overall site distribution (Figure 232) as unrepresentative.

Be that as it may, Pre-Dorset and Maritime Archaic settlement in the Hebron region is concentrated in two

central places. Harp Isthmus on the south side of Hebron Fjord has several Pre-Dorset localities, including over 30 visible structures (Fitzhugh 1984:23), while minor traces of Maritime Archaic occur nearby. North of Hebron, Nulliak Cove-1 is a repeatedly occupied Late Maritime Archaic site with the remains of 27 longhouses and four burial mounds. The site is believed to have been used as a seasonal staging area for expeditions to the Ramah chert sources further north. Radiocarbon dates for Nulliak range from 4300-3500 B.P. (Fitzhugh 1981, 1984, 1985a). A Pre-Dorset component is also present. Localities of both cultures are found at Jerusalem Harbour, between Hebron and Nulliak. The area between Jerusalem Harbour and Harp Isthmus lacks distinct sites of both cultures, although minor surface indications are present. It is possible, however, that traces of Maritime Archaic and Pre-Dorset occupation are hidden under Inuit and Moravian settlement accumulations at the abandoned Hebron mission, a circumstance that may create an impression of greater spatial partitioning than was actually the case. Two small Pre-Dorset components are situated about 40 km inside Hebron fjord, not far from a tunnel valley and lake which lead deep into the interior. One of these, Nuvotanâluk-1, contains one or two Pre-Dorset dwelling structures and associated lithic scatters located on the same beach ridge as, and only 20 m distant from, a 90 m long Ramah chert flake scatter. The latter did not contain clearly diagnostic tools, but a probable flake point fragment and some slate flakes, along with the linear configuration of the scatter, suggest a Late Maritime Archaic affiliation. The other site, Siugakuluk-2, contained traces of a Pre-Dorset dwelling along with Early Pre-Dorset tools and a diagnostic Intermediate Indian Saunders Complex side-notched biface and a possible Intermediate Indian convex based biface (Hood 1998a).

As noted by Fitzhugh (1984), the concentration of Pre-Dorset and Maritime Archaic settlement in two outer coast "enclaves" at Harp Isthmus and Nulliak Cove, separated by about 25 km, gives the impression of micro-territoriality within the overall distributions of the two cultures. The range of radiocarbon dates from Nulliak suggest the site was used prior to the Pre-Dorset colonization as well as during most of the period of Early Pre-Dorset occupation of northern Labrador. Thus, Nulliak was a well-established place that Pre-Dorset newcomers would have to relate to. On the other hand, the existence of sites with remains from both cultures, such as at Jerusalem Harbour and Nuvotanâluk, raises questions about the territorial model. Both cultures were inclined to use at least some of the same sites and probably for the same purposes. Even if these sites were radiocarbon dated, however, contemporaneity or lack thereof could not be established given the range of error inherent in current dating techniques.

It is important to point out that in the Hebron area the Late Maritime Archaic people were operating near their ecological limit and at the extreme northern end of their social network. Although they were able to make effective use of the area north of the tree line, they apparently did so as seasonal visitors rather than as year-round residents. This limitation has important consequences for their relations with the Pre-Dorset people who, we assume, eventually became year-round inhabitants of the region.

Saglek Bay to Ramah Bay

Moving further north, Saglek Bay is probably the best surveyed portion of northern Labrador besides the Nain region, thanks to several years of survey by Tuck (1975), Smithsonian researchers (Fitzhugh 1980) and Thomson (1981, 1982, 1983, 1984, 1985, 1986, 1989). Saglek contains many Pre-Dorset localities but only a few definite Late Maritime Archaic sites (Figure 232). Nonetheless, there is at least a hint of territorial enclaves here as well. A major concentration of Pre-Dorset activity at St. John's Harbour on the south side of Saglek may represent a central place similar to Harp Isthmus at Hebron. One locality has seven dwelling structures while a larger site nearby extends for 300 m

along a terrace. A couple of Maritime Archaic stemmed point fragments were also collected from these localities (Thomson 1982:16, 1986:19). On the north side of Saglek Bay, Saglek Site A (Tuck 1975:76-81) contains the remains of a Maritime Archaic longhouse feature (Fitzhugh 1985b:50). At Rose Island Site Q, a Late Maritime Archaic component dated 3890±110 B.P. is stratigraphically overlain by a Pre-Dorset component dated 3830±115 B.P. (Tuck 1975:54, 57). Both Maritime Archaic components were presumably small staging camps for trips to or from Ramah Bay.

Between Saglek and Ramah Bay there are sporadic Pre-Dorset sites, but no definitive Late Maritime Archaic sites. There must be Maritime Archaic quarrying activity in Ramah Bay, but it is difficult to demonstrate directly given the lack of diagnostic tools in the quarry debitage (Gramly 1978; Lazenby 1980).

PALEOENVIRONMENTAL CONSIDERATIONS

Paleoenvironmental information from pollen analysis (Fitzhugh and Lamb 1985; Short 1978) is of insufficient chronological resolution to provide a detailed context for the cultural boundary situation within the 4000-3500 B.P. period. The treeline, which today lies at Napaktok Bay (Elliot and Short 1979), seems to have been close to its present location during this time period (Fitzhugh and Lamb 1985:363), but it was not a critical limiting factor for Indian settlement. The shrub-tundra of the Hebron-Saglek district is a more relevant northern boundary for Maritime Archaic seasonal occupations (Fitzhugh 1985a:88; Fitzhugh and Lamb 1985:363). If a longer time span is considered, however, there are changes in the pollen record in the 5000-4000 B.P. range that provide a context for discussing why Middle/Late Maritime Archaic activity seems limited in the Nain and Okak regions.

Figure 233 presents alder (*Alnus*) and spruce (*Picea*) pollen percentages for the period 6000-2500 B.P. from the Nain Pond core analyzed by Short (1978:25-31); the raw data were acquired from the

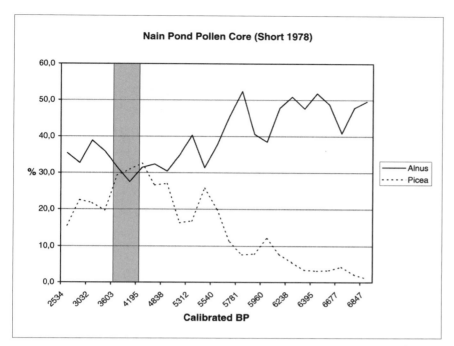

Nain Pond Pollen Core (Short 1978)

233/ Pollen percentages for alder (Alnus) and spruce (Picea) in the Nain region from 6800-2500 calBP. Period of Maritime Archaic/Pre-Dorset overlap marked in gray. Data from Short (1978) via the NOAA database.

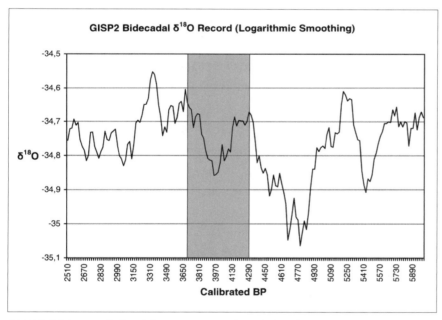

GISP2 Bidecadal δ¹⁸O Record (Logarithmic Smoothing)

234/ GISP2 ice core bidecadal oxygen isotope (δ18O) data from 5800-2500 calBP, with logarithmic smoothing. Period of Maritime Archaic/Pre-Dorset overlap marked in gray. Stuiver et al. (1995), data from the NOAA database.

(1978:28) original discussion of the dating of vegetation changes in the core was largely based on extrapolation from other cores, particularly Ublik Pond in the Okak region. The B.P. dates in the NOAA data base presumably were projected from estimated sediment accumulation rates, so given the potential for dating error the pollen profiles should be considered as depicting general time trends rather than precisely dated zones. Note that Figure 233 uses *calibrated* B.P. dates; the NOAA uncalibrated dates were converted to enable comparison with the ice core data presented below.

Short (1978:31) dated the transition to spruce woodland in the Nain area as occurring between 5700-4400 calB.P., possibly with an earlier first stage of spruce colonization of the inner coastal zone and a later migration onto the interior plateau. Subsequent reduction in spruce pollen combined with increases in alder, birch and clubmoss suggest a reduction of forest cover and an increase in the shrub-tundra component, related to climatic cooling (Short 1978:31). Generally speaking, Figure 233 suggests overall warming and expansion of spruce forest until ca. 3600 calB.P., followed by a cooling period with spruce forest reduction and an increase in the alder component. But looking more closely,

NOAA (National Oceanic and Atmospheric Administration) internet paleoclimatology database. The core has eight radiocarbon dates, but there are serious problems with date reversals. Short's and taking the B.P. dates for granted, the core suggests a flip-flop sequence with a 5600-5400 calB.P. warming trend marked by a drop in alder and an increase in spruce, followed by a 5400-4800 calB.P. cooling marked by an alder peak coupled with a spruce drop. The latter cooling corresponds with the period for which we have minimal evidence for Maritime Archaic presence in the Nain and Okak regions: 5300-4600 calB.P. (4600-4100 uncalibrated B.P.).

Given the poor chronological resolution in the pollen data and their insensitivity to short-term climate changes that might have strong impacts on humans, it is useful to marshall another proxy indicator of climate variability: the oxygen isotope data from the GISP2 ice core from Greenland (Stuiver et al. 1995). Figure 234 presents a logarithmic smoothing of bidecadal $\delta^{18}O$ isotope data from 6000-2500 calB.P., as derived from the NOAA internet paleoclimatology database. From 5300-4950 calB.P. there was a relatively warm period, followed by a cooling from 4950-4670 calB.P., with particularly sharp cooling ca. 4790 calB.P. and 4670 calB.P.. The pollen data are more-or-less consistent with the latter cooling, but are seemingly contrary to the former warming period; poor dating resolution in the pollen core may account for the anomaly. In any event, the cooling episode partly corresponds with the lack of Maritime Archaic settlement in the Nain and Okak regions between 5300-4600 calB.P. (4600-4100 uncalibrated B.P.). The ice core shows a warming trend from 4600-4370 calB.P., leading to a warm peak 4370-4150 calB.P.. This warm period spans most of the Rattlers Bight Phase (4500-3700 calB.P.; 4100-3500 uncalibrated B.P.). A cooling episode follows from 4150-3810 calB.P., corresponding with the Early Pre-Dorset occupation. After an overall warmer but variable trend from 3810-3330 calB.P., there is a shift to somewhat cooler conditions after 3200 calB.P..

While it is difficult to project how these climatic cycles would affect important variables such as the distribution of sea ice and game resources, the point is that the time period discussed in this chapter was marked by significant variations in climate. Consequently, the lack of Late Maritime Archaic settlement in the Nain and Okak regions may not have been the result of competitive exclusion relations with Pre-Dorset, but instead a consequence of the Maritime Archaic having withdrawn from year-round habitation of these regions during the preceding centuries because of climate-related environmental factors. If so, Pre-Dorset might have colonized an open habitat, thereby blocking a Maritime Archaic resettlement of the Nain and Okak regions.

A NOTE ON OTHER CULTURAL VARIABLES

Although the focus in this chapter is on the interrelationship between the Late Maritime Archaic and Early Pre-Dorset in northern Labrador, cultural dynamics in central and southern Labrador should also be considered. During the centuries preceding the Rattlers Bight Phase a southern Labrador Maritime Archaic variant— the Black Island Complex— intruded into the Hamilton Inlet region. Fitzhugh (1975:125) chooses to date the Complex to ca. 4200 B.P., but most of the radiocarbon dates span a period of 4900-4100 B.P. (Fitzhugh 1975:123). The apparent shifts in the geographical distribution of the northern Labrador Maritime Archaic in the period 5000-4000 B.P. therefore need to be seen relative to the cultural intrusion on the central coast, not simply as a response to environmental change.

A related issue is the sudden disappearance of the northern Maritime Archaic as a recognizable archaeological entity ca. 3500 B.P. (the latest radiocarbon date is from a burial mound at Nulliak Cove-1; Fitzhugh 1981) and its replacement in central and northern Labrador by the so-called Intermediate Indian complexes (Fitzhugh 1972; Nagle 1978). The earliest dates for the Intermediate Indian Saunders Complex are ca. 3500 B.P. (Nagle 1978:142). In central and northern Labrador, 3500 B.P. is viewed as a time of cultural discontinuity between the Maritime Archaic and

Intermediate Indians, with changes in tool typology, lithic raw materials and settlement patterns. The Intermediate Indian complexes exhibit less intensive use of the outer coast and a greater orientation towards the inner coast and interior, as indicated by site locations and the use of interior cherts. In southern Labrador, however, the southern branch Late Maritime Archaic may have developed *in situ in*to the Intermediate Indian complexes (Madden 1976).

The economic and social demands placed on the northern Maritime Archaic by their interaction with Pre-Dorset, in conjunction with cultural intrusions along their southern boundary, may have contracted their spatial distribution and severely affected their ability to reproduce their cultural system. Already operating near their ecological limits and in a potential competitive situation with Pre-Dorset, their maintenance of a long-distance procurement system for Ramah chert may have led to organizational over-extension, resulting in cultural collapse. The question is whether that collapse was marked by local extinction or simply a reduction in social "complexity" and rapid re-organization into a more interior-oriented cultural system that has remained archaeologically invisible because of the lack of research in the interior.

Brief mention should also be made of later Pre-Dorset relationships with Intermediate Indians during the period 3500-3000 B.P., although the empirical basis for the discussion is considerably weaker. There are relatively few radiocarbon dates for Late Pre-Dorset in Labrador and the limited typological changes in tools make it difficult to recognize change until ca. 3200 B.P., when facial grinding of burins and notching of endblades and burins became common (Cox 1978, 1988). A few Pre-Dorset sites in the Nain and Okak regions can be slotted into the 3500-3000 B.P. span either by radiocarbon dates or typology. In the Nain region there is Double Island Cove-1, Structure 2 (Chapter 12), and Nukasusutok-2 (Cox 1978:99; Fitzhugh 2002). At Okak there is Nuasornak-2, Structures 1, 3 and 4 (Cox 1988), Okak-4 (Cox

1977:204-206, 1978:104), Okak-6 (Cox 1977:217-224) and Green Island-6 (Cox 1977:125). The overall impression, though, is of lower site density than in Early Pre-Dorset. Too few sites are known to evaluate whether Late Pre-Dorset settlement patterns were essentially the same as Early Pre-Dorset. There are few Pre-Dorset sites south of Nain, the southernmost being recorded at Cape Aillik, near Makkovik on the central coast (Fitzhugh 1981:8). The Cow Head site on the west coast of Newfoundland (Tuck 1978) contains a small amount of Late Pre-Dorset material stylistically similar to that from Okak-4 in northern Labrador, presumed to date ca. 3000 B.P.. The Cow Head material indicates Late Pre-Dorset people made a rapid colonization foray through central and southern Labrador about that time.

Intermediate Indian Saunders Complex sites occur along the central coast and as far north as Hebron Fjord (Nagle 1978; Hood 1998). Although there are relatively few localities, they are more frequent in the Nain and Okak regions than both Late Maritime Archaic and Late Pre-Dorset sites. Saunders Complex sites north of Davis Inlet contain mostly Mugford chert (Nagle 1978:139), which was derived from sources on the northern edge of the Okak region. Both settlement distribution and raw material usage therefore indicate that Intermediate Indian groups moved rather extensively along the north-central coast of Labrador. Although the data are scanty, it is likely there was some spatial overlap with Late Pre-Dorset and that social boundary questions are also relevant in this time period.

NAVIGATION 1:
AN ECOLOGICAL NARRATIVE

The Pre-Dorset colonization of the northernmost tip of Labrador occurred into an open habitat, but once they moved south of Ramah Bay they entered a region that was used seasonally by the Maritime Archaic. South of the tree-line, Pre-Dorset encountered regions that in earlier periods were the center of year-round Maritime

Archaic occupation, but which were only sparsely populated or seasonally exploited by the Indians at the time of cultural contact. The southern limit of Early Pre-Dorset settlement in the Nain area suggests further southward colonization was blocked by permanent Maritime Archaic settlement in the Voisey's Bay/Davis Inlet region.

Although the two cultures had broadly similar settlement patterns, they probably had different organizational strategies for resource procurement and mobility. The resident Maritime Archaic populations had built up detailed knowledge of the Labrador coast and its resources and had regular mobility patterns along with a repertoire of tested alternatives to cope with variations in resource availability. Their increasing technological and social dependence on Ramah chert during the fifth millennium B.P. was sustained by a raw material procurement system involving long-distance forays on the part of large multi-family groups. In contrast, Pre-Dorset colonizers would have been in more of a "search" mode, moving through a series of new environments on a "familiarization tour," learning about resource distributions and natural conditions. Pre-Dorset might extend by analogy their knowledge of other areas to Labrador, but their frequent discovery of anomalies would necessitate a flexible foraging and organizational repertoire.

The general similarities in the two cultures' subsistence-settlement strategies (niche overlap) imply a significant potential for interference competition on at least a seasonal basis. The settlement pattern data indicate that the Maritime Archaic and Pre-Dorset used at least some of the same resource patches, sometimes from the same site. The differing organizational strategies of the two cultures, however, might result in different rankings of site preference. Maritime Archaic large group expeditions would require aggregation sites to be located near places where high resource return rates could sustain multi-family longhouse groups, such as good spring/fall harp sealing stations or predictable caribou hunting locales. Although Pre-

Dorset might be drawn to the same high-return locations, their smaller group sizes, exploratory foraging repertoire and less culturally-anchored relationship with space would allow them more flexibility in choosing alternative locations if they discovered their top-ranked locale was already in use by the Maritime Archaic. In contrast, shifting to lower-ranked locales was not an easy option for large Maritime Archaic groups that found Pre-Dorset people ensconced in traditional Maritime Archaic sites, although the large Indian groups might have encouraged Pre-Dorset interlopers to reconsider their camping options.

These place selection dynamics may have shifted over time. Early in the Pre-Dorset colonization process, when they lacked knowledge of resource distributions, their settlement strategies may have involved "refuging" at less optimal resource locales or "floating" through the interstices of Maritime Archaic settlement. This might be considered as asymmetric competition with Maritime Archaic dominance relegating Pre-Dorset to secondary locations. But as Pre-Dorset gained knowledge of resource distributions they might have been able to block Maritime Archaic use of optimal locations in areas where the Maritime Archaic were only seasonal visitors. Thus the likelihood of interference competition might have increased over time. If Maritime Archaic settlement was often highly patch-selective, then even modest activity by Pre-Dorset groups at key locations could leave the Maritime Archaic vulnerable to interference effects, while the smaller scale and more organizationally flexible Pre-Dorset groups may have been less vulnerable.

Potential competitive relations could be mitigated either by some form of spatial partitioning or non-overlapping temporal scheduling of resource use. Fitzhugh's (1984) model suggested territorial behavior on the part of both cultures, organized at both the macro- and micro-scales. Evaluation of the archaeological and paleoenvironmental data, however, suggests that tendencies towards macro-territoriality may be only a partial or indirect consequence of a competitive situation. The southern boundary of Pre-Dorset activity might be a historic artifact of Maritime Archaic abandonment of year-round settlement in the Nain and Okak areas during the fifth millennium B.P., which provided Pre-Dorset with a relatively open habitat to colonize. Once that colony was established, the southern boundary with the Maritime Archaic was maintained by exclusion while interference competition was a seasonal phenomenon in the Nain to Ramah Bay regions. But given the very limited presence of Maritime Archaic in the Nain and Okak regions the potential for competition would have been greater in the more northerly areas.

Micro-territoriality was probably the primary resource partitioning strategy for reducing interference competition. Temporal scheduling seems less likely since both cultures' subsistence procurement focused on similar resource peaks, such as the harp seal migrations, which had relatively limited time windows that would require spatial partitioning of access rather than temporally sequential access. The strongest evidence for micro-territoriality comes from the Hebron region, with its marked concentrations of Pre-Dorset localities at Harp Isthmus and Maritime Archaic activity at Nulliak Cove. Some sites in both the outer and inner portions of the Hebron region contain traces of both cultures, but contemporary versus sequential use cannot be established given the limits of existing dating techniques. In Saglek Bay there is also a hint of similar micro-territorial concentrations.

A somewhat different spatial pattern is found in the Nain region. Here there are many small Pre-Dorset settlements, but also three or four localities that might be considered as repeatedly used central places, though not on the scale of Harp Isthmus or St. John's Harbour. The only significant Late Maritime Archaic site in the region is Attu's Bight, which lies only 1.8 km from the Attu's Point Pre-Dorset central place. Radiocarbon dates for the two sites do not support contemporaneity, but circumstantial evidence from stratigraphy and shoreline sequences maintain the remote possibility of temporal overlap. The Attu's

Bight Maritime Archaic site was most likely a seasonal transit camp used by groups moving north-south along the coast using the protected inner passage of Port Manvers Run as a travel route. Interestingly, the Run also contains one of the major concentrations of Pre-Dorset sites in the Nain region and may have channeled Pre-Dorset settlement movements between the outer coast at Thalia Point and the inner bay region at Webb Bay. Consequently, Late Maritime Archaic groups, perhaps based south of the Nain region near Voisey's Bay, "floated" through the interstices of a Pre-Dorset "territory," either on their way to and from Ramah Bay or on brief seasonal foraging trips to a specific place on Webb Bay.

The geographical proximity of the Attu's Point and Attu's Bight sites has several possible interpretations, depending on the likelihood of contemporaneity. If contemporary, proximity could indicate only mild avoidance behavior or even quasi-mutualism in a low-competition situation in which both cultures exploited virtually the same resource patch. Or, proximity might be the result of non-simultaneous but broadly-contemporary occupation resulting from temporal scheduling of occupation in different seasons (e.g., Maritime Archaic in the spring, Pre-Dorset in the fall). If the sites are non-contemporary, and the 4000 B.P. dates from the Maritime Archaic locality mark its terminal use-phase, the proximity of the two sites might indicate Pre-Dorset usurpation of a previous Maritime Archaic resource patch and central place. None of these possibilities can be evaluated thoroughly given the currently thin dating situation, but the non-contemporaneous alternative bears some weight.

The foregoing discussion framed the social boundary problem in somewhat static terms. The Pre-Dorset colonization of Labrador was treated largely as a single culture-historical event, implicitly as an *en masse* appropriation of a geographical macro-region over a short period of time. In most accounts of Arctic prehistory, once the culture-historical unit is present in a geographical region colonization is treated as a *fait accom-*

pli and there is little further concern with the dynamics of the process. Similarly, once the culture contact situation is established, social boundary maintenance comes into play and macro- and micro-territories are formed and maintained. But both colonization and boundary relations can be understood as more complex and discontinuous spatial and temporal processes. Pre-Dorset movement into and within Labrador could be seen as consisting of multiple colonization events on small geographical scales and as not necessarily involving contemporary occupation of contiguous regions or a neat sequential filling of regions from north to south. Colonization events could include unstable "cycling" movements involving repeated re-colonization episodes in particular regions. These cycles could represent either failed colonization attempts or deliberate short term strategies to avoid Maritime Archaic populations. Likewise, Maritime Archaic settlement strategies were treated as largely the same over the period in question, but they could have involved cycles of greater and lesser activity in the various regions, responding to shifts in Pre-Dorset actions. These short-term cycles might be largely unrecognizable archaeologically, but they would result in periodic "re-shuffling" of previous spatial relations. Consequently, the Maritime Archaic/Pre-Dorset boundary relationship might have been one of highly contingent spatial and social relations, marked by continual re-negotiation rather than static equilibrium.

NAVIGATION 2:
A SOCIAL AND IDEOLOGICAL
LANDSCAPE NARRATIVE

The preceding narrative used the ecological relations of energy extraction and settlement strategies as an entry point into the boundary *problematique*. An alternative narrative takes the entry point of landscape as a cultural construct, an arena for action structured by social relationships and ideological meanings. Its starting block is the distinction between the Maritime Archaic as an established population and the Pre-

Dorset as colonizers, a contrast previously expressed in ecological terms but also one with important phenomenological implications. There are probably important differences in landscape practices between populations that have been established in an area for many generations and those that have newly arrived.

The ca. 4000 year Maritime Archaic presence in northern Labrador was surely marked by the development of a culturally-defined landscape that intertwined social practices with places and paths. Some of these places were repeatedly used habitation sites that came to bear traces of a "built environment" in the form of pit-houses, longhouses, burial mounds, cemeteries, caches, slab pavements, etc. These physical traces, perhaps especially the graves, connected cultural memory with place, providing a link with past generations and precedents for contemporary action. In other words, they constituted part of long-term cultural structures. Elsewhere it was argued that spatially anchored practices combined with a high degree of seasonal mobility were important for structuring Maritime Archaic social relations; investment in place sustained "complexity" processes that otherwise tend to be associated with more sedentary systems (Hood 1995:99).

Other significant places consisted of unmodified portions of the natural environment that contained meanings derived from cultural tradition and ongoing experience. It seems likely that the Ramah chert quarries had meaning beyond simply being a source of lithic material. Located as they were at the extreme northern periphery of the Maritime Archaic world, necessitating long and potentially risky procurement expeditions, the process of acquiring the material and the places experienced along the paths to and from the sources may have been associated with an elaborate set of symbolic meanings and practices. Furthermore, given that Ramah chert became the exclusive lithic raw material for the Late Maritime Archaic, was circulated thousands of kilometers to the south and was associated with mortuary rituals, it is likely that the material had a symbolic loading that permeated a wide range of social practices (cf., Loring 2002).

This social and ideological landscape was not static, but was slowly transformed physically over time as a result of land uplift and topographic changes as well as being transformed conceptually and practically during the course of shifts in demography and social relations. Nonetheless, we might posit a set of long-term structures entwining both landscape and social practices, structures that provided precedents, guidelines and legitimation for social action.

In contrast to Maritime Archaic engagement with long-term landscape structures, the Pre-Dorset colonizers experienced movement though what was for them *terra incognita.* They entered new landscapes for which they had no pre-existing cognitive maps, no knowledge of resource distributions, no coded network of known places or paths to relate to. They had to act without structural precedents, except insofar as they could extend analogies from previous experience elsewhere. Flexible resource-searching practices would enhance subsistence-related knowledge, but in so doing the Pre-Dorset were also engaged in constructing a culturally meaningful landscape by building up an archive of experiences with places and paths. In this process, Pre-Dorset's consistent use of Mugford cherts would provide a spatial anchor for the process of landscape construction and perhaps a diacritical material culture contrast with the long-established Maritime Archaic use of Ramah chert (Fitzhugh 1984:22). Also, although the establishment of central places for settlement may have been premised first and foremost on resource availability, repeated occupation of certain places would provide additional reference points for construction of a network of places and paths in the landscape.

Pre-Dorset activity in an established Maritime Archaic landscape would not only interfere with Maritime Archaic resource extraction, but might hinder or prevent the enactment of important Maritime Archaic social practices that were linked to specific places. As discussed previously, even modest interference effects from Pre-Dorset could have threatened Maritime Archaic social reproduction, since the latter may already have been operating near their organizational limit in northern Labrador. But the settlement pattern data suggest the operation of spatial partitioning mechanisms for mitigating interference effects in the regions of seasonal overlap between the two cultures. In the first narrative these mechanisms were referred to as "territoriality" in its traditional sense of geographically defined packages, but here that term will be nuanced by returning to Ingold's (1986) discussion of the dialectical relationship between tenure and territoriality.

An alternative reading of the micro-territoriality suggested for northern Labrador is that it was not structured as control of broad blocks of contiguous space so much as by the tenure of specific *places* along specific cultural paths. This seems most clear in the case of the Maritime Archaic, with sites like Nulliak Cove being used repeatedly over several centuries, resulting in the accumulation of visible features in the landscape, including ancestral burials. These places were repositories of cultural memories and important prompts for the enactment of cultural practices, some of which were crucial for sustaining the temporary corporate units of co-residential longhouses (Hood 1995:95). In other words, the places were dispersed nodes in a network that bound Maritime Archaic groups into a historical relationship with their landscapes. Maritime Archaic claims to tenure over these places, perhaps involving intensified ritualization, may have become more crucial when the seasonally-used landscapes in northern Labrador were colonized by year-round Pre-Dorset inhabitants. Tenure of *place* might also clarify the proximity of the Maritime Archaic Attu's Bight and Pre-Dorset Attu's Point sites in the Nain area (assuming they were at least partly contemporary), in that tenure of these two places could be maintained by their respective cultures without implying control over a surrounding two-dimensional geographical package. But contemporary tenure of *place* would also necessitate a negotiated appropriation of *resources* to minimize mutual interference, the process Ingold (1986) termed "territoriality." This could also be an alternative reading of the central place patterns at Hebron and Saglek.

While Maritime Archaic landscape use might have prioritized the assertion of tenure over well-established places and ensuring passage along the paths between these places— reproducing a system of existing relations— Early Pre-Dorset's landscape use was likely marked by a more flexible "place-making" mode. Without long-term historical linkages to a network of places and paths, and with a social organization consisting of small, easily dispersed family units, Early Pre-Dorset could more easily establish new places and had the option of moving to less resource-optimal locations if faced with direct competition for places with the larger Maritime Archaic residential groups. Consequently, Early Pre-Dorset boundary maintenance strategies could be more negotiable than those of the Maritime Archaic. Such strategies resemble Ingold's (1986) "territoriality": resource appropriation strategies aimed at minimizing interference in extraction processes and which are situationally contingent, responding to changes in the natural and social environments. Once a regular network of Pre-Dorset places became established (on a generational time scale), *territorial* resource appropriation practices would be supplemented by social relations of *tenure* based on the assertion of historical connections with the landscape. These shifts over time in the way resources were appropriated, and how they were enfolded in social relations, were fundamental to the dynamics of landscape construction in both cultures.

CONCLUSION

This chapter had two goals. The first was to discuss the culture-historical problem of Maritime Archaic/Pre-Dorset social boundaries within the context of two different theoretical entry points. It is debatable whether the problem has been advanced much beyond the preliminary model proposed by Fitzhugh (1984), but it is hoped that a slightly fuller and updated view of the settlement pattern data has been provided and that the alternative interpretative frameworks will encourage further assessment of the problem from multiple perspectives. The second goal was to use the culture-historical problem to reflect on the dilemma of working in the tension area between different archaeological "paradigms" or ontologies. The two theoretical entry points were formulated as independent interpretative frames without any explicit effort to build bridges between them. Although there are clearly domains of overlap where ecological variables and social strategies slide together, there is no point-to-point congruence that would permit the development of a coherent "third way" narrative or conceptual edifice. The needed language simply does not exist, at least not yet. But using "landscape" as a common platform for discussion may further the possibility of a social practice ecology that has been hinted at in recent attempts to rehabilitate the role of Nature in the theoretical landscape (e.g., Crumley 1994; Descola and Pálsson 1996; Ingold 2000; Scoones 1999).

Concluding Remarks

15

This volume binds together a variety of individual site studies. As noted in the Introduction, the objective was not to formulate a synthetic culture-history for the Nain region because a large amount of archaeological material remains to be presented by other researchers. Instead, the goal was to provide a series of analyses and commentaries that would make the most out of the material available while being informed by current concerns in archaeological theory and method. The different sections or chapters were to some extent conceived as separate essays, although the social structuration of space was an underlying theme that wove its way in and out. Consequently, the resulting product is not a well-integrated unity but a quilt of different colored pieces, some of which are stitched in more tightly than others. The chapters that highlighted theory and method were designed to contrast major contemporary archaeological perspectives in order to illuminate different parts of the conceptual landscape. No synthesis was attempted since the tensions between these perspectives resist resolution in a unified text. Addressing these tensions will undoubtedly vex some of us for the next archaeological generation or two. In any event, the conclusions drawn from the studies presented herein were modest in scope and need to be pursued further with a larger set of comparative data.

Given the nature of the archaeological data utilized here, the primary focus was on problems of site structure as seen through studies of spatial patterning. The major effort was directed towards the Early/Middle Maritime Archaic site Nukasusutok-5, while other analyses were conducted at the Dorset site Nukasusutok-12 and the Pre-Dorset sites Attu's Point and Port Manvers Run-1. These analyses were guided by the methodological strategies outlined in Chapter 3, one for Maritime Archaic sites, another for Paleoeskimo localities. The strategies attempted to play off model-based interpretation— involving assumptions about longhouses, axial features and indoor/outdoor hearth patterns— against model-independent pattern recognition techniques such as k-means cluster analysis. Some form of "middle-range theory" was considered to be essential for justifying behavioral inferences, irrespective of whether the interpretative goal was functional analysis or the exploration of social practice and meaning. So how did this approach succeed in the site studies?

At Nukasusutok-5, the longhouse and inside/outside hearth models provided useful frameworks for investigating the spatial patterning, suggesting the presence of "behavioral modules" or rectangular structures at Area 2A, possibly an outside hearth with a concentric fire-cracked rock distribution at Area 2B, and part of another behavioral module or rectangular structure at Area 2C. The model-independent quantitative methods did not reveal much patterning that would contradict or amplify the model-based interpretations. Overall, although it was possible to generate useful insights into various micro-level behaviors, it proved difficult to link these together into unambiguous meso/macro-level interpretations beyond suggesting the presence of "behavioral modules." The conclusions regarding actions and practices remain distant from a sense of the people and society that produced them, ending up with the "faceless blobs" lamented by Tringham (1991).

The ambiguous result is a consequence of two factors. First, the formation history of the site involved an uncertain number of re-occupations that might have generated palimpsest effects and aeolian processes might have complicated the spatial structure. Second, we do not know enough about variations in Maritime Archaic dwelling features and site structure. The "longhouse model" primes us to look for linear hearth and debitage distributions and rectangular structures (e.g., Aillik, Nulliak Cove), but the model has not been elaborated in sufficient detail to capture the full range of spatial dynamics. Furthermore, there are other Maritime Archaic features on the landscape that have not received much attention, but which may be dwelling related. In sum, a systematic comparative study of Maritime Archaic dwelling features and site structure patterns is needed to provide firm reference points for future analyses.

Spatial analysis of the Paleoeskimo sites was in some cases facilitated by the presence of well-preserved axial structures (e.g., Attu's Point L-7, Nukasusutok-12) and in other cases hindered by obvious disturbance. Cluster analysis was sometimes helpful in distinguishing tool groupings that otherwise would be visually ambiguous, but the small tool sample sizes posed difficulties for understanding activity patterning. The tool distributions did not indicate much spatial patterning attributable to activity specialization or gender. The Attu's Point Pre-Dorset site exhibited tendencies toward the spatial separation of Mugford chert and slate reduction, suggesting deliberately structured social practices. Refitting studies are needed to better understand how the deposition and circulation of raw materials relates to individual actions within and outside of dwellings. One of the Dorset axial structures at Nukasusutok-12 displayed a degree of behavioral symmetry in the use of hearths at each end of the feature. Given the relatively large size of the feature, two co-residential domestic units might be inferred.

The regional level of spatial structuration was also addressed in several chapters, although in somewhat different ways. The Early/Middle Maritime Archaic settlement patterns contemporary with Nukasusutok-5 were not treated systematically. Instead, Nukasusutok-5 was used to illustrate some of the methodological problems inherent in inter-site comparison. Nukasusutok-5 provides a good example of the multi-occupation complexity that might be expected on the highly attractive raised tombolo beaches of northern Labrador. Imagine a similar occupation history at a dozen other Early/Middle Maritime Archaic sites and it is not hard to grasp why it was difficult to sort out the chronology of the *Naksak* Complex. These site formation conditions require that inter-assemblage comparisons conducted either for the purposes of chronology building or settlement pattern studies must pay attention to the nature of the units being compared. It is not only a question of avoiding chronologically mixed samples; we also must ensure that we compare meaningful "behavioral modules" rather than eclectic samples of poorly contextualized materials. But Nukasustok-5 also shows how difficult it may be to isolate and understand a context.

The discussions of Pre-Dorset settlement patterns in the Nain area (Chapters 13 and 14) were hampered by a lack of comparable collections and quantitative data, so inferences regarding site seasonality and function were impressionistic. A combination of geographical location, dwelling remains and lithic assemblage content was used to suggest that Attu's Point was a spring/fall site used within a coast/inner bay annual round. The linear hearths encountered at Port Manvers Run-1 and the pit structure at Double Island Cove-1 exemplify the need to document a wider range of Pre-Dorset features in order to capture variations in site structure and function. Interpretation of the lithic assemblages associated with individual Pre-Dorset features must be situated within the regional system of technological organization. The curation and reduction staging practices inferred from the Attu's Point lithic materials were only local segments of a geographically dispersed decision chain in which people responded to a changing array of seasonal, situational and social variables, as well as raw material availability. In contrast to the Pre-Dorset context, the treatment of Dorset

CHAPTER 15

settlement patterns in Chapter 10 was facilitated by better information on Dorset feature types with different seasonal implications (semi-subterranean houses, tent dwellings) and quantitative data from several Dorset lithic assemblages in the Nain area. The Nukasusutok-12 Ramah chert materials could therefore be positioned within the overall system of Dorset technological organization.

In contrast to the rather faceless, primarily behavioral, interpretation of pre-contact site structure, the 18th-19th century Inuit material outlined in Chapter 11 opened up the realm of people and agency. The ethnohistoric sources provided a baseline for interpreting the social strategies used by Inuit men and women to deal with changing economic and social relations during a critical juncture of the Contact Period. The Nukasusutok-8 communal house settlement could be related to real people documented in written sources, although the archaeological record of the site itself is sadly deficient. Some of the site inhabitants were well-known "big-men" involved in the baleen trade with Europeans, and the quantity of European goods found in two of the graves on Nukasusutok Island may imply such individuals. However, the graves also indicated that the Contact Period was not just a story of big-*man* traders, since considerable quantities of European goods in two female graves suggested that women also attained distinctive social identities.

Contact Period settlement patterns in the Nain area were outlined in terms of seasonal and functional variability. But the settlement history of Nukasusutok-8 also points to changes in the *meaning* of place that occurred during the late 18th and early 19th centuries after the establishment of the Moravian mission. During this time, the Nukasusutok settlement was transformed from being one of several winter communities in an Inuit landscape to being an isolated "heathen" outpost that symbolized resistance to Christianity and Moravian-controlled life at the mission village of Nain. The case study illustrates the potential for Contact Period archaeology to explore the structuration of space in all its dimensions: economic, social and ideological.

Explicitly theoretical interpretation was brought to bear on Late Maritime Archaic and Pre-Dorset social boundary relations in Chapter 14 because that subject provides good raw material for illustrating the tensions between processual and post-processual understandings of adaptation and landscape. These archaeologies often appear trapped on either side of the Nature/Culture dualism, with one failing to see beyond behaviors optimized relative to energy acquisition and the other entirely ignoring the food quest in preference for interpretation of human actors' experience of a symbolically meaningful landscape. As things stand today, we lack a theoretical language to bridge these differences, but the term "landscape" can serve as a platform for dialogue between estranged archaeologies. The discussion presented in Chapter 14 presented alternative entry points to the Maritime Archaic and Pre-Dorset boundary situation based on evolutionary ecology and a structuration approach. Each narrative was a partial reading that activated different concepts relevant to human practices in the landscape. Empirically, the material culture provided rather equivocal information on contact and interaction between the two cultures, but the site distribution data suggested some degree of spatial partitioning of the landscape. Understanding this interaction must take into account both potential competition for resources and cultural differences between the landscape relations practiced by an established population with an entrenched network of significant places, and those practiced by a colonizing population that lacked a long-term historical relationship with the land.

There are surely many blind spots in this work, some the result of thin or missing data, others undoubtedly self-inflicted. Attentive readers hopefully will discern these deficits and treat them as challenges to improve the empirical, methodological and theoretical dimensions of archaeology in the Nain region and elsewhere in Labrador.

Summer activities in Nain: char fishing, July 2004. Not shown: the author on rinse detail. (Photo: B. Hood)

References Cited

Anderson, H. A., M. L. Berrow, V. C. Farmer, A. Hepburn, J. D. Russell, and A. D. Walker
1982 A Reassessment of Podzol Formation Processes. *Journal of Soil Science* 33:125-136.

Andrefsky, William
1998 *Lithics. Macroscopic Approaches to Analysis.* Cambridge University Press.

Anschuetz, Kurt F., Richard H. Wilshusen, and Cherie L. Scheick
2001 An Archaeology of Landscapes: Perspectives and Directions. *Journal of Archaeological Research* 9:157-211.

Appelt, Martin, Hans Christian Gulløv, and Hans Kapel
1998 The Gateway to Greenland. Report on the Field Season 1996. In *Man, Culture and Environment in Ancient Greenland,* edited by Jette Arneborg and Hans Christian Gulløv, pp. 136-153. Danish Polar Center Publication No. 4. Danish National Museum and Danish Polar Center, Copenhagen.

Appelt, Martin, and Hans Christian Gulløv (editors)
1999 *Late Dorset in High Arctic Greenland.* Danish Polar Center Publication No. 7. Danish National Museum and Danish Polar Center, Copenhagen.

Aronson, Jerrold L., Rom Harré, and Eileen Cornell Way
1995 *Realism Rescued. How Scientific Progress is Possible.* Open Court, Chicago and Lasalle.

Audouze, Françoise
1987 Des modèles et des faits: les modèles de A. Leroi-Gourhan et de L. Binford confrontés aux résultats récents. *Bulletin del la Société Préhistorique Française* 84(10-12):343-352.

Auger, Réginald
1991 *Labrador Inuit and Europeans in the Strait of Belle Isle: From the Written Sources to the Archaeological Evidence.* Collection Nordicana No.55, Centre d'études nordiques, Université Laval, Québec .

Bamforth, Douglas B.
1991 Technological Organization and Hunter-Gatherer Land Use: A California Example. *American Antiquity* 56:216-234.

Barsalou, Lawrence W.
1983 Ad Hoc Categories. *Memory & Cognition* 11(3):211-227.

Barth, Fredrik
1969 Introduction. In *Ethnic Groups and Boundaries,* edited by Fredrik Barth, pp. 9-38. Little, Brown and Company, Boston.

Bell, Trevor
1997 Application of Sea Level History and Geomorphology to Historic Resources Mapping in the Voisey's Bay Region, Labrador. Appendix A In *Voisey's Bay 1996 Environmental Baseline Technical Data Report: Historic Resources,* by Yves Labrèche, Fred Schwarz and Bryan Hood. Voisey's Bay Nickel Company, St. John's.

Bender, Barbara (editor)
1993 *Landscape: Politics and Perspectives.* Berg, Oxford.

Bernstein, Richard J.
1983 *Beyond Objectivism and Relativism: Science, Hermeneutics, and Praxis.* University of Pennsylvania Press, Philadelphia.

Binford, Lewis R.
1978a Dimensional Analysis of Site Structure: Learning from an Eskimo Hunting Stand. *American Antiquity* 43:330-361.

1978b *Nunamiut Ethnoarchaeology.* Academic Press, New York.

1979 Organization and Formation Processes, Looking at Curated Technologies. *Journal of Anthropological Research* 35:255-273.

1980 Willow Smoke and Dog's Tails: Hunter-Gatherer Settlement Systems and Archaeological Site Formation. *American Antiquity* 45:4-20.

1981 *Bones: Ancient Men and Modern Myths.* Academic Press, New York.

1982 Objectivity-Explanation-Archaeology, 1981. In *Theory and Explanation in Archaeology,* edited by Colin Renfrew, Michael J. Rowlands and Barbara A. Segraves, pp. 125-138. Academic Press, New York.

1983 *In Pursuit of the Past: Decoding the Archaeological Record.* Thames and Hudson, New York.

1987 Researching Ambiguity: Frames of Reference and Site Structure. In *Method and Theory for Activity Area Research,* edited by Susan Kent, pp. 449-512. Columbia University Press, New York.

1991 When the Going Gets Tough, the Tough Get Going: Nunamiut Local Groups, Camping Patterns and Economic Organisation. In *Ethnoarchaeological Approaches to Mobile Campsites. Hunter-Gatherer and Pastoralist Case Studies,* edited by C. S. Gamble and W. A. Boismier, pp. 25-138. International Monographs in Prehistory, Ethnoarchaeological Series 1, Ann Arbor.

Bird, Junius B.

1945   *Archaeology of the Hopedale Area, Labrador.* Anthropological Papers of the American Museum of Natural History, Volume 39: Part 2.

Blankholm, Hans Peter

1991   *Intrasite Spatial Analysis in Theory and Practice.* Aarhus University Press.

Boles, Bruce, Gerald J. Chaput, and Frank R. Phillips

1980   *Offshore Labrador Biological Studies 1979: Seals. A Study and Review of the Distribution and Ecology of Pinnipeds in Labrador.* Atlantic Biological Services, St. John's.

Bourdieu, Pierre

1970   La maison Kabyle ou le monde renversé. In *Échanges et communications, tome II,* edited by Jean Pouillon and Pierre Maranda, pp. 739-758. Mouton, The Hague.

Brain, Jeffrey P.

1979   *Tunica Treasure.* Papers of the Peabody Museum of Archaeology and Ethnology, Volume 71, Cambridge.

Brice-Bennett, Carol

1977   Land Use in the Nain and Hopedale Regions. In *Our Footprints are Everywhere,* edited by Carol Brice-Bennett, pp. 97-203. Labrador Inuit Association, Nain.

1981   *Two Opinions: The Inuit and Moravian Missionaries in Labrador.* Unpublished M.A. Thesis, Department of Anthropology, Memorial University of Newfoundland, St. John's.

Briggs, Jean L.

1974   Eskimo Women: Makers of Men. In *Many Sisters: Women in Cross-Cultural Perspective,* edited by Carolyn J. Matthiasson, pp. 261-304. The Free Press, New York.

Bronk-Ramsey, Christopher

2005   *OxCal Program v3.10.* Oxford Radiocarbon Accelerator Unit.

Cabak, Melanie

1991   *Inuit Women as Catalysts of Change: An Archaeological Study of 19th Century Northern Labrador.* Unpublished M.A. Thesis, Department of Anthropology, University of South Carolina, Columbia.

Cabak, Melanie, and Stephen Loring

2000   "A Set of Very Fair Cups and Saucers": Stamped Ceramics as an Example of Inuit Incorporation. *International Journal of Historical Archaeology 4:1-34.*

Callahan, Errett

1987   *An Evaluation of the Lithic Technology in Middle Sweden During the Mesolithic and Neolithic.* AUN 8, Societas Archaeologica Upsaliensis, Uppsala.

Callahan, Errett, Lars Forsberg, Kjel Knutsson, and Christina Lindgren

1992   Frakturbilder. Kulturhistoriska kommentarer till det säregna sönderfallet vid bearbetning av kvarts. *TOR* 24:27-63.

Canada Soil Survey Committee, Subcommittee on Soil Classification

1978   *The Canadian System of Soil Classification.* Canadian Department of Agriculture Publication 1646. Supply and Services Canada, Ottawa.

Carothers, John H., and Fabian M. Jaksić

1984   Time as a Niche Difference: the Role of Interference Competition. *Oikos* 42:403-406.

Carr, Christopher

1984   The Nature of Organization of Intrasite Archaeological Records and Spatial Analytic Approaches to their Investigation. *Advances in Archaeological Method and Theory* 7:103-222.

1987   Dissecting Intrasite Artifact Palimpsests Using Fourier Methods. In *Method and Theory for Activity Area Research,* edited by Susan Kent, pp. 236-291. Columbia University Press, New York.

1991   Left in the Dust: Contextual Information in Model-Focused Archaeology. In *The Interpretation of Archaeological Spatial Patterning,* edited by Ellen M. Kroll and T. Douglas Price, pp. 221-256. Plenum Press, New York.

Carsten, Janet, and Stephen Hugh-Jones

1995   Introduction: About the House— Lévi-Strauss and Beyond. In *About the House. Lévi-Strauss and Beyond,* edited by Janet Carsten and Stephen Hugh-Jones, pp. 1-46. Cambridge University Press.

Chi, Michelene T. H.

1992   Conceptual Change Within and Across Ontological Categories: Examples from Learning and Discovery in Science. In *Cognitive Models of Science,* edited by Ronald N. Giere, pp. 129-186. Minnesota Studies in the Philosophy of Science Volume 15, University of Minnesota Press, Minneapolis.

Clark, Peter U., and William W. Fitzhugh

1990   Late Deglaciation of the Central Labrador Coast and Its Implications for the Age of Glacial Lakes Naskaupi and McLean and for Prehistory. *Quaternary Research* 34:296-305.

1992   Postglacial Relative Sea Level History of the Labrador Coast and Interpretation of the Archaeological Record. In *Paleoshorelines and Prehistory: An Investigation of Method,* edited by Lucille Lewis Johnson, pp. 189-213. CRC Press, Boca Raton.

Cox, Steven L.

1976   *Prehistoric Settlement and Culture Change at Okak, Labrador.* Unpublished Ph.D. Dissertation, Department of Anthropology, Harvard University, Cambridge.

1978   Palaeo-Eskimo Occupations of the North Labrador Coast. *Arctic Anthropology* 15(2):96-118.

1988   Pre-Dorset Occupations of Okak Bay, Labrador. *The Northern Raven* 7(3):1-3.

n.d.   A Pre-Dorset Sequence from Nuasornak Island, Okak Bay, Labrador. Manuscript on file, Archaeology Section, Culture Heritage Division, St. John's.

2003   Palaeoeskimo Structures in the Okak Region of Labrador. *Études/Inuit/Studies* 27(1-2): 417-433.

Cox, Steven L., and Arthur Spiess

1980 Dorset Settlement and Subsistence in Northern Labrador. *Arctic* 33:659-669.

Crumley, Carol L. (editor)

1994 *Historical Ecology. Cultural Knowledge and Changing Landscapes.* School of American Research Press, Santa Fe.

Cziesla, Erwin

1990 *Siedlungsdynamik auf steinzeitlichen Fundplätzen. Metodische Aspekte zur Analyse latenter Strukturen.* Studies in Modern Archaeology Volume 2. Holos, Bonn.

Cziesla, E., S. Eickhoff, N. Arts, and D. Winter (editors)

1990 *The Big Puzzle. International Symposium on Refitting Stone Artifacts. Studies in Modern Archaeology 1.* Holos, Bonn.

Damkjar, Eric

2000 A Survey of Late Dorset Longhouses. In *Identities and Cultural Contacts in the Arctic,* edited by Martin Appelt, Joel Berglund and Hans Christian Gulløv, pp. 170-180. Danish National Museum and Danish Polar Center, Copenhagen.

Davidson, Donald A.

1987 Podzols: Changing Ideas on their Formation. *Geography* 72:122-128.

Davies, H. M.

1974 Geology of Nukasorsuktokh Island. In *The Nain Anorthosite Project, Labrador: Field Report 1973,* edited by S. A. Morse, pp. 81-95. Contribution No.13, Geology Department, University of Massachusetts, Amherst.

Dekin, Albert A.

1976 Elliptical Analysis: An Heuristic Technique for the Analysis of Artifact Clusters. In *Eastern Arctic Prehistory: Paleoeskimo Problems,* edited by Moreau S. Maxwell, pp. 79-88. Memoirs of the Society for American Archaeology No. 31.

Descola, Philippe, and Gísli Pálsson (editors)

1996 *Nature and Society. Anthropological Perspectives.* Routledge, London.

Desrosiers, Pierre M., and Noura Rahmani

2003 Analyse spatiale et architecture du site dorsétien GhGk-63 (Kuujjuarapik, Nunavik). *Études/Inuit/Studies* 27(1-2):131-153.

Dobres, Marcia-Anne

2000 *Technology and Social Agency.* Blackwell, Oxford.

Dyson-Hudson, Rada, and Eric A. Smith

1978 Human Territoriality: An Ecological Reassessment. *American Anthropologist* 80:21-41.

Edwards, Paul N.

1994 Hyper Text and Hypertension: Post-Structuralist Critical Theory, Social Studies of Science and Software. *Social Studies of Science* 24:229-278.

Ellen, Roy

1996 Introduction. In *Redefining Nature. Ecology, Culture and Domestication,* edited by Roy Ellen and Katsuyoshi Fukui, pp. 1-36. Berg, Oxford.

Elliott, Deborah L., and Susan K. Short

1979 The Northern Limit of Trees in Labrador: A Discussion. *Arctic* 32:201-206.

Enloe, James G., Francine David, and Timothy S. Hare

1994 Patterns of Faunal Processing at Section 27 of Pincevent: The Use of Spatial Analysis and Ethnoarchaeological Data in the Interpretation of Archaeological Site Structure. *Journal of Anthropological Archaeology* 13:105-124.

Environment Canada

2002 Canadian Climate Normals 1961-1990: Hopedale. Http://www.msc-smc.ec.gc.ca/ climate/climate_normals_1990/show_normals_e.cfm

Fauconnier, Gilles, and Mark Turner

2002 *The Way We Think. Conceptual Blending and the Mind's Hidden Complexities.* Basic Books, New York.

Fitzhugh, William W.

1972 *Environmental Archeology and Cultural Systems in Hamilton Inlet, Labrador. A Survey of the Central Labrador Coast from 3000 BC to the Present.* Smithsonian Contributions to Anthropology Number 16, Washington D.C.

1973 Smithsonian Archaeological Investigations on the Central Labrador Coast in 1973: A Preliminary Report. *Canadian Archaeological Association Bulletin* 5:78-89.

1975 A Maritime Archaic Sequence from Hamilton Inlet, Labrador. *Arctic Anthropology* 12(2):117-138.

1976a Preliminary Culture History of Nain, Labrador: Smithsonian Fieldwork, 1975. *Journal of Field Archaeology* 3:123-142.

1976b Paleoeskimo Occupations of the Labrador Coast. In *Eastern Arctic Prehistory: Paleoeskimo Problems,* edited by Moreau S. Maxwell, pp. 103-118. Memoirs of the Society for American Archaeology No. 31.

1977a Population Movement and Culture Change on the Central Labrador Coast. In *Amerinds and Their Paleoenvironments in Northeastern North America,* edited by Walter S. Newman and Bert Salwen, pp. 481-497. Annals of the New York Academy of Sciences 288.

1977b Indian and Eskimo/Inuit Settlement History in Labrador: An Archaeological View. In *Our Footprints are Everywhere,* edited by Carol Brice-Bennett, pp. 1-42. Labrador Inuit Association, Nain.

1978a Maritime Archaic Cultures of the Central and Northern Labrador Coast. *Arctic Anthropology* 15(2):61-95.

1978b Winter Cove-4 and the Point Revenge Occupation of the Central Labrador Coast. *Arctic Anthropology* 15(2):146-174.

1980 Preliminary Report on the Torngat Archaeological Project. *Arctic* 33:585-606.

1981a Boulder Pits to Longhouses: Settlement and Community Pattern Development in the Labrador Maritime Archaic. Paper Presented to the Annual Meeting of the Canadian Archaeological Association, Vancouver.

1981b   Smithsonian Archaeological Surveys, Central and Northern Labrador, 1980. In *Archaeology in Newfoundland & Labrador 1980,* edited by Jane Sproull Thomson and Bernard Ransom, pp. 26-47. Historic Resources Division, Department of Culture, Recreation and Youth, Government of Newfoundland and Labrador, St. John's.

1984   Residence Pattern Development in the Labrador Maritime Archaic: Longhouse Models and 1983 Surveys. In *Archaeology in Newfoundland & Labrador, 1983,* edited by Jane Sproull Thomson and Callum Thomson, pp. 6-47. Historic Resources Division, Government of Newfoundland and Labrador, St. John's.

1985a   The Nulliak Pendants and Their Relation to Spiritual Traditions in Northeast Prehistory. *Arctic Anthropology* 22(2):87-109.

1985b   Early Maritime Archaic Settlement Studies and Central Coast Surveys. In *Archaeology in Newfoundland & Labrador, 1984,* edited by Jane Sproull Thomson and Callum Thomson, pp. 48-78. Historic Resources Division, Government of Newfoundland and Labrador, St. John's.

1986   Maritime Archaic Field Studies in Central Labrador and Notes on Northwest Corners. In *Archaeology in Newfoundland & Labrador, 1985,* edited by Jane Sproull Thomson and Callum Thomson, pp. 54-65. Historic Resources Division, Government of Newfoundland and Labrador, St. John's.

1987   Archaeological Ethnicity and the Prehistory of Labrador. In *Ethnicity and Culture,* edited by Réginald Auger, Margaret F. Glass, Scott MacEachern and Peter H. McCartney, pp. 141-153. Proceedings of the Eighteenth Annual Conference of the Archaeological Association of the University of Calgary, Calgary.

1994   Staffe Island 1 and the Northern Labrador Dorset-Thule Succession. In *Threads of Arctic Prehistory: Papers in Honour of William E. Taylor, Jr.,* edited by David Morrison and Jean-Luc Pilon, pp. 239-268. Archaeological Survey of Canada Mercury Series Paper 149, Canadian Museum of Civilization, Ottawa.

1997   Biogeographical Archaeology in the Eastern North American Arctic. *Human Ecology* 25:385-418.

2002   Nukasusutok-2 and the Paleoeskimo Transition in Labrador. In *Honoring our Elders. A History of Eastern Arctic Archaeology,* edited by William W. Fitzhugh, Stephen Loring and Daniel Odess, pp. 133-162. Contributions to Circumpolar Anthropology 2, National Museum of Natural History, Smithsonian Institution, Washington D.C.

2006   Settlement, Social and Ceremonial Change in the Labrador Maritime Archaic. *The Archaic of the Far Northeast,* edited by David Sanger and M.A.P. Renouf. Pp. 47-82. Orono: University of Maine Press.

Fitzhugh, William W., and H. F. Lamb

1985   Vegetation History and Culture Change in Labrador Prehistory. *Arctic and Alpine Research* 17:357-370.

Flenniken, J. Jeffrey

1981   *Replicative Systems Analysis: A Model Applied to the Vein Quartz Artifacts from the Hoko River Site.* Washington State University Laboratory of An-thropology, Reports of Investigations No. 59. Hoko River Archaeological Project Contribution No. 2.

Fox, Manasse

1979   Nukagek Unatannigik (The Brother's War). *Them Days* 4:14.

Galison, Peter

1996   Computer Simulations and the Trading Zone. *In The Disunity of Science. Boundaries, Contexts, and Power,* edited by Peter Galison and David J. Stump, pp. 118-157. Stanford University Press, Stanford.

Gamble, Clive

1999   *The Paleolithic Societies of Europe.* Cambridge University Press.

Gargett, Rob, and Brian Hayden

1991   Site Structure, Kinship, and Sharing in Aboriginal Australia: Implications for Archaeology. In *The Interpretation of Archaeological Spatial Patterning,* edited by Ellen M. Kroll and T. Douglas Price, pp. 11-32. Plenum Press, New York.

Gero, Joan M.

1991   Genderlithics: Women's Roles in Stone Tool Production. In *Engendering Archaeology. Women and Prehistory,* edited by Joan M. Gero and Margaret W. Conkey, pp. 163-193. Blackwell, Oxford.

Giddens, Anthony

1979   *Central Problems in Social Theory. Action, Structure and Contradiction in Social Analysis.* University of California Press, Berkeley.

1984   *The Constitution of Society.* University of California Press, Berkeley.

Giere, Ronald N.

1994   The Cognitive Structure of Scientific Theories. *Philosophy of Science* 61:276-296.

Giffen, Naomi Musmaker

1930   *The Roles of Men and Women in Eskimo Culture.* University of Chicago Press, Chicago.

Golovnev, Andrei V., and Gail Osherenko

1999   *Siberian Survival. The Nenets and Their Story.* Cornell University Press, Ithaca.

Gordon, Bryan C.

1996   *People of Sunlight, People of Starlight. Barrenland Archaeology in the Northwest Territories of Canada. Archaeological Survey of Canada Mercury Series Paper 154,* Canadian Museum of Civilization, Ottawa.

Gordon, Diana

1980   Reflections on Refuse: A Contemporary Example from James Bay, Quebec. *Canadian Journal of Archaeology* 4:83-98.

Gramly, Richard Michael

1978   Lithic Source Areas in Northern Labrador. *Arctic Anthropology* 15(2):36-47.

Greenacre, Michael J.

1993   *Correspondence Analysis in Practice.* Academic Press, London.

Grigor'ev, Gennadii Pavlovich

1967 A New Reconstruction of the Above-Ground Dwelling of Kostenki. *Current Anthropology* 8:344-349.

1993 The Kostenki-Avdeevo Archaeological Culture and the Willendorf-Pavlov-Kostenki-Avdeevo Cultural Unity. In *From Kostenki to Clovis. Upper Paleolithic—Paleo-Indian Adaptations,* edited by Olga Soffer and N. D. Praslov, pp. 51-65. Plenum Press, New York.

Grønnow, Bjarne

1994 Qeqertasussuk— The Archaeology of a Frozen Saqqaq Site in Disko Bugt, West Greenland. In *Threads of Arctic Prehistory: Papers in Honour of William E. Taylor, Jr.,* edited by David Morrison and Jean-Luc Pilon, pp. 197-238. Archaeological Survey of Canada Mercury Series Paper 149, Canadian Museum of Civilization, Ottawa.

Grønnow, Bjarne, and Jens Fog Jensen

2003 *The Northermost Ruins of the Globe. Eigil Knuth's Archaeological Investigations in Peary Land and Adjacent Areas of High Arctic Greenland.* Meddelelser om Grønland, Man & Society 29.

Grønnow, Bjarne, and Morten Meldgaard

1991 De første vestgrønlændere. *Tidsskriftet Grønland* 39(4-7):103-144.

Guemple, Lee

1986 Men and Women, Husbands and Wives: The Role of Gender in Traditional Inuit Society. *Études/Inuit/Studies* 10(1-2):9-24.

Gulløv, Hans Christian

1983 *Fortidsminner i Nuuk kommune— inuit-kulturens bopladser.* Kalaallit Nunaata katersugaasivia and Nationalmuseet, Nuuk.

1997 *From Middle Ages to Colonial Times.* Meddelelser om Grønland, Man and Society 23.

Gulløv, Hans Christian, and Hans Kapel

1988 De palæoskimoiske kulturer i Nuuk Kommune. In *Palæoeskimoisk Forskning i Grønland,* edited by Tinna Møbjerg, Bjarne Grønnow and Helge Schultz-Lorentzen, pp. 39-58. Aarhus Universitetsforlag, Aarhus.

Harp, Elmer Jr.

1963 *Evidence of Boreal Archaic Culture in Southern Labrador and Newfoundland.* National Museum of Canada, Bulletin No. 193, Ottawa.

1976 Dorset Settlement Patterns in Newfoundland and Southeastern Hudson Bay. In *Eastern Arctic Prehistory: Paleoeskimo Problems,* edited by Moreau S. Maxwell, pp. 119-138. Memoirs of the Society for American Archaeology No. 31.

Harré, Rom

2002 *Cognitive Science. A Philosophical Introduction.* Sage Publications, London.

Harré, Rom, and Michael Krausz

1996 *Varieties of Relativism.* Blackwell, Oxford.

Hawkes, E. W.

1916 *The Labrador Eskimo.* Geological Survey of Canada Memoir 91, Anthropological Series No. 14, Department of Mines, Ottawa.

Haakanson, Sven David, Jr.

2000 *Ethnoarchaeology of the Yamal Nenets: Utilizing Emic and Etic Evidence in the Interpretation of Archaeological Residues.* Unpublished Ph.D. Dissertation, Department of Anthropology, Harvard University, Cambridge.

Hayden, Brian

1980 Confusion in the Bipolar World: Bashed Pebbles and Splintered Pieces. *Lithic Technology* 9:2-7.

Hayden, Brian, Nora Franco, and Jim Spafford

1996 Evaluating Lithic Strategies and Design Criteria. In *Stone Tools. Theoretical Insights into Human Prehistory,* edited by George Odell, pp. 9-45. Plenum Press, New York.

Henriksen, Georg

1973 *Hunters in the Barrens. The Naskapi on the Edge of the White Man's World.* Institute of Social and Economic Research, Memorial University of Newfoundland, St. John's.

Hietala, Harold J.

1984 *Intrasite Spatial Analysis in Archaeology.* Cambridge University Press.

Hiller, James

1971 Early Patrons of the Labrador Eskimos: The Moravian Mission in Labrador, 1764-1805. In *Patrons and Brokers in the Eastern Arctic,* edited by Robert Paine, pp. 74-97. Institute of Social and Economic Research, Memorial University of Newfoundland, St. John's.

Hirsch, Eric and Michael O'Hanlon (editors)

1995 *The Anthropology of Landscape: Between Space and Place.* Clarendon Press, Oxford.

Hodder, Ian

1982 *Symbols in Action. Cambridge University Press.*

1987 The Meaning of Discard: Ash and Domestic Space in Baringo. In *Method and Theory for Activity Area Research,* edited by Susan Kent, pp. 424-448. Columbia University Press, New York.

1990 *The Domestication of Europe.* Basil Blackwell, Oxford.

1999 *The Archaeological Process. An Introduction.* Blackwell, Oxford.

2001 Introduction: A Review of Contemporary Theoretical Debates in Archaeology. In *Archaeological Theory Today,* edited by Ian Hodder, pp. 1-13. Polity Press, Cambridge.

Hodder, Ian, and Clive Orton

1976 *Spatial Analysis in Archaeology.* Cambridge University Press.

Hood, Bryan C.

1981 *The Maritime Archaic Occupation of Nukasusutok Island, Nain, Labrador.* Unpublished M.A. Thesis, Department of Anthropology, Trent University, Peterborough.

1986 Nukasusutok-12: Early/Middle Dorset Axial Structures From the Nain Region, Labrador. In *Palaeo-Eskimo Cultures in Newfoundland, Labrador and Ungava,* pp. 49-64. Reports in Archaeology No.1, Memorial University of Newfoundland, St. John's.

1988 Sacred Pictures, Sacred Rocks: Ideological and Social Space in the North Norwegian Stone Age. *Norwegian Archaeological Review* 21(2):65-84.

1993 The Maritime Archaic Indians of Labrador: Investigating Prehistoric Social Organization. *Newfoundland Studies* 9:163-184.

1995 Circumpolar Comparison Revisited: Hunter-Gatherer Complexity in the North Norwegian Stone Age and the Labrador Maritime Archaic. *Arctic Anthropology* 32(2):75-105.

1998a Archaeological Surveys Between the Nain and Hebron Regions, Northern Labrador, 1997. Report Submitted to the Cultural Heritage Division, Department of Tourism and Culture, St. John's. http://nfmuseum.com/9721Ho.htm.

1998b Theory on Ice: the Discourse of Eastern Canadian Arctic Paleo-Eskimo Archaeology. *Acta Borealia* 15(2):3-58.

2000 Pre-Dorset/Maritime Archaic Social Boundaries in Labrador. In *Identities and Cultural Contacts in the Arctic,* edited by Martin Appelt, Joel Berglund and Hans Christian Gulløv, pp. 120-128. Danish National Museum and Danish Polar Center, Copenhagen.

Hood, Bryan C., and Gary Baikie

1998 Mineral Resource Development, Archaeology and Aboriginal Rights in Northern Labrador. *Études/Inuit/Studies* 22(2):7-29.

House, John H., and David L. Ballenger

1976 *An Archaeological Survey of the Interstate 77 Route in the South Carolina Piedmont.* Institute of Archaeology and Anthropology, University of South Carolina, Columbia.

Ingold, Tim

1986 *The Appropriation of Nature.* University of Iowa Press, Iowa City.

1993 The Temporality of the Landscape. *World Archaeology* 25(2):152-174.

1996 Hunting and Gathering as Ways of Perceiving the Environment. In *Redefining Nature. Ecology, Culture and Domestication,* edited by Roy Ellen and Katsuyoshi Fukui, pp. 117-155. Berg, Oxford.

2000 *The Perception of the Environment: Essays on Livelihood, Dwelling and Skill.* Routledge, London.

Jackson, M. L.

1958 *Soil Chemical Analysis.* Prentice-Hall, Englewood Cliffs.

Jensen, Jens Fog

1994 Den to-delte bolig- en rumlig analyse af et midtergangsildsted og dets oldsagsinventar. *Grønlandsk kultur og samfunds forskning* 94: 66-87. Ilisimatusarfik/Atuakkiorfik, Nuuk.

1996 Paleo-Eskimo Sites and Finds in Skjoldungen District, South East Greenland. In *The Paleo-Eskimo Cultures of Greenland,* edited by Bjarne Grønnow, pp. 143-169. Danish Polar Center, Copenhagen.

Johnson, J. Peter Jr.

1969 Late Glacial Origin of the Sandbanks, Webb Bay, Labrador. *Canadian Geographer* 13(2): 99-112.

1985 Geomorphic Evidence and the Upper Marine Limit in Northern Labrador. In *Our Geographic Mosaic: Research Essays in Honour of G. C. Merrill,* edited by D. B. Knight, pp. 70-91. Carleton University Press, Ottawa.

Jordan, Peter

2003 *Material Culture and Sacred Landscape. The Anthropology of the Siberian Khanty.* Altamira Press, Walnut Creek.

Jordan, Richard H.

1974 Preliminary Report on Archaeological Investigations of the Labrador Eskimo in Hamilton Inlet in 1973. *Man in the Northeast* 8:77-89.

1977 Inuit Occupation of the Central Labrador Coast Since 1600 AD. In *Our Footprints are Everywhere,* edited by Carol Brice-Bennett, pp. 43-48. Labrador Inuit Association, Nain.

1978 Archaeological Investigations of the Hamilton Inlet Labrador Eskimo: Social and Economic Responses to European Contact. *Arctic Anthropology* 15(2):175-185.

1980 Preliminary Results from Archaeological Investigations on Avayalik Island, Extreme Northern Labrador. *Arctic* 33:607-627.

Jordan, Richard H., and Susan A. Kaplan

1980 An Archaeological View of the Inuit/European Contact Period in Central Labrador. *Études/Inuit/Studies* 4(1-2):35-45.

Julien, Michèle, Claudine Karlin, and Pièrre Bodu

1987 Pincevent: Où en est le modèle théorique aujourd'hui? *Bulletin de la Société Préhistorique Française* 84(10-12): 335-342.

Kaplan, Susan A.

1983 Economic and Social Change in Labrador Neo-Eskimo Culture. Unpublished Ph.D. Dissertation, Department of Anthropology, Bryn Mawr College, Bryn Mawr.

1985 European Goods and Socio-Economic Change in Early Labrador Inuit Society. In *Cultures in Contact. The European Impact on Native Cultural Institutions in Eastern North America, A.D. 1000-1800,* edited by William W. Fitzhugh, pp. 45-69. Smithsonian Institution Press, Washington D.C.

Karklins, Karlis

1992 *Trade Ornament Usage Among the Native Peoples of Canada. A Source Book.* Studies in Archaeology, Architecture and History, National Historic Sites, Canadian Parks Service, Environment Canada, Ottawa.

Karlin, C., and M. Julien

1994 Prehistoric Technology: A Cognitive Science? In *The Ancient Mind. Elements of a Cognitive Archaeology,* edited by Colin Renfrew and Ezra B. W. Zubrow, pp. 152-164. Cambridge University Press.

REFERENCES CITED

Keddy, Paul A.

1989   *Competition.* Chapman and Hall, London.

Keene, Arthur S.

1983   Biology, Behavior and Borrowing: A Critical Examination of Optimal Foraging Theory in Archaeology. In *Archaeological Hammers and Theories,* edited by James A. Moore and Arthur S. Keene, pp. 137-155. Academic Press, New York.

Kelly, Robert L.

1988   The Three Sides of a Biface. *American Antiquity* 53:717-734.

1995   *The Foraging Spectrum. Diversity in Hunter-Gatherer Lifeways.* Smithsonian Institution Press, Washington D.C.

Kennedy, John C.

1995   *People of the Bays and Headlands. Anthropological History and the Fate of Communities in the Unknown Labrador.* University of Toronto Press, Toronto.

Kidd, Kenneth E., and Martha Ann Kidd

1970   A Classification System for Glass Beads for the Use of Field Archaeologists. *Canadian Historic Sites, Occasional Papers in Archaeology and History* 1:45-89.

Kintigh, Keith W., and Albert Ammerman

1982   Heuristic Approaches to Spatial Analysis in Archaeology. *American Antiquity* 47:31-63.

Klein, Richard G.

1969   *Man and Culture in the Late Pleistocene. A Case Study.* Chandler, San Francisco.

Knuth, Eigil

1967a   *Archaeology of the Musk Ox Way.* Contributions du Centre d'Études Arctiques et Finno-Scandinaves No. 5. Paris.

1967b   The Ruins of the Musk Ox Way. *Folk* 8-9: 191-219.

1968   The Independence II Bone Artifacts and the Dorset-evidence in North Greenland. *Folk* 10:61-80.

1983   The Northernmost Ruins of the Globe. *Folk* 25:5-21.

Knutsson, Kjel

1998   Convention and Lithic Analysis. In *Third Flint Alternatives Conference at Uppsala,* edited by Lena Holm and Kjel Knutsson, pp. 71-93. Occasional Papers in Archaeology 16, Department of Archaeology and Ancient History, Uppsala University.

Koetje, Todd A.

1987   *Spatial Patterns in Magdalenian Open Air Sites from the Isle Valley, Southwestern France.* B.A.R. International Series 346, Oxford.

1994   Intrasite Spatial Structure in the European Upper Paleolithic: Evidence and Patterning from the SW of France. *Journal of Anthropological Archaeology* 13:161-169.

Kramer, Finn Erik

1996   Akia and Nipisat I: Two Saqqaq Sites in Sisimiut District, West Greenland. In *The Paleo-Eskimo Cultures of Greenland. New Perspectives in Greenlandic Archaeology,* edited by Bjarne Grønnow, pp. 65-96. Danish Polar Center, Copenhagen.

Kuhn, Thomas S.

2000   *The Road Since Structure. Philosophical Essays 1970-1993.* Edited by James Conant and John Haugeland. University of Chicago Press, Chicago.

Kuijt, Ian, William C. Prentiss, and David L. Pokotylo

1995   Bipolar Reduction: An Experimental Study of Debitage Variability. *Lithic Technology* 20:116-127.

Labrèche, Yves, Fred Schwarz, and Bryan Hood

1997   *Voisey's Bay 1996 Environmental Baseline Technical Data Report: Historic Resources.* Voisey's Bay Nickel Company, St. John's.

Lacelles, Bruce, Roland Bol, and David Jenkins

2000   The Role of 14C Dating in Ironpan Formation. *The Holocene* 10:281-285.

Landes, Ruth

1968   *Ojibwa Religion and the Midéwiwin.* University of Wisconsin Press, Madison.

Latour, Bruno

1993   *We Have Never Been Modern.* Translated by Catherine Porter. Pearson Education, Harlow.

Lazenby, M. E. Colleen

1980   Prehistoric Sources of Chert in Northern Labrador: Field Work and Preliminary Analyses. *Arctic* 33:628-645.

1984   *Ramah Chert Use Patterns in the Maritime Archaic Period in Labrador.* Unpublished M.A. Thesis, Department of Anthropology, Bryn Mawr College, Bryn Mawr.

Leacock, Eleanor B., and Nan A. Rothschild (editors)

1994   *Labrador Winter. The Ethnographic Journals of William Duncan Strong, 1927-1928.* Smithsonian Institution Press, Washington D.C.

LeBlanc, Raymond

1992   Wedges, Pieces Esquillees, Bipolar Cores and Other Things: An Alternative to Shott's View of Bipolar Industries. *North American Archaeologist* 13(1):1-14.

LeBlanc, Sylvie, and Murielle Nagy (editors)

2003   Architecture paléoesquimaude/Paleoeskimo Architecture. *Études/Inuit/Studies* 27(1-2).

LeMoine, Genevieve, James Helmer, and Bjarne Grønnow

2003   Late Dorset Architecture on Little Cornwallis Island, Nunavut. *Études/Inuit/Studies* 27(1-2):255-280.

Leroi-Gourhan, André, and Michel Brézillion

1972   *Fouilles de Pincevent. Essai d'analyse ethnographique d'un habitat Magdalénien.* VIIe supplément à Gallia Préhistoire. CNRS, Paris.

Lévi-Strauss, Claude

1963   *Structural Anthropology.* Basic Books, New York.

Loring, Stephen G.

1983   An Archaeological Survey of the Inner Bay Region Between Nain and Davis Inlet, Labrador: A Report of 1982 Fieldwork. In *Archaeology in Newfoundland & Labrador 1982,* edited by Jane Sproull Thomson and Callum Thomson, pp. 32-56. Historic Resources Division, Government of Newfoundland and Labrador, St. John's.

1985   Archaeological Investigations into the Nature of the Late Prehistoric Indian Population in Labrador: A Report on the 1984 Field Season. In *Archaeology in Newfoundland & Labrador 1984*, edited by Jane Sproull Thomson and Callum Thomson, pp. 122-153. Historic Resources Division, Government of Newfoundland and Labrador, St. John's.

1989   Tikkoatokak (HdCl-1): A Late Prehistoric Indian Site Near Nain. In *Archaeology in Newfoundland & Labrador 1986*, edited by Callum Thomson and Jane Sproull Thomson, pp. 32-56. Historic Resources Division, Government of Newfoundland and Labrador, St. John's.

1992   *Princes and Princesses of Ragged Fame: Innu Archaeology and Ethnohistory in Labrador.* Unpublished Ph.D. Dissertation, Department of Anthropology, University of Massachusetts, Amherst.

1998   The Archaeology of Eskimo Hütte (IkDb-2): Inuit Sovereignty in the Torngat. *Études/Inuit/Studies* 22(2):53-76.

2001   Archaeology with the Innu at Kamistastin. *Arctic Studies Center Newsletter* 9:10-11.

2002   "And They Took Away the Stones from Ramah": Lithic Raw Material Sourcing and Eastern Arctic Archaeology. In *Honoring Our Elders: A History of Eastern Arctic Archaeology*, edited by William W. Fitzhugh, Stephen Loring and Daniel Odess, pp.163-185. Contributions to Circumpolar Anthropology 2, National Museum of Natural History, Smithsonian Institution, Washington D.C.

Loring, Stephen, and Steven L. Cox
1986   The Postville Pentacostal Groswater Site, Kaipokok Bay, Labrador. In *Palaeo-Eskimo Cultures in Newfoundland, Labrador and Ungava*, pp. 65-93. Reports in Archaeology No.1, Memorial University of Newfoundland, St. John's.

Lothrop, Jonathan, and Richard Michael Gramly
1982   Pièce Esquillée from the Vail Site. *Archaeology of Eastern North America* 10:1-22.

Luedtke, Barbara E.
1999   Gunflints in the Northeast. *Northeast Anthropology* 57:27-43.

Lysaght, A.M.
1971   *Joseph Banks in Newfoundland and Labrador, 1776. His Diary, Manuscripts and Collections.* Faber and Faber, London.

MacDonald, George F.
1968   *Debert. A Palaeo-Indian Site in Central Nova Scotia.* Anthropology Papers No.16, National Museums of Canada, Ottawa.

Madden, Marcie
1976   *A Late Archaic Sequence in Southern Labrador.* Unpublished M.A. Thesis, Department of Anthropology, Memorial University of Newfoundland, St. John's.

Martijn, Charles A., and Norman Clermont (eds.)
1980   Les Inuit du Québec -Labrador méridional. The Inuit of Southern Québec -Labrador. *Études/Inuit/Studies* 4(1-2).

Masterman, Margaret
1970   The Nature of a Paradigm. In *Criticism and the Growth of Knowledge*, edited by Imre Lakatos and Alan Musgrave, pp. 59-89. Cambridge University Press.

Maxwell, Moreau S.
1985   *Prehistory of the Eastern Arctic.* Academic Press, Orlando.

McGhee, Robert
1971   An Archaeological Survey of Western Victoria Island, N.W.T., Canada. *National Museum of Canada Bulletin* 232:158-191.

1979   *The Palaeoeskimo Occupations at Port Refuge, High Arctic Canada.* Archaeological Survey of Canada Paper No. 92, National Museums of Canada, Ottawa.

1996   *Ancient People of the Arctic.* UBC Press, Vancouver.

McGhee, Robert, and James A. Tuck
1975   *An Archaic Sequence from the Strait of Belle Isle, Labrador.* Archaeological Survey of Canada Mercury Series Paper No. 34, National Museums of Canada, Ottawa.

Meyer, J., and E. Montague
1993   Soapstone Reconnaissance Survey in the Okak Area, Northern Labrador. *Newfoundland Department of Mines and Energy, Geological Survey Branch, Current Research Report* 93-1:357-361.

1994   Soapstone in the Hopedale Area. *Newfoundland Department of Mines and Energy, Geological Survey Branch, Current Research Report* 94-1: 273-278.

1995   Dimension Stone in Labrador. *Newfoundland Department of Mines and Energy, Geological Survey Branch, Current Research Report* 95-1:153-158.

Mikalsen, Tor
2001   *Teltliv i Grønlands steinalder. Romlig analyse av steinartefakter på Saqqaqboplasser.* Unpublished Hovedfag Thesis, Institute for Archaeology, University of Tromsø.

Moore, T. R.
1976   Sesquioxide-Cemented Soil Horizons in Northern Quebec: Their Distribution, Properties and Genesis. *Canadian Journal of Soil Science* 56:333-344.

Morlan, Richard E.
2001-2005   Canadian Archaeological Association Radiocarbon Database (CARD). Http://www.canadianarchaeology.ca/radiocarbon/card/card.htm.

Morphy, Howard
1995   Landscape and the Reproduction of the Ancestral Past. In *The Anthropology of Landscape. Perspectives on Place and Space*, edited by Eric Hirsch and Michael O'Hanlon, pp. 184-209. Clarendon Press, Oxford.

Morse, Stearns A.

1971   Operational Report. In *The Nain Anorthosite Project, Labrador: Field Report 1971,* edited by Stearns A. Morse, pp. 73-100. Contribution No. 9, Geology Department, University of Massachusetts, Amherst.

Møbjerg, Tinna

1998   The Saqqaq Culture in the Sisimiut Municipality Elucidated by the Two Sites Nipisat and Asummiut. In *Man, Culture and Environment in Ancient Greenland,* edited by Jette Arneborg and Hans Christian Gulløv, pp. 98-118. Danish Polar Center Publication No. 4. Danish National Museum and Danish Polar Center, Copenhagen.

1999   New Adaptive Strategies in the Saqqaq Culture of Greenland, c. 1600-1400 BC. *World Archaeology* 30:452-465.

Nagle, Christopher L.

1978   Indian Occupations of the Intermediate Period on the Central Labrador Coast: A Preliminary Synthesis. *Arctic Anthropology* 15(2):119-145.

1984   *Lithic Raw Materials Procurement and Exchange in Dorset Culture Along the Labrador Coast.* Unpublished Ph.D. Dissertation, Department of Anthropology, Brandeis University, Waltham.

1986   Flaked Stone Procurement and Distribution in Dorset Culture Sites Along the Labrador Coast. In *Palaeo-Eskimo Culture in Newfoundland, Labrador and Ungava,* pp. 95-110. Reports in Archaeology No.1, Memorial University of Newfoundland, St. John's.

National Oceanic and Atmospheric Administration (NOAA)

2003   WDC for Paleoclimatology. Http://www.ngdc. noaa.gov/paleo/data.html.

Nelson, Margaret C.

1991   The Study of Technological Organization. *Archaeological Method and Theory* 3: 57-100.

Nersessian, Nancy J., and Hanne Andersen

1997   Conceptual Change and Incommensurability: A Cognitive-Historical View. *Danish Yearbook of Philosophy* 32:111-151.

O'Connell, James F.

1987   Alyawara Site Structure and Its Archaeological Implications. *American Antiquity* 52:74-108

Odell, George H.

1996   Economizing Behavior and the Concept of "Curation." In *Stone Tools. Theoretical Insights into Human Prehistory,* edited by George H. Odell, pp. 51-80. Plenum Press, New York.

Odgaard, Ulla

2001   *Ildstedet som livscentrum. Aspekter af arktiske ildsteders funktion og ideologi.* Unpublished Ph.D. dissertation, Institute for Prehistoric Archaeology, Medieval Archaeology, Ethnography and Social Anthropology, Aarhus University.

2003   Hearth and Home of the Palaeo-Eskimos. *Études/Inuit/Studies* 27(1-2):349-374.

Olsen, Bjørnar

1998   Saqqaq Housing and Settlement in Southern Disko Bay, West Greenland. *Acta Borealia* 15(2):81-128.

Parry, William J., and Robert L. Kelly

1987   Expedient Core Technology and Sedentism. In *The Organization of Core Technology,* edited by Jay K. Johnson and Carol A. Morrow, pp. 285-304. Westview Press, Boulder.

Pearson, Michael Parker, and Colin Richards

1994   Ordering the World: Perceptions of Architecture, Space and Time. In *Architecture and Order. Approaches to Social Space,* edited by Michael Parker Pearson and Colin Richards, pp. 1-37. Routledge, London.

Penney, Gerald

1997   Historic Resources Overview Assessment of One Diamond Drill Site for NDT Ventures. Manuscript on File, Archaeology Section, Cultural Heritage Division, St. John's.

Periodical Accounts (P.A.)

1790-1811   *Periodical Accounts Relating to the Missions of the Church of the United Brethren, Established Among the Heathen.* Volumes 1-5. London.

Perlès, Catherine

1992   In Search of Lithic Strategies. A Cognitive Approach to Prehistoric Chipped Stone Assemblages. In *Representations in Archaeology,* edited by Jean-Claude Gardin and Christopher S. Peebles, pp. 223-247. Indiana University Press, Bloomington and Indianapolis.

Plumet, Patrick

1985   *Archéologiede l'Ungava: le site de la Pointe aux Bélougas (Qilalugarsiuvik) et les maisons longues Dorsétiennes.* Collection Paléo-Québec No. 18, Laboratoire d'archéologie de l'Université du Québec à Montréal, Montréal.

1989   Le foyer dans l'Arctique. *Actes du colloque de Nemours 1987, Memoires du Museé de préhistoire d'Ile de France* 2:313-325.

Preucel, Robert W., and Ian Hodder

1996   Communicating Present Pasts. In *Contemporary Archaeology in Theory. A Reader,* edited by Robert W. Preucel and Ian Hodder, p. 3-20. Blackwell, Oxford.

Raab, L. Mark, Robert F. Cande, and David W. Stahle

1979   Debitage Graphs and Archaic Settlement Patterns in the Arkansas Ozarks. *Mid-Continental Journal of Archaeology* 4:167-182.

Ramsden, Peter, and Maribeth Murray

1995   Identifying Seasonality in Pre-Dorset Structures in Back Bay, Prince of Wales Island, NWT. *Arctic Anthropology* 32(2):106-117.

Renfrew, Colin

1989   Comments on Archaeology into the 1990s. *Norwegian Archaeological Review* 22(1):33-41.

Renouf, M. A. P.

1977   A Late Paleo-Indian and Early Archaic Sequence in Southern Labrador. *Man in the Northeast* 13:35-44.

1993   Palaeoeskimo Seal Hunters at Port au Choix, Northwestern Newfoundland. *Newfoundland Studies* 9:185-212.

Richling, Barnett

1993   Labrador's "Communal House Phase" Reconsidered. *Arctic Anthropology* 30(1):67-78.

Rowley, Graham, and Susan Rowley

1997   Igloolik Island Before and After Jørgen Meldgaard. In *Fifty Years of Arctic Research. Anthropological Studies from Greenland to Siberia*, edited by R. Gilberg and H. C. Gulløv, pp. 269-276. Publications of the National Museum of Denmark, Ethnographical Series Vol. 18, Copenhagen.

Ryan, B.

1990   Geological Map of the Nain Plutonic Suite and Surrounding Rocks (Nain-Nutak, NTS 14Sw). Newfoundland Department of Mines and Energy, Geological Survey Branch, Map 90-44, Scale 1:500000.

Ryan, B., R. J. Wardle, C. F. Gower, and G. A. G. Nunn

1995   Nickel-Copper-Sulphide Mineralization in Labrador: The Voisey Bay Discovery and Its Exploration Implications. *Newfoundland Department of Mines and Energy, Geological Survey Branch, Current Research Report* 95-1:177-204.

Sahlins, Marshall D.

1963   Poor Man, Rich Man, Big-Man, Chief: Political Types in Melanesia and Polynesia. *Comparative Studies in Society and History* 5:285-303.

Samson, Gilles

1978   Preliminary Cultural Sequence and Palaeo-Environmental Reconstruction of the Indian House Lake Region, Nouveau-Quebec. *Arctic Anthropology* 15(2):186-205.

Savelle, James M.

1984   Cultural and Natural Formation Processes of a Historic Inuit Snow Dwelling Site, Somerset Island, Arctic Canada. *American Antiquity* 49:508-524.

Sayer, Andrew R.

1992   *Method in Social Science: A Realist Approach.* Second Edition. Routledge, London.

2000   *Realism and Social Science.* Sage, London.

Schiffer, Michael B.

1972   Archaeological Context and Systemic Context. *American Antiquity* 37:156-165.

1987   *Formation Processes of the Archaeological Record.* University of New Mexico Press, Albuquerque.

2000   Social Theory in Archaeology: Building Bridges. In *Social Theory in Archaeology,* edited by Michael B. Schiffer, pp. 1-13, University of Utah Press, Salt Lake City.

Schlanger, Nathan

1994   Mindful Technology: Unleashing the *chaîne opératoire* for an Archaeology of Mind. In *The Ancient Mind. Elements of Cognitive Archaeology,* edited by Colin Renfrew and Ezra B. W. Zubrow, pp. 143-151. Cambridge University Press.

Schledermann, Peter

1976   Thule Communal Houses in Labrador. *Arctic* 29:27-37.

1990   *Crossroads to Greenland. Komatik Series No. 2,* The Arctic Institute of North America, Calgary.

Schoener, T. W.

1974   The Compression Hypothesis and Temporal Resource Partitioning. *Proceedings of the National Academy of Sciences USA* 71:4169-4172.

Scoones, I.

1999   New Ecology and the Social Sciences: What Prospects for a Fruitful Engagement? *Annual Review of Anthropology* 28:479-507.

Séguin, Jocelyne

1995   La Structuration de l'espace des sites d'habitation et des ateliers de taille. *Archéologiques* 9:33-46.

Short, Susan K.

1978   Palynology: A Holocene Environmental Perspective for Archaeology in Labrador-Ungava. *Arctic Anthropology* 15(2):9-35.

Shott, Michael J.

1989   Bipolar Industries; Ethnographic Evidence and Archaeological Implications. *North American Archaeologist* 10:1-24.

Simek, Jan F.

1984   *A K-Means Approach to the Analysis of Spatial Structure in Upper Paleolithic Habitation Sites.* BAR International Series 205, Oxford.

Spencer, Robert F.

1959   *The North Alaskan Eskimo. A Study in Ecology and Society. Bureau of American Ethnology Bulletin 171, Washington.*

Speth, John D., and Gregory A. Johnson

1976   Problems in the Use of Correlation for Investigation of Tool Kits and Activity Areas. In *Cultural Change and Continuity,* edited by Charles Cleland, pp. 35-75. Academic Press, New York.

Spielmann, Katherine Ann

1986   Interdependence Among Egalitarian Societies. *Journal of Anthropological Archaeology* 5:279-312.

Spiess, Arthur

1978   Zooarchaeological Evidence Bearing on the Nain Area Middle Dorset Subsistence-Settlement Cycle. *Arctic Anthropology* 15(2):48-60.

Stapert, Dick

1989   The Ring and Sector Method: Intrasite Spatial Analysis of Stone Age Sites, with Special Reference to Pincevent. *Palaeohistoria* 31:1-57.

Stapert, Dick, and Lykke Johansen

1996   Ring & Sector Analysis, and Site 'IT' on Greenland. *Palaeohistoria* 37/38:29-69.

StatSoft, Inc.

2002   *Electronic Statistics Textbook.* StatSoft, Tulsa. http://www.statsoft.com/textbook/stathome.html.

Steinbring, Jack H.

1981   Saulteaux of Lake Winnipeg. In *Handbook of North American Indians. Volume 6. Subarctic,* edited by June Helm, pp. 244-255. Smithsonian Institution Press, Washington D.C.

Stevenson, Marc G.

1991   Beyond the Formation of Hearth-Associated Artifact Assemblages. In *The Interpretation of Archaeological Spatial Patterning*, edited by Ellen M. Kroll and T. Douglas Price, pp. 269-299. Plenum Press, New York.

Steward, Julian H.

1955   *Theory of Culture Change. The Methodology of Multilinear Evolution.* University of Illinois Press, Urbana.

Stewart, T. Dale

1939   Anthropometric Observation on the Eskimos and Indians of Labrador. *Field Museum of Natural History Anthropology Series* 31(1):1-163.

Stopp, Marianne P.

1997   Long-Term Coastal Occupancy Between Cape Charles and Trunmore Bay, Labrador. *Arctic* 50(2):119-137.

2002   Reconsidering Inuit Presence in Southern Labrador. *Études/Inuit/Studies* 26(2):71-106.

Strong, William Duncan

1930   A Stone Culture from Northern Labrador and Its Relation to the Eskimo-Like Cultures of the Northeast. *American Anthropologist* 32:126-144.

Stuiver, Minze, Pieter. M. Grootes, and Thomas F. Braziunas

1995   The GISP2 ^{18}O Climate Record of the Past 16,500 Years and the Role of the Sun, Ocean and Volcanoes. *Quaternary Research* 44:341-354.

Sutherland, Patricia

2003   Variability and Change in Palaeo-Eskimo Architecture: A View from the Canadian High Arctic. *Études/Inuit/Studies* 27(1-2):191-212.

Sutton, Douglas, Bryan Hood, and William Fitzhugh

1981   In Quest of Dorset Subsistence Strategies: 1980 Excavations at Okak-1 and No-Name Island, Labrador. In *Archaeology in Newfoundland & Labrador 1980,* edited by Jane Sproull Thomson and Bernard Ransom, pp. 48-57. Historic Resources Division, Government of Newfoundland and Labrador, St. John's.

Tanner, Adrian

1979   *Bringing Home Animals. Religious Ideology and Mode of Production of the Mistassini Cree Hunters.* Institute of Social and Economic Research, Memorial University of Newfoundland, St. John's.

Tanner, Väinö

1944   *Outlines of the Geography, Life and Customs of Newfoundland-Labrador.* Acta Geographica Fenniæ 8 (1, parts 1,2). Helsinki.

Taylor, J. Garth

1966   Field Notes. Site Survey in the Nain-Okak Area, Northern Labrador. Manuscript No. 713, Archaeological Survey of Canada Archives.

1969   William Turner's Journeys to the Caribou Country with the Labrador Eskimos in 1780. *Ethnohistory* 16(2):141-164.

1974   *Labrador Eskimo Settlements of the Early Contact Period.* Publications in Ethnology No. 9, National Museums of Canada, Ottawa.

1976   *The Inuit Middleman in the Labrador Baleen Trade.* Unpublished Manuscript.

1979a   Tuglavina. In *Dictionary of Canadian Biography, Volume 4,* edited by F. G. Halpenny, p. 740. University of Toronto Press, Toronto.

1979b   Indian-Inuit Relations in Eastern Labrador, 1600-1976. *Arctic Anthropology* 16:49-58.

1983   The Two Worlds of Mikak. Part I. *The Beaver,* Outfit 314:3:4-13.

1984   The Two Worlds of Mikak. Part II. *The Beaver,* Outfit 314:4:18-25.

1985   The Arctic Whale Cult in Labrador. *Études/Inuit/Studies* 9(2):121-132.

1988   Labrador Inuit Whale Use During the Early Contact Period. *Arctic Anthropology* 25(1):120-130.

1989   Shamanic Sex Roles in Traditional Labrador Inuit Society. In *Shamanism: Past and Present,* edited by M. Hoppál, O. J. von Sadovszky, pp. 297-306. ISTOR Books, Budapest—Los Angeles/Fullerton.

1990   The Labrador Inuit Kashim (Ceremonial House) Complex. *Arctic Anthropology* 27(2):51-67.

Thagard, Paul

1992   *Conceptual Revolutions. Princeton University Press, Princeton.*

Thomson, J. Callum

1981   Preliminary Archaeological Findings From Shuldham Island, Labrador, 1980. In *Archaeology in Newfoundland & Labrador 1980,* edited by Jane Sproull Thomson and Bernard Ransom, pp. 5-25. Historic Resources Division, Government of Newfoundland and Labrador, St. John's.

1982   Archaeological Findings from Saglek Bay, 1981. In *Archaeology in Newfoundland & Labrador 1981,* edited by Jane Sproull Thomson and Bernard Ransom, pp. 5-31. Historic Resources Division, Government of Newfoundland and Labrador, St. John's.

1983   Maritime Archaic Longhouses and Other Survey Results from Outer Saglek Bay, Northern Labrador, August 1982. In *Archaeology in Newfoundland & Labrador 1982,* edited by Jane Sproull Thomson and Bernard Ransom, pp. 3-31. Historic Resources Division, Government of Newfoundland and Labrador, St. John's.

1984   Maritime Archaic Occupation of Big Island, Saglek Bay: A Preliminary Report. In *Archaeology in Newfoundland & Labrador 1983,* edited by Jane Sproull Thomson and Bernard Ransom, pp. 48-54. Historic Resources Division, Government of Newfoundland and Labrador, St. John's.

1986   Caribou Trail Archaeology: 1985 Investigation of Saglek Bay and Inner Saglek Fjord. In *Archaeology in Newfoundland & Labrador 1985,* edited by Jane Sproull Thomson and Bernard Ransom, pp. 9-53. Historic Resources Division, Government of Newfoundland and Labrador, St. John's.

1989   The Caribou Trail Continues: A Survey of White Point, Between Saglek and Hebron. In *Archaeology in Newfoundland & Labrador 1986,* edited by Jane Sproull Thomson and Bernard Ransom, pp. 27-51. Historic Resources Division, Government of Newfoundland and Labrador, St. John's.

Tilley, Christopher
1994   *A Phenomenology of Landscape.* Berg, Oxford.
1999   *Metaphor and Material Culture.* Blackwell, Oxford.

Tringham, Ruth E.
1991   Households with Faces: The Challenge of Gender in Prehistoric Architectural Remains. In *Engendering Archaeology. Women and Prehistory,* edited by Joan M. Gero and Margaret W. Conkey, pp. 93-131. Blackwell, Oxford.

Trudel, François
1980   Les relations entre les français et les Inuit au Labrador méridional, 1660-1760.*Études/Inuit/Studies* 4 (1-2):135-145.

Tuck, James A.
1971   An Archaic Cemetery at Port au Choix, Newfoundland. *American Antiquity* 36:343-358.
1975   *Prehistory of Saglek Bay, Labrador: Archaic and Palaeo-Eskimo Occupations.* Archaeological Survey of Canada Mercury Series Paper No. 32, National Museums of Canada, Ottawa.
1976   *Ancient People of Port au Choix. The Excavation of an Archaic Indian Cemetery in Newfoundland.* Institute of Social And Economic Research, Memorial University of Newfoundland, St. John's.

Tuck, James A., and Robert McGhee
1975   Archaic Cultures in the Strait of Belle Isle Region, Labrador. *Arctic Anthropology* 12(2):76-91.

Turner, Lucien M.
1894   *Ethnology of the Ungava District, Hudson Bay Territory.* Eleventh Report of the Bureau of Ethnology, Smithsonian Institution, 1889-1890:159-350.

Ucko, Peter J., and Robert Layton (editors)
1999   *The Archaeology and Anthropology of Landscape. Shaping Your Landscape.* Routledge, London.

VanStone, James W.
1985   *Material Culture of the Davis Inlet and Barren Ground Naskapi: The William Duncan Strong Collection.* Fieldiana Anthropology, New Series No. 7.

Wandsnider, LuAnn
1996   Describing and Comparing Archaeological Spatial Structures. *Journal of Archaeological Method and Theory* 3:319-384.

Way, Jacob Edson III
1978   *An Osteological Analysis of a Late Thule/Early Historic Labrador Eskimo Population.* Unpublished Ph.D. Dissertation, Department of Anthropology, University of Toronto.

Wenner, Carl-Gösta
1947   Pollen Diagrams from Labrador. *Geografiska Annaler* 29:137-373.

Wheeler, E. P.
1953   *List of Labrador Eskimo Place Names.* National Museum of Canada Bulletin No. 131, Ottawa.

Whitelaw, Todd M.
1991   Some Dimensions of Variability in the Social Organisation of Community Space Among Foragers. In *Ethnoarchaeological Approaches to Mobile Campsites. Hunter-Gatherer and Pastoralist Case Studies,* edited by C. S. Gamble and W. A. Boismier, pp. 139-188. International Monographs in Prehistory, Ethnoarchaeological Series 1, Ann Arbor.
1994   Order Without Architecture: Functional, Social and Symbolic Dimensions in Hunter-Gatherer Settlement Organization. In *Architecture & Order. Approaches to Social Space,* edited by Michael Parker Pearson and Colin Richards, pp. 217-243. Routledge, London.

Whiteley, William H.
1979   Mikak. In *Dictionary of Canadian Biography, Volume 4,* edited by F. G. Halpenny, pp. 536-537. University of Toronto Press, Toronto.

Wiens, J. A.
1977   On Competition and Variable Environments. *American Scientist* 65:590-597.

Woollett, James M.
1999   Living in the Narrows: Subsistence Economy and Culture Change in Labrador Inuit Society During the Contact Period. *World Archaeology* 30:370-387.

Wyatt, A. G. N.
1934   Surveying Cruises of H.M.S Challenger off the Coast of Labrador in 1932 and 1933. *Geographical Journal* 84:33-53.

Wylie, Alison
1989   Archaeological Cables and Tacking: The Implications of Practice for Bernstein's 'Options Beyond Objectivism and Relativism'. *Philosophy of Social Science* 19:1-18.
2000   Questions of Evidence, Legitimacy, and the (Dis)Union of Science. *American Antiquity* 65:227-237.

Yates, Timothy
1989   Habitus and Social Space: Some Suggestions About Meaning in the Saami (Lapp) Tent ca. 1700-1900. In *The Meanings of Things. Material Culture and Symbolic Expression,* edited by Ian Hodder, pp. 249-262. Unwin Hyman, London.

Yellen, John E.
1977   *Archaeological Approaches to the Present: Models for Reconstructing the Past.* Academic Press, New York.

Yodzis, Peter
1978   *Competition for Space and the Structure of Ecological Communities.* Lecture Notes in Biomathematics 25. Springer-Verlag, Berlin.

Zimmerly, David William
1975   *Cain's Land Revisited. Culture Change in Central Labrador 1775-1972.* Institute of Social and Economic Research, Memorial University of Newfoundland, St. John's.

Index

OTHER TITLES IN THE SERIES

Contributions to Circumpolar Anthropology

Vol. 1: *Gateways: Exploring the Legacy of the Jesup North Pacific Expedition,*1897-1902. Edited by Igor Krupnik and William W. Fitzhugh. Arctic Studies Center, National Museum of Natural History, Smithsonian Institution, Washington, DC. 2001. xvi+335 pp.

Vol. 2: *Honoring Our Elders: A History of Eastern Arctic Anthropology.* Edited by William W. Fitzhugh, Stephen Loring, and Daniel Odess. Arctic Studies Center, National Museum of Natural History, Smithsonian Institution, Washington, DC. 2002. xvi+319 pp.

Vol. 3: *Akuzilleput Igaqullghet/Our Words Put to Paper: Sourcebook in St. Lawrence Island Yupik Heritage and History.* Edited by Igor Krupnik, Willis Walunga, and Vera Metcalf. Compiled by Igor Krupnik and Lars Krutak. Arctic Studies Center, National Museum of Natural History, Smithsonian Institution, Washington, DC. 2002. 464 pp.

Vol. 4: *Constructing Cultures Then and Now: Celebrating Franz Boas and the Jesup North Pacific Expedition.* Edited by Lauren Kendall and Igor Krupnik. Arctic Studies Center, National Museum of Natural History, Smithsonian Institution, Washington, DC. 2003. xviii+364 pp.

Vol. 5: *Taymyr: The Archaeology of Northernmost Eurasia.* By Leonid P. Khlobystin. Edited by William W. Fitzhugh and Vladimir V. Pitulko. Arctic Studies Center, National Museum of Natural History, Smithsonian Institution, Washington, DC. 2005. xxvii+235 pp.

Vol. 6: *Northern Ethnographic Landscapes: Perspectives from Circumpolar Nations.* Edited by Igor Krupnik, Rachel Mason, and Tonia Horton. Arctic Studies Center, National Museum of Natural History, Smithsonian Institution, Washington, DC. 2004. xvi+446 pp.